Journey
to Healing

Journey to Healing

Aboriginal People with Addiction and Mental Health Issues

WHAT HEALTH, SOCIAL SERVICE AND JUSTICE WORKERS NEED TO KNOW

Edited by Peter Menzies and Lynn F. Lavallée
Foreword by Elder Vern Harper

camh

Centre for Addiction and Mental Health
Centre de toxicomanie et de santé mentale

Library and Archives Canada Cataloguing in Publication

Journey to healing: Aboriginal people with addiction and mental health issues: what health, social service and justice workers need to know / edited by Peter Menzies and Lynn Lavallée; foreword by Vern Harper.

Includes bibliographical references and index.

ISBN 978-1-77114-159-8 (PRINT)
ISBN 978-1-77114-160-4 (PDF)
ISBN 978-1-77114-161-1 (HTML)
ISBN 978-1-77114-162-8 (ePUB)

1. Native peoples—Counseling of—Canada. 2. Native peoples—Services for—Canada. 3. Mental healing—Canada. 4. Native peoples—Mental health—Canada. 5. Native peoples—Mental health services—Canada. 6. Native peoples—Drug use—Canada. 7. Native peoples—Canada—Social conditions. I. Menzies, Peter, 1953–, editor of compilation. II. Lavallée, Lynn, 1966–, editor of compilation. III. Centre for Addiction and Mental Health, issuing body.

RC451.5.I5J69 2014361'.0608997071   C2013-908401-0   C2013-908402-9

This publication may be available in other formats. For information about alternative formats or other CAMH publications, or to place an order, please contact Sales and Distribution:
Toll-free: 1 800 661-1111
Toronto: 416 595-6059
E-mail: publications@camh.ca
Online store: http://store.camh.net
Website: www.camh.ca

This book was produced by CAMH Publications.

4175a/06-2014/P600

Acknowledgments

Developing and producing this book required the collective effort of many dedicated and wise people. Our first thanks go out to the authors who devoted their learning, insight and time to writing and responding to edits and reviews of their chapters. To all, we say *chi miigwetch*–thank you–for your patience with the long process, for your enduring support of this project and especially for the contribution of your knowledge and guidance. To Elder Vern Harper, we say *ay hay*–thanks in Cree–for his foreword. His words remind us that though we may walk on different paths, we walk this world together, always sharing a view of the same sun and moon.

Next, we thank those who generously volunteered their time and expertise to review and comment on chapters. In alphabetical order: Kathy Absolon, Judith G. Bartlett, Alison Benedict, Nicole Blackman, Carrie Bourassa, Leslie Brown, Ed Connors, Marlyn Cook, Robert Cooke, Sheila Cote-Meek, Rick Csiernik, Yasmin Dean, Rosa Dragonetti, Corrine Fox, Bonnie Freeman, Anne George, Gaye Hanson, Robert Harding, Michael Anthony Hart, Elaine Herbert, Gus Hill, Barbara Hurford, Randy Jackson, Bonnie Jeffery, Shelly Johnson, Andrea Kennedy, Alexandra King, Malcolm King, Kathy Langlois, Grant Larson, Renee Linklater, Paul S. Links, Glen Lowry, Darrel Manitowabi, David C. Marsh, Paul Masotti, Blair McFarland, L. Jane McMillan, Taima Moeke-Pickering, Jane Moseley, Christopher Mushquash, Bill Mussell, Julie Pelletier, Priya Raju, Allison Reeves, Johanne Renaud, Jean-Paul Restoule, Luciana Rodrigues, Hugh Shewell, Wally Sinclair, Brenda Stade, Qwul'sih'yah'maht (Robina Thomas), Shayna Watson, Joanne Whitty-Rogers and Art Zoccole.

The driving force behind this book, from original concept to print production, was Michelle Maynes, product developer at CAMH. Her support and organizational skills kept us focused, and her patience and tenacity brought the project safely home.

We are also indebted to the professional editors whose feedback helped the authors to further develop and refine their work. Thanks especially to Louise MacKenzie, who helped many of the authors to craft ideas and whose humour and willingness to learn created a supportive environment for all, and to Hema Zbogar, whose high standards for precision and clarity brought a sparkling polish to the final drafts. Thanks also to Julie Bedford, Diana Ballon, Jackie Dulson, Margaret McClintock, Lynn Schellenberg, Laurie Thomas and Jacquelyn Waller-Vintar for their excellent work.

And finally, thanks to Mara Korkola for her thoughtful and sensitive design and typesetting of the cover and text; to Kelly Coleman, for her careful proofreading; and to Judy Dunlop, for taking on the challenge of compiling the index with enthusiasm and skill.

We are also grateful for the financial support of the Access and Transitions Program of CAMH.

Contents

Part 1: History and Experience

Part 2: Foundations of Healing

Part 3: Meeting the People

Part 4: Issues and Approaches

Part 5: Providing Services to Aboriginal Communities

Preface

PETER MENZIES AND LYNN F. LAVALLÉE

Healing for Aboriginal peoples has always been grounded in tradition. It means more than healing in the curative, individually focused sense of mainstream Western medicine. It means restoring well-being among individuals and communities by recuperating and renewing traditional practices that recognize Aboriginal peoples' inherent resilience and vitality and that restore their collective strength and identity.

Restoring well-being and identity also means that people choose for themselves who will accompany them on their healing journey, and how. Some Aboriginal people prefer traditional approaches and traditional healers. Others opt for treatment via mainstream services. Still others seek help that combines aspects of both.

The title of this book, *Journey to Healing*, reminds us that healing is a process. As helpers, we need to be mindful of this. There are no quick solutions to resolve issues that have been created over a lifetime for individuals—and over centuries for Aboriginal peoples. We need both individual and collective healing. Healing is a journey the helper embarks on with the client, be it for a few hours, months or even years. Healing is sacred and requires helpers to be in the moment with their clients, as well as with clients' ancestors. We say ancestors because we believe we carry their spirits with us and that these spirits are a part of the healing journey. The journey involves not only the individual, but also families, communities, nations and the entire country. It means building partnerships between Aboriginal communities and mainstream organizations, and using both Western and Aboriginal healing approaches. The journey to healing means learning from one another and believing each person is the expert in his or her life and needs.

This book offers various Aboriginal perspectives on the issues—there is no single Aboriginal perspective, given the diverse background and experiences of Aboriginal people across Canada. Readers may also notice that some of the Aboriginal authors place themselves in their writing. They use this approach because Aboriginal peoples have a strong oral tradition. Before the arrival of Europeans, stories and information were shared in this way. People started by identifying themselves, their family and their place of origin to show how they were related to the story. The story was not seen as an isolated event, but rather, as being connected to the person sharing it. Even today, Aboriginal researchers often locate themselves within the context of their research findings.

This book is divided into five parts: **Part 1: History and Experience** provides the context that underpins the health disparities and other issues that Aboriginal individuals, families and communities experience today. **Part 2: Foundations of Healing** presents different frameworks for working with Aboriginal clients, which can involve traditional, mainstream or merged approaches. **Part 3: Meeting the People** focuses on the unique issues and needs of specific groups, such as youth, men, women, two-spirit people and older adults. **Part 4: Issues and Approaches** examines specific mental health and addiction issues, as well as housing, homelessness and domestic violence, and strategies for addressing them. **Part 5: Providing Services to Aboriginal Communities** explores the uniqueness and complexities of urban and remote Aboriginal communities and discusses ways to deliver health care services in these different settings, as well as how training and partnerships can meet the unique needs of Aboriginal people in these different environments.

We have tried to create a comprehensive picture of the issues affecting contemporary Aboriginal people, but given the complexity of issues, it is impossible to cover everything in one volume. We encourage you to explore topics not covered in this book to enrich your understanding as we all strive to provide contemporary solutions to long-standing problems.

A NOTE ON TERMINOLOGY

This book uses various terms to refer to the Indigenous inhabitants of Canada. Some language is rooted in law and legislation and some is based in community practice and how Aboriginal peoples define themselves. This book does not alter historical and legal usages of terms and respects authors' preferences in how they identify themselves and their communities, or the communities they discuss. Readers will notice, too, that authors use their preferred spelling for terms that can vary, such as the names of some peoples.

The title of this book and many of the chapters use the term **Aboriginal people** to refer collectively to Inuit, Métis and First Nations people, the three groups recognized in the Canadian Constitution as the descendents of the original people of North America. Some authors use "First peoples," "Indigenous peoples" or "Native peoples" rather than "Aboriginal peoples" as a collective term.

Inuit are the Aboriginal people of Arctic Canada, which includes the Inuvialuit region of the Northwest Territories, Nunavut, Nunavik (northern Quebec) and Nunatsiavut (northern Labrador).

Métis are people of mixed First Nation and European ancestry whose original settlements included parts of what we now know as the Northwest Territories, Nunavut, Ontario, Quebec and Alberta, as well as most of Saskatchewan and all of Manitoba.

The term **First Nations** has been adopted widely to replace the term **Indians**, which was used to describe the original inhabitants of Canada south of the Arctic and continues to be used as a legal term in the Indian Act. **Status Indian** is a legal term for those who are included on the federal Indian Register and are entitled to certain rights and benefits under the law. Status Indians are also referred to as **registered Indians**. **Treaty Indians** are status Indians who are members of First Nations that signed treaties with the Crown. **Non-status Indians** are those who have a biological link to a First Nation but who are unable to prove their status or have lost their status rights. Non-status Indians are not entitled to the same rights and benefits as status Indians.

The term **First Nation** is also used to refer to the name of a community, to replace the word "band," which is used in the Indian Act.

Visit the Journey to Healing web page at www.camh.ca/journeytohealing for related information and updates.

Foreword

VERN HARPER

The coming together of Aboriginal and mainstream Western ways of dealing with addiction and mental health issues is important in the healing journey of our Aboriginal communities. It is important because we need to learn about our identity in order to heal, and Aboriginal approaches to healing deal with identity. Our Native culture is passed on to us by our ancestors—it is who we are—but we live in the dominant Western culture. We need to understand both cultures so we can make good choices that will benefit us. This dual perspective is often ignored in mainstream addiction and mental health treatment models. But in the course of working with Aboriginal people who have mental health and addiction challenges, I have witnessed them becoming healthy through learning about their identity and culture and working with mainstream Western counsellors.

I worked for more than 10 years as the Elder of the Aboriginal Service at the Centre for Addiction and Mental Health (CAMH) in Toronto. I introduced Aboriginal ways of healing, such as the purification ceremony and the purification lodge. These ceremonies are commonly known as smudging and sweat lodges, but informal names miss the true meaning of these ceremonies. For many people, "sweat lodge" evokes images of a sauna; it doesn't convey the sacredness of the ceremony. If we are going to use the "white man's language," we need to use it in a meaningful way. A sweat lodge is in fact a purification lodge. Another inaccurate term is "peace pipe." There's no such thing. That's John Wayne, Hollywood propaganda. The correct term is "prayer pipe." In my teachings, the prayer pipe is equivalent to the Bible. It's our bible and it's all we need. The lodge is our synagogue, our church, our cathedral. It is natural and connected to the land.

At CAMH, bringing together Aboriginal and mainstream approaches to healing was sometimes a challenge because different concepts and values underlie each approach. But bringing these perspectives together has helped the people we serve. It has prepared them to heal and deal with their addictions. Joining these approaches has made a difference because for most of our people, mental health challenges and addiction have a lot to do with identity.

When Peter Menzies approached me about being the Elder for the Aboriginal Service, I wondered why he chose me. When he explained, it was clear that he was listening to his spirit. He knew that I had become a spiritual person, a spiritual Elder, and that's why he wanted me. I felt I knew Peter by connecting with his spirit. Peter is a strong Indian man. He believes that our people have to learn to live with and understand both Aboriginal and mainstream Western culture. That's what I respect, and that's what I do.

Peter had the strength to advocate for a full-time Elder, which allowed for the role to have real meaning. He was strong in his conviction and clear about the conditions I would need to serve our people well. One condition was that I would serve as a traditional Elder. Ours is an oral culture and Peter ensured that I would not have to write reports. He also pushed for full recognition of the Elder's role, insisting that I receive a good salary, not an honorarium.

What is the Elder's role? An Elder, as far as I'm concerned, helps people stay on the right road. What the Elder has that others don't have is life experience and spiritual development. Most people think that Elders are old, but not all of us are. I once met a 14-year-old Elder. He was recognized as a wise and spiritual man.

People ask me, "What gives you the right to do what you do?" And I respond, "I have the 'Cree'dentials." Seriously, though, I never asked to be an Elder, but when I realized that the people wanted me for that role I felt an obligation to them. And I thought, "If they're going to see me as an Elder, I don't want to be just an Elder—I want to be a good one."

I want to share some key teachings that are important for both our own people and those who work with them. First, I have learned through my teachers and experience that Indian women are much stronger than Indian men. I believe one reason is that Indian women know who they are. When they bond together, nothing will ever break that bond. Indian women have one of the most important things in our belief and culture: they have the fire of life. Our mothers tell us who we are. It took me a long time to really understand that and recognize that I am the son of my mother, a beautiful, strong Indian woman. I acknowledge that I come from her and that my grandmother was also a strong Indian woman. It is women who are the life-givers.

It is also important to acknowledge that we are spirit beings. People tend to see themselves as humans with spirit. But our belief system as Native people tells us that although we emerge from our mother's womb in the form of a physical body, we are spirit first; this physical world is not our home. We are here only for a very short time. The longer I live—I have been here 80 winters—the more I realize how short our time in this physical world really is. My body will go back into the earth from which I came, but my spirit will go home to the spirit world.

When I prepare a sacred altar, I include the four sacred elements—fire, water, wind and earth. The first element, fire, represents women, the life-givers. They have the fire of life. When a woman gives birth, her water breaks. Water, the second element, is the blood of Mother Earth. She needs this blood as we need water. When we emerge from the womb, we take our first breath of air—the third element, wind. Earth, Mother Earth, is the fourth element. In our culture, "mother" is a very important word— grandmother, mother, Mother Earth. For Native people, connection to the land is spiritual, sacred. We believe that all things have energy, all things are living, everything has spirit. That is the significance of the land. Even an old table contains life energy in the wood from which it is formed. And so our ceremonies incorporate Mother Earth.

When mainstream Western counsellors are dealing with Native clients something is missing. What is missing is the Native perspective—where we are coming from—and acknowledgment that we are spiritual beings. I see myself not as a religious person but as a spiritual person. People who are spiritual don't need a religion. The purification lodge is their church and the prayer pipe is their bible.

I would like to share some other thoughts related to the work that counsellors do. I see harm reduction as a positive thing. Sometimes people are not allowed into treatment or into a group unless they are clean or sober. But if I do not allow them to come in I'm rejecting them, I'm judging them. Still, I do have certain, I guess you could call them, rules. The people I work with have to behave themselves. I keep things simple and they respond to it. They respond to the kindness. Our culture is based on kindness, on love of the land, love of the people, and that's what I offer. My new work is on the street. I get out of the vehicle and sit with people. When others ask them why they respond to me, they say, "We know from his experience and his time with us that he loves us and we've got to learn to love him."

As an Elder, I believe it is important to walk the red road, especially when working with people who have mental health and addiction challenges. By walking the red road I mean being free of alcohol and other drugs and being sober minded—physically, mentally, emotionally and spiritually—in order to be a spiritual person. And that means total abstinence from substances.

A final teaching I will share is about tobacco. Tobacco is a medicine, an herb. We use tobacco to pray. It helps us return our essence to Mother Earth, from whom we come. We are taught that when tobacco is used properly, it will not cause harm. But now this medicine has been chemically treated. Smoking cigarettes is not using tobacco as a sacred medicine. It is using this herb improperly, not respecting it, and this causes harm. Yet smoking is culturally accepted and tobacco addiction is widespread. I have seen that it is the hardest addiction in the world to overcome.

I also see how we have been defeathered, our culture and identity stripped away. My uncle wanted to take me after my mother died when I was a toddler. But I was denied my relatives by Indian Affairs. I was denied my relatives when I was put in a shelter and in a foster home. I wanted to be with my family, but Indian Affairs, the government and the church wouldn't allow it. So I spent a lifetime trying to connect with my family, and I have. One reason for having the many children and grandchildren I have is to pass on who I am. I have always chosen Indian wives to give me Indian children. I prayed that my daughters would meet the right person so they would give me Indian grandchildren. The whole purpose of foster homes and residential schools was to defeather us, denying us of our culture. I was denied my culture and it has been very difficult for me. But as an Elder recognized by the people, I wear my feathers proudly.

Part 1

History and Experience

Chapter 1

Speaking from the Heart

CHERYLE PARTRIDGE

Waynaboozhoo, Aanii, Kwe kwe, Sago, Wachiya, Tansi, Kia ora, Bonjour.
Greetings.

Baybaamoosay-Kwe n'dishinaakaaz.
I was gifted with the spirit name "Woman who leaves healing tracks."

Migizi n'dodem.
I am a member of the Eagle dodem.

N'winiizhoo Midewiwin Kwe.
I am a second-degree Midewiwin woman.

Anishinaabe miinwaa Botwatomi n'dow.
I am of Ojibwe and Pottawatomi descent.

Wasauksing miinwaa N'Swakamok n'doonjibaa.
I am from Wasauksing First Nation, and I live and work in Sudbury, Ontario.

This is a glimpse at how Anishinaabek introduce ourselves. We try to include others by greeting them in their language if possible. In this way we show respect and inclusivity.

We begin a meeting, conference or ceremony with a prayer or invocation. Here is a prayer written by members of my home community.

Wasauksing Anamaawin

Mishomsinaan, Waabanong, gmiigwechwendimigoo maanda
  minobimaadiziwin,
jeh aanji kendimaang nishinaabemwin.
Mishomsinaan, Zhaawanong, gmiigwechwendimigoo, jeh
  minobimaadiziwaat,
jeh mshkowendimowaat niijaansinaanik.
Mishsomsinaan, Epgishmog, gmiigwechwendimigoo,
  mshkowendimowin,
Gchindendimowin, miinwaa jeh mshkowendimowaat kinah
  ndanwemaagnidak.
Mishomsinaan, Giiwedinong, zhewenim eh aakzijig jeh minoyaawaat,
miigwech minobimaadiziwin.
Mishomis Schkaawbewis, gmiigwechwendimigoo, jeneh waamdamaang
  gehnizhaayaang. Nokmis, widookooshnong jeh zhawendimaangedwaa
  nwiijeh bemaadizijig.
Schkaakmiikwe, gmiigwechwendimigoo maanda mniss endaayaang,
miinwaa kinah emiizyaang.
Gzhiminido gen giin, gmiigwechwendimigoo maanda
  Anishinaabemaadziwen
miinwaa kinah bimaadiziwen.

Wasauksing Prayer

Grandfather to the East, we give thanks for the Good Life,
That we relearn our language.
Grandfather to the South, we give thanks that our children have
  good health,
That they be strong.
Grandfather to the West, we give thanks for our strength, for
  happiness and the strength of all our families.
Grandfather to the North, pity those who are suffering, that they
  too have good health,
Thank you for all good health.

> Grandfather who walks the day sky, we give thanks that we have
>   good direction.
> Grandmother who walks the night sky, help us to have compassion
>   for the lives of others.
> Mother Earth, we give thanks for this island that we live on, for all
>   that you provide. Great forgiving spirit, to you we give thanks for
>   our Anishinaabe ways,
> For all of life itself.

I am a modern Ojibwe woman, and I have returned to the traditional and cultural ways of the Anishinaabe, which includes joining the Three Fires Midewiwin Lodge[1] and embracing its traditional healing practices. I have been attending Midewiwin ceremonies for the past 24 years and have never been so fulfilled— spiritually, emotionally, physically, mentally and intellectually. The Midewiwin teachings are transformative. I was transformed from someone who had been tentatively practising her culture to someone who proudly and eagerly partakes of all that is offered within the ceremonial lodge and the Aboriginal community. I became curious about the Midewiwin when my brother-in-law and his first cousin began attending ceremonies. I saw them change from being people who liked to party to being more serious-minded, responsible individuals. The changes were dramatic enough to draw remark, but also subtle because these men had always been kind, gentle and respectful; now they were even more so.

My curiosity about Midewiwin deepened when I took classes in Native studies with Professor James Dumont, who spoke about its teachings. There was a vibrant Midewiwin society here in Sudbury, and I began participating in sweats, teachings and ceremonies near the small town of St. Charles. One of our members had a large plot of farmland nearby where we held some of our seasonal ceremonies.

Midewiwin has been around for thousands of years. Members follow the old ways of living. We do not use foreign substances, such as alcohol or other drugs. We follow the Teachings of the Seven Grandfathers as closely as we can and try to attend spring ceremonies in Wisconsin. Our members live in Ontario, Manitoba, Saskatchewan, Michigan, Minnesota, Wisconsin and many other places. The teachings and traditions are spiritual and we respect and believe in them inherently.

I remember the first time I attended spring ceremonies in Bad River, Wisconsin. I was in awe at all the smiling, genuinely happy Anishinaabek I met. They recognized that I was "new" and went out of their way to make me feel welcome. All the sights, sounds, smells and feelings are still with me. It was then that I knew for certain that this was a way of life I wanted to follow as long as I lived. As I began to seriously pursue this way of life, I realized that it was familiar to me. It was inherent in my blood memory.

---

1 "Three Fires" refers to the Ojibwe, Odawa and Pottawatomi Nations. *Midewiwin* means "heart way."

The words of Toulouse (2006) resonated with me:

> The land and all that she provides is our way of life and the root of our cosmology. . . . All that is important in our sense and perception of the world around us is grounded in the earth beneath our feet. (p. 41)

That familiarity was there, the feeling of having heard those words before. They transported me to a journey I made in 1993 to attend the World Indigenous Peoples Conference on Education in Australia. Arriving at the airport in Sydney, I pictured the globe, and there I was, standing on the Australian continent upside down. I thought to myself, "Here is this little Anishinaabe-kwe from Wasauksing First Nation, a speck really, standing on the other side of the world upside down." That moment was one of the most humbling experiences of my life. What I was doing was identifying myself in relation to my home on Turtle Island (North America). It goes to show that no matter where you find yourself in the world, you are still you. You travel with your life experiences, your body's experiences and your relatives' and ancestors' experiences.

I would like to share a story about a visit I made to Mexico. We were a group of doctoral students who had been taken to a sacred site in the mountains. Our guide suggested that we start making our way down the mountain before it got dark. Everyone seemed to be well on their way, leaving the guide and me to descend together. (I was not nicknamed "Turtle" by my uncles for my quickness of movement!) A couple of large raindrops fell, and soon we were in the midst of a tropical, torrential downpour. Our little path was now a fast-moving river. I have to admit, I was starting to panic. "Hold my hand and step where I step," said the guide. I did as I was told. But then I heard murmurings coming from the bushes and small trees along the path. They were comforting me, telling me not to be afraid. I was instantly taken from panic to calmness by listening to my relatives the "standing people" (plants). I can relive that moment whenever I begin to feel nervous, and then calmness descends.

McKay (2002) described the relationships that are at the core of our spirituality: "Indigenous spirituality around the world is centred on the notion of our relationship to the whole Creation. We call the earth 'our mother.' The animals are 'our brothers and sisters.' Even what biologists describe as inanimate, we call our 'relatives'" (p. 28). In our Native studies class, Professor Dumont explained that these relatives could live without us, but we humans could not live without them. That was one of my "aha" moments. Even though I instinctively knew we were related, I felt a new sense of respect and reverence.

My experiences hint at some of the perspectives that many Aboriginal people share. The most profound perspective involves connection to the land. Lyons (1985) described that relationship:

> That is why we are here; he (Creator) put us in this land. He did not put the white people here; he put us here with our families, and by

that I mean the bears, the deer, and the other animals. . . . We share
land in common, not only among ourselves but with the animals and
everything that lives in our land. (p. 19)

Aboriginal peoples have inhabited this land since time immemorial. Our teachings, which have been passed down from generation to generation, for countless generations, tell us that this is where we belong. It is probably why we have never sailed the
oceans looking for new places to settle and call home, as the Europeans did. We knew
our home was here on Turtle Island. We accepted that and were more than happy
to stay, and to discover, remember and pass on the knowledge of our territory to
future generations.

It is important to understand the relationship that existed in the time before
contact, and still does, between Aboriginal peoples and the other inhabitants of this
great land—plants, animals, water, rocks, everything above and below the surface of
Mother Earth (as the land was called by the people who lived here). The Lakota Sioux
spiritual leader Fools Crow called these relationships "linkages": "Mind, body and
spirit are linked together. People, other creatures, and the rest of Creation are linked
together. Thinking in dimensions like these . . . stretches and expands the mind"
(Fools Crow, as cited in Mails, 1991). In other words, Aboriginal peoples considered
themselves related to everything and everyone, and they respected the environment as
they respected one another.

Prior to contact, Aboriginal peoples lived as one with the land, the sky, the
water, the plants, the animals, the winds and one another. There was no territory not
occupied by Aboriginal peoples. As Elder Benton-Banai (2002) explained, "We . . . have
a history that goes back 50,000 years on this continent which is now known as North
America, but which has always been known to us as Turtle Island" (p. 16). Their
territories were vast. Most peoples were hunters and gatherers and gave the earth
time to rest and recover from their hunting of animals and gathering of berries,
medicinal plants and other necessities. They believed they would always occupy
the lands they were born on, their parents had been born on and in which their
ancestors were buried.

Aboriginal peoples were shaped by their relationship with Mother Earth; they
adapted to their specific environments. Those who lived near the oceans, rivers and
lakes built their relationships with the water for transportation, trading and food, as
well as using land-based resources for shelter and clothing. Those who lived in the
Arctic built their relationships with the snow and ice in the winter and depended on
the abundant mammals and sea life. During the short summer, they harvested the
plants and berries that grew in their territory. Those who lived on the plains depended
on their relationships with the buffalo and local plants. They were mainly nomadic
and travelled with the seasons, living on the plains during the summer and moving
to higher ground that provided vegetation and protection during the harsh winters.
Those who lived in mixed woodland settings based their relationship on hunting the

plentiful deer, moose, bear, beaver and rabbit. They harvested the wild rice and farmed small root vegetables, squash and maize.

Aboriginal peoples have always been researchers. We would have certainly perished had we not learned how to live on Turtle Island's back, with its countless environmental quirks. As Battiste and Henderson (2000) explained, Aboriginal peoples were carriers of the knowledge of their local environments: "Indigenous knowledge . . . is the expression of the vibrant relationships between the people, their ecosystems, and the other living beings and spirits that share their lands" (p. 42).

We had systems in place that ensured our survival and that of our environment. In our families, each member was considered important. Within our communities everyone was treated with respect, from the tiniest baby, who was a gift from G'chi-Manido[2], to the oldest member, to whom G'chi-Manido had given the gift of long life. Each person had a special place within the community circle. When we know where we belong, when we know where we come from, who our ancestors are, when we know our extended family and our roles, when we know the patterns that exist within our territory and that an unseen power exists and cares for all of Creation, then we can be assured that our mental health is in balance.

Aboriginal peoples are diverse and have different beliefs, depending on what part of Turtle Island they inhabit. However, we also share some common beliefs or world views: everything in the world is connected; unseen spiritual powers exist and affect all things; everything constantly changes in recurring cycles; humans need to be in harmony with one another and with nature (Reed, 1999).

The notion of reciprocity is one which is of particular importance. Dickason (2006) used the term "reciprocating forces," which implies that reciprocity happens naturally. It also happens consciously when we give thanks to G'chi-Manido, the Great Spirit, the Creator for the blessings we have received. We are thankful for the air we breathe, the water we drink, the land we live and walk upon, for the plants that provide our food and fuel, for the animals that provide our clothing, shelter and food. Today we can purchase much of what we need, but we must still be thankful for it. We have a standing joke in our home: when my partner returns from shopping, he says, "It was a good hunting trip," and we have a chuckle.

We can reciprocate in the form of a daily prayer or invocation—through spoken words or thoughts. G'chi-Manido hears these thoughts as though they had been shouted to the universe. (One does not have to wait until a certain hour, on a certain day, in a certain building, to communicate reciprocity to G'chi-Manido.) We also demonstrate reciprocity in the physical sense; for example, sacred tobacco is offered to the earth to give thanks to strawberry plants for giving up their fruits so we can have some sweet sustenance. Knudtson and Suzuki (1992) called such gestures "the living circle of reciprocity" (p. 88).

Before Europeans arrived in North America, Aboriginal peoples had established a

---

2   *G'chi-Manido* is another name for the Great Spirit or Creator.

strong cultural foundation that included:
- a carefully chosen geographical location considering allies and safety
- distinctive, self-caring and self-sustaining family units that included extended family
- use of local resources for shelter, clothing, transportation, storage and fuel
- systems of planning for year-round sustenance needs
- systems (e.g., clans) that ensured the holistic good governance of family systems
- a high value placed on Elders' life experiences and knowledge to educate
- a high value placed on life and all its stages, from the womb through to death
- use and development of a spoken language
- ceremonies to celebrate and honour G'chi-Manido / Great Spirit, as well as special community events
- use of natural features and formations of the environment when providing directions (Mussell, 2005, p. 105).[3]

With this strong cultural foundation, Aboriginal peoples were able to care for their families, extended families and Elders. Each person had a role to play and tried to fulfil its responsibilities. Elders were the teachers, storytellers and carriers of the knowledge of their people. The medicine people and healers used Mother Earth's pharmacy to heal sickness; they depended on their dreams and visions to counsel people.

I often mention spiritual aspects of life throughout this narrative. The Aboriginal world view is holistic; when we talk about being "in balance," it encompasses the spiritual, mental, physical and emotional aspects of ourselves (Assembly of First Nations, 1994; Bopp et al., 1985; Nabigon, 2006). Being in balance means "exercising the total capacity of body, mind, heart and experience in total responsiveness and total relationship to the whole environment" (Dumont, 2006, p. 25). Mussell and colleagues (1991) traced this value to before the time of contact with Europeans: "The value of balance for holistic health was fundamental, and was honoured in all activities throughout life. The culture had well-established practices for teaching the people how to maintain balance and how to right the balance when it was upset" (p. 20). Mussell and colleagues (1991) described how this balance is transmitted from mother to child:

> From conception, the fetus would benefit from the self-discipline of the mother who provided a balanced environment for her unborn through her moderation in eating, drinking, working, expression of emotions, positive thinking and spiritual practices. From birth the child was shown that balance was important and extremes of behaviour were unacceptable. (p. 20)

Mussell and colleagues (1991) explained how this balance can be disturbed: "Over-focusing or under-focusing on any one aspect upsets the balance of the four. Thus *mental* health . . . is inseparable from *emotional, physical* and *spiritual* health" (p. 19).

---

3   For a discussion about the elements of this cultural foundation, see chapter 14.

The medicine wheel, a concept used by some First Nations, has been used to convey the notions of wholeness, balance and inclusion. It is depicted as a circle divided by two straight lines to form four equal parts. Its teachings symbolize many concepts, ideas and values. One concept is the cardinal directions, with the four parts of the wheel representing north, south, east and west. "The symbolic importance of the cardinal directions to wholeness is pivotal," according to Hart (2002, p. 40). Regnier (1994) elaborated on this concept:

> Whenever one stands in the world, there are always four equal directions. Without all the directions, the world is incomplete and cannot be. It is the unity of these directions that makes the whole a reality. Each direction relies on the existence of the other directions for its own identity as a direction. Each direction reflects differences in the world (plenitude) and sets out the possibility for interconnectedness. (p. 132)

Other important concepts that can be articulated through the medicine wheel teachings include:
- the four human aspects: spiritual, emotional, physical and mental/intellectual
- the four stages of life: birth/infancy, childhood/youth, adulthood and senior/elder/death
- the four races of human: red, yellow, black and white
- the four primary elements: mineral/earth, fire, water and wind/air
- the four seasons: spring, summer, fall and winter
- the four sacred medicines: tobacco, cedar, sage and sweetgrass
- the four aspects of Indigenous intelligence: way of seeing, way of relating, way of thinking, way of being
- the five human characteristics: feelings, relationships, respect, caring and healing
- the "five rascals" of human characteristics: inferiority, envy, resentment, apathy and jealousy
- plants, animals and the cosmos.

Each of these elements is part of a living whole, which is not complete without all these elements. It is not possible to compartmentalize any aspect of the medicine wheel: "One of the hallmarks of an Aboriginal approach to healing is the focus on holism, specifically a consideration of the spiritual, mental, physical, and emotional aspects of the person" (Hill & Coady, 2003, p. 46). In the succinct words of Bopp and colleagues (1985), "The Medicine Wheel turns forever" (p. 9).

The sense of balance valued in Aboriginal cultures was profoundly affected by the appearance of Europeans on Turtle Island. The oral tradition of the Anishinaabe mentions their arrival: Seven prophecies were brought to the Anishinaabe by seven prophets many hundreds of years ago. These prophecies came to be known as the Seven Fires. Below I recount the Fourth Fire, as presented by Benton-Banai (1988).

Originally, the Fourth Fire was given to our ancestors by two prophets, although they came as one. They told our people of the coming of the "light-skinned race," what we now know as the white race. One of the prophets said that we would know the future of our people by which face the newcomers were wearing. If they came wearing the face of *nee-kon'-i-win* (brotherhood), then there would come a time of positive change for our future generations. We would recognize the face of brotherhood if the light-skinned race came with no weapons, only its knowledge and a handshake. Our two nations would join together and form one mighty nation. It would be joined by two other nations to forge the mightiest nation of all. The second prophet warned us to beware of the light-skinned race if they wore the face of *ni-boo-win* (death). The prophet explained that the two faces look very much alike, so if they came carrying weapons, if they looked like they were suffering, then beware, because they could fool you. Their hearts could be filled with greed for the land and its abundant resources. The prophet said, "Do not accept them in total trust. You shall know that the face they wear is the one of death if the rivers run with poison and fish become unfit to eat. You shall know them by these many things" (Benton-Banai, 1988, pp. 89–90).

We are now in a different and rapidly changing era, in which anything is possible. I cannot emphasize enough the hope and optimism that Aboriginal people have for the next seven generations. Our current reality is that we have regained our footing on Mother Earth and we are confidently stepping into the future. We are restructuring our Aboriginal society with our vision of self-government, cultural revitalization, language renewal and peace-building with the inhabitants of Turtle Island. These are realities that will rebuild our cultural foundation. Aboriginal youth have started to regain their voices by way of the Idle No More movement, which is mobilizing people across the nation and across the globe. LaDuke (1999) provided a glimpse into the hope and faith we have in the ancient traditions:

> The last 150 years have seen a great holocaust. There have been more species lost in the past 150 years than since the Ice Age. During the same time, Indigenous peoples have been disappearing from the face of the earth. Over 2,000 nations of Indigenous peoples have gone extinct in the western hemisphere and one nation disappears from the Amazon rainforest every year.
>
> There is a direct relationship between the loss of cultural diversity and the loss of biodiversity. Wherever Indigenous peoples still remain, there is also a corresponding enclave of biodiversity. Trickles of rivers still running in the Northwest are home to the salmon still being sung back by Native people. The last few Florida panthers remain in the presence of traditional Seminoles, hidden away in the great cypress swamps of the Everglades. (p. 1)

As is our tradition, this narrative began with a prayer. And it will end with one. This prayer that I wrote reminds us that we have much to be thankful for, today and every day.

Giving Thanks[4]

Waynaboozhoo G'chi-Manido
Greetings Great Spirit

Waynaboozhoo Mishoomisag miinwaa Nookmisag
Greetings Grandfathers and Grandmothers

Waynaboozhoo kiinwaa nemdibiyek
Greetings to all of you who sit in these directions

Odi Waabanong
East

Odi Zhaawanong
South

Odi Epingiishmok
West

Odi Giiwedinong
North

G'chi-Miigwech for all you do for all of us who reside on *Shkagamik-Kwe* (Mother Earth)

G'chi-Miigwech for all you do to keep our *n'biish* (waters) clean and sparkling for the generations

G'chi-Miigwech for all you do to keep our air clean and pure for the generations

G'chi-Miigwech for all you do to keep *Shkagamik-Kwe* alive and well for the generations

---

4 "Giving Thanks," by C. Partridge, 2012, *Native Social Work Journal, 8,* p. i. Reprinted with permission.

G'chi-Miigwech for all you do to keep our *ishpiming* (Sky World) revolving in our sacred circular motion

For all these things we say *Miigwech, Miigwech, Miigwech, Miigwech* (Thank you).

References

Assembly of First Nations. (1994). *Breaking the Silence: An Interpretive Study of Residential School Impact and Healing as Illustrated by the Stories of First Nations Individuals*. Ottawa: Author.

Battiste, M. & Henderson, J.Y. (2000). *Protecting Indigenous Knowledge and Heritage: A Global Challenge*. Saskatoon, SK: Purich.

Benton-Banai, E. (1988). *The Mishomis Book: The Voice of the Ojibway*. Hayward, WI: Indian Country Communications.

Benton-Banai, E. (2002). *Ojibwemowin*: Ojibwe oral tradition. In T.D. Peacock & M. Wisuri (Eds.), *Ojibwe* Waasa Inaabidaa: *We Look in All Directions* (pp. 14–37). Afton, MN: Afton Press.

Bopp, J., Bopp, M., Brown, L. & Lane, Jr., P. (1985). *The Sacred Tree* (2nd ed.). Lethbridge, AB: Four Worlds International Institute for Human and Community Development.

Dickason, O.P. (2006). *A Concise History of Canada's First Nations*. Toronto: Oxford University Press.

Dumont, J. (2006, October 18). *Indigenous intelligence*. Public lecture at the University of Sudbury, Sudbury, ON.

Hart, M.A. (2002). *Seeking Mino-Pimatisiwin: An Aboriginal Approach to Helping*. Halifax, NS: Fernwood.

Hill, G. & Coady, N. (2003). Comparing Euro Western counseling and Aboriginal healing methods: An argument for the effectiveness of aboriginal approaches to healing. *Native Social Work Journal, 5*, 44–63.

Knudtson, P. & Suzuki, D. (1992). *Wisdom of the Elders*. Toronto: Stoddart.

LaDuke, W. (1999). *All Our Relations: Native Struggles for Land and Life*. Cambridge, MA: South End Press.

Lyons, O. (1985). Traditional Native philosophies relating to Aboriginal rights. In M. Boldt & J.A. Long (Eds.), *The Quest for Justice: Aboriginal Peoples and Aboriginal Rights* (pp. 19–24). Toronto: University of Toronto Press.

Mails, T.E. (1991). *Fools Crow: Wisdom and Power*. Tulsa, OK: Council Oak Books.

McKay, S. (2002). Rooted in Creation. In J. Bird, L. Land & M. Macadam (Eds.), *Nation to Nation: Aboriginal Sovereignty and the Future of Canada* (rev. ed.; pp. 27–33). Toronto: Irwin.

Mussell, W.J. (2005). *Warrior-Caregivers: Understanding the Challenges and Healing of First Nations Men*. Retrieved from Aboriginal Healing Foundation website: www.ahf.ca

Mussell, W.J., Adler, M.T. & Nicholls, W.M. (1991). *Making Meaning of Mental Health Challenges in First Nations: A Freirean Approach*. Chilliwack, BC: Salishan Institute Society.

Nabigon, H. (2006). *The Hollow Tree: Fighting Addiction with Traditional Native Healing*. Montreal: McGill-Queen's University Press.

Partridge, C. (2012). Giving Thanks. *Native Social Work Journal, 8*, i.

Reed, K. (1999). *Aboriginal Peoples: Building for the Future*. Toronto: Oxford University Press.

Regnier, R. (1994). The sacred circle: A process pedagogy of healing. *Interchange: A Quarterly Review of Education, 25*, 129–144.

Toulouse, P.R. (2006). *Anishinabek Research Practices: Sharing a Living Story*. M'Chigeeng, ON: Kenjgewin Teg Educational Institute.

ABOUT THE AUTHOR

Cheryle Partridge, BSW, MSW, RSW, is an Anishinaabe-kwe from Wasauksing First Nation. She is very proud of the roles she plays within her family: daughter, sister, niece, cousin, auntie, partner, mother, grandmother, great-grandmother. She has been a lifelong advocate for social justice for Aboriginal people who strives to live and abide by the Teachings of the Seven Grandfathers and the teachings of the Three Fires Midewiwin Lodge. Cheryle teaches in the School of Native Human Services at Laurentian University in Sudbury, Ontario. Her interests lie in traditional knowledge, culture and tradition, mental health and residential schools.

Chapter 2

Setting the Foundation: A Brief History of Colonization in Canada

DAVID LONG

More than 400 years of European colonialism—the "colonial project"—has contributed to an array of health and social problems for First Nations, Métis and Inuit[1] in Canada (Cooke & Long, 2011). At the time of European contact, the Aboriginal peoples of North America had adapted to the land and diversified into hundreds of self-governing tribal groups with well over 50 languages (Dickason & McNab, 2009). Each group had its own culture and traditions, and while some tribes and communities were fairly settled, most pre-contact peoples in North America lived a semi-nomadic hunting, fishing and gathering way of life. The world view of most of these groups was Indigenous, meaning that they experienced "all their relations" with living and non-living beings and entities in cyclical, holistic and spiritual terms (Bopp et al., 1984). Certainly one of the keys to understanding the brief socio-historical account offered in this chapter is that colonially induced health and social problems have often made realizing the unique, self-governing visions of Aboriginal peoples a daunting and at times seemingly impossible task. Nonetheless, Aboriginal peoples have never simply been passive victims of the European colonial project (Lux, 1992; Royal Commission on Aboriginal Peoples [RCAP], 1996). It is also important to understand that it has been Aboriginal peoples' commitment to honouring the sacredness of all their relations, including their relation with the land, that has enabled them to maintain hope

---

1 For definitions of these terms, see the preface.

in the face of the countless physical, social, economic and political challenges they have encountered, both before and after European contact (Long, 2011).

Early Effects of Colonialism: Warfare and Disease

Prior to European contact, most societies of the First peoples[2] of North America were well organized, culturally distinct and economically self-sufficient. Indeed, it was the "intelligent manipulation of nature backed by supportive social structures" that made "survival possible under extremely difficult conditions" (Dickason & McNab, 2009, p. 30). Despite their rich and diverse cultures, these First peoples shared the Indigenous view that they inhabited a materially, socially and spiritually integrated world ecosystem in which, ideally, humans exist in equal and respectful relationships with every living and non-living being and entity in Creation (Bopp et al., 1984).

This perspective stands in stark contrast to the world view of 16th-century Western Europeans, for whom the relationship between humans and nature was drawn largely from the Judeo-Christian teaching that humans have dominion over the earth and every living thing. In part to legitimize the colonial expansion of their empires, the French and the British developed various measures to quantify a people's humanness and level of civilization. These included mode of obtaining food (hunting and gathering versus agriculture); dietary practices; apparent lack of political structure and reasoned thought; indifference to suffering and cruelty; language and the lack of writing; housing; nudity and cannibalism (Dickason, 1984). Given their measures of civilization and the obvious bias that informed their observations of the First peoples they encountered, French and British explorers, missionaries and government representatives commonly referred to these people as "relatively innocent children of nature" at best, or "savages" at worst (Dickason, 1984). Defining First peoples in this way helped to justify attempts by Europeans to Christianize or "civilize" *l'homme sauvage*, which they hoped in the end would eradicate "the Indian problem altogether" (LaRocque, 2012, p. 83). In other words, the myth of the savage became a key element in the ideology of Europeans who were committed to furthering their colonial empires by conquering the First peoples of Canada through whatever means they could (Dickason, 1984).

The Aboriginal population, estimated to be at about 500,000 at the time of European contact (RCAP, 1996), declined significantly soon after the arrival of Europeans, and for some peoples, the decline toward extinction was as high as 50 to 90 per cent (Adams, 1995; Dickason & McNab, 2009). One reason for this was violence and warfare between Europeans and Aboriginal peoples, as well as among Aboriginal groups (Romaniuc, 2000). The formation of alliances with Europeans escalated wars between certain Aboriginal groups, which fought one another over the right to gain political favour with their European allies or to have access to European goods and

---

2   The term *First peoples* is commonly used when speaking about First Nations and Inuit, and sometimes includes Métis.

weapons.[3] As more and more Aboriginal groups adopted the use of European guns and swords in battle, Aboriginal death rates increased accordingly.

The rapid decline of the Aboriginal population soon after European arrival was also a consequence of Aboriginal people's lack of immunity to diseases of European origin, such as smallpox, tuberculosis, influenza and measles (Waldram, 1997). Successive waves of these infectious diseases devastated Aboriginal populations across the East Coast, as well as in much of Upper and Lower Canada throughout the 16th, 17th and 18th centuries (Cook, 1973; Wesley-Esquimaux & Smolewski, 2004). Beginning in the early 1870s, it took a mere 10 years for tuberculosis to become the primary cause of death among First Nations living on the western plains (Kelm, 1998). This pattern of post-contact relations had the same devastating effects on many Aboriginal groups in the Americas (Cook, 1998).

While lack of immunity to certain diseases of European origin devastated the Aboriginal population, other factors played a significant role in its rapid decline (Daschuk et al., 2006). For one, disease epidemics both increased the number of deaths and decreased the number of births among affected tribes. In her examination of the impact of the 1918 influenza epidemic on some prairie Indian groups, Lux (1992) suggested that poor living conditions and nutrition and lack of access to proper medical care contributed to high death rates compared with non-Aboriginal populations.[4] Undernourishment was another factor that contributed to low disease resistance (Tough, 1996). Traditional diets were altered as Europeans displaced Aboriginal peoples from their lands and killed off the animals traditionally used for food and furs. As a result, Aboriginal peoples had little choice but to pay for imported European foods, which had much lower nutritional value than their traditional foods. Traditional health resources were also altered as Elders and medicine people lost their power and credibility (as they were unable to help dying people), while missionaries and European-trained medical professionals became the "expert" health providers (Wesley-Esquimaux & Smolewski, 2004). From contact to the mid-1900s, medical professionals and government officials exacerbated health problems by largely ignoring the impact European diseases were having on Aboriginal people and communities (Kelm, 1998; Lux, 1992).

The analyses of Cook (1998), Adams (1995), Alfred (1999) and Wesley-Esquimaux and Smolewski (2004) clearly indicate that the term "genocide" can be legitimately applied to colonialism in Canada. Colonial correspondence and other official documents confirm that many government and church officials were committed to "exterminating" Indigenous languages and cultures, and that the serious bodily and mental harm their policies and practices inflicted were of genocidal proportions. Even

---

3   Although war and fighting among Aboriginal groups involved killing, some Aboriginal groups took prisoners of war as slaves (Dickason & McNab, 2009). Much less is currently known about European practices of slavery, although Adams (1995) argued that slavery resulted in the disappearance and death of relatively large numbers of Aboriginal people.
4   Marshall's (1996) analysis of the decline and eventual extinction of the Beothuk tribe of Newfoundland provides rather sobering insight into the devastating social, economic, political and eventually mortal consequences of an ongoing colonial project of calculated violence carried out against one particular tribe of Aboriginal people.

in the face of widespread colonial destruction, Aboriginal leaders showed wisdom, resolve and political acumen when negotiating the terms of official relations between their people and colonial governments.

The Colonial Imprint in Early Treaty and Trade Relations

The First peoples of the land that was to become Canada were well versed in the treaty-making process long before European explorers, fur traders or settlers arrived in North America (Dickason, 2011). Although many treaties between First peoples were oral, written agreements such as pictographs and two-row wampum belts were often used to record conflict resolutions and to formalize trade and marriage arrangements between tribes (Belanger & Newhouse, 2011; Dickason & McNab, 2009). When the Europeans arrived, the First peoples used their experience in trade and treaty relations in their dealings with these newcomers.

Treaty agreements with First peoples were very important to the French and British, who had begun to develop the fur trade in Eastern Canada and the Maritimes by the mid-17th century. Europeans recognized that success in the fur trade required the help and co-operation of First peoples, and so their initial treaties with them were mostly economic in nature. The rapid spread of the fur trade indicates that, at least initially, there were economic benefits for all involved. Europeans obtained the furs they needed through Aboriginal peoples' knowledge of the land and its animals, and First Nations peoples and Inuit gained access to European goods such as weapons, gunpowder, agricultural tools, blankets and cooking utensils (Dickason & McNab, 2009). The mutual benefits of trade relations were communicated through the early treaties, and it is evident that those involved recognized from the very beginning that treaty agreements were expressions of mutual respect between trading partners. The fur trade did not come without cost, however, as it soon contributed to numerous social and political problems within and between Aboriginal communities. For example, competition for trade increased tensions and divisions between many already divided tribes (Rich, 1991). These tensions and divisions increased substantially as the fur trade declined, as did the economic hardships for those who had come to depend on the income and goods they received from their European trading partners (Adams, 1989).

Trade-based treaties were replaced by peace and friendship treaties at the beginning of the 18th century. Europeans intent on settling in North America soon recognized the importance of developing peaceful relations with the local Aboriginal peoples (Dickason & McNab, 2009). In the Maritimes, for example, peace and friendship treaties were used to end hostilities and encourage co-operation between the British and First Nations. The French also signed treaties with Inuit and numerous First Nations with whom they had been in conflict for a number of years (Rich, 1991).

Peace and friendship treaties served another purpose for the British and French. Tensions had been rising for some time between the two European rivals over control of the land, and they both saw peace and friendship treaties as ways to develop stronger military alliances with their First Nations treaty partners (Taylor, 1991).

Nonetheless, colonial development has always taken more than a few unjust twists and turns. Soon after defeating the French in the Seven Years War (1754–1763 in North America), the British began replacing peace and friendship treaties with treaties based on territorial rights (Miller, 2004). Unfortunately for the First Nations, the British regarded this new approach to treaty making as a means to extinguish First Nations' inherent land rights (Dickason & McNab, 2009). The Canadian government continued this approach soon after Confederation in 1967 by signing 11 numbered treaties[5] with First Nations between 1871 and 1921.[6] Most of the numbered treaties stipulated that First Nations cede their interest in large tracts of their lands throughout the Prairies, the North and northwestern Ontario, which became "Crown land," in return for smaller tracts of land, which became "reserves" (Taylor, 1991). Each numbered treaty promised that every registered member of a treaty First Nation would retain the right to hunt and fish on its home reserve or on unoccupied Crown land and receive a small annuity and various goods (Taylor, 1991).[7]

After acquiring these large tracts of land, the government intensified the expansion of European settlement across Canada by constructing the Canadian Pacific Railway and by offering generous land grants to European immigrants (Dickason & McNab, 2009). The railway delivered significant numbers of European settlers to the western prairies, and it was not long before rapidly growing new communities and towns began encroaching on traditional First Nations territories. The destructive patterns of colonial expansion also played out on the Prairies: over-hunting of buffalo and other animals by European settlers and trappers soon depleted the traditional food sources of many First Nations (Dickason & McNab, 2009). This, combined with forced displacement; the introduction of "foreign" diseases; drastic changes in diet; and the loss of traditional sources of identity, healing and leadership had devastating effects on First Nations populations (Lux, 1992; Wesley-Esquimaux & Smolewski, 2004).[8]

Relations between First Nations and Government

While government support to establish settlements throughout Western and Northern Canada in the late-19th and early-20th centuries affected First Nations, Inuit and

---

5   These are also called the Land Cession or Post-Confederation Treaties.

6   Not all First Nations signed treaties. Many First Nations in Western Canada, particularly British Columbia, had no formal written agreements with the Canadian government.

7   Most of the treaties also mention the provision of educational services, although only Treaties 7 and up include a "medicine chest" (i.e., health services) provision.

8   As noted later in this chapter, a very similar story played out among Inuit in Canada's North.

Métis, two legal documents have had the most far-reaching effects on the lives of Aboriginal peoples in Canada. The first was the Royal Proclamation of 1763, a decree by King George III, which claimed ownership of British territory in North America and established guidelines for European settlement of Aboriginal territories. The proclamation prohibited settlers from claiming land occupied by First Nations, and clearly stated that only the Crown could buy land from "said Indians." Further, it acknowledged that the British agreed to protect and deal fairly with "the Indians" in terms of their land (Dickason, 2011). While First Nations have long argued that the proclamation affirms their sovereignty as well as title to their lands, those who read the document through colonial eyes see it as one of the first legal documents to establish the fiduciary relationship[9] between the British Crown and First Nations.

In 1867, the British North America (BNA) Act transferred responsibility for First Nations from the British to the Canadian government. Section 91(24) established that the federal government had legislative jurisdiction over "Indians and lands reserved for the Indians." In order to consolidate many different pieces of legislation that concerned First Nations, the government passed the Indian Act in 1876. Among other things, the act legally defined who was allowed to claim Indian status in Canada, the rights and obligations that accompanied that status, the structure of Canada's reserve system and the nature of Indian "self-government." The Indian Act also granted the federal government power to:
• prohibit many traditional ceremonies
• specify how Indian bands would elect their leaders and administer their affairs
• expropriate portions of reserve lands for roads, railways and other public works
• lease out uncultivated reserve lands to non-Indians for farming or pasture
• move an entire reserve if it was deemed expedient
• remove Indian children from their communities and send them to residential schools (RCAP, 1996, pp. 235–308).

The Indian Act thus served to take away self-governance and self-determination from First Nations. While a number of amendments to the act in 1884 granted First Nations wider powers over local government and raising money, other amendments took away most of those powers by stipulating that an Indian agent must serve as chairman of each band council.[10] Thus, Indian agents had immense power over everyday life on the reserves. The Indian Act stayed in place until 1951, when revisions to it lifted the bans on many traditional ceremonies and removed certain regulations that had prevented First Nations peoples from moving away from or back to their reserves.

The Indian Act also established different relationships between the Canadian government and various Aboriginal groups by specifying that only members of Indian bands that had signed treaties with the government would be entitled to the rights and

---

9 Fiduciary responsibility means that one party acknowledges its legal obligation to protect and care for the assets and/or rights of another, and to act in the best interest of another rather than for its own benefit or profit.
10 An Indian agent was a Canadian government official authorized to oversee the implementation of the Indian Act with respect to a particular Aboriginal reserve or band.

benefits described in the act. Such individuals are still referred to as registered Indians or status Indians. Despite the fact that Inuit and Métis (often called "half-breeds") had been acknowledged in many government reports and documents, the Indian Act made it clear that the federal government was willing to accept fiduciary responsibility only for registered status Indians (Belanger & Newhouse, 2011; Wall, 2000).[11]

According to the Truth and Reconciliation Commission of Canada (2012), the first and most overwhelmingly destructive expression of formal governmental "support" for Aboriginal peoples was residential schooling. The federal government had joined forces with Christian churches to promote the value of a "civilized" education for Aboriginal children, and the vision that informed their efforts was unapologetically colonial. They were convinced that "civilizing" Aboriginal children could only be achieved by removing them from all family and community influences and re-socializing them into the Western way of life (Hare, 2011).[12] While residential schooling is now receiving a great deal of public attention, it is but one of the many areas of governmental responsibility for First Nations addressed in the Indian Act. As the Idle No More movement sought to point out, the sweeping power that the Indian Act established over virtually every area of the lives of First Nations peoples provided the government with a permanent, legally sanctioned foothold for the colonial project in Canada. As noted below, this project has also significantly affected the lives of Inuit, Métis and non-status Indians.

Recognition for Inuit, Métis and Non-Status Indians

Apart from a relatively brief early foray into trading with Inuit, European and Canadian colonizers had taken little interest in the North. Thus, Inuit had remained largely insulated from colonial influences before and during the residential school experiment. Things changed just prior to the Second World War, when the Canadian government started building airbases and more permanent settlements to establish a strategic military and civilian presence in the region. Northern development continued into the mid-1950s through the Canadian government's High Arctic relocation program, which introduced educational, health and economic development services in a number of permanent locations throughout the North. Not surprisingly, the rapid influx of Europeans into these regions depleted traditional food sources and displaced many small, nomadic communities (Dickason & McNab, 2009; Romaniuc, 2000). Most Inuit gradually settled in these administrative centres to gain access to food and government services, and so within a relatively short period of time their traditional

---

11 The fourth major Aboriginal population group is non-status Indians. Unlike with status Indians and Inuit, the rights of Métis and non-status Indians were not fully recognized by the Canadian government until 2013, when the courts decided that the federal government has a fiduciary responsibility to them as Aboriginal people under section 35 of the Canadian Constitution.

12 For a discussion about residential schools, see chapter 3.

hunting and gathering way of life all but came to an end (Dickason & McNab, 2009).

The changes Inuit experienced were similar to those experienced by Aboriginal groups in the south. Profound changes in their social and economic circumstances also contributed to unemployment, poverty and food insecurity among Inuit. Rates of serious illness and death increased rapidly due to lack of immunity to diseases of European origin (Romaniuc, 2000), their inability to afford the extremely expensive but unhealthy European food (Wesley-Esquimaux & Smolewski, 2004) and the lack of specialized health care in northern nursing stations (Willows et al., 2009). Growing dependence on Western medicine and health care also seriously undermined the roles of traditional healers and medicines, which served to gradually strip away the traditional sense of community identity among Inuit (Cooke & Long, 2011).

Despite the many problems caused by the establishment of Canadian military and administrative settlements in the North, and although the Supreme Court of Canada had affirmed Inuits' right to be included in the Indian Act in 1939, the Canadian government paid relatively little attention to Inuit rights and made little effort to work with them to establish a territory for them until the late 1960s. In 1969, the government appointed a commissioner of Native claims and also provided funding to Aboriginal associations that were interested in making a claim (Dickason & McNab, 2009). A number of associations soon formed to pursue their land claims in the North, including the Inuit Tapirisat of Canada in 1971 and the Northern Quebec Inuit Association in 1972. Their efforts were bolstered by three 1973 court decisions that acknowledged that Aboriginal title to their lands was a right stemming from their long-term use and occupation of lands prior to European colonization. The territory of Nunavut was finally established in 1999 when the Nunavut Act was passed (Wall, 2000).

Métis are another Aboriginal group that has realized full constitutional recognition during the last 30 years. Métis are people born from the unions of Aboriginal women and European men. As Métis women and men intermarried, they eventually developed into a distinct Aboriginal nation with a shared history, culture, language, kinship connections and traditional territories based largely in western and northwestern Canada (Wall, 2000). When Manitoba entered Confederation in 1870, section 31 of the Manitoba Act stated that 1.4 million acres in the province was to be reserved for Métis. Under section 31, Métis individuals were entitled to 160 acres of land or a scrip (certificate of land grant) valued at either $160 or $240, depending on the age of the applicant. Unfortunately for Métis, government policy allowed scrips to be sold to anyone. This allowed for a great deal of unscrupulous buying and selling of scrip and scrip lands by "middlemen," who benefitted economically by speculating on land that could have provided a potential homeland with Aboriginal title for Métis (Augustus, 2005). The government's woefully complicated and disorganized approach to the administration of scrip policy also meant that many Métis individuals were denied the land to which they were entitled (Tough, 1996). It is clear that government representatives failed to consider Métis ways of life throughout the development and implementation of scrip policy, and that they did little to guarantee Métis land rights or to help Métis successfully address the social, political and economic challenges they were facing (Tough, 1996). It is also clear that the government was far more concerned with the settling of land in the northwest by agriculturalists than it was with protecting Aboriginal title and reserving a land base for Métis (Augustus, 2013).

Despite long-standing disagreements between the federal and provincial governments in Canada over who is responsible for Métis (Wall, 2000), the Métis Nation was formally recognized as an Aboriginal people when Parliament passed the Constitution Act in 1982. The Province of Alberta and the Federation of Métis Settlement Associations eventually signed the Alberta-Métis Settlements Accord in 1989, which secured Métis ownership of lands they had historically used and occupied in Alberta (Wall, 2000). The Métis National Council signed a framework agreement with the federal government in 2005 to establish Métis self-government, and on January 8, 2013, the federal court ruled that the Aboriginal rights of Métis and non-status Indians were covered under section 35 of the Constitution Act. Although the ruling potentially entitles non-status Indians and Métis to negotiate for tax exemptions as well as for government support in such areas as education and health, the government immediately appealed the court's decision, and so it remains to be seen how this decision will affect these two Aboriginal groups.

Looking Back and Moving Forward

The final RCAP (1996) report discussed in detail how European colonization and the implementation of the Indian Act contributed to the loss of traditions and languages; family and community disruption; high rates of chronic disease, disability and comparatively shorter life spans compared with non-Aboriginal people; relatively low levels of education, high rates of unemployment and serious economic disparity within as well as between Aboriginal communities. The report asserted that, given the many acute and chronic health consequences of colonization, a full and hopeful response requires the visions, strengths and wisdom of both Indigenous and non-Indigenous peoples (Brant Castellano, 2011; Cooke & Long, 2011; Couture, 2011; Long, 2004; Wesley-Esquimaux & Smolewski, 2004).

The RCAP (1996) report also described the many negative social, economic, political and legal consequences of the Indian Act. One of the major inequities enshrined in the act was discrimination against registered Indian women. The act stipulated that only registered Indians were entitled to live on their home reserves, which meant that any registered Indian woman who married a non-Indian man not only lost her registered Indian status; she also had no choice but to move off her reserve (Voyageur, 2011). In 1985, Bill C-31 was passed as an amendment to the Indian Act to address this discrimination (Native Women's Association of Canada, 1986).[13] As a result, thousands of First Nations women—and their children—regained their registered Indian status. Despite Bill C-31, the B.C. Court of Appeal ruled in *McIvor v. Canada* (2009) that the Indian Act still discriminated between registered Indian men and women. The federal government addressed the limitations of Bill C-31 by passing Bill C-3, the Gender Equity in Indian Registration Act (Aboriginal Affairs and Northern Development Canada, 2011). When it took effect in 2011, approximately 45,000 eligible grandchildren of women who had lost status immediately became entitled to register their Indian status (Merchant Law Group, 2011). Even with this positive development, some Aboriginal groups and nations consider Bill C-3 as yet another failure of the government to "respect the right of First Nations to control the determination of our collective and individual identities" (Chiefs in Ontario, 2010, p. 1).

These and other inequities between Aboriginal peoples and the rest of Canada have led many, including the grand chief of the Assembly of First Nations, Shawn Atleo, to call for the Indian Act to be abolished and for the Department of Aboriginal Affairs and Northern Development to be dismantled (Galloway, 2011). Although there is widespread agreement that the Indian Act is a thoroughly racist piece of legislation, it is also the one official document in Canadian law that paradoxically (and somewhat ironically) protects the unique constitutional rights of Aboriginal peoples (Belanger & Newhouse, 2011; Cardinal, 1969). Belanger and Newhouse (2011) noted that numerous provincial and Supreme Court decisions supporting these rights over the past 40 years have helped to shed light on the unique relationship between Aboriginal peoples and the rest of Canada, which has in turn clarified the federal government's fiduciary responsibility to First Nations, Inuit, Métis and non-status Indians. They also noted that while court decisions have consistently ruled in favour of Aboriginal sovereignty and acknowledged Aboriginal peoples' inherent right to self-government, there is widespread consensus that official relations between Aboriginal peoples and the rest of Canada remain deeply flawed, and that no quick fix will remedy the devastating effects of more than 400 years of colonialism.

Despite the many differing opinions on how to move this relationship forward, an increasing number of people agree that reconciliation and healing will occur when the relationship between Aboriginal peoples and the rest of Canada is characterized by respect for the uniqueness, dignity and sovereignty of all peoples (Belanger & Newhouse, 2011; Truth and Reconciliation Commission of Canada, 2012). As many chapters in this book attest, Aboriginal peoples and all others in Canada will experience hope in facing the physical, social and spiritual harms caused by more than four centuries of colonialism as we learn to walk and heal together on the land we all call home.

---

13 Bill C-31 also instituted other changes that are beyond the scope of this chapter.

References

Aboriginal Affairs and Northern Development Canada. (2011). Gender Equity in Indian Registration Act (Bill C-3) comes into force on January 31, 2011 [Press release]. Retrieved from www.aadnc-aandc.gc.ca

Adams, H. (1989). *Prison of Grass: Canada from a Native Point of View*. Saskatoon, SK: Fifth House.

Adams, H. (1995). *A Tortured People: The Politics of Colonization*. Penticton, BC: Theytus Books.

Alfred, T. (1999). *Peace, Power, Righteousness: An Indigenous Manifesto*. Toronto: Oxford University Press.

Augustus, C. (2005). *The Scrip Solution: The North West Métis Scrip Policy, 1885–1887* (Unpublished master's thesis). University of Calgary, Alberta.

Augustus, C. (2013). *Métis Scrip*. Retrieved from http://scaa.sk.ca/ourlegacy/exhibit_scrip

Belanger, Y. & Newhouse, D. (2011). The Canada problem in Aboriginal politics. In D. Long & O. Dickason (Eds.), *Visions of the Heart: Aboriginal Issues in Canada* (3rd ed.; pp. 353–380). Toronto: Oxford University Press.

Bopp, J., Bopp, M., Brown, L. & Lane, P. (1984). *The Sacred Tree*. Lethbridge, AB: Four Worlds Development.

Brant Castellano, M. (2011). Elders' teachings in the twenty-first century: A personal reflection. In D. Long & O. Dickason (Eds.), *Visions of the Heart: Aboriginal Issues in Canada* (3rd ed.; pp. 35–54). Toronto: Oxford University Press.

Cardinal, H. (1969). *The Unjust Society: The Tragedy of Canada's Indians*. Vancouver: Douglas & McIntyre.

Chiefs in Ontario. (2010). *Bill C-3 and the Indigenous Right to Identity*. Retrieved from http://64.26.129.156/misc/CIO.pdf

Cook, N.D. (1998). *Born to Die: Disease and New World Conquest, 1492–1650*. Cambridge, UK: Cambridge University Press.

Cook, S.F. (1973). The significance of disease in the extinction of the New England Indians. *Human Biology, 45*, 485–508.

Cooke, M. & Long, D. (2011). Moving beyond the politics of Aboriginal well-being, health and healing. In D. Long & O. Dickason (Eds.), *Visions of the Heart: Aboriginal Issues in Canada* (3rd ed.; pp. 292–327). Toronto: Oxford University Press.

Couture, J. (2011). The role of Elders: Emergent issues. In D. Long & O. Dickason (Eds.), *Visions of the Heart: Aboriginal Issues in Canada* (3rd ed.; pp. 18–34). Toronto: Oxford University Press.

Daschuk, J.W., Hackett, P. & MacNeil, S. (2006). Treaties and tuberculosis: First Nations people in late 19th-century Western Canada—a political and economic transformation. *Canadian Bulletin of Medical History, 23*, 307–330.

Dickason, O. (1984). *The Myth of the Savage and the Beginnings of French Colonialism in the Americas*. Edmonton: University of Alberta Press.

Dickason, O. (2011). Towards a larger view of Canada's history: The Native factor. In D. Long & O. Dickason (Eds.), *Visions of the Heart: Aboriginal Issues in Canada* (3rd ed.; pp. 1–17). Toronto: Oxford University Press.

Dickason, O. & McNab, D. (2009). *Canada's First Nations: A History of Founding Peoples from Earliest Times* (4th ed.). Toronto: Oxford University Press.

Galloway, G. (2011, July 12). Scrap Indian Act to forge a new deal, AFN chief urges Ottawa. Retrieved from *Globe and Mail* website: www.theglobeandmail.com

Hare, J. (2011). Learning from indigenous knowledge. In D. Long & O. Dickason (Eds.), *Visions of the Heart: Aboriginal Issues in Canada* (3rd ed.; pp. 91–112). Toronto: Oxford University Press.

Kelm, M.E. (1998). *Colonizing Bodies: Aboriginal Health and Healing in British Columbia, 1900–50*. Vancouver: UBC Press.

LaRocque, E. (2012). Conversations with Olive Dickason: A tribute to a national treasure. *Native Studies Review, 21* (2), 31–35.

Long, D. (2004). On violence and healing: Aboriginal experiences, 1969–1993. In J.I. Ross (Ed.), *Violence in Canada: Socio-political Perspectives* (2nd ed.; pp. 40–77). New Brunswick, NJ: Transaction.

Long, D. (2011). Introduction. In D. Long & O. Dickason (Eds.), *Visions of the Heart: Aboriginal Issues in Canada* (3rd ed.; pp. 1–11). Toronto: Oxford University Press.

Lux, M. (1992). Prairie Indians and the 1918 influenza epidemic. *Native Studies Review, 8* (1), 23–33.

Marshall, I. (1996). *A History and Ethnography of the Beothuk*. Montreal: McGill-Queen's University Press.

McIvor v. Canada (Registrar of Indian and Northern Affairs), [2009] B.C.J. 669. Retrieved from www.courts.gov.bc.ca

Merchant Law Group. (2011). 45,000 Canadians wronged notwithstanding the adoption of Bill C-3 [Press release]. Retrieved from www.merchantlaw.com/classactions/assets/pdf/pressrelease.pdf

Miller, J.R. (2004). *Lethal Legacy: Current Native Controversies in Canada*. Toronto: McClelland & Stewart.

Native Women's Association of Canada. (1986). *Guide to Bill C-31: An Explanation of the 1985 Amendments to the Indian Act*. Ottawa: Author.

Rich, E.E. (1991). Trade habits and economic motivation among the Indians of North America. In J.R. Miller (Ed.), *Sweet Promises: A Reader in Indian–White Relations in Canada* (pp. 158–179). Toronto: University of Toronto Press.

Romaniuc, A. (2000). Aboriginal population of Canada: Growth dynamics under conditions of encounter of civilizations. *Canadian Journal of Native Studies, 20*, 95–137.

Royal Commission on Aboriginal Peoples (RCAP). (1996). *Report of the Royal Commission on Aboriginal Peoples. Vol. 1: Looking Forward, Looking Back*. Ottawa: Canada Communication Group.

Taylor, J.L. (1991). Canada's Northwest Indian Policy in the 1870s: Traditional promises and necessary innovations. In J.R. Miller (Ed.), *Sweet Promises: A Reader in Indian–White Relations in Canada* (pp. 207–211). Toronto: University of Toronto Press.

Tough, F. (1996). *As Their Natural Resources Fail: Native Peoples and the Economic History of Northern Manitoba, 1870–1930*. Vancouver: UBC Press.

Truth and Reconciliation Commission of Canada. (2012). *They Came for the Children: Canada, Aboriginal Peoples, and Residential Schools*. Retrieved from www.trc.ca/websites/trcinstitution/index.php?p=580

Voyageur, C. (2011). Contemporary First Nations women's issues. In D. Long & O. Dickason (Eds.), *Visions of the Heart: Aboriginal Issues in Canada* (3rd ed.; pp. 213–237). Toronto: Oxford University Press.

Waldram, J.B. (1997). *The Way of the Pipe: Aboriginal Spirituality and Symbolic Healing in Canadian Prisons*. Peterborough, ON: Broadview Press.

Wall, D. (2000). Aboriginal self-government in Canada: The cases of Nunavut and the Alberta Métis settlements. In D. Long & O. Dickason (Eds.), *Visions of the Heart: Aboriginal Issues in Canada* (2nd ed.; pp. 143–165). Toronto: Harcourt Canada.

Wesley-Esquimaux, C.C. & Smolewski, M. (2004). *Historic Trauma and Aboriginal Healing*. Retrieved from Aboriginal Healing Foundation website: www.ahf.ca

Willows, N.D., Veugelers, P., Raine, K. & Kuhle, S. (2009). Prevalence and sociodemographic risk factors related to household food security in Aboriginal Peoples in Canada. *Public Health Nutrition, 12,* 1150–1156.

ABOUT THE AUTHOR

David Long has been a professor of sociology at The King's University College in Edmonton since 1989. Along with his teaching and research interests in Aboriginal/non-Aboriginal relations, men's health and well-being, and fathering, David works extensively with men's groups, human service organizations and government in developing support services for disadvantaged populations. He is also on a national steering committee to establish a nationwide support network for fathers and their families. The third edition of *Visions of the Heart: Aboriginal Issues in Canada,* which he co-edited with Olive Dickason, was published by Oxford University Press in 2011.

Chapter 3

Residential Schools for Aboriginal Children in Canada

EILEEN ANTONE

> There is no doubt that the effects of residential schools live on today.
> It is our responsibility as [N]ative people to rectify this. We have
> suffered from the negative things that were passed to us—abuse,
> anger, fear, shame, and hurt. But now we know what has caused
> this and as a community we need to harness our strength and
> the knowledge that comes from our teachings. (Farris, as cited in
> Hodgson, 2008, p. 367)

Over a century of forced assimilation, thousands of Aboriginal children were
removed form their homes and placed in Canadian residential schools, and the voices
of Aboriginal peoples in Canada were silenced. This chapter describes the historical
context and conditions of residential schools. It highlights the continued negative
impact of residential schools on Aboriginal communities. It also discusses how the
residential school experience has had a profound effect on the mental health of
Aboriginal peoples and how traditional ways of wellness and well-being are required
to restore our communities to a balanced way of life.[1]

---

1   For more discussion about the residential schools and their impact, see chapter 5.

Traditional Education

Residential schooling was not a traditional form of education for Aboriginal children in Canada. Before contact with the European people, children in Aboriginal communities were educated by their parents and extended family to have a good mind. Children were taught roles and responsibilities in the traditional languages and cultures of their nations, and through their relationship to the natural world around them. Various methodologies were used such as modelling roles and telling stories and legends to teach about the many ceremonies and different medicines that were used to maintain the well-being of the people (Kirkness, 1995; Knockwood, 1992). Spirituality was central to the teachings of Aboriginal people. As Seton and Seton stated in *The Gospel of the Redman* (1977), "The Redman has the most spiritual civilization the world has ever known. . . . His measure of success is 'How much service have I rendered to my people?' . . . His mode of life, his thought, his every act are given spiritual significance" (as cited in Kirkness, 1999, p. 14).

The practice of incorporating cultural beliefs and spirituality into Aboriginal teachings began to shift with European contact. In his poem "Education," Anishnawbe spiritual teacher Arthur Solomon (1990) explained how example, experience and storytelling were vital characteristics of the lifelong learning process, which was based on respect for all of creation. Solomon (1990) stated: "But in the course of history there came a disruption. And then education became 'compulsory miseducation' for another purpose, and the circle of life was broken and the continuity ended" (p. 79). It was this "miseducation" that was imposed by the residential school system in Canada for more than 100 years.

The Mis-education Begins

When the Europeans arrived, they brought with them another way of life, which caused profound changes to Aboriginal peoples' traditional ways of being. According to Harrison (2009), the colonial objective was to assimilate Aboriginal people into Canadian society "by taking [Aboriginal] children away from their families and communities . . . to eradicate all vestiges of their language, culture and spirituality through the school system" (p. 151).This colonial objective was rooted in the erroneous view of Aboriginal peoples as "'simple savages' in an unformed state of nature waiting to be moulded by a civilizing hand" (Dickason, 1992, p. 165).

Attempts at civilizing Aboriginal people began in 1620 with the *Récollets* (Dickason, 1992), a French branch of the Roman Catholic order. They instituted two programs to educate, and thus convert, Aboriginal peoples. The first program sent selected Aboriginal children to France to learn the French language and culture. It was hoped that, upon their return, these children would influence their own people to adopt the

French culture and, in turn, encourage an increase in French settlements (Dickason, 1992, p. 165). In 1881 LeClercq wrote: "To civilize them it was necessary first that the French should mingle with them and habituate them among us, which could be done only by an increase to the colony" (pp. 110–111).

The second program started by the Récollets was a boarding school funded by people in France. This school became the earliest of the recorded residential school experiments (National Aboriginal Health Organization [NAHO], 2008), with missionaries coming from Europe to teach in the boarding schools established to convert Aboriginal people to the ways of Christianity (Kirkness, 1995). These school experiments were the basis for the conversion of Aboriginal people. "Civilization" and Christianization of Aboriginal peoples were the major goals of these mission schools (Canadian Encyclopedia, n.d.). In 1629, the Récollets withdrew from New France and closed their school when the people in France deemed it unsuccessful (Royal Commission on Aboriginal Peoples [RCAP], 1996).

The Jesuits then assumed the role the Récollets had abandoned, "with the same goal of building conversion allies within First Nations communities" (NAHO, 2008, p. 9). According to Abé (2011), "The schools for Amerindians taught no useful secular subjects, but only theology and prayer that were alien to Amerindian life" (p. 115). They also removed Indigenous boys from their parents. In 1639, the Ursuline nuns and the hospital nuns arrived in New France to set up elementary school systems where Aboriginal girls were also enrolled. In 1676, Marguerite Bourgeoys, an Ursuline nun, later known as Mother du Saint-Sacrement, established a boarding school, which was the first domestic training for girls. The purpose of this school was to train young female Aboriginal students to be subservient, submissive and obedient. This instruction began the process of creating an economic class of the lowest order, and marked the continual silencing and erosion of Aboriginal voices and ways of being (Awakening Our Spirit, n.d.). These schools not only removed Aboriginal children from their homes: they offered minimal education in ways to advance the students' economic self-sufficiency.

The Driving Forces

The interest of missionaries in "saving souls" and gaining favour with God by converting "heathens" to Christianity was the basis of early formal education for Aboriginal people. Although the first attempts at assimilative residential school programming failed to convert Aboriginal peoples, many forces came together in the 18th and 19th centuries to establish Indian residential schools, including Christian missionary aspirations and the oppressive Eurocentric ideology of European settlers.

After the English victory on the Plains of Abraham in 1759, when Britain gained control of North America from the French, the Anglican Church gained authority and was adopted by some Mohawk people and others who were loyal to the Crown during the War of Independence. As Canada's European population increased in the 19th century, churches of many denominations sprang up, including the Presbyterian and Methodist churches, which were also involved in missionary work with Aboriginal peoples. Although early residential schools were built by Christian organizations, the colonial government supported their ongoing costs.

Church and State Partnership

The first schools for North American Indian children, including boarding schools, were set up by churches with permission and support from the colonial government or the Hudson's Bay Company. The Mohawk Institute, started in 1828 in Brantford, Ontario, on the Six Nations Reserve, was one of the first residential schools. The school was established by the Anglican Church as the Mechanics' Institute, a day school for Aboriginal boys from the Six Nations Reserve, which was funded by Society for the Propagation of the Gospel in New England, also known as the New England Company, an independent missionary society. Three years later, it was turned into a residential school when it began to take in boarders. Then in 1834, the year generally taken as the founding date of the Anglican Church residential schools in Canada, girls were also admitted as students to this facility (Anglican Church of Canada, 2008).

William Case, president of the Upper Canadian Methodists, set up another small residential school in 1828. It was built on Grape Island, an Ojibwe settlement in the Bay of Quinte, and later became the Alnwick School at Alderville First Nation, until it was closed in 1860. These first two schools were not a part of the residential school system that was developed after Confederation; they were instead independent schools affiliated with Anglican and Wesleyan churches and run by missionary societies to Christianize and civilize Aboriginal people.

The education system for Aboriginal people changed after Confederation in 1867. Canadian government officials developed an "aggressive assimilation" policy for church-run, government-funded industrial schools, which later became known as residential schools ("A History," 2008). It was believed that the best chance for Aboriginal people to succeed was for them to learn English and adopt Christianity and Canadian customs. The ultimate purpose of the residential schools was thus to eradicate all facets of Aboriginal culture with the children's assimilation into the body politic of Canadian society.

At the time of Confederation, there were just two Indian residential schools in Canada—the Mohawk Institute and Mount Elgin Residential School in Muncey, Ontario, originally established by Ojibwe leader Reverend Peter Jones. About two residential schools were established per year, with the number growing to 64 schools by 1904. When 13 more residential schools sprang up in the next three years, the senior clerk in charge of education proclaimed, "The clergy seem to be going wild on the subject of Indian education and it is time some limit should be fixed to their demands" (RCAP, 1996). By 1931, there were 80 residential schools, and during the residential school era, there were more than 130 residential schools in Canada. In 1996 when the last residential school closed, 150,000 Aboriginal students had attended these schools established by the Catholic, Anglican, Methodist or Presbyterian churches (Legacy of Hope Foundation, 2003).

The Indian Act: Making the Agenda Explicit

In 1876, the Indian Act, which was both racist and paternalistic, was passed with the fundamental purpose of assimilating Aboriginal peoples, primarily through residential schools.[2] The Indian Act was amended in 1884 to make boarding schools mandatory for all Aboriginal children aged between six and 15 years. The new requirements of the act also granted the government the power to arrest, transport or detain children at school, and appointed Indian agents the right to fine or jail those parents who did not co-operate. An Oneida woman who attended residential school in Brandon, Manitoba, during the 1920s described how she and her brother agreed to go with the Indian agent to the school, because they did not want to make life difficult for their father who was unwell. The siblings believed the agent when he told them that Christian people ran the school, so they would be well fed, well clothed and well educated. In reality, there was "no[thing] Christian about it (the residential school)" (Antone, 1997, p. 139). The children were often hungry and constantly punished for speaking their traditional language (Antone, 1997, p. 139).

Prime Minister John A. Macdonald explained his rationale for having Aboriginal children separated from their parents and put into residential schools. In 1883, he told the House of Commons:

> When the school is on the reserve, the child lives with his parents who are savages; he is surrounded by savages, and though he may learn to read and write, his habits and training and mode of thought are Indian. He is simply a savage who can read and write. (Macdonald, as cited in Truth and Reconciliation Commission of Canada, 2012, p. 6)

In the early years of Confederation, the government had wanted large industrial residential schools to be located far from the reserves, but due to the high cost of these schools, they instead opted for boarding schools for younger children, which became known as residential schools (Barman et al., 1986), and were placed close to reserves. Because of poor funding, the churches began to rely increasingly on student labour: the schools' curriculum combined a half day of limited basic education with practical

---

2   For more discussion about the Indian Act, see chapter 2.

training and/or child labour in agriculture, crafts or household duties intended to prepare students for their future on the lower outer edge of Canadian society.

This residential school system, with its horrifically oppressive practices, is unparalleled in its failure to educate or assimilate Aboriginal children in North America. Kirkness (1995) stated:

> The period from around 1870 to the early 1980s in which boarding/ residential schools operated in Canada is considered the time of greatest oppression for our people, a period of cultural disruption marked by efforts of assimilation which today are viewed more as tactics of extermination. (p. 30)

Residential School Conditions

Throughout the 19th and 20th centuries, children at these underfunded schools were forced to live in overcrowded and unhealthy conditions. "Dormitories, for Aboriginal children in a disgraced system, were disease 'breeding grounds'" (Canadian Press, 2013). The draconian conditions of the schools, and the children's exposure to European diseases, created a "trail of disease and death [that went] almost unchecked by any serious efforts on the part of the Department of Indian Affairs" (Bryce, 1922, p. 14).

CULTURAL AND SPIRITUAL LOSS

Aboriginal people were abused and forcibly stripped of their culture at a formative and vulnerable point in their lives. Upon arrival at the schools, the children's heads were shaved, despite the belief among many Aboriginal communities that long hair was symbolic of awareness and power, and should only be cut when mourning the death of a family member. Student Charlie Bigknife recalled having his hair cut off at the File Hills School in Saskatchewan, and then being told, "Now you are no longer an Indian" (Truth and Reconciliation Commission of Canada, 2012, p. 22). After arriving at the schools, the children's clothes and sacred items were also taken away and burned, and they were forced to wear residential school uniforms instead. These uniforms were poorly suited for the weather, and children were often overheated or freezing as a result. The buildings were formidable structures that were typically dark and dreary, and thus intimidating to the children.

Other practices also served to dehumanize and isolate Aboriginal children from their culture, and from a sense of their identity and connection to a spiritual life. For example, faculty and staff forced them to abandon their traditional languages. Many former residents relate the pain they had to endure when a needle was pushed through their tongue because they spoke the language of their home. The children were also forced to abandon their traditional songs and dances, despite the fact that, in many communities, language was used to transmit culture, including traditional roles and responsibilities, and spirituality. Being stripped of their language was devastating, and meant that they could not conduct the traditional ceremonies that brought health and healing. Disconnecting Aboriginal people from their way of life damaged the identity of many Aboriginal people and continues to affect their health and well-being today. Because of the residential schools experiences, subsequent generations were raised to believe that Aboriginal ceremonies, languages, stories, songs, dances and ways of being were the ways of the devil. Consequently, many Aboriginal people learned to be ashamed of their language and culture, which has had a major impact on their mental health.

DISCIPLINE AND ABUSE

Aboriginal children also endured shame and suffering as a result of the abuses perpetuated at residential schools, which they carry into adulthood The abuse broke many children's spirit, impeding them from growing up to be emotionally, physically, mentally and spiritually whole. Many have turned to alcohol to help them deal with their pain. Alcohol addiction led to the collapse of many Aboriginal communities, which then led to what is referred to as "the '60s scoop," a time beginning in the 1960s when the child welfare system removed Aboriginal children from their families without the consent of their families or bands—and the parents felt helpless to intervene.[3] With the children's apprehension, they were no longer in the community to receive teachings from the Elders, so the natural life cycle of interaction between children and Elders was diminished.

Many examples exist in residential school literature to describe the physical, mental and sexual abuse experienced by Aboriginal children. One residential school survivor described his experience, illustrating the abusive discipline many children suffered and their fear of retribution:

> Shortly after I arrived at St. Anne's residential school, I remember being in the dining room having a meal. I got sick and threw up on the floor. Sister Mary Immaculate slapped me many times before she made me eat my vomit. So I did, I ate all of it. And then I threw up again, for the second time. Sister Mary Immaculate slapped me and told me again to eat my vomit. I ate it, half of it, and then I was told to go to the dorm. (Wesley, 2010, p. 98)

When this survivor was 12 years old, he recalled what happened when a friend kicked him under the table and he pulled off his friend's shoe:

---

3   For more discussion about Aboriginal children in the child welfare system, see chapter 4.

> Sister Mary Immaculate caught me. She . . . hit me on my head with
> the heavy shoe. She hit me about fifty times. I passed out for a while. I
> was not allowed to report the incident, and I was not allowed to go to
> the clinic. The beating left a large lump on the back of my neck, at the
> top of my spine (which has never gone away). For many, many days
> I had a hard time walking or playing because it hurt. I had a regular,
> severe nosebleed that kept coming back for months. (Was this person
> working for the church and Jesus?) (Wesley, 2010, p. 98)

Although Aboriginal children faced such abuse, they were unable to turn to their
fellow students or family members for help. Boys and girls were separated, so brothers
and sisters rarely interacted. This policy further weakened family and community ties
and isolated individuals, thus compounding the negative effects of the abuse.

GOVERNMENT RESPONSE TO ABUSE

Evidence suggests that the Department of Indian Affairs was unwilling to interfere in
the churches' running of the residential schools. Department of Indian Affairs official
Martin Benson complained in 1897 that the church had "too much power" and, in
1903, that the department had "a certain amount of hesitancy in insisting on the church
authorities taking the necessary action" (Milloy, 1999, p. 23). Inspector W. Graham
commented:

> Where the churches are concerned there is no use sending an adverse
> report, as the department will listen to excuses from incompetent
> Principals of the schools more readily than to a report from our
> Inspectors based on the facts as they find them. (as cited in Milloy,
> 1999, p. 147)

As a result of the church and state partnership, the "Department of Indian Affairs
maintained the fiction of care" and the churches' contribution was "marked by the
persistent neglect and abuse of children" (Milloy, 1999, p. 147). Despite Aboriginal
people being wards of the federal government, Canada failed to protect them.

Change in the Relationship between the Government and Aboriginal Peoples

Many Aboriginal people gave up their Indian status to participate in the First and
Second World Wars and in the Korean War, but when they returned home they
continued to be treated as second-class citizens. Recognizing that they were not being

treated like other returning soldiers, the veterans forced the government to revise its racist policies toward Indigenous people of Canada. In 1946, a special joint parliamentary committee of the Senate and House of Commons was formed to review Canada's policies and the management of Indian affairs (Aboriginal Affairs and Northern Development Canada [AANDC], 2011). For three years, the committee received briefs and representations from First Nations, missionaries, school teachers and federal government administrators. This was one of the "first occasions where First Nation leaders and Elders were able to address parliamentarians directly instead of through the intermediary of the Department of Indian Affairs" (AANDC, 2011, p. 9). At this time Aboriginal people explicitly rejected their assimilation into non-Aboriginal society. As a result of the committee, the Department of Indian Affairs made changes to the educational component of the residential school system in the 1950s and 1960s (RCAP, 1996). Although the last residential school was closed in the late 1990s, the effects of these schools continue to ripple through Aboriginal communities. In 2008, Prime Minister Steven Harper apologized to the Aboriginal peoples of Canada for the mis-education that was forced upon them (Prime Minister of Canada, 2008). Assembly of First Nations leader Phil Fontaine formally responded to the government's apology with the following statement:

> For the generations that will follow us, we bear witness today in this House that our survival as First Nations peoples in this land is affirmed forever. . . . We heard the Government of Canada take full responsibility for this dreadful chapter in our shared history. We heard the prime minister declare that this will never happen again. Finally, we heard Canada say it is sorry. (Canwest News Service, 2008, ¶5, 8–9)

There was mixed reaction to the government's apology among Aboriginal people. Stan Beardy, grand chief of the Nishnawbe Aski Nation, stated:

> This apology does not erase the pain endured by survivors, nor does it fix the broken families, Nations or promises that were a result of the residential school system, but it is an important first step towards reconciliation between the Government of Canada and First Nations. (Wawatay News Online, 2008, ¶8)

Bernice Falkus, an Osoyoos Indian band member who attended residential school in Kamloops for eight years in the 1950s (and was only allowed to go home to visit family in the summer) said she still has nightmares from her experiences, and questioned how genuine Harper's words actually were (Flexhaugrn, 2008).

The various churches involved in the residential school system have also issued apologies: the Oblates of Mary Immaculate in 1991, the Anglican Church in 1993, the

Presbyterian Church in 1994 and the Roman Catholic Church in 2009. The United Church of Canada gave a general apology in 1986 and then gave a formal apology for the church's participation in the residential school system in 1998.

Despite the many abuses perpetrated against them, Aboriginal communities across Canada are in the process of restoring traditional teachings of spiritual wellness and well-being. They are working to overcome the negative impact of their assimilative experiences, which includes addressing addiction and mental health issues that have weakened the basic social structures of Aboriginal society.

Restoring Aboriginal Spirituality

In 1998, the Aboriginal Healing Foundation (AHF) was created to manage the federal government's one-time grant of $350 million to help individuals and communities heal from the physical and sexual abuse that occurred in residential schools. This healing fund was a component of *Gathering Strength: Canada's Aboriginal Action Plan* (Minister of Indian Affairs and Northern Development, 2000). One of the large projects that resulted from this fund was the Indian Residential School Museum of Canada, situated in the former Portage Indian School on Long Plain Reserve in Manitoba. Although the AHF funded large projects, many other healing activities also took place across the country, such as engaging with Elders and participating in ceremonies, one-on-one counselling, talking circles, traditional medicine, workshops, conferences, land-based activities, residential treatment, parenting skills training, family counselling, alternative medicine and Western therapies. According to AHF, participants in these activities indicated in a survey that they had developed new relationships and gained self-awareness, knowledge and cultural reclamation. Many participants indicated that they felt better about themselves because they found inner strength, improved their self-esteem, and were able to work through their trauma (AHF, 2006). AHF gave many grants to Aboriginal organizations across Canada to help individuals and communities heal the wounds left by the residential school experience.[4]

Researchers have been studying the legacy of residential schools in Aboriginal communities and have found that the Western paradigm of health differs from Aboriginal world views. This difference forms a barrier to Western practitioners providing effective mental health support services for Aboriginal people seeking help from formally trained counsellors, including those who may be trained in cross-cultural or multicultural approaches (Steward, 2008). Steward (2008) also found that counsellors can best help clients by addressing culture when looking at their healing needs. Creating healing models for the health and well-being of Aboriginal people is not an easy task. Waldram (2008) found that effective treatment programs must accommodate a wide variety of Aboriginal people, regardless of their cultural heritage; their

---

4 For a more detailed discussion about the Aboriginal Healing Foundation, see chapter 31.

knowledge of Aboriginal language; and their familiarity with Aboriginal spiritual traditions, Christianity or absence of spirituality.

Mussell and Martin (2006) suggested a positive link between the healing of individuals and their families in the move toward community health and well-being. The healing process engages traditional cultural ways, beliefs, values and ceremonies that nurture and affirm identity. This begins the circle of healing: "As our communities and families become stronger they are better able to support the health and wellness . . . of individual[s]" (Mussell & Martin, 2006, p. 10).

The degrading and abusive experiences perpetuated by the assimilative residential school system have long-term consequences. Many residential school survivors and subsequent generations struggle to regain balance and health in the aftermath. We need to continue our traditional ways of achieving wellness and well-being to restore our communities to a balanced way of life.

All my relations.

References

Abé, T. (2011). *The Jesuit Mission to New France: A New Interpretation in the Light of the Earlier Jesuit Experience in Japan.* Leiden, Netherlands: Koninklijke Brill NV.

Aboriginal Affairs and Northern Development Canada (AANDC). (2011). *A History of Indian and Northern Affairs Canada.* Retrieved from www.aadnc-aandc.gc.ca

Aboriginal Healing Foundation (AHF). (2006). *The Aboriginal Healing Foundation Summary Points of the AHF Final Report.* Retrieved from www.fadg.ca/downloads/rapport-final-eng.pdf

A history of residential schools in Canada. (2008). Retrieved from CBC News website: www.cbc.ca/news/canada/a-history-of-residential-schools-in-canada-1.702280

Anglican Church of Canada. (2008). *The Mohawk Institute—Brantford, ON: Mission and Justice Relationships.* Retrieved from www.anglican.ca/relationships/trc/histories/mohawk-institute

Antone, E. (1997). *In Search of Voice: A Collaborative Investigation on Learning Experiences of Onyota'a:ka* (Unpublished doctoral dissertation). University of Toronto, Toronto.

Awakening Our Spirit. (n.d.). *History of Indian Residential Schools. (Cold Lake Native Friendship Centre and the Cold Lake Community Reconciliation and Healing Project).* Retrieved from http://209.15.218.187/~montreal/sites/default/files/history_of_indian_residential_schools.pdf

Barman, J., Hébert, Y. & McCaskill, D. (1986). The legacy of the past: An overview. In J. Barman, Y. Hébert & D. McCaskill (Eds.), *Indian Education Volume 1: The Legacy* (pp. 1–22). Vancouver: UBC Press.

Bryce, P.H. (1922). *The Story of a National Crime: Being an Appeal for Justice to the Indians of Canada.* Retrieved from Internet Archive website: www.archive.org/stream/storyofnationalc00brycuoft#page/n5/mode/2up

Canadian Encyclopedia. (n.d.). Education of Aboriginal people. Retrieved from www.thecanadianencyclopedia.com/en/article/aboriginal-people-education/www.thecanadianencyclopedia.com

Canadian Press. (2013, February 18). At least 3,000 died in residential schools, research shows. Retrieved from CBC News website: www.cbc.ca/news/canada/story/2013/02/18/residential-schools-student-deaths.html

Canwest News Service. (2008, June 11). AFN leader Phil Fontaine's response to the House of Commons on Wednesday. Retrieved from www.canada.com/vancouversun/news/story.html?id=4f3fddf0-f3e7-43d4-a9a0-f6ebfbdb6f20

Dickason, O.P. (1992). *Canada's First Nations: A History of Founding Peoples from Earliest Times*. Don Mills, ON: Oxford University Press.

Flexhaugrn, A. (2008, June 18). Osoyoos Indian band has mixed feelings on residential schools apology. Retrieved from Osoyoos Times website: www.osoyoostimes.com

Harrison, P. (2009). Dispelling ignorance of residential schools. In G. Younging, J. Dewar & M. DeGagné (Eds.), *Response, Responsibility, and Renewal: Canada's Truth and Reconciliation Journey* (pp. 149–161). Retrieved from Aboriginal Healing Foundation website: www.ahf.ca

Hodgson, M. (2008). Reconciliation: A spiritual process. In M. Brant Castellano, L. Archibald & M. DeGagné (Eds.), *From Truth to Reconciliation: Transforming the Legacy of Residential Schools* (pp. 361–379). Retrieved from Aboriginal Healing Foundation website: www.ahf.ca

Kirkness, V.J. (1995). Aboriginal peoples and tertiary education in Canada: Institutional responses. *London Journal of Canadian Studies, 11*, 28–40. Retrieved from www.canadian-studies.net/lccs/LJCS/Vol_11/Kirkness.pdf

Kirkness, V.J. (1999). Aboriginal education in Canada: A retrospective and a prospective. *Journal of American Indian Education, 39* (1), 14–30. Retrieved from http://jaie.asu.edu/v39/V39I1A2.pdf

Knockwood, I. (1992). *Out of the Depths*. Lockport, NS: Roseway Publishing.

LeClercq, C. (1881). *First Establishment of the Faith in New France*. Retrieved from Internet Archive website: http://ia600508.us.archive.org/0/items/firstestablishme01lecl/firstestablishme01lecl.pdf

Legacy of Hope Foundation. (2003). About us. Retrieved from www.legacyofhope.ca/about-residential-schools/establishment-closure

Milloy, J. (1999). *A National Crime: The Canadian Government and the Residential School System—1879 to 1986*. Winnipeg: University of Manitoba Press.

Minister of Indian Affairs and Northern Development. (2000). *Gathering Strength: Canada's Aboriginal Action Plan*. Ottawa: Minister of Public Works and Government Services Canada.

Mussell, B. & Martin, N. (2006, February). *Pathways to Healing: A Mental Health Toolkit for First Nations People*. Retrieved from Canadian Collaborative Mental Health Initiative website: www.ccmhi.ca/en/products/toolkits/documents/EN_PathwaystoHealing.pdf

National Aboriginal Health Organization (NAHO). (2008). *First Nations/Inuit/Métis Health Human Resource Inventory: First Nations, Inuit and Métis Education History from a HHR Perspective*. Retrieved from www.naho.ca/documents/naho/english/pdf/hhr_Aboriginal_education.pdf

Prime Minister of Canada. (2008). Prime Minister Harper offers full apology on behalf of Canadians for the Indian Residential Schools system. Retrieved from www.pm.gc.ca

Royal Commission on Aboriginal Peoples (RCAP). (1996). *Report of the Royal Commission on Aboriginal Peoples. Vol. 1: Looking Forward, Looking Back*. Ottawa: Canada Communication Group.

Seton, E. & Seton, J.M. (1977). *The Gospel of the Redman*. Winnipeg, MB: Mary Scorer Books.

Solomon, A. (1990). Education. In M. Posluns (Ed.), *Songs for the People: Teachings on the Natural Way* (p. 79). Toronto: NC Press.

Steward, S. (2008). Promoting Indigenous mental health: Cultural perspectives on healing from Native counsellors in Canada. *International Journal of Health Promotion and Education, 46* (2), 49–56.

Truth and Reconciliation Commission of Canada. (2012). *They Came for the Children: Canada, Aboriginal Peoples, and Residential Schools*. Retrieved from www.trc.ca/websites/trcinstitution/index.php?p=580

Waldram, J.B. (2008). The models and metaphors of healing. In J.B. Waldram (Ed.), *Aboriginal Healing in Canada: Studies in Therapeutic Meaning and Practice* (pp. 1–8). Ottawa: Aboriginal Healing Foundation.

Wawatay News Online. (2008, June 26). Reaction to Harper's apology. Retrieved from www.wawataynews.ca/node/13502

Wesley, A. (2010). A survivor's story: O Ke che manido. In D. Balia & K. Kim (Eds.), *Edinburgh 2010. Vol. 2: Witnessing to Christ Today* (pp. 97–99). Retrieved from Edinburgh 2010 website: www.edinburgh2010.org/fileadmin/files/edinburgh2010/files/Resources/Witnessing%20to%20Christ%20Today.pdf

ABOUT THE AUTHOR

Eileen Antone, emeritus, University of Toronto, is a member of the Oneida of the Thames First Nation, Turtle Clan. She is former director of Aboriginal studies at the Centre for Aboriginal Initiatives at the University of Toronto. She served as a faculty member with what was then the department of Adult Education, Community Development, and Counselling Psychology, as well as with the Transitional Year Programme. Dr. Antone's research, professional writing, teaching and field development focus on Aboriginal knowledge and traditional ways of being.

Chapter 4

Child Welfare

PETER MENZIES

A range of social and economic federal public policies has contributed to the separation of Aboriginal children from their families. This experience is well documented in the nine volumes of findings of the 1996 Royal Commission on Aboriginal Peoples (RCAP). For more than 100 years, Canada's residential schools systematically undermined Aboriginal culture and disrupted generations of families, contributing to a general loss of language and culture in subsequent generations. The RCAP reported that many Aboriginal children were raised in institutional settings that failed to provide them with the knowledge and skills necessary to raise their own families (Fournier & Crey, 1997).

The devastating effects of the residential school system are far reaching and continue to significantly affect Aboriginal communities. The RCAP (1996a) found that the percentage of Aboriginal children in care is six times that of children in the general population.

This chapter reviews how public policies have contributed to a disproportionate number of Aboriginal children coming into contact with child welfare authorities in Canada. It also assesses the impact government policies continue to have on Aboriginal children, their families and their communities.

Historical Context

In 1876, the federal government passed the Indian Act under the guise of protecting and "civilizing" Aboriginal peoples in Canada. This paternalistic legislation gave the government the power to regulate and administer the lives of status Indians and

Aboriginal reserve communities. It imposed governing structures in the form of tribal bands and established the federal government's fiduciary responsibility toward Aboriginal peoples. The Indian Act treated Aboriginal peoples in Canada as children rather than as full citizens.

In the 1880s, the government began to establish residential schools across Canada, and in 1920, the Indian Act made it mandatory for all First Nations children to attend these schools.[1] This federally funded school system was used to support the government's assimilative policies:

> Marching out from the schools, the children, effectively re-socialized, imbued with the values of European culture, would be the vanguard of a magnificent metamorphosis: the "savage" was to be made "civilized," made fit to take up the privileges and responsibilities of citizenship. (RCAP, 1996b, p. 335)

It is estimated that from the 1840s until 1996, 150,000 Aboriginal children, including status Indian, Métis and Inuit, were placed in residential schools across Canada (Commission to Promote Sustainable Child Welfare, 2011). In 2005, about 85,975 residential school survivors were still living, with an average age of 57 years. For the first time in decades, survivors are sharing the impact of their experiences with their families, their communities and other Canadians (Truth and Reconciliation Commission of Canada, 2012).

The residential school system separated families and undermined the ways Aboriginal culture was taught and sustained. As a result, it contributed to a general loss of language and culture in subsequent generations. Many of the children returning from residential schools to their home communities were described as "poorly educated, angry, abused strangers" (Fournier & Crey, 1997, p. 82). Many found themselves becoming parents without the skills necessary to provide for their children's healthy development (Beaucage, 2011; Galley, 2010). Without appropriate parenting models, many Aboriginal parents lacked the necessary knowledge to raise their children; instead, children were introduced to dysfunctional models of behaviour (Brant, 1990; Grant, 1996; Van de Sande, 1995). Napier (2000) concluded that "the bonds between many hundreds of Aboriginal children and their families and nations were bent and broken, with disastrous results" (p. 3). Many parents themselves experienced the negative effects of having been placed in the residential school system:

> Eventually these same children became parents but instead of drawing upon the richness of the knowledge of their Elders, family and community to parent, they drew upon their experiences of residential

---

1 For a discussion about the residential schools, see chapter 3.

school and thus were often too authoritarian or were too lax and disorganized in their parenting. (Bennett et al., 2005, p. 18)

While residential schools no longer operate, the legacy of more than 100 years of institutionalized assimilation continues to contribute to a crisis within Aboriginal families and communities. As parents and grandparents struggle with issues resulting from historical abuses, neglect and cultural isolation, their children and grandchildren face removal from their homes through a different government policy instrument: child welfare. The legacy of residential schools contributed to unsafe environments in Aboriginal communities and the federal government stepped in to protect children in another way.

Child Welfare Policies

Before the 1950s, the federal government had limited involvement in child welfare issues in Aboriginal communities. Government staff only became involved if a life-or-death situation was reported, or if a federal Indian agent determined that parents were not competent to provide care for their children. In such cases, Aboriginal children were placed in residential schools (Armitage, 1993; Timpson, 1990). After the Second World War, increasing urbanization and migration of Aboriginal people to urban centres brought Aboriginal families to the attention of social welfare authorities. Social workers and other helping professionals witnessed the deplorable conditions that First Nations people faced in their communities. High levels of poverty, poor housing and deteriorating health conditions provoked a new wave of social concern (Bennett et al., 2005).

The Canadian Welfare Council and the Canadian Association of Social Workers made a joint presentation during the sitting of the Special Joint Committee of the Senate and House of Commons (1946–1948), demanding that Aboriginal people receive the same services available to non-Aboriginal people, including child welfare services provided by the provinces. Both organizations condemned the use of residential schools as homes for children and stated that neglected Aboriginal children lacked the protection that was generally afforded to non-Aboriginal children under social legislation. They also recommended against the development of a parallel, federally operated Native child welfare system, and instead recommended the full assimilation of Indians into Canadian life. They concluded that the best way to improve the situation was to extend the services of the provincial departments of health, welfare and education to the residents of reserves. The committee accepted the argument, and changes to the Indian Act ensued (Armitage, 1995).

In 1951, section 88 of the Indian Act was amended to allow provincial laws to apply to Aboriginal peoples (Palmer & Cooke, 1996). Provincial and territorial governments were given power over child welfare services for Aboriginal communities across Canada. Section 88 set out that:

> Subject to the terms of any treaty and any other Act of Parliament, all laws of general application from time to time in force in any province are applicable to and in respect of Indians in the province, except to the extent that those laws are inconsistent with this Act or any order, rule, regulation or by-law made there under, and except to the extent that those laws make provision for any matter for which provision is made by or under this Act. (Indian Act, 1951, c. 149, s. 87)

Despite these changes and advocacy efforts, from 1951 until the late 1960s, the federal government and the provinces and territories were locked in funding disputes related to Aboriginal peoples that hampered improvements. The federal government funded on-reserve services under the authority of the Indian Act. While the federal government accepted its constitutional responsibility for Aboriginal people living on reserves, the different levels of government continued to argue over financial responsibility for Aboriginal people who chose to live off reserves. The provincial and territorial governments claimed that on- and off-reserve First Nations people were the financial responsibility of the federal government.

This political wrangling significantly affected the lives of off-reserve First Nations families who were unable to secure social benefits, including welfare and housing, during this time. The needs of First Nations children would be met only if the federal government's Indian agent and a provincial or territorial child welfare worker perceived the matter as critical (Timpson, 1990).

The public policy vacuum during this period created even more hardships for Aboriginal people. Hawthorn (1966) noted the deteriorating health and economic conditions in First Nations communities during this time. This included a death rate from tuberculosis that was 14 times higher than the rate among the general population; an infant mortality rate of 180 per 1,000 compared with 54 per 1,000 in the general population; serious problems of malnutrition; and dilapidated, unsanitary and overcrowded housing. The brief also noted the disruption of family units caused by the residential school system; exclusion from old age pensions; and the lack of adequate adoption, foster home and juvenile delinquent treatment practices.

The establishment of the Canada Assistance Plan in 1966 allowed for a significant expansion of provincial child welfare services by providing federal cost-sharing to offset provincial costs (Bull, 1991). As a consequence, the proportion of Aboriginal children in care began to increase dramatically across the country. Under this system, the welfare of Aboriginal children was assessed according to provincial and territorial child welfare standards. However, no funding amendment was made for preventative measures to help deal with the psychological trauma Aboriginal people experienced in the residential schools. Parents did not receive support to deal with their traumas and improve their parenting skills, but their children, once in care, attained the same standard of living as other Canadian children:

> Social services such as counselling, homemakers and child care were not available to intact aboriginal families from either the provinces or federal Health and Welfare. Only when aboriginal families were split apart and their children made legal wards—inducted into the mainstream—could aboriginal children count on attaining a standard of living even remotely approximating that enjoyed by other Canadian children. (Fournier et al., 1997, p. 84)

Because provincial and territorial child welfare agencies took a crisis intervention approach to child welfare, Aboriginal children were permanently removed from their homes and placed in foster care or made Crown wards (Andres, 1981; Johnston, 1983; Richard, 2004; Timpson, 1990). These arrangements were poor substitutes for the support in the traditional Aboriginal community or home, but by the late 20th century, that structure had been so weakened that for many Aboriginal people it had ceased to exist. In other words, the residential school system had undermined many Aboriginal traditional practices around parenting skills and the involvement of extended families.

However, in 1969, widespread demonstrations and co-ordinated efforts by Aboriginal groups prevented further federal devolution of responsibilities to the provinces and territories for Aboriginal programs and services, as proposed in the federal government's white paper (Timpson, 1990). However, by that time, the child welfare system was well established in its role as a new instrument of colonization (Armitage, 1995; Hudson & McKenzie, 1981).

Advocacy Efforts

The period from the 1950s until the 1980s was one of struggle for Aboriginal communities in Canada. Deplorable reserve conditions and mental health and addiction issues arising from the residential school system perpetuated the use of the child welfare model. A 1972 National Indian Brotherhood briefing to the federal government detailed increasing concerns about the lack of preventative social programs in First Nations communities. Other public policy researchers echoed the demand for more culturally appropriate services within communities struggling to address growing social issues.

Sanders (1978) alerted government policy-makers to the increasing number of Aboriginal children coming to the attention of child welfare authorities in his 1978 report on behalf of the Canadian Council on Children and Youth. Hepworth (1980) completed a study on behalf of the Canadian Council on Social Development regarding foster care and adoption, a study that detailed the extent to which Aboriginal children were being removed from their homes in disproportionate numbers to non-Aboriginal children in every province across Canada.

While these documents identified a disproportionate number of Aboriginal children among child welfare clients, it was Patrick Johnston's (1983) report for the Canadian Council on Social Development that quantified the depth of the impact child welfare policies were having on Aboriginal communities across Canada. Johnston introduced the term "the '60s scoop" to describe the overwhelming number of Aboriginal children permanently removed from their homes and communities during this period and placed in foster care or made Crown wards. In his examination of provincial data across Canada, Johnston found that Aboriginal children were highly overrepresented in the child welfare system: Manitoba, Yukon and Saskatchewan had more than 50 per cent of Aboriginal children in care. Johnston also noted that the overwhelming majority of Aboriginal children placed for adoption were adopted by non-Aboriginal parents: The proportion of status Indian children adopted by non-Indians during that period ranged from 84.9 per cent in 1972 to 71.4 per cent in 1975. Between 1977 and 1981, that figure was consistently around 75 per cent (Johnston, 1983).

In 1985, Justice Edwin Kimelman's (1984) inquiry into adoptions and placement of First Nations and Métis children in Manitoba validated these findings. Based on the first-hand testimony of Aboriginal children and adults who were removed from their birth families and home communities, the inquiry confirmed the claims of Aboriginal peoples that their communities were being destroyed by a child welfare system, operating under the guise of providing for the best interest of the children.

Changes to Child Welfare Policies

Ongoing advocacy from Aboriginal leaders, band councils and others concerned about the growing rate of child welfare apprehensions in Aboriginal communities prompted the federal government to take action in the late 1970s and early 1980s. The federal government created the First Nations Child and Family Services program in the 1970s. This program transferred the administration of child and family services from provinces or territories to local bands, and decentralized services and funding.

This decentralization of child welfare services required new funding provisions. Services on reserves were negotiated on a case-by-case basis, with child welfare mandates approved through the provincial/territorial authority under a delegated service model. Under this model, each province and territory authorized First Nations agencies to provide a range of child welfare services to First Nations children and families. These services were to be provided in accordance with provincially recognized child welfare legislation. In some cases, limited services were also provided to Aboriginal families living off reserves. Funding arrangements continued to be made through the federal government, with some provinces providing minimal cost sharing. As a result, First Nations child welfare services varied within and across provinces and territories (Blackstock, 2003).

Shifting control over child welfare systems from federal and provincial jurisdictions to local communities allowed for the infusion of culturally congruent programs and services. The number of Aboriginal child welfare agencies grew from four in 1981 to 30 in 1986 (Armitage, 1995). As the Aboriginal demand for self-governance in child welfare matters grew, the federal government recognized that a more systematic response was needed. A moratorium was placed on the development of First Nations–delivered child welfare services in 1986. After five years of review, the federal government introduced a national child welfare policy in 1991 that included a funding formula for First Nations child and family service agencies. The policy set out the funding framework for on-reserve child and family services (McDonald et al., 2000). Based on this new funding formula, additional child welfare agencies were established in First Nations communities across Canada.

The RCAP (1996a) acknowledged that Canada's child welfare policy had caused great hardship to Aboriginal families and communities. It concluded that the percentage of Aboriginal children in care was six times that of the general population. To compound this situation, the RCAP found that placement of children in non-Aboriginal foster care homes was as high as 90 per cent in some provinces (RCAP, 1996a). It also identified the federal government's fiduciary responsibility to support Aboriginal nations and their communities in restoring Aboriginal families to a state of health and wholeness, and concluded that the best interest of Aboriginal children would only be served if both Aboriginal and non-Aboriginal agencies worked together to achieve this objective. It also recommended that block funding be provided to child welfare agencies mandated by Aboriginal governments or communities to facilitate the restoration of Aboriginal families (RCAP, 1996a).

The momentum for self-directed child welfare services within First Nations communities suffered a significant setback in 1999 when the federal government ceased to provide inflationary cost increases for new services. As a result, all funding for child welfare services on reserves was frozen. The impact of this action gained public attention with the release in June 2000 of the Joint National Policy Review final report from the Assembly of First Nations and the Department of Indian and Northern Affairs (McDonald et al., 2000). The document described how status children on First Nations reserves received 22 per cent less funding for child welfare than other children. Without adequate, stable funding, preventative services and enhanced education and training for culturally appropriate social work interventions could not be supported.

As we entered the new millennium, the number of Aboriginal families involved with child welfare services continued to grow, demonstrating the intergenerational impact of child welfare policy development in Canada. Despite earlier advocacy efforts to decentralize and provide culturally congruent child welfare services within Aboriginal communities, Aboriginal children continue to be overrepresented in the child welfare system. The National Advisory Committee on First Nations Child and Family Services was established in 2000 as a joint initiative of the Assembly of First Nations and Indian and Northern Affairs Canada to address the growing child welfare crisis in First Nations communities. Over the next four years, attempts were made to develop an action plan for the recommendations identified in the Joint National Policy Review (McDonald et al., 2000). In 2004, the First Nations Child and Family Caring Society of Canada (FNCFCS) was commissioned to conduct an extensive review of federal child welfare policies. Over the next two years, it presented both crisis and long-term response options for child welfare issues in First Nations communities to Indian and Northern Affairs Canada.

Despite the robustness of the reports and the call to action to avert deepening the crises facing families residing in Aboriginal communities, the federal government did not take action. As a result, the Assembly of First Nations and FNCFCS launched a Canadian human rights complaint against the federal government—an unprecedented action. The complaint cited racial discrimination against First Nations children resulting from the government's First Nations Child and Family Services Program. In 2007, federal funding to the Assembly of First Nations for the work of the National Advisory Committee was terminated. The case is currently before the Canadian Human Rights Tribunal.

Understanding Child Welfare as a Colonialist Tool

Like the residential institutions to which children's parents, grandparents and great-grandparents had been sent, the foster care and adoption system created another generation of children who have been subjected to psychological, emotional, sexual and physical abuse. During the 1960s, isolation from their families and Aboriginal identity was intensified when some children were sent for adoption to the United States and Europe (Bagley et al., 1993). Lederman (1999) observed:

> Children's Aid Societies perpetuated the same belief as residential schools: that a well-meaning White, cultural institution was better than a Native child's family and community. Many, perhaps even most, of the child welfare workers were compassionate and well-intentioned. But, however well-meaning Children's Aid Society intrusions may have been, they further continued the traumatization of Native people and likely compounded it. (p. 64)

In Palmer and Cooke (1996), Sally Palmer recalled her work as an inexperienced Children's Aid Society worker:

> The CAS worker, who came to the community weekly, would move the children into long-term foster homes in the non-Native community. Little attempt was made to let parents know what was happening: it was assumed that the foster carer or someone else would tell parents that their children had been placed. When parents did not contact the agency asking to see their children, the agency assumed they were not interested. (p. 713)

A number of child welfare studies in Canada and the United States describe the long-term effects of removing Aboriginal children from their birth families and placing them in non-Aboriginal homes (Couchi & Nabigon, 1994; Frideres, 1998; Locust, 1999). For many Aboriginal people, the connection between spiritual, emotional, physical and mental well-being was disrupted.

Some argue that child welfare is an extension of the assimilation process of Aboriginal peoples. Monture (1989) suggested that child welfare legislation is racist in that it applies standards that are not culturally relevant to Aboriginal peoples and shows no respect for Aboriginal values of parenting, which includes extended families.

Hudson and McKenzie (1981) suggested that social workers have only considered Aboriginal child welfare through a colonialist lens, with external bodies exercising power and decision-making authority over Aboriginal peoples with no regard for Aboriginal culture, including parenting. Concerns about cultural and social impacts were simply not considered in the decision-making process and most parental consent was obtained without full information or dialogue.

Carriere (2009) and Richard (2004) argued that Canada's current child welfare system operates from the "best interest of the child"—a concept rooted in Anglo-European values and in conflict with Aboriginal values related to the extended family and the interest of community. Richard (2004) noted:

> The "best interests of the child" principle has evolved over time, through policy, social work practice and the courts, to become the primary consideration in planning for a child. While the principle seems self evident and culturally neutral it is defined subjectively through a value, knowledge and practice context that is decidedly Anglo European. The notion of the child and her best interests, as separate and distinct from her family, community and culture, is one that has its roots in the individualist orientation of European culture. (p. 102)

Families that came into contact with this system were seen from this lens regardless of their culture. Bull (1991) also argued that the right of individuals is a Western ideology and is expressed through the child welfare system over the needs of the community.

A Complicated Issue

The issues that Aboriginal communities face in the wake of the residential schools and child welfare policies cannot be understood in isolation. For example, psychological issues are compounded by systemic poverty and cultural confusion.

Brant (1993) identified three factors within the Aboriginal experience in Canadian society as significant contributors to mental illness among Aboriginal peoples: poverty, powerlessness and anomie—a feeling of being disconnected from any particular cultural group. This last factor is linked to the fact that long-term separations created confusion and value conflict for the children. They were taken from their homes but not provided with an alternative home in which they could positively identify.

Locust (1999) coined the term "split feathers" to describe the Aboriginal children adopted or placed in foster care outside their culture who develop long-term psychological problems. Forced to assume the values of another culture that derided their own belief system, children were left in a cultural vacuum, relating neither to mainstream culture nor to their own community. As adults, a number of former residential school students and child welfare system survivors have significantly higher rates of anxiety disorders, alcohol and other substance use problems, depression, suicide and low self-esteem than the general population (Beisner & Attneave, 1982; Gagné, 1998; Hodgson, 1990; Mussell et al., 1991).

My own experience in the child welfare system highlights some of these points. I was sent to several foster homes, receiving homes and group homes. I experienced abuse and witnessed other children being abused. Staff would use racial slurs ("That wagon burner never listens"). As a child, I believed I had nowhere to go and no one to trust. I was alone, unloved, uncared for and confused about who I was. I ran away many times from these safe places and sought the comfort of solvents and other illegal drugs. I developed an "I don't care" attitude and participated in high-risk behaviours without considering the consequences.

It is also important to reflect on the systemic conditions that continue to exacerbate child welfare rates in Aboriginal communities. Endemic poverty, limited access to appropriate health care and substandard housing have only aggravated the conditions that require intervention by external authorities. In their comprehensive investigation into the overrepresentation of Aboriginal children in the care of Canadian child welfare agencies, Trocmé and colleagues (2004) made the following observation:

> Aboriginal families have statistically significantly less stable housing, greater dependence on social assistance, younger parents, more parents who were maltreated as children, and higher rates of alcohol and drug abuse. They are more likely to be investigated for neglect or emotional maltreatment. . . . Higher rates of placement among

Aboriginal children are statistically explained by a combination of
family, child, caregiver, and maltreatment characteristics. (p. 594)

Noting the divergent socio-economic conditions among First Nations communities across Canada, the Assembly of First Nations (2011) called for "funding, standards, and programs which take into account community specific contexts in order to
address the real needs of First Nations children and families" (p. 12).

Currently, there are 125 Aboriginal child and family service agencies in Canada,
including 84 First Nations agencies mandated to conduct child welfare investigations.
In line with the federal directive, these agencies have developed culturally appropriate,
community-based approaches to child and family service provision, which emphasize
prevention and support efforts to maintain bonds between family members and the
community (Blackstock, 2003; McKenzie & Flette, 2003).

Despite these efforts, more Aboriginal children are placed in out-of-home
care today than were placed in residential schools at the height of their operation
(Blackstock, 2003). Department of Indian Affairs and Northern Development data
confirms that between 1995 and 2001, the number of registered (status) Indian children
entering care rose to 71.5 per cent nationally (McKenzie, 2002). A 2003 study found that
across Canada, 30 to 40 per cent of children in care were Aboriginal (Farris-Manning &
Zandstra, 2003). Most disheartening is the fact that in 2011, of the roughly 30,000 children aged 14 years and under who were in foster care, 48.1 per cent were Aboriginal.
Moreover, 14,225 or 3.6 per cent of Aboriginal children were in foster care, compared
with 0.3 per cent of non-Aboriginal children (Statistics Canada, 2013). As the political
wrangling over financial support for the effective delivery of culturally appropriate
child welfare services for Aboriginal families continues to unfold, it is Aboriginal children and their parents who continue to bear the brunt of inequitable service delivery.
Despite the federal government's apology for not recognizing the discriminatory and,
some say, genocidal policies of the residential school system, it is possible that the persistent failure of government leaders to address current child welfare needs will result
in future apologies. Instead of seeking ways in which to mitigate their responsibilities,
the federal and provincial governments need to recognize the right and authority of
Aboriginal peoples in identifying the pathway forward for their own children, for their
families and, ultimately, for Aboriginal communities in Canada.

Conclusion

Canadian social policies have created institutions that eradicated Aboriginal value
systems that had existed for thousands of years and replaced them with doctrines
that continue to disrupt life for Aboriginal peoples. Canada's public policy toward
Aboriginal peoples has continually sought to assimilate them into mainstream culture.

Instead of emphasizing the importance of interconnectedness between individuals and the world around them, colonization has effectively cut Aboriginal people adrift from nurturing community environments and supplanted extended family support with arm's length service providers. Federal policies have weakened the family support structure that is vital to the Aboriginal home and have created conditions that put children at increased risk of being removed from their family and community of birth.

Ongoing advocacy efforts by national organizations such as the FNCFCS of Canada continue to push for restoring equitable funding to Aboriginal child welfare organizations. At the same time, organizations such as the Association of Native Child and Family Services Agencies of Ontario must maintain their advocacy efforts for self-governance in other areas of social policy in order to restore Aboriginal children to their families and communities.

On a personal note, at age 28, I decided to return to my First Nation to discover my roots. I was afraid to make this journey because I felt that I would not be accepted by my community. But the opposite happened: the community feasted at my return home. Many of my family members thought I had died. I know that I am one of the lucky ones to return home. Many of my Aboriginal brothers and sisters who went through experiences similar to mine never went back home or had a home to go back to.

References

Andres, R. (1981). The apprehension of Native children. *Ontario Indian, 46*, 32–37.

Armitage, A. (1993). Family and child welfare in First Nation communities. In B. Wharf (Ed.), *Rethinking Child Welfare in Canada* (pp. 131–171). Toronto: McClelland & Stewart.

Armitage, A. (1995). *Comparing the Policy of Aboriginal Assimilation: Australia, Canada and New Zealand*. Vancouver: UBC Press.

Assembly of First Nations. (2011). *Kiskisik Awasisak: Remember the Children. Understanding the Overrepresentation of First Nations Children in the Child Welfare System*. Retrieved from http://cwrp.ca/publications/2280

Bagley, C., Young, Y. & Scully, A. (1993). *International and Transracial Adoptions: A Mental Health Perspective*. Burlington, VT: Avebury.

Beaucage, J. (2011). *Children First: The Aboriginal Advisor's Report on the Status of Aboriginal Child Welfare in Ontario*. Retrieved from Ontario Ministry of Children and Youth Services website: www.children.gov.on.ca

Beisner, M. & Attneave, C. (1982). Mental disorders among Native American children: Rates and risk periods for entering treatment. *American Journal of Psychiatry, 139*, 193–198.

Bennett, M., Blackstock, C. & De La Ronde, R. (2005). *A Literature Review and Annotated Bibliography on Aspects of Aboriginal Child Welfare in Canada* (2nd ed.). Retrieved from First Nations Child and Family Caring Society of Canada website: www.fncaringsociety.com

Blackstock, C. (2003). First Nations child and family services: Restoring peace and harmony in First Nations communities. In K. Kufeldt & B. McKenzie (Eds.), *Child Welfare: Connecting Research Policy and Practice* (pp. 331–343). Waterloo, ON: Wilfrid Laurier University Press.

Brant, C. (1990). Native ethics and rules of behaviour. *Canadian Journal of Psychiatry, 35*, 534–539.

Brant, C. (1993). Suicide in Canadian Aboriginal peoples: Causes and prevention. In Royal Commission on Aboriginal Peoples (Chair), *The Path to Healing: Report on the National Round Table on Aboriginal Health and Social Issues*. Ottawa: Royal Commission on Aboriginal Peoples.

Bull, L.R. (1991). Indian residential schooling: The native perspective. *Canadian Journal of Native Education, 18* (Suppl.), 1–64.

Carriere, J. (2009). *You Should Know That I Trust You . . . Phase 2*. Retrieved from Ministry of Children and Family Development (British Columbia) website: www.mcf.gov.bc.ca/adoption/pdf/ cultural_planning_phase_2.pdf

Commission to Promote Sustainable Child Welfare. (2011). *Aboriginal Child Welfare in Ontario: A Discussion Paper*. Toronto: Minister of Child and Youth Services.

Couchi, C. & Nabigon, H. (1994). A path towards reclaiming birth culture. In F. Shroff (Ed.), *The New Midwifery* (pp. 41–50). Toronto: LPC InBook.

Farris-Manning, C. & Zandstra, M. (2003). *Children in Care in Canada: A Summary of Current Issues and Trends with Recommendations for Future Research*. Retrieved from Child Welfare League of Canada website: http://cwrp.ca

Fournier, S. & Crey, E. (1997). *Stolen from Our Embrace: The Abduction of First Nation Children and the Restoration of Aboriginal Communities*. Toronto: Douglas & McIntyre.

Frideres, J. (1998). *Aboriginal Peoples in Canada: Contemporary Conflicts* (5th ed.). Toronto: Prentice Hall Allyn & Bacon Canada.

Gagné, M. (1998). The role of dependency and colonialism in generating trauma in First Nations citizens. In Y. Danieli (Ed.), *International Handbook of Multigenerational Legacies of Trauma* (pp. 355–372). New York: Plenum Press.

Galley, V.J. (2010). *Summary Review of Aboriginal Over-Representation in the Child Welfare System*. Retrieved from Saskatchewan Child Welfare Review Panel website: http://saskchildwelfarereview.ca/ final-report.htm

Grant, A. (1996). *No End of Grief: Indian Residential Schools in Canada*. Winnipeg, MB: Pemmican Publications.

Hawthorn, H.B. (Ed.). (1966). *A Survey of the Contemporary Indians of Canada: Economic, Political, Educational Need and Policy: Part 1*. Ottawa: Indian and Northern Affairs Canada.

Hepworth, P. (1980). *Foster Care and Adoption in Canada*. Ottawa: Canadian Council on Social Development.

Hodgson, M. (1990). *Impact of Residential Schools and Other Root Causes of Poor Mental Health*. Edmonton, AB: Nechi Institute on Alcohol and Drug Education.

Hudson, P. & McKenzie, B. (1981). Child welfare and Native people: The extension of colonialism. *The Social Worker, 49*, 63–66, 87–88.

Indian Act ("An Act respecting Indians"), R.S. (1951, c. I-5).

Johnston, P. (1983). *Native Children and the Child Welfare System*. Toronto: Lorimer.

Kimelman, E. (1984). *Report on the Adoption of Native Children*. Winnipeg, MB: Government of Manitoba.

Lederman, J. (1999). Trauma and healing in Aboriginal families and communities. *Native Social Work Journal, 2* (1), 59–90.

Locust, C. (1999). Split feathers: Adult American Indians who were placed in non-Indian families as children. *Pathways, 14* (1), 1–5.

McDonald, R.J., Ladd, P., Blue Hills Training and Management, Keystone Consulting, Semanganis, H., Poirier Communications, . . . Assembly of First Nations. (2000). *Joint National Policy Review Final Report*. Retrieved from First Nations Child and Family Caring Society of Canada website: www.fncfcs.com/sites/default/files/docs/FNCFCS_JointPolicyReview_Final_2000.pdf

McKenzie, B. (2002). *Block Funding Child Maintenance in First Nations Child and Family Services: A Policy Review*. Winnipeg, MB: Kahnawake Shakotiia'takenhas Community Services.

McKenzie, B. & Flette, E. (2003). Community building through block funding in Aboriginal child and family services. In K. Kufeldt & B. McKenzie (Eds.), *Child Welfare: Connecting Research, Policy and Practice* (pp. 343–353). Waterloo, ON: Wilfrid Laurier University Press.

Monture, P. (1989). A vicious circle: Child welfare and the First Nations. *Canadian Journal of Women and the Law, 3*, 1–17.

Mussell, W., Nicholls, W. & Adler, M. (1991). *Making Meaning of Mental Health Challenges in First Nations*. Chilliwack, BC: Salishan Institute Society.

Napier, D. (2000, May 2). Sins of the fathers. *Anglican Journal*. Retrieved from www.anglicanjournal.com/articles/sins-of-the-fathers-6853

National Indian Brotherhood. (1972). *Indian Control of Indian Education*. Retrieved from Assembly of First Nations website: http://64.26.129.156/calltoaction/Documents/ICOIE.pdf

Palmer, S. & Cooke, W. (1996). Understanding and countering racism with First Nations children in out-of-home care. *Child Welfare, 75*, 709–725.

Richard, K. (2004). A commentary against Aboriginal to non-Aboriginal adoption. *First Peoples Child & Family Review, 1*, 101–109.

Royal Commission on Aboriginal Peoples (RCAP). (1996a). *Report of the Royal Commission on Aboriginal Peoples. Vol. 3: Gathering Strength*. Ottawa: Canada Communication Group.

Royal Commission on Aboriginal Peoples (RCAP). (1996b). *Report of the Royal Commission on Aboriginal Peoples. Vol. 1: Looking Forward, Looking Back*. Ottawa: Canada Communication Group.

Sanders, D. (1978). *Admittance Restricted*. Ottawa: Canadian Council on Children and Youth.

Statistics Canada. (2013). *National Household Survey, 2011: Aboriginal Peoples in Canada—First Nations People, Métis and Inuit*. (Catalogue no. 99-011-X2011001). Ottawa: Minister of Industry.

Timpson, J.B. (1990). Indian and Native special status in Ontario's child welfare legislation. *Canadian Social Work Review, 7*, 49–68.

Trocmé, N., Knoke, D. & Blackstock, C. (2004). Pathways to the overrepresentation of Aboriginal children in Canada's child welfare system. *Social Service Review, 78*, 577–600.

Truth and Reconciliation Commission of Canada. (2012). *They Came for the Children: Canada, Aboriginal Peoples, and Residential Schools*. Retrieved from www.trc.ca/websites/trcinstitution/index.php?p=580

Van de Sande, A. (1995). Native and mainstream parenting programs. *Native Studies Review, 10* (1), 1–20.

ABOUT THE AUTHOR

Peter Menzies, BA, BSW, MSW, PhD, is a member of the Sagamok Anishnawbek First Nation. He is a private consultant working primarily with First Nations communities in Ontario. Before establishing his private practice, Peter spent 14 years building culturally congruent mental health and addiction programs in partnership with urban and rural First Nations communities through the Centre for Addiction and Mental Health in Toronto. Peter is an assistant professor in the Department of Psychiatry at the University of Toronto and an adjunct professor in the Faculty of Social Work at Laurentian University in Sudbury. He received the Centre for Equity in Health and Society's Entrepreneurial Development and Integration of Services Award in 2005, and the Kaiser Foundation's Excellence in Indigenous Programming Award in 2011.

Part 2

Foundations of Healing

Chapter 5

Intergenerational Trauma

PETER MENZIES

Increasing evidence shows that more than a century of assimilative government policies has resulted in personal, familial and community trauma for Aboriginal peoples in Canada. The institutions and systems, such as residential schools, implemented as a result of these policies attempted to eradicate Aboriginal perspectives and values and replace them with ideological systems that continue to undermine life for Aboriginal peoples. Generations of people continue to be affected by the traumas of abuse, state-enforced separation and racist devaluation of culture.

This chapter reviews the evolving literature on intergenerational trauma and explores how culturally appropriate therapeutic interventions need to be informed by the history of Aboriginal peoples in Canada. Based on my own experience as a social work practitioner and therapist, the infusion of culturally appropriate healing strategies within therapeutic responses is a viable model for addressing the mental health needs of Aboriginal people.

Historical Context

The Canadian government has used a number of mechanisms to assimilate Aboriginal communities. Between 1840 and 1996, approximately 150,000 Aboriginal children were placed in the Indian residential school system for the purpose of assimilation, segregation and integration into Canadian society (Troniak, 2011). Separation from their families for months, even years, at a time resulted in children losing their language, culture and spiritual beliefs, as well as their sense of belonging to a family, community and nation. The abuses these children experienced are well documented in the reports of the 1996 Royal Commission on Aboriginal Peoples ([RCAP], 1996). In addition to being segregated by the residential school system, generations of Aboriginal children were also removed from their homes by child welfare systems. As a result, many Aboriginal people have been left without the necessary personal and community resources to address health problems in order to achieve harmony in their daily lives. This is evidenced by the following facts:

- In 2000, suicide was the leading cause of death among First Nations people aged 10 to 44 years. Almost one-quarter of all deaths among First Nations youth aged 10 to 19 were due to suicide (Health Canada, 2005).
- Aboriginal women are three times more likely to be victims of spousal violence than non-Aboriginal women (Chansonneuve, 2007).
- Alcohol-related deaths among Aboriginal people are six times higher than among the general population (Tremblay, 2009).
- In 2005, injection drug users accounted for a higher proportion of new human immunodeficiency virus infections among Aboriginal people than among the general population (53 per cent and 14 per cent, respectively) (Health Canada, 2009).
- First Nations children are in the care of child welfare authorities at rates disproportionate to those of other populations (Assembly of First Nations, 2006).

The abuses experienced and witnessed by generations of children have led to significant rates of mental health issues, such as depression, substance use problems and personality disorders, among Aboriginal people (Corrado & Cohen, 2003). The trauma of state-enforced separation has affected the ability of many Aboriginal people to achieve balance in their physical, mental, emotional and spiritual well-being. When subsequent generations continue to be affected by government policies that erode individual, family and community well-being, the ensuing trauma experienced by members of one generation affect the health and well-being of the next generation. This is intergenerational trauma.

From Systemic to Personal Trauma

Historical social policies and their resulting trauma have affected multiple generations of Aboriginal people (Chansonneuve, 2007). While the effects are experienced by individuals, my professional experience in the field of social work has led me to conclude that personal experiences are very much linked to family history and community experiences.

As mentioned in chapter 4, which discusses child welfare, anomie is a contributing factor to mental health problems among Aboriginal people in Canada (Brant, 1993). Anomie is a feeling of being disconnected from any particular cultural group. For Aboriginal people, anomie is linked to the residential school experience. Attending these schools for long periods away from their families and being immersed in a different culture created confusion and value conflict for the children.

The child welfare system had similar effects. Several studies have described the long-term effects of removing Aboriginal children from their birth families and placing them in non-Aboriginal homes (Couchi & Nabigon, 1994; Frideres, 1998; Locust, 1999). Because they were forced to assume the values of another culture that derided their own belief system, children were left in a cultural vacuum; they could relate neither to mainstream culture nor to their own community (Locust, 1999). Locust (1999) coined the term "split feathers" to refer to these children. Many Aboriginal children who were adopted or placed in foster care outside of their culture developed long-term psychological problems (Sinclair, 2011).

As adults, residential school and child welfare system survivors have higher rates of anxiety disorders, alcohol and other substance use problems, depression, suicide and low self-esteem compared with the general population (Chansonneuve, 2007; Corrado & Cohen, 2003; Gagné, 1998; Hodgson, 1990; Sinclair, 2011). Recently, psychologists developed the term "residential school syndrome" to describe the constellation of symptoms, similar to those of posttraumatic stress disorder (PTSD), experienced by residential school survivors (Brasfield, 2001). Residential school syndrome is the result of experiencing and witnessing physical, sexual, mental and emotional abuse over many generations.

PTSD is a diagnosis often given to Aboriginal people struggling with various issues (Söchting et al., 2007). As described in the *Diagnostic and Statistical Manual of Mental Disorders* (American Psychiatric Association, 2013), PTSD involves exposure to one or more traumatic events, such as war, terrorism, torture and actual or threatened physical or sexual violence, or to catastrophic medical events or serious accidents. A person may also develop PTSD as a result of witnessing, or even simply hearing about, these traumatic events happening to other people. Experiences of PTSD symptoms may vary. Some people relive the event through vivid, involuntary memories ("flashbacks") of the event or through dreams, and they may have emotional and behavioural symptoms. Others may experience negative thoughts, an inability to experience pleasure, or anxiety and restlessness. Yet others may become aggressive, reckless or self-destructive.

While PTSD and associated disorders focus on the individual's response to trauma, a diagnosis of PTSD for Aboriginal individuals does not acknowledge the conditions that have created and that perpetuate the trauma within families and across generations (Brave Heart & DeBruyn, 1998; Duran et al., 1998). Given the far-reaching consequences of public policy concerning Aboriginal peoples in Canada, it is important to understand that trauma affects more than just the individual; it affects multiple generations, entire families and whole communities (Kirmayer et al., 2003).

Defining Intergenerational Trauma

Both mainstream and Aboriginal mental health practitioners have challenged the practice of diagnosing disorders such as PTSD among Aboriginal people (Waldram,

1997). These diagnoses ignore the role of culture and intergenerational or community trauma and do not connect the person's experience to broader, systemic conditions that perpetuate and exacerbate the problems the person is facing. Researchers suggest that a diagnosis based on understanding intergenerational trauma—trauma that is passed down behaviourally from generation to generation—allows for better healing outcomes (Phillips, 1999; Whitbeck et al., 2004).

Several researchers have argued that focusing on individual trauma does not adequately address the complex Aboriginal experience. Kirmayer and colleagues (2000) suggested that it is often difficult for individuals to see their personal trauma as evidence of family and community trauma:

> Individual events are part of larger historical formations that have profound effects for both individuals and communities—effects that are harder to describe. These damaging events were not encoded as declarative knowledge but rather "inscribed" on the body or else built into ongoing social relations, roles, practices and institutions. (p. 613)

Duran and Duran (1995) were also critical of the focus on individual trauma, arguing that the diagnostic process fails to situate the person within his or her community's historical perspective. They suggested that many Aboriginal people are experiencing intergenerational PTSD:

> Many of the problems facing Native American people today—such as alcoholism, child abuse, suicide, and domestic violence—have become part of the Native American heritage due to the long decades of forced assimilation and genocidal practices implemented by the federal government. (p. 35)

The residential school experience is a key component of the forced assimilation experienced by Aboriginal peoples. In a discussion of the sociological etiology of intergenerational trauma among First Nations peoples, Gagné (1998) concluded that the effect of the residential school experience was felt beyond the generation that attended the school. Residential school survivors often became abusers, and thus, subsequent generations became victims (Mussell, 2005).

Gagné (1998) proposed that colonialism planted the "seed of trauma" for many First Nations communities. When experienced by more than one generation, personal trauma becomes institutionalized within a family. Where multiple families within a community experience similar life events, the community is left without the resources it needs to effectively address the resultant social consequences. As a result, entire Aboriginal communities are affected by the isolation, sadness, anger, hopelessness and pain of intergenerational trauma (Hodgson, 1990; Kirmayer et al., 2007).

The cumulative impact of trauma experienced by both children and their parents as a result of Canada's residential school policy continues to have consequences for subsequent generations of children. Phillips (1999) summarized the intergenerational impact of trauma:

> If we do not deal with our trauma, we inadvertently hand it down to the next generation . . . if we're angry and act angry all the time to others, our kids will think that's normal and do the same. If we ignore each other and deprive each other of love and affection in our relationships, our kids see and feel that deprivation of love and might think it's normal. (p. 6)

The theory of intergenerational trauma provides a framework for understanding the origins and context of individual maladaptive behaviours. Although it does not isolate the elements that help identify possible healing strategies, the theory improves understanding of symptomology. When symptoms such as depression, alcohol use problems and family violence are addressed in isolation of their precipitating cause, they are only superficially redressed. It is vital to understand individual behaviour in the context of a more generalized condition within the social infrastructure in which the trauma survivor exists. This deeper cultural understanding of intergenerational trauma and actual symptoms is necessary to move beyond temporary or partial solutions in order to address the malignant causes (Waldram, 2004).

Linking Cultural Loss to Symptomology

Residential school survivors and others in Aboriginal communities share common mental health experiences. The intergenerational trauma they experience correlates with their personal symptomology to reveal a complex picture without simple solutions.

Brave Heart (1998) examined the concepts of intergenerational trauma in her American-based study of the Lakota people. She found that many of the people interviewed for the study exhibited a number of symptoms associated with trauma. Brave Heart documented common somatic issues, including depression, psychic numbing, substance use problems, low affect, hypervigilance, suicide ideation, low self-esteem, victim identification, anger and hurt. She also documented other common symptoms that related to membership in the Lakota community, including identification with the dead, survivor guilt, loyalty to ancestral suffering and the deceased, distortion and denial of Native genocide and living life as if in more than one era, in the past and present.

While Brave Heart's (1998) research identified the psychological symptoms of historical trauma, she did not make the connection between the symptoms and their historical source. Whitbeck and colleagues (2004) were able to quantify and qualify a link between historical loss and unresolved grief and the emotional responses they elicit. In their exploratory study of American Indians, they developed two scales related to historical trauma: the Historical Loss Scale, which measures how often a person has thoughts pertaining to historical loss, and the Historical Loss Associated Symptoms Scale, which measures how often a person experiences certain emotions in thinking about these losses. Historical loss was identified as loss of land, language, culture, spiritual ways, family and family ties, self-respect, trust, people through early death and children's loss of respect for Elders and traditional ways. In the symptoms scale, emotional responses associated with historical loss include sadness, depression, anger, anxiety, nervousness, shame, loss of concentration, isolation or distance from other people, loss of sleep, rage, discomfort around white people, fear or distrust of the intentions of white people, feeling as though the loss is happening again and feeling like avoiding places or people. The scales link the theory of intergenerational trauma with symptoms experienced by trauma survivors.

In another exploratory study, Menzies (2009) examined the link between intergenerational trauma and homelessness among Aboriginal men in Canada. From the narratives of these men, Menzies identified common issues along four axes: individual, family, community and nation. The men consistently identified a range of personal somatic symptoms and a sense of social anomie. Their social histories included isolation from their birth, adoptive or foster families. Few men reported having experienced long-term attachments in their adult lives. Along the family axis, the men described chaotic and dysfunctional family lives with chronic or episodic family violence, including physical, sexual, emotional and verbal abuse of children by adults in the household, and a lack of emotional bonding with siblings and extended family members. Many grew up in homes that denied their own cultural heritage and where negative stereotypes of Aboriginal people were often propagated within the family of birth or the caregiver environment. The men reported open abuse of alcohol and other substances by parents and other adults in the home. Along the community axis, poverty, poor health care and lack of organization were reported by men who grew up within their birth family. Many described feelings of low self-esteem due to the public ridicule they experienced in institutional settings such as at school and at work, and even through media such as television shows. Having to hide one's cultural heritage was common among the men because of the public stereotypes associated with being Aboriginal.

The exploratory studies of Whitbeck and colleagues (2004) and Menzies (2009) have helped to build an understanding that individual behaviours are gestated in historical loss and trauma. These studies suggested that healing strategies must look beyond individual symptomology and focus more holistically on community healing. While researchers continue to explore how symptoms are linked to their historical causes, in my own practice, I see a growing number of people seeking help to address the pain of their symptoms.

Traditional Healing

Given the importance of the historical links between individual and community trauma, it is not surprising that there is increasing demand for services based on Aboriginal values and culture. Traditional approaches to healing acknowledge intergenerational trauma and mental health symptoms, and allow individuals, families and communities to access holistic healing strategies. Western approaches to mental health practice, including models of trauma and psychology that focus on the individual, must recognize the value of traditional methods of healing. Clinicians must look beyond the existing toolkit for dealing with issues such as depression, substance use problems and PTSD. Traditional approaches may be more effective for Aboriginal people because they address trauma from a strength-based approach, which emphasizes the strengths of the individual, family or community rather than focusing on deficits. This approach recognizes protector factors and facilitates finding solutions built on identified strengths (O' Connell, 2006).

Brave Heart (2005) argued that therapeutic interventions for intergenerational trauma require therapists to understand the concept of historical unresolved grief and appreciate that the healing context must consider the extended kin network that supports identity and history:

> Our underlying premise in this healing model rests on the importance of extended kin networks which support identity formation, a sense of belonging, recognition of a shared history, and survival of the group. Clinicians must be trained specifically in the concept of historical unresolved grief as well as address their own unresolved grief issues. (p. 70)

The therapeutic intervention must allow people to make the connection between the past, present and future. It must help them to become conscious of circumstances related to their pain and encourage them to heal themselves. This understanding gives Aboriginal people the "courage to initiate healing" (Brave Heart, 2005, p. 76).

Brave Heart (2005) advocated incorporating traditional ceremonies into the healing process to address unresolved grief. This includes ceremonies that recognize the pain experienced by multiple generations as a result of the loss of land, language and culture. These ceremonies need to be positive in order to help participants transcend their pain, achieve personal wellness and ultimately contribute to community transformation.

In his examination of attachment disorders precipitated by trauma, McCormick (1997) supported the use of traditional ceremonies as a way of reconstructing the individual's relationship with his or her culture. He proposed that traditional rites of passage, such as the vision quest ceremony, can help people develop healthy attachments, which had been destroyed by colonizing influences. The vision quest, which usually involves seclusion in nature, fasting and dreaming, allows the person to enter into a meditative state and find a pathway to healing. The person emerges from the ceremony with a new sense of awareness and identity, and is welcomed back to the community in celebration. In a therapeutic context, the role of the therapist, rather than being that of a surrogate attachment figure, is to support the person on his or her healing journey and to "act as a facilitator to enable the client to establish the needed 'secure base'" (McCormick, 1997, p. 21).

The medicine wheel can serve as a guide to the healing process. Wellness can only be achieved if there is balance and synergy among the four components of the self—physical, spiritual, emotional and mental—as represented by the medicine wheel (Hart, 2002). When one component is out of balance, the resulting imbalance among the remaining components can cause distress. A person who is depressed may turn inward and away from his or her spirituality, causing feelings of hopelessness. The person may not eat properly, which disrupts physical well-being. If mental depression forces the person into isolation, he or she will lose the emotional benefits of interacting with others. This synergy also applies to families and communities, which must seek to balance themselves around the medicine wheel.

Denham (2008) advocated the use of oral traditions, including narratives and dialogue, in the healing process and challenged the Western mental health model's deficit approach to therapeutic interventions with Indigenous populations:

> The exact resilience transmission or acquisition process was initially unclear. . . . Specifically, the way narratives are constructed and told, in addition to their contents or meaning, communicate specific resilience strategies. This resilience process is facilitated by not only consistent reminders of who they are as Native people, but also the strong circle of oral traditions and narratives contributed by each family member to the larger family circle. (p. 293)

The strength-based approach to wellness inherent in Aboriginal traditions promotes intergenerational healing by addressing the root causes of mental health issues in Aboriginal communities. Traditional approaches to healing and promoting health empower Aboriginal people and help them address issues arising from colonization and intergenerational trauma. This approach to healing strengthens communities in distress.

Clinical Application

At the Centre for Addiction and Mental Health in Toronto, work is under way to bring together traditional Aboriginal mental health and addiction services and mainstream

Western interventions. Building on the premise that culturally congruent service delivery promotes healing, especially for people seeking support, the Aboriginal Service provides clients with access to mainstream interventions, coupled with the support of Indigenous therapists and an Elder. As part of an interdisciplinary team, clients get the care they need to sustain them physically, mentally, emotionally and spiritually. Cultural support is available to Aboriginal clients in order to ground their healing within the healing of the community. This includes sweat lodge ceremonies, working with the Elder, vision quests, naming ceremonies and access to Aboriginal therapists. In this model, Indigenous health care practices are supported by the mainstream health care system and vice versa. This cultural support strengthens the bonds between individuals and the Aboriginal community, restoring competency and confidence to the community:

> The need is paramount for programs that support the development of Aboriginal peoples and allow us, as a community, to enhance our knowledge and skills so that we can provide support to community members through health care services, education, public policy, the justice system, and other important elements of our nation's social infrastructure. (Menzies, 2009, p. 21)

After more than 30 years as a social work practitioner and therapist, I have leveraged various approaches to meet the needs of people who seek help in addressing the symptoms of trauma at an individual level. I have used mainstream approaches such as brief solution-focused therapy, informed trauma practice, psychotherapy, dream work and cognitive-behavioural therapy, as well as traditional practices.

One of the cultural practices that I use with Aboriginal clients is to recount traditional Nanabush stories or teachings. In Ojibway teaching, Nanabush was sent to the Anishinaabe people to teach them how to live a good life. Nanabush's mother was Anishinaabe-kwe and his father was a spirit. Nanabush's stories or teachings can provide insight and spiritual help to people struggling with life. Before we examine these stories, the client and I explore what problems the client might be experiencing and determine strategies to help resolve them, which may include attending an addiction treatment centre. When the client is comfortable with me and we have developed a trusting relationship, and with the client's permission, I focus on one part of the client's problem and tell a Nanabush story that I believe best fits the client's situation. I tell the client that once I give the story it belongs to him or her as set out in Ojibway teachings. I ask the client to consider how the story might apply to his or her situation. Many clients are confused at first about how to apply the stories to their problem, so together we discuss the possible meaning of the story. Eventually, clients start applying what the story might mean to them, and through this process, they learn about their culture, identity and spirituality, and develop insights and ideas about how to address the problem.

This is a long process that requires a lot of patience while the client figures out how the story relates to himself or herself. Ojibway teachings tell us that we must not interfere with a person's development, so only with the person's permission can we help to interpret the meaning of the story as it applies to the problem. In fact, we can give the story, but clients do not have to tell us what the story might mean to them. As an Aboriginal therapist, I use my personal knowledge of Aboriginal culture and Ojibway teachings to inform my practice. A challenge for non-Aboriginal therapists working with Aboriginal clients is to find ways to collaborate with traditional healers rather than try to assume this role themselves (Lavallée, 2010). By leveraging the cultural richness of storytelling within the context of mainstream psychotherapeutic practice, a skilled Aboriginal therapist can use the strengths of both perspectives to support healing among Aboriginal clients.

Conclusion

For more than 100 years, Aboriginal peoples in Canada have been subjected to colonialist social policies that undermined their traditional values, beliefs, customs and community structures. While recent efforts demonstrating a commitment to addressing historical injustices are welcomed, Aboriginal people continue to experience a quality of life that is distinctly different from that of other people in Canada. Historical injustices continue to affect individuals, families and communities. Intergenerational trauma has emerged from the body of work related to PTSD and related disorders to reflect the ongoing transmission of trauma from one generation to the next. Therapeutic interventions for individuals with symptoms of intergenerational trauma need to consider the historical context that has shaped symptoms and behaviours. Traditional methods of healing can be used in conjunction with mainstream Western-based approaches to better address the complex needs of Aboriginal people.

References

American Psychiatric Association. (2013). *Diagnostic and Statistical Manual of Mental Disorders* (5th ed.). Washington, DC: Author.

Assembly of First Nations. (2006). *Leadership Action Plan on First Nations Child Welfare*. Ottawa: Author.

Brant, C. (1993). Suicide in Canadian Aboriginal peoples: Causes and prevention. In Royal Commission on Aboriginal Peoples (Chair), *The Path to Healing: Report on the National Round Table on Aboriginal Health and Social Issues*. Ottawa: Royal Commission on Aboriginal Peoples.

Brasfield, C.R. (2001). Residential school syndrome. *BC Medical Journal, 43*, 78–81.

Brave Heart, M. (1998). The return to the sacred path: Healing the historical trauma and historical unresolved grief response among the Lakota through a psychoeducational group intervention. *Smith*

College Studies in Social Work, 68, 280–305.

Brave Heart, M. (2005). *From Intergenerational Trauma to Intergenerational Healing: A Teaching about How It Works and How We Can Heal.* Colorado Springs, CO: White Bison.

Brave Heart, M. & DeBruyn, L.M. (1998). The American Indian holocaust: Healing historical unresolved grief. *American Indian and Alaska Native Mental Health Research, 8* (2), 60–82.

Chansonneuve, D. (2007). *Addictive Behaviours among Aboriginal People in Canada.* Retrieved from Aboriginal Healing Foundation website: www.ahf.ca

Corrado, R.C. & Cohen, I.M. (2003). *Mental Health Profiles for a Sample of British Columbia's Aboriginal Survivors of the Canadian Residential School System.* Retrieved from Aboriginal Healing Foundation website: www.ahf.ca

Couchi, C. & Nabigon, H. (1994). A path towards reclaiming birth culture. In F. Shroff (Ed.), *The New Midwifery* (pp. 41–50). Toronto: LPC InBook.

Denham, A. (2008). Rethinking historical trauma: Narratives of resilience. *Transcultural Psychiatry, 45,* 391–414. DOI: 10.1177/1363461508094673

Duran, E. & Duran, B. (1995). *Native American Postcolonial Psychology.* New York: State University of New York Press.

Duran, E., Duran, B., Yellow Horse Brave Heart, M. & Yellow Horse-Davis, S. (1998). Healing the American Indian soul wound. In Y. Danieli (Ed.), *International Handbook of Multigenerational Legacies of Trauma* (pp. 341–354). New York: Plenum Press.

Frideres, J. (1998). *Aboriginal Peoples in Canada: Contemporary Conflicts.* Toronto: Prentice Hall Allyn & Bacon Canada.

Gagné, M. (1998). The role of dependency and colonialism in generating trauma in First Nations citizens: The James Bay Cree. In Y. Danieli (Ed.), *Intergenerational Handbook of Multigenerational Legacies of Trauma* (pp. 355–371). New York: Plenum Press.

Hart, M. (2002). *Seeking Mino-Pimatisiwin: An Aboriginal Approach to Healing.* Halifax, NS: Fernwood.

Health Canada. (2005). *A Statistical Profile on the Health of First Nations in Canada for the Year 2000.* Ottawa: Author.

Health Canada. (2009). *A Statistical Profile on the Health of First Nations in Canada: Self-Rated Health and Selected Conditions, 2002 to 2005.* Ottawa: Author.

Hodgson, M. (1990). *Impact of Residential Schools and Other Root Causes of Poor Mental Health.* Edmonton, AB: Nechi Institute on Alcohol and Drug Education.

Kirmayer, L., Brass, G.M., Holton, T., Paul, K., Simpson, C. & Tait, C. (2007). *Suicide among Aboriginal People in Canada.* Retrieved from Aboriginal Healing Foundation website: www.ahf.ca

Kirmayer, L., Brass, G.M. & Tait, C.L. (2000). The mental health of Aboriginal peoples: Transformations of identity and community. *Canadian Journal of Psychiatry, 45,* 607–616.

Kirmayer, L., Simpson, C. & Cargo, M. (2003). Healing traditions: Culture, community and mental health promotion with Canadian Aboriginal peoples. *Australasian Psychiatry, 11,* 15–23.

Lavallée, L.F. (2010). Blurring the boundaries: Social work's role in Indigenous spirituality. *Canadian Social Work Review, 27,* 143–146.

Locust, C. (1999). Split feathers: Adult American Indians who were placed in non-Indian families as children. *Pathways, 14* (1), 1–5.

McCormick, R. (1997). An integration of healing wisdom: The vision quest ceremony from an attachment theory perspective. *Guidance & Counselling, 12* (2), 18–21.

Menzies, P. (2009). Homeless Aboriginal men: Effects of intergenerational trauma. In J.D. Hulchanski, P. Campsie, S. Chau, S. Hwang & E. Paradis (Eds.), *Finding Home: Policy Options for Addressing Homelessness in Canada* [e-book]. Retrieved from www.homelesshub.ca/FindingHome

Mussell, W. (2005). *Warrior-Caregivers: Understanding the Challenges and Healing of First Nations Men*. Retrieved from Aboriginal Healing Foundation website: www.ahf.ca

O'Connell, D. (2006). *Brief Literature Review on Strength-Based Teaching and Counselling*. Retrieved from Metropolitan Action Committee on Violence against Women and Children website: www.metrac.org

Phillips, G. (1999, November). *How we heal*. Paper presented at the National Stolen Generations Conference, Gold Coast, Australia.

Royal Commission on Aboriginal Peoples. (1996). *Report of the Royal Commission on Aboriginal Peoples. Vol. 1: Looking Forward, Looking Back*. Ottawa: Canada Communication Group.

Sinclair, R. (2011). Identity lost and found: Lessons from the sixties scoop. *First Peoples Child & Family Review, 3* (1), 65–82.

Söchting, I., Corrado, R., Cohen, I., Ley, R. & Brasfield, C. (2007). Traumatic pasts in Canadian Aboriginal people: Further support for a complex trauma conceptualization? BC *Medical Journal, 49*, 320–326.

Tremblay, P. (2009, March). *Getting it right: Using population-specific, community-based research to advance the health and well-being of First Nations, Inuit and Métis in Canada*. Paper presented at the 3rd International Meeting on Indigenous Child Health, Albuquerque, New Mexico.

Troniak, S. (2011). *Addressing the Legacy of Residential Schools (Background Paper)*. Retrieved from Parliament of Canada website: www.parl.gc.ca/Content/LOP/ResearchPublications/2011-76-e.pdf

Waldram, J. (1997). The Aboriginal peoples of Canada. In I. Al-Issa & M. Tousignant (Eds.), *Ethnicity, Immigration and Psychopathology* (pp. 169–187). New York: Plenum Press.

Waldram, J. (2004). *Revenge of the Windigo: The Construction of the Mind and Mental Health of North American Aboriginal Peoples*. Toronto: University of Toronto Press.

Whitbeck, L., Adams, G., Hoyt, D. & Chen, X. (2004). Conceptualizing and measuring historical trauma among American Indian people. *American Journal of Community Psychology, 33*, 119–130.

ABOUT THE AUTHOR

Peter Menzies, BA, BSW, MSW, PhD, is a member of the Sagamok Anishnawbek First Nation. He is a private consultant working primarily with First Nations communities in Ontario. Before establishing his private practice, Peter spent 14 years building culturally congruent mental health and addiction programs in partnership with urban and rural First Nations communities through the Centre for Addiction and Mental Health in Toronto. Peter is an assistant professor in the Department of Psychiatry at the University of Toronto and an adjunct professor in the Faculty of Social Work at Laurentian University in Sudbury. He received the Centre for Equity in Health and Society's Entrepreneurial Development and Integration of Services Award in 2005, and the Kaiser Foundation's Excellence in Indigenous Programming Award in 2011.

Chapter 6

Indigenous Ways of Helping

MICHAEL ANTHONY HART

We, the Indigenous peoples of Turtle Island[1], have our own ways of helping. They are based in our own ways of being in, experiencing, feeling, contemplating and understanding our world. Some Indigenous people assume their responsibilities by learning and carrying their gifts and sharing them to help others. These are serious responsibilities that have been threatened by colonialism. Fortunately, the commitment of these Indigenous helpers has been strong enough that our ways are beginning to flourish again and are being sought by more and more people, both Indigenous and non-Indigenous, as their chosen means of healing and change. In light of this growing positive influence (Fleming & Ledogar, 2008; Manitowabi & Shawande, 2011), people working in helping professions such as social work, psychology, nursing, counselling and medicine need to support the growth of Indigenous helping practices by making space for them and learning about them (Hart, 2002; Hill, 2003).

The purpose of this chapter is to help those in the caring professions understand Indigenous helping practices. I begin with a general overview of Indigenous ways of being in, experiencing, feeling and understanding the world. This overview cannot capture all the dynamics and complexities of Indigenous ways, but it can help readers recognize and support these ways. I then discuss helping processes that reflect Indigenous ways of being, particularly in central Turtle Island. The chapter concludes with a discussion of the influences colonization has had on Indigenous ways of being and helping practices. It also describes how helping professionals can work in an anti-colonial, indigenist manner to create and maintain space for Indigenous helping practices and decolonizing processes.

---

1 The name Turtle Island originates in the historical stories of several Indigenous nations and refers to the land that is now generally known as North America.

Being in, Experiencing, Feeling and Understanding the World

As McCormick (2009) suggested, "to communicate with and provide counselling services to Aboriginal people, providers must understand the traditional worldview of Aboriginal people" (p. 338). However, it is important to recognize that there is no single Indigenous way of being in the world. Because there are many different Indigenous peoples in Canada, there are many Indigenous ways of being in, experiencing, feeling and understanding the world. When working with a particular people on Turtle Island, it is important to find out about their world view, since the true source of understanding must come from those people themselves. However, there are many common elements in Indigenous peoples' ways: the central place of spirituality; significance of relationships; respect for individual development; connection to previous generations; continued reliance on traditional practices; emphasis on sharing and community; significance of knowledge keepers, namely Elders, as the main link for future generations; and wholistic[2] understanding. These elements are introduced below, but true understanding requires immersion in Indigenous ways.

THE CENTRAL PLACE OF SPIRIT

Indigenous ways of being in the world recognize the central place of spirit (Anderson, 2011; Hart, 2008a, 2009; Kirmayer et al., 2009). All life—people, animals, plants and other entities—contains spirit (Cajete, 2000). Spirit must be respected regardless of its form or location (Bopp et al., 1985). To respect spirit means that, as human beings, we do not hold ourselves higher than other life forms; that we honour how other life forms share their gifts, which stem from the spiritual essence; and that we honour our own spirit by sharing our gifts with other life forms in ways that properly recognize their roles and contributions (Hart, 2008a, 2009; Young et al., 1989).

SIGNIFICANCE OF RELATIONSHIPS

Indigenous peoples recognize that spirit connects all life (Aikenhead & Michell, 2011; Frideres, 2011; Hart, 2002, 2008a, 2009). We recognize that this interconnection is present in many ways: it exists within people (each person's spirit, emotional, mental and physical aspects interconnect) and between people; it exists between people and other animals, people and the elements, people and the land, and people and the spiritual realm. Life does not happen without relationships. Thus, to fully respect and

---

2 "Wholistic" is spelled with a *w* to respect the wishes of some Elders who would like to visually distance the concept from the word "holy" and emphasize the concept of wholeness.

honour spirit and, in turn, life, we must nurture the relationships we have with ourselves, with other people, with other animals, with the elements and with the spiritual realm. We refer to these others as our "relations." Our relationships with them are key to our well-being. How we treat our relations influences how they affect us because we are directly connected to them through spirit.

RESPECTFUL INDIVIDUALISM

Because spirit lies within all individual life, we must respect all people (Cordova, 2007; Hart, 2008a, 2009). We show respect by providing space for them to develop their own internal connections to their spirit and, through these connections, to uncover their gifts that they can share with other life (Cordova, 2007; Ermine, 1995). If we impose our will on others, we may interfere with their processes of connecting with spirit and developing their gifts. For example, a parent who decides his or her child should be a doctor has interfered with the child's self-discovery process. In general, if we interfere, we are getting in the way of what the Creator had in mind for the person. By understanding spirit, we come to know how we are going to contribute to the well-being of all life, including the people of the community. Indeed, it is well understood that individual well-being and community well-being are interconnected (Anderson, 2011; Cordova, 2007). As such, respectful individualism is quite different from the mainstream concept of individualism, which focuses only on the self without much attention to others (Gross, 2003). The Indigenous concept is based on the assumption that by being provided significant space for their development, individuals will act on their commitment to their community and orientate their gifts toward the well-being of the community.

CONNECTION TO PREVIOUS GENERATIONS AND CONTINUED RELIANCE ON TRADITIONS

Some people have undergone processes to connect with their sense of spirit and the spirit found in all life, and to determine what gifts they have and develop them (Anderson, 2011; Couture, 2011). This development is evident in the way these people live their lives. Not everyone demonstrates such personal development, but those who do have been recognized and are sought by others to provide guidance (Couture, 2011). Their knowledge, experience and guidance are passed down to them from previous and older generations as teachings for younger generations to consider (Frideres, 2011). Some of the processes involved in this development are many, many generations old and have become the tested means—the traditions—that are carefully emulated by people seeking to improve their lives. By following traditions, we connect to past generations, and by passing on these traditions, we connect to future generations.

SHARING AND COMMUNITY

While all forms of life have gifts, some Elders say that the only beings who do not innately understand their gifts are humans. By connecting to spirit, reaching back to past generations and carefully following the traditions laid down for us, we can understand and develop our gifts (Bopp et al., 1985). These gifts can be used in many ways, including to help or hinder other life (Young et al., 1989). In honouring and respecting spirit, we are encouraged to share our gifts in ways that benefit all life (Frideres, 2011). When we share our gifts, communities are developed and maintained. In turn, we receive support and develop a wider sense of purpose through these communities (Cordova, 2007). We also develop our faith in others and ourselves, as we believe what motivates people is the desire to experience *mino-pimatisiwin* (a Cree term for "the good life," which is the idea that all aspects of a person's life are interconnected and attended to so they are balanced and work in harmony) and the desire to contribute to the well-being of all. This belief reflects a high value on sharing and communalism (Cardinal & Hildebrandt, 2000; Hart, 2008a, 2009).

INDIGENOUS KNOWLEDGE KEEPERS

By walking through these processes, some people have developed their gifts and sense of purpose and have contributed to the well-being of their families and communities (Couture, 2011; Ellerby, 2001). Their experiences and contribution are recognized by the community, and people seek them for guidance. These individuals hold particular roles, such as Elder, knowledge keeper, traditional teacher, medicine person and spiritual adviser. Their knowledge and abilities are central to maintaining Indigenous ways of being, experiencing and understanding. While highly respected, they recognize the vastness of what is yet to be learned and how insignificant human beings are in the whole scheme of life. This belief helps them maintain a deep sense of humility, a value that is greatly appreciated by Indigenous communities.

WHOLISTIC UNDERSTANDING

Indigenous knowledge focuses on wholism (Aikenhead & Michell, 2011; Bopp et al., 1985; Pritchard, 1997) and related concepts, which are reflected in the medicine wheel (Hart, 2002). The medicine wheel is often depicted as a circle divided into four equal quadrants. The circle represents the whole and the four quadrants represent the grouping of different components in life. The four quadrants are identical; together they represent balance in life. The lines dividing the circle represent the relationships between different aspects of life; where the two lines cross represents the place where all aspects of life are in harmony. This medicine wheel concept is often used as a foundation for understanding the four stages of life, the four aspects of human beings, various key groups of life and the four directions (Cordova, 2007; Hart, 2002).[3] All four components must be included and given equal importance. In our lives, we need to consider the most wholistic picture possible: we must give attention to ourselves and others in ways that reflect all aspects of the medicine wheel, namely wholeness, relationship, balance and harmony.

This brief overview provides only a glimpse of a few elements that are central to Indigenous helping processes. However, recognizing these elements can assist helping professionals in letting go of practices that are based on positivistic empiricism, categorization and hierarchies. Doing so may avoid the unintentional, but destructive, colonial prejudice that often happens when developing an understanding of Indigenous helping processes.

Indigenous Helping Processes

Indigenous helping processes based on our ways of being in, experiencing and understanding the world intertwine the personal experience within community and spiritual interactions. Helping processes often include doing physical activities such as dancing, sharing ideas and experiences that touch people on an emotional level, telling stories that encourage people to reflect and engaging in meditative activities such as praying and listening deeply. All of these activities are associated with personal spiritual connection and support people in undertaking personal journeys. People do not make personal journeys in isolation. Each person is on a different journey but also shares that journey with others and is supported by friends, family and the community. These people in turn are supported by the person's growth and healing (Garrett et al., 2011).

Many Indigenous helping processes are based on identifying and developing values that stem directly from Indigenous ways of being, experiencing and understanding the world. These processes are often facilitated by Elders who are able to use what they have learned from many decades of life experience. They include ceremonies, which have been passed through many generations, as well as medicines, which have a more wholistic meaning. Medicine includes not only remedies for physical ailments, but also activities that influence people's emotional, mental and spiritual aspects. In addition, Elders have developed well-respected skills, including oration, storytelling and deep listening. The following sections examine features of the helping process.

VALUES AS GUIDELINES

In the helping process, Elders often introduce values associated with *mino-pimatisiwin* as guidelines for people to follow. These values include respect, sharing, honesty, faith, strength of character, kindness, humility and thankfulness (Cardinal & Hildebrandt,

---

3 Medicine wheel teachings are also discussed in chapters 1, 7, 9, 15 and 28.

2000; Hart, 2002). They are often learned through stories, both personal stories and legends that describe characters acting in ways that reflect the values or that describe characters experiencing difficulties because they have acted in ways that are contrary to the values. An example is the Anishinaabek Teachings of the Seven Grandfathers, which highlight the values of respect, honesty, truth, humility, strength, love and wisdom (Benton-Banai, 1988). The values are also discussed through pictures and models such as the Cree teepee teachings that outline 15 fundamental values, including hope, respect, humility, happiness, good child rearing, faith, kinship and love. Younger generations learn the values by observing older generations and by doing activities that facilitate the spiritual, emotional and cognitive understandings of the values.

ROLE OF ELDERS

Through decades of personal development and learning, contributing to the well-being of others and participating in Indigenous helping practices, Elders have become our "professionals." They support healing and growth by serving as role models, sharing traditional Indigenous knowledge and acting as guides and facilitators (Anderson, 2011; Couture, 2011; Hart, 2002). They become recognized as Elders by their communities through the ways they have met life challenges, lived the values of the people, learned the teachings of previous generations and acted to support their families and communities (Menzies et al., 2010). In other words, Elders model those attributes that have helped them in their own lives and that can help others heal and move toward *mino-pimatisiwin*. Through lifelong active learning, self-reflection and listening to older generations, Elders have become the prime knowledge keepers (Ellerby, 2001). Often this knowledge includes understanding how to guide people in developing the values that can help them overcome difficulties. Elders are keepers of traditional stories and of their own personal stories of self-development. In telling these stories, they provide culturally based ways to help people heal and grow. Through facilitating traditional ceremonies and acting on the wisdom given to them by their inner guides, Elders provide contexts for individuals, families and communities within which to heal and learn (Hart, 2002; Menzies et al., 2010).[4]

TRADITIONAL CEREMONIES AND PRACTICES

Central to Indigenous healing processes are numerous ceremonies that have been developed over many generations to help people wholistically connect with other life, and to promote healing and self-development. These ceremonies include lodge ceremonies, ceremonial dances and pipe ceremonies. Indigenous healing practices include fasting, feasting and smudging.

---

4 For more discussion about the role of Elders, see chapter 7.

Lodge Ceremonies

Of the wide variety of ceremonial lodges, perhaps the most familiar one is the sweat lodge. Sweat lodges are facilitated fairly consistently, but some Indigenous nations have many types of sweat lodges, each with its own set of teachings and processes (Bruchac, 1993; Bucko, 1999; Young et al., 1989). In the northern part of Turtle Island, the physical sweat lodge is usually a dome-shaped structure, formed by small trees and covered by blankets or canvas tarps (Bucko, 1999). The covering is designed to stop light from entering the lodge. Rocks are heated in a nearby fire and are brought into the lodge to provide heat. The details of how the lodge is constructed and facilitated come from the teachings followed by the lodge keeper. Sweat lodge facilitators spend years studying sweat lodge teachings from other knowledge carriers, usually Elders, who have developed this knowledge. Sweat lodges support healing and personal growth when they are conducted by individuals who deeply understand the ceremony (Livingston, 2010; Wagemakers Schiff & Moore, 2006). Many other lodges, including smoke lodges, night lodges and shake tents, provide similar healing and guidance. Common features of lodge ceremonies include the focus on spirit, group participation and understanding the lodge's cultural meaning.

Ceremonial Dances

Many First Nations have ceremonial dances, which support healing and growth. They include sun dances, chicken dances, warrior dances and spirit dances (Dion, 1994; Pritchard, 1997). The facilitator has learned the processes involved in the ceremonies over an extended period of time. Each of the ceremonial processes requires the participation of the people seeking help and guidance, primarily through dancing, singing, deep meditation or prayer. Some dances require significant time commitments or physical sacrifices. These commitments and sacrifices are key aspects of healing and growth.

Pipe Ceremonies

Pipe ceremonies play a central role in healing and helping among Indigenous peoples in central Turtle Island, as well as in many other territories (Manitoba First Nations Education Resource Centre [MFNERC], 2008; Paper, 1988; Young et al., 1989). Sacred pipes usually carved from wood or stone are involved in these ceremonies that focus on deep meditation and prayer through which participants acknowledge and reach out to the spiritual realm. These ceremonies are often facilitated by pipe carriers, who have been given this task by their Elders, communities or traditional teachers. Pipe carriers are often Elders. Different pipe carriers may have similar teachings. In other circumstances, they can carry specific teachings associated with particular pipes. Overall, these teachings promote healing and growth by providing direction about conduct that leads to *mino-pimatisiwin*. Pipe carriers use their pipes to help participants learn from these teachings. The ceremonies are regularly facilitated as part of many lodges and dances.

Fasting

While fasting is a ceremony in itself, it often accompanies certain lodges and dances. It involves abstaining from food and water for a specified period of time, usually four days. Because fasting involves a significant sacrifice, it must be facilitated by individuals who have learned the ceremony thoroughly, usually through apprenticeship (Anderson, 2011; McPherson & Rabb, 1993). The facilitator must be well prepared to ensure the safety of participants. A fasting ceremony includes particular processes and protocols based on teachings that are common to many Indigenous nations, as well as teachings specific to particular nations, communities and facilitators. As with the other ceremonies, people fast to promote healing and growth. More specifically, they often fast to develop spiritual insight and connection, and self-awareness and knowledge, and to contribute to community well-being (McPherson & Rabb, 1993).

Feasting

Feasting has been structured as a ceremony since time immemorial. It is regularly associated with other ceremonies, such as sun dances, walking out ceremonies and naming ceremonies (Pritchard, 1997). Food is prepared in particular ways. For example, people preparing the food must not eat any of it as it is being prepared. Some nations have specific protocols; for example, the food must be prepared from scratch, which ensures it is fresh. Another example is that the prepared food cannot be thrown out, which ensures nothing is wasted (MFNERC, 2008). In feasting, we recognize that we are eating with or on behalf of our ancestors. Thus, foods that our ancestors would have eaten should be part of the meal whenever possible.

Smudging

Smudging is a basic but essential process in lodges, dances and other ceremonies (MFNERC, 2008; Pritchard, 1997). Smudging uses certain plants, either individually or in a mixture. The plants are dried and lit to smoulder. People take in the smoke that the smouldering plants emit by moving their hands toward themselves in a gentle washing motion. This cleanses the mind, heart, body and spirit. The smoke is understood to carry the person's thoughts and feelings to a higher spiritual power. Smudging is also used to cleanse an area or item to prepare it for use in a positive, supportive manner, such as in a ceremony. It may be conducted as a ceremony in and of itself, but is almost always part of other ceremonies.

PLANT MEDICINES

Indigenous healing processes include the wholistic use of plants (Marles et al., 2000). Individuals are trained in their preparation and use for specific physical conditions. Plants are also used for more wholistic purposes, such as in smudging, which helps people centre and cleanse themselves emotionally, spiritually, physically and mentally

(MFNERC, 2008). In some Indigenous cultures, a person may offer tobacco to an Elder, which indicates the person is making a formal request, such as asking for help in understanding or overcoming a personal challenge.

ORATION, STORIES AND LISTENING

Many Indigenous cultures focus on using words and sound as medicines in helping and healing (McLeod, 2007; Pritchard, 1997; Simpson, 2011; Whidden, 2007). Elders are often very careful about how they express themselves: they understand the influence their wording may have (Pritchard, 1997). Many well-respected Elders are great orators. Elders and other people in helping positions may share their stories if recounting a personal life event can help someone who is trying to make a choice in similar circumstances. Stories also include legends that have been passed from generation to generation. Some legends recount the exploits of cultural heroes, such as Nanaboozoo in Anishnaabe stories and Wesakechahk in Cree stories. These stories teach about the natural world and healing activities, and provide life lessons, such as that actions have consequences. Singing also promotes healing (Whidden, 2007). It is seen as an important medicine that can help people regain balance. As such, singing is an integral part of many ceremonies. Similarly, Indigenous healing emphasizes the importance of listening: people are encouraged to listen rather than to make themselves heard over others. On a spiritual level, people are encouraged to keep themselves open to hearing the spirit that touches their heart when they are meditating or praying.

These aspects of Indigenous healing used in many parts of Turtle Island are snapshots of Indigenous ways of being. Indigenous ways of helping are being used today. They are based on ways of being that are different from those of the settler societies. In order to best serve Indigenous clients, helping professionals must learn about these healing practices and about Indigenous ways of being in, experiencing, feeling, contemplating and understanding the world.

Recognizing Diverse Ways of Being

We must shift from the attitude that Indigenous people need to choose between either Indigenous or mainstream ways of being and move toward a more nuanced understanding that people can express themselves in various ways. Through my interactions with many Indigenous people I have learned that some are strong in their Christian faith, others are steeped in Indigenous spirituality, and still others have been denied the opportunity to understand themselves as members of a people. Some Indigenous people are strict followers of non-Aboriginal ways of being in the world, whereas others know only their Indigenous traditions and culture. Still others combine these two ways of being in the world, for example, an Indigenous teenager who listens to rap music, dances pow wow, practises Buddhist meditation and participates in sweat lodge ceremonies with her grandparents. However, I would suggest that what helping professionals understand the least is Indigenous understandings that lie at the root of most Indigenous peoples' ways of being in the world, regardless of diversity of self-expression. Without this understanding, helping professionals will rely on their default position that is based in non-Indigenous perspectives and practices. By relying on this default position, they ignore or unconsciously marginalize Indigenous understandings and practices.

Helping professionals must appreciate the diversity in Indigenous communities and be ready to provide services that reflect and support Indigenous peoples' ways of being in the world whenever appropriate. Otherwise, they risk perpetuating the colonial oppression that Indigenous peoples have experienced.

Indigenous Helping Practices and Colonial Oppression

While it has been suggested that Indigenous concepts and practices are beginning to be accepted by helping professions in Canada, too often these concepts and practices are considered secondary to non-Indigenous ones (Hart, 2002; Sinclair 2004). Indigenous helping practices have not been well regarded by mainstream social services and health organizations. I have seen organizations, agencies and individuals work to stop even basic Indigenous practices from being incorporated into their workplace, even though they serve a large number of Indigenous people.

This kind of situation contributes to the colonialism that continues to exist in Canada. Colonialism is a process through which Indigenous peoples

> face the imposition, from genocide to assimilation to marginaliza-
> tion, of views, ideas, beliefs, values, and practices by other peoples at
> the cost of our lives, views, ideas, beliefs, values, practices, lands, and
> resources. It includes when we, as a peoples of this land, are stopped,
> hindered, cajoled, and/or manipulated from making decisions about
> our lives, individually and as a group, because of being a person of a
> peoples of this land. (Hart, 2008b, n.p.)

As professionals, we have an obligation to consider how we can best move away from such oppression and better serve Indigenous people. Such movement requires us to engage in several processes. First, we must look honestly at ourselves to see how we contribute to oppression, both as professionals and as individuals. This process entails learning about such concepts as privilege, whiteness, oppression, colonialism, racism and marginalization, and examining how we contribute to them. Second, overcoming colonialism requires us to learn about our relationship with members of the oppressed group. This involves understanding such concepts as cultural awareness, cultural sensitivity, cultural competence and cultural safety.[5] We cannot stop at simply developing awareness or being sensitive. We need to make ourselves competent helpers who provide culturally safe practice for Indigenous people seeking help. Third, we need to learn about Indigenous peoples' world views and practices. Ideally, this knowledge will lead us to support people when they make changes in their lives in ways that reflect their culture. It will also help us to create physical, conceptual and emotional space for those Indigenous peoples who wish to reflect and use Indigenous knowledge and practices.

Conclusion

It is clear for us as Indigenous peoples that our own helping practices must remain. These practices are deeply rooted in our helping philosophies and ways of being in the world. While we recognize that non-Indigenous society has made its own contributions to ways of helping, some of which we may accept, our own helping practices need more space and support. This chapter has highlighted some of these practices. The onus is now on each of us to continue to respectfully develop our understanding and wisdom so we will be best able to support Indigenous people, and potentially ourselves, in the healing process. Indeed, overcoming the legacy of colonial oppression requires such action on all accounts.

References

Aikenhead, G. & Michell, H. (2011). *Bridging Cultures: Indigenous and Scientific Ways of Knowing Nature*. Don Mills, ON: Pearson Education.

Anderson, K. (2011). *Life Stages and Native Women: Memory, Teachings, and Story Medicine*. Winnipeg: University of Manitoba Press.

Benton-Banai, E. (1988). *The Mishomis Book: The Voice of the Ojibway*. Saint Paul, MN: Red School House.

Bopp, J., Bopp, M., Brown, L. & Lane, P. (1985). *The Sacred Tree*. Lethbridge, AB: Four Worlds International Institute for Human and Community Development.

Bruchac, J. (1993). *The Native American Sweat Lodge: History and Legends*. Freedom, CA: Crossing Press.

Bucko, R.A. (1999). *The Lakota Ritual of the Sweat Lodge: History and Contemporary Practice*. Lincoln: University of Nebraska Press.

Cajete, G. (2000). *Native Science: Nature Laws of Interdependence*. Santa Fe, CA: Clear Light.

Cardinal, H. & Hildebrandt, W. (2000). *Treaty Elders of Saskatchewan: Our Dream Is That Our Peoples Will One Day Be Clearly Recognized as Nations*. Calgary, AB: University of Calgary Press.

Cordova, V.F. (2007). *How It Is: The Native American Philosophy of V.F. Cordova*. In K.D. Moore, K. Peters, T. Jojola & A. Lacy (Eds.). Tucson: University of Arizona Press.

---

5 For discussions about cultural competence and cultural safety, see chapters 10 and 30.

Couture, J.E. (2011). The role of Native Elders: Emergent issues. In D. Long & O.P. Dickason (Eds.), *Visions of the Heart: Canadian Aboriginal Issues* (3rd ed.; pp. 31–48). Don Mills, ON: Oxford University Press.

Dion, J.F. (1994). *My Tribe the Crees*. Calgary, AB: Glenbow-Alberta Institute.

Ellerby, J.H. (2001). *Working with Aboriginal Elders: An Introductory Handbook for Institution-Based and Health Care Professionals Based on the Teachings of Winnipeg-Area Aboriginal Elders and Cultural Teachers* (2nd ed.). Winnipeg, MB: Native Studies Press.

Ermine, W. (1995). Aboriginal epistemology. In M. Battiste & J. Barman (Eds.), *First Nations Education in Canada* (pp. 101–112). Vancouver: UBC Press.

Fleming, J. & Ledogar, R.J. (2008). Resilience and Indigenous spirituality: A literature review. *Pimatisiwin: A Journal of Aboriginal and Indigenous Community Health, 6* (2), 47–64.

Frideres, J.S. (2011). *First Nations in the Twenty-First Century*. Don Mills, ON: Oxford University Press.

Garrett, M.T., Torres-Rivera, E., Brubaker, M., Portman, T.A.A., Brotherton, D., . . . Grayshield, L. (2011). Crying for a vision: The Native American sweat lodge as therapeutic intervention. *Journal of Counseling and Development, 89*, 318–325. DOI: 10.1002/j.1556-6678.2011.tb00096.x

Gross, L.W. (2003). Cultural sovereignty and Native American hermeneutics in the interpretation of the sacred stories of the Anishinaabe. *Wicazo Sa Review, 18*, 127–134.

Hart, M.A. (2002). *Seeking* Mino-Pimatisiwin: *An Aboriginal Approach to Helping*. Halifax, NS: Fernwood.

Hart, M.A. (2008a). Critical reflection on an Aboriginal approach to helping. In J. Coates, M. Grey & M. Yellowbird (Eds.), *Indigenous Social Work around the World: Towards Culturally Relevant Education and Practice* (pp. 129–140). Aldershot, UK: Ashgate Press.

Hart, M.A. (2008b). *Understanding oppression: An Aboriginal perspective*. Paper presented at the Understanding Oppression: Becoming an Ally Community Workshop, Winnipeg, MB.

Hart, M.A. (2009). Anti-colonial indigenist social work: Reflections on an Aboriginal approach. In R. Sinclair, M.A. Hart & G. Bruyere (Eds.), *Wicihitowin: Aboriginal Social Work in Canada*. Halifax, NS: Fernwood.

Hill, D.M. (2003). *Traditional Medicine in Contemporary Contexts: Protecting and Respecting Indigenous Knowledge and Medicine*. Ottawa: National Aboriginal Health Organization.

Kirmayer, L.J., Brass, G.M. & Valaskakis, G.G. (2009). Conclusion: Healing/intervention/tradition. In L.J. Kirmayer & G.G. Valaskakis (Eds.), *Healing Traditions: The Mental Health of Aboriginal Peoples in Canada* (pp. 440–472). Vancouver: UBC Press.

Livingston, R. (2010). Medical risks and benefits of the sweat lodge. *Journal of Alternative and Complementary Medicine, 16*, 617–619. DOI: 10.1089/acm.2008.0381

Manitoba First Nations Education Resource Centre (MFNERC). (2008). *First Nations Teachings & Practices*. Winnipeg, MB: Manitoba First Nations Education Resource Centre.

Manitowabi, D. & Shawande, M. (2011). The meaning of Anishinabe healing and wellbeing on Manitoulin Island. *Pimatisiwin: A Journal of Aboriginal and Indigenous Community Health, 9*, 441–458.

Marles, R.J., Clavelle, C., Monteleone, L., Tays, N. & Burns, D. (2000). *Aboriginal Plant Use in Canada's Northwest Boreal Forest*. Vancouver: UBC Press.

McCormick, R. (2009). Aboriginal approaches to counselling. In L. Kirmayer & G. Valaskakis (Eds.), *Healing Traditions: The Mental Health of Aboriginal Peoples in Canada* (pp. 337–354). Vancouver: UBC Press.

McLeod, N. (2007). *Cree Narrative Memory: From Treaties to Contemporary Times*. Saskatoon, SK: Purich.

McPherson, D.H. & Rabb, D. (1993). *Indians from the Inside: A Study in Ethnometaphysics*. Thunder Bay, ON: Lakehead University Centre for Northern Studies.

Menzies, P., Bodnar, A. & Harper, V. (2010). The role of the Elder within a mainstream addiction and mental health hospital: Developing an integrated paradigm. *Native Social Work Journal, 7*, 87–107.

Paper, J. (1988). *Offering Smoke: The Sacred Pipe and the Native American Religion.* Moscow: University of Idaho.

Pritchard, E.T. (1997). *No Word for Time: The Way of the Algonquin People.* San Francisco: Council Oak Books.

Simpson, L. (2011). *Dancing on Our Turtle's Back: Stories of Nishnaabeg Re-creation, Resurgence and New Emergence.* Winnipeg, MB: Arbeiter Ring.

Sinclair, R. (2004). Aboriginal social work education in Canada: Decolonizing pedagogy for the seventh generation. *First Peoples Child and Family Review, 1*(1), 49–61.

Wagemakers Schiff, J. & Moore, K. (2006). The impact of the sweat lodge ceremony on dimensions of well-being. *American Indian and Alaska Native Mental Health Research, 13* (3), 48–69.

Whidden, L. (2007). *Essential Song: Three Decades of Northern Cree Music.* Waterloo, ON: Wilfrid Laurier Press.

Young, D., Ingram, G. & Swartz, L. (1989). *Cry of the Eagle: Encounters with a Cree Healer.* Toronto: University of Toronto Press.

ABOUT THE AUTHOR

Michael Anthony Hart is a member of Fisher River Cree Nation. He is the father of two boys and is committed to providing them a way life that reflects Cree ways of being. He is deeply committed to the well-being of Indigenous peoples, cultures and knowledge. Michael has worked in the areas of child welfare, addiction, and family and individual therapy. He does volunteer work in community development and facilitating cultural events. He is the Canada Research Chair in Indigenous Knowledges and Social Work, and an associate professor in the Faculty of Social Work at the University of Manitoba. His research focuses on Indigenous ways of helping.

Chapter 7

The Role of Elders in the Community

SUSAN MANITOWABI

Elders have always occupied a special position in society. These spiritual and cultural leaders have "painstakingly accumulated reservoirs of personal experience, knowledge, and wisdom—or compassionate insight," which they "freely offer to living generations of their people in an effort to help them connect harmoniously with their past, present, and future" (Suzuki & Knudston, 1992, p. 224).

Traditionally, Elders help their communities in a variety of ways: they provide cultural teachings, share knowledge of the language and of the medicines, and offer spiritual teachings and wisdom. This role is evolving. Elders are being sought for guidance and advice not only by Aboriginal communities, but by non-Aboriginal communities, as well. For example, in a discussion about bridging traditional and mainstream Western science, Colorado (1988) described the importance of consulting Elders because of their knowledge of the natural environment. Elders were also key contributors during the consultation process conducted by the Royal Commission on Aboriginal Peoples (1996).

This chapter discusses what it means to be an Elder, highlights the roles Elders play in Aboriginal communities and explores the emerging roles of Elders in non-Aboriginal communities. It also provides practical information about how to make effective use of Elders, listening and appreciating their knowledge, understanding and teachings in a respectful manner that is consistent with cultural protocols.

What It Means to Be an Elder

There are many ways to define "elder." Often, the term refers to a person of greater age or seniority. Colorado (1988) distinguished between Elders and older adults, noting that in Aboriginal cultures, all older people are recognized for the lessons they have to offer based on their life experiences.[1] Not all older adults are considered Elders, but they are still important members of the community and should be meaningfully involved in it. Anishinaabe teachings tell us that every member of the community has something to offer, even the youngest child.

What sets Elders apart is their specialized knowledge of the cosmos, their ability to learn from their experiences and interpret them in traditional terms, and their capacity for understanding and centring themselves in relation to the universe and imparting that learning to others (Colorado, 1988; Hart, 2002). In Aboriginal communities, an Elder is a person that community members seek for spiritual and cultural leadership and for their knowledge of some aspect of tradition. Elders are acknowledged for their life experiences and, as experts on life, can provide guidance to younger people.

Elders know what it means to be an Aboriginal person, as well as having a deep understanding of Aboriginal philosophies and world views as handed down in ceremonies and traditional teachings. Traditional philosophy contains teachings about *mino-pimatisiwin* (how to live a healthy life) and how to have a strong sense of identity (Hart, 2002). Aboriginal communities usually call upon their Elders to help make decisions about a range of issues, including health, community development and governmental negotiations regarding land use and self-government (Stiegelbauer, 1996).

Elders are not necessarily older people. Many young people have become Elders, recognized for the "gifts" they carry or respected for the work they have done in their communities (Edge & McCallum, 2006). For example, a community may recognize a young person as an Elder through having learned the teachings of the Pipe or the sweat lodge. These young Elders may also follow a traditional lifestyle based on the teachings of *mino-pimatisiwin*.

CHARACTERISTICS OF ELDERS

Elders embody various characteristics (Colorado, 1988; Edge & McCallum, 2006; Hart, 2002; Nabigon, 2006; Stiegelbauer, 1996). In general, they
• are well-known and well-respected
• maintain good reputations in their communities
• hold specialized knowledge about the traditions, ceremonies, teachings, stories and legends, and the process of life
• are able to transmit culture and teachings

---

1   For more discussion about older Aboriginal adults, see chapter 13.

• are able to provide counselling
• speak the nation's language
• know their teachings, culture, traditions and spiritual ceremonies and live by them
• have progressed through all stages of life (although not always)
• are recognized by the community for their wisdom and ability to help
• have a range of knowledge and skills.

Elders are the personification of tradition, whatever their specific expertise or training. They are symbols of Aboriginal culture, not only in their words and actions, but in their very being. They can draw upon their knowledge and wisdom to help others understand the teachings and to heal individuals and communities.

How Elders Become Recognized by the Community

Elders are usually recognized by an Aboriginal community as having knowledge and understanding of the traditional culture of the community, including the physical manifestations of the culture, as well as its spiritual and social traditions (Couture, 2000). Aboriginal communities recognize Elders for a number of reasons: their greater age and stage in life, social contributions, family standing, wisdom and ability to contribute to the welfare of the community (National Aboriginal Health Organization [NAHO], 2008; Swinomish Tribal Mental Health Project, 2002). Often, it is because of the choices they make or the lifestyle they lead that they are recognized by the community. Becoming an Elder is not something that happens overnight. It is a process.

Becoming an Elder can happen quite naturally by being involved with the community's teachings and living a traditional way of life (Nabigon, 2006). It can evolve by developing an interest in cultural practices and apprenticing with an Elder, but it can also happen suddenly as a result of going through extreme life experiences (Stiegelbauer, 1996). In any case, becoming an Elder involves a learning process precipitated by an event (personal, spiritual or political) that motivated a person to return to the traditional way—to learn the teachings and ceremonies by practising them (Stiegelbauer, 1996).

Roles of Elders within Aboriginal Communities

The roles that Elders play among First Nations, Métis and Inuit are similar. Significant differences in teachings and cultural protocols exist within these three groups, but for the purposes of this chapter, I discuss Elder roles that are common to all Aboriginal peoples.

Elders are often looked to as role models for the community—as teachers and keepers of traditional knowledge and history; as wise counsel, spiritual guides and advisers; as holders of ceremonial practice; and as advisers in community decision making (Edge & McCallum, 2006; Hart, 2002; Stiegelbauer, 1996; Swinomish Tribal Mental Health Project, 2002). Elders have a social responsibility to transmit their cultural knowledge (Johnston, 1976) and to point people toward their rituals so they can become more aware of themselves and their place within the natural world (Colorado, 1988). Elders are teachers to the grandchildren and all young people because of their wisdom, greater life experience, historical perspective and close ties to traditional ways (Swinomish Tribal Mental Health Project, 2002).

ELDERS AS ROLE MODELS

Being an Elder requires modelling traditional approaches to speaking, teaching and working with others. Elders must mirror traditional values in everything they do, and follow a traditional lifestyle in their relationships and in their approach to work. They are role models for all members of their families, the community and the nation, showing them how to live a traditional life (Stiegelbauer, 1996).

ELDERS AS TEACHERS AND ADVISERS

In its broadest sense, teaching means passing on knowledge. Anyone who imparts knowledge or helps people to understand is considered a teacher. Therefore, the role of teacher does not fall solely to Elders. However, Elders as teachers have a special responsibility to share their teachings with the community. The community recognizes the lifelong learning that Elders have undergone and the teachings they hold by inviting them to give their teachings at community gatherings and ceremonies.

Elders are often referred to as our "grandparents"—as *mishoomis* (grandfather) or *nookomis* (grandmother). Not all grandparents are considered Elders. However, the traditional role of grandparents influences how Anishinaabe people view their Elders. For example, grandparents were the primary teachers of children. They taught children about their culture, family history and relationships, and about socially acceptable behaviour. Growing up, I spent many long hours with my grandmother. She taught me our family history and would tell stories about relatives who had passed on and how they were related to my family. She would share with me how the memory of our ancestors was kept alive by naming children after them.

Being Anishinaabe-kwe (an Aboriginal woman) from Manitoulin Island in Ontario, the medicine wheel teaching on the special relationship between grandparents and grandchildren was explained to me in the following way: The medicine wheel is a sacred symbol that contains many teachings. One of the teachings is about relationships. The medicine wheel depicts four periods of the lifespan: infancy, youth, adulthood and elderhood (see Figure 7-1).

FIGURE 7-1

Four Stages of Life

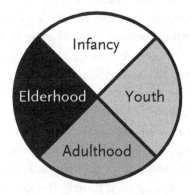

The infant and the adult sit opposite each other on the medicine wheel, as do the youth and the Elder. The infant and the adult have a close relationship: the parent is usually the primary caregiver and has the greatest influence on the infant, especially during the first six years of life. Youth can be a time of turmoil and conflict, especially with parents, so it is natural for youth to seek out other sources of support, often their grandparents. As a youth, I spent a great deal of time with my grandmother, and now, as a grandmother myself, I spend a lot of time with my granddaughter. This is a special time, mutually beneficial, as we do chores together and I provide a caring, listening ear as we work through my granddaughter's struggles.

Elders are increasingly being sought out by both Aboriginal and non-Aboriginal organizations for their expertise as advisers on traditional practices and cultural knowledge and protocols. The Native Canadian Centre of Toronto (2010) uses Elders from the Taam Kaadinakiijik Advisory Circle to provide guidance for its programs. Anishnawbe Health Toronto (n.d.) includes Elders in the healing services it provides. Elders also provide guidance and counselling to the Northern Ontario School of Medicine (2011). Other universities are approaching Elders, such as Dr. Cecil King from the University of Saskatchewan, to teach and sit on graduate committees or to be part of their faculties. For example, Margaret Lavallée is Elder-in-residence at the University of Manitoba (University of Manitoba, 2013).

ELDERS AS HEALERS

Since Elders have reached an optimum place of healing, by being centred on the medicine wheel and having achieved balance and wholeness, they are able to assist people with their healing journeys. Mussell (2005) described healing as a process that involves "grieving the significant losses in one's life that have inhibited growth and development and contributed to personal difficulties" (p. 11). Healing does not refer only to the process of helping individuals recover from an illness or solve a problem; it also refers to the process that is required when there is a sense of being disconnected, imbalanced and in disharmony with the natural world (Absolon, 1993; Hart, 2002; Ross, 1996). Thus, the healing process can involve guidance, often from an Elder, who helps to restore "the person, community and nation to wholeness, connectedness and balance" (Regnier, 1994, p. 135). Elders are able to communicate teachings in a meaningful way that facilitates the healing journey.

Elders facilitate the healing process by helping individuals to build self-knowledge and increase their skills and knowledge of the external world in order to positively modify their capacity to manage life's challenges (Mussell, 2005). Genuine listening is very important in the healing process; healing emerges from dialogue: the person tells the Elder what is wrong and how the Elder can help, and the Elder explains what needs to be done. Storytelling can also be used to help the Elder understand the person's suffering. By listening to the person's story, the Elder can understand the situation, and the story can provide clues about what caused it (Mehl-Madrona, 2009).

Listening to dreams is an important part of healing. When I was a young adult, I shared a dream I had had with my Elder. In the dream, I was trying to cross a river when a vicious storm came up, making the crossing difficult. The Elder asked if I made it to the other side of the river, to which I replied "yes." Then he related to me that I would experience some challenges in life, but that I would overcome them.

It is said that when we dream our spirit travels, sometimes into the future, where we can see what will happen. An example is when you approach an Elder with tobacco and the Elder acknowledges that he or she has been waiting for you and knows why you are there. Elders, being so close to the spirit world, work with the spirits who provide them with guidance about how to help people.

ELDERS AS CULTURAL AND SPIRITUAL COUNSELLORS

Elders provide counselling, support and guidance based on what they have learned from their life experiences. They can provide cultural teachings to help people address issues stemming from the historical degradation of their culture and to help people who are striving toward *mino-pimatisiwin* (Hart, 2002). Counselling focuses on learning from one's experience; working toward maintaining a balance among the spiritual, emotional, mental and physical aspects of being; reconnecting to traditional ways; and seeking harmony within the self to facilitate healing and growth (Long & Dickason, 1998).

ELDERS AS CONDUCTORS OF CEREMONIES

Because of their knowledge of culture, ceremonies and traditions, Elders are often called upon to conduct ceremonies (e.g., pipe, naming, sweetgrass, sweat lodge, fasting) (Stiegelbauer, 1996). Ceremonies can take place in various settings: sacred grounds, outdoors, community agencies (schools, offices, institutions) or other private locations. There are usually protocols around each ceremony, so it is wise to speak with the Elder conducting the ceremony about what to expect.

Elders usually work with the spirits when they conduct ceremonies. They call upon the spirits of our ancestors to assist in the ceremony. Elders know how to call these spirits in and, more importantly, how to send them back. This special knowledge comes from experience and having worked alongside other healers, helpers, medicine people and Elders who know how to work with spirit.

ELDERS IN COMMUNITY WORK

Elders as knowledge keepers of traditions, beliefs, ceremonies and philosophies can provide guidance and advice around creating culturally appropriate or culturally based programs (Stiegelbauer, 1996). For example, friendship centres use Elders to provide cultural and spiritual counselling. The mission of the National Association of Friendship Centres is to improve the quality of life of Aboriginal people living in urban areas, while emphasizing Aboriginal cultural distinctiveness. Friendship centres refer individuals to Elders or bring Elders into the program to provide cultural teachings and counselling (National Association of Friendship Centres, 2013).

ELDERS IN CONFLICT RESOLUTION AND MEDIATION

Elders may be asked to help Aboriginal organizations or communities resolve a conflict. Smudging[2] and saying prayers helps both sides to approach the issue with good intentions and clear minds. By facilitating discussion and establishing protocols, the Elder helps both sides to listen to and hear one another. Elders draw upon their experience to help clarify the issues and move the discussion forward toward a resolution.

An example of this mediation role is the Community Council Program, an Aboriginal-run justice diversion project operated by Aboriginal Legal Services of Toronto (Warry, 2008). The Crown attorney refers cases involving Aboriginal offenders to this program. A panel of Aboriginal volunteers, community leaders and Elders helps both offenders and victims reach agreements about the most culturally appropriate ways to resolve disputes and reconcile differences.

ELDERS IN HEALTH CARE

Elders play an important role in the health of Aboriginal communities. For example, Aboriginal health access centres (AHAC) provide a combination of traditional healing,

---

2   Smudging is a ceremony that involves cleansing the mind, ears, eyes, mouth, heart and body with smoke from burning medicines—sage, sweetgrass, tobacco and cedar.

primary care, cultural programs, health promotion programs, community development initiatives, and social support services to First Nations, Métis and Inuit communities (Association of Ontario Health Centres, n.d.).

The Noojmowin Teg Health Centre (NTHC) on Manitoulin Island in Ontario has made great strides in braiding together traditional and Western approaches to health and wellness. This health centre has formed a Traditional Healing Advisory Committee made up of Elders and representatives from the seven First Nations communities it serves. The committee supports the Traditional Healing Program and its co-ordinator (AHAC, 2010).

When the voices of Elders are present in Aboriginal health care settings, clients feel safer about accessing traditional supports and ceremonies. NTHC, which was already using traditional healers and Elders, deemed it necessary to develop a policy about traditional activities. In 2006, it released a bicultural traditional healing services policy and program manual (NTHC, 2007), which AHACS across the country have adapted (AHAC, 2010). Formalizing the Elder role is a testament to its importance within health care organizations that serve Aboriginal people.

ELDERS IN RESEARCH

Research involving Aboriginal people has undergone a paradigm shift—from researcher as expert to researcher as facilitator of research, which is shaped by Elders and others in the community. Researchers now routinely seek out Elders for wisdom and guidance, as well as for ongoing feedback throughout the research process (Moeke-Pickering et al., 2006).

Ethical guidelines for research involving Aboriginal populations have been developed in response to Aboriginal demand for more control over the types of research conducted among their people, and the research methods used. For example, the Manitoulin Anishinabek Research Review Committee developed the *Guidelines for Ethical Aboriginal Research* (GEAR) in consultation with Elders (NTHC, 2003a). The *Ethics and Research Review Workbook* (NTHC, 2003b) that accompanies the guidelines includes a section that incorporates the principles of ownership, control, access and possession outlined by NAHO (2005). The principles ensure that research projects are culturally appropriate, that the rights of individuals and communities are protected and that ethical guidelines for research with Aboriginal people are followed. The GEAR document has become a model for other Aboriginal organizations and communities that are interested in establishing similar guidelines.

Ethical guidelines for research also exist at the national level. The *Tri-Council Policy Statement: Ethical Conduct for Research Involving Humans* (Canadian Institutes of Health Research, Natural Sciences and Engineering Research Council of Canada & Social Sciences and Humanities Research Council of Canada, 2010) includes a section on research with First Nations, Inuit and Métis. In it, the authors recognize the role of Elders and other knowledge holders, and advocate their meaningful participation in the design and execution of research, and the interpretation of findings. Elders should also play a significant role in developing research proposals and grant applications because they have access to community networks and can provide ethical guidance and advice to researchers about how to interpret findings in the context of traditional knowledge.

How to Find Elders

A good place to find Elders is through your local community, whether that is a First Nation or urban Aboriginal community. If you would like to approach an Elder from a First Nation community, get to know its members, since it is through the community that Elders come to be recognized. If you are in an urban community, contact the local friendship centre, Métis association, AHAC or other Aboriginal organization. For example, in Toronto, you might visit Anishnawbe Health Toronto, the Native Canadian Centre or Aboriginal Legal Services. If you are in Sudbury, the N'Swakamok Native Friendship Centre, Shkagamik-Kwe Health Centre or Métis Association of Ontario may be helpful. Each community provides a similar array of services.

Getting to know the Aboriginal community is essential to ensuring you connect with a "true" Elder. There are individuals who claim to be Elders: they may attend ceremonies, sit around a drum and sing, have sacred items (smudge bowl, eagle feathers), wear ceremonial clothing, have an Indian name and identify as a healer or medicine person. They may look and act like an Elder, but the difference is that an Elder is recognized by the community. Those who claim to be Elders without this recognition may still be on their healing journey and could put people who come to them in jeopardy. We cannot always be sure whether people are working in a good way or not. Therefore, it is important to build trusting relationships, listen to what the community says about the person and examine that person's reputation before engaging his or her services.

How to Approach Elders

There is no single correct way to approach Elders, but there are some common practices. These widely accepted protocols are described in various resources, such as those produced by Anishnawbe Health Toronto (2000), NAHO (2008), the Northern Ontario School of Medicine (2011) and the Council on Aboriginal Initiatives (2012) at the University of Alberta.

There are many ways to approach Elders, but the following list presents some basic guidelines:
• Be respectful of the Elders and of yourself.
• Provide an offering or gift (e.g., tobacco, fabric, clothing, fur, firewood, food).

• Explain why you have come to the Elder—to ask a question or to ask for help.
• Do not use alcohol or other drugs when visiting with an Elder.
• Avoid approaching an Elder when on your moon time (menstrual cycle).[3]

Tobacco is the gift most commonly offered to Elders (although groups such as Inuit may not follow these tobacco teachings). Tobacco can be offered in any form: one cigarette from a pack, a pack of cigarettes, a pouch of tobacco or loose tobacco wrapped in a small square of cloth (called a "tobacco tie"). Typically the person holds the tobacco in the left hand—the hand closest to the heart—and then makes the request. Acceptance of the tobacco means the Elder has accepted the request and a sacred contract has been formed. The presentation of tobacco signifies that the conversation in some way concerns the spirit. Elders view this exchange as the person's willingness to listen and take seriously the help being offered. The Elder may smoke the tobacco or burn it, which signifies calling on the Creator for guidance. Tobacco also indicates a sacred trust, thus ensuring confidentiality between the Elder and the person.

How to Work with Elders

Elders can be involved at various levels of decision making and service provision. At a macro level, they can serve as consultants or advisers to government and Aboriginal organizations around issues relating to the environment and traditional knowledge. They can be cultural advisers, provide assistance in land claim settlements, and advocate Aboriginal rights and self-government. At the meso level, Elders can assist Aboriginal communities, agencies and organizations in community development work; act as cultural advisers to programs and services; and contribute to developing policies related to Aboriginal peoples. Elders can also offer services to non-Aboriginal agencies and organizations. They can act as bridges between Aboriginal and Western world views by providing advice for these organizations, offering cross-cultural training and influencing the way services are provided. Many non-Aboriginal organizations are now trying to provide services in culturally appropriate ways, which requires creating space for Elders and developing policies about how to involve them. At the micro level, the level of service delivery, Elders can provide services alongside agency workers, who can refer clients to Elders or themselves seek their services.

---

3   Some people may find this guideline offensive or sexist if they are not familiar with traditional teachings. The moon cycle is a gift to women, a time to celebrate life and the special role women play in being able to bring life into the world. Because women have the ability to give life, moon time is considered a time of great power. In acknowledgment of this power, women refrain from preparing foods or medicines, taking part in ceremonies or using the Pipe and other sacred items during moon time. Moon time is a time for renewal, a time for women to relax.

COLLABORATING WITH AGENCY WORKERS

Some agencies have a roster of Elders they can call upon. The organization may have protocols for approaching Elders or policies and procedures about the services Elders can provide. For example, NTHC (2007) has a traditional healing services policy and program manual that guides this involvement. Agencies may collaborate with Elders in various ways. They may invite Elders to share their teachings; offer counselling and advice to clients; provide advice about service delivery; conduct opening and closing prayers at workshops and conferences; and lend on-site support at workshops and conferences dealing with sensitive issues, such as sexual abuse, substance use problems or residential school experiences.

It is important that the agency first build a relationship with the Elder, since it is through this process that the Elder learns about the agency's scope of services and what it expects from the Elder. Establishing a relationship also helps agencies learn and understand what gifts the Elder has so they can optimize what the Elder offers the agency and its clients.

REFERRING CLIENTS TO ELDERS

Agencies may refer clients to Elders for cultural teachings, counselling, ceremonies, conflict resolution, mediation or problem solving. They must first ask the Elder whether he or she can provide the required service, and the client must consent to the referral before it is made. It is good practice for an agency worker to escort the client to the Elder to make proper introductions. Workers can prepare clients for the visit by explaining the Elder's role and ways the Elder may respond (Hart, 2002). This preparation helps to alleviate any fears clients may have and gives them an opportunity to ask questions and express concerns they may have about working with an Elder.

SEEKING AN ELDER FOR PERSONAL SUPPORT

People working in health and social services may sometimes want the services of an Elder for themselves because their work can be very stressful. Vicarious trauma is an occupational hazard for social workers, nurses, psychologists, psychiatrists and others who are repeatedly exposed to clients' difficult stories and problems. Workers need to learn self-care to prevent or minimize vicarious trauma. Elders can offer support by helping workers achieve and maintain the harmony and balance necessary for *mino-pimatisiwin*. This helps to prevent other problems, such as turning to alcohol or other drugs, which in turn lead to more problems.

Conclusion

Elders play an important, ever-evolving role in Aboriginal society. This chapter provided an overview of who Elders are, the roles they play and how to access their services. As self-determination continues to grow among Aboriginal communities, their members will increasingly rely on the wisdom and guidance of Elders.

We, in the Aboriginal community, often assume that our Elders will always be there. Lately, I have been saddened by the passing of so many Elders; I wonder who is going to take up those important roles. My mother, who served as an Elder for many years, echoed this sentiment. She believed that it is time for the next generation to take up the torch. It is a lack of confidence rather than a lack of knowledge that prevents the next generation from assuming these roles. My mother has joined the spirit world, and the task of transmitting our knowledge and culture now falls to my generation. It is time to take up those responsibilities, to connect with the surviving Elders, to build those relationships with the cosmos and to continue the cycle of life.

References

Aboriginal Health Access Centres (AHAC). (2010). *Aboriginal Health Access Centres: Our Health, Our Future*. Retrieved from Association of Ontario Health Centres website: http://aohc.org/aboriginal-health-access-centres

Absolon, K. (1993). *Healing as Practice: Teachings from the Medicine Wheel*. Victoria, BC: Wunska Network.

Anishnawbe Health Toronto. (n.d.). *Services & Programs*. Retrieved from www.aht.ca/services-and-programs

Anishnawbe Health Toronto. (2000). *Approaching a Traditional Healer, Elder or Medicine Person*. Retrieved from www.aht.ca/images/stories/TEACHINGS/ApproachingElderHealer.pdf

Association of Ontario Health Centres. (n.d.). Aboriginal Health Access Centres. Retrieved from http://aohc.org

Canadian Institutes of Health Research, Natural Sciences and Engineering Research Council of Canada & Social Sciences and Humanities Research Council of Canada. (2010). *TCPS 2: Tri-Council Policy Statement: Ethical Conduct for Research Involving Humans*. Retrieved from Panel on Research Ethics, Government of Canada website: www.pre.ethics.gc.ca

Colorado, P. (1988). Bridging Native and Western science. *Convergence, 21* (2–3), 49–68.

Council on Aboriginal Initiatives. (2012). *Elder Protocol and Guidelines*. Retrieved from Office of the Provost and Vice-President (Academic), University of Alberta website: www.provost.ualberta.ca

Couture, J. (2000). Elder/healer: The elements of promise. *Forum on Corrections Research, 12* (1), 38–39.

Edge, L. & McCallum, T. (2006). Métis identity: Sharing traditional knowledge and healing practices at Métis Elders' gatherings. *Pimatisiwin: A Journal of Aboriginal and Indigenous Community Health, 4*, 83–115.

Hart, M.A. (2002). *Seeking Mino-Pimatisiwin: An Aboriginal Approach to Helping*. Halifax, NS: Fernwood.

Johnston, B. (1976). *Ojibway Heritage*. Toronto: McClelland & Stewart.

Long, D. & Dickason, O.P. (1998). *Visions of the Heart: Canadian Aboriginal Issues*. Toronto: Thompson Nelson.

Mehl-Madrona, L. (2009). What traditional Indigenous Elders say about cross-cultural mental health training. *Explore (NY), 5* (1), 20–29. DOI: 10.1016/j.explore.2008.10.003

Moeke-Pickering, T., Hardy, S., Manitowabi, S., Mawhiney, A., Faries, E., Gibson-van Marreweijk, K., ... Taitoko, M. (2006). *Keeping Our Fire Alive: Towards Decolonising Research in the Academic Setting*. Retrieved from World Indigenous Nations Higher Education Consortium website: www.win-hec.org/docs/pdfs/TMoeke%20final.doc.pdf

Mussell, W.J. (2005). *Warrior-Caregivers: Understanding the Challenges and Healing of First Nations Men*. Retrieved from Aboriginal Healing Foundation website: www.ahf.ca

Nabigon, H. (2006). *The Hollow Tree: Fighting Addiction with Traditional Native Healing*. Montreal: McGill-Queen's University Press.

National Aboriginal Health Organization (NAHO). (2005). *Ownership, Control, Access, and Possession (OCAP) or Self-Determination Applied to Research: A Critical Analysis of Contemporary First Nations Research and Some Options for First Nations Communities*. Retrieved from www.naho.ca/documents/fnc/english/FNC_OCAPCriticalAnalysis.pdf

National Aboriginal Health Organization (NAHO). (2008). *An Overview of Traditional Knowledge and Medicine and Public Health in Canada*. Retrieved from www.naho.ca/documents/naho/publications/tkOverviewPublicHealth.pdf

National Association of Friendship Centres. (2013). Our mission. Retrieved from http://nafc.ca

Native Canadian Centre of Toronto. (2010). Taam Kaadinakiijik Advisory Circle. Retrieved from www.ncct.on.ca/taamkaadinakiijik.php

Noojmowin Teg Health Centre (NTHC). (2003a). *Guidelines for Ethical Aboriginal Research: A Resource Manual for the Development of Ethical and Culturally Appropriate Community-Based Research within the First Nations Communities in the Manitoulin Area*. Retrieved from www.noojmowin-teg.ca/SitePages/MARRC.aspx

Noojmowin Teg Health Centre (NTHC). (2003b). *Ethics and Research Review Workbook*. Retrieved from www.noojmowin-teg.ca/SitePages/MARRC.aspx

Noojmowin Teg Health Centre (NTHC). (2007). *Traditional Healing Services Policy and Program Manual*. Little Current, ON: Author.

Northern Ontario School of Medicine. (2011). *Elders Handbook: How the Medical School Works with and Engages Aboriginal Elders*. Retrieved from www.nosm.ca

Regnier, R. (1994). The sacred circle: A process pedagogy of healing. *Interchange, 25*, 129–144.

Ross, R. (1996). *Returning to the Teachings: Exploring Aboriginal Justice*. Toronto: Penguin Books.

Royal Commission on Aboriginal Peoples. (1996). Traditional health and healing (Appendix 3A). In *Report of the Royal Commission on Aboriginal Peoples. Vol. 3: Gathering Strength* (pp. 325–340). Ottawa: Canada Communication Group.

Stiegelbauer, S.M. (1996). What is an elder? What do elders do? First Nation Elders as teachers in culture-based urban organizations. *Canadian Journal of Native Studies, 16*, 1, 37–66.

Suzuki, D.T. & Knudtson, P. (1992). *Wisdom of the Elders: Sacred Native Stories of Nature*. Toronto: Stoddart.

Swinomish Tribal Mental Health Project. (2002). *A Gathering of Wisdoms: Tribal Mental Health—A Cultural Perspective* (2nd ed.). LaConner, WA: Swinomish Tribal Community.

University of Manitoba. (2013). Elder-in-residence. Retrieved from http://umanitoba.ca

Warry, W. (2008). *Ending Denial: Understanding Aboriginal Issues* (2nd ed.). Toronto: University of Toronto Press.

ABOUT THE AUTHOR

Susan Manitowabi, PhD candidate, is originally from Wiigwaskinaga (Whitefish River First Nation) but through marriage is now a member of Wikwemikong Undeced Indian Reserve. She has four children and five granddaughters. She is an assistant professor in the School of Indigenous Relations at Laurentian University in Sudbury, where she is completing her PhD through the School of Rural and Northern Health. Her research interests include traditional Aboriginal healing practices, Aboriginal mental health and issues related to violence against women.

Chapter 8

Harm Reduction

DENNIS WARDMAN

A few months ago, Jenny, a First Nations woman in her late 30s, came to my clinic. She was an intravenous heroin user, living with her boyfriend who was also using, and sustained her habit through work in the sex trade. She was experiencing depression and was estranged from her family. She wanted to improve her situation, but was far from ready to stop using heroin. After considering the possible options, she decided to start methadone maintenance treatment (MMT), which helps individuals reduce their dependence on opioids. She also began working with a psychotherapist. I connected Jenny with community service agencies to help her obtain housing, income and other supports. These measures allowed Jenny to begin rebuilding her life without needing to stop using heroin immediately.

A Pragmatic Philosophy

The methadone maintenance treatment Jenny used to reduce her use of heroin is a harm reduction strategy. Harm reduction is an approach to public health that aims to reduce the negative health, social and economic consequences of using alcohol and other drugs. It accepts that drug use is part of most societies, and focuses on improving the quality of life and well-being of individuals and communities, rather than on eliminating the use of drugs. In a harm reduction program, abstinence is not a requirement for obtaining services or treatment. Harm reduction respects people's desires, rights and responsibilities to control their own lives; values their strengths; and empowers them to make their own decisions by giving them information about reducing harms, and the means to protect themselves (Canadian Aboriginal AIDS Network [CAAN], 1998).

Harm reduction has proven much more effective than law enforcement in reducing drug use. In Vancouver, which has been a leader in implementing harm reduction programs, among people who use drugs, methadone maintenance treatment increased from 11.7 per cent in 1996 to 54.5 per cent in 2008 and has remained stable since; injection drug use cessation has increased from 0.4 per cent in 1996 to 46.6 per cent in 2011; and there has been a significant decrease in syringe sharing and related HIV and hepatitis C transmissions. These results were achieved while illicit drugs remained easily accessible and affordable (Urban Health Research Initiative, 2013).

Central to harm reduction is the principle that individuals who use drugs, and communities affected by drug use, must be involved in the design and implementation of policies and programs. Thus, there is no one formula for harm reduction; strategies range from needle exchange programs to reduce needle sharing and the risk of HIV transmission among injection drug users to designated-driver programs to reduce alcohol-related traffic fatalities. Harm reduction programs benefit individuals by reducing infections, disease, accidents and death, and benefit families and communities by diminishing social harms such as violence and crime, and promoting the reintegration of previously marginalized members of society (CAAN, 1997).

Harm reduction also recognizes that the realities of poverty, racism, past trauma and other social inequalities affect people's vulnerability to and capacity for effectively dealing with drug-related harms. For Aboriginal people, this aspect of harm reduction is particularly relevant, as the colonialist policies of domination and assimilation have resulted in many traumas and inequities: broken families and communities, disconnection from traditional culture, racism and discrimination, political disempowerment, and severe and continuing socio-economic disparities. These are the root cause of rates of harms from the use of alcohol and other drugs in Aboriginal populations that are well above the national average (Dell, 2008).

Harm reduction shares a number of key features with traditional Aboriginal culture—its approach is holistic, and respect for one another and the importance of community are central concepts. Many essential understandings of harm reduction are relevant when working with Aboriginal populations, including the importance of not imposing one's own values, recognizing strengths, encouraging empowerment and autonomy and appreciating the role of socio-economic factors in harmful substance use. There are also some significant cultural differences that must be acknowledged. Traditional Aboriginal approaches to healing begin with the spiritual rather than the physical realm, and while harm reduction accepts drug use as normal in a society, the use of drugs is not a part of traditional Aboriginal cultures. Finally, the impact of colonialism must be understood in any consideration of the health of Aboriginal people.

The notion of empowerment and choice is at the heart of harm reduction initiatives, and at the heart of Aboriginal participation in harm reduction initiatives. This encompasses empowerment not just as individuals, but as bands, tribes, nations and peoples. The importance of culturally relevant programs is a recurring theme in studies of harm reduction and Aboriginal populations. In order for health services for Aboriginal people to be effective, they must incorporate Aboriginal culture and traditions and an understanding of Aboriginal history. They must be relevant to the clients' world views and values, and like all harm reduction initiatives, they must acknowledge the capacity and responsibility of individuals and communities for creating their own health and healing.

Throughout the rest of this chapter, profiles are presented of programs that take a harm reduction approach in order to illustrate various issues related to harm reduction.

A Holistic Approach

Anishnawbe Health Toronto (www.aht.ca) *provides holistic health care to Aboriginal people using both traditional and Western approaches. It works with individuals on a broad range of issues, including substance use, abuse, effects of the residential school system, heritage identity, adoption and foster care issues, self-esteem and relationship issues. Respect, autonomy and non-judgmental, compassionate support are foundations of the program. Clients make their own choices about health care and define their own healing paths. Central understandings are that sickness begins in the spirit, and then affects the mind, emotions and body; wellness is a state of balance and harmony. Practitioners include Elders and medicine people, and spiritual ceremonies offered include the sweat lodge, shaking tent, full moon ceremony, naming ceremony, clan feasts, pipe ceremony and vision quests.*

While there are many diverse Aboriginal cultures within Canada, most share some basic concepts and principles. Aboriginal world views and concepts of health are holistic and centre on the interconnectedness and interdependence—and the sacredness—of all life. All objects and processes in the natural world, both living and inanimate, are to be treated with deep respect. Traditional Aboriginal cultures teach values such as humility, honesty and truth that enable people to live in harmony with all of Creation. Individuals, communities and nations are not seen as separate from one another: what happens to each affects the others. The mental, physical, spiritual and emotional are interconnected parts of life that interact in a dynamic process. Health is a state of balance and harmony among all aspects of personal and collective life.

Harm reduction's approach to personal and social health is also holistic. It views the individual not alone but as a member of a family, community and society, with each influencing the others, and it considers a client's whole life and history, not just his or her dependence on drugs. In conducting a needs assessment, the practitioner and client together look at all dimensions of the client's life and how they interconnect and interplay with one another, in order to identify needs and goals. Included in the assessment are the key determinants of health, such as income and social status, social support networks, education and literacy, employment and working conditions, social and physical environments, personal health practices and coping skills, healthy child development, health services, gender and culture (Canadian Harm Reduction Network & Canadian AIDS Society, 2008). Practitioners aim to understand the client's whole relationship to drug use and not simply treat the symptoms (Centre for Addiction and Mental Health, 2002).

Conducting a Needs Assessment

In a harm reduction needs assessment, practitioners help clients identify the goals that will define their healing journey and access their strengths, gifts and inner resources that will support them in achieving these goals. Client self-determination is paramount with this approach. Tools such as the transtheoretical (stages of change) model and decisional (pros and cons) balance sheet can help clients to focus their thinking and begin exploring their reasons for using drugs; the impact of drug use on their lives and on those of family and friends; ways other than substance use in which they can meet their needs; and their resistance to change. The medicine wheel, a symbol originating in Prairie First Nations cultures, which is now part of many other Aboriginal traditions and has been adopted by mainstream social service agencies, is another useful needs assessment model to assist clients in identifying their goals. The medicine wheel can also help illustrate and guide clients' healing journeys.

Goals may include protecting against overdose, reducing drug use, exploring treatment options, starting treatment, improving general health, addressing other health care needs or undergoing counselling. Other examples of goals include accessing supported employment, housing and other services; connecting with family members; volunteering; and building knowledge about drug use. It may be that harm reduction measures can be tied in with other programming; for example, a client who comes to a clinic for tuberculosis checkups might also receive addiction counselling and treatment. The practitioner can give referrals to support services, provide medical information about the client's drug use and its impact on health, and encourage the client to reflect on the role drug use plays in his or her life. The client will be comfortable participating in this discussion if it is confidential, non-judgmental and not tied to legal or other negative consequences. Engaging the client in decision making and developing strategies for change promotes empowerment.

While the practitioner can help the client to clarify goals and set priorities, the goals that emerge from the needs assessment arise from, and are decided on by, the client. At this stage, most clients are not yet ready or able to stop using drugs, and a harm reduction approach does not require this. Instead, practitioners support clients by validating their lack of readiness, acknowledging that the decision is theirs, encouraging self-exploration and explaining the risks of continued use. The practitioner respects the choices made by the client and helps him or her to deal with any adverse consequences that may result from less than optimal choices.

As well as providing clients with access to information and the means to protect themselves, the practitioner helps the client to develop healthy coping skills and strategies to reduce reliance on drugs, deal with stressful life events and strengthen personal relationships. Together, the practitioner and client review the goals on an ongoing basis. It is an active and empowering process in which clients can improve their decision-making skills and learn to assume responsibility for their personal and social health.

Working with Aboriginal People

Insite (http://supervisedinjection.vch.ca) *in Vancouver's Downtown Eastside is Canada's only supervised injection facility. Since opening its doors in 2003, Insite has been a safe, health-focused place where people inject drugs and connect to health care services—from primary care to treat disease and infection, to addiction counselling and treatment, to housing and community supports. About 25 per cent of the clientele is Aboriginal, and some of the staff are Aboriginal. About half of the people who use Insite are homeless, live in shelters or have significant mental health issues. Insite has 12 injection booths where clients inject pre-obtained illicit drugs under the supervision of nurses and health care staff. It supplies clean injection equipment such as syringes, cookers, filters, water and tourniquets. Nurses also provide other health care services, such as wound care and immunizations. If an overdose occurs, the team members, led by a nurse, intervene immediately. Since Insite opened, there has never been a fatality at the site, and overdoses in the vicinity of the site have decreased by 35 per cent, compared to a nine per cent decrease in the city overall. Unlike in other cities, the number of new HIV infections among injection drug users in Vancouver has shrunk every year of Insite's operation, despite major population growth.*

The Western Aboriginal Harm Reduction Society (WAHRS) (www.vandu.org/groups. html#wahrs) *is an all-Aboriginal group located in Vancouver's Downtown Eastside. It is run and directed by Aboriginal people who have used or currently use alcohol or other drugs. As well as hepatitis C and HIV/AIDS, alcohol use is another major problem in this neighbourhood, involving not only hard liquor and beer, but substitutes such as rubbing alcohol, mouthwash and Lysol. This use is causing many health problems, including mental health–related difficulties. One WAHRS initiative is an alcohol maintenance program in which people are not forced to stop drinking immediately, but instead are offered beer to consume in managed doses. Once they are on this maintenance program, the next step can be a withdrawal management or treatment centre. The latest initiatives of this client-driven group include distributing shoes and winter boots to help clients avoid foot problems, reclaiming Indigenous culture and increasing client access to traditional activities and healing, providing peer counselling and conducting user-driven research.*

More than half (54 per cent) of Aboriginal people live in urban areas (Statistics Canada, 2008). Most larger urban communities have harm reduction programs, but for First Nations, Inuit and Métis, obtaining services that are culturally relevant can be more difficult. Harm reduction programs in urban centres are usually targeted at the general population; yet for most Aboriginal clients, it is important, even essential, to have services that incorporate—and the support of people who understand and appreciate—their own culture, history and circumstances (Wardman & Quantz, 2006).

Many Aboriginal people are uncomfortable with the health care system and may not access non-Aboriginal services, where they may experience harsh judgment and discrimination from health care providers. Mainstream health services often do not provide services that respond to the cultures and priorities of Aboriginal people, and often do not understand the specific dynamics of Aboriginal ill health. The demand for Aboriginal staff in programs serving Aboriginal populations, particularly in urban centres, greatly outstrips supply across the country, but non-Aboriginal practitioners, with the help of their Aboriginal clients and others in the Aboriginal community, can build the required knowledge and awareness. In doing so, they help to create a healing process centred on shared learning that opens up new levels of understanding for both client and practitioner. While for some Aboriginal people working with Aboriginal service providers is beneficial for building trust, many others will welcome the opportunity to work with non-Aboriginal staff who are open-minded and non-judgmental, and who respect and value Aboriginal peoples and their cultures and heritage (Wardman & Quantz, 2006).

Cultural identity is a source of meaning, strength and resilience for Aboriginal peoples. While not all Aboriginal clients wish to embrace their traditions, most see connection to their traditional culture as central to well-being. Traditions and beliefs can vary widely between individuals, communities and groups. For example, there are more than 200 First Nations in British Columbia alone, representing more than 30 languages and 40 major cultural groups, and cultural differences also exist between communities within these major groups. It is important to learn about and respect each client's culture and values and to be familiar with cultural resources. The client is the practitioner's best source of assistance in developing cultural competence (Weaver, as cited in Verniest, 2006). Aboriginal agencies, friendship centres or community leaders can also help identify local resources, such as sweat lodges and other ceremonies, Elders, and Aboriginal counsellors, social workers and medical staff.[1]

---

1 General approaches to cultural competence and cultural safety are also discussed in chapter 10 on women and chapter 30 on training.

Traditional Aboriginal healing focuses on the spiritual. Wellness flows from living in harmony with the world. An Aboriginal healer guides the individual through a process of self-discovery to understand his or her nature in relation to the world, and how and why his or her life is out of balance. The healing journey may involve spiritual components such as sweats, ceremonies and fasts (where alcohol and other drugs are not permitted), traditional medicines and teachings, talking circles and counselling. Spiritual beliefs and ceremonies vary between tribal groups. Many Aboriginal clients want to learn more about and practise their own spiritual traditions, the practice of which the Canadian government once made illegal. Reclaiming spirituality is part of reclaiming identity. Practitioners can assist these clients by connecting them with local Elders or organizations that embrace traditional spirituality.[2]

Aboriginal cultures value storytelling as a source of insight and wisdom. Listening to clients' stories will unearth some of the emotional stresses in their lives, whether they arise from current traumas such as abuse, unemployment or homelessness, or from historical trauma such as residential school experiences—either their own or those of family members. Attempting to mask deep-seated emotional pain can be at the heart of drug use, and the client will need help in processing the difficult emotions that surface during the recovery process. In helping a client to identify needs, listening with empathy and curiosity is essential. Being unhurried, asking about home communities and personal histories, having a genuine desire to understand the person as an individual and taking the time to listen without interrupting build trust. It is particularly important to understand the layers of stigma experienced by Aboriginal people who use drugs. They are doubly stigmatized by mainstream society through negative stereotypes about people who use drugs and about Aboriginal peoples, and because of their drug use, they are often not accepted in their own communities. It is important to speak frankly to clients about discrimination.

Practitioners need to be aware of cultural differences in communication styles: long silences are considered acceptable and valuable; direct eye contact with someone who is speaking may be seen as a sign of disrespect; nodding signifies understanding, not necessarily agreement; and words spoken softly are considered the most emphatic. Aboriginal clients may be reluctant to respond to direct questions; due to a sense of disempowerment arising from residential school experiences, they may feel fear, mistrust or discomfort asking questions of someone perceived to be an authority figure. As well, English may not be the client's first language, in which case an interpreter may be needed.

Family is very important to Aboriginal peoples, and a common goal for clients is to reconnect with family members. Members of a client's extended family will often want to be present at assessment or counselling sessions. They can be helpful in understanding the client's history, needs and wishes, and their support will be important in the client's recovery. Often clients want to appear strong for the sake of their family,

---

2   For a discussion about Aboriginal ways of helping, see chapter 6. For more about the role of Elders, see chapter 7.

which can motivate them to get help in dealing with their drug dependence, but it can also prevent them from seeking help out of a desire not to appear weak. Other family members may also have dependence issues or be drug dealers, and there may be codependent patterns that can sabotage a client's recovery. For example, out of an understandable desire not to see a family member suffer, a parent or sibling will pay for clothes, rent, food and other essentials, thus enabling the client to spend money on drugs. Counselling may be necessary to help families recognize and address enabling behaviour. This can be challenging because sharing and assisting others are cultural norms. Additionally, many lack parenting and family skills because of residential school and other interventions, which significantly disrupted families.

Harm reduction practitioners working with Aboriginal clients need to understand the history of colonialism, its socio-economic impacts on Aboriginal peoples in general, and its connection to many health problems, including present-day high levels of harmful substance use in Aboriginal populations, in order to help clients critically examine how their lives have been, and continue to be, shaped by social, economic and historical forces.[3] This can empower clients by helping to reduce the internal blame and shame that often defeat efforts at recovery (Verniest, 2006). One good place to start for insight into the relationship between Canada and Aboriginal peoples and an overview of ongoing issues is *Highlights of the Report on the Royal Commission on Aboriginal Peoples* (Royal Commission on Aboriginal Peoples, 1996).

Abstinence and Harm Reduction

The National Native Alcohol and Drug Abuse Program (NNADAP) is a Health Canada program established to help First Nations and Inuit communities set up and operate culturally relevant programs aimed at reducing the harmful use of alcohol and other drugs. NNADAP now supports 52 residential treatment centres and more than 550 prevention and aftercare programs across Canada, almost all of which are staffed, operated and controlled by Aboriginal people and organizations. Programs include cultural and spiritual events and activities. Most NNADAP treatment centres have a strong focus on abstinence and the Alcoholics Anonymous philosophy, partly because abstinence models were the norm when the NNADAP program was established in the 1970s, but also because many First Nations, Inuit and Métis individuals and communities adhere to models of abstinence and prohibition for cultural reasons (Health Canada, n.d.).

Twelve-step programs such as those offered by many NNADAP treatment centres have been invaluable in helping many Aboriginal people overcome dependence on alcohol and other drugs. An Aboriginal client of mine with a 30-year narcotic dependence who went to a NNADAP centre reported feeling that, for the first time in his life, he was with

---

3   See chapter 2 for a discussion about colonialism and how it has affected the health and well-being of Aboriginal people.

people who truly understood him and why he did what he did. However, only a small percentage of people who use drugs are ready to stop using and enter such programs, and dropout rates are often high. For other clients, harm reduction is often the best alternative, but because harm reduction focuses on reducing immediate harms to the client and community, rather than on helping the client to abstain, it is often seen as incompatible with Aboriginal culture.

Recreational drug use and drug dependence were brought to Aboriginal communities by Europeans. Prior to contact, Aboriginal people used controlled amounts of tobacco, alcohol and psychoactive substances for ceremonial and ritualistic purposes only. Thus, there was no need to develop strategies to reduce harm from substance use. Because of this history, and because the use of alcohol and other drugs has had such a devastating effect on the lives of Aboriginal people, there is strong support for abstinence in Aboriginal communities; often, it is seen as the only legitimate approach to treatment of drug dependencies. Individuals who use substances such as alcohol or injection drugs, or replacement drugs such as methadone, are viewed as being out of balance and often face stigma from their communities. As well, many addiction counsellors working in Aboriginal communities were once dependent on alcohol or other drugs themselves, and thus often advocate abstinence (Wardman & Quantz, 2006).

Unlike in harm reduction, abstinence models typically do not allow for moderate or reduced substance use. However, the two approaches need not be considered mutually exclusive. Some programs offer clients both harm reduction strategies and support for abstinence. Common to both approaches is the goal of assisting individuals and communities with the harms they are experiencing because of problematic substance use. Viewing harm reduction and abstinence as allies addressing a common problem allows for a broader range of solutions that can then be tailored to the unique and varied needs of individuals and communities.

Working with Aboriginal Communities

All Nations Hope AIDS *Network (*ANH*)* (www.allnationshope.ca) *in Saskatchewan is a network of Aboriginal people, organizations and agencies that offers support and services to First Nations, Métis and Inuit families and communities living with* HIV/AIDS *and hepatitis C. Most new cases of* HIV *in Saskatchewan are Aboriginal injection drug users.* ANH *provides educational workshops and training about* HIV/AIDS, *hepatitis C and two-spirited people to Aboriginal individuals and communities in Saskatchewan. The network offers training for front-line workers dealing with at-risk populations and those working with Aboriginal women with substance dependencies during their child-bearing years, and peer-based training for inmates in correctional systems that includes components of both traditional teachings and basic* HIV/AIDS *information.* ANH *supports harm reduction services such as needle exchange and methadone maintenance. Its publications include a* *harm reduction guide and a video for front-line workers dealing with Aboriginal people who disclose that they are newly diagnosed or living with HIV/AIDS. Anyone with questions about HIV/AIDS and hepatitis C can send ANH an anonymous e-mail and receive information.*

Remote, reserve and rural communities have limited access to many health services, especially harm reduction programs, and programs to assist individuals who use drugs generally focus on alcohol and tobacco rather than injection drugs or the mismanagement of prescription opioids. There are almost no safer use programs such as needle exchanges or condom distribution; few counsellors have a background in harm reduction; and access to MMT is often an issue because there is a shortage of prescribing physicians, nurses lack training in MMT, and the cost to ship methadone from distant pharmacies is high. To access harm reduction services, people must travel long distances to urban centres, often on a frequent basis (Wardman & Quantz, 2006).

In small communities, among both service providers and community members, there is often a lack of understanding of harm reduction, its effectiveness and its potential value to the community (Dell et al., 2010). Few of the nurses and counsellors who work in remote communities and on reserves have been trained in harm reduction or in specific interventions such as MMT. The risk of HIV transmission from Aboriginal injection drug users to others in their home communities who do not use drugs is high, due to frequent travel by injection drug users to and from urban areas, reserves and prisons; yet awareness in Aboriginal communities of HIV and the risks it poses for those communities is generally very low (CAAN, 1998). Nurses typically provide stellar service, but like other health professionals, may have neither the time to seek service information and support nor knowledge of who could provide information relevant to their local situation.

There are also many competing needs. Harm reduction gives priority to the most urgent needs of individuals and communities, and to the most immediate and realistic goals to reduce harms; both the costs and benefits of interventions must be considered in setting priorities. Many remote, reserve and rural communities face multiple pressing health and social problems, including unemployment, substandard housing, unclean water and other risks to health, and addressing these needs must be given priority. There may also be a lack of human resources to get projects up and running. As well, the complex arrangements between federal, provincial and local governments and agencies for funding Aboriginal health services have led to fragmentation of services and make it difficult to plan, co-ordinate and fund new services, including harm reduction programs (Landau, 1996).

Also, because abstinence is the preferred treatment model for people who use drugs in most Aboriginal communities, there is often a stigma attached to drug use that extends to individuals with dependencies, particularly injection drug users who use harm reduction programs. Harm reduction programs may be viewed as an admission of failure—as a last option after abstinence has failed. Communities can also fear that harm reduction services may attract injection drug users. Thus, for the individual, there are often not the medical and community supports needed, and the shame arising from the stigmas associated with drug use creates an additional barrier to accessing what supports there may be. For injection drug users with HIV or who have spent time in prison, the stigmatization and shame are even greater, and because in small communities service providers and other program participants are usually people the person knows, the lack of confidentiality can deter people from accessing services for safer drug use or HIV testing (CAAN, 1998; Wardman & Quantz, 2006).

Lack of control over important dimensions of living in itself contributes to ill health. A central principle of harm reduction is that individuals who use substances and communities affected by substance use must be involved in designing and developing harm reduction policies and programs. This is particularly important for Aboriginal communities, given their histories of disempowerment and the wide diversity of cultures and traditions, languages and geographies. Harm reduction is also about choice, respect and autonomy, and again, these principles apply not just to individuals, but also to communities. The need for Aboriginal peoples to exercise control over their own health and social services and for non-Aboriginal health and social services agencies to start seeing Aboriginal peoples as partners in the design, development and delivery of health services were stressed by the Royal Commission on Aboriginal Peoples (1996). Aboriginal people want to exercise their own judgment and understanding about what makes people healthy, and their own skills in solving health and social problems. Many Aboriginal communities have already made considerable commitments toward the treatment and prevention of substance use problems. Thus, decisions about the appropriateness of harm reduction programs must begin at the community level, and programs must be directed by communities and their members (CAAN, 1998; Dell et al., 2010; Wardman & Quantz, 2006).

In Aboriginal cultures, collective decisions are arrived at by consensus, which means that for a harm reduction program to be introduced and implemented, there must be consensus in the community that this is an appropriate and viable approach (Gliksman et al., 2007). Education is needed to help communities become more aware of the value of harm reduction programs, why they are needed, and how they can fit with existing programs. Community leaders, Elders, service providers and the general community all have important roles to play in this process. Educational initiatives must acknowledge that cultural differences as well as commonalities exist between traditional and harm reduction approaches. Harm reduction, rather than focusing on what is wrong, focuses on building on strengths and resilience to heal and empower individuals and communities. This offers a positive starting point for dialogue with Aboriginal communities on the potential benefits of introducing harm reduction services (Wardman & Quantz, 2006).

Blood Ties Four Directions Centre (http://bloodties.ca) in Whitehorse, Yukon, offers free, confidential needle exchange, safer crack use kits and hygiene supplies, as well as counselling, drop-in services, hot meals, an outreach nurse, a housing advocate, HIV/AIDS and hepatitis C education and information workshops. Forty-one per cent of the injection drug users and 74 per cent of the crack users it serves are from First Nations. Its No Fixed

Address outreach van, built from an old ambulance, operates six nights per week, distributing new injection equipment, safer crack use kits, hygiene supplies, and condoms and lube, and also provides food and beverages, clothing, support and referrals. The van program, which is supported by community volunteers, small business owners and several not-for-profit organizations, is widely accepted. A coalition of four local organizations shares ownership of the van program, which has ensured continuity of service, even though some of the organizations have lost funding. The coalition has proved an effective way of uniting agencies, individuals and community members to address a problem within the community. It has allowed information about harm reduction to be disseminated across a wide and diverse range of people and has helped to gain support for controversial issues such as the Safer Crack Kit Program (Canadian Harm Reduction Network & Canadian AIDS Society, 2008).

To accommodate individual differences and goals, harm reduction programs must be flexible and provide a wide range of options. There are many harm reduction approaches, programs and materials that could potentially benefit Aboriginal communities, ranging from materials for safer use and opioid replacement therapies to overdose prevention and social justice projects. In small communities, new harm reduction services will often need to be integrated into existing programs. Basic training in harm reduction for all service staff, including those not directly working in harm reduction services, could be valuable. Mobile harm reduction services may be possible in some communities with access to roads. Providing further education for nursing-station staff, using telehealth services to communicate with prescribing physicians, and enabling nurses to dispense methadone are some possibilities for remedying the problem of access to MMT. Telehealth is also an option when counsellors with the appropriate background are not available in the community. Using nurses from outside the community and keeping the records outside the community could help to overcome issues of confidentiality. Different measures will be appropriate for different communities.

Finally, program evaluation is important to determine the needs for, access to, and effectiveness and appropriateness of harm reduction services in Aboriginal communities (Centre for Addiction and Mental Health, 2002; Dell & Lyons, 2007; Wardman & Quantz, 2006). Due to the difficulty in doing research in remote communities where there are often language barriers, relevant research is still in short supply. Evaluations must be culturally relevant for Aboriginal peoples and should be conducted by and with Aboriginal communities and organizations (Dell et al., 2010).

Revisiting Jenny's Story

As Jenny reduced her heroin use and worked to understand the dark turn her life had taken, it was painful for her to acknowledge the suffering she had caused herself and others. But with regular counselling and a lot of encouragement and support, she has made many positive life changes in just three months. She has stopped all heroin use, ended the relationship with her boyfriend and is no longer working in the sex trade. She has also stopped smoking and regularly attends 12-step meetings. She now lives in her own home and is reaching out to her family after many years of no contact. Some family members are wary of her because of past disappointments, but Jenny is persevering. She is also looking into vocational training options and has hopes for a future when she will no longer be dependent on social assistance.

Jenny's situation is not perfect, and neither is the world in which she is attempting to recreate her life. Substance use problems among First Nations people are symptomatic of a breadth of social ills and inequalities that have persisted for generations. Harm reduction approaches to drug use will not solve these complex issues, but what they can do is allow for a broader spectrum of solutions to a greater number of people. Used in conjunction with abstinence approaches, they have the potential to attract and keep more people who use drugs in treatment, thereby substantially reducing the pain and distress experienced by people and their communities. And perhaps, at least for now, that is as perfect as it gets.

References

Canadian Aboriginal AIDS Network (CAAN). (1997). *Walk with Me Pathways to Health Harm Reduction Service Delivery Model*. Retrieved from http://caan.ca

Canadian Aboriginal AIDS Network (CAAN). (1998). *Joining the Circle: An Aboriginal Harm Reduction Model: A Guide for Developing a Harm Reduction Program in Your Community: Phase I*. Ottawa: Author.

Canadian Harm Reduction Network & Canadian AIDS Society. (2008). *Learning from Each Other: Enhancing Community-Based Harm Reduction Programs and Practices in Canada*. Retrieved from www.cdnaids.ca

Centre for Addiction and Mental Health. (2002). *CAMH and Harm Reduction: A Background Paper on Its Meaning and Applications for Substance Use Issues*. Retrieved from www.camh.ca

Dell, C.A. (2008). Harm reduction and abstinence—more alike than different? *Visions Journal, 5* (1), 21–22. Retrieved from www.heretohelp.bc.ca

Dell, C.A. & Lyons, T. (2007). *Harm Reduction Policies and Programs for Persons of Aboriginal Descent*. Retrieved from Canadian Centre on Substance Abuse website: www.ccsa.ca

Dell, C.A., Lyons, T. & Cayer, K. (2010). The role of "Kijigabandan" and "Manadjitowin" in understanding harm reduction policies and programs for Aboriginal peoples. *Native Social Work Journal, 7*, 109–137.

Gliksman, L., Rylett, M. & Douglas, R.R. (2007). Aboriginal Community Alcohol Harm Reduction Policy (ACAHRP) Project: A vision for the future. *Substance Use & Misuse, 42*, 1851–1866.

Health Canada. (n.d.). *First Nations and Inuit Health: National Native Alcohol and Drug Abuse Program.* Retrieved from www.hc-sc.gc.ca

Landau, T.C. (1996). The prospects for a harm reduction approach among Aboriginal people in Canada. *Drug and Alcohol Review, 15,* 393–401.

Royal Commission on Aboriginal Peoples. (1996). *People to People, Nation to Nation: Highlights from the Report of the Royal Commission on Aboriginal Peoples.* Retrieved from Aboriginal Affairs and Northern Development Canada website: www.aadnc-aandc.gc.ca

Statistics Canada. (2008). *Aboriginal Peoples in Canada in 2006: Inuit, Métis and First Nations, 2006 Census.* (Catalogue no. 97-558-XIE.) Ottawa: Minister of Industry.

Urban Health Research Initiative. (2013). *Drug Situation in Vancouver* (2nd ed.). Retrieved from British Columbia Centre for Excellence in HIV/AIDS website: www.cfenet.ubc.ca/sites/default/files/uploads/news/releases/war_on_drugs_failing_to_limit_drug_use.pdf

Verniest, L. (2006). Allying with the medicine wheel: Social work practice with Aboriginal peoples. *Critical Social Work, 7* (1). Retrieved from www1.uwindsor.ca/criticalsocialwork/allying-with-the-medicine-wheel-social-work-practice-with-aboriginal-peoples

Wardman, D. & Quantz, D. (2006). Harm reduction services for British Columbia's First Nation population: A qualitative inquiry into opportunities and barriers for injection drug users. *Harm Reduction Journal, 3.* DOI: 10.1186/1477-7517-3-30

ABOUT THE AUTHOR

Dennis Wardman is a First Nations person from the Key First Nation in Saskatchewan. He completed medical school, followed by a fellowship in Community Medicine in Alberta, and is the first Aboriginal person in Canada to have completed this fellowship. He is board certified by the American Board of Addiction Medicine. Dr. Wardman worked with the First Nations and Inuit Health Branch, BC Region, as director of the Health Promotion and Disease Prevention Directorate. He practises clinical addiction medicine in the Vancouver area and is also a health researcher in the area of Aboriginal people and addiction issues.

Part 3

Meeting the People

Chapter 9

In Search of Identity: Supporting Healing and Well-Being among Youth

LYNN F. LAVALLÉE AND KELLY ANNE FAIRNEY

I suffered from addiction for many years. I started to drink and smoke weed when I was about 12 years old. By the time I was 14, I was selling and doing drugs. It numbed my pain and I felt accepted by others. It made me feel superior to but weaker than others all in the same moment. I was the one everyone needed, and after a while, it became a way of life. I was good at being a hustler. I could get anything I wanted. But it came with a price. I paid the price many times to save myself and my friends from a bad outcome. I had completely lost myself and had nothing to live for. I didn't give myself one ounce of respect because I was so focused on escaping.

My life has been full of mental, sexual, physical and emotional abuse. I was molested as a child, raped at 17, and again at 20. Experiencing sexual abuse was just another reason to continue on my destructive path. I was so beaten down that I had no love for myself, and it was very hard to love another. Because of my history with men, it was difficult to maintain a positive relationship of any kind. I ended up hurting a lot of people and didn't care because I didn't have the emotion or ability to do so.

One day, after being high for days on end, I needed an escape. I
realized I could no longer live this way or I would die. I didn't love
myself enough to stop using, but I thought that if I had something
else to live for, to love, I would find the strength to get clean. My
boyfriend and I decided to have a baby. My incentive for living was
clear as day. I got pregnant and enrolled in school. I made it my goal
to get clean and provide my son with everything he needed to lead
a healthy, happy life. It was no longer about me anymore. I had to
be responsible and provide for my child. I am proud to say that I
have been clean since 2008. I have graduated from college and am
working full time as a child and youth worker. My son is beautiful,
healthy and happy. He is the best thing that has ever happened to me.
If it weren't for him, I would be dead by now. He will always be my
motivation and my light.

Everyone has the capacity to overcome addiction—they just need to
find the incentive that will give them the strength to carry them through.

Kelly Anne Fairney's story illustrates the significant challenges Aboriginal youth face
that place them at risk for addiction and mental health issues. This chapter focuses on
some of the issues within a Canadian context. We also examine promising practices
and recommendations for working with this population, which emphasize youth as
agents of change in their own lives through cultural and spiritual activities.

Defining Youth

Specific age ranges for defining youth vary. The United Nations Permanent Forum on
Indigenous Issues (United Nations, 2009) defines youth as people aged 15 to 24 years.
Many Aboriginal youth employment programs set the age at 29 years and under. The
Canadian census and the Canadian judicial system define youth as under age 18. To
accommodate these age variations, this literature review included the search terms
"youth" and "young adult," and examined the literature about youth aged between
15 and 29 years.

An important consideration when discussing Aboriginal youth programming
is that the Aboriginal population is younger than the general population. In 2011,
the median age of Aboriginal and non-Aboriginal people was 28 years and 41 years,
respectively (Statistics Canada, 2013). In addition, 18.2 per cent of the Aboriginal
population was between the ages of 15 and 24 years compared with 12.9 per cent of the
general population (Statistics Canada, 2013), while almost 30 per cent were under 15.
The percentage of children under age 15 and the percentage of youth between age 15

and 24 in the non-Aboriginal population were more evenly distributed (16.5 per cent and 12.9 per cent, respectively) (Statistics Canada, 2013). This translates into more youth per population requiring services in Aboriginal communities compared with non-Aboriginal communities.

YOUTH AS DEFINED BY OUR ELDERS' TRADITIONAL TEACHINGS

Defining youth in Aboriginal populations must consider traditional teachings related to the lifespan, which focus not on age, but on cycles throughout life. This approach is reflected in the medicine wheel, where the first part of the life cycle emphasizes learning and the second part emphasizes teaching (Figure 9-1). Youth encompasses adolescence and young adulthood, where learning and teaching merge. As the basic premise of the medicine wheel is that everything is connected and flowing, there is no specific age definition for youth.[1] This is why some Aboriginal youth programs extend the age beyond 30 years.

FIGURE 9-1

Lifespan in the Medicine Wheel

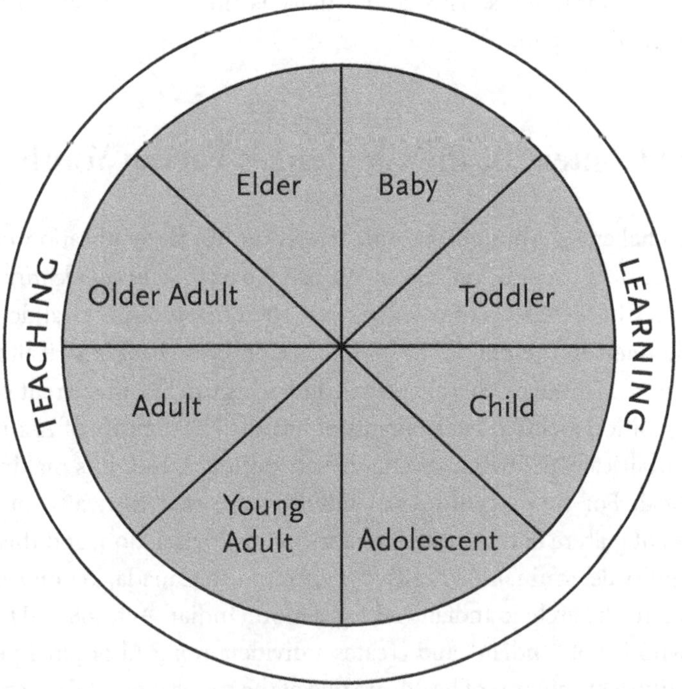

---

1   Traditional teachings vary across nations. For example, Ojibwe teachings may be quite different than Mohawk teachings. Those mentioned in this chapter reflect the authors' heritages, experiences and teachings about the lifespan captured from many Elders. It should also be noted that not all Aboriginal people follow traditional teachings.

Past and Present Roles of Aboriginal Youth

In our experience with traditional teachings, people of all age groups—children, youth and older adults—play significant roles in society. In traditional societies, youth was a period of discovery and learning from adults in preparation for adulthood. Colonization, in particular the residential school experience, disrupted this pattern for First Nations, Métis[2] and Inuit. Many children were taken from their families and did not return until they were 16 years old (Wesley-Esquimaux & Smolewski, 2004). Parenting and adult roles no longer involved teaching children life lessons because there were no children to teach. Upon returning home from residential schools, many children were unable to relate to the lifestyle of their communities and were often unable or unwilling to speak their traditional languages (Norris, 1998). This caused a disruption in the learning cycle in the communities, which created an intergenerational scar that is still felt by many Aboriginal people (Menzies, 2008).

Today, youth from troubled homes are often forced to grow up too quickly, disrupting the learning cycle. Kelly's story at the beginning of this chapter reflects the path of many Aboriginal youth who are experiencing far more than they should during childhood and adolescence. The traditional teachings of the life cycle emphasize that programs that help youth must involve everyone along the lifespan and focus on positive parenting (Menzies, 2008). Since we are all connected, we need to heal collectively as families and communities. This connectivity is the premise behind the medicine wheel teachings of lifespan.

Historical Context of the Challenges Facing Youth

Many of the challenges Aboriginal youth face relate to the eradication of Indigenous culture and identity during colonization. We use the term *political identity determinants of health* to refer to the effects of colonization. The notion of political determinants of health usually refers to the politics of health care policies (People's Health Movement, n.d.; Prince, 2012). However, this chapter includes historical and current colonial legislation in the political identity determinants of health. The identity of Aboriginal people in Canada is politically defined, making identity political, and thus making Aboriginal people political. For them, politics and identity are tied to health outcomes. The historical loss of culture and identity is tied to colonial legislation, and this we define as a political identity determinant of health; for example, in Canada, identity for Aboriginal peoples is tied to the archaic Indian Act legislation (Indian Act, 1985). The act dictates who is and who is not "Indian" and creates a divide among Aboriginal peoples. These political identity determinants of health are one of the root causes of the issues Aboriginal

---

2   Although some argue that Métis did not attend residential schools, many scholars have collected evidence that some Métis children did (e.g., Chartrand et al., 2006). However, the majority of residential school attendees were First Nations people.

youth experience today. Addiction and mental health issues are *symptoms of colonization* and its resulting intergenerational grief and trauma (Menzies, 2008). Although many Aboriginal people and youth have begun to heal from the trauma of colonization and are breaking the cycle of ill health and dysfunction, many individuals, families and communities remain unhealthy. Some of the issues Aboriginal youth face include urbanization, high dropout rates in high school, unemployment, early pregnancy, suicide, incarceration, and alcohol and other substance use problems.[3]

This section examines some of the challenges Aboriginal youth experience and provides the statistics behind those challenges. Although statistics can sometimes promote prejudice and discrimination, we cannot ignore them. It is important to frame the statistics in such a way that does not perpetuate stereotypes. This is often done by acknowledging the impacts of colonization and social determinants that create inequity and significant challenges, rather than blaming the individual.

URBANIZATION

The 2006 census showed that 60 per cent of First Nations people live off reserves and 76 per cent of those live in urban centres. This compares with 69 per cent for Métis and 17 per cent for Inuit (Statistics Canada, 2008). Youth move to urban areas for a variety of reasons: employment, education, excitement or to follow friends. Kirmayer and colleagues (2009) discussed the implications of rapid cultural change as a source of psychological trauma for Aboriginal people who have moved to cities. However, many Aboriginal people have lived in urban centres for generations, so cultural change does not fully explain the psychological trauma experienced by urban Aboriginal youth.

Specific challenges may differ depending on the region. For example, the challenges for youth in Regina may be vastly different from those of youth in Toronto. In a large multicultural city such as Toronto, Aboriginal youth might "blend in" more, which may buffer some of the racism and discrimination that Aboriginal people experience. In contrast, those who live in predominantly white urban centres such as Regina (Statistics Canada, 2009) may experience more racism and discrimination. Differences also exist from city to city around employment opportunities and the availability of Aboriginal programming and housing. Mental health and addiction programs for youth must take into account the varying circumstances of both the individual and the community in which the person lives.

PRECIOUS CHILDREN HAVING PRECIOUS CHILDREN

An Anishinaabe traditional teaching tells us that children are a precious gift. This means that all parents, regardless of age, must be supported. However, statistics

---

3 For a discussion about suicide, see chapter 21.

show a difficult road ahead for young parents. Aboriginal women are having children at a younger age compared with non-Aboriginal women. The 2006 census (Statistics Canada, 2008) found that 26 per cent of Inuit children, 27 per cent of off-reserve First Nations children and 22 per cent of Métis children under age 6 had mothers who were aged between 15 and 24 years compared with eight per cent of non-Aboriginal children under age 6 (O'Donnell & Wallace, 2011).

When we talk with young parents, we need to share the Anishinaabe teaching about the precious gift of children and be supportive and nurturing. As Kelly described in her personal story, having a child can be an extremely rewarding experience that provides both mothers and fathers with a strong incentive to give their children the best life possible. In Kelly's case, this meant overcoming her addiction and changing many aspects of her life. We must stress that having a child is not a treatment for addiction or mental health issues. The point is that there needs to be an internal motivation to change.

INCARCERATION

The statistics on the incarceration of Aboriginal youth aged between 12 and 17 years are discouraging. Since the judicial system classifies adults as those 18 years and older, statistics on the incarceration of youth over 17 are difficult to obtain. Statistics Canada (Munch, 2012) data for 2010–2011 indicates that Aboriginal youth represent six per cent of Canada's youth, but in the correctional system, 34 per cent of all female youth and 24 per cent of male youth were Aboriginal. This data does not include Saskatchewan, Nova Scotia, Quebec, British Columbia and the Northwest Territories (Munch, 2012). Perreault (2009) found that the ratio of Aboriginal to non-Aboriginal youth incarceration is 7.7:1 nationally, and 26.1:1 in Saskatchewan. If the Statistics Canada (Munch, 2012) data had included Saskatchewan, the Northwest Territories and some of the other provinces, the statistics might have shown even higher rates of incarceration among Aboriginal youth.

This higher involvement with the correctional system can be explained partially by the greater tendency for youth in general to be in conflict with the law and by the relatively young age of the Aboriginal population compared with the non-Aboriginal population (Perreault, 2009). There is also a connection between incarcerated youth and substance use problems: 56 per cent of incarcerated Aboriginal youth have substance use problems (Latimer & Foss, 2005). Moreover, on average, incarcerated Aboriginal youth are two academic years behind incarcerated non-Aboriginal youth, and 89 per cent attend alternative schools (Corrado & Cohen, 2002).

Racism and discrimination within the judicial system affect incarceration rates (Satzewich, 1998; York, 1990). Racism targeted at individuals, systemic racism, ideological or cultural racism, and discrimination by police and the justice system all contribute to the high number of incarcerated Aboriginal youth (Roy, n.d.). First Nations people are three times more likely to be charged and sent to court compared with the general population, and 18 per cent of First Nations people are released on full parole compared with 42 per cent of the general inmate population (York, 1990). These outcomes may reflect not only racism by police and the courts, but also the existence of relatively few Aboriginal people working in the judicial system (Satzewich, 1998; York, 1990).

To decrease incarceration rates of Aboriginal youth, systemic racism and discrimination need to be addressed by developing nationwide anti-racism educational programs for people working in correctional institutions, the courts and police departments. This recommendation addresses a systemic issue, racism, and such systemic issues need to be addressed in order to have a positive effect on youth. We cannot simply focus on the individual when systemic social and political determinants of health remain poor for Aboriginal people, particularly Aboriginal youth.

ALCOHOL AND OTHER SUBSTANCE USE PROBLEMS

The statistics on alcohol and other substance use problems classify adults as 18 years and older, so data for young people aged between 18 and 29 is not presented in this chapter. The statistics presented here include some adult statistics.

Contrary to the stereotype, Aboriginal people drink less often and abstain from alcohol more often than non-Aboriginal people. Only 17.8 per cent of Aboriginal people report drinking weekly compared with 44 per cent of non-Aboriginal people (Dell & Lyons, 2007; National Native Addictions Partnership Foundation & Thatcher, 2000). However, First Nations people who do drink, do so more heavily, which may contribute to the stereotype (First Nations Information Governance Centre, 2007). In the North, Inuit also drink less often, but have a higher rate of binge drinking (Nunavik Inuit Health Survey, 2004). Further research is required to determine whether these patterns exist among Métis, and also to distinguish between heavy drinking and binge drinking.

The younger average age and lower socio-economic status of Aboriginal people compared with non-Aboriginal people may account for some of the differences between the two populations in terms of alcohol use problems (National Native Addictions Partnership Foundation & Thatcher, 2000). Young age and lower socio-economic status are both factors that contribute to alcohol use problems.

Aboriginal youth are at higher risk of using cannabis and illicit drugs compared with other youth (Tonkin, 2005; Tu et al., 2008). Using solvents to get high is also more common among Aboriginal youth (Coleman et al., 2001). However, Dell and Lyons (2007) noted that perceptions of the prevalence of solvent use may be inflated due to the media, particularly to repeated showings of media clips of Innu youth inhaling gasoline. A Manitoba study that compared the use of substances among off-reserve First Nations and Métis youth and non-Aboriginal youth found that Aboriginal youth had higher rates of substance use and that their use of LSD and marijuana was three times higher than that of non-Aboriginal youth (Gfellner & Hundleby, 1995). Erickson and Butters (2005) noted that substance use statistics for Aboriginal youth can vary greatly by region and tribal background. This is an important consideration when analyzing the statistics and developing programs.

While the statistics paint a negative picture of Aboriginal youth, we cannot ignore the challenges that our youth face. However, we need to acknowledge the systemic issues that contribute to these statistics. We also need to capitalize on the strengths and resilience of our youth, as illustrated by Kelly-Anne's story: she overcame many of the challenges of her childhood and, as you will read later, now helps other youth on their healing journeys.

Holistic Promising Practices

Within a universalist framework for mental health and addiction programs, programs can be designed for all people. A contextual and developmental framework posits that programs need to be designed and delivered in the context of the individual's social location, culture and developmental stage (Iarocci et al., 2009; Kim, 2000). Examples of contextual and developmental programs offered at the Centre for Addiction and Mental Health in Toronto include treatment programs for gay men, Spanish-speaking adults and Aboriginal men and women. The rationale for a contextual and developmental approach to mental health and addiction programs is the need to address systemic and societal challenges unique to specific populations. For example, while Aboriginal and non-Aboriginal youth undoubtedly have similar challenges, programs designed specifically for Aboriginal youth can address some of the unique challenges these youth face.

CULTURE AS AN INDIGENOUS FORM OF COGNITIVE-BEHAVIOURAL THERAPY

Collectively, Aboriginal peoples are going through a healing process. Their ability to connect to their culture, identity and one another contributes to their resilience. As a community, we can heal collectively and succeed as individuals. In the lifespan teachings, youth generally look to older generations, such as parents and grandparents, for guidance and direction. This means that the healing of Aboriginal people of all ages is essential to the well-being of youth.

In his seminal work on psychosocial development, Erik Erikson (1968) theorized that youth establish their individual identities based on their thoughts, feelings, personal interests and opinions. While general theories have emerged around identity development among ethnic adolescents (Phinney, 1993), there are unique differences between Aboriginal youth and other ethnic minority youth. Aboriginal youth may have a confused sense of identity rooted in historical events such as the residential schools and Indian Act dictates around identity, as well as in current stigma associated with self-identifying as Aboriginal. These experiences have had a significant impact in shaping identity and young people's acceptance of and pride in their unique heritage.

It is important that programs for Aboriginal youth incorporate spiritual values and traditions, and include Aboriginal role models. In our review of promising practices, we found that most treatment centres for Aboriginal youth incorporate culture as a primary component in their programs (Table 9-1). Programs encompassing cultural identity are critical to healing from or coping with addiction and mental health issues.

TABLE 9-1

Treatment Centres Serving Youth

TREATMENT CENTRE	LOCATION
Athabasca Alcohol and Drug Abuse Project	Saskatchewan
Carrier Sekani Family Services (Najeh Bayou)	British Columbia
Kainaiwa Adolescent Treatment Centre	Alberta
Leading Thunderbird Lodge	Saskatchewan
Lone Eagle Treatment Centre	Atlantic Region
Mi'kmaw Lodge Treatment Centre	Atlantic Region
Oh Shki Be Ma Te Ze Win	Ontario
Saulteaux Healing and Wellness Centre	Saskatchewan
White Buffalo Treatment Centre	Saskatchewan
Wilp Si'Satxw House of Purification	British Columbia
Young Spirit Winds Treatment Program	Alberta

Cognitive-behavioural therapy (CBT), rational emotive behaviour therapy and motivational enhancement therapy are typical Western treatments for substance use problems (Willenbring, 2010). They help people to change their thought processes and how they see the world. We argue that cultural traditions and, for the Anishinaabek, ceremonies such as traditional drumming, singing and dancing; birthing and naming ceremonies; and sweats, fasts and vision quests are an Indigenous form of CBT that not only affect the individual, but heal us collectively. As with CBT, participating in ceremonies changes the way people view the world, themselves and their communities. It offers motivation for change similar to that provided in motivational enhancement therapy. Rather than viewing culture as an "add-on" in addiction treatment and mental health programs for Aboriginal youth, we advocate using culture front and centre. Kelly Anne's story of reconnecting to her roots by finding employment at an Aboriginal health agency reflects the importance of a cultural approach to healing.

This past year I have learned something very important. I want to share it because there are so many people out there with similar stories. This is my message of hope to all the youth who have lost themselves, just as I had.

I was given the opportunity to work at an Aboriginal organization, Anishnawbe Health Toronto. It is a non-profit organization dedicated to enhancing the lives and well-being of our community. They offer a wide range of services, including traditional healing.

I never imagined that my time there would change my life as it did. I reconnected to my roots. I always knew I was Aboriginal, but never really understood what that meant. Colonization has set our culture back and now we are all in a healing process and we need to capture what was taken from us. I learned so much in such a short time. On my second day, a young girl came in and asked for guidance from one of the healers on how to forgive someone and let go. I felt that the teaching for this young girl was a teaching I needed to hear myself. The healer told her that she needed to ask the Great Spirit to forgive for her. The healer explained that we are living out our stories, and our spirit accepted this life before we were even born. If we ask our spirit to forgive, it will; we just need to be willing to let go.

After I heard this, things seemed to make sense. This was the first time in 20 years that I felt at peace with my past. How could I be mad and hold resentment toward others when I had made the choice to accept my life before it even started? When I think about my life and the horrible things I have been through, I still wouldn't change anything because those things define me as a person. I have a purpose in life. I might have needed to go through those things to carry out the rest of my story. After work, I felt overwhelmed and happy. It felt so good to make sense of things. I was intrigued and fully embraced the culture. I received my spirit name, colours and clan. I also brought my son in to get the same. I started smudging every day and praying.

The one thing that really made me believe is when I started taking some medicines. I wanted to stop taking my painkillers, which I had been taking for almost a decade. I offered my tobacco and received a medicine that would take all the poison out of my blood. The healer told me that if I chose to take this medicine and go a traditional route, I would not be able to take anymore pills for pain. The first thing that went through my mind was the experience of withdrawal.

I had tried to stop taking the painkillers before and I got extremely sick. The healer asked me to take some time to think about it, but I didn't need to—I was willing to stop. When I got the medicine, I took it home, smudged it and myself, and asked my spirit to take away my sickness.

The next morning I woke up, smudged, went to work and felt great. I stopped taking my pills without any sickness or withdrawal. I was able to manage my chronic pain and feel good about it. I was amazed. In one week, I overcame my addiction to prescription pills and let go of 20 years of built-up anger. I was on the path of spirituality to reconnect with myself. I was ready to accept my life so that I could move on. I had been desperately searching for something to guide me. I believe that everything happens for a reason, and there was a reason why I started working in an Aboriginal organization.

Today, I take part in ceremonies. I volunteer when I can. I am a presence in my community. Being connected makes me feel accepted and has given me a sense of belonging. It is very hard to walk through life feeling alone. What I learned is that I will never be alone. I will always have my spirit with me to guide me through the good times and the bad.

Kelly Anne's story illustrates the importance of moving beyond a focus on the individual addiction and appreciating how culture can play a key role in healing. This means that addiction and mental health programs for Aboriginal youth need to focus holistically on the family. Youth are more than their addiction or behaviour. Addictions and some mental health issues are symptoms of colonization. We need to move beyond simply treating symptoms and focus on promoting holistic well-being. There are also programs that do not focus on addictions or mental health issues but that have a positive impact on youth and play a preventative role. For example, Kelly Anne describes a program at Anishnawbe Health Toronto that incorporates culture and has an impact on many levels.

The Oshkii Okitchiidak youth program at Anishnawbe Health Toronto is run by experienced social workers who have devoted their lives to helping our youth stay in school to become outstanding, respected and contributing members of society. They work with the parents to assess the needs of the youth and work as a team to give our youth a safe place to learn who they are. I think these types of programs are important because the focal point is culture. Moccasin workshops, berry picking and beading workshops are all ways to teach youth where they come from. We need to instil in our youth the importance of what being Aboriginal really means. We are one big family and being connected to one another the way we are is a very special gift that we all possess. When youth have realized that others do care and that help is there, they will be more willing to tap into these resources when they are facing challenges.

Conclusion

Addressing the challenges that Aboriginal youth face requires recognizing the social and political identity determinants of health and their impact on mental health and substance use issues. Understanding how these determinants of health are linked to conflicted feelings about Aboriginal identity, particularly for youth, is critical. Although including techniques such as CBT and motivational interviewing in addiction and mental health programs can be useful, helping Aboriginal youth identify with a strong Aboriginal community is most important in the healing process. Exploring some of the positive things that are happening among Aboriginal youth, such as the resurgence of drumming, singing—including Native hip hop—and dancing groups, will help to challenge stereotypes about Aboriginal youth.

Nationwide educational campaigns about the historical legacies and current injustices that have contributed to the ill health of Aboriginal youth, as well as about the positive activities that happen in Aboriginal communities, will also challenge negative stereotypes. While we acknowledge that youth will be ready in their own time to heal, it is important that programs and traditional activities be widely available and publicized so youth know that their communities are welcoming and non-judgmental, and are waiting to encourage the next generation. Traditional activities and ceremonies, such as sweats, fasting and vision quests, can help to change thoughts and behaviours, and can become our cognitive-behavioural therapies that promote well-being and cultural pride among Aboriginal youth.

References

Chartrand, L.N., Logan, T.E. & Daniels, J.D. (2006). *Métis History and Experience and Residential Schools in Canada.* Retrieved from Aboriginal Healing Foundation website: www.ahf.ca/downloads/metiseweb.pdf

Coleman, H., Charles, G. & Collins, J. (2001). Inhalant use by Canadian Aboriginal youth. *Journal of Child and Adolescent Substance Abuse, 10* (3), 1–20.

Corrado, R.R. & Cohen, I.M. (2002). A needs profile of serious and/or violent Aboriginal youth in prison. *Forum on Corrections Research, 14* (3), 20–24.

Dell, C.A. & Lyons, T. (2007). *Harm Reduction Policies and Programs for Persons of Aboriginal Descent.* Retrieved from Canadian Centre on Substance Abuse website: www.ccsa.ca

Erickson, P.G. & Butters, J.E. (2005). How does the Canadian juvenile justice system respond to detained youth with substance use associated problems? Gaps, challenges and emerging issues. *Substance Use & Misuse, 40,* 953–973.

Erikson, E. (1968). *Identity: Youth and Crisis*. New York: Norton.

First Nations Information Governance Centre. (2007). *First Nations Regional Longitudinal Health Survey (RHS) 2002/03: The Peoples' Report* (rev. 2nd ed.). Retrieved from www.fnigc.ca

Gfellner, B.M. & Hundleby, J.D. (1995). Patterns of drug use among native and white adolescents: 1990–1993. *Canadian Journal of Public Health, 86*, 95–97.

Iarocci, G., Root, R. & Burack, J.A. (2009). Social competence and mental health among Aboriginal youth: An integrative developmental perspective. In L.J. Kirmayer & G. Guthrie Valaskakis (Eds.), *Healing Traditions: The Mental Health of Aboriginal Peoples in Canada* (pp. 80–108). Vancouver: UBC Press.

Indian Act ("An Act respecting Indians"), R.S.C. (1985, c. I-5). Retrieved from http://laws-lois.justice. gc.ca/eng/acts/I-5/page-1.html

Kim, U. (2000). Indigenous, cultural, and cross-cultural psychology: A theoretical, conceptual, and epistemological analysis. *Asian Journal of Social Psychology, 3*, 265–287. DOI: 10.1111/1467-839X.00068

Kirmayer, L.J., Tait, C.L. & Simpson, C. (2009). The mental health of Aboriginal peoples in Canada: Transformations of identity and community. In L.J. Kirmayer & G. Guthrie Valaskakis (Eds.), *Healing Traditions: The Mental Health of Aboriginal Peoples in Canada* (pp. 3–35). Vancouver: UBC Press.

Latimer, J. & Foss, L.C. (2005). The sentencing of Aboriginal and non-Aboriginal youth under the *Young Offenders Act*: A multivariate analysis. *Canadian Journal of Criminology and Criminal Justice, 47*, 481–500.

Menzies, P. (2008). Developing an Aboriginal healing model for intergenerational trauma. *International Journal of Health Promotion and Education, 46*, 41–48.

Munch, C. (2012). *Youth Correctional Statistics in Canada, 2010/2011*. (Statistics Canada catalogue no. 85-002-X). Retrieved from www.statcan.gc.ca

National Native Addictions Partnership Foundation & Thatcher, R. (2000). *NNADAP Renewal Framework*. Retrieved from http://nnapf.com/wp-content/uploads/2012/02/original-renewal-framework.pdf

Norris, M.J. (1998). Canada's Aboriginal languages. *Canadian Social Trends, 51*, 8–16. (Statistics Canada catalogue no. 11-008). Retrieved from www.statcan.gc.ca/pub/11-008-x/1998003/article/4003-eng.pdf

Nunavik Inuit Health Survey. (2004). *Alcohol, Drug Use and Gambling among the Inuit of Nunavik: Epidemiological Profile*. Retrieved from Institut national de santé publique du Québec website: www. inspq.qc.ca/pdf/publications/resumes_nunavik/anglais/AlcoholDrugUseAndGamblingAmongTheInuitOfNunavik.pdf

O'Donnell, V. & Wallace, S. (2011). First Nations, Métis and Inuit women. *Women in Canada: A Gender-Based Statistical Report*. (Statistics Canada catalogue no. 89-503-X). Retrieved from www. statcan.gc.ca

People's Health Movement. (n.d.). *Political Management of Health Determinants: Addressing Unhealthy Policies*. Retrieved from World Health Organization website: www.who.int/social_determinants/ resources/egypt.pdf

Perreault, S. (2009). The incarceration of Aboriginal people in adult correctional services. *Juristat, 29* (3). (Statistics Canada catalogue no. 85-002-X). Retrieved from www.statcan.gc.ca

Phinney, J.S. (1993). A three-stage model of ethnic identity development in adolescence. In. M.A. Bernal & G.P. Knight (Eds.), *Ethnic Identity: Formation and Transmission among Hispanics and Other Minorities* (pp. 61–80). New York: State University of New York Press.

Prince, M.J. (2012, February). *Political determinants of health care policy in Canada*. Paper presented at the Social Dimensions of Health Program Colloquium, University of Victoria, Victoria, BC.

Roy, J. (n.d.). *Racism in the Justice System*. Retrieved from Canadian Race Relations Foundation website: www.crr.ca/divers-files/en/pub/faSh/ePubFaShRacJusSys.pdf

Satzewich, V. (1998). *Racism and Social Inequality in Canada: Concepts, Controversies and Strategies of Resistance.* Toronto: Thompson Educational Publishing.

Statistics Canada. (2008). *Aboriginal Peoples in Canada in 2006: Inuit, Métis and First Nations, 2006 Census.* (Catalogue no. 97-558-XIE). Ottawa: Minister of Industry.

Statistics Canada. (2009). Population by selected ethnic origins, by Census metropolitan areas (2006 Census) (Regina) (table). *2006 Census of Population.* Retrieved from www.statcan.gc.ca/tables-tableaux/sum-som/l01/cst01/demo27s-eng.htm

Statistics Canada. (2013). *National Household Survey, 2011: Aboriginal Peoples in Canada—First Nations People, Métis and Inuit.* (Catalogue no. 99-011-X2011001). Ottawa: Minister of Industry.

Tonkin, R.S. (2005). *British Columbia Youth Health Trends: A Retrospective, 1992–2003.* Retrieved from McCreary Centre Society website: www.mcs.bc.ca/pdf/AHS-Trends-2005-report.pdf

Tu, A.W., Ratner, P.A. & Johnson, J.L. (2008). Gender differences in correlates of adolescents' cannabis use. *Substance Use and Misuse, 43,* 1438–1463. DOI: 10.1080/10826080802238140

United Nations. (2009). *State of the World's Indigenous Peoples.* Retrieved from www.un.org/esa/socdev/unpfii/documents/SOWIP_web.pdf

Wesley-Esquimaux, C. & Smolewski, M. (2004). *Historic Trauma and Aboriginal Healing.* Retrieved from Aboriginal Healing Foundation website: www.ahf.ca

Willenbring, M.L. (2010). The past and future of research on treatment of alcohol dependence. *Alcohol Research and Health, 33* (1/2), 55–63.

York, G. (1990). *The Dispossessed: Life and Death in Native Canada.* Toronto: Little, Brown and Company.

ABOUT THE AUTHORS

Kelly Anne Fairney is an Anishinaabe Métis youth who was born in Toronto and grew up in small rural towns north of the city. She currently lives in Penetanguishene, Ontario. She has battled with addiction and draws on her own experiences in her work. She recently completed the Child and Youth Worker degree program at Georgian College in Orillia, graduating with honours.

Lynn F. Lavallée, BA, MSC, PHD, is Anishinaabe Métis born in Sudbury, Ontario. She moved to Toronto as a child and grew up in the social housing development Regent Park. As a youth and young adult she faced mental health challenges. Lynn has a BA in psychology and kinesiology, an MSC in community health and a PHD in social work. She is an associate professor at Ryerson University, as well as associate director of the School of Social Work and chair of the Research Ethics Board. Her research interests include the holistic well-being of Indigenous peoples, social and political determinants of health and Indigenous research ethics.

Chapter 10

Ensuring a Culturally Safe Practice in Working with Aboriginal Women

CRISTINE REGO AND REBEKAH REGO

> The woman is the foundation on which nations are built. She is the
> heart of her nation. If that heart is weak, the people are weak. If her
> heart is strong and her mind is clear, then the nation is strong and
> knows its purpose. The woman is the center of everything.
> — Art Solomon, Ojibway Elder (1990)

It is critical that all service providers and helpers understand the challenges and complexities Aboriginal women face in maintaining their health and well-being, as well as that of their families and communities. Equally important is recognizing Aboriginal women's individual strengths in the face of a changing landscape, in which their entire identities and traditional ways of life within the family have been challenged by the dominant Western culture. People who provide health and social services to Aboriginal women must develop strategies to understand and effectively work with women on their healing journeys. Service providers must apply an Aboriginal world view that draws on the expertise of Elders and incorporates traditional healing ceremonies and other Aboriginal teaching and practices to ensure their interactions with Aboriginal women are culturally informed.

The Loss of Traditional Roles with Colonization

The status of Aboriginal women changed dramatically with the introduction of the Indian Act. This federal legislation allowed the government to set aside lands to be occupied and used exclusively by "Indians" while outlawing traditional ceremonies and spiritual practices.[1] Assimilationist policies such as the residential school system further eroded traditional ways of life. In traditional societies, women were responsible for ensuring health and balance in their families and communities, and acted as life givers and caretakers. The women assumed care of the children, the family, the home and, in part, the health of the community, while men were the providers of food, clothing and shelter. According to Jacobs (2000), men were traditionally respected for their physical strength, while women were valued for their mental strength.[2] Both were respected for their spiritual strength.

The Indian Act also contributed to the loss of women's power through the relocation of their traditional lands and ultimately the loss of their traditional roles in community governance. Women became subservient to the patriarchal processes enforced by Indian agents.[3] They no longer had a say in governance matters or community decisions, could not own or inherit land from their husbands, relied on external sources for support and saw their children taken away and sent to residential schools.

Aboriginal women lost not only their political power, but also the opportunity to mother their children. The residential schools removed children from their families, a practice whose legacy continues to be felt today: the Royal Commission on Aboriginal Peoples ([RCAP], 1996a) found that the percentage of Aboriginal children in care is six times that of children in the general population. Moreover, the residential schools failed to provide children with the knowledge and skills they would need to raise their own families. Instead, the schools systematically undermined Aboriginal culture and disrupted generations of families. Mothers who lost their children to the residential schools were left to grieve, with no opportunity to maintain an attachment with their children. These women often experienced violence in their relationships and in the community due to alcohol and other substance use problems.

Analysis of the population data collected by Human Resources and Skills Development Canada ([HRSDC], 2009) indicated a growing number of Aboriginal teenage mothers, and a greater proportion of Aboriginal single-parent families—16 per cent compared to 12 per cent in the general population. Moreover, 80 per cent of single Aboriginal parents are female (HRSDC, 2009).

From the time women are born, laws established by a European male-dominated system determine their identities. Under the Indian Act, an Aboriginal woman would lose her Indian status if she married a non-Aboriginal man, as would any children

---

1 For a discussion about the history of colonization and its effects, see chapter 2.

2 For more discussion about the traditional roles of Aboriginal men, see chapter 11.

3 An Indian agent was a Canadian government official authorized to oversee the implementation of the Indian Act with respect to a particular Aboriginal reserve or band.

born from that relationship, and she would be forced to leave the community (Furi & Wherrett, 1996). The act dismantled not only the communities themselves, but also the strong supportive role that women had within them.

Bill C-31, which passed into law in April 1985, was an attempt to amend the Indian Act and bring it in line with gender equality under the Canadian Charter of Rights and Freedoms. The modifications to the act included significant changes to Indian status and band membership to address gender discrimination. The bill restored Indian status to people who had been forcibly disenfranchised by previous discriminatory provisions, and allowed bands to control their own band membership as a step toward self-government. Women who had lost their status for marrying a man who was not Aboriginal qualified to have their status reinstated. However, the bill fell short in limiting how their children and subsequent grandchildren could obtain status. Despite this shortcoming, the modifications were intended to help Aboriginal women re-establish a connection to their community and recognize their traditional roots. But Bill C-31 failed to address the historical impact on women and communities.

The communities' collective grieving, which began with the Indian Act, continues today, as women struggle to restore balance within their families and communities. Aboriginal women continue to be one of the most victimized groups in Canadian society, discriminated against based on their race, gender and class.

Healing from Colonization

Assisting Aboriginal women in understanding how colonization has affected them will help them move toward decolonization—a process where colonized people reclaim their traditional culture, redefine themselves as a people, reassert their distinct identity and in turn move along on their healing journey. If Aboriginal women can heal, they can in turn support healing in the family and community.

Understanding the effect of assimilationist practices on Aboriginal women's lives and communities informs both practice and program development. Self-awareness needs to occur on an individual level for the healing journey to begin. These insights will enhance the way in which service providers can support these women on their healing journeys. Health providers need to be better educated about how environmental factors contribute to improved health and healing (Kleinman, 2006). Equally important is for health providers to understand the role history has played in the healing journey.

Despite the challenges, Aboriginal women continue to persevere and recognize the importance of their role in keeping the family and community healthy. More Aboriginal women are graduating from post-secondary schools and some are pursuing political positions of power.

As Aboriginal women deal with the wounds of colonization, they face mental health and substance use problems and non-communicable diseases such as high blood pressure and diabetes. According to the Prairie Women's Health Centre of Excellence (Wilson,

2004), Aboriginal women have lower life expectancy, elevated morbidity rates and higher suicide rates compared with non-Aboriginal women. The First Nations Regional Longitudinal Health Survey (First Nations Information Governance Centre, 2005) found that while rates of suicidal ideation were similar in First Nations women and men (33 per cent and 29 per cent, respectively), 19 per cent of women reported having attempted suicide at least once, compared to 13 per cent of men. Among First Nations youth aged 12 to 17 years, girls were more likely than boys to be at a normal weight or underweight (62 per cent versus 55 per cent), but they were more likely to be dissatisfied with their weight (13 per cent versus 6 per cent). Girls also felt less balanced mentally and physically than boys.

Aboriginal women living on reserves also experience significantly higher rates of coronary heart disease, cancer, cerebrovascular disease and other chronic illnesses than non-Aboriginal women (Waldram et al., 2000). Compared to other Canadians, First Nations, Inuit and Métis children and their families experience major disparities in the social determinants of health: overall, they have less education and experience poorer health, as well as being more likely to experience inadequate or unsafe housing and unemployment (Smylie & Adomako, 2009).

According to a statistical profile of Aboriginal women in Canada from the 2006 census (Statistics Canada, 2008), Aboriginal women have more post-secondary and university education than Aboriginal men, but less education than both non-Aboriginal men and women (see Figure 10-1).

FIGURE 10-1

Level of Education, Non-Aboriginal and Aboriginal Populations, Age 25–65 Years, 2006 (Percentages)

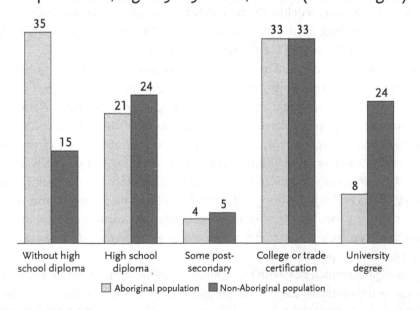

Source: Statistics Canada (2008)

Aboriginal women have lower levels of education than non-Aboriginal women, but they are more educated than in the past. Yet despite higher educational attainment in recent years, more than 36 per cent of Aboriginal women, compared to 17 per cent of non-Aboriginal women, live in poverty, according to the 2006 census (Statistics Canada, 2008). Moreover, although Aboriginal women are attaining higher levels of education, the 2006 census (Statistics Canada, 2008) found that their income level remains lower than that of Aboriginal men and non-Aboriginal people (see Figure 10-2).

FIGURE 10-2

Average Individual Income for the Population 15 years and Over by Aboriginal Group and Gender, 2006

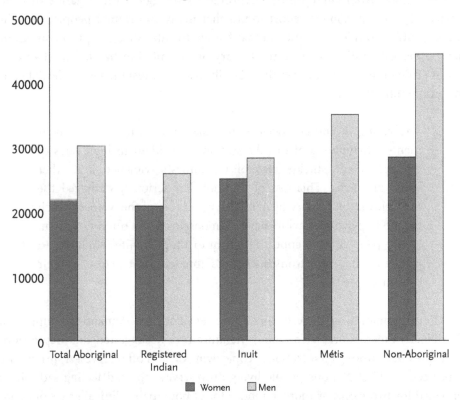

Source: Statistics Canada (2008)

Overall, trends indicate that Aboriginal women continue to earn less than non-Aboriginal men and women, in part because they are often employed on reserves in positions that rely on transfer payments from the federal government with restricted budgets.

TRAUMA AND ABUSE

Aboriginal women experience higher rates of substance use, sexual trauma, domestic violence, criminal activity and incarceration. Aboriginal overrepresentation in federal institutions rose by 20 per cent between 1998 and 2008 (Public Safety Canada, 2008). Even more disturbing is the number of federally incarcerated Aboriginal women: an increase of 131 per cent over the same period. Between 2007 and 2008, 33 per cent of women in federal penitentiaries were Aboriginal (Public Safety Canada, 2008).

Intergenerational trauma and the fast growth of younger Aboriginal populations are reflected in higher rates of suicides, teen pregnancies, and mental health and addiction issues. In her literature review on intergenerational trauma, mental health, violence against women, addiction and homelessness, Goudreau (2012) stated that, in many cases, Aboriginal women continue to struggle with negative historical impacts. The RCAP (1996b) report found that many Aboriginal people, including women, suffer from low self-esteem that has led to substance use problems, among many other difficulties, because the history of assimilation has led to shame and lack of pride in their cultural identity. Hamilton and Longstaffe (1987) described the impact of cultural loss:

> The razing of Indian societies and their traditions is well documented. Symptoms of this dislocation are evident in high rates of unemployment, suicide, alcoholism, domestic violence, and other social problems. This loss of tradition has seriously damaged the oral means of preserving cultural norms, and the values which prohibit deviant behaviors have been obscured and often forgotten. Native peoples often appear reluctant to adopt "white" solutions to problems that stem from the latter's apparent destruction of their societies. (p. 8)

The combination of these factors creates an increased demand for support for Aboriginal women. Christian's (2009) literature review suggested that depression is highly prevalent among First Nations people living on and off reserves. Approximately 30 per cent of First Nations people living on reserves reported feeling sad, blue or depressed for two weeks or more, an indicator of potentially clinical levels of depression. Social and psychological problems, and issues related to intergenerational trauma, are more common among Aboriginal than non-Aboriginal people, as a result of the residential school experience (Corrado & Cohen, 2003).[4] The fact that more single-parent homes are led by Aboriginal women only compounds the stress these women experience.

---

4 For more discussion about the residential schools and intergenerational trauma, see chapters 3 and 5, respectively.

According to the 2009 General Social Survey on Victimization, Aboriginal women compared to their non-Aboriginal counterparts, are three times as likely to report being the victims of spousal violence and are eight times more likely to be killed by their spouse after a separation (Brennan, 2011). The survey also found that almost 67,000 (13 per cent) of Aboriginal women aged 15 years and older living in the provinces stated that they had been violently victimized.[5] However, since the data is based on self-disclosure, the rate of victimization may be higher because many women are reluctant to disclose these experiences for fear of reprisal or because of the degree of violence, often involving weapons (Brennan, 2011).

Aboriginal women are also overrepresented in the sex trade. This puts them at an increased risk of harm, violence and sexually contracted diseases. An HIV outreach worker in Sudbury, Ontario, explained that young women are forced into the sex trade to support their children or a drug habit (personal communication, June 21, 2003).

Like other examples of the marginalization and discrimination experienced by Aboriginal women, these statistics illustrate Aboriginal women's vulnerability in our society and the historical and current injustices they have faced. This vulnerability is fuelled by social and economic marginalization and a history of oppressive government policies.

Working with Aboriginal Women

CULTURAL COMPETENCE

Practising cultural competence will help service providers empower the women they are working with. Cultural competence is the understanding of cultural distinctions, taking into consideration the beliefs, values, activities and customs of distinct population groups. In the health field, there are often prescribed ways of talking about health and the human body, and a common medical terminology that can be alienating and disempowering for people who are unfamiliar or uncomfortable with this language. Furthermore, people with a history of shame and sexual abuse may not be open to discussing their body.

Cultural competence usually refers to health practitioners' skills, knowledge and attitudes, whereas culture safety or culturally safe practice are more all-encompassing terms that also include the experience of the client, and respect the interaction between, and experiences of, both the client and the practitioner.

CULTURAL SAFETY

By incorporating cultural safety into a culturally competent practice, helpers (e.g., counsellors, social workers, doctors, other allied health staff) move progressively

---

5   Data from the Northwest Territories, Yukon and Nunavut was not collected in the report.

beyond cultural awareness, cultural sensitivity and cultural competence. Cultural safety equalizes the power imbalance between the helper and the person seeking help on the healing journey. For Indigenous people, healing is traditionally viewed as a lifelong journey rather than as an individual problem to be fixed. The concept of cultural safety was developed in the 1980s in New Zealand in response to the Maori people's discontent with nursing care. Maori nursing professionals and Maori national organizations supported the theory of cultural safety, which incorporates the political ideas of self-determination and decolonization (National Aboriginal Health Organization, 2006). A culturally safe way of working with Aboriginal women promotes self-determination and decolonization, unlike the biomedical model of health care where the helper is the expert in the relationship.

Fulcher (1998) defined cultural safety as:

> That state of being in which the [individual] knows emotionally that her/his personal wellbeing, as well as social and cultural frames of reference, are acknowledged—even if not fully understood. Furthermore, she/he is given active reason to feel hopeful that her/his needs and those of her/his family members and kin will be accorded dignity and respect. (p. 133)

The person receiving the service decides whether the service is culturally safe. Power thereby shifts from the provider to the person in need of service. This process provides an opportunity for the helper to understand the inherent power imbalance in health service delivery and recognize the intergenerational impact on the Aboriginal woman client (Spence, 2001). A key feature of culturally safe practice is that the practitioner embarks on a journey of self-reflection to understand that she or he is a bearer of culture and therefore has biases and values that affect the interaction. What differentiates cultural safety from cultural competence is the helper's process of self-reflection.

A practice that promotes cultural safety allows Aboriginal history to provide the context for how to work with Aboriginal women. Browne and colleagues (2000) described developing culturally safe practice as the process of respecting nationality, culture, age, sex and political and religious beliefs. Culturally safe practice establishes trust with the person seeking help. By practising culturally safe care, the helper reinforces the validity of the person's knowledge and reality in an environment where the person feels safe sharing feelings and safety concerns during the healing process.

Culturally safe practice ensures that communication with the person is respectful and does not humiliate, alienate or dissuade her or him from accessing necessary care. The helper can encourage the person to share past experiences of feeling that a sense of safety was breached and how it made the person feel.

The helper should recognize the power imbalance inherent in the helping relationship and acknowledge that the person may be from a different culture.

Historically, Aboriginal people have been controlled by policies and practices established and enforced by those outside their culture. Helpers need to know how to change their practice to ensure they do not unconsciously exert that power. It may require that they interact differently with clients, for example, by not telling them what is best for them, but rather, by helping clients determine what course of treatment will work best for them. The challenge for the helper is ensuring meaningful participation despite the challenge of practising cultural safety in a mainstream health care system.

Culturally safe practice provides a framework for practice that encourages service providers, regardless of their own cultural backgrounds, to engage in communication and practices that consider the social, linguistic, political and cultural realities of the people with whom they are working (Mental Health Commission of Canada, 2009).

Approaches to Healing

Saleebey (2006) stated that everything the helper does should be based on facilitating the discovery and enhancement, exploration and use of clients' strengths and resources in helping them achieve their goals and realize their dreams. Clients are generally the experts on which types of helping strategies will help them—and which will not. Rapp (2006) suggested that clients are most successful when they identify and use their strengths, abilities and assets.

According to Saleebey (2006), important concepts underlying a strengths-based approach to healing include:
• believing in the potential of the client
• having dialogue with the client to establish a relationship and foster collaboration as a way to nurture trust and not reproduce oppressive practices
• helping clients become more empowered by trusting their wisdom and perspective
• recognizing the healing and wholeness that comes from the clients' internal resources
• maintaining hope and optimism that are necessary in the process of healing and transformation, and belief in the possibility of change
• promoting membership to build a sense of belonging and inclusion
• promoting adaptability and resilience from a strengths perspective, which helps clients identify how far they have come on their journey.

Aboriginal women should have the option of accessing treatment that combines traditional healing with conventional social work practice (Baker & Cunningham, 2004). Differences in Western and Aboriginal approaches to healing can bring valuable perspectives to shape practice and open new pathways of understanding (Blackstock, 2009). The practice needs to adhere to principles that include respect, safety, accessibility and relevance, confidentiality and privacy, inter-agency collaboration and consultation, and evaluation. This will ensure that traditional principles remain a part of the intervention. A strong collaborative approach that includes both Aboriginal and non-Aboriginal service providers, along with traditional and non-traditional helpers, ensures respect for holistic approaches to healing and allows for continuum-of-care services (Clark, 2006).

There are limitations to exclusively relying on a Western or biomedical model of healing when working in a culturally safe manner. Despite the diversity among First Nations people, there tend to be similar ways of viewing the world and of understanding interpersonal interactions. An Aboriginal world view respects the interrelatedness of past with present and future. Within the Aboriginal world view, history is an important part of what informs an understanding of the individual and the world in which she revolves. By contrast, a Western world view is a more fragmented hierarchical perspective on the system that views healing in direct relationship to the physical. With this more limited world view, treatment often addresses only physical aspects of the problem and how it appears in the present, while ignoring past influences. In contrast, the Aboriginal world view embraces a response that promotes balance among the four parts of the self: spiritual, emotional, physical and cognitive or mental. The healing journey is directed by the individual and is continually in motion (Vukic et al., 2011).

A CIRCLE OF SUPPORT

Family and community members act as a natural support system in Aboriginal communities. A circle of support can include immediate family members, extended family members, close friends, community members, health professionals and peer support workers. Both the members of the circle of support and their roles can change over time and vary across different cultural settings (Mental Health Commission of Canada, 2009). In urban centres, this support system can be lacking, which can diminish a woman's sense of belonging (McCormick & Amundson, 1997). The person seeking help and the helper should together consider who is best suited to be included in a circle of support. Encourage the client to include helpful supporters and to avoid toxic partners who could be a source of stress. Without positive support systems, and a result of other noted factors, Aboriginal women are vulnerable to being surrounded by people who may not put their best interests first.

TRADITIONAL HEALING PRACTICES

Unlike Western medicine, which separates the body from the mind by focusing on the physical presentation, traditional healing is holistic because it considers the person's emotional, mental, spiritual and physical well-being. Traditional healing aims to restore balance using ceremony, faith and belief, which are important parts of the traditional healing process. This form of healing is considered a way of living or a way of approaching life (Native Women's Association of Canada, 2007).

Displaying Aboriginal visual and written material creates an environment that encourages disclosure of culture and implies that you are familiar with the client's culture. But avoid making assumptions about spirituality when working with Aboriginal women. The woman may practise a traditional lifestyle, incorporate both traditional and non-Aboriginal culture, and identify as Aboriginal, but not participate in a traditional lifestyle due to her spiritual beliefs. Or she may not identify as an Aboriginal because she has assimilated into Western ways or rejected traditional ways of living. How the woman identifies can be tied to self-esteem—to her pride in knowing who she is and where she comes from (Witko, 2006).

Ask the woman if she participates in any traditional ceremonies. As the helper, ensure you have access to an Elder or traditional worker who can act as a consultant, work collaboratively with you or, at the very least, assist you in the information-gathering process. Explore other treatment options for handling stress and dealing with problems beyond attending office appointments (e.g., the medicine wheel, sweat ceremonies, sharing circles, healing circle, cedar baths, traditional healers such as Elders, and storytelling).[6]

Zellerer (2003), Kiyoshki (2003), Recollet and colleagues (2009) and Cheers and colleagues (2006) highlighted the importance of incorporating spirituality and rituals such as smudging ceremonies, talking circles, sweat lodge ceremonies and the medicine wheel into Aboriginal programming because these processes are integral to Aboriginal ways of healing. Men and women perform many customs and practices separately (Aboriginal Services Branch, 2009).

For some women, knowing and following the teachings of the medicine wheel[7] is one way to help restore balance in their lives; however, not all Aboriginal cultures use the wheel, so it is important to find out whether the wheel is culturally relevant to the woman you are helping.

The healing that comes with following the teachings is about making a lifelong commitment to a healing journey. The teachings are as useful today as they were in the past for our ancestors. The teachings are meant to guide behaviour and how one interacts with the world.

ADDRESSING BARRIERS TO HEALING

Be aware of any challenges in providing services to Aboriginal women, and ensure that processes are in place to help them manage these challenges. Barriers to care can include:
• poor history with the organization (e.g., the woman has been turned away by the organization before or has heard about previous complaints of racist treatment being dismissed, rationalized or minimized

---

6   For more discussion about traditional approaches to healing, see chapter 6.
7   For more discussion about the medicine wheel, see chapters 1, 6, 7, 9, 15 and 28.

- the impact of colonization, which has left a legacy of paternalistic policies where the health care system does not see the woman seeking help as having credible information to participate in a treatment plan that respects her world view
- difficulty accessing services (e.g., work, child care or transportation issues that prevent the woman from attending appointments). Does the woman have a partner who supports her in following through on the treatment plan? Is safety an issue for her or her children?

Approaches to healing that are grounded in culturally safe practices will go a long way in supporting Aboriginal women on their journeys toward health and balance.

Practice Tips

- Educate yourself on cultural ways of healing.
- Familiarize yourself with the area you are working in and the different First Nation, Métis and Inuit populations within the area.
- Educate yourself about culturally relevant service organizations and service providers in your area.
- Establish partnerships with these organizations and service providers so you are able to identify how your client's needs fit within the framework of their programs to make appropriate referrals.
- Offer appropriate resources to help Aboriginal women on their healing journeys.
- Allow for time to build trust. Establishing trust with clients is crucial due to the mistrust developed over generations of oppression.
- Unless there is imminent danger to someone, screen for "red flags" or issues of concern that you will follow up on later for further exploration. Note that certain things, such as having weapons in the house, may be normal for many First Nations people, for whom hunting has been part of a traditional lifestyle, and thus does not necessarily pose a threat.
- Pay close attention to verbal and non-verbal communication. Is the client making eye contact, and if not, why not? How is the client holding her body? Does the client laugh when she discusses the issues? Be aware that laughter is a healing medicine in some Aboriginal cultures when used appropriately.
- Respect long periods of silence. Silence allows the client to gather her thoughts and find the strength to voice her concerns. Collectively, women have lost their voice through colonialist oppression. They are beginning to find it again, but need to be supported in a kind and gentle way that encourages them to share.
- Understand that it may take more than one meeting for the woman to tell her story. Your patience is critical.
- Critically analyze yourself as a bearer of culture and how those biases and assumptions affect your work with other groups.

Conclusion

Aboriginal women continue to struggle against challenges from the past. Despite gains in education and health, more work needs to be done in practice and research to ensure that the needs of Aboriginal women are not ignored. Social policy that promotes inclusion and self-determination will work to remove the vestiges of discrimination that continue today. Embracing a culturally safe way of providing support to women on their healing journey will help them to embrace the future with strength, perseverance and hope.

References

Aboriginal Services Branch. (2009). *Working with Aboriginal People and Communities: A Practice Resource*. Retrieved from Family and Community Services, New South Wales Government website: www.community.nsw.gov.au

Baker, L. & Cunningham, A. (2004). *Helping Women Survive: Supporting Woman Abuse Survivors as Mothers: A Resource Planning Guide*. Toronto: Ontario Women's Directorate.

Blackstock, C. (2009). Why addressing the over-representation of First Nations children in care requires new theoretical approaches based on First Nations ontology. *Journal of Social Work Values and Ethics, 6* (3), 1–18.

Brennan, S. (2011). *Violent Victimization of Aboriginal Women in the Canadian Provinces, 2009.* (Statistics Canada catalogue no. 85-002-X). Retrieved from www.statcan.gc.ca

Browne, A.J., Fiske, J.A. & Thomas, G. (2000). *First Nations Women's Encounters with Mainstream Health Care Services and Systems*. Retrieved from B.C. Centre of Excellence for Women's Health website: http://bccewh.bc.ca/publications-resources/documents/firstnationsreport.pdf

Cheers, B., Binell, M., Coleman, H., Gentle, I., Miller, G., Taylor, J. & Weetra, C. (2006). Family violence: An Australian indigenous community tells its story. *International Social Work, 49* (1), 51–63. DOI: 10.1177/0020872806059401

Christian, T-M. (2009). *Alberta NNADAP Regional Needs Assessment: Final Report*. Retrieved from National Native Alcohol and Drug Abuse Program website: http://nnadaprenewal.ca/wp-content/uploads/2012/01/Alberta_RNA_Final-Report.pdf

Clark, R.L. (2006). Healing the generations: Urban American Indians in recovery. In T.M. Witko (Ed.), *Mental Health Care for Urban Indians: Clinical Insights from Native Practitioners* (pp. 83–99). Washington, DC: American Psychological Association.

Corrado, R.R. & Cohen, I.M. (2003). *Mental Health Profiles for a Sample of British Columbia's Survivors of the Canadian Residential School System*. Ottawa: Aboriginal Healing Foundation.

First Nations Information Governance Centre. (2005). *First Nations Regional Longitudinal Health Survey (RHS) 2002/03: Results for Adults, Youth and Children Living in First Nations Communities*. Retrieved from www.fnigc.ca

Fulcher, L.C. (1998). Acknowledging culture in child and youth care practice. *Social Work Education: The International Journal, 17* (3), 321–338. DOI: 10.1080/02615479811220321

Furi, M. & Wherrett, J. (1996). *Indian Status and Band Membership Issues*. Library of Parliament. Retrieved from www.parl.gc.ca/content/lop/researchpublications/bp410-e.htm

Goudreau, G. (2012). *Aboriginal Women's Initiative Literature Review: A Review of the Literature on Intergenerational Trauma, Mental Health, Violence against Women, Addictions and Homelessness among Aboriginal Women of the North* (NOWSOPE). Retrieved from YWCA Canada website: www.ywcacanada.ca

Hamilton, B. & Longstaffe, S. (1987). *A New Justice for Indian Children: Final Report of the Child Advocacy Project.* Winnipeg, MB: Child Protection Centre, Children's Hospital.

Human Resources and Skills Development Canada (HRSDC). (2009). *Summative Evaluation: Aboriginal Human Resources Development Agreements—Final Report, July 2009.* Retrieved from Employment and Social Development Canada website: www.esdc.gc.ca

Jacobs, B. (2000). *International Law: The Great Law of Peace* (Unpublished master's thesis), University of Saskatchewan, Saskatoon.

Kiyoshki, R. (2003). Integrating spirituality and domestic violence treatment: Treatment of Aboriginal men. *Journal of Aggression, Maltreatment and Trauma 7*, 137–256. DOI: 10.1300/J146v07n01_10

Kleinman, A. (2006). *What Really Matters: Living a Moral Life amidst Uncertainty and Danger.* New York: Oxford University Press.

McCormick, R.M. & Amundson, N.E. (1997). A career-life planning model for First Nations people. *Journal of Employment Counseling, 34*, 171–179. DOI: 10.1002/j.2161-1920.1997.tb00467

Mental Health Commission of Canada. (2009). *Toward Recovery and Well-Being: A Framework for a Mental Health Strategy for Canada.* Retrieved from www.mentalhealthcommission.ca

National Aboriginal Health Organization. (2006). *Fact Sheet: Cultural Safety.* Retrieved from www.naho.ca/documents/naho/english/Culturalsafetyfactsheet.pdf

Native Women's Association of Canada. (2007). *Aboriginal Women and Traditional Healing: An Issue Paper.* Retrieved from Labrador and Aboriginal Affairs Office website: www.laa.gov.nl.ca/laa/naws/pdf/nwac_traditional_healing-jun1607.pdf

Public Safety Canada. (2008). *2008 Corrections and Conditional Release Statistical Overview.* Retrieved from www.publicsafety.gc.ca/cnt/rsrcs/pblctns/2008-ccrs/index-eng.aspx

Rapp, R.C. (2006). The strengths perspective and persons with substance abuse problems. In D. Saleebey (Ed.), *The Strengths Perspective in Social Work Practice* (4th ed.; pp. 77–96). Boston: Allyn & Bacon.

Recollet, D., Coholic, D. & Cote-Meek, S. (2009). Holistic arts-based group methods with Aboriginal women. *Critical Social Work, 10* (1). Retrieved from www1.uwindsor.ca/criticalsocialwork/holistic-arts-based-group-methods-with-aboriginal-women

Royal Commission on Aboriginal Peoples (RCAP). (1996a). *Report of the Royal Commission on Aboriginal Peoples. Vol. 3: Gathering Strength.* Ottawa: Canada Communication Group.

Royal Commission on Aboriginal Peoples (RCAP). (1996b). *People to People, Nation to Nation: Report of the Royal Commission on Aboriginal Peoples. Vol. 4: Perspectives and Realities.* Ottawa: Canada Communication Group.

Saleebey, D. (Ed.). (2006). *The Strengths Perspective in Social Work Practice* (4th ed.). Boston: Allyn & Bacon.

Smylie, J. & Adomako, P. (Eds.). (2009). *Indigenous Children's Health Report: Health Assessment in Action.* Retrieved from Centre for Research on Inner City Health, St. Michael's Hospital website: www.stmichaelshospital.com/crich/wp-content/uploads/ichr_report-web.pdf

Solomon, A. (1990). *Songs for the People: Teachings on the Natural Way.* Toronto: NC Press.

Spence, D.G. (2001). Hermeneutic notions illuminate cross-cultural nursing experiences. *Journal of Advanced Nursing, 35*, 624–630. DOI: 10.1046/j.1365-2648.2001.01879.x

Statistics Canada. (2008). *Educational Portrait of Canada, Census 2006*. (Catalogue no. 97-560-X2006001). Retrieved from www12.statcan.ca/census-recensement/2006/as-sa/97-560/pdf/97-560-XIE2006001.pdf

Vukic, A., Gregory, D., Martin-Misener, R. & Etowa, J. (2011). Aboriginal and Western conceptions of mental health and illness. *Pimatisiwin: A Journal of Aboriginal and Indigenous Community Health, 9* (1), 65–86.

Waldram, J.B., Herring, D.A. & Young, T.K. (2000). *Aboriginal Health in Canada: Historical, Cultural, and Epidemiological Perspectives*. Toronto: University of Toronto Press.

Wilson, A. (2004). *Living Well: Aboriginal Women, Cultural Identity and Wellness: A Manitoba Community Project*. Retrieved from Prairie Women's Health Centre of Excellence website: www.pwhce.ca/pdf/livingWell.pdf

Witko, T.M. (2006). An introduction to First Nations people. In T.M. Witko (Ed.), *Mental Health Care for Urban Indians: Clinical Insights from Native Practitioners* (pp. 3–16). Washington, DC: American Psychological Association.

Zellerer, E. (2003). Culturally competent programs: The first family violence program for Aboriginal men in prison. *Prison Journal, 83*, 171–190. DOI: 10.1177/0032885503083002004

ABOUT THE AUTHORS

Cristine Rego is a member of Lac Seul First Nation. She is a registered social worker who has worked for more than 20 years with organizations that have touched Aboriginal women's lives. She is an experienced crisis and trauma worker whose research interests include capacity building, community and individual health, addiction and mental health, violence against women, Aboriginal professional education and cultural safety. She is a regular speaker about issues affecting Aboriginal people, such as intergenerational trauma and suicide awareness. She also incorporates storytelling in her sessions in keeping with her traditional understandings.

Rebekah Rego is pursuing a degree in contemporary studies with an Indigenous focus at Wilfrid Laurier University in Waterloo, Ontario, and plans to then study law. Rebekah continues to advocate positive change in relationships with Aboriginal youth and different systems. Her research includes developing a culturally appropriate response to cyberbullying for Aboriginal youth.

Chapter 11

Aboriginal Men: Reclaiming Our Place

ROD MCCORMICK, MIKE ARNOUSE AND PATRICK WALTON

In 1744, Iroquois Chief Canassatego responded to an offer from the College of William and Mary in Virginia to continue to educate young Iroquois men at the college's Indian School, established with the goal of assimilating Native Americans into the colonists' culture:

> Several of our young people . . . were instructed in all your sciences; but when they came back to us, they were bad runners, ignorant of every means of living in the woods, unable to bear either cold or hunger, knew neither how to build a cabin, take a deer, nor kill an enemy, spoke our language imperfectly, were neither fit for hunters, warriors, or counselors. (Canassatego, in Deloria & Junaluska, 1976)

With these words, Chief Canassatego illustrated how the traditional roles of Aboriginal men were being eradicated through European colonial influence. Almost 300 years later, we as Aboriginal men continue to be weighed down with baggage accumulated over centuries of oppression that wiped out our culture and identity. Each time we experience another personal loss or trauma in our current lives, we add to the load. And so it goes.

This chapter discusses the challenges Aboriginal men face so we can then address them and move forward. We are on a healing journey to reconnect with our culture, identity, children, families, communities, the land and our unique roles. As with many traditional ways of telling stories, the chapter is divided into three parts: where have we come from, where are we now and where are we going.

Where Have We Come From?

As Chief Canassatego described, Aboriginal men had long been connected to the land as hunters, gatherers or farmers. This deep connection with nature and Creation fulfilled many of their physiological, safety, belonging, esteem and self-actualization needs, as described in Maslow's (1962) hierarchy of needs framework. In many traditional Aboriginal cultures, it was also the male's responsibility to teach the skills of farming, hunting and fishing, and to be a warrior and guardian of the family and community. Chief Dan George described this responsibility in a story he told his grandson:

> I wanted to give something of my past to my grandson. So I took him into the woods, to a quiet spot. Seated at my feet he listened as I told him of the powers that were given to each creature. He moved not a muscle as I explained how the woods had always provided us with food, homes, comfort, and religion. He was awed when I related to him how the wolf became our guardian, and when I told him that I would sing the sacred wolf song over him, he was overjoyed. In my song, I appealed to the wolf to come and preside over us while I would perform the wolf ceremony so that the bondage between my grandson and the wolf would be lifelong. (cited in George & Helmut, 2003, p. 112)

Aboriginal men were guardians of their families and communities. *Yucwemínmet*, which means "protector of the community" in Secwepemctsin, the language of the Secwepemc[1], was translated into English as "warrior," someone who was primarily a fighter. However, the Secwepemc warrior fought not only to defend the community, but also to protect the weak, the sick and the helpless. One author (Arnouse) describes the role of men in Secwepemc culture:

> As far as I can remember, the more traditional way of thinking for men is as protectors: protect the ones who are unable to take care of themselves and take care of the children. Women took a larger role than men with very young children, but men were more involved as boys grew older. Men and women combined to take care of the children. By the time a boy's voice changed, he already should have known how to take care of the family and the community.

---

1 The Secwepemc, known in English as the Shuswap people, are a First Nations people residing in British Columbia.

Many Aboriginal communities included both men and women as hunters, warriors and counsellors, and as mentors for children. Preparation for these traditional roles included speaking the language and learning survival skills. What children learned and how they were mentored were key to cultural survival.

THE CHILD IS FATHER OF THE MAN

Many Aboriginal cultures emphasize relationships and connections to others and to Creation (McCormick, 2009a). Some believe that newborn babies are directly connected to the Creator and to ancestors, and that they will lose those connections as they grow older if they are not respected and nourished. Fathers traditionally played an important role in building and strengthening these connections in their children.

The influence of fathers in the family and community extended to subsequent generations of sons and fathers. The idea that this paternal influence carries forward for generations cuts across world views. The line "The Child is father of the Man" from William Wordsworth's poem "My heart leaps up when I behold" can have many meanings. To us, the words describe how childhood experiences—good or bad—shape the man, and how fathers have the opportunity to learn from and teach their own children. Those children will then go on to father healthier men. The poem engenders hope that the ripple effect from father to son can be positive, an experience markedly different from that of Aboriginal men, scarred through centuries of colonialism.

THE EFFECTS OF COLONIZATION

The most obvious and immediate effects of colonization were epidemics of infectious disease.[2] In 1492, an estimated 30 million people lived in what is now North America. By the end of the 17th century, disease had reduced the population to about 8 million people ("La catastrophe démographique," 2007). Forced relocation of communities to "reserves" prevented nomadic cultures from pursuing their livelihoods and maintaining their ways of life. Traditional lands were destroyed and polluted in the Europeans' quest for natural resources, such as minerals and lumber. The destruction of forests and rivers affected the traditional roles of Aboriginal men as hunters, fishermen and providers. Loss of land meant loss of traditional cultural and self-sustaining ways of life (Miller, 1992).

Colonialist policies and practices also rapidly eroded Aboriginal ways of healing, including herbalism and spiritual healing (Warry, 2000). For example, the Indian Act prohibited traditional healing ceremonies (O'Neil, 1993). Cultural practices such as drumming, sweats and potlatches were often banned, and spiritual practices were replaced wherever possible with Christianity. The colonizers used this disconnection

---

2   For a detailed discussion about the history of colonialist policies and practices, see chapter 2.

from culture and spiritual practices as a strategy for assimilating Aboriginal peoples.

One of the most devastating colonialist policies was the residential school system.[3] Residential schools removed children from their parents and communities, separating them from their culture, identity, childhood, relationships, language, spirituality and land (Milloy, 1999). The experience has created an intergenerational legacy of trauma still felt today that includes denigrated cultures and, among individuals, low self-esteem, fractured identity, sexual abuse and poor parenting skills.[4] Residential school survivors and subsequent generations are left with limited knowledge of their languages and cultures, and how to parent and teach their own children. Smoking, drinking and using other drugs have become the rites of passage into adulthood for many Aboriginal boys, who also learned to behave in a passive-aggressive way (Mussell, 2005).

Where Are We Now?

Colonialist practices and policies eroded men's sense of personal and cultural identity. Mussell (2005) identified seven consequences of colonization that First Nations males continue to experience today:
• problems with acceptance and trust
• relative comfort with rejection
• difficulty with emotional expression
• few teaching and learning skills
• difficulties relating to youth, both male and female
• problems with intimacy
• problems filling the role of provider.

Compared with the general population, Aboriginal men experience much higher rates of school dropout, unemployment, injury, poverty, suicide, incarceration, addiction, homelessness and depression (Health Canada, 2005). They also struggle with trauma, abuse and parenting issues.

TRAUMA AND GRIEF

Unresolved trauma and grief are the culprits in many of the mental health struggles of Aboriginal men. According to Herman (1997), trauma undermines the basic sense of trust that is normally established in the first few years of life and leaves the person feeling abandoned, alienated and disconnected, which will affect future relationships. Most Aboriginal men (and women) in Canada are either survivors of residential schools or have experienced secondary trauma, having been raised by residential

---

3   For more discussion about the residential schools and their impact, see chapter 3.
4   For more discussion about intergenerational trauma, see chapter 5.

school survivor parents who lacked parenting skills because they did not have positive role models (Ing, 2001; Vedan, 2002).

The impact of colonization-induced trauma is well documented. Brave Heart (2005) described historical trauma as collective emotional and psychological injury over the lifespan and across generations, the result of a cataclysmic history of genocide. Wexler (2006) found a link between this legacy of trauma and mortality-related issues: the most significant factor accounting for life expectancy differences between males aged 15 to 24 years living in Inuit Nunangat and the rest of Canada was injury, particularly self-inflicted injury. (The largest factors for Inuit females were malignant neoplasm and respiratory disease at ages 65 to 79.)

Aboriginal men also show signs of survivor guilt, a clinical diagnosis based on a phenomenon originally identified among Jewish Holocaust survivors (Brave Heart & DeBruyn, 1998). In 1994, survivor guilt was removed from the *Diagnostic and Statistical Manual of Mental Disorders* as a recognized specific diagnosis and redefined as a significant symptom of posttraumatic stress disorder (American Psychiatric Association, 1994).

ABUSE

Most of the clients that one author (McCormick) assessed in his work as a consulting psychologist to a First Nations addiction treatment centre were victims of sexual or physical abuse. Staff at First Nations treatment centres have reported that up to 90 per cent of men coming for treatment disclose having been sexually abused (Royal Commission on Aboriginal Peoples [RCAP], 1996). The psychological effects of sexual abuse are fairly universal. They range from fear, panic attacks, sleep problems, nightmares, irritability, outbursts of anger and sudden shock reactions when being touched to lowered self-confidence, self-respect and respect for one's body. Other common effects of sexual abuse are substance use problems, excessive involvement in work or sports, depression, self-destructive behaviour and prostitution (Herman, 1997).

ALCOHOL AND OTHER SUBSTANCE USE PROBLEMS

Research has demonstrated that cultural breakdown is strongly linked with alcohol use problems (Duran & Duran, 1995; Smith et al., 2009; Wexler, 2006; York, 1990).[5] Pedigo (1983) argued that substance use is a survival mechanism for Aboriginal people, whose culture and values have suffered due to assimilation. Whatever the reasons, the effects of alcohol and other drugs on Aboriginal men have been devastating: almost three-quarters of deaths caused by accidents and violence, such as suicide, homicide and fires, have been linked to alcohol (York, 1990).

---

5   For a discussion about Aboriginal approaches to addressing alcohol use problems, see chapter 15.

Traditional Indigenous peoples perceive alcohol as a spiritual entity that has destroyed their ways of life (Duran & Duran, 1995). Alcohol "spirits" are used as substitutes for the spirit residing in Aboriginal people who are connected to their people, culture and Creator. Wing and colleagues (1995) found that many Aboriginal people believe that alcohol use problems are caused by a lack of spirituality. According to Duran and Duran (1995), alcohol "continually wages war within the spiritual arena, and it is in the spiritual arena that the struggle continues" (p. 139).

DIFFICULTIES WITH FATHERHOOD AND PARENTING

When the residential schools closed, many provincial child welfare authorities permanently removed Aboriginal children from their homes and placed them in foster care or made them Crown wards.[6] Approximately 40 per cent of children in foster care are Aboriginal, although Aboriginal people make up less than three per cent of the Canadian population (Farris-Manning & Zandstra, 2003). Many Aboriginal children live in single-parent households, approximately 90 per cent of which are headed by women (Steffler, 2008).

Traditionally, children were seen as being at the centre of the community, surrounded by a circle of mothers that was enclosed within a circle of grandparents and an outermost circle of men to protect the inner circles. The residential schools erased traditional Aboriginal child-raising practices. We must revive them, and we must relearn and resume our traditional roles as men. For many fathers who are first- and second-generation survivors of residential schools, raising children is something they feel they are doing blind, with no positive role models, few resources and little support (National Collaborating Centre for Aboriginal Health [NCCAH], 2011).

Where Are We Going?

In 2011, the NCCAH hosted a conference in Ottawa about Aboriginal fathers in communities, programs, research and policies. Grand Chief Edward John of the B.C. First Nations Summit stated that First Nations, Inuit and Métis fathers are one of the "greatest untapped resources in the lives of Aboriginal children" (NCCAH, 2011, ¶1). The main message was that fathers must be invited back into their family and community circles, and that their healing journeys must be supported to promote the health of children, families and communities.

It took centuries of assimilationist policies to get Aboriginal communities to where they are today. Now we need to heal. One author (Arnouse) asks: "Is the system coming from Europe going to destroy us eventually? If we follow our own ways, given to us

---

6   For a more detailed discussion about the child welfare system, see chapter 4.

by the Creator, through our stories and ceremonies, then we will outlast the system imposed on us." All of our ceremonies—sweats, Elder stories, songs and prayers—are about heart, mind, body and spirit. We need to undo the assimilation and revitalize Aboriginal culture and language. From our experiences and observations, the path to wellness for many Aboriginal men begins with connecting to our spirit and culture.[7] In a study examining the facilitation of healing among Aboriginal people in British Columbia, McCormick (1995) confirmed that reconnecting to family, community, culture, nature and spirituality was the primary source of healing. Thus, strategies to help men heal need to include ways to empower them and connect them to nature, their ancestors, their families and their cultures.

EMPOWERMENT AND CONNECTION TO NATURE

Healing from trauma and abuse is a huge task for Aboriginal men. Because these experiences stripped us of power, we need to find ways to feel empowered again. Empowerment can come from cleansing, reconnection and asking others for help. Although trauma can be healed through empowerment, it takes time, courage and resources. An important resource for men in this process is getting support from other men.

Connecting with nature is also healing because many Aboriginal people feel a spiritual connection with the land. All elements of Creation are considered equal in the eyes of the Creator. Connection to nature, which may be experienced by going out on the land and engaging in traditional land-based activities, can help people to feel part of something larger than themselves, and to feel stronger, more grounded, less lonely and more secure (McCormick, 2009b; McCormick & Gerlitz, 2009).

CONNECTION TO ANCESTORS AND CULTURE

Resilience in Aboriginal communities has a collective aspect, combining spirituality, family strength, guidance from Elders, ceremonial ritual, oral traditions, identity and support. These connections extend to ancestors, who may be present in memory, stories and ceremonial practices. Ancestors, sometimes referred to personally as "grandfather" or "grandmother," require attention and must be honoured. In return, they provide a sense of connectedness across time. Health and wellness are achieved when a person has a moral and spiritual relationship with ancestors and others in the family and community, as well as with the larger web of relations that makes up the world. "All my relations" means that everything is connected—stars, the universe, the earth and every creature, including humans (McCormick, 2012).

One important goal of therapy for Aboriginal people is to reaffirm cultural values, what LaFromboise and colleagues (1990) called "retraditionalization." A study

---

7   For more discussion about Aboriginal ways of helping and healing, see chapter 6.

about Aboriginal addiction counselling in British Columbia suggested a therapeutic framework that emphasizes personal and cultural identity (Anderson, 1993). In a study examining recovery of personal meaning, understanding traditional Aboriginal knowledge and culture, and maintaining or relearning Aboriginal languages, emerged as major themes (More, 1985). According to Duran and Duran (1995), the most effective treatment models are those that incorporate traditional Aboriginal beliefs and practices. The Round Lake Treatment Centre in British Columbia, which provides substance use counselling, acknowledges the crucial role of traditional teachings in its program motto, "Culture is treatment." By focusing on Aboriginal knowledge, initiatives for Aboriginal health can reflect the wisdom of those who stand to benefit from them (RCAP, 1996).

Men who seek healing may find guidance through the Teachings of the Seven Grandfathers, which come from the Anishnaabe people. The seven teachings are honesty (*gwekwaadiziwin*), humility (*dbaadendiziwin*), truth (*debwewin*), wisdom (*nbwaakaawin*), love (*zaagidwin*), respect (*mnaadendimowin*) and bravery (*aakwade'ewin*). Men can also be guided by Elders, who promote self-understanding by imparting cultural teachings through stories and shared activities (Halfe, 1993).[8] This incorporation of self or identity within traditional ideology gives people the strength to cope in the mainstream environment (Axelson, 1993).

Canada is witnessing a renaissance of traditional healing ways among Aboriginal peoples (Waldram et al., 1995). In a study of residential school survivors in the Cariboo region of British Columbia, researchers found that 45 per cent of those surveyed consulted Elders for advice and 41 per cent accessed a sweat lodge ceremony as part of their use of mental health services; two-thirds of respondents used traditional healing activities for mental health (Cariboo Tribal Council, 1991). A study involving 500 Aboriginal addiction counsellor trainees found that 27 per cent used Aboriginal healing activities as an integral part of their own healing (Nechi Institute on Alcohol and Drug Education & Research Centre, 1992). Wyrostock and Paulson (2000) found that the majority of Aboriginal students in their study participated in various traditional healing practices.

McCormick (1995) interviewed 50 Aboriginal people in British Columbia to find out what strategies, what he called "critical incidents," they used to help them heal. Although participants reported some critical incidents that reflected Western approaches, most of them reported traditional approaches to healing. The 437 critical incidents were divided into 14 categories: participating in ceremonies, expressing emotion, learning from a role model, establishing a connection with nature, doing exercise, engaging in challenging activities, establishing a social connection, gaining an understanding of the problem, establishing a spiritual connection, obtaining help and support from others, doing self-care, setting goals, anchoring the self in tradition and helping others. These categories can be used as a guide when planning programs to help men heal.

---

8 For more discussion about the role of Elders in healing, see chapter 7.

CONNECTION TO COMMUNITY AND FAMILY

Community involvement is central to the success of substance use intervention strategies for Aboriginal people (Edwards & Edwards, 1988; Smith et al., 2010). The community must acknowledge that a substance use problem exists and be committed to addressing it. As the central institution in Aboriginal societies (RCAP, 1996), the family also plays an important role in prevention and treatment, and in determining positive and negative behaviours (Trotter & Rolf, 1997). In the traditional Aboriginal family, norms of sharing and mutual support provide a safety net for each member. Johnson and Johnson (1993) found that family involvement was the second most effective intervention after spiritual support that Aboriginal people with substance use problems identified: 48 per cent indicated that family was their main motivation for committing to being sober.

SPIRITUALITY

Aboriginal perspectives on mental health are more holistic than in the Western medical-based model (Locust, 1988).[9] Spirit plays as big a role as the mind and body in sickness and wellness (Hammerschlag, 1988).[10] Medicine Eagle (1989) described spirit as the essence of healing. In the words of Dugan (1985), "It is to the Great Spirit, perceived everywhere, that the Aboriginal turns to in times of need" (p. 110). Anderson (1993) found that spirituality was an important component of a culturally sensitive approach to counselling Aboriginal people. Many Aboriginal healing ceremonies emphasize this spiritual aspect; for example, in the vision quest ceremony, the person makes contact with his or her spiritual identity (Hodgson & Kothare, 1990). The Hopi people of the southwestern United States believe that civilization will come to an impoverished end when the spirit, or its symbol, is owned and not felt (Hammerschlag, 1993). For Western counselling approaches to be effective with Aboriginal people, they "must re-examine religion and transcendental ways of understanding the world" (LaFromboise et al., 1990, p. 648). In doing so, Western counsellors might find that they are providing better care for non-Aboriginal clients, as well.

FATHERHOOD

There are many factors that help Aboriginal men to be positively involved fathers and to sustain connections with their children (Ball & George, 2006). Research shows that actively involved fathers can make a difference in their children's lives. Paternal involvement leads to better emotional and psychological health in children, as well as higher academic achievement and better social skills. Fathers experience less distress,

---

9 For more discussion about Aboriginal perspectives on mental health, see chapter 14.

10 For more discussion about the role of spirituality in mental health and healing, see chapter 6.

lower rates of substance use problems, improved marital stability and happiness, and greater capacity for attachment (Ball & George, 2006). Fathers would benefit from support programs that are not mother-centric and that are staffed by father-support workers. Facilitating the development of fatherhood skills involves helping fathers develop realistic expectations and providing long-term support. It is also important for fathers to co-parent their children with the mother and extended family. In many traditional Aboriginal communities, everyone who comes to the marriage ceremony, not just the couple, shares in the commitment to raise the children and guide the couple.

OUTCOMES OF HEALING

Healing is reflected in five outcomes: balance, belonging or connectedness, cleansing, empowerment and discipline (McCormick, 1995). Balance, as defined by Aboriginal teachings such as the medicine wheel, means keeping the mental, physical, emotional and spiritual parts of the self in balance. Belonging, or connectedness, means attaining or maintaining connection with sources of meaning and guidance beyond the self, such as family, community, culture, nation, the natural world and the spiritual world. Cleansing means identifying and expressing emotions in a good way. Empowerment involves attaining and maintaining mental, physical, emotional and spiritual strength. Discipline, received through traditional teachings, means accepting responsibility for one's actions.

Final Thoughts

Many Aboriginal men are making the journey to reconnect with their culture and identity; their children, families and communities; and the land. They are developing strategies to deal with the pain of cultural dislocation and the legacy of trauma. These strategies rely on the community and family to provide culturally appropriate support for healing. Traditional cultural values, ceremonies and healing techniques provide the knowledge and skills people need to develop and maintain a meaningful connection with Creation. This sounds beautiful, but the reality is that many challenges arise in making these changes and in healing and revitalizing our Aboriginal cultures. Our work is far from complete.

Dick Lourie's poem "forgiving our fathers" complements Wordsworth's poem discussed earlier in this chapter that expresses hope for positive father engagement. For us, the message is that as Aboriginal men we must confront our past and overcome the anger and denial around all that was done wrong by our fathers. Confronting and understanding these past wrongs creates the opportunity to forgive both our fathers and ourselves. Parenting our own children in a good way gives us the opportunity to re-parent ourselves. By forgiving our fathers, we can enable the child to become the father of the man.

forgiving our fathers[11]

maybe in a dream: he's in your power
you twist his arm but you're not sure it was
he that stole your money   you feel calmer and you decide to let
him go free

or he's the one (as in a dream of mine)
I must pull from the water but I never
knew it or wouldn't have done it until
I saw the street-theater play so close up
I was moved to actions I'd never before taken

maybe for leaving us too often or
forever when we were little   maybe
for scaring us with unexpected rage
or making us nervous because there seemed
never to be any rage there at all

for marrying or not marrying our mothers
for divorcing or not divorcing our mothers
and shall we forgive them for their excesses
of warmth or coldness   shall we forgive them

for pushing or leaning for shutting doors
for speaking only through layers of cloth
or never speaking or never being silent

in our age or in theirs or in their deaths
saying it to them or not saying it—
if we forgive our fathers what is left

References

American Psychiatric Association. (1994). *Diagnostic and Statistical Manual of Mental Health Disorders* (4th ed.). Washington, DC: Author.

Anderson, B.M. (1993). *Aboriginal Counselling and Healing Processes* (Unpublished master's thesis). University of British Columbia, Vancouver.

---

11 From *Ghost Radio* (p. 48), by Dick Lourie, 1998, Brooklyn, NY: Hanging Loose Press. © Dick Lourie. Reprinted with permission.

Axelson, J.A. (1993). *Counseling and Development in a Multicultural Society* (2nd ed.). Pacific Grove, CA: Brooks/Cole.

Ball, J. & George, R. (2006, March 22). *Policies and practices affecting Aboriginal fathers' involvement with their children*. Presented at the 2nd Tri-annual Aboriginal Policy Research Conference, Ottawa.

Brave Heart, M.Y. & DeBruyn, L.M. (1998). The American Indian holocaust: Healing historical unresolved grief. *American Indian and Alaskan Native Mental Health Research, 8* (2), 60–82. DOI: 10.5820/aian.0802.1998.60

Brave Heart, M.Y.H. (2005). From intergenerational trauma to intergenerational healing: A teaching about how it works and how we can heal. *Wellbriety!, 6* (6), 2–8. Retrieved from White Bison website: www.whitebison.org/magazine/2005/volume6/wellbriety!vol6no6.pdf

Cariboo Tribal Council. (1991). Faith misplaced: Lasting effects of abuse in a First Nations community. *Canadian Journal of Native Education, 18*, 161–197.

Deloria, V., Jr. & Junaluska, A. (1976). *Great American Indian Speeches: Volume 1* [Audiobook on CD]. New York: Caedmon.

Dugan, K.M. (1985). *The Vision Quest of the Plains Indians: Its Spiritual Significance*. Lewiston, NY: Edwin Mellen Press.

Duran, E. & Duran, B. (1995). *Native American Postcolonial Psychology*. Albany: State University of New York Press.

Edwards, E.D. & Edwards, M.E. (1988). Alcoholism prevention/treatment and Native American youth: A community approach. *Journal of Drug Issues, 18* (1), 103–114.

Farris-Manning, C. & Zandstra, M. (2003). *Children in Care in Canada: Summary of Current Issues and Trends with Recommendations for Future Research*. Retrieved from National Alliance for Children and Youth website: www.nationalchildrensalliance.com/nca/pubs/2003/Children_in_Care_March_2003.pdf

George, D. & Helmut, H. (2003). *The Best of Chief Dan George*. Surrey, BC: Hancock House.

Halfe, L. (1993). Native healing. *Cognica, 26* (1), 21–27.

Hammerschlag, C.A. (1988). *The Dancing Healers: A Doctor's Journey of Healing with Native Americans*. San Francisco: HarperCollins.

Hammerschlag, C.A. (1993). *The Theft of the Spirit: A Journey to Spiritual Healing with Native Americans*. New York: Simon & Schuster.

Health Canada. (2005). *A Statistical Profile on the Health of First Nations in Canada for the Year 2000*. Ottawa: Author.

Herman, J.L. (1997). *Trauma and Recovery: The Aftermath of Violence—From Domestic Abuse to Political Terror*. New York: Basic Books.

Hodgson, J. & Kothare, J. (1990). *Vision Quest: Native Spirituality and the Church in Canada*. Toronto: Anglican Book Centre.

Ing, N.R. (2001). *Dealing with Shame and Unresolved Trauma: Residential School and Its Impact on the 2nd and 3rd Generation Adults* (Unpublished doctoral dissertation). University of British Columbia, Vancouver.

Johnson, J. & Johnson, F. (1993). Community development, sobriety and after-care at Alkali Lake Band. In Royal Commission on Aboriginal Peoples (Chair), *The Path to Healing: Report of the National Round Table on Aboriginal Health and Social Issues* (pp. 133–135). Retrieved from Union of B.C. Indian Chiefs website: www.ubcic.bc.ca

"La catastrophe démographique" (The demographical catastrophe). (2007, July/August). *L'Histoire, 322.*

LaFromboise, T.D., Trimble, J.E. & Mohatt, G.V. (1990). Counseling intervention and American Indian tradition: An integrative approach. *The Counseling Psychologist, 18*, 628–654. DOI: 10.1177/0011000090184006

Locust, C. (1988). Wounding the spirit: Discrimination and traditional American Indian belief systems. *Harvard Educational Review, 58*, 315–331.

Lourie, D. (1998). *Ghost Radio*. Brooklyn, NY: Hanging Loose Press.

Maslow, A.H. (1962). *Toward a Psychology of Being*. Princeton, MA: D. Van Nostrand.

McCormick, R.M. (1995). The facilitation of healing for the First Nations people of British Columbia. *Canadian Journal of Native Education, 21*, 251–322.

McCormick, R.M. (2009a). All my relations. In Canadian Institute for Health Information (Ed.), *Mentally Healthy Communities: Aboriginal Perspectives* (pp. 3–8). Retrieved from Canadian Institute for Health Information website: www.cihi.ca

McCormick, R. (2009b). Aboriginal approaches to counselling. In L. Kirmayer & G.G. Valaskakis (Eds.), *Healing Traditions: The Mental Health of Aboriginal Peoples in Canada* (pp. 337–354). Vancouver: UBC Press.

McCormick, R. (2012). Ohen:ton Karihwatehkwen. *CrossCurrents: The Journal of Addiction and Mental Health, 16* (1), 28.

McCormick, R. & Gerlitz, J. (2009). Nature as healer: Aboriginal ways of healing through nature. *Counselling and Spirituality, 28* (1), 55–72.

Medicine Eagle, B. (1989). The circle of healing. In R. Carlson & B. Shield (Eds.), *Healers on Healing* (pp. 58–62). New York: Penguin Putnam.

Miller, J.R. (1992). *Sweet Promises: A Reader on Indian–White Relations in Canada*. Toronto: University of Toronto Press.

Milloy, J.S. (1999). *A National Crime: The Canadian Government and the Residential School System, 1879–1986*. Winnipeg: University of Manitoba Press.

More, J.M.D. (1985). *Cultural Foundations of Personal Meaning: Their Loss and Recovery* (Unpublished master's thesis). University of British Columbia, Vancouver.

Mussell, W.J. (2005). *Warrior-Caregivers: Understanding the Challenges and Healing of First Nations Men*. Retrieved from Aboriginal Healing Foundation website: www.ahf.ca

National Collaborating Centre for Aboriginal Health (NCCAH). (2011). *With Dad: Strengthening the Circle of Care*. Retrieved from www.nccah-ccnsa.ca

Nechi Institute on Alcohol and Drug Education & Research Centre. (1992). *The Eagle Has Landed: Data Base Study of Nechi Participants, 1974–1991*. Edmonton, AB: Author.

O'Neil, J.D. (1993). Aboriginal health policy for the next century. In Royal Commission on Aboriginal Peoples (Chair), *The Path to Healing: Report of the National Round Table on Aboriginal Health and Social Issues* (pp. 156–157). Retrieved from Union of B.C. Indian Chiefs website: www.ubcic.bc.ca

Pedigo, J. (1983). Finding the "meaning" of Native American substance abuse: Implications for community prevention. *The Personnel and Guidance Journal, 61*, 273–277.

Royal Commission on Aboriginal Peoples (RCAP). (1996). *People to People, Nation to Nation: Highlights from the Report of the Royal Commission on Aboriginal Peoples*. Retrieved from Aboriginal Affairs and Northern Development Canada website: www.aadnc-aandc.gc.ca

Smith, A., Leadbeater, B. & Clark, N. (2010). Transitions to adulthood for vulnerable youth in British Columbia, Canada. *Relational Child and Youth Care Practice, 23*, 16–23.

Smith, A., Stewart, D., Peled, M., Poon, C., Saewyc, E. & McCreary Centre Society. (2009). *A Picture of Health: Highlights from the 2008 B.C. Adolescent Health Survey*. Retrieved from McCreary Centre Society website: www.mcs.bc.ca/pdf/AHSIV_APictureOfHealth.pdf

Steffler, J. (2008). Aboriginal peoples: A young population for years to come. In *Horizons: Hope or Heartbreak: Aboriginal Youth and Canada's Future* (pp. 13–20). Ottawa: Policy Research Initiative.

Trotter, R.T. & Rolf, J.E. (1997). Cultural models of inhalant use among Navajo youth. *Drugs and Society, 10* (2), 39–59.

Vedan, R.W. (2002). *How Do We Forgive Our Fathers: Angry/Violent Aboriginal / First Nations Men's Experiences with Social Workers* (Unpublished doctoral dissertation). Simon Fraser University, Burnaby, BC.

Waldram, J.B., Herring, D.A. & Young, T.K. (1995). *Aboriginal Health in Canada: Historical, Cultural, and Epidemiological Perspectives.* Toronto: University of Toronto Press.

Warry, W. (2000). *Unfinished Dreams: Community Healing and the Reality of Aboriginal Self-Government.* Toronto: University of Toronto Press.

Wexler, L.M. (2006). Inupiat youth suicide and culture loss: Changing community conversations. *Social Science and Medicine, 63,* 2938–2948.

Wing, D.M., Crow, S.S. & Thompson, T. (1995). An ethnonursing study of Muscogee (Creek) Indians and effective health care practices for treating alcohol abuse. *Family and Community Health, 18* (2), 52–64.

Wyrostock, N.C. & Paulson, B.L. (2000). Traditional healing practices among First Nations students. *Canadian Journal of Counselling, 34* (1), 14–24.

York, G. (1990). *The Dispossessed: Life and Death in Native Canada.* Toronto: Little, Brown and Company.

ABOUT THE AUTHORS

Mike Arnouse is an Elder-in-residence at Thompson Rivers University in Kamloops, B.C. He is a Secwepemc Elder from the Adams Lake Band.

Rod McCormick, PhD, is a member of the Mohawk Nation (Kanienkehake). He recently moved his extended family from the University of British Columbia in Vancouver to the traditional territory of the Secwepemc people in Kamloops, where his partner and two youngest children are members of the Kamloops Indian band. He is a professor and holds the B.C. Regional Innovation Chair in Aboriginal Early Childhood Development at Thompson Rivers University.

Patrick Walton is an associate professor in the School of Education at Thompson Rivers University in Kamloops, B.C. He is from Saskatchewan and has French-Canadian, English and Aboriginal ancestry.

Chapter 12

Beyond LGBT: Two-Spirit People

DOE O'BRIEN-TEENGS AND LAVERNE MONETTE

> Growing up in the James Bay Region in the 70s and 80s, the culture was heavily influenced by Christianity. I never heard the term "two-spirit people" until 1999 when I moved to Toronto. I was thrilled and spiritually moved when I learned that there was a place for us in the past. It means a lot to me. — *Doe O'Brien-Teengs*

The term *two spirit* is a fairly recent one. It was adopted in the early 1990s by a group of two-spirit people who had been meeting every year, alternating between Canada and the United States (Deschamps, 1998). The group felt that terms such as *lesbian, gay, bisexual, transgendered* and *intersexed* did not completely capture who two-spirit people are; rather, they described only sexual orientation or physical attraction, not the whole physical, spiritual, emotional and mental self. The group felt that the term two spirit reflected spirituality and the traditional roles of the people to whom it refers. The term has been defined in different ways, but most commonly as people who have male and female spirits co-existing within themselves (Deschamps, 1998).

Some Aboriginal people do not refer to themselves as two spirit, perhaps because they have never heard the term or because they prefer to describe themselves as gay, lesbian, bisexual, intersexed, transgendered, transsexual, queer, questioning or try-sexual (will try anything). Some South American Indigenous people refer to themselves as "two-hearted." For ease of reference, we use the term two spirit in this chapter, on the understanding that it encompasses all of these other terms. The beauty of the term, too, is that you can use it or not.

Throughout the chapter, we provide reflections on our own lived experiences as two-spirit women, in addition to citing research about the experiences of other two-spirit people.

History

Prior to the arrival of the Europeans, homophobia was not common among Aboriginal peoples on Turtle Island (North America). Two-spirit people were created by the Creator and therefore were a gift to the people. Difference was not seen as something to stamp out, but as a gift to the community, often with a sacred meaning (Deschamps, 1998; Gunn Allen, 1986; Williams, 1986).

In many Aboriginal communities, two-spirit men were quite diverse. Some dressed as women and engaged in women's roles, while others dressed as men and engaged in men's roles. Some took husbands and some did not. Some were sexually active with their own sex and others were celibate. Two-spirit men were mediators, teachers, child care workers, healers, artists and warriors, and held important ceremonial and economic roles. Two-spirit women were also very diverse. Some were called "manly-hearted women" (Gunn Allen, 1986) and were warriors and married other women. They were also hunters, healers, mediators, mothers and medicine people. They performed roles appropriate to their interests and skills, much like two-spirit people do today (Brown, 1997; Deschamps, 1998; Jacobs et al., 1997; O'Brien-Teengs, 2008; Roscoe, 1991; Williams, 1986).

Many Indigenous peoples in North and Central America have terms in their languages for two-spirit people:
• Blackfoot: *Aakíí'skassi* (male-bodied)
• Blackfoot: *Saahkómaapi'aakííkoan* (female-bodied)
• Cree: *Aayahkwew* (male-bodied)
• Cree: *înahpîkasoht* (female-bodied)
• Crow: *Bade*
• Flathead: *Ma'kali* (male-bodied)
• Inuit: *Sipiniq* (male-bodied)
• Lakota: *Winkte*
• Mexico: *Vestido*
• Micmac: *Geenumu gesallagee* (male-bodied)
• Mohave: *Hwame*
• Navaho: *Nadle*
• Ojibwe: *Gizhemanido-kwe* and *ogokwe/ogowkwe-nini*
• Paiute: *Moroni Noho*
• Shoshone: *Tainna Wa'ippe*

• Zapotec: *Muxe*
• Zuni: *Lhamana*

When the Europeans arrived, they documented the acceptance of two-spirit people in the communities through letters and reports back to Europe. They were horrified, particularly by the ease of sexual expression and acceptance of sexual diversity among Aboriginal peoples. The Europeans had arrived after centuries of killing people who did not conform to Christian conventions. Sexual activity was condoned only within marriage between a man and a woman. Same-sex sexual intimacy was considered pagan and offensive. Two-spirit people were routinely killed, not only because the colonizers needed to eliminate the spirituality of the peoples they were colonizing, but also because they were offended by their culture and sexuality (Reding, 2000).

Homophobia (an umbrella term that includes homophobia, lesbophobia, transphobia and heterosexism) has taken hold in Aboriginal communities since colonization. Mihalik (as cited in Banks, 2003) defined homophobia in this way:

> any belief system that supports negative myths and stereotypes about homosexual people, or any of the varieties of negative attitudes that arise from fear or dislike of homosexuality. The irrational fear of, or aversion to, homosexuals and homosexuality. Homophobics react to homosexuals as enemies to be feared, hated and actively repressed. (p. 6)

Homophobia is a learned behaviour ranging from mere dislike and intolerance to name calling, beatings (gay bashing) and murder.

Heterosexism is defined as

> a belief system that values heterosexuality as superior to, and/or more natural than, homosexuality. It does not acknowledge the existence of non-heterosexuals. It believes that heterosexuality is normative and that non-heterosexuality is deviant and intrinsically less desirable. Heterosexists react to homosexuals as unfortunate, devalued individuals. (Mihalik, as cited in Banks, 2003, p. 6)

Impact of Colonization on Acceptance of Sexual Diversity

Contact with Europeans has led to devastating results for Aboriginal peoples. Colonization; the residential school experience; "the '60s scoop," in which children were removed from their homes by the child welfare system; and loss of culture and lands has affected every Aboriginal person in Canada.[1] Political leaders in Aboriginal

---

1 For detailed discussions about colonization, residential schools and "the '60s scoop," see chapters 2, 3 and 4, respectively.

communities, particularly women, were disempowered. Spiritual leaders were under-mined and devalued. Social and economic systems were destroyed. The land was stolen. Culture, language and ceremonies came under attack. Two-spirit people were killed. For example, in 1594, the Spanish explorer Vasco Núñez de Balboa condemned Indigenous people found guilty of sodomy to be eaten alive by dogs (Williams, 1986). Open acceptance and expressions of sexuality and diverse sexual orientations went underground and in most places came to be forgotten by many Aboriginal peoples and even some current traditionalists. Heterosexism became the cultural norm.

It is important to note that the residential school system is the most likely source of the greatest suppression of Aboriginal sexual views. The residential school system led to the homophobia that exists in our communities through the Christian dogma that infused the schools, but also, and most damagingly, through the legacy of sexual abuse perpetrated at the schools. "How confusing it must have been for many of the students to have been taught that sex is for procreation upon marriage by the same people who committed violent sexual acts against them" (Barlow, 2009, p. 11).

Current Issues Facing Two-Spirit People

Two-spirit people today suffer from double or triple oppression in mainstream society. Two-spirit men are reviled for their sexual orientation and for being Aboriginal people. Two-spirit women are under attack for their sexual orientation, for being Aboriginal people and for being women. Widespread homophobia in Aboriginal and non-Aboriginal communities is harming the mental health of two-spirit people.

Many two-spirit people have to leave their home communities because of homopho-bia and fear of violence. Furthermore, Banks (2003) found that gay, lesbian and bisexual youth account for 30 per cent of completed youth suicides, and that the number of deaths by suicide in Canada by people who are gay, lesbian or bisexual ranges from 859 to 968 every year (Banks, 2003). Health Canada (2006) reported that the suicide rate among First Nations youth is five to seven times that of non-Aboriginal youth. There is no reliable research on two-spirit youth and suicide, but anecdotal evidence suggests that suicidal ideation is common and that the actual suicide rate is very high.

> Working for both 2-Spirited People of the 1st Nations and the Ontario Aboriginal HIV/AIDS Strategy for 13 years, I have taken many calls from two spirit people who were desperate to hear a friendly voice and both myself and my coworkers tried to talk the individuals out of suicide. And even so, in the year 2012, we lost two of our transgendered two spirit community members to suicide in Toronto. — *Doe*

Suicide happens in rural and reserve communities, as well, as described by "Mary":

> A friend of mine attended a funeral in northwestern Ontario of an Oji-Cree youth who killed herself. She was a trans woman in a community that did not believe or follow Aboriginal cultural traditions. The community was very strong in Pentecostal Christian beliefs, which left no place for her to identify herself in a healthy and proud manner. She experienced both homophobia and transphobia. The moment that struck my friend the most was when another youth went to the casket with an eagle feather and prayed over her body in tears. No one stopped him. One wonders whether the community recognized the loss of life was not hers alone, but the entire community who lost what she had to offer by living among them. (O'Brien-Teengs, 2008, p. 22)

Many two-spirit people flee to the cities; there they experience racism, lack of employment opportunities, more homophobia and lack of community support in the urban Aboriginal community (Monette et al., 2001; O'Brien-Teengs & Travers, 2006). When young two-spirit people go to urban centres, they are often not prepared for what will face them and do not know how to keep safe from social predators and HIV infection (O'Brien-Teengs & Travers, 2006). Many are alienated from other members of the Aboriginal community due to homophobia, and often do not even meet other Aboriginal two-spirit people socially or professionally because they fear being identified as a two-spirit person (O'Brien-Teengs, 2008). Banks (2003) found that gay, lesbian and bisexual people with high internalized homophobia engaged in more risky sexual behaviours than did their counterparts with lower internalized homophobia. Moreover, those with higher internalized homophobia were less affiliated with the gay community and therefore had less access to safer sex messaging and resources (p. 37).

Colonization, paternalism, racism, homophobia, misogyny and culture loss continue to affect two-spirit people. In a world where heterosexism is the rule, two-spirit people are dismissed as expressing a "lifestyle choice," when they are merely being who they are. Aboriginal people who are two spirited and living in Aboriginal communities are likely to be isolated, either through hiding their identity or by experiencing various levels of social violence because of their identity. Lack of family and community support and understanding are contributing factors in long- and short-term health outcomes (Brotman & Levy, 2008; Jacobs et al., 1997; Monette et al., 2001; O'Brien-Teengs, 2008).

During the late 1980s, HIV/AIDS started to hit the newly established two-spirit community in Toronto. Two-spirit men were the first and hardest hit by the epidemic in the Aboriginal community, and dread of the disease added yet another layer of stigma and discrimination to that which two-spirit people experienced. Families and communities rejected Aboriginal people living with HIV/AIDS (APHA) out of fear and ignorance. Very few culturally appropriate resources were available. Most AIDS service organizations were established by and for gay white men. The organization 2-Spirited People of the 1st Nations had to step in and develop services and programs for APHAS. It became the first Aboriginal AIDS service organization in Canada (Deschamps, 1998). Research in the United States by Walters and colleagues (2000) found that trauma experienced by American Indian and Alaska Natives was a factor in predicting HIV vulnerability due to HIV risk behaviours. Duran and Walters (2004) found that culturally specific HIV programming and support had holistic benefits for American Indian and Alaska Natives.

Many two-spirit people describe the early days of the HIV/AIDS epidemic as a time when they had to "pick up their medicine bundles[2]." The entire two-spirit community was engaged in the fight for survival against the epidemic. Care teams had to be set up to care for APHAS. Ceremonies had to be conducted, and funerals arranged. Many political and spiritual leaders would not participate or assist in these activities. Some members of Aboriginal communities were afraid that letting APHAS come home would infect the community and that burying an APHA in his or her home community would infect the ground water with HIV, which, of course, is impossible, as the virus cannot survive outside of a living human host. AIDSphobia was added to the list of phobias that led to discrimination against two-spirit people in the Aboriginal community.

The loss of APHAS to early death added another layer to two-spirit people's multi-generational loss. For those two-spirit people who continue to be active in the AIDS movement, the loss has been compounded over the past 25 years. It is one of several factors implicated in mental health issues and substance use in the two-spirit community.

Two-spirit people are already vulnerable to stress and mental health issues; living with HIV/AIDS is another issue that can cause substance use and mental health problems. Depression is common among APHAS, as is using substances to self-medicate (Jackson & Reimer, 2005). In a study about care, treatment and support issues conducted by the Canadian Aboriginal AIDS Network, 54.4 per cent of APHAS surveyed needed or used one or more mental health or counselling services. Moreover, 60.5 per cent needed or used one or more substance use services, including addiction treatment, harm reduction and needle exchange programs. Addiction treatment programs were accessed by 47.2 per cent of survey respondents. About 40 per cent of APHAS surveyed did not have their needs met. The single most commonly cited barrier to care (16.1 per cent) was lack of confidentiality and privacy (Monette et al., 2001).

These experiences led to the creation of 2-Spirited People of the 1st Nations and two-spirit people banding together for mutual support:

> I met Art Zoccole, the first openly two-spirit person I ever met in Toronto, through work with First Nations organizations in the early 1980s. In the late 1980s, I was involved with Native Earth Performing

---

2   A medicine bundle refers to becoming active within an Aboriginal spiritual tradition. It can be figurative, or it can literally be a bundle that contains sacred items, such as a drum or tobacco.

Arts, then the only Native theatre company in Canada. As a board member I met Rene Highway, Tomson Highway and other two-spirit people in the performing arts. Rene told me that Art was trying to get together all the two-spirit people we knew in Toronto to set up a social support network and urged me to come to the meeting. In January of 1989, a group of about 25 or more two-spirit people and their supporters and partners came to the 519 Church Street Community Centre for a "tea and bannock." This was the first ever meeting of two-spirit people and it took off like a raging fire. We talk-ed about issues and shared stories and laughed so hard my stomach was sore for days after. It was such a momentous event in our lives to be out as gay, lesbian, whatever, and to have support and respect for who we were. It was also the birthplace of 2-Spirited People of the 1st Nations, the only two-spirit agency in Canada. — *LaVerne*

Working with Two-Spirit People

If your goal is to work effectively with two-spirit people who have substance use or mental health issues or both, a cautionary note is in order. This chapter will help you understand the basics, but you need to do considerably more research in order to achieve your goal. (As a starting point, refer to this chapter's Resources section for a list of service providers who work with two-spirit people.)

If there are any rules for working with two-spirit people, the first one would be to work with the person in his or her current situation, respectfully and with compassion. Everyone is unique and has different life experiences. Some two-spirit people may be "out" to their families and communities, and others may not be. Some may have sup-portive families, and others may have experienced rejection. As "Jen" describes:

> I'm still kind of estranged from both communities in a sense because, I don't know, my own personal issues. I didn't grow up in a Native com-munity, but I have never been around other two spirited people. . . . I only actually started kind of getting more involved in the two spirited people when I came to Toronto, which was back in 2003. There was the odd gay man here and there . . . that's why when I first came out I dressed as a woman because I didn't want to fall into those stereotypes of being that bull dyke and what not, but it's inevitable. . . . I've always been like that, and it's good for me to accept that. I'm a handsome woman, I'm not a pretty girl. (O'Brien-Teengs, 2008, p. 26)

The second rule for working with two-spirit people would be to ensure that the person's privacy is protected. One major reason why two-spirit people do not seek assistance when they know they need it is concern about privacy and confidentiality. In a survey of two-spirit men, respondents were reluctant to access social services because they felt unwelcome, were afraid of social service organizations or were afraid of discrimination because of their sexual orientation (Monette et al., 2001). Deschamps (1998) described this reluctance to seek help:

> We are not likely to turn to many organizations that are supposedly responding to the needs of a community. Our issues of safety are much more sensitive. We know that if we walk into an organization in the "lesbian and gay community" we may not be welcome because our traditions are too foreign and our skin is too brown. We cannot walk into a Native organization as easily as other people because we don't know whether we'll be sneered at or accepted. We only know that it is a risk. (p. 14)

Even in large urban centres, Aboriginal people are still connected to one another and their home communities. It is not uncommon for a client to know the receptionist at an agency as someone from his or her home community; it can also happen with counsellors, youth workers and other staff the client meets. Two-spirit people who left their communities in rural or northern regions to escape homophobia may encounter people they know who still harbour negative attitudes toward two-spirit people, and the discrimination may continue. Respecting everyone's right to non-judgmental services will ease the tension for two-spirit people who have experienced many negative experiences in their lives because of who they are.

In your work with two-spirit people, check your own attitude about homosexuality. Being two-spirited and wanting to express your whole self is not a mental health issue. In the fight against discrimination and violence toward two-spirit people, more knowledge and role models who are welcoming and open to all Aboriginal people are needed. Banks (2003) noted studies which have shown that people who know one or more people who are not heterosexual demonstrate less hostility toward all people who are not heterosexual. Children learn from watching their parents or guardians and from the guidance they give. It is time that cultural traditions such as the Teachings of the Seven Grandfathers are brought to Aboriginal children, parents, service providers and community members, at social gatherings and in workplaces, so that honesty, humility, truth, wisdom, love, respect and bravery[3] become incorporated into daily living and the way we treat one another. Everyone should be included in the circle. In the words of Deschamps (2008), "We, as two-spirited people, identify ourselves very strongly as members of the First Nations. We take an interest in the future of our Nations and wish to play

---

3   These are Cree and Ojibwe teachings. Other First Nations have similar guiding principles.

an active role in that future" (p. 14).

Substance use among Aboriginal two-spirit people is a symptom of deeper issues. It is the impact of heterosexism that causes depression, suicidal ideation and self-medicating. It is the pain of culture loss and multi-generational post- and current traumatic stress that leads to self-medication. It is the despair caused by the ongoing, state-sanctioned oppression of Aboriginal peoples. Merely referring someone to addiction treatment does not resolve these issues. How will the person deal with the ongoing pain of internalized homophobia or rejection by friends, family or community without the substance that he or she is using to cope with the pain? How can the person feel hope for the future when nothing has substantially changed in her or his life or in the lives of Aboriginal people?

Many Canadians believe that colonialism is a thing of the past, that Aboriginal people should "just get over it."[4] But colonialism continues in the daily lives of Aboriginal people, who are treated like backward children in need of constant supervision. Aboriginal service providers need to decolonize their attitudes. The first step is to acknowledge and understand that Aboriginal people are still living in a colonized state and that the Indian Act is still in effect. Our grandparents who signed the treaties were still living off the land as our ancestors had been doing for thousands of years. The demands of Aboriginal nations for self-government and cultural survival are based upon standing treaties that have been abrogated by the Canadian state, which treats what should be a nation-to-nation relationship as a custodial one.

As well, many of the beliefs held by many Aboriginal people about our traditions have been influenced by Christianity and Catholicism. The residential school system was implemented to mould the minds of children, and thus change our cultures and peoples (Gunn Allen, 1986). Historically, Aboriginal cultures were not as judgmental as they are now. Because many of our grandparents attended residential schools, they are viewing a culture through a lens that they did not create, but that was imposed upon them as children. Heterosexism and homophobia were not part of our cultures of the past; they are a product of the belief systems of the colonizing peoples.

To better serve your two-spirit clients, explore and learn about resources available in their area for Aboriginal and two-spirit people. Ensure that your referrals are appropriate. If an agency or service has homophobic or stereotypical attitudes, this would be a huge setback in your client's healing journey.

While two-spirit people often seek therapy or counselling to deal with their problems, many do not. Counselling or therapy is not sufficient to address all the issues two-spirit people may be experiencing. They also need:
• positive, accurate information that challenges myths and stereotypes about the causes of homosexuality and about two-spirit people
• a sense of history about the beauty of Aboriginal peoples and particularly about two-spirit history and traditions

---

4   For a discussion about cultural competence and cultural safety, see chapter 31.

- a historical understanding of why Aboriginal peoples are where we are today
- peer support
- positive role models, including health and social service providers and Elders
- assistance in asserting their human rights
- safer sex information
- other practical supports around housing, social assistance, education and training, employment and life skills development
- information about Aboriginal cultural ceremonies, such as sweat lodges and talking circles in which they can participate.

Conclusion

Two-spirit people today are starting to relearn and reclaim their place in contemporary Aboriginal cultures. It will take some time, but with every sharing circle that teaches about two-spirit history, and every ceremony that includes two-spirit people, all of our peoples will be healed and become able to lead productive and healthy lives. There are many two-spirit people who have worked and continue to work for our communities. There are two-spirit people in our families and among our friends. It is important that they are recognized as integral parts of our communities, and they will always want to be.

As "Kimberly" shares:

> We spend so much time trying to find our differences. We focus so much on our differences that we overlook the similarities and the common ground where we can all meet each other. And I think it is incredibly important that we do that: that we spend more energy finding what we have in common than what we don't have in common. You know, so if people could change their focus, move their energy a bit towards unification. (O'Brien-Teengs, 2008, p. 27)

Resources

The organizations listed here serve the needs of two-spirit people. You can visit their websites for more information. It is also a good idea to research organizations in your area.

2-Spirited People of the 1st Nations
www.2spirits.com
2-Spirited People of the 1st Nations provides support to two-spirit people, as well as those living with and affected by HIV/AIDS. Support comes in many ways, such as

practical support, social gatherings, education to community and outreach programs. As with any Aboriginal agency, they are specialized, but they also deal with all issues that result from ongoing colonization.

Canadian Aboriginal AIDS Network (CAAN)

www.caan.ca

CAAN provides up-to-date information on Aboriginal issues in Canada relating to HIV/AIDS, and maintains a network of agencies within Canada.

Canadian Rainbow Health Coalition (CRHC)

www.rainbowhealth.ca

The CRHC provides leadership and advocacy for LGBT people and their families in Canada, and is an avenue for shared resources and support.

Equality for Gays and Lesbians Everywhere (Egale)

http://egale.ca

Egale Canada is a national LGBT human rights organization and participates in events and advocacy promoting human rights and healthy living for LGBT people and their friends and families.

Ontario Aboriginal HIV/AIDS Strategy (OAHAS)

www.oahas.org

OAHAS provides education and support to Aboriginal individuals and communities regarding HIV/AIDS and related issues. It operates in urban centres throughout Ontario.

PFLAG Canada

www.pflagcanada.ca

PFLAG is a strong network of support for friends and families of LGBT people in Canada. People can create their own PFLAG group in their region.

References

Banks, C. (2003). *The Cost of Homophobia: Literature Review on the Human Impact of Homophobia in Canada*. Saskatoon, SK: Community–University Institute for Social Research. Retrieved from www.usask.ca

Barlow, K. (2009). *Residential Schools, Prisons, and HIV/AIDS among Aboriginal People in Canada: Exploring the Connections*. Retrieved from Aboriginal Healing Foundation website: ww.ahf.ca

Brotman, S. & Levy, J. (2008). *Intersections: Cultures, sexualités et genres*. Quebec City: Presses de l'Université de Québec.

Brown, L.B. (Ed.). (1997). *Two Spirit People: American Indian Lesbian Women and Gay Men*. Binghamton, NY: Harrington Park Press.

Deschamps, G. (1998). *We Are Part of a Tradition: A Guide on Two-Spirited People for First Nations Communities*. Toronto: 2-Spirited People of the 1st Nations.

Duran, B. & Walters, K. (2004). HIV/AIDS prevention in "Indian Country": Current practice, indigenist etiology models, and postcolonial approaches to change. *AIDS Education and Prevention, 16*, 187–200.

Gunn Allen, P. (1986). *The Sacred Hoop: Recovering the Feminine in American Indian Traditions*. Boston: Beacon Press.

Health Canada. (2006). *First Nations & Inuit Health—Suicide Prevention*. Retrieved from www.hc-sc.gc.ca

Jackson, R. & Reimer, G. (2005). *Canadian Aboriginal People Living with HIV/AIDS: Care, Treatment and Support Issues*. Retrieved from Canadian Aboriginal AIDS Network website: www.caan.ca

Jacobs, S., Thomas, W. & Lang, S. (1997). *Two-Spirit People: Native American Gender Identity, Sexuality, and Spirituality*. Urbana: Board of Trustees of the University of Illinois.

Monette, L., Albert, D. & Waalen, J. (2001). *Voices of Two-Spirited Men*. Retrieved from 2-Spirited People of the 1st Nations website: www.2Spirits.com

O'Brien-Teengs, D. (2008). *Two Spirit Women* (2nd ed.). Retrieved from 2-Spirited People of the 1st Nations website: www2Spirits.com

O'Brien-Teengs, D. & Travers, R. (2006). "River of life, rapids of change": Understanding HIV vulnerability among two-spirit youth who migrate to Toronto. *Canadian Journal of Aboriginal Community-Based HIV/AIDS Research, 1*, 17–28.

Reding, A.A. (2000). *Mexico: Update on Treatment of Homosexuals*. Washington, DC: INS Resource Information Center, U.S. Citizenship and Migration Services.

Roscoe, W. (1991). *The Zuni Man-Woman*. Albuquerque: University of New Mexico Press.

Walters, K., Simoni, J.M. & Harris, C. (2000). Patterns and predictors of HIV risk among urban American Indians. *American Indian and Alaska Native Mental Health Research, 9* (2), 1–21.

Williams, W.L. (1986). *The Spirit and the Flesh: Sexual Diversity in American Indian Culture*. Boston: Beacon Press.

ABOUT THE AUTHORS

Doe (Doris) O'Brien-Teengs is a two-spirit Mushkego Cree/Irish Canadian woman who worked for 2-Spirited People of the 1st Nations for seven years and the Ontario Aboriginal HIV/AIDS Strategy for almost 14 years. She is currently pursuing her PhD in education at Lakehead University in Thunder Bay, Ontario. She is a writer, as well as the mother of two children, and wife to her partner of 13 years.

LaVerne Monette was a strong two-spirit Métis and Ojibwe woman. She was born in Winnipeg, Manitoba, and raised in Thunder Bay, Ontario. She was trained as a lawyer, and helped to create the Canadian Aboriginal AIDS Network and the Ontario Aboriginal HIV/AIDS Strategy (OAHAS), for which she became the provincial co-ordinator, and then executive director when OAHAS incorporated in 2005. She passed away on December 1, 2010, leaving a legacy of advocacy and leadership as a two-spirit woman.

Chapter 13

Older Adults: Shedding Light on an Invisible Population

MARK W. ROSENBERG AND KATHI WILSON

If you were to ask a non-Aboriginal person to describe an older Aboriginal person, it is likely that one of two images would emerge. The first would be an image of a man with long white hair in traditional buckskins, perhaps Chief Dan George, arguably Canada's most famous Aboriginal actor. It is a positive image of the wise Elder. The other common image is a negative one: a homeless person in an inner-city alley with a long history of experiencing discrimination, abuse, alcohol problems, street violence and now dementia. Both stereotypes have a small recognizable kernel of reality at their heart, but the images are distorted through lack of information and an unfocused gaze. And neither image bears much resemblance to the arguably equally stereotypical, but perhaps less conflicted, images the average Canadian may have of older non-Aboriginal people in their communities.

The experiences and circumstances of older Aboriginal people in Canada are more complex than the stereotypes indicate, but a fuller picture can be difficult to obtain. Demographics are one lens through which we may get a sense of a population, although statistics cannot convey the dimensions and textures of individual lives. Unlike the young and working-age Aboriginal populations who are the focus of most research and public policy discussions and debates in Canada, older Aboriginal people have received almost no attention in either the academic or grey literature from researchers, practitioners and policy-makers. In the seminal works of Waldram and colleagues (1995) and Young (1988) on Aboriginal health in Canada, the terms "aging," "older," "elder," "elderly" and "seniors" are not even listed in the indexes. Nor is there any mention of health care issues particularly affecting older people, including aging-associated diseases such as dementia and arthritis, and the need for home care, long-term care or nursing homes. From this perspective, the older Aboriginal population is virtually invisible. The goal of this chapter is to shed some light on the health and social circumstances of older Aboriginal people in Canada.

The chapter is organized into six sections, focusing on demographics; traditional roles; the importance of place; health and health care; social issues; and challenges and solutions. For older Aboriginal adults, the issues raised in each section are interlocking pieces of a puzzle framed by the history of the colonialist and discriminatory treatment they have experienced. Older Aboriginal men and women are *survivors* of a lifetime of experiences with residential schools, and of callous treatment from bureaucracies at every level of government. They have also endured years of living within or alongside non-Aboriginal communities that preferred to treat their Aboriginal residents and neighbours as out of sight and out of mind.

A Demographic Profile

The population of older Aboriginal men and women is growing steadily, so that issues affecting older adults will become even more critical in the years to come. Three important demographic points provide context for this chapter:
• The older Aboriginal population currently makes up a small but important proportion of the Aboriginal population.
• The older Aboriginal population is growing rapidly and will continue to grow in the coming decades.
• As the older Aboriginal population ages, it is increasingly dominated by older women.
In the 2011 National Household Survey (NHS), Statistics Canada (2013) reported a total Canadian population of 32.8 million, with 1.4 million (4.3 per cent) self-identifying as Aboriginal:
• First Nations only: 851,560 (60.8 per cent)
• Métis only: 451,795 (32.3 per cent)
• Inuit only: 59,455 (4.2 per cent)
• multiple Aboriginal identities: 11,415 (0.8 per cent)
• Aboriginal identities not included elsewhere: 26,475 (1.9 per cent) (Statistics Canada, 2013, pp. 4–5).
According to the 2011 NHS (Statistics Canada, 2013), the Aboriginal population is a very young one: almost 50 per cent of Aboriginal people are under age 24 years, compared with 30 per cent in the Canadian population as a whole. Only about six per cent of the Aboriginal population in 2011 was 65 and older, compared with 14 per cent of the non-Aboriginal population. The age groups used in the survey were 0 to 24, 25 to 64 and 65 and older. The 2006 census, which used more detailed age breakdowns, reported that people older than 55 made up about 12 per cent of the

Aboriginal population, compared with 25 per cent of the total population (Statistics Canada, 2008).

The Aboriginal population is the fastest-growing segment of the Canadian population. It grew by 20 per cent between 2006 and 2011, compared with a five per cent increase in the non-Aboriginal population (Statistics Canada, 2013). There is a trend toward aging in both populations, though the Aboriginal population is aging more slowly—all age groups with a growth rate higher than 20 per cent were above age 60 (Statistics Canada, 2013). Similarly, between 2001 and 2006, the Aboriginal population increased by 20 per cent, with the 44+ group growing the fastest, while the total Canadian population grew by only six per cent (Statistics Canada, 2008). Population projections suggest that the number of people aged 65 and older in Canada will nearly double within two decades, and that the older Aboriginal population will grow at an even more accelerated rate (Statistics Canada, 2011).

The differences in the proportions of old and young between the Aboriginal and non-Aboriginal populations reflect higher fertility rates and shorter life expectancy of the First Nations, Métis and Inuit populations. In 2017, the life expectancy for the total Canadian population is projected to be 79 years for men and 83 years for women (Michalowski et al., 2005). The projected life expectancy for Aboriginal people is significantly lower: for Métis and First Nations, 73 to 74 years for men and 78 to 80 years for women; and for Inuit, 64 years for men and 73 years for women. As in the non-Aboriginal population, the sex ratio of older Aboriginal women to older Aboriginal men increases with age. In the older Aboriginal population in 2006, the sex ratios for the 55-to-64 and the 65+ age cohorts were 1.06 (106 women to 100 men) and 1.20 (120 women to 100 men), respectively (Michalowski et al., 2005).

To date, the older Aboriginal population has received limited attention from researchers and policy-makers. One reason for this may be that the Aboriginal population is so young compared with the general population. As the older Aboriginal population continues to grow, fuller recognition and understanding of its needs and of appropriate approaches to addressing them become more pressing.

Traditional Roles

Older Aboriginal people have long been the holders of traditional, historical and cultural knowledge and wisdom in their communities. The expectation was that older individuals would be taken care of by their families, and by other community members more generally. This role still exists in many places. However, out-migration, illness and incarceration of Aboriginal parents have created new roles for older Aboriginal people in their communities. For example, relatively large proportions of older Aboriginal people, in contrast to older non-Aboriginal people, take care of grandchildren. The 2011 NHS (Statistics Canada, 2013) reported that 2.7 per cent of Aboriginal children live with one or both grandparents where no parents are present, and 9.1 per cent live in multi-generational families with at least one parent and grandparent. For non-Aboriginal children, the rates are 0.4 per cent and 3.4 per cent, respectively.

For older Aboriginal people who live away from their traditional communities (e.g., First Nations people living off-reserve or Inuit who have migrated south), especially those in the largest urban centres, where older Aboriginal people are concentrated, traditional roles and expectations often break down because of separation from family members and a lack of traditional community structures and culturally sensitive and appropriate services. As a result, older Aboriginal people living outside their traditional communities face a unique set of challenges linked to their Aboriginal identity, in addition to other challenges that all older adults face.

The Importance of Place

The challenges of researching the everyday lives of older Aboriginal adults now go well beyond extrapolating from the experiences of small numbers of older people who live in isolated northern communities or in the far North. The geography of where older Aboriginal people live and under what conditions has become increasingly complex. In a report on the health of First Nations people, Health Canada (2009) classified First Nations communities as either remote isolated, isolated, semi-isolated or non-isolated. (The profile did not include Aboriginal communities in the Northwest Territories or Nunavut, Inuit communities of northern Quebec, bands under the James Bay and Northern Quebec Agreement or Métis.) Of the 626 First Nations communities profiled, 405 (65 per cent) were non-isolated—accessible by road and less than 90 kilometres from physician services. In other words, the majority of First Nations communities are located in southern Canada. Furthermore, these southern Aboriginal communities are not primarily in rural areas or on isolated reserves, but rather in urban areas.

More than half of Aboriginal people in Canada, including almost half of older Aboriginal adults, now live in urban centres, ranging from large cities to communities with populations above 10,000 (Statistics Canada, 2008). The majority of Aboriginal people living in urban areas reside in Winnipeg, Edmonton, Vancouver, Calgary and Toronto. An exception to this urban trend is Inuit, few of whom live in urban centres in the south. Urban migration of Aboriginal people is a long-term trend that is magnified by the increasing growth rate of the Aboriginal population. As well, more and more older Aboriginal people are being forced to move to cities due to the lack of health care services and facilities in their rural and northern communities (Kaufert, 1999; Kaufert et al., 1999). This trend stands in stark contrast to the non-Aboriginal older population, which is encouraged to age in place. Moving out of one's home and community contradicts the scientific literature and the dominant policy view that aging in place is generally more supportive of healthy aging.

One of the inevitabilities of aging is the increasing likelihood that the older one gets the more likely one will end up alone, as spouses, siblings, relatives and friends die. Thus, living alone is a relatively common experience among older Aboriginal adults, as it is among their non-Aboriginal counterparts. Among older Aboriginal adults, about 19 per cent of the 55-to-64 age group live alone, and almost 29 per cent of the 65+ age group live alone. The percentages among older non-Aboriginal people are about 15 per cent and 27 per cent, respectively (Statistics Canada, 2008).

There is no readily available data to interpret differences in access to services among older Aboriginal people living in their traditional communities or away from them. We can hypothesize that older Aboriginal people who live in their traditional communities are more likely to have stronger formal and informal social networks to ameliorate the negative consequences of living alone (e.g., loneliness and depression); on the other hand, many traditional communities have few if any formal services for older people who live alone. In contrast, urban centres are likely to offer formal services for older people (although whether they are welcoming of older Aboriginal people is a whole other question). In these larger centres, however, older Aboriginal people are more likely to find themselves even more socially isolated than their non-Aboriginal counterparts. In the extreme, there are those older Aboriginal people who are homeless.

The basic housing conditions in which older Aboriginal people live stand in stark contrast to the basic conditions experienced by older non-Aboriginal people. Rosenberg and colleagues (2009) asked older Aboriginal adults to self-evaluate their homes. They found that 23.4 per cent of older Aboriginal people aged 55 to 64 and 21.1 per cent aged 65 and older said the housing in which they lived in 2006 needed major repairs. In comparison, among their non-Aboriginal counterparts in the two age groups, only 5.8 per cent and 5.1 per cent, respectively, said their homes required major repairs.

The importance of place in relation to the issues facing older Aboriginal men and women can be summarized in four points. First, it is now likely that more than half of the older Aboriginal population lives in urban Canada, and this proportion will continue to increase. Second, a substantial percentage of the older Aboriginal population lives alone, similar to the non-Aboriginal population, an arrangement that frequently creates challenges, not only for the older people themselves, but also for their formal and informal service providers. Living alone does not necessarily mean living in social isolation, though social isolation is indeed a problem for many people who live alone. A third issue related to the importance of place is the high number of older Aboriginal people who live in housing that needs major repairs, which is significantly less common among their non-Aboriginal counterparts. Living in a home that requires major repairs often raises day-to-day expenses, such as heating costs. It can exacerbate existing health conditions, such as respiratory problems, which are aggravated by living in homes with a mould problem. Living under these conditions can also have a negative emotional impact on the person. Finally, these three issues individually and in combination pose a challenge to healthy aging and aging in place for older Aboriginal people.

Health and Health Care

Comparing the health of older Aboriginal people and their non-Aboriginal counterparts, we found that as both groups grew older, they were more likely to assess their health as fair or poor rather than good, very good or excellent (Rosenberg et al., 2009). The difference between the two populations was that among older Aboriginal adults, almost 40 per cent of those aged 55 to 64 and 45 per cent of those aged 65 to 74 assessed their health as fair or poor—almost 20 percentage points higher than those for the matching cohorts of older non-Aboriginal people. A second health difference involved the number of chronic conditions each group experienced. Among Aboriginal people aged 75 and older, only 15 per cent reported having no chronic conditions, and 41 per cent reported three or more chronic conditions. Among non-Aboriginal people in that same age group, 21 per cent reported having no chronic conditions and only 23 per cent reported having three or more chronic conditions. A third health difference related to the occurrence of specific health conditions. For example, among those 75 and older, 23 per cent of Aboriginal people reported having diabetes, compared with 13 per cent of non-Aboriginal people. This higher prevalence also held true in the 55-to-64 and 65-to-74 age groups and for other conditions such as arthritis, heart disease, cancer and stroke (Rosenberg et al., 2009).

Taken together, this data clearly shows that older Aboriginal people are more likely to be in poor health than their non-Aboriginal counterparts. Providing health care poses unique challenges in communities where the number of older Aboriginal people who need specialized services is likely to be small and the difficulties of either delivering the services in situ or sending people to specialists in urban areas is challenging due to the lack of specialized transportation services, long distances and difficult winter driving conditions. In urban areas, a key issue is whether older Aboriginal people who require specialized services can find health providers who are culturally sensitive to their unique needs.

The poorer health status of older Aboriginal adults can be explained by understanding how the social determinants of health (e.g., employment, housing, education, nutrition), negative health behaviours, racism and the residential school experience affect mental and physical health. Below, we focus on negative health behaviours. Later in the chapter, we discuss the unquantifiable effects that the history of racism and residential schools has had on the health of older Aboriginal people.

The use of tobacco products among Aboriginal peoples is a complex issue because of tobacco's significance in traditional ceremonies. However, there are distinct differences in smoking rates between Aboriginal and non-Aboriginal older adults. According to data compiled by Health Canada (2009) with the assistance of the First Nations Information Governance Committee, among First Nations people aged 60 and older who live on a reserve, 23.5 per cent reported being daily smokers and 4.6 per cent reported being occasional smokers. This is compared with 10.6 and 1.8 per cent, respectively, among non-Aboriginal people from this age group.

Excessive alcohol use is a risk factor for reduced longevity and many chronic diseases, including diabetes, cardiovascular disease and some forms of cancer. Although rates of alcohol use problems are generally lower in older populations than younger ones, older adults are more vulnerable to the harmful effects of alcohol because their bodies process alcohol more slowly, and intoxication can lead to falls. It is difficult to find data comparing alcohol use among older Aboriginal people with that among older non-Aboriginal people, but a general picture is available. Both the 2006 Aboriginal Peoples Survey (APS) (Statistics Canada, 2009) and the 2005 Canadian Community Health Survey (CCHS) (Statistics Canada, 2005) asked the following question: "During the past 12 months how often did you drink alcoholic beverages?" About 15 per cent of Aboriginal people aged 55 and older chose either the response category "4 to 6 times a week" or "every day," compared with 26 per cent of older non-Aboriginal people. Statistics Canada (2009) also classified respondents as regular drinkers (one alcoholic beverage once a month or more), occasional drinkers (less than once a month) or non-drinkers. Comparing Aboriginal and non-Aboriginal people aged 55 and older, 44 versus 56 per cent were regular drinkers, 21 versus 18 per cent were occasional drinkers and 35 versus 26 per cent were non-drinkers (Figure 13-1).

FIGURE 13-1

Alcohol Consumption: Older Aboriginal and Non-Aboriginal Persons Compared

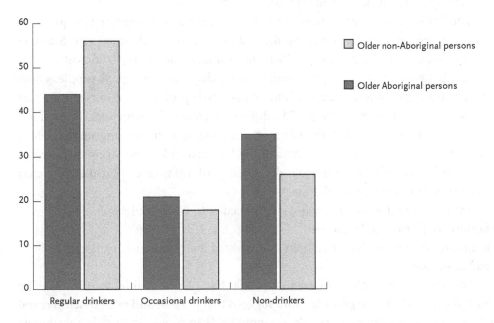

Source: Statistics Canada, 2005, 2009

There are various ways to interpret the statistics presented in Figure 13-1. The data shows a slightly lower overall rate of alcohol consumption by older Aboriginal people compared with older non-Aboriginal people. This finding challenges the general public perception that all Aboriginal people are more likely to consume alcohol than non-Aboriginal people. We should point out that these statistics do not capture people who have serious alcohol use problems. As statistically representative household surveys that do not include people with no fixed address or who are in prison, the 2006 APS (Statistics Canada, 2009) and 2005 CCHS (Statistics Canada, 2005) are likely to have excluded people with severe alcohol use problems. As well, both surveys excluded people living on reserves in the provinces and in First Nations communities in the territories.

Older Aboriginal people often receive inadequate medical care, for a variety of reasons. The health care services and facilities in remote and isolated communities are often quite limited. Older adults may have limited mobility and access to transportation. Aboriginal people in general may face delays and procedural blocks in obtaining health care caused by federal and provincial and territorial wrangling over jurisdiction (Aboriginal health care is paid for by the federal government, with provincial and territorial governments delivering services). Older Aboriginal people may have difficulty navigating the health care system due to language, cultural and educational barriers, and therefore underuse the services that are available. For example, the 2006 APS (Statistics Canada, 2009) found that 45 per cent of Aboriginal people over age 55 years, and 55 per cent over 65, claim an Aboriginal language as their mother tongue; 12 per cent over 65 speak neither French nor English, and in the North, this number is much higher (Statistics Canada, 2009).

The limited data we have on access to health care services measured by questions such as "Have you seen a physician in the past 12 months?" in the 2006 APS (Statistics Canada, 2009) and the 2005 CCHS (Statistics Canada, 2005) shows almost no differences between older Aboriginal people and older non-Aboriginal people. Older Aboriginal adults, however, are much more likely to report seeing a nurse in the past 12 months (Rosenberg et al., 2009). This difference likely reflects the much greater use of nurses on reserves and at clinics and emergency rooms in urban communities where older Aboriginal people receive care, and the fact that older non-Aboriginal people are much less likely to see a nurse independently of a physician and therefore may discount their interactions with nurses.

Types of care that are generally more particular to older adults are:
• home care (formal and informal)
• long-term care in residential settings (i.e., assisted living and nursing homes)
• palliative care.

Obviously, where older Aboriginal people live makes a difference in thinking about these services. The grey literature suggests that in rural and remote settings and on reserves, older Aboriginal people are more likely to receive culturally appropriate informal care from immediate and extended family and other band members, but that these settings often lack formal home care services, long-term residential care and palliative care. As a consequence, older Aboriginal people who need these kinds of care are "shipped out" to facilities that can provide these services, the closest often hundreds of kilometres from their home communities. Older adults who are sick or dying may find themselves socially isolated and tended to by non-Aboriginal health care workers who cannot communicate with them in their own language or provide culturally appropriate care. Kaufert (1999) and Kaufert and colleagues (1999) found that in these situations, physicians may fail to divulge all the care options and that it may be difficult to translate information about biomedical issues for older Aboriginal patients and their families. As well, these researchers pointed out cultural differences in how Aboriginal and non-Aboriginal families discuss and make end-of-life decisions with older family members, which may generate tension with medical staff. Aboriginal families tend to seek consensus, rather than base decisions on a majority vote or on the advice of an authority figure; this approach requires time for discussion to ensure that everyone feels comfortable with the decision. While a non-Aboriginal family might focus on the need to make a prompt decision so treatment can proceed, an Aboriginal family might be more concerned with ensuring an effective decision-making process.

For older Aboriginal people who live in urban settings, there is often no band structure to provide the informal network of support that exists on reserves, and even informal family networks may be more attenuated, or non-existent. While proximity to services is likely not an issue in urban settings, social isolation, lack of culturally appropriate services and language barriers are issues that both older Aboriginal people living in cities and those on reserves face.

Social Issues

Family violence, substance use problems and suicide are among the social issues any older adult may experience. It has proven remarkably difficult to determine how many people have experienced these and other social issues (e.g., grief, accidents, theft) or to find ways to effectively intervene in a community or neighbourhood where violence or abuse is part of the everyday social climate. It is also difficult to compare the experiences of older Aboriginal people with those of their non-Aboriginal counterparts because data is not always available for older non-Aboriginal adults. However, a picture is beginning to emerge. The 2006 APS (Statistics Canada, 2009) asked respondents whether certain social issues were a problem for Aboriginal people in the communities or neighbourhoods where they lived. The results for older Aboriginal people aged 55 years and older were as follows:
- alcohol abuse (64.3 per cent)
- drug abuse (61.5 per cent)
- family violence (51.2 per cent)
- suicide (36.4 per cent).

Because there were no equivalent surveys done among non-Aboriginal residents of these communities, we do not know whether their experience is different.

Some important research exists on elder abuse among the older Aboriginal population. Although much of her data is from the 1990s, Dumont-Smith (2002) documented the issue of elder abuse and its effects on older Aboriginal people at the national level. Cyr and colleagues (2004) identified various forms of abuse experienced by older Aboriginal people in the Toronto area. Ship and Tarbell (1997) identified social isolation (physical, social, spiritual, mental-emotional), depression, anxiety, fear, grief and abuse as having a negative effect on the health of older Aboriginal adults.

A survey of health care workers in 210 First Nations communities conducted by the National Aboriginal Health Organization ([NAHO], 2010) identified elder abuse as an issue, among other problems. Respondents reported the following key social issues affecting older Aboriginal people:
• elder abuse, including financial abuse (most often cited), as well as emotional, spiritual, physical and sexual abuse (65 per cent)
• isolation (54 per cent)
• inadequate housing (27 per cent) or lack of long-term-care facilities (27 per cent)
• loss of culture (24 per cent)
• inadequate transportation (23 per cent)
• lack of services (20 per cent) (NAHO, 2010, p. 2).

Challenges, Solutions and Conclusions

In many ways, the health, health care and social issues confronting older Aboriginal people are the same issues all older people face. However, the unique historical and geographical context in which these issues occur for older Aboriginal adults makes the challenges more complex and solutions more difficult to find.

The community health care workers interviewed in the NAHO study (2010) were asked to identify programs or services that are needed in the community to improve the overall health of older Aboriginal adults. Respondents indicated the following needs:
• housing (54 per cent)
• social programs (34 per cent)
• improved or expanded existing programs (20 per cent)
• facilities for older adults (16 per cent)
• specialized health care providers (14 per cent)
• mental health programs (10 per cent)
• meals on wheels programs (8 per cent)
• programs to address elder abuse (7 per cent)
• physical activity and fitness programs (6 per cent)

• assistive devices (5 per cent)

• medications (4 per cent) (NAHO, 2010, p. 2).

These suggestions, as far as they go, are reasonable and achievable and should be implemented. What is missing, however, is recognition of the challenges that may confront older Aboriginal people and that are specific to where these older adults live. To service a region that includes remote communities, where the number of older Aboriginal adults in any one community is small and where the number who require long-term care or specialized care providers is even smaller, does one build a regional long-term care facility staffed with specialized care providers, knowing that moving an older Aboriginal person to such a facility might exacerbate feelings of social isolation from family and friends? In urban communities, where there is less likelihood that a band structure exists and where older Aboriginal people are more likely to be socially isolated, how does one identify older Aboriginal adults who are vulnerable and encourage them to take advantage of services that have been designed for older adults, not older Aboriginal people? How can health care providers make culturally sensitive services for older Aboriginal adults a priority when culturally sensitive services are needed for other larger groups of older adults who also face cultural barriers to services? Finally, even if we could address these issues, how would any of these improvements be funded, especially in this period of fiscal restraint at the federal and provincial and territorial levels?

These are difficult questions to answer. The first step, however, is to develop a much better understanding of the unique needs of older Aboriginal adults in the context of their histories and geographies. If aging in place as the best way of achieving healthy aging is the goal of non-Aboriginal older adults, supported by all levels of government, it should include Aboriginal older adults. Achieving such a goal will require strategies that reflect the unique needs of older Aboriginal people living in traditional communities and those in urban centres, and that acknowledge the deep impact of racism and residential schools on all Aboriginal people.

References

Cyr, R., Native Canadian Centre of Toronto & Ontario Coalition of Senior Citizens' Organizations. (2004). *Breaking the Cycle of Violence: Preventing Violence against Seniors in the Aboriginal Community*. Toronto: Native Canadian Centre of Toronto & Ontario Coalition of Senior Citizens' Organizations.

Dumont-Smith, C. (2002) *Aboriginal Elder Abuse in Canada*. Retrieved from Aboriginal Healing Foundation website: www.ahf.ca

Health Canada. (2009). *A Statistical Profile of the Health of First Nations in Canada. Determinants of Health, 1999 to 2003*. Retrieved from www.hc-sc.gc.ca

Kaufert, J. (1999). Cultural mediation in cancer diagnosis and end of life decision-making: The experience of Aboriginal patients in Canada. *Anthropology & Medicine, 6*, 405–421.

Kaufert, J., Putsch, R.W. & Lavellée, M. (1999). End-of-life decision-making among Aboriginal Canadians: Interpretation, mediation, and discord in the communication of bad news. *Journal of Palliative Care, 15*, 31–38.

Michalowski, M., Low, S., Verma, R.P.B., Germain, M. & Grenier, C. (2005). *Projections of the Aboriginal Populations, Canada, Provinces and Territories.* (Statistics Canada catalogue no. 91-547-XIE). Ottawa: Minister of Industry.

National Aboriginal Health Organization (NAHO). (2010). *Perspectives of Front Line Staff on Health Issues and Community Service Needs for First Nations Seniors.* Retrieved from www.naho.ca/documents/fnc/english/2011_frontline_staff_perspectives.pdf

Rosenberg, M.W., Wilson, K., Abonyi, S., Wiebe, A., Beach, K. & Lovelace, R. (2009). *Older Aboriginal Peoples in Canada: Demographics, Health Status and Access to Health Care.* Retrieved from Research on Social and Economic Dimensions of an Aging Population, McMaster University website: http://socserv.mcmaster.ca/sedap/p/sedap249.pdf

Ship, S.J. & Tarbell, R. (1997). Our nations' elders speak—Ageing and cultural diversity: A cross-cultural approach. *In Touch, 7* (4), 1–33.

Statistics Canada. (2005). *Canadian Community Health Survey, Cycle 3.1.* Ottawa: Minister of Industry.

Statistics Canada. (2008). *Aboriginal Peoples in Canada in 2006: Inuit, Métis and First Nations, 2006 Census.* (Catalogue no. 97-558-XIE). Ottawa: Minister of Industry.

Statistics Canada. (2009). *2006 Aboriginal Peoples Survey.* (Catalogue no. 89-637-XWE). Ottawa: Minister of Industry.

Statistics Canada. (2011). *Population Projections by Aboriginal Identity in Canada, 2006 to 2031.* (Catalogue no. 91-552-XWE). Ottawa: Minister of Industry.

Statistics Canada. (2013). *National Household Survey, 2011. Aboriginal Peoples in Canada: First Nations People, Métis and Inuit.* (Catalogue no. 99-011-X2011001). Ottawa: Minister of Industry.

Waldram, J.B., Herring, D.A. & Young, T.K. (1995). *Aboriginal Health in Canada: Historical, Cultural, and Epidemiological Perspectives.* Toronto: University of Toronto Press.

Young, T.K. (1988). *Health Care and Cultural Change: The Indian Experience in the Central Subarctic.* Toronto: University of Toronto Press.

ABOUT THE AUTHORS

Mark W. Rosenberg is a professor of geography and cross-appointed as a professor of public health sciences at Queen's University in Kingston, Ontario. He is also the Canada Research Chair in Development Studies. He received his undergraduate training at the University of Toronto and his graduate training at the London School of Economics and Political Science in the United Kingdom. He has carried out numerous studies about older Aboriginal and non-Aboriginal populations and is particularly interested in their access to health and social services.

Kathi Wilson is a professor of geography at the University of Toronto Mississauga. Her main area of research is Aboriginal health, with particular focus on migration and health, and access to health and social services. She is an advocate of community-based and collaborative research partnerships.

Part 4

Issues and Approaches

Chapter 14

Mental Health from an Indigenous Perspective

BILL MUSSELL

This chapter presents an Indigenous perspective on mental health and addiction challenges to inform efforts in finding effective strategies for working with individuals, families and communities in urban, rural and isolated settings. It describes the evolution of the relationship between government and First peoples since contact. It also describes the peoples' skilful adaptation to lifeways imposed on them, and their reliance upon traditional values, beliefs and practices as they experienced these upheavals. It identifies resources they drew upon, including the core values and assumptions of their own communities, which were key to their survival, and explores how understanding this history and perspective may guide the practice of health, justice, education and social service professionals. It is a story about movement toward increasing humanization and self-determination.

Indigenous Perspective on Wellness

Most people in First Nations, Inuit and Métis communities see mental health and addiction in terms of wellness. They consider the terms "mental health" and "mental illness" reflective of a Western paradigm characterized by dualism, negative labelling and a focus on deficits. In fact, these terms do not exist in their traditional languages. Wellness, in their view, is more readily identified with wholeness and the importance of building on strengths. Indigenous peoples see mental wellness as a continuum from minimal to optimal. A person's place on the continuum at any given time is a result of many internal and external converging factors. Accordingly, this chapter speaks of mental wellness, rather than mental health or illness.

Achieving mental wellness is a lifelong journey. Wellness requires a balance of body, mind and spirit. Its elements include self-esteem, personal identity, cultural identity and relational capacity, all of which are shaped in interaction with the social, physical, economic and political environment. In an Indigenous context, mental wellness must be defined in terms of the values and beliefs of Inuit, Métis and First Nations people.

While there is great diversity among Indigenous cultures, I believe they hold in common certain core values. The core values include a respect for autonomy and self-determination at all levels: individual, family, community and nation. They also share fundamental principles and assumptions. One principle is that we are spiritual, mental, emotional, social and physical beings who are gifted with opportunities throughout our existence on this material plane to find and live our purpose. An assumption is that each person is of value and is inherently good, and brings to the world unique gifts. The journey toward wholeness and actualization of one's gifts requires nurturing relationships and a context that sustains and supports development. Health practitioners and social and justice workers can better address First Nations, Inuit and Métis wellness challenges if they know about and respect Indigenous peoples' enduring cultural beliefs.

The current state of First Nations, Inuit and Métis peoples' wellness is rooted in the historically oppressive relationship between Indigenous and mainstream communities. Indigenous peoples were viewed as not fully human, and their cultures disparaged. This perception still underlies and shapes the relationship between Canadian social systems, including the mental health system, and First Nations, Inuit and Métis people. Those who work with Indigenous people need to understand the links between Indigenous peoples' wellness, or lack of it, and the persistent social and political inequities they continue to experience. Informing one's practice in this way requires a capacity for self-reflection and critical thinking.

Cultural Foundations for Mental Wellness

Long before the arrival of settlers, First peoples of North America created their own cultures, which were living and functional whole systems complete with norms, values, standards of behaviour, social structures and culturally dictated interaction patterns. Each culture had unique concepts of birth, death, health, illness and healing. Culture has been defined as "the whole complex of relationships, knowledge, languages, social institutions, beliefs, values and ethical rules that bind a people together and give a collective and its individual members a sense of who they are and where they belong" (Royal Commission on Aboriginal Peoples [RCAP], 1995, p. 25).

Belief in the Creator and the spiritual dimensions of life permeated all aspects of life. The cultures valued and honoured relationships between all created beings, and especially those between people. Values informed all aspects of life—spiritual beliefs and practices, kinship patterns, social arrangements and communication networks—and included norms that regulated personal, familial and social conduct. Culture was transmitted through the structures and practices of family and community life. Ways of living on the land, strong social networks and extended families remain core cultural strengths shared among all Indigenous cultures.

Culturally informed values underpin strategies for healthy living and serve as the foundation for wellness. Brant Castellano (2005) affirms this:

> When Aboriginal people speak about maintaining and revitalizing their cultures they are not proposing to go back to igloos and tipis and hunter-gatherer lifestyles. They are talking about restoring order to daily living in conformity with ancient and enduring values that affirm life. (p. 3)

Values continue to guide successful adaptations to ever-changing environments.

Ancestors of First Nations people in Canada understood that all facets of Creation were interrelated and mutually responsible parts of the whole, with constant and necessary give and take between the physical, the mental, the emotional and the spiritual, and between the individual, the family and the culture (Swinomish Tribal Mental Health Project, 1991). Their world view is holistic and features living in harmony with nature, valuing the rights of the collective and living co-reliantly, as opposed to depending on others. Being self-caring and self-sufficient prepares and equips one to live in "sharing and caring ways"—to be reciprocal, and thereby to help sustain a community of care that is the foundation of health, well-being and transmission of culture.

Families create the foundation for self-care, self-determination, mutual aid, bravery and learning (wisdom). From the time of their birth, children are included in family activities in ways that enable them to see, experience and understand how all things come together (Ross, 1996). Through inclusion and genuine communication, new family members learn to meet their needs and those of others, to understand cause and effect and to integrate new information. They learn responsibility and accountability. Traditional ways of teaching and learning were a discovery process in which knowledge was transmitted experientially. The learners' capacities to make sense of both inner and outer worlds were nurtured, activated and seen to be of benefit to the whole community.

Raised in a safe, caring and respectful environment, human beings learn to value their own lives and those of all other creations of the Great Spirit (another term for the Creator), including plants and animals. They learn to believe in their ability to make informed decisions, choices and other kinds of judgments. They pay attention to their intuitiveness and use it as a guide in their daily lives. They believe in their ability to modify themselves and convey this belief to others. Song, dance, ceremony and other processes of caring and sharing enrich the sense of inner wholeness, togetherness and purpose on this earth. Honouring femaleness, maleness and two-spiritedness begins early in life. In our traditional communities, all are viewed and treated as sacred.

Land is healing for First Nations, Inuit and Métis, who relate to it as home, as a resource and as an educational experience. Land is a place or territory where family members reside and foster their unique culture and livelihoods in the presence of ancestors. Land is steeped in values and becomes a landscape made familiar by shared stories. Land also offers profound learning experiences for young people who engage, from time to time, in back-to-the-land rituals where they learn about living off the land and the importance of co-operation, collaboration, harmonization, clear communication and co-reliance. Such activities build relationships between younger people and their seniors, through which the transmission of culture takes place.

As an outcome, mental wellness is relational: strength and security are based in family and community. Mental wellness is cultivated in a social context, and embodied in group traditions, laws, customs and everyday practices that foster and maintain health in every dimension. In this view of mental wellness, principles of connectedness, togetherness, holism and cultural ways of knowing, and core cultural institutions such as family, clan and community are honoured. Individual well-being is strongly connected to the health and wellness of the family and community. Enduring values and practices of ancestors provided a foundation, not only for identity, but also for making necessary adaptations to inevitable changes and challenges in life. This way of viewing health is very different from the Western perspective that features individualism over the importance of the collective.

In the Indigenous world, the well-being of the individual is inseparable from that of the social collective and the whole of Creation. Mental unwellness is the outcome of a rupture in "right relations" that may be due to forces that deprive or overwhelm or both. To the Western-trained eye, resulting disharmony can be easily attributed to the individual versus the contextual realities. Privileged biomedical approaches based on the Western world view crowd out understandings and associated strategies of First Nations, Inuit and Métis people.

Disruption of Cultural Foundations

Colonization brought changes to First Nations, Inuit and Métis communities. It attacked, undermined and devalued their world view while also drastically altering living conditions. Through their governments, churches and residential schools, the colonizers attempted to impose their lifestyle, values and beliefs upon the people. All aspects of life deteriorated, due to the introduction of foreign diseases and alcohol, the imposition of the reserve system and prohibitions against spiritual practices and speaking traditional languages. In short, colonization brought negative, extreme and rapid changes to Indigenous life at the same time as it denied the validity of, and access to, the tools traditionally used by First Nations, Inuit and Métis to cope with changes.

"Graduates" of the residential school system share stories of personal and collective physical, emotional, intellectual and spiritual deprivation. These young people not only lost meaningful contact with their families and communities; they were even forbidden to interact with their own brothers and sisters at the schools and were not allowed to speak the languages they learned at home. These harsh rules compounded their isolation and loneliness, which could not be alleviated through the "sharing and caring" they would normally have from their loved ones (parents and grandparents, brothers and sisters, aunts, uncles and cousins). Food was rationed so that the children were hungry; poor nutrition impaired their physical growth. Similarly, their unmet emotional needs impaired their emotional development, resulting in poor self-esteem, a growing sense of hopelessness and an increasing inability to handle the stressors connected with learning based on a foreign system.

The residential school prohibition against speaking Indigenous languages and their replacement with English imposed a Western lens and filter through which to make meaning of life, and denied access to the world view imbedded in the mother tongue. Furthermore, the schools' Western pedagogy required students to become passive, dependent learners. This learning experience stood in contrast to the traditional discovery process in which knowledge was transmitted experientially.

How can children who experience chronic hunger, who feel lost and miss family and community, who long for friendship and support possibly begin to focus on what a teacher or anyone else tries to teach? Those children know nothing about their personal powers of perception or their feelings, or about critical thinking and taking action; they lack the tools, energy and skills to learn about the external world as portrayed by the school curriculum. What personal, social and other competencies would these children bring home as 16-, 17- or 18-year-olds?

Youngsters returning to their communities from residential schools came back to crowded living conditions and poverty. In my home territory, I remember people struggling to survive because jobs were limited, housing was scarce and poor, and mutual aid within the community was minimal. Alcoholics Anonymous was in its infancy, and social welfare programs were not yet established. People distrusted one another and lacked personal and social skills; families lived in isolation from one another. The community's earlier vitality, nurtured through togetherness, shared activities and work projects, and an optimistic belief in what the future might hold, faded into the past. Other than in a few self-caring and self-determining families, collective life no longer cultivated or sustained Indigenous knowledge, new learning, family health and wellness, safety and hopefulness.

The ramifications of the residential school experience continue to be felt in communities. Too often people struggle to cope with stressors without the support of values, beliefs and strategies that could guide them in their efforts. When people lack physical and emotional safety and security, their fear, anxiety and anger build. In these states it is very difficult for people to act in caring, rational ways, or to learn, be reflective and create the understanding of themselves and their world that is needed to bring about positive change.

In spite of the damage done by the residential school system—disrupted community life, broken families, top-down bureaucratic ways of life, loss of traditional languages, institutionalized and foreign education, an imposed governance system, isolation and the absence of health and social support—First Nations, Inuit and Métis people continued to survive, discovering and implementing strategies for adaption and change. Such strategies included, and continue to include, Euro-Western medicines and practices, and increasingly, more and more knowledge, values and practices that are embedded in their respective heritages.

The legacy of these destructive forces in the lives of contemporary Indigenous people is seen in low scores on measures of social determinants of health: income, employment and working conditions, food security, environment and housing, economic development, education and literacy, social support and connectedness, healthy behaviour and access to health care. Poor social determinants of health for Indigenous people are exacerbated by racism and discrimination (Hyman, 2009). These prejudiced perceptions are rooted in settlers' false beliefs that First Nations, Inuit and Métis were less than human and their cultures primitive. These discriminatory attitudes continue to shape the relationships between First peoples and Canadian social systems, including the mental health system.

Restoring and Sustaining Mental Wellness

Today's First Nations, Métis and Inuit families possess lifestyles that fit somewhere on a continuum between "somewhat traditional" and "mostly Western." Their acculturation experiences over the past four and five generations have emphasized materialism and individual rights, and de-emphasized mutual aid and togetherness. At the same time, core aspects of a traditional world view continue to be central to Indigenous peoples:
• Each person is of value and goodness and brings gifts.
• Each person has spiritual, physical, emotional and intellectual dimensions.
• All people are interconnected.
• No one can reach potential wholeness without experiencing nurturing interpersonal relationships throughout all life stages.
• (Positive) mental wellness is the outcome of a variety of forces affecting a person's life.
• Each person is cultural and has the capacity to embrace life.

Over the past 50 years, Indigenous peoples have demonstrated success in their efforts to restore mental wellness through programs and services based on these beliefs. Increased government funding made it possible for communities to shift from survival mode to taking collective, community-driven action.

In the early 1960s, I recall our political leaders writing briefs to request education and training opportunities so more of their community members could qualify for employment, improved health and housing services, and recognition of the long denial of title to the land. This last point was vital to the people, because restrictions to living off the land (hunting, trapping, fishing, harvesting natural foods) and to entering the wage economy (ranching, logging, farming, fishing) were stripping them of their identity as providers, caregivers, leaders and stewards of the land. As well, the existing health, welfare, housing, education and other social services were not adequate to support self-care, personal growth and social development. At best, health, welfare and social services were crisis oriented.

In this context, First Nations in British Columbia were provided with funds to administer their own affairs, subject to government supervision and approval. Communities with larger populations were able to hire a home-school co-ordinator, a health worker and perhaps a drug and alcohol worker. Many community members expected such service providers to "fix the problem" because they were acculturated to dependence through their residential school and associated institutionalization.

Effects of the history of institutionalization have taken years to change and continue to have a strong presence in our everyday lives: on the one hand, people assume the role as experts of their needs, but on the other hand, they decline to take responsibility for anything, instead allowing others to "make history" for them. Over the years I have heard leaders lament how hard it is to wipe out residential school training that taught us to be helpless and hopeless. Thus, restoring mental wellness in families and communities has been highly challenging, but, as we have discovered, not out of reach.

Programs and services in First Nations and Inuit communities in crisis often run in survival mode and have insufficient resources; the heaviness of life's burdens spurs people to find relief from the stressors rather than try to understand why they live as they do. However, when these programs can be supplemented with external funding and associated technical and professional assistance, some community members discover mutual concerns, needs and hopes, and decide to work collaboratively for improved health and wellness. Without such incentives and supports, destructive life forces find no collective resistance, so living as victims continues.

Evidence for these observations can be found by examining government-funded programs, such as the National Native Alcohol and Drug Abuse Program (NNADAP), the Native Human Services Program, the Salishan Institute Society and the Aboriginal Healing Foundation. The NNADAP was approved in 1982 and included both treatment and community-based prevention programs. In its early years, programming was based on the medical model of addiction as a disease. The focus was on the presenting problem, not the underlying factors that shaped the personal and social life of the "drinker." Aftercare supports were minimal, and the usual 28-day treatment program was not sufficient to address a lifetime of trauma. With First Nations and Inuit leadership, the program has begun to integrate Western and Indigenous approaches, ways of knowing, wisdom and healing practices, resulting in more effective treatment and aftercare strategies, with more people managing to maintain sobriety and assume citizenship responsibilities.

Education and training offered by the Native Human Services Program in British Columbia dealt with colonization and its consequences, such as violence, abuse and intergenerational trauma. The focus was on personal, social and structural issues and change strategies. This unique program was funded by the Department of Indian Affairs (Pacific). It acknowledged that First Nations people were needed to deliver health, education, social development, recreation and addiction services in communities.

Another contribution to transformative education was made by the Salishan Institute Society. From 1988 to 1998, with funding from Health Canada (Pacific), the organization designed and delivered educational programs for hundreds of NNADAP workers and community health representatives who were expected to address a wide range of complex physical and mental health and addiction needs in their resource-poor, and often rural and isolated, communities. Salishan courses featured honouring the Great Spirit, studying the teachings of Elders, learning personal and community history, linking major challenges in life with colonizing practices, and developing strategies for family restoration and community change. Participants gained or regained their agency, learning to live as subjects of life, rather than as objects or victims of life; this outcome was the result of transformative education at its best.

The Aboriginal Healing Foundation (AHF) promoted, supported and helped to implement community-designed and -driven, culturally based programs that featured holistic healing and the revitalization of practices contributing to wellness of individuals, families and communities. In its work, the AHF demonstrated that mental health issues are a serious threat to the survival and health of First Nations, Inuit and Métis communities; and that suicidal and other self-destructive behaviours, such as problems with alcohol and other drugs, and violence, were direct and indirect consequences of colonization in First Nations, Inuit and Métis lives (RCAP, 1995). Now that AHF has closed down, many communities do not have access to supports for mental wellness programs based on traditional values and practices.

In summary, opportunities to explore the history of colonization and its deleterious effects have been accessible to some communities only since the 1980s. In British Columbia, such work has focused on restoring aspects of personal growth and development and attending to other damaging consequences of the oppressive residential school system. Indigenous and non-Indigenous educators delivering training at the community level over the last 30 years have facilitated learning and personal growth by supporting grieving and healing, and by building wellness pathways. These include self-care strategies, learning how to learn, nurturance through relationship-building, dialogue, mutuality, co-reliance and experiencing the outcomes of making one's own history.

These strategies have contributed to a growing understanding of how change takes place and the recognition that we, as Indigenous people, have to take charge of our own grieving, healing and personal growth. More and more of us are discovering that imbalance in our communities lies in our powerlessness relative to the social institutions that dominate every aspect of our lives—from the way we are educated and make a living to the way we are governed, a reality articulated by RCAP. We are challenged with rebuilding whole communities, as well as with restoring our families' ability to nurture caring, respectful, law-abiding human beings (RCAP, 1996).

Each of the programs described above provided pathways to wellness through reconnecting participants with their cultural heritage. Because First Nations, Inuit and Métis people have experienced interference with their access to their own knowledge through the residential school experience, it is especially important that they have opportunities to reconstruct and reconnect with this heritage. All human beings benefit from knowing who they are, what they are and to whom they belong, and that they are appreciated and valued throughout life. Such knowledge contributes to their ability to achieve inner peace and self-acceptance, and to create social balance and harmony in their lives.

When Indigenous people have meaningful opportunities to learn about their family and community history through sharing and discussing personal stories based on early memories, especially of relationships with family and other community members, this facilitates the discovery of forgotten lessons, affirms personal identity and connects people to themselves and to others. Such a discovery process may bring a whole range of feelings—tears of sadness, tears expressing pain and shame, tears of joy. Within a context of personal safety, acceptance, understanding and love, the natural expression of powerful feelings helps people gain insight into their inner lives that dissolves barriers to personal change.

Improving Effectiveness of Practitioners

Culturally based practices are those that work through the strengths of the individual, family and community. The practitioner should not expect to make changes in isolation. Change is essentially a collective and emergent process that involves connecting services the practitioner provides with those already in place in the community. It requires networking, collaborating and relationship building. It is facilitated through becoming known to the community and understanding its lifeways by participating in gatherings such as sports events, health fairs, community dinners and celebrations. Such participation reveals the worlds of experience possessed by older adults and those in the middle years, especially those willing to share their cultural knowledge. Through relationships with such people, it becomes possible to find ways to harmonize Euro-Western practices with the values, traditions and healing approaches of the community being served.

The practitioner is clearly not an expert in the life of the person he or she is expected to assist. Therefore, the practitioner must be ready to learn from the help seeker and to look beyond the "presenting problem" to the broader social contexts of the help seeker. Practitioners should know that contemporary life for many First Nations, Inuit and Métis people is difficult for the following reasons:

- Making a living is out of reach for most people, with many dependent upon social assistance.
- Social assistance fails to cover the cost of living in many First Nations and Inuit locations, especially rural and remote ones.
- Housing conditions are poor and often unsafe, and good housing is always in short supply.
- Financial resources for housing construction are virtually unattainable for most people living on reserves.
- Unmanageable stressors contribute to personally destructive, risky and socially unacceptable behaviour.
- Programs and services are not designed to break cycles of poverty.

There are many barriers to positive personal and social change in most communities, including distrust of one another and distrust of the health care system; lack of knowledge, insight or critical thinking on the part of community members; and scarcity of role models. Specifically, the following factors contribute to the complexity of making social change:

- Sharing personal feelings and thoughts was not cultivated in the residential school system, which has impaired relationships between peers and across generations.
- People are more familiar with indifference and negativity than with positive regard and genuine person-to-person interaction.
- Few people live in a world where others share an unfailing belief in people's ability to change; they live in a world of distrust.
- Only today are some of our members learning to assert themselves, identify problems and be proactive (without anger).
- Many people find any assessment process intimidating because of unfamiliar communication patterns and language.
- Articulating their life experience often takes a highly unwelcome conscious effort, particularly for those for whom English is a second language or whose trauma predates language acquisition. Therefore, other modalities, such as storytelling, spontaneous art or role play, may be useful.
- Fear of the stigma associated with a diagnosis of mental illness weighs heavily in many First Nations, Inuit and Métis families. How will the person diagnosed be treated by the community? Such concern often keeps people away from mental health service providers.

Mental health care providers can take steps to help meet these challenges in the following ways:

- Appreciate that most rural and isolated villages do not have on-site service providers dedicated to mental health and addiction issues. These communities have poor general access. Some treatment options simply may not be affordable. For these reasons, it is important to build capacity by working through the community's or family's natural inclination to help one another, focusing on self-help and mutual aid, to affirm or reaffirm inherent strengths.

• Remember that most First Nations, Inuit and Métis people live in close-knit, yet often distrusting, communities where there is little privacy. Most service buildings are centrally located; some residents can see all who come and go from them. If the conditions of the workspace are not private, consider doing personal work with those seeking help outside of the office.

• Familiarize people with service systems and how to navigate them, as needed.

• Recognize that people have survived without systematic and organized mental health and other services; they have done so through lived life experience, generation to generation, and therefore possess significant strengths.

• Consider how the person, family or group deals with everyday challenges; help them identify what works and why, and build upon such strengths.

• Help people to clarify their values and set priorities; help them to distinguish between real or lived values and ideal ones.

• Encourage people to express feelings honestly; model honesty and honourable and respectful behaviour.

• Allow people time to tell their stories; both talking and listening are healing.

• Be familiar with traditional and modern ways of doing trauma work and try to do this work in small groups.

• Promote social cohesion and sustained mutual support and togetherness by working through individual and collective strengths and by finding natural leaders and learning from them.

• Include families in work with an individual because the family is the primary resource that will still be in the person's life long after you have gone. It is important to give each family member equal time and opportunity to talk because these meetings may be the only time they are all together.

• Help families to make choices most suited to their strengths and lifestyle. When working with children, involve both parents and regard them as equally important. Invite them to tell their own story, in their own words, thereby helping them discover what they know.

• Remember that the people you are serving may have different perceptions than you of health, illness, death and birth; of "the good life," adversity, success and good and bad. Take the time to understand their point of view.

• Be prepared to make a long-term commitment to those who seek your help. This is important because health care and other practitioners often come and go without ever building any kind of relationship that can make a difference.

• If you receive an offer of employment, do a careful assessment of forces that support good work as you understand it and negative forces that may constrain your chances to make a difference in the proposed job. For example, if you are expected to think and make decisions on behalf of help seekers, but are trained to mobilize self-care and responsibility, you may face resistance and possible dismissal, depending on the expectations of the chief and council as usually represented by the band or senior paid manager.

• Promote self-reflection and encourage balancing negative memories with positive ones.

Conclusion

First Nations, Inuit and Métis people are moving away from historical oppression toward self-determination and wellness. Mainstream social systems, including the Euro-Western model of mental health and addiction, do not sufficiently address Indigenous needs. Practitioners who work with First Nations, Inuit and Métis people must have a high degree of cultural competence and be willing to work with traditional healing practices unique to each community, and sometimes with other modalities to functionally integrate them with their own orientation. When First Nations, Inuit and Métis people choose to seek help, they are looking for relationships they can trust; they relate to people, not the systems that employ them. Practitioners must be willing to learn from help seekers and to remember that each person has a network that is personally significant. Harmonization of Indigenous and Western ways to address mental health and wellness challenges in Indigenous contexts can make a positive difference for both service recipients and service providers, as well as others in their respective networks.

References

Brant Castellano, M. (2005, October). *The ethical community: An anchor for identity and mental health*. Paper presented at the 2005 conference of the Canadian Association for Suicide Prevention and the National Native Mental Health Association of Canada, Ottawa.

Hyman, I. (2009). *Racism as a Determinant of Immigrant Health*. Retrieved from Metropolis website: www.metropolis.net/pdfs/racism_policy_brief_e.pdf

Ross, R. (1996). *Returning to the Teachings: Exploring Aboriginal Justice*. Toronto: Penguin Books.

Royal Commission on Aboriginal Peoples (RCAP). (1995). *Choosing Life: Special Report on Suicide among Aboriginal People*. Ottawa: Canada Communication Group.

Royal Commission on Aboriginal Peoples (RCAP). (1996). *Report of the Royal Commission on Aboriginal Peoples. Vol. 3: Gathering Strength*. Ottawa: Canada Communication Group.

Swinomish Tribal Mental Health Project. (1991). *A Gathering of Wisdoms: Tribal Mental Health—A Cultural Perspective*. LaConner, WA: Swinomish Indian Tribal Community.

ABOUT THE AUTHOR

Bill Mussell wrote this chapter drawing on his upbringing as a status First Nation person in a Coast Salish village, his volunteer work during university with the executive of the North American Indian Brotherhood and his professional work in probation, parole and post-secondary teaching. Bill was instrumental in establishing the Salishan Institute Society in 1988 and continues to serve as its principal educator. He has also provided leadership in the development of social workers, teachers, community health educators, leaders and mental health practitioners, and has filled major roles in regional and national non-governmental organizations, such as the Native Mental Health Association of Canada.

Chapter 15

Using Storytelling in Alcohol Use Intervention

CHRISTOPHER MUSHQUASH

In Canada, Aboriginal people were first exposed to alcohol by explorers, fur traders and merchants, beginning in the Eastern regions during the 1670s (Brady, 2000). Since then, alcohol has created many challenges for Aboriginal people in Canada and has greatly affected the health and well-being of our communities. These challenges have long been recognized, not only in the epidemiological data (e.g., Health Canada, 2009), but, more importantly, by Aboriginal communities themselves. The profound changes colonialism and aggressive assimilation policies forced upon Aboriginal peoples have led to a wide range of health disparities (Loppie Reading & Wien, 2009) and the use of alcohol. There has been a growth in Aboriginal-specific literature discussing mental health (e.g., Kirmayer & Valaskakis, 2009), addictive behaviours (e.g., Chansonneuve, 2007) and rebuilding and renovating alcohol prevention strategies in Aboriginal communities (e.g., Thatcher, 2004). The purpose of this chapter is to discuss ways in which health professionals and service providers can work with Aboriginal clients to help manage their alcohol use.

One could argue that Western intervention approaches alone have been insufficient. While there has been a call toward developing interventions that combine traditional Aboriginal and Western healing strategies and practices, there have until now been few clear examples of this integration in action. Combining these sometimes disparate-seeming approaches is notably complex. This chapter presents examples of the integration of storytelling with Western treatment concepts and culturally relevant metaphors. It also describes the similarities between the sacred medicine wheel and one Western conceptualization of mental health, namely, Beck's cognitive theory

(Beck, 1976). The focus here is largely on individual and group therapeutic approaches to treatment. The full continuum of services needed to help people experiencing alcohol use disorders is outside the scope of this chapter but requires equally careful consideration.

In *The Truth about Stories*, Thomas King (2003) makes the point that "the truth about stories is that that's all we are" (p. 2). One goal for alcohol treatment in our communities would be to create a new story—one that builds upon our strengths, strategies and capacities for wellness. To begin this discussion, I offer one such story, "The Boy and the Canoe":

> There was once a community, a strong and healthy community. The community had a rich history and culture. There were stories and ceremonies. There were medicines. The people in the community had learned how to live in balance and how to heal themselves when the balance was upset. Every person contributed to the wellness of the community.
>
> In this community there was a very large canoe. The canoe was so large, in fact, that all of the people in the community could travel together. Everyone had their very own paddle. The children had small paddles, the right size, so that they could help even though their hands were small and their arms were not yet strong. The adults in the community had broad paddles, so that their strength could benefit everyone. The Elders brought their knowledge and medicines on the journeys.
>
> This story is about something that happened in the community.
>
> There was a boy among these people who was well known and liked by everyone. He was adventurous and headstrong. Sometimes his youthful impulses would get the better of him and he would find himself in trouble. It was never very bad, just little things, here and there. Once, he got lost while following a group of older boys, though this story is not about that time. The community would always help the boy when he had lost his way. The Elders would have ceremonies and pray with him, and the people together would gather whatever was needed to help the boy heal.
>
> One day, as fall approached, the community was talking about how to organize themselves to travel to winter camp. They discussed the supplies they would need, when they would leave, and how long the journey would take. They discussed the importance

of listening to Mother Earth and of travelling when it was safe. That night, the boy dreamt of wonderful places far away where he could have exciting adventures. He awoke. As he lay thinking about the upcoming journey to winter camp, he felt angry. He did not like having to work to help prepare camp or the supplies for hunting trips. He did not like cutting wood and singing with the drum group. He had an idea. Before the summer camp was packed and the community ready to leave, he would take the canoe out exploring.

The boy decided he must travel alone. The Elders would not be able to paddle strong enough. They would want to bring their medicines and have ceremonies, which would slow him down. The children were too small to paddle, hunt, fish or gather supplies. Their constant singing would become tiresome. And the others would not understand what he wanted and, stronger than him, might paddle the canoe back to shore. So the boy began preparing, in secret, for his adventure. He did not talk with the Elders about his need to seek new and exciting experiences, and he did not ask others for help readying the supplies. Instead, he would do this himself, and then everyone would be impressed with his courage.

One evening, when the moon was at the top of her travels through the night sky, the boy set forth. He packed what he needed into the canoe. He quietly pushed the canoe from the shore and climbed in. The water was calm and the wind was still. The canoe seemed to drift effortlessly, the boy hardly paddling. He was pleased with himself. As he drifted to sleep, he imagined how exciting his great adventure would be.

As the morning came, the sky was dark and there was a cold wind coming from the North, which made the waters rough. It made the canoe difficult to paddle. Although his arms were tiring, the boy still had plenty of strength. He did not know that the canoe was drifting and that he was not in control of its direction. The boy realized that he was using his small-person's paddle. He grabbed another paddle from the bottom of the canoe, one that belonged to his uncle, thinking, "I am an adult now and deserve to use a big paddle."

The boy did not look back. The canoe drifted further and further away from shore. The water was getting deeper and the waves were getting more dangerous. The boy was scared but tried to be brave.

Although he did not know what he was seeking, he was sure he would find something interesting.

The boy drifted for a long time. He was using a grown person's paddle but did not have the strength to pull it through the water. He struggled to paddle, but only drifted further away. Sometimes he would think that it was time to go home. He would try to turn the canoe around. The nose of the canoe would turn slightly back toward shore, but he did not have the strength to turn the canoe all the way around. He drifted further away. Soon he found it hard to remember the faces of people from his community. He forgot the stories the Elders told. He forgot the songs that the children sang. He was very lonely and began to think about sinking the canoe so that he would not have to drift anymore.

One night, the boy awoke to great waves crashing at the canoe. A terrible storm was coming. From his canoe, it looked like the world dropped off, like a cliff, just ahead of him. The boy decided that it was time to make a great effort to change. He put down his uncle's paddle and took up his own. He accepted that it was made properly for him; it fit his hands, and he was able to paddle much better with it. He tried again to turn the canoe. It took a lot of effort. He paddled, and paddled, and paddled.

Days passed, maybe years, but the boy did not give up. Instead, when his arms were already tired from paddling, he worked even harder to turn the canoe toward shore. Turning the canoe around was the most difficult part. Little by little, stroke-by-stroke, it slowly became easier. He continued paddling toward his home. In the distance he could hear drumming and singing. The community had gathered and was calling! Now his spirit was full of energy. He could hear the songs and could smell the smoke from the fire they had lit for him. He was proud to be from such a loving community. Finally, the boy could see the fire on the shore. But he saw something else that surprised him. Many people from the community were paddling out in their own canoes to meet him. One by one, they joined him on his journey and paddled beside him. Some helped tow him ashore. With their help, the canoe was now moving very quickly. With every beat of the drum the boy became stronger. His heart beat more proudly. He knew that he was coming home.

Once they were all ashore, the community showed their love for the boy. There was dancing and feasting. As the night went on and the drums grew quiet, a group gathered in a circle with the Elders and the others in the community. They called for the boy to join them. They talked for hours. The Elders shared their medicine with him. The boy shared his feelings with the Elders and together they prepared for a new kind of journey. We should all visit this community. The people who live there have much to share with us.

The purpose of our traditional stories is to transmit knowledge in a way that is meaningful. The story of "The Boy and the Canoe" creates a narrative around addiction and the healing journey. The story introduces concepts such as community based knowledge, traditional healing practices, risk factors, responsibility, decision making, motivation, social support, relapse prevention, recovery, and community- and self-forgiveness (among others). This is one example of how to create a narrative that can share therapeutic concepts and strategies in a more engaging, relevant and memorable way than is possible through a simple listing of concepts and strategies or common psychoeducational approaches. Using storytelling as a way of introducing issues related to alcohol treatment is limited only by the imagination of the storyteller. However, it is important that this approach does not present as disingenuous. It is vital to avoid stereotypical representations of "Aboriginal stories" and to work in collaboration with clients to approach content in a personally meaningful manner. To ensure cultural relevance, consider engaging Elders and other cultural helpers within the treatment process to help develop stories to share with clients that are informed by culture, and to provide wisdom in choosing when stories might be appropriate.

Indigenous and Western Models of Health

The sacred medicine wheel, used by some First Nations, illustrates the complex interconnected relationships among the various aspects of health (see Figure 15-1). By maintaining balance across the physical, mental, emotional and spiritual domains, a person can experience wellness. The profundity of this holistic model of health must not be overlooked. Our ancestors' awareness and understanding as they observed relationships and developed this model of health are remarkable. While it is now widely accepted that wellness operates within a holistic framework (e.g., the determinants of health), this is a relatively recent development in Western medicine and, particularly, in thinking about causes and strategies to address mental health problems. Beck's (1976) cognitive theory of depression (see Figure 15-2) was derived from a clinical understanding of the relationships between thoughts, feelings and actions, and from which cognitive-behavioural therapy (CBT) emerged. I focus on CBT as an example, since it has become a commonly used intervention model. While other treatment modalities might be more appropriate for some First Nations peoples (e.g., narrative approaches), clinicians should match useful treatment modalities with client characteristics, symptoms and preferences. A cursory examination of these two models shows that there are potentially useful conceptual similarities between the mental, emotional and physical categories of the medicine wheel and the cognitive, emotional and behavioural categories of CBT.

FIGURE 15-1

Holistic Framework of Health as Represented by the Medicine Wheel

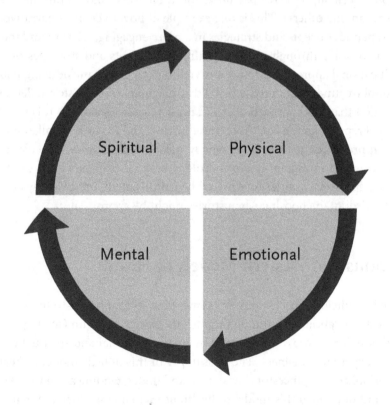

FIGURE 15-2

Beck's (1976) Cognitive Model of Depression

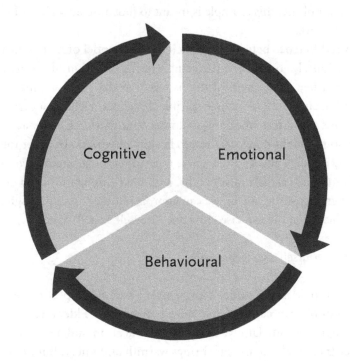

The convergence of these two models may have many potential benefits for Aboriginal people. First, CBT is a well-established, empirically tested mode of therapy that includes assessment, clinical conceptualization and treatment, with emphasis on the circular nature of evidence-based practice; that is, CBT is a highly individualized, formulation-driven approach that is continually evaluated, reassessed and reformulated as treatment proceeds (Persons et al., 2001). While the purpose here is not to present CBT methods, it is important to describe the theoretical model underpinning the approach because aspects of it may be similar to notions of balance and wellness within the medicine wheel. Where similarities exist and are validated by the appropriate cultural knowledge keepers (e.g., Elders), opportunities emerge for its use as a relevant teaching tool.

CBT is based on the idea that thoughts, feelings and actions are connected; that is, thoughts lead to emotions, which in turn lead to behaviours. It is recognized also that emotions can lead to thoughts, particularly among younger children, but may not always represent a therapeutic access point. While we may have little control over the outside world and others, we can learn to manage our thoughts in such a way as to lead to fewer negative emotions and decrease the likelihood of engaging in problematic behaviours.

For example, suppose a person has learned to cope with feelings of hopelessness by using alcohol. This person might experience negative thoughts about life, which in turn lead to low mood and feelings of hopelessness, and then drinking to feel better. This cycle will continue until the person learns healthier ways to cope with negative feelings. While simplistic, this example is meant to illustrate how alcohol use might fit into a CBT framework.

An obvious difference between a medicine wheel model of mental health and the cognitive-behavioural model is the medicine wheel's inclusion of a spiritual component. However, a key component of CBT is teaching the client coping skills, which, depending on the client, could include spiritual practices. Helping a person recognize negative thoughts that affect emotions, and intervening in such a way as to encourage positive behaviour and thinking, can lead to healthy outcomes. In order to help clients develop healthy coping skills and recognize their inherent strengths, we must convey the importance of such skills and strengths, and make opportunities to develop these skills and strengths possible. Again, we can approach these topics through storytelling and imagery, such as in the exercise "Imagine Yourself as a Teepee:"

Imagine yourself as a teepee . . .

. . . Each pole in the teepee represents a particular aspect of health. For example, we can imagine poles representing Elders' teachings, our languages, our family, clean water, education and so on. In the teepee there is also a fire. Fire brings warmth and safety. But fire is to be respected, because it can also harm.

Now, imagine removing teepee poles, one by one. First, we remove Elders' teachings. Next, we remove language, and then family support. As we continue removing different aspects of health, the teepee becomes very unstable. It is no longer in balance. Finally, it falls into the fire.

If we don't ensure that we have aspects of our health in balance, we, like the teepee, become unstable and can fall. When we feel ourselves falling, we reach out for the closest thing to brace ourselves. These closest things are our coping skills. We can also use these things as teepee poles when others have been removed, to help us maintain balance. Even when our coping skills are harmful, such as using alcohol, the coping serves as a teepee pole to keep us out of the fire. Whenever we remove a teepee pole, even if it is an unhealthy coping skill, we must ensure that we replace it with something else. Otherwise we are still at risk of upsetting the balance and of falling and reaching out for the easiest or most familiar item to grab for support.

With the metaphor of the teepee, we approach the issue of healthy coping skills, supports and personal strengths in a way that illustrates the consequences of removing previously learned coping skills. If a client uses alcohol to help manage emotions and is seeking to make changes and develop healthy ways of coping, we must work together with the client to develop new "teepee poles" that can be used to maintain balance. We may also consider opportunities to introduce traditional and spiritual healing methods as coping strategies, thus opening a dialogue within CBT on how a person might engage in cultural healing aspects and spirituality as a way of avoiding alcohol. For example, traditional practices such as drumming, singing and sweat lodge ceremonies have been used as spiritually based treatment approaches in many treatment centres in Canada.

Another promising approach to addictive behavioural change is through motivational interviewing (MI) (Miller & Rollnick, 1991). MI works to change behaviour through a client-centred approach that involves exploring ambivalence and working to resolve it. MI techniques can help clients develop insight into the discrepancy between their current state and their goals; in this case, what they want in life and how their alcohol use is related to (or compromising) their larger values. As with CBT, MI also rests upon important clinical concepts that overlap with Aboriginal healing concepts. Expressing empathy, being curious and non-judgmental, being comfortable with ambivalence, avoiding argument, being comfortable with resistance, supporting self-efficacy and asking questions without making statements are all important MI techniques and also cultural values. These therapeutic aspects again overlap with many traditional Aboriginal values and beliefs. For example, these principles are embedded in the Seven Sacred Teachings—love, respect, courage, honesty, wisdom, humility and truth—the aspirational ways of living for which many Aboriginal peoples strive. By exploring similarities between essential therapeutic skills and Aboriginal values (e.g., the Seven Sacred Teachings), or more specifically, the values of their Aboriginal clients, clinicians can develop more meaningful therapeutic relationships. Clinicians should use meaningful cultural frameworks such as the Seven Sacred Teachings to develop treatment goals with clients on their healing journey. Necessary in treatment planning is the ability of the clinician to navigate this process in a manner that is culturally appropriate and culturally sincere, while meeting the client's personal expectations and goals.

Finally, comorbid or other conditions should be carefully considered in treatment planning. Given the complex history of many Aboriginal clients, including high rates of trauma and intergenerational trauma associated with a history of residential schooling, and past and ongoing exposure to violence and abject poverty, clients understandably often have complex clinical presentations. It is not uncommon to work with clients who have had difficult experiences stemming from disrupted attachments during childhood, multiple foster placements, trauma during childhood and adulthood, and physical, emotional or sexual abuse. In some cases, problematic alcohol use presents clinically as a symptom rather than a discrete addictive disorder. While clients often present for treatment of their alcohol use problems, treatment that focuses less on the alcohol use and more on the wider range of symptoms that clients are experiencing, and on the conditions in their lives that lead them to use alcohol, may be more effective. By addressing the contributors of addictive behaviour, clinicians can decrease absolute symptom levels that predict the use of alcohol.

Moving Forward

Alcohol treatment for Aboriginal people is experiencing a practical cultural paradigm shift from disease and abstinence-based models to culturally consistent healing approaches. Continued attention to the cultural values underlying addiction treatment approaches is important. In the past, addiction prevention and treatment services in Aboriginal communities have focused on abstinence-based models—that is, on models that viewed alcohol addiction as a disease or moral failing—largely as a result of historical mainstream addiction treatment favouring this approach. Treatment has operated under the assumption that the only alternative to problematic drinking is absolute abstinence from alcohol. This treatment philosophy is probably most familiar as the Alcoholics Anonymous (AA) or 12-step approach (Alcoholics Anonymous, 2001), in which alcohol addiction is viewed as a disease a person has for life. AA encourages clients to partner with others in recovery, achieve spiritual growth and abstain from alcohol use. While this treatment program has been successful for some Aboriginal people, many find the 12-step approach unsatisfactory. For example, abstinence versus alcoholism creates a false dichotomy in which these two categories are mutually exclusive and exhaustive without acknowledging or considering alternatives. As well, some people find the 12-step programs incongruent with their traditional Aboriginal beliefs; while the idea that the AA member must surrender to a higher power to enable change and recovery allows in theory for the person's own conceptualization of that higher power, in practice, there is often a Christian focus in the program that some people may not find compatible with traditional Aboriginal spiritual beliefs, or that may be reminiscent of previous difficult experiences related to the church (e.g., residential school attendance).

More recently, there has been discussion of prevention and treatment service development within Aboriginal communities based on the philosophy of harm reduction. Harm reduction conceptualizes addiction not as a problem that is ethically or disease-based, but as a behavioural disorder, in which alcohol use exists on a continuum from abstinence to excess, with moderate and controlled drinking as an acceptable treatment outcome. The goal of this approach is to reduce the harms associated with alcohol use in a way that respects the client's personal goals for treatment. This approach recognizes that abstinence may be the ideal outcome, but that there are alternatives to reduce harm (van der Woerd et al., 2010). While some Aboriginal people may feel that harm reduction is inconsistent with traditional beliefs and values (e.g., that the use of alcohol is not part of our ways), others believe that there are similarities between the philosophies of harm reduction and traditional values, that is, in respecting the choices of individuals, families and communities, and in accepting people "where they are at" (Dell & Lyons, 2008).

While contextual information is integrated within some intervention strategies (e.g., CBT), the primary focus of Western therapeutic practices is to effect change in the individual, focusing on measureable, often dichotomous, outcomes (e.g., client X relapsed / did not relapse). This individualistic focus might be a poor fit for Aboriginal clients who identify with their culture and community in a more collective way. If treatment providers offer a dominantly Western intervention approach that makes clients uncomfortable—such as an approach that focuses too much on the individual at the expense of family and community—clients may feel that the treatment providers do not understand their experiences (or values or goals) in a way that will allow treatment to be of benefit. Such a predominantly Western approach will limit relevance and thus affect "buy-in" to the treatment. Instead, community-based and community-centred intervention approaches aimed at helping clients prevent future alcohol-related harms are promising. Under the current system (e.g., attending a treatment centre), providing community-based aftercare initiatives that support clients upon their return home is also important, and is a topic that deserves its own chapter.

Finally, possibly the most interesting and exciting development in alcohol treatment for Aboriginal people in Canada has been the development and implementation of a culturally based framework for addiction treatment on reserves: Honouring Our Strengths (Health Canada et al., 2011). This new framework emerged from a comprehensive, community-driven consultation process and outlines a continuum of care with six key elements:
• community development, prevention and health promotion
• early identification, brief intervention and aftercare
• secondary risk reduction
• active treatment
• specialized treatment
• care facilitation.

In addition, six key supports to the continuum of care are also identified in the framework:
• workforce development
• governance and co-ordination of and within systems
• addressing mental health needs
• performance measurement and research
• pharmacological approaches
• accreditation.

Perhaps most important in the development of Honouring Our Strengths was the inclusion of culture at the centre of the framework. With the implementation of this new framework, we will be able to observe benefits as the use of cultural approaches in treating addiction among Aboriginal people gains widespread acceptance and use.

Future Considerations

Spillane and Smith (2007) presented a theory of alcohol use risk for American Indian peoples living on reservations. Although flaws have been identified in their two central arguments—namely, that reservation-dwelling American Indians have higher rates of problem alcohol use than non–American Indians or those living off reservations, and that this pattern of alcohol use comes from the lack of "standard life reinforcers" (see Beals et al., 2009)—Spillane and Smith have outlined a number of limitations in previous research addressing issues related to risk factors for alcohol use. First, they highlight a historical tendency toward non-holistic measurement and research through the examination of single variables in isolation with no or very limited consideration of the role of multiple variables in drinking risk. Second, there is a lack of cultural appropriateness in that variables identified in non-Aboriginal people have been applied to Aboriginal people without a sufficient consideration of the likely contextual differences that exist between groups. A third limitation of previous research is that not enough consideration has been given to distinguishing between high average levels of drinking in Aboriginal communities and individual differences in drinking levels. That is, as a group, some communities might have relatively high levels of drinking, but among the individuals in that group, there is great variation—including non-drinkers. Finally, little distinction has been made between Aboriginal people living on reserves and those living in urban centres with respect to overall risk for alcohol use problems.

These same limitations apply to literature specific to Aboriginal peoples in Canada. While a growing amount of research is happening in our communities, it will be essential to balance the wishes of communities with the research agenda. Three major Canadian research organizations have developed a policy statement that includes policies for conducting Aboriginal health research in ethical ways (Canadian Institutes of Health Research, Natural Sciences and Engineering Research Council of Canada & Social Sciences and Humanities Research Council of Canada, 2010). The policy statement will help researchers and communities develop meaningful research relationships. This development represents a step forward for Aboriginal communities and researchers, with great promise for developing knowledge to help improve the health of Aboriginal people. Respectful dialogue and repairing strained relationships between Aboriginal communities and researchers will enable the exploration of meaningful questions to not only address the limitations in current research, but also to most benefit our communities.

Finally, the language we use to describe issues related to alcohol and addiction in our communities can convey a great deal of meaning, sometimes unintended. To that end, rather than discussing alcohol abuse within Aboriginal cultures, a more accurate focus might be on the culture of alcohol use within some Aboriginal communities. By being specific with the language while discussing ideas and developing intervention, treatment and research, we can reorient ourselves toward a more accurate understanding of the problems. This specificity should take into consideration the contexts of problematic alcohol use in communities in which we are partnered in research or delivering clinical services. Attention to the specifics creates a respectful dialogue that acknowledges the differences and challenges that exist within a community while respecting the unique conditions in which communities exist.

Conclusion

In Canada, there are many different Aboriginal groups, all with different languages and cultures. While some similarities exist, it is important to respect the diversity of our communities and not operate under the assumption that all communities are the same. Western approaches to intervention and treatment have much to offer Aboriginal healing approaches, but the opposite is also true—Aboriginal approaches have much to offer Western approaches. Only a few examples of overlap between Aboriginal healing, cognitive-behavioural approaches and motivational interviewing approaches have been presented in this chapter. However, consideration and discussion of additional approaches (e.g., narrative or other story-based methods, and culture-based approaches) are warranted and represent other potential next steps in the treatment of Aboriginal mental health and addiction. Ultimately, matching appropriate treatment modalities with appropriate clients in the context of culture and history and individual needs would represent an important shift in treatment of problematic alcohol use among Aboriginal people. There may be circumstances in which CBT approaches are inappropriate or not relevant.

Implicit in the discussion, but which must be made explicit, is the need for research to determine the effectiveness of treatment approaches with First Nations, Inuit and Métis peoples. As is often the case, service providers of all backgrounds are left wondering (at best) or not considering (at worst) whether a particular treatment is likely to be more effective or appropriate for an Aboriginal person. In the absence of careful methods and research, the risk of harm is also a concern. Carefully exploring the relationships between different approaches to treatment can provide knowledge that will benefit Aboriginal clients struggling with alcohol. Storytelling and the use of cultural metaphors can help convey important therapeutic concepts in a way that is relevant to some Aboriginal clients. Celebrating the diversity among Aboriginal peoples' experiences and acknowledging the great healing traditions within all Aboriginal cultural groups will be important in developing and maintaining meaningful relationships as we work together to improve the health of our communities.

Finally, moving away from deficits-based language and treatment programming that focuses on alcohol use disorders as a discrete phenomenon, and moving toward treatment models more congruent with our realities and our conceptualizations of health, will ensure that intervention, planning and delivery target much more than what might be simply a symptom of a number of underlying processes occurring at the individual, family, community and environmental levels. Mainstream clinical conceptualizations must be expanded to include culture-based conceptualizations of mental health and addiction. If a client or community understands that alcohol use is related to a broad set of determinants, including historical trauma, exposure to violence, poverty, oppression and individual-level variables (e.g., hopelessness), then clinicians must expand their conceptualizations and intervene in a manner that respects the wisdom in these cultural understandings. It is hoped that careful attention to community and client needs as they relate to healing from a long legacy of colonialism, as well as the current neo-colonial environment, will improve outcomes in addressing alcohol use problems and promoting wellness.

References

Alcoholics Anonymous. (2001). How it works. In *Alcoholics Anonymous: The Story of How Many Thousands of Men and Women Have Recovered from Alcoholism* (4th ed.; pp. 58–71). New York: Alcoholics Anonymous World Services.

Beals, J., Belcourt-Dittloff, A., Freedenthal, S., Kaufman, C., Mitchell, C., Whitesell, N., . . . Walters, K. (2009). Reflections on a proposed theory of reservation-dwelling American Indian alcohol use: Comment on Spillane and Smith (2007). *Psychological Bulletin, 135*, 339–343.

Beck, A.T. (1976). *Cognitive Therapy and the Emotional Disorders.* New York: International Universities Press.

Brady, M. (2000). Alcohol policy issues for indigenous people in the United States, Canada, Australia, and New Zealand. *Contemporary Drug Problems, 3*, 435–509.

Canadian Institutes of Health Research, Natural Sciences and Engineering Research Council of Canada & Social Sciences and Humanities Research Council of Canada. (2010). *Tri-Council Policy Statement: Ethical Conduct for Research Involving Humans* (2nd ed.). Retrieved from Interagency Advisory Panel on Research Ethics website: www.ethics.gc.ca

Chansonneuve, D. (2007). *Addictive Behaviours among Aboriginal People in Canada.* Retrieved from Aboriginal Healing Foundation website: www.ahf.ca

Dell, C.A. & Lyons, T. (2008). *Harm Reduction for Special Populations in Canada: Harm Reduction Policies and Programs for Persons of Aboriginal Descent.* Retrieved from Canadian Centre on Substance Abuse website: www.ccsa.ca

Health Canada. (2009). *A Statistical Profile on the Health of First Nations in Canada: Determinants of Health, 1999–2003.* Retrieved from www.hc-sc.gc.ca

Health Canada, Assembly of First Nations & National Native Addictions Partnership Foundation. (2011). *Honouring Our Strengths: A Renewed Framework to Address Substance Use Issues among First Nations People in Canada.* Retrieved from http://nnapf.com

King, T. (2003). *The Truth about Stories: A Native Narrative.* Toronto: House of Anansi Press.

Kirmayer, L.J. & Valaskakis, G.G. (Eds.). (2009). *Healing Traditions: The Mental Health of Aboriginal Peoples in Canada.* Vancouver: UBC Press.

Loppie Reading, C. & Wien, F. (2009). *Health Inequalities and Social Determinants of Aboriginal Peoples' Health.* Prince George, BC: National Collaborating Centre for Aboriginal Health.

Miller, W.R. & Rollnick, S. (1991). *Motivational Interviewing: Preparing People to Change Addictive Behaviour.* New York: Guilford Press.

Persons, J.B., Davidson, J. & Tompkins, M.A. (2001). *Essential Components of Cognitive-Behavior Therapy for Depression.* Washington, DC: American Psychological Association.

Spillane, N.S. & Smith, G.T. (2007). A theory of reservation-dwelling American Indian alcohol use risk. *Psychological Bulletin, 133*, 395–418.

Thatcher, R. (2004). *Fighting Firewater Fictions: Moving beyond the Disease Model of Alcoholism in First Nations.* Toronto: University of Toronto Press.

Van der Woerd, K.A., Cox, D.N., Reading, J. & Kmetic, A. (2010). Abstinence versus harm reduction: Considering follow-up and aftercare in First Nations addictions treatment. *International Journal of Mental Health and Addiction, 8*, 374–389.

ABOUT THE AUTHOR

Christopher Mushquash, PhD, is an assistant professor in the Department of Psychology at Lakehead University in Thunder Bay, and in the Division of Human Sciences at the Northern Ontario School of Medicine. He completed his PhD in clinical psychology at Dalhousie University, and the northern pre-doctoral residency in the Department of Clinical Health Psychology at the University of Manitoba. Dr. Mushquash is Ojibway and a member of Pays Plat First Nation. In 2013, he received the Canadian Psychological Association President's New Researcher Award for exceptional contributions to psychological knowledge in Canada. His research and clinical work focus on culturally appropriate addiction and mental health assessment and intervention for First Nations people.

Chapter 16

Fetal Alcohol Spectrum Disorder and Indigenous Peoples of Canada

CAROLINE L. TAIT*

In 1973, American researchers introduced the diagnostic category fetal alcohol syndrome (FAS) to describe birth anomalies associated with prenatal alcohol exposure (Jones & Smith, 1973). Shortly afterwards, Canadian researchers completed a handful of clinical and community-based studies (e.g., Asante & Nelms-Matzke, 1985; Robinson et al., 1987) that shaped the direction of national research and public health programs for FAS. This chapter reflects on the evolution of the diagnostic category in Canada over the past four decades and the implications this has had for First Nations and other Indigenous groups. I draw upon my FAS-related research and advisory experience and various studies I have completed with Indigenous communities and stakeholders. This chapter shares some of my observations about the "social life" of the diagnostic label FAS, analyzing the impact on Indigenous women and their children of a label that is too often applied to them within the human services sector[1] without diagnostic confirmation. I have witnessed both the benefits of a medical diagnosis of FAS, as well as the stigma, surveillance, scrutiny and personal losses experienced by Indigenous women as a result of the label. After years of research, I remain wary of arguments that make a direct correlation between rates of FAS and social problems experienced by Indigenous

* Support for the research and preparation of the manuscript was provided by CIHR grant: Technologies of potential change: Tracking the impact of Saskatchewan's Child Welfare Reform using theoretical and applied ethics. Funding reference no. EOG-115690.

1 In general, the human services sector includes education, justice, social welfare and health.

peoples, even though I agree that some Indigenous groups are at elevated risk for the illness, and that a national strategy for prevention, intervention and diagnosis is required in any country where prenatal alcohol exposure is a health issue.

What Is Fetal Alcohol Spectrum Disorder?

The umbrella term fetal alcohol spectrum disorder (FASD) refers to a subgroup of related conditions including fetal alcohol syndrome (FAS), partial FAS (PFAS) and alcohol-related neurodevelopment disorders (ARND) (Chudley et al., 2005). While distinct diagnostic criteria exist for each condition, they are all caused by prenatal alcohol exposure, with binge drinking and alcohol dependence being strong indicators of elevated risk. Using the broader term FASD is consistent with the observation that prenatal alcohol-related effects exist along a continuum from mild to severe birth defects. Despite the introduction of clinical guidelines (Chudley et al. 2005), controversy remains about the threshold levels at which alcohol exposure becomes dangerous to the developing fetus and about whether alcohol exposure alone is sufficient to cause the observed effects (Abel, 1998). The hallmark features of FAS are a characteristic set of facial features, evidence of growth deficiency and evidence of structural or organic brain dysfunction. Of these anomalies, the "facial gestalt" is thought to be clinically unique, and central nervous system dysfunction the most significant effect (Stratton et al., 1996).

Consistent application of the classifications across clinical settings has historically proven to be difficult (Abel, 1998). For example, clinicians had trouble distinguishing between cognitive and behavioural effects caused by prenatal alcohol exposure and those resulting from disorders with similar expressions, or from children being exposed repeatedly to negative environmental factors. Growth retardation was also linked to other risk factors, such as maternal tobacco use and poor maternal nutrition, while the facial features of FAS were found to occur naturally in certain populations, including some Indigenous populations (Abel, 1998). Because of diagnostic challenges, significant attention focused on identifying biological and behavioural markers specific to FASD, standardizing clinical guidelines and obtaining widespread consensus of best practice approaches for identification, prevention and treatment across the lifespan. While notable gains have been made in understanding FASD, these challenges continue to preoccupy FASD research, diagnostics and treatment.

In Canada, several barriers exist in assessing FASD. These include the high costs of assessment, a shortage of trained diagnostic teams and some local or regional settings where physicians are less familiar with FASD and therefore do not feel comfortable making a diagnosis. The recent inclusion of FAS in the *Diagnostic and Statistical Manual of Mental Disorders* (American Psychiatric Association, 2013) has increased the attention of psychiatrists to FASD, as collectively they have been slower than other specialties to embrace the diagnosis in their assessments. While diagnostics have improved, barriers to assessment, particularly for adolescents and adults, suggest that most people with FASD are never diagnosed (Tait, 2009). For Indigenous and other groups living in rural and remote areas, added barriers exist, including high travel costs for attending assessments and follow-up treatment, and a lack of local interventions and supports that may be more readily available in urban centres.

Epidemiology of FASD in Indigenous Populations

In Canada, as in all parts of the world, it has been difficult to determine prevalence and incidence rates of FAS and, more generally, FASD. This difficulty is due, in part, to the diagnostic challenges associated with assessment at birth and over the lifespan, as well as to the absence of a strong, Canadian-based epidemiological understanding of FASD. Estimates for Canada are based on U.S. prevalence and incidence rates, themselves drawn from only a handful of studies. Furthermore, the data that is based in Canada is mainly drawn from studies targeting First Nations populations.

With the introduction of the FAS diagnosis in the 1970s, Canadian researchers focused their attention on clinical populations with high numbers of Indigenous children and on First Nations communities. Developmental pediatricians led these studies (Asante & Nelms-Matzke, 1985; Robinson et al., 1987), and while they drew attention to the risks of maternal alcohol use problems in First Nations in northern regions, their focus ignored data showing that a larger percentage of non-Indigenous women in Canada used alcohol (e.g., Addiction Research Foundation of Ontario, 1996; Poole, 1997; Statistics Canada, 1993), and that First Nations women made up only a small percentage of the overall female Canadian population at risk. In contrast to the research focus in Canada, American researchers emphasized the "democratization" of FASD to illustrate how, regardless of ethnic, racial and socio-economic status, all pregnant women who drank alcohol were at equal risk for giving birth to a child with FASD (Armstrong & Abel, 2000; Tait, 2003a).

By the late 1990s, information coming from the media, health promotion and public health messaging, and national and international FASD conferences linked FASD to elevated social problems in Indigenous populations. High rates of suicide, violence, sexual assault, unemployment, school dropout, teen pregnancy, gang involvement and incarceration were increasingly attributed to cognitive and behavioural problems caused by FASD playing out at a population level (Dophin, 2002; Roberts, 1998). A circular argument emerged, whereby the existence of individual and social "dysfunction" experienced by Indigenous peoples who had lived through generations of colonial assaults, including the residential school system, was invoked as evidence that rates of FASD were extremely high in this population (reserve, remote and urban). In turn, FASD was used as an explanatory framework for the elevated rates of individual and social "dysfunction" found among the same populations, while ignoring the negative impact of colonization. This unfair inference of a direct causal link between FASD and social problems in Indigenous populations occurred in contexts where medical assessments for FASD were virtually absent and fuelled perceptions that rates of FASD in Indigenous communities were out of control. In one example, a leading American researcher, citing a study conducted in a First Nation community in Canada, went so far as to suggest that a given population would experience a loss of culture—the very essence of what it means to be human—if FASD rates were high enough (Streissguth, 1997).

As knowledge about FASD grew, researchers and clinicians pushed for government recognition that a health crisis was unfolding in Indigenous communities across the country. Curiously, the same researchers paid virtually no attention to prenatal alcohol exposure and the occurrence of FASD in the general population. This bias has shaped Canadian research of FASD and in turn has influenced government policies, public health strategies and health care systems across the country.

By the early 1990s, as the risks associated with prenatal alcohol exposure became better known, Indigenous peoples, specifically in Western Canada, took ownership of the problem, seeking answers about local incidence and prevalence rates. Because there were few, if any, individuals medically assessed for FASD in most Indigenous communities, speculation about who had the illness was common. This was partially fuelled by federal government funding that asked First Nations communities to define and estimate their problems and incidences of FASD in order to access funding (Tait, 2009). Local negotiations of the problem included lay estimates of FASD rates, non-medical labelling of individuals suspected of having FAS and "train the trainer" programs that left human services sector workers believing FASD was an epidemic in Indigenous communities. Added to the growing concern about FAS rates was a public health message warning that all levels of prenatal alcohol were dangerous to the developing fetus. In some instances, claims were made that upwards of 50 per cent of children in certain First Nations communities were alcohol affected (Square, 1997). Such claims were used to support calls by Indigenous health care leaders for more government funding (although funding was not necessarily forthcoming), and provided an explanation for individual and social dysfunction—which, supposedly, could be alleviated in a single generation if pregnant women abstained from alcohol (Tait, 2003b, 2007). Governments seemed to respond to the calls with great concern, creating expert committees and allocating funding for prevention, intervention and diagnosis. However, the amount of funding was limited, piecemeal and short-term, and no national strategy emerged.

The "G" Case and FASD Prevention

Already marginalized because of poverty, stigma and racism, Indigenous women receiving social assistance have been hardest hit by the negative societal backlash of a

public health message describing FASD as 100 per cent preventable. The backlash escalated in 1997 when the Supreme Court of Canada agreed to hear the case of "Ms. G"
(*Winnipeg Child and Family Services [Northwest Area] v. G. [D.F.]*, 1997), a pregnant
First Nation woman who lived in Winnipeg. Ms. G was a chronic glue sniffer, and as
a result of her addiction, all of her children had been permanently removed from her
care by child and family services. Knowing about her current pregnancy, child welfare
workers convinced Ms. G to enter residential addiction treatment; however, a bed
could not be secured until four days later, at which time Ms. G changed her mind
about going into treatment. This sparked a series of court requests by child and family
services that Ms. G be detained and mandated to attend residential treatment. The
case eventually made its way to the Supreme Court, where various interveners argued
for and against court-ordered treatment. For the most part, the arguments focused on
whether the courts recognized the rights of the fetus, and because prenatal glue sniffing
was not attached to identified birth defects, FAS became the medical diagnostic basis
upon which arguments for court-mandated treatment were made (Tait, 2009).

The Supreme Court ruled against court-mandated addiction treatment or other
forms of detainment for pregnant women, upholding previous rulings that the fetus
was not a person and therefore could not be afforded the same protections given to
Canadian citizens. Yet despite the ruling, the case became a lightning rod for public
opinion, and an undeniable unease (and at times outrage) grew across the country and
across the political spectrum as Canadians became increasingly aware of the risks associated with prenatal alcohol and other drug exposure (Wente, 2000, 2001). Journalist
reports of the "G" case, such as those of Chisholm (1996) and Coyne (1997), solidi-
fied the link between prenatal substance use problems and Indigenous women in the
imagination of the Canadian public. This was then extended to government bureau-
crats in health and social services ministries, who through policies and interventions
reinforced the idea that Indigenous women basically defined the category of women at
risk for giving birth to a child with FASD. In a new, albeit familiar, way, disadvantaged
Indigenous women were conceived as being a great risk to their children's well-being—
a risk that not only left their children disabled for life, but was defined as being "100
per cent preventable." This message ushered in a new era of increased surveillance and
regulation of the behaviour of Indigenous women, perpetuating trauma and stigma
across generations (Tait, 2003b).[2]

Fortunately, after the Supreme Court struck down court-mandated treatment,
provincial and territorial health regions prioritized pregnant women for residential
and other forms of addiction treatment. Less positively, child and family service
agencies pursued their own "preventative" measures to coerce pregnant women to
accept addiction treatment. Pregnant women (particularly those on social assistance

---

2   Historically, Indigenous women and men have been portrayed as unfit parents by settler society. For example, government
policies that facilitated the removal of generations of Indigenous children to residential schools were based upon the premise
that Indigenous parents could not raise their children properly. The "'60s scoop" began decades of high rates of placement of
Indigenous children in foster and adoptive homes by government child welfare agencies, a practice that continues to this day.

who were identified as using substances) in different parts of the country were told that their babies would be apprehended at birth if they did not complete addiction treatment. If they were parenting other children, actual or threatened apprehension of these children was used as leverage to "urge" them into treatment (Tait, 2000, 2003a). In many instances, residential treatment consisted of 28-day programs, which ended prior to the woman giving birth. While women were encouraged to attend aftercare treatment, this was not always available, and even if it was, the women generally returned to the same circumstances they left before treatment. In some instances, fears of apprehension resulted in "high-risk" women concealing their pregnancies by avoiding addiction outreach and prenatal services entirely. For other women, the threat or actual apprehension of their children escalated their substance use, thereby increasing the risk to the pregnancy (Tait, 2000, 2003b).

The moral panic that grew in the media and within federal, provincial and territorial health and child and family services departments as the "G" case unfolded did not translate into meaningful expansion of addiction services for pregnant women at highest risk, that is, those who are alcohol dependent and those who regularly binge drink (Tait, 2008). Almost two decades after the "G" case, Canada has realized some significant gains in primary prevention of FASD, but sadly, all levels of government have failed to provide appropriate interventions to meet the needs of pregnant women who are most at risk, whether Indigenous or not. While there are certainly areas of promise and success in FASD prevention and treatment, addiction services for all women in Canada continue to be underfunded, underdeveloped and under-resourced, and in some cases they simply do not exist at all (Dell & Roberts, 2005; Poole, 1997; Tait, 2003a).

Prevention of FASD

For Indigenous populations, the profile of alcohol use characteristically features a large population of abstainers and a smaller population of individuals who are alcohol dependent or engage in regular binging. In this latter group, use of tobacco and illegal drugs is high, as is engagement in a high-risk lifestyle, where individuals are susceptible to violence, accidental injury, sexually transmitted diseases and endemic poverty (Poole, 2007; Tait, 2003a). These factors contribute to poor birth outcomes, as well as to compromised maternal health and risk of premature maternal death (Abel, 1998).

The consensus in the research literature is that women at greatest risk for giving birth to a child with FASD are either alcohol dependent or frequent binge drinkers (Abel, 1998; Dell & Roberts, 2005; Roberts & Nanson, 2000). When a woman has other risk factors—advanced maternal age, having given birth more than twice, previous birth of a child with FASD, poor nutrition, chronic poverty, little or no prenatal care, insecure housing, domestic violence, social isolation and alcohol-related illness—the probability that she will deliver a child with FASD rises significantly (Abel, 1998). Risk can be compounded further for Indigenous women due to geographical isolation and remoteness; governmental jurisdictional barriers and disputes over health care; involvement with the criminal justice system; racism and stigma; and structural and psychological barriers that prevent women from accessing or completing addiction treatment and receiving appropriate aftercare supports (Tait, 2000, 2003b). Prevention strategies that target women at highest risk, whether or not they are Indigenous, would significantly reduce incidence rates of FASD. A first step in this effort would include expanding addiction treatment strategies that address structural and geographical barriers and bolster services specifically for this subgroup of women. Fortunately, Canada has a sound research base that is informed by addiction workers and front-line experts, and by the voices of the women themselves (Dell & Roberts, 2005; Poole, 2007; Tait, 2000). Unfortunately, however, co-ordination and improvement of services for this high-risk population has been piecemeal and is characterized by pilot projects or short-term initiatives (Poole, 2007; Tait, 2000, 2008). Exceptions do exist, for example, in Vancouver, Toronto and Winnipeg; however, in general, support services and inter-ventions lack sufficient and sustainable funding required to significantly decrease rates of FASD and improve maternal health.

Factors that may not be considered in this context by government policy-makers and health ministries are the myriad of problems that pregnant women most at risk for substance use problems commonly deal with. Residential treatment is based on the philosophy that intense therapy and support in a safe and secure environment gives pregnant women an opportunity to address their substance use problems, decrease their stress and focus on being healthy and having a healthy baby. However, entering residential treatment does not mean that the stressors and commitments that preg-nant women have cease to need their attention. For example, pregnant women can be regularly pulled away from residential therapy because of the need to keep medical appointments, meet with their social worker or the social worker(s) of their children, consult lawyers about custody issues or outstanding charges and attend court. Dealing simultaneously with these issues and with needing to schedule required appointments and find transportation to and from them not only pulls women out of treatment, but can contribute to relapse, increased stress and other mental health problems. In many programs, pregnant women who relapse are asked to leave treatment, just like any other residential client.

PREVENTION OF FASD THROUGH CONTRACEPTION

In the 1990s, FASD prevention strategies targeting impoverished Indigenous women expanded to include pregnancy prevention. Depo-Provera became the contraception of choice for "at-risk" Indigenous women because it involved a single injection every three months. Unlike more active forms of contraception such as birth control pills, which women must take daily, or condoms, the use of which must be negotiated each time a woman has sex, Depo-Provera involves passive decision making by Indigenous women in their reproductive health. Health care providers commonly advise its use rather than other forms of contraception because they believe Depo-Provera is a more effective resource for preventing both pregnancy and FASD. However, as a prevention option, Depo-Provera does not prevent sexually transmitted infections, nor does it compel governments to expand addiction services for women (Tait, 2003b).

A second, more permanent strategy is to offer women tubal ligation right after they give birth. The timing of the offer and the gravity of the decision ignores the fact that women may agree to sterilization out of a sense of guilt and shame about their substance use and the prenatal impact on their newborn (Tait, 2000, 2003b). Important to note is that pressure placed on women to agree to sterilization is not necessarily accompanied by pressure (or even suggestion) by health and social workers to begin addiction treatment as an alternative preventative measure (Tait, 2000, 2013). Some Indigenous women in long-term addiction recovery who agreed to a tubal ligation when they were using reported experiencing severe loss and regret about their decision once their lives stabilized (Tait, 2000, 2003b). For women who "agree" to sterilization, not having children in their care or ever becoming pregnant again makes them essentially invisible to health and social service programming unless they experience a severe health crisis (Poole, 1997; Tait, 2000, 2003b, 2013). Consequently, premature death due to alcohol-related illness or violence increases dramatically for these women if they do not have support to seek services for addiction, mental health and other needs (Abel, 1998; Fournier & Crey, 1997; Tait, 2003b). Coercive practices, even if they are believed to be justifiable, can have enormous negative impacts, particularly on Indigenous women who are overrepresented in the social welfare system (Poole, 1997; Tait, 2000, 2003b, 2013). While family planning is essential in supporting these women, it must be done within an ethical context that recognizes their vulnerabilities, autonomy and rights as health care consumers.

BEST PRACTICE MODELS

As with other populations, FASD prevention in Indigenous populations is complex. Experiences within Indigenous communities illustrate that pregnancy is an opportune time to work with women, particularly through the creation of culturally safe and supportive environments that respect the woman as a mother-to-be, and include her ideas and input in determining what will work for her in reducing her substance use (Poole, 1997, 2007; Tait, 2000). While best practice models have been identified, their implementation has not always been smooth (Tait, 2008). Problems arise when government funders fail to provide appropriate funding, training and timelines for Indigenous communities to set up, run and evaluate programs (Tait, 2000, 2008). As well, Indigenous health care leaders and front-line workers report that they and the vulnerable populations they serve are set up for failure when governments do not adhere to evidence-based guidelines for implementing best practice models when they plan funding (Tait, 2008; Tait & Cuthand, 2011a, 2011b), or when they fail to allow time and resources to create or modify interventions so they are culturally appropriate and effective.

Unfortunately, there are no measures within government policies that require adherence to evidence-based guidelines or to practices that are accountable to program recipients and their communities. As a result, government departments are free to modify best practice models based on their funding and timeline constraints. The resultant watering down of best practice models that can occur raises serious ethical questions about the potential harm to vulnerable populations (Tait, 2008). For example, if the length or components of a particular program are modified to suit funding or time constraints, there is a risk of losing the very essence of what makes that program fit a best practice model (Tait, 2008). Further, such modifications mean that it is highly unlikely that opportunities will be made available to adapt programming to suit local needs (e.g., adequately adapting an urban-based model to a rural or remote setting). Key questions arise within this context: are vulnerable individuals and communities placed at unacceptable risk when government departments modify evidence-based prevention and intervention models for FASD or other illnesses? Are government departments capable of weighing the therapeutic (biomedical or Indigenous knowledge) implications when they decide to modify or "water down" an evidence-based or best practice model?

A further consideration is the co-ordination (or lack thereof) between addiction, mental health and outreach supports with social and child welfare, and justice systems. For more than a decade, researchers have illustrated a clear link between adversarial child welfare practices (and related involvement with the justice system) and increased substance use by pregnant women, arguing that co-ordinated efforts that support pregnant women to parent their children is a "best practice" measure to prevent FASD (Poole, 1997, 2007; Tait, 2000, 2003a, 2003b, 2007).

Prevention of FASD has been a public health priority in most rural, reserve and urban Indigenous communities for the better part of three decades. When given the opportunity, First Nations, Inuit and Métis have built upon their existing culturally based programming in addiction and maternal and child health, and interwoven FASD prevention into the continuum of care for pregnant women and women dealing with substance use problems. Over the years, federal, provincial and territorial governments have granted funding for a range of initiatives that span primary, secondary and tertiary care. These include poster prevention campaigns, education workshops, training for front-line prevention workers and mentoring models of relational care for women. On many occasions, Indigenous people have successfully modified outside programming to reflect local cultural beliefs, practices and priorities, and socio-environmental circumstances. However, they point out that significant gaps and barriers exist in tertiary prevention. These are in part due to governments prioritizing primary and secondary prevention initiatives that target *all* pregnant women, rather than prioritizing and investing in more specialized (and prolonged) services targeting pregnant women struggling with binge drinking and addiction (Poole, 1997; Tait, 2003b, 2007).

Living with FASD[3]

The research, public health and lay literature commonly describe living with FASD as a lifelong sentence of limited potential characterized by psychological, emotional and social suffering (Barnett, 1997; Boland et al., 1998, 2000; Conry & Fast, 2000; Koptie, 2013). Unfortunately, individuals diagnosed with FASD are often marked by multiple risk factors beginning at birth and continuing into adulthood. Some of the most devastating early environmental factors include an unstable home life in which the child experiences neglect or abuse, abandonment, multiple foster placements and a lack of support programming in school and at home. For individuals experiencing these risk factors, FASD over the lifespan can be one of a number of negative factors affecting their quality of life (Koptie, 2013). Other factors can include mental health stressors and disorders such as chronic anxiety, schizophrenia, bipolar disorder, conduct or attention-deficit disorders, hyperactivity, depression, low self-esteem, substance use problems and poor social networks (Streissguth, 1997; Streissguth et al., 1997).

Although life can be difficult for people with FASD, quality of life can be improved through early diagnosis and intervention, a stable home environment and adequate educational and social supports (Fuchs et al., 2010; Streissguth, 1997; Streissguth et al., 1997). There is better access to supports in urban than in rural or reserve communities, but in all contexts more supports are needed. It is unclear whether other socio-environmental factors, such as a strong cultural identity and involvement in cultural and spiritual practices, community involvement and supports, and extended kinship ties, play a role in positive outcomes. Also, there is a limited understanding about whether and to what degree FASD symptoms and the associated stigma exacerbate or dissipate risk in different social settings. These gaps call for further research in order to enhance supports for Indigenous people with FASD.

Parenting a child with FASD can be challenging for biological parents with insufficient supports and for foster or adoptive parents who are either unaware of the child's condition or have no experience in parenting a child with FASD. Due to increased awareness and better diagnostic tools, screening and assessment for FASD in newborns and children is occurring more frequently. Early assessment and diagnosis, combined with proper support for the child and parents, have been shown to produce better short- and long-term outcomes (Fuchs et al., 2010; Streissguth 1997; Streissguth

---

3   I purposely do not discuss Indigenous community interventions for people with FASD because these are varied and for the most part unevaluated. In most instances, interventions are also co-located with other supports for children, youth and adults with developmental and behavioural problems, reflecting the necessity experienced by Indigenous health care decision-makers to take a global (and pragmatic) approach to support, given the multiple and varied needs of their people and the chronic under-resourcing of mental health and addiction services.

et al., 1997). When children with FASD are not diagnosed, their condition can be mistaken for "bad" or inappropriate behaviour, and this misunderstanding can be extremely frustrating and confusing for parents, teachers and other caregivers. Living without a diagnosis can be just as frustrating and difficult for the individual, no matter what age. Depending on the severity of the illness and the compounding health and environmental factors, people with FASD face a daily struggle, with problems escalating as they age. The strain on parents and other family members can be enormous without a diagnosis to help them understand the causes underlying their loved ones' struggles, and how best to support them.

That said, unless proper supports are in place, the utility of a diagnosis is limited, if not meaningless. The biggest challenge facing health care professionals and caregivers is providing supports specifically tailored to people who have FASD, particularly those who live in remote and isolated communities and/or in situations of extreme poverty and social disruption. Without proper supports, the risk factors for such children are compounded. As they grow into adolescence and adulthood, they and their caregivers are placed at significant risk to experience a range of problems that become increasingly difficult to address. In relation to larger societal costs, upfront investment in FASD prevention and early diagnosis and intervention will not only yield significant financial benefit, but will also garner more positive individual, family and societal gains.

Conclusion

While alcohol can affect the health of a developing fetus, FASD has evolved as a label that stigmatizes and further marginalizes Indigenous women, their children and their communities. Making a direct causal link between FASD and the social suffering manifested in high rates of Indigenous poverty, family instability, alcohol use problems and incarceration ignores the historical conditions that have shaped the present-day context in which Indigenous peoples live. FASD is but one (and certainly not a primary one) of many factors that contribute to social ills found only among a subgroup of First Nations, Inuit and Métis.

In truth, the story of FASD in Canada is interwoven with the history of Indigenous peoples and settler society (Tait, 2003a, 2013). In our efforts to understand the illness, we cannot ignore this broader context because it reveals the increased medicalization of Indigenous social suffering on the part of governments, special interest groups and the medical community. As a category, FASD should never be used as a sweeping explanatory framework to explain away processes of colonization, Western imperialism, structural violence and their resulting outcomes. To do so negates the history of Indigenous peoples and instead places responsibility and blame on Indigenous women.

While we must make every effort to prevent FASD and to assist those who suffer from this illness, we also need a balanced approach to address this problem, one that is grounded in the expertise and knowledge of Indigenous peoples and the experiences of women struggling with addiction and people living with FASD. Indeed, my research has examined how First Nations and Métis peoples have taken hold of the problem of FAS and emerged as national leaders in prevention and intervention supports. When combined with knowledge from these individuals and communities of expertise, appropriate government commitment, as well as treatment and support founded in evidence-based practice, will go a long way in addressing the problem of FASD.

Finally, provision of programs and services across the continuum of care must be grounded in ethical policies and practices that consider first and foremost the protection of those most vulnerable. Each time a policy or programming decision for FASD prevention or intervention services is made, policy-makers must ask the following questions:

• How will this policy or program affect the lives of those most vulnerable?
• What supports must be in place to ensure that no harm comes to those targeted by this policy and program?
• How can clients be protected from harm at moments of transition out of programs that provide support to them?

Thoughtfully developed ethical policies and programs will translate into better outcomes for at-risk women, their children and their communities, whether Indigenous or not.

References

Abel, E.L. (1998). *Fetal Alcohol Abuse Syndrome*. New York: Plenum Press.

Addiction Research Foundation of Ontario. (1996). *The Hidden Majority: A Guidebook on Alcohol and Other Drug Issues for Counsellors Who Work with Women*. Toronto: Author.

American Psychiatric Association. (2013). *Diagnostic and Statistical Manual of Mental Disorders* (5th ed.). Washington, DC: Author.

Armstrong, E.M. & Abel, E.L. (2000). Fetal alcohol syndrome: The origins of a moral panic. *Alcohol & Alcoholism, 35*, 276–282. DOI: 10.1093/alcalc/35.3.276

Asante, K.O. & Nelms-Matzke, J. (1985). *Report on the Survey of Children with Chronic Handicaps and Fetal Alcohol Syndrome in the Yukon and Northwest British Columbia*. Ottawa: Health and Welfare Canada.

Barnett, C.C. (1997). A judicial perspective on FAS: Memories of the making of Nanook of the North. In A.P. Streissguth & J. Kanter (Eds.), *The Challenges of Fetal Alcohol Syndrome: Overcoming Secondary Disabilities* (pp. 134–145). Seattle: University of Washington Press.

Boland, F.J., Burrill, R., Duwyn, M. & Karp, J. (1998). *Fetal Alcohol Syndrome: Implications for Correctional Service*. Ottawa: Correctional Service Canada.

Boland, F.J., Duwyn, M. & Serin, R. (2000). Fetal alcohol syndrome: Understanding its impact. *Forum on Correctional Research, 12* (1), 16–18.

Chisholm, P. (1996, August 19). Does a fetus have rights? *Maclean's,* 16–19.

Chudley, A.E., Conry, J., Cook, J.L., Loock, C., Rosales, T. & LeBlanc, N. (2005). Fetal alcohol spectrum disorder: Canadian guidelines for diagnosis. *Canadian Medical Association Journal, 172*, S2–S21.

Conry, J. & Fast, D.K. (2000). *Fetal Alcohol Syndrome and the Criminal Justice System*. Vancouver: Fetal Alcohol Syndrome Resource Society & Law Foundation of British Columbia.

Coyne, A. (1997, November 4). Court's conundrum. *Montreal Gazette*, p. B3.

Dell, C.A. & Roberts, G. (2005). *Alcohol Use and Pregnancy: An Important Canadian Public Health and Social Issue*. Ottawa: Health Canada.

Dophin, R. (2002, June 11). No simple solutions to Native problems. *Calgary Herald*, p. A9.

Fournier, S. & Crey, E. (1997). *Stolen from Our Embrace: The Abduction of First Nations Children and the Restoration of Aboriginal Communities*. Toronto: Douglas & McIntyre.

Fuchs, D., Burnside, L., Marchenski, S. & Mudry, A. (2010). Children with FASD-related disabilities receiving services from child welfare agencies in Manitoba. *International Journal of Mental Health & Addiction, 8*, 232–244. DOI: 10.1007/s11469-009-9258-5

Jones, K.L. & Smith, D.F. (1973). Recognition of the fetal alcohol syndrome in early infancy. *The Lancet, 2*, 999–1001.

Koptie, S. (2013). Alcohol is a great destroyer: A call for insight on ceremonial approaches for coping with FASD. *First Peoples Child & Family Review, 8* (1), 17–24.

Poole, N. (1997). *Alcohol and Other Drug Problems and BC Women: A Report to the Minister of Health from the Minister's Advisory Council on Women's Health*. Victoria, BC: Ministry of Health & Ministry Responsible for Seniors.

Poole, N. (2007). Policy highlight: A women-centred framework for the prevention of fetal alcohol spectrum disorder. In N. Poole & L. Greaves (Eds.), *Highs and Lows: Canadian Perspectives on Women and Substance Abuse* (pp. 289–298). Toronto: Centre for Addiction and Mental Health.

Roberts, D. (1998, November 2). Native murder rate in Manitoba alarming, study shows. *Globe and Mail*, p. A3.

Roberts, G. & Nanson, J. (2000). *Best Practices: Fetal Alcohol Syndrome / Fetal Alcohol Effects and the Effects of Other Substance Use during Pregnancy*. Ottawa: Health Canada.

Robinson, G.C., Conry, J.L. & Conry, R.F. (1987). Clinical profile and prevalence of fetal alcohol syndrome in an isolated community in British Columbia. *Canadian Medical Association Journal, 137*, 203–207.

Square, D. (1997). Fetal alcohol syndrome epidemic on Manitoba reserve. *Canadian Medical Association Journal, 157*, 59–60.

Statistics Canada. (1993). *Language, Tradition, Health, Lifestyle and Social Issues*. (Catalogue no. 89-533-XPB). Ottawa: Ministry of Industry.

Stratton, K., Howe, C. & Battaglia, F.C. (Eds.). (1996). *Fetal Alcohol Syndrome: Diagnosis, Epidemiology, Prevention, and Treatment*. Washington, DC: National Academy Press.

Streissguth, A.P. (1997). *Fetal Alcohol Syndrome: A Guide for Families and Communities*. Toronto: Paul H. Brooks.

Streissguth, A.P., Barr, H.M., Kogan, J. & Bookstein, F.L. (1997). Primary and secondary disabilities in fetal alcohol syndrome. In A.P. Streissguth & J. Kanter (Eds.), *The Challenge of Fetal Alcohol Syndrome: Overcoming Secondary Disabilities* (pp. 25–39). Seattle: University of Washington Press.

Tait, C.L. (2000). *A Study of the Service Needs of Pregnant Addicted Women in Manitoba*. Winnipeg, MB: Prairie Women's Health Centre of Excellence.

Tait, C.L. (2003a). *Fetal Alcohol Syndrome among Canadian Aboriginal Peoples: Review and Analysis of the Intergenerational Links to Residential Schools*. Retrieved from Aboriginal Healing Foundation website: www.ahf.ca

Tait, C.L. (2003b). *The Tip of the Iceberg: The "Making" of Fetal Alcohol Syndrome in Canada*. (Unpublished doctoral dissertation). McGill University, Montreal, Quebec. Retrieved from McGill

University website: www.mcgill.ca/files/namhr/Tait-2003.pdf

Tait, C.L. (2007). *A Critical Analysis of Fetal Alcohol Spectrum Disorder(s) Prevention in Canadian First Nations Communities*. Prepared for the Assembly of First Nations, Ottawa.

Tait, C.L. (2008). Ethical programming: Toward a community-centred approach to mental health and addiction programming in Aboriginal communities. *Pimatisiwin: A Journal of Indigenous and Aboriginal Community Health, 6* (1), 29–60.

Tait, C.L. (2009). Disruptions in nature, disruptions in society: Indigenous peoples of Canada and the "making" of fetal alcohol syndrome. In L.J. Kirmayer & G. Valaskakis (Eds.), *Healing Traditions: The Mental Health of Aboriginal Peoples in Canada* (pp. 196–220). Vancouver: UBC Press.

Tait, C.L. (2013). Resituating the ethical gaze: Government morality and the local worlds of impoverished Indigenous women. *International Journal for Circumpolar Health*, 72. DOI: 10.3402/ijch. v72i0.21207

Tait, C.L. (Writer/Producer) & Cuthand, D. (Producer). (2011a). *Child Welfare: Do You Find This Unethical, Partner?* [Motion picture]. Saskatoon, SK: Blue Hill Productions.

Tait, C.L. (Writer/Producer) & Cuthand, D. (Producer). (2011b). *Child Welfare: The State as Parent* [Motion picture]. Saskatoon, SK: Blue Hill Productions.

Wente, M. (2000, October 7). Our poor ruined babies: The hidden epidemic. *Globe and Mail*, p. A17.

Wente, M. (2001, February 1). Finally, we're talking about FAS. *Globe and Mail*, p. A13.

Winnipeg Child and Family Services (Northwest Area) v. G. (D.F.), [1997] 3 S.C.R. 925. Retrieved from http://scc.lexum.org/decisia-scc-csc/scc-csc/scc-csc/en/item/1562/index.do

ABOUT THE AUTHOR

Caroline Tait, PhD, is an associate professor in the Department of Psychiatry at the University of Saskatchewan. She received her PhD in medical anthropology from McGill University in Montreal in 2003 and completed post-doctoral studies in the Division of Social and Transcultural Psychiatry in 2004. She is the recipient of individual and interdisciplinary team grants in the areas of FASD prevention, ethics, ethics and child welfare, knowledge translation, Indigenous mental health and addiction, resilience and community-based research. She is Métis from MacDowall, Saskatchewan.

Chapter 17

Prescription Opioid Misuse

JONATHAN RAJEEVAN BERTRAM

The misuse of prescription drugs, particularly opioids, is a growing health problem worldwide. Since the mid-1990s, both therapeutic use and misuse of prescription opioids in Canada have grown exponentially, along with the rates of harms associated with misuse. Opioid misuse occurs across the general population and in all age groups, but it is especially prevalent in some Aboriginal communities (Webster, 2013). The reasons are complex and involve many variables. The historical trauma, dislocation, disempowerment and socio-economic disparities experienced by Aboriginal peoples related to colonization play a central role in this vulnerability to substance use disorders. Solutions to opioid misuse must be multi-dimensional and involve individuals, communities, the medical profession and health services and government.

Opioids and Harms Related to Misuse

Opioids are a family of drugs used primarily for pain relief. They include the opiates, morphine, codeine and thebaine, which are natural alkaloids found in the opium poppy; semi-synthetic opioids, such as heroin, oxycodone and hydromorphone, which are derived from opiates; and synthetic opioids, such as fentanyl and methadone. Opioids bind to receptor molecules on the surface of nerve cells in the brain and reduce the perception of pain.

When opioids are prescribed and used appropriately, they are valuable therapeutic tools for people experiencing pain, but they also have a high potential for harm. Opioids can produce strong feelings of euphoria, cause sedation and slow down breathing. Taking too large a dose can cause breathing to stop, and the danger of overdose increases when opioids are combined with other drugs, especially alcohol or benzodiazepines. Opioids are usually used orally or transdermally in clinical settings; the risk of overdose increases when opioids are taken in other ways, such as snorting, crushing or injecting.

Overdose, accidental death and suicide, fetal exposure and increased risks of hepatitis C and HIV/AIDS are some of the harms related to opioid misuse. In some First Nations communities, misuse has led to increased crime, violence, family breakdown, spousal and child abuse or neglect, and overall community deterioration (Chiefs of Ontario, 2010).

Demographics

Canada has the second-highest per capita consumption of prescription opioids in the world (International Narcotics Control Board [INCB], 2013). For the periods 2000–2002 and 2008–2010, the country's consumption of prescription opioids tripled (INCB, 2011). In 2011, 16.7 per cent of Canadians aged 15 years and older and 14.3 per cent of youth under age 15 used prescription opioids (Health Canada, 2012).

There is little national data available on prescription opioid misuse and related harms, but data from Ontario indicates the nature and scope of the problem. Between 1991 and 2004, opioids were implicated in almost half of all deaths in Ontario involving alcohol or other drugs, and the annual number of opioid-related deaths almost doubled, from 13.7 to 27.2 per million (Dhalla et al., 2009). Almost all these deaths also involved at least one non-opioid central nervous system depressant, such as benzodiazepines or alcohol, and were deemed by the Coroner to be largely unintentional. Over this same period, both opioid prescriptions and dosages increased significantly. From 1991 to 2007, opioid prescriptions in Ontario increased by 29 per cent; notably, oxycodone prescriptions rose by more than 850 per cent to constitute a third of all opioid prescriptions (Dhalla et al., 2009).

For the periods 2005–2006 and 2010–2011 in Ontario, the number of emergency room visits related to opioid use more than doubled (Expert Working Group on Narcotic Addiction, 2012). From 2004 to 2009, admissions to substance use treatment programs for prescription opioids doubled (Fischer et al., 2010). By 2010–2011, almost one in five people seeking treatment for a substance use disorder at the Centre for Addiction and Mental Health (CAMH) in Toronto identified opioids as the problem substance (Ialomiteanu et al., 2012). From 2001 to 2011, enrolment in methadone maintenance treatment (MMT) in Ontario quadrupled, an increase thought to be largely driven by people who were misusing prescription opioids (Fischer & Argento, 2012).

ABORIGINAL COMMUNITIES

Substance use problems in Aboriginal communities involve a variety of legal and illegal substances, including alcohol, benzodiazepines, cocaine and crystal meth, but the misuse of prescription opioids has been a particularly overwhelming problem. Here again, research data is sparse. As early as 1994–1995, data from the National Native Alcohol and Drug Abuse Program (NNADAP) indicated the growing misuse of prescription drugs among First Nations and Inuit; in the early 2000s, 35 per cent of social service workers at NNADAP treatment programs identified prescription drug misuse as a problem in their communities. In 2008, the Chiefs of Ontario undertook a needs assessment of the region's services for people with substance use disorders. In all of the 30 focus groups held as part of this study, health professionals, treatment centre staff and clients reported prescription drug misuse as a problem they were facing, with 28 groups specifically referencing oxycodone or other prescription opioids (Chiefs of Ontario, 2010).

In its 2012 report to Ontario's Minister of Health and Long-Term Care, the Expert Working Group on Narcotic Addiction reported that for the period 2008–2009, the number of emergency room visits for opioid-related disorders by members of Ontario First Nations was almost fives times that of the general population; by 2010–2011, the rate was almost 15 times as high. In 2009, Nishnawbe Aski Nation, which represents 49 First Nations communities in northern Ontario, declared a state of emergency: more than half of adults in these communities were misusing opioids (Nishnawbe Aski Nation, 2013). In 2012, the band officials and health staff of Cat Lake First Nation in northwestern Ontario estimated the rate of prescription drug misuse among on-reserve adults and youth at 70 per cent.

Sources of Prescription Opioids

Most opioids are obtained from doctors' prescriptions, either directly, or indirectly through family members or friends (Brands et al., 2004; Fischer et al., 2006). Until relatively recently, physicians were reluctant to prescribe opioids because of the high risk of misuse and overdose, but aggressive promotion by pharmaceutical companies and a natural desire on the part of physicians to relieve suffering led to opioids being widely used to treat chronic non-cancer pain. As the level of opioid prescribing rose, so did related rates of mortality and admissions to emergency departments or treatment facilities for substance use (Dhalla et al., 2009; Novak et al., 2004).

The fastest rise in prescribing levels was seen with long-acting oxycodone (OxyContin), added to the Ontario Drug Benefit Formulary in 2000. A fivefold increase in oxycodone-related mortality followed (Dhalla et al., 2009). OxyContin delivers oxycodone in a time-released format to provide 12-hour relief from pain. Because of the time-release feature, OxyContin was thought to pose less risk of misuse and overdose than other prescription opioids. However, a single OxyContin tablet contains a large amount of oxycodone (from 10 to 80 milligrams in Canada), which is twice as potent an analgesic as morphine. Enough is released right after ingestion to produce euphoria, and when a tablet is crushed and then snorted, injected or ingested, the full dose, intended for release over 12 hours, is released all at once. Unlike Percocet, which contains oxycodone in a smaller amount (5 milligrams), OxyContin does not contain acetaminophen, which has a high risk of toxicity. These features made OxyContin a popular drug to misuse.

Most opioids are prescribed by family physicians, who often lack adequate training in pain management and substance use disorders. Opioid-related deaths are concentrated among the patients of a small number of high-opioid prescribers. In Ontario, Dhalla and colleagues (2011) found that the 20 per cent of family physicians who prescribed opioids most frequently issued opioid prescriptions 55 times more often than the 20 per cent who prescribed opioids least frequently.

Prescription opioids can be misused by those to whom they are prescribed in a number of ways. These include deliberately using a higher-than-recommended dose; using opioids in combination with other substances to enhance euphoria or alleviate withdrawal; tampering with the medication (by crushing it) to achieve a faster and stronger effect; and obtaining multiple prescriptions from different physicians, known as "double-doctoring." One study found that 40 per cent of prescription opioid overdose mortalities occurred in individuals who double-doctored (Shield et al., 2013). The problem has been exacerbated by a lack, until recently, of effective provincial systems for monitoring prescription duplication and double-doctoring, and no national surveillance system.

A number of other factors related to access have contributed to the rise in prescription opioid misuse in Aboriginal communities. High rates of diseases associated with chronic pain, such as diabetes, arthritis, rheumatism, heart disease and cancer, lead to higher levels of opioid prescribing. Furthermore, overprescribing opioids occurs to a greater degree among First Nations than among the general population. In Ontario in 2007, 591 opioid prescriptions were dispensed per 1,000 members of the general population, with 197 of these for oxycodone formulations (Dhalla et al., 2009); 898 opioid prescriptions were dispensed per 1,000 First Nations individuals, with 119 of these for oxycodone (Health Canada, 2010). Many Aboriginal people have multiple risk factors for substance use disorders (see "Risk Factors and Comorbidities" section). Finally, it is difficult for law enforcement to stop the influx of prescription drugs into remote communities due to health privacy laws and because these drugs are legal when used as prescribed. Economic incentives for dealers are high, and the risk of arrest and prosecution low.

In 2012, Health Canada delisted OxyContin, leaving OxyNEO (a tamper-resistant version) available for people with existing prescriptions and for cancer and palliative-care patients. Some provinces subsequently removed OxyContin from their formularies. Surprisingly, Health Canada then approved generic long-acting oxycodone, which the U.S. Food and Drug Administration refused to approve (however, generic long-acting oxycodone is not included on the Non-Insured Health Benefits [NIHB] program drug benefit list). OxyContin use has dwindled as a result of its delisting, but opioid misuse has not. Reports from across Canada indicate an increase in the use of generic oxycodone and heroin, hydromorphone and fentanyl, all of which are more potent than oxycodone (Canadian Centre on Substance Abuse & Canadian Community Epidemiology Network on Drug Use, 2013). In order to avoid the misery of opioid withdrawal, many people have simply chosen a new drug. In remote communities without treatment facilities and with minimal access to other medical services, the epidemic of opioid dependence merely continues in other forms.

Assessment and Diagnosis

Treatment of substance use disorders begins with a diagnosis and an assessment of comorbidities, concurrent disorders and pain. Some symptoms of substance use disorders and other mental disorders are similar, making diagnosis and treatment complex. Patients entering treatment for a substance use disorder should also be screened for other mental disorders, and vice versa. In Aboriginal communities, it is also important to consider the social and historical determinants of health, such as poverty and trauma, which are also risk factors for substance use disorders (Bombay et al., 2009).

The *Diagnostic and Statistical Manual of Mental Disorders* (American Psychiatric Association, 2013) lists 11 criteria for making a diagnosis of opioid use disorder. They include wanting to cut down or stop using but not managing to do so; experiencing cravings to use; and failing to carry out important roles at home, school or work because of opioid use. At least two criteria must be met for the diagnosis, and the severity of the disorder increases as more criteria are met.

SCREENING TOOLS

Substance use screening tools such as the CAGE and Walid–Robinson Opioid-Dependence questionnaires for adults, and the CRAFFT questionnaire for children and youth, can help health care practitioners identify the need for specialized assessment. The CAGE questionnaire was designed to identify the possibility of an alcohol use disorder, but it can also screen for opioid use disorders. The CRAFFT tool screens people under the age of 21 for alcohol and other substance use disorders simultaneously. These questionnaires can also help people become more aware of and reflect on some of the potential risks and consequences of their substance use.

RISK FACTORS AND COMORBIDITIES

Risk factors for substance use disorders include a genetic predisposition; early exposure to drugs; a history of mental disorders, including substance use disorders, or a family history of such disorders; chronic pain; trauma; and exposure to stressful environmental or social conditions.

Substances such as alcohol, nicotine and opioids can result in long-lasting changes in areas of the brain involved with pleasure and reward, which can increase the person's vulnerability to future substance misuse (Gould, 2010). These changes occur in some of the same brain areas that are disrupted in other mental disorders, such as depression and anxiety, and many studies have found a high rate of comorbidity between substance use disorders and certain other mental disorders. A person with a substance use disorder is approximately twice as likely to have a mood or anxiety disorder as someone without a substance use disorder, and vice versa. While in some cases this comorbidity is the result of a drug causing symptoms of a mental disorder, or of the person using the drug to treat symptoms of a mental disorder, it can also be caused by shared risk factors (CAMH, 2010).

Stressful experiences can result in individual differences in behaviour, mental processes and mental health that exacerbate the person's response to future stress. Stressful and traumatic experiences are associated with substance use disorders and other mental disorders, such as depression, anxiety and posttraumatic stress disorder (PTSD) (Bombay et al., 2009). Individuals can also be vulnerable to changes in their environment during fetal development, childhood and adolescence, but these changes can occur at any time in the lifespan, and can be passed down from parent to child, even persisting for multiple generations.

Some social determinants of health, such as poverty, unemployment, poor housing, homelessness, lack of education and being located far from health services are correlated with a higher risk for substance use disorders. Poverty and unemployment can be consequences of substance misuse, but they also create conditions that make substance misuse more likely.

Opioids are often prescribed to manage chronic pain, which is itself a risk factor for opioid use disorders (Boscarino et al., 2011). Pain is the most common reason why Canadians seek health care (Schopflocher et al., 2011). People with chronic pain often also have mental health disorders, including PSTD (Bosco et al., 2013). Other research links chronic pain with low socio-economic status and lack of education (Goldberg & McGee, 2011).

Many Aboriginal people in Canada have most or all of these risk factors for substance use or concurrent disorders. Compared with the general Canadian population, Aboriginal people have higher rates of chronic diseases often associated with pain, and of mental disorders such as depression, PTSD and anxiety. Most Aboriginal people experience dire socio-economic inequities and ongoing stigmatization and discrimination, resulting in high levels of stress, particularly for children growing up in these conditions. Finally, generations of First Nations, Métis and Inuit have dealt—and are still dealing—with the immense trauma and related harms to health caused by colonialism.[1] The high rates of substance use and other mental health issues found in many Aboriginal communities today are linked to the accumulated individual and communal pain and stresses of these traumas, and while there are thriving Aboriginal communities, many are struggling under this legacy (Bombay et al., 2009; Health Canada et al., 2011; NACPDM, 2013).

WITHDRAWAL

All long-term opioid users, including those who take their medication as prescribed, become physically dependent on the opioid, and will experience withdrawal symptoms if they reduce or abruptly stop the drug. While physical dependence alone is not sufficient to indicate a substance use disorder, it is useful to understand the phenomenon because it is often while experiencing withdrawal that a person presents for help.

Withdrawal symptoms for opioids include restlessness and involuntary leg movements, muscle and joint pain, anxiety and insomnia, nausea, vomiting and diarrhea, cold flashes with goose bumps, runny nose and tears and an elevated heart rate. Unlike alcohol or benzodiazepine withdrawal, opioid withdrawal is rarely fatal in people who are in generally good health and have access to medical treatment, but it can be extremely physiologically and psychologically painful. The onset of withdrawal usually coincides with the half-life of a drug—the amount of time it takes for the body to eliminate half of the initial dose. The half-life of different opioids varies, ranging from one to two days; withdrawal will generally peak from three to five days after the drug was last taken.

Treatment

No one treatment is effective for all people with opioid use disorder. The two main treatment options are maintenance drug therapies using methadone or buprenorphine, and behaviour-oriented counselling; a combination of the two is generally most effective (National Institute on Drug Abuse, 2010). The treatment plan should also consider concurrent disorders, including pain and other mental health and substance use problems. Treatment for Aboriginal people may incorporate both mainstream and traditional approaches. Prescription drug misuse is a relatively new phenomenon and most treatment facilities lack specialized expertise in treating related disorders. Wait times for treatment are often very long.

---

1   For a discussion about the history of colonization and how it has affected the health and well-being of Aboriginal people, see chapter 2. To read more about intergenerational trauma, see chapter 5.

MANAGEMENT OF ACUTE OVERDOSE AND WITHDRAWAL

Naloxone is the most commonly used treatment for opioid overdose. It rapidly reverses the respiratory depression and sedation caused by opioid intoxication. In British Columbia, take-home naloxone kits can be made available to those who misuse opioids, and training in the use of these kits given to health workers and those in band offices (Toward the Heart, 2012). In acute opioid withdrawal, the person can be symptomatically managed or stabilized using methadone or buprenorphine in a supervised setting on a dose determined by careful titration with reference to established guidelines, as well as by the person's symptoms of withdrawal. There is emerging evidence for home inductions using buprenorphine that may not require supervised treatment to the extent that supervision is currently provided (Lee et al., 2009).

MAINTENANCE THERAPY

MMT involves long-term prescribing of methadone, along with providing counselling, case management and other medical and mental health services. Methadone alleviates opioid withdrawal symptoms and reduces cravings. It also alleviates chronic pain. As a long-acting opioid, it need only be administered once a day. People on MMT need to see their health care provider regularly. Regular visits, particularly during early treatment, allow medication consumption to be closely monitored and dosage to be adjusted. These visits provide structure and opportunities for counselling. Tolerance to methadone develops relatively slowly. MMT has been found to reduce the risk of use of other opioids, overdose, injection drug–related diseases and illegal activity, and it improves physical and mental health, social functioning and retention in treatment programs (College of Physicians and Surgeons of Ontario, 2011). Pregnant women who use opioids regularly are often treated with methadone to avoid the risk of opioid withdrawal, which increases the risk of miscarriage or premature birth.

In recent years, the availability of MMT in Canada has improved, but not yet to the extent needed. Physicians must apply to Health Canada and their provincial medical regulatory body for permission to prescribe methadone, and MMT must be medically supervised. Often, in the initiation stage of treatment, clients must travel to a clinic each day to take their medication. Access to MMT can be particularly difficult in remote and rural areas, due to a lack of prescribing physicians, health workers who are not trained in MMT and high transportation costs to access the drug.

When taken as prescribed, methadone is safe; however, as with any opioid, it can be misused—using too much or selling or giving it to someone for whom it was not prescribed. Because individual levels of tolerance to methadone vary and because the drug works very slowly, there is a danger of inadvertent overdose, especially when methadone is combined with other drugs. Of particular concern are benzodiazepines, commonly prescribed to treat anxiety in people with opioid use disorder and mental health comorbidities. Benzodiazepines have sedating effects and can interact fatally with opioids. Another problem is that it can be difficult to taper off methadone. These issues have created concern among leaders and members of some Aboriginal communities about the use of methadone. Because substance use and misuse are viewed as legacies of colonialism, not part of traditional culture, some Aboriginal communities oppose treatment that involves the long-term use of an opioid.

A lesser known maintenance treatment, buprenorphine, available as Suboxone (buprenorphine and naloxone), became available in Canada in 2008. Administered in pill form as opposed to a liquid, Suboxone offers some advantages over methadone. It takes less time to arrive at an appropriate dose, is more difficult to misuse than methadone and has a lower overdose potential (Wolff, 2005). These features have made Suboxone a more appealing replacement therapy in communities lacking the health services or infrastructure required for an MMT program. A number of pilot Suboxone programs have been launched in First Nations communities in northern Ontario (e.g., Uddin, 2013).

Another medication, naltrexone, blocks opioid receptors and prevents the body from responding to opioids. As this can cause precipitated withdrawal, naltrexone is generally only used as an alternative or complementary treatment where maintenance therapy has reached completion or is not indicated.

Approaches to Intervention

Solutions to the complex problem of prescription drug misuse must be multi-faceted. Early identification and intervention are critical. Also needed are expanded treatment options and harm reduction programs; improved education and training opportunities for front-line workers; increased support for public education and prevention initiatives; and strengthened prescription-monitoring programs and regulation to improve prescribing practices.

Interventions for First Nations, Inuit and Métis individuals and communities must involve both stakeholders and decision makers; be culturally relevant, community-based and resilience-focused; and reflect the social, cultural and economic diversity of Aboriginal communities (Health Canada et al., 2011). Better collaboration among federal, provincial and territorial governments and First Nations governments is needed to improve policies, programs and services.

SYSTEMIC INITIATIVES

Many groups and organizations are contributing to the development of a comprehensive approach to prescription drug misuse in Canada, including among Aboriginal communities. The Canadian Centre on Substance Abuse led the development of the

National Prescription Drug Misuse Strategy (NACPDM, 2013). The National Native Alcohol and Drug Abuse Program (NNADAP) Renewal Process aims to develop a new program framework informed by culture, evidence and needs. Health Canada's Prescription Drug Abuse Coordinating Committee is working in partnership with First Nations and provinces and territories to develop projects and initiatives. In 2013, the Federal/Provincial/Territorial Working Group on Prescription Drug Abuse was formed with the goal of enhancing intergovernmental collaboration and leadership on prescription drug issues.

HEALTH CARE PRACTITIONER EDUCATION

Better education of prescribers, dispensers and other members of health care teams will help to limit the exposure of vulnerable individuals to high doses of opioids that are prescribed and subsequently misused, and will reduce the volume of prescription opioids accessible through diversion. More emphasis is needed on educating health care practitioners about the complexities of substance use disorders, in particular comorbidities and concurrent disorders; pain management and alternatives to opioids; the historical and socio-economic causes of substance use and other mental disorders in Aboriginal populations; and the important role that culture plays in healing.

MONITORING, REGULATION AND FUNDING LIMITS

The provinces have strengthened their prescription-drug monitoring and surveillance systems in recent years, but a national system is not yet in place. Changes have been made to the listing status of some opioids, particularly oxycodone. Changes to funding policies of third-party payers, such as the NIHB program, workers' compensation boards and private insurers are also being used to improve prescribing practices.

CULTURALLY RELEVANT PROGRAMS

Culturally relevant programs take a holistic approach to treating substance use problems and incorporate traditional cultural activities and ways of healing. Such programs have been found to support resilience, encourage health-enhancing behaviours and reduce levels of substance use problems among Aboriginal people (Jiwa et al., 2008; NACPDM, 2013). To gain community support, treatment approaches must respect Aboriginal values: for example, because substance use is not part of traditional culture and some Aboriginal communities see maintenance therapy as merely replacing one drug with another, tapering, rather than long-term MMT, must be considered a possibility.

Both traditional and mainstream Western approaches to healing and wellness have valuable contributions to make to pain management and the treatment of substance use and other mental health issues. A number of treatment programs in Canada incorporate traditional practices and activities; for example, CAMH's Aboriginal Service provides 21-day programs at its Toronto site for local and distance clients that include both traditional Aboriginal forms of healing and non-Aboriginal therapeutic modalities. More such programs are needed.

Community-Based Programs

Intermediate- and long-term day and residential treatment programs have been mainstays in the management of substance use problems for decades. The value of intensive inpatient programs (which usually run from 21 to 28 days but can last up to a year or more) is their ability to control the person's environment over a sufficient period of time for the person to build the skills required to avoid relapse and manage moods and cravings. For those in remote communities, participation in residential programs means travelling long distances and being away from one's family, community and workplace. People usually return from treatment to the same situations and stresses, with little or no access to aftercare, and relapse rates are high. In contrast, community-based programs foster connectedness to family, community and culture, all of which are associated with health and recovery. They also promote understanding of substance use problems and approaches to treatment within communities (Jiwa et al., 2008).

COMMUNITY MOBILIZATION

In Constance Lake First Nation in Ontario, 46 per cent of people reported misusing prescription drugs in 2005, and the community was plagued with related problems. The community mobilized to address these issues. In 2006, it established an on-reserve methadone clinic along with a tapering-off program, and provided counselling to everyone in the program. To discourage drug trafficking, Constance Lake collaborated with local law enforcement to implement bylaws to prevent unauthorized people from entering the reserve. The results were reduced rates of crime and violence, more stable families and much improved social functioning for people in the program. Ongoing initiatives include establishing a treatment and wellness centre for people with substance use problems and a counselling and support program for family members (Chiefs of Ontario, 2010).

A community becomes mobilized when its members recognize a shared problem and then develop and implement community-based solutions that reflect the community's resources and values. Such initiatives require strong community engagement and leadership and sufficient funding to develop sustainable programming. Which interventions are possible will depend partly on the community's stage of readiness for intervention.

In-school, parenting/family and low-threshold outreach programs can help to acclimatize the community, young and old, to the challenges of substance use recovery, as well as to reduce the stigma often associated with drug use in Aboriginal communities. Drug-user peer networks and Narcotics Anonymous and Alcoholics Anonymous programs, which can be strong sources of information and support, often require approval by community leaders.

One approach that shows promise is the community mobile treatment (CMT) model, developed in 1984 to assist several First Nations communities in British Columbia that were experiencing dire rates of alcohol use problems. The CMT model involves one to two years of work by community members and leaders to promote a culture of sobriety and a supportive environment for people in recovery, followed by 21 to 28 days of CMT and aftercare programming. In essence, the communities themselves become treatment facilities. In the B.C. communities where CMT was first used, up to 75 per cent of community members received treatment, and a survey conducted six months after treatment in the community of Anahim Lake reported a 75 per cent abstinence rate (Wiebe & Huebert, 1996). Similar interventions in other parts of Canada suggest that this approach holds promise for communities facing problems with other substances, including prescription drugs (Jiwa et al., 2008).

Conclusion

Ultimately, a commitment is needed from all Canadians to acknowledge and work together with Aboriginal peoples to repair the legacies of colonialism, including residential schools, and to address the environmental and social inequities among Aboriginal populations that increase the risk of substance use, including opioid misuse, as well as other mental health issues.

References

American Psychiatric Association. (2013). *Diagnostic and Statistical Manual of Mental Disorders* (5th ed.). Washington, DC: Author.

Bombay, A., Matheson, K. & Anisman, H. (2009). Intergenerational trauma: Convergence of multiple processes among First Nations peoples in Canada. *International Journal of Indigenous Health, 5* (3), 6–47.

Boscarino, J.A., Rukstalis, M.R., Hoffman, S.N., Han, J.J., Erlich, P.M., Ross, S., . . . Stewart, W.F. (2011). Prevalence of prescription opioid-use disorder among chronic pain patients: Comparison of the DSM-5 vs. DSM-4 diagnostic criteria. *Journal of Addictive Diseases, 30,* 185–194. DOI: 10.1080/10550887.2011.581961

Bosco, M.A., Gallinati, J.L. & Clark, M.E. (2013). Conceptualizing and treating comorbid chronic pain and PTSD. *Pain Research and Treatment, 2013* (174728). DOI: 10.1155/2013/174728

Brands, B., Blake, J., Sproule, B., Gourlay, D. & Busto, U. (2004). Prescription opioid abuse in patients presenting for methadone maintenance treatment. *Drug and Alcohol Dependence, 73,* 199–207.

Canadian Centre on Substance Abuse & Canadian Community Epidemiology Network on Drug Use. (2013, April). Misuse of opioids in Canadian communities. *CCENDU Bulletin*. Retrieved from Canadian Centre on Substance Abuse website: www.ccsa.ca

Centre for Addiction and Mental Health (CAMH). (2010). *Concurrent Substance Use and Mental Health Disorders: An Information Guide*. Retrieved from www.camh.ca

Chiefs of Ontario. (2010). *Prescription Drug Abuse Strategy: "Take a Stand."* Retrieved from www. chiefs-of-ontario.org

College of Physicians and Surgeons of Ontario. (2011). *Methadone Maintenance Treatment: Program Standards and Clinical Guidelines*. Retrieved from www.cpso.on.ca

Dhalla, I.A., Mamdani, M.M., Gomes, T. & Juurlink, D.N. (2011). Clustering of opioid prescribing and opioid-related mortality among family physicians in Ontario. *Canadian Family Physician, 57* (3), e92–e96.

Dhalla, I.A., Mamdani, M.M., Sivilotti, M.L.A., Kopp, A., Qureshi, O. & Juurlink, D.N. (2009). Prescribing of opioid analgesics and related mortality before and after the introduction of long-acting oxycodone. *Canadian Medical Association Journal, 181*, 891–896. DOI: 10.1503/cmaj.090784

Expert Working Group on Narcotic Addiction. (2012). *The Way Forward: Stewardship for Prescription Narcotics in Ontario*. Retrieved from Ministry of Health and Long-Term Care website: www. health.gov.on.ca

Fischer, B. & Argento, E. (2012). Prescription opioid related misuse, harms, diversion and interventions in Canada: A review. *Pain Physician, 15* (Suppl. 3), ES191–ES203.

Fischer, B., Nakamura, N., Rush, B., Rehm, J. & Urbanoski, K. (2010). Changes in and characteristics of admissions to substance use treatment related to problematic prescription opioid use in Ontario, 2004–2009. *Drug and Alcohol Dependence, 109*, 257–260. DOI: 10.1016/j.drugalcdep.2010.02.001

Fischer, B., Rehm, J., Patra, J. & Firestone Cruz, M. (2006). Changes in illicit opioid use across Canada. *Canadian Medical Association Journal, 175*, 1385–1387. DOI: 10.1503/cmaj.060729

Goldberg, D.S. & McGee, S.J. (2011). Pain as a global public health priority. *BMC Public Health, 11*, 770. DOI: 10.1186/1471-2458-11-770

Gould, T.J. (2010). Addiction and cognition. *Addiction Science & Clinical Practice, 5* (2), 4–14.

Health Canada. (2010). *NIHB Ontario Region—Prescription Drug Trends: A Ten-Year Analysis*. Retrieved from Chiefs of Ontario website: www.chiefs-of-ontario.org/sites/default/files/files/NIHB%20 Ontario%20Region%20Prescription%20Drug%20Trends%20A%20Ten-Year%20Analysis_0.pdf

Health Canada. (2012). *Canadian Alcohol and Drug Use Monitoring Survey: Summary of Results for 2011*. Retrieved from www.hc-sc.gc.ca

Health Canada, Assembly of First Nations & National Native Addictions Partnership Foundation. (2011). *Honouring Our Strengths: A Renewed Framework to Address Substance Use Issues among First Nations People in Canada*. Retrieved from http://nnapf.com

Ialomiteanu, I.A., Adlaf, E.M., Hamilton, H. & Mann, R.E. (2012). *CAMH Monitor eReport: Addiction and Mental Health Indicators among Ontario Adults, 1977–2011*. Retrieved from Centre for Addiction and Mental Health website: www.camh.ca

International Narcotics Control Board (INCB). (2011). *Narcotic Drugs: Estimated World Requirements for 2012—Statistics for 2010*. New York: United Nations.

International Narcotics Control Board (INCB). (2013). *Narcotic Drugs: Estimated World Requirements for 2013—Statistics for 2011*. New York: United Nations.

Jiwa, A., Kelly, L. & St. Pierre-Hansen, N. (2008). Healing the community to heal the individual: Literature review of aboriginal community-based alcohol and substance abuse programs. *Canadian Family Physician, 54*, 1000–1000.e7.

Lee, J.D, Grossman, E., DiRocco, D. & Gourevitch, M.N. (2009). Home buprenorphine/naloxone induction in primary care. *Journal of General Internal Medicine, 24*, 226–232. DOI: 10.1007/s11606-008-0866-8

National Advisory Council on Prescription Drug Misuse (NACPDM). (2013). *First Do No Harm: Responding to Canada's Prescription Drug Crisis.* Retrieved from Canadian Centre on Substance Abuse website: www.ccsa.ca

National Institute on Drug Abuse. (2010.) *Comorbidity: Addiction and Other Mental Illnesses.* Retrieved from www.drugabuse.gov/sites/default/files/rrcomorbidity.pdf

Nishnawbe Aski Nation. (2013). Mental Health and Addictions: Prescription Drug Abuse. Retrieved from http://nanhealth.sims.sencia.ca

Novak, S., Nemeth, W.C. & Lawson, K.A. (2004). Trends in medical use and abuse of sustained-release opioid analgesics: A revisit. *Pain Medicine, 5*, 59–65.

Schopflocher, D., Taenzer, P. & Jovey, R. (2011). The prevalence of chronic pain in Canada. *Pain Research & Management, 16*, 445–450.

Shield, K.D., Jones, W., Rehm, J. & Fischer, B. (2013). Use and nonmedical use of prescription opioid analgesics in the general population of Canada and correlations with dispensing levels in 2009. *Pain Research & Management, 18*, 69–74.

Toward the Heart. (2012). BC's Take Home Naloxone Program. Retrieved from http://towardtheheart.com/naloxone

Uddin, F. (2013). Hope in Fort Hope: First Nations community is winning the battle against prescription drug abuse. *Canadian Family Physician, 59*, 391–393.

Webster, P.C. (2013). Indigenous Canadians confront prescription opioid misuse. *The Lancet, 381*, 1447–1448. DOI: 10.1016/S0140-6736(13)60913-7

Wiebe, C. & Huebert, K.M. (1996). Community mobile treatment. What it is and how it works. *Journal of Substance Abuse Treatment, 13*, 23–31.

Wolff, K. (2005). Substance misuse: Substitution drugs (methadone and buprenorphine). In J. Payne-James, R.W. Byard, T.S. Corey & C. Henderson (Eds.), *Encyclopaedia of Forensic and Legal Medicine* (pp. 157–162). Oxford, UK: Elsevier.

ABOUT THE AUTHOR

Jonathan Rajeevan Bertram, BSC (Hon), MD, is an addiction medicine physician at the Centre for Addiction and Mental Health under the Addiction Medicine Service, as well as the Aboriginal Northern Provincial Service. He is engaged in First Nations outreach, especially in northern Ontario, where he educates clinicians about the principles of addictive behaviour and addiction treatment. He also runs a clinical practice in pain, family medicine and addiction in Bowmanville. He is a graduate of the University of Western Ontario Family Medicine Program and completed his PGY3 addiction medicine fellowship at the University of Toronto.

Chapter 18

Inhalant Use

DEBRA DELL AND CAROL HOPKINS

This chapter explores inhalant use among Aboriginal people within the context of historical oppression that has led to substance use and mental health problems. It discusses current ideas about the causes of inhalant use, including predisposing factors and co-existing mental health problems. A case study illustrates the complexity of issues involved in assessing and treating inhalant use among Aboriginal people. We also examine approaches to assessment, treatment and intervention that reflect the unique perspectives and needs of Aboriginal people, as well as discussing deterrent strategies.

Inhalants and Inhalant Use Disorder

Inhalants are a class of substances that are taken into the body through the lungs by breathing. They enter the bloodstream and move quickly to the heart and brain, resulting in rapid alteration of central nervous system functioning. The terms *inhalant abuse*,[1] *volatile substance abuse*, *huffing* and *sniffing* all describe the activity of deliberately inhaling volatile fumes to get a mind-altering, euphoric high (MacLean, 2005). Common inhalants used for this purpose include aerosols, such as hairspray or electronic dusting sprays, and volatile solvents, such as paint thinners, gasoline and correction fluid.

Inhalant use carries numerous health risks. Depending on the specific substance, inhalants have been linked to cell damage in all organs of the body, including the brain, as well as to blood disorders (National Inhalant Prevention Coalition, n.d.). The shocking nature of inhalant use has led to the widely held idea that inhalants cause

---

1   This chapter uses the term *inhalant use* to avoid the judgmental implication of the word "abuse."

permanent brain damage. Fortunately, science is beginning to show that brain cell and brain function recovery are possible following a period of abstinence (Dingwall et al., 2011). There is some indication that the claim of irreparable damage is linked to a time when many inhalants contained lead, which causes permanent brain damage (Cairney et al., 2013).

The *Diagnostic and Statistical Manual of Mental Disorders* ([DSM], American Psychiatric Association, 2013) includes a diagnostic category called inhalant use disorder. The 10 diagnostic criteria include repeated use of the inhalant despite knowing it is causing serious personal harm and continuing to use despite experiencing social or interpersonal problems related to use. In terms of severity, meeting two of the 10 criteria over a 12-month period indicates a mild disorder, four to five indicates a moderate disorder and more than six indicates a severe disorder.

A Picture Out of Focus

In terms of the prevalence of inhalant use, the data may be misleading. Although inhalant use occurs across socio-economic groups, most studies focus on specific user groups, which can be stigmatizing and may reduce the generalizability of findings to other groups. Research seems to suggest that inhalant use occurs predominantly in Aboriginal populations (Howard et al., 2008; Sakai et al., 2004). However, the point is seldom made that most Canadian research on inhalant use focuses on these populations. Canadian prevalence data may also be skewed because widespread media attention to inhalant use among Aboriginal youth has led to epidemiological studies that focus on the Aboriginal population, with the findings then being erroneously extended to the general Canadian population. This may also be the case in the United States, where surprisingly high rates of inhalant use in the general population were reported in national surveys. Inhalants came second to marijuana as the most commonly used substances by students in grades 8 and 10 (Wu et al., 2004). Skewing the picture further is the fact that reductions in inhalant use in Indigenous populations are rarely reported. Yet Beauvais, Wayman and colleagues (2002) found that among three ethnic groups studied for more than a decade, Native Americans showed the greatest reduction in rates of inhalant use.

A further concern is that the success of inhalant use treatment programs for Aboriginal youth in Canada has received little attention, even though this population is frequently identified in research and the media as being disproportionately affected by inhalant use (Howard et al., 2008; Sakai et al., 2004).

Reinforcing this negative picture is the fact that much research about inhalant use focuses on co-existing psychiatric conditions and the serious consequences of inhalant use, including organ and brain damage and behavioural unpredictability. These studies generally highlight poor prognosis and a clientele that does not respond well to treatment. This negative focus may unintentionally create a sense of hopelessness and pessimism around inhalant use intervention and treatment.

Correcting the Focus

Applied to Aboriginal people, the DSM diagnosis of inhalant use disorder is fraught with complications because the diagnostic criteria do not consider environmental context; for example, meeting the criterion of failing to fulfil important obligations at school or employment might be due to the actual lack of school or employment opportunities in the community rather than to the person's inhalant use alone. Failing to understand inhalant use disorder within the context of colonization and the intergenerational trauma and pervasive stress this experience has created for entire communities leads to inappropriate interventions. Similarly, some scholars have challenged that the diagnosis of posttraumatic stress has been compromised by unacknowledged cultural differences (Phillips, 2010). People are more than any DSM diagnosis they receive. For Aboriginal people, using diagnostic categories and criteria that focus on individual behaviour, disconnected from environmental, cultural and historical factors, does not create an accurate picture of the problem. Strategies for assessing and treating inhalant use among Aboriginal people require cultural competence that is embedded in an understanding of the historical and social contexts in which problems have developed, and must recognize Aboriginal healing capacities and practices.

Waldram (2004) highlighted the importance of challenging accepted conceptual paradigms, which in mainstream Western health care tend to focus on individual factors, rather than the broader context in which problems develop:

> What we as researchers and clinicians think we know affects people's lives, *Aboriginal* peoples' lives, in profound ways, and if we have it wrong the consequences—erroneous diagnoses, ineffective or damaging treatment, stereotyping and stigmatization of individuals and whole communities—can be dire indeed. (p. 8)

The long history of colonization experienced by Aboriginal peoples has had destructive consequences, which include many mental health and substance use issues. Rapid cultural change, oppression and intergenerational trauma have affected the mental health of those who lived through or were exposed to these events, and the legacy of unresolved emotions is felt by younger generations (Smye & Browne, 2002).[2] Given this traumatic history, inhalant use among Aboriginal people should be viewed as a social issue that affects entire communities and often multiple generations.

---

2   For more discussion about the history of colonization in Canada and how it has affected Aboriginal peoples, see chapter 2. To read more about intergenerational trauma, see chapter 5.

Ivey and colleagues (2005) described a therapeutic approach called developmental counselling and therapy (DCT), which views severe client distress as a logical response to developmental history. Through this therapeutic lens, we can view inhalant use among Aboriginal people as a logical response to a traumatic history—inhalant use becomes an attempt to cope with this legacy. Significantly, the culture of Aboriginal peoples and their unique culture-based therapeutic practices have persisted despite the devastating effects of colonization. Successful programs for Aboriginal youth who use inhalants have combined culture-based practices with mainstream Western approaches. Helping youth to situate their trauma within the context of colonization and addressing this trauma with culture-based practices are foundational therapeutic principles to the programs of the Youth Solvent Addiction Committee (YSAC), a network of 10 First Nations inhalant-specific residential treatment centres across Canada. First Nations peoples developed these programs, which show extremely promising results (Erickson & Butters, 2005). Whereas Western diagnostic models tend to label inhalant use solely as pathology, recognizing the roles that historical grief, oppression and trauma contribute to this behaviour may help clients find a new path to healing.

Predisposing Factors

The long history of colonization that Aboriginal peoples have experienced has led to psychosocial factors that may increase the risk of using inhalants. In terms of social risk factors, people who use inhalants often come from areas of extreme poverty and unemployment, and often have limited school success or connection to schools (Siqueira & Crandall, 2007; YSAC, 2008). In terms of psychological risk factors, people who use inhalants often have higher than average rates of suicide attempts, have experienced multiple traumas such as abuse and neglect, and have other family members with addictions (Howard et al., 2008; Kelly et al., 2002; Siqueira & Crandall, 2007; YSAC, 2008).

Mosher and colleagues (2004) suggested that people who use inhalants represent a fundamentally different category of drug users because solvents are legal products that can be obtained easily and inexpensively, and since thousands of products containing these substances are available in homes and at school, using them to get high is easy to conceal (e.g., Mehta, 2006; Mosher et al., 2004). In the authors' experience, the fact that these substances often induce hallucinations that bring emotional relief seems to be a more important factor than their low cost and high availability. Unfortunately, there is little research examining the relationship between pre-existing emotional issues or the desirability of the induced hallucinations and the probability of inhalant use. Addressing inhalant use among Aboriginal people requires examining the impact of historical oppression, trauma and multiple levels of grief.

For some people who use inhalants, grief, loneliness and fear figure prominently as emotional drivers for continued use. They use inhalants to deal with unpleasant emotions in the real world. From the stories shared by many youth in YSAC programs, inhalant intoxication causes what appears to be a controllable hallucination, in which the user can choose what scenario to hallucinate and with whom to interact in the scenario. For example, the scenario might be a family gathering in which a deceased, much-loved friend appears, and with whom the user converses. After this hallucination, the person may describe having felt a sense of relief from grief and a desire to pursue ongoing hallucinations to maintain a relationship with the family or the deceased friend. The person thinks that maintaining this connection is possible only through inhalant intoxication.

Cause or Consequence? Mental Health Problems

Substance use problems have consistently been observed to co-exist with mental health problems. According to the Council on Drug Abuse (2009), 53 per cent of people with substance use problems have co-occurring mental health concerns. It is not clear whether the occurrence of comorbid mental health issues differs between people who use inhalants and those who use other substances.

Two general theories have been developed to explain concurrent mental health and substance use problems. The self-medication theory posits that people use substances to cope with underlying mental health and emotional issues (Suh et al., 2008). The common-factor model suggests that addiction and mental health issues often co-exist because they share biopsychosocial risk factors (Muesner et al., as cited in Hawkins, 2009). With inhalant use, it is difficult to determine the validity of either theory because it is rare that a mental health assessment has been conducted before it is known that a person is using inhalants. In their study, Evren and colleagues (2006) stated that they had limited ability to determine whether comorbid mental health issues are the cause or consequence of inhalant use. Similarly, Howard and colleagues (2008) were unable to show whether comorbid mental health issues are an effect of or an antecedent to inhalant use. Ron (as cited in Evren et al., 2006) argued that inhalant use does not cause psychiatric comorbidities, but rather, that inhalant use is more common among people with existing mental health problems, and that depressive symptoms are more accurately explained as symptoms of withdrawal from the inhalant.

Mental health disorders most commonly comorbid with inhalant use include generalized anxiety disorder (GAD), mood disorders, personality disorders, and schizophrenia and other psychoses. Below we describe the links between these disorders and inhalant use.

GENERALIZED ANXIETY DISORDER

The defining clinical feature of GAD is sustained and excessive worry to the point that it interferes with functioning in a variety of life domains. Physical manifestations include tension, fatigue, concentration problems, sleep problems and irritability (Sadock & Sadock, 2007). Evren and colleagues (2006) reported that 76 per cent of people seeking treatment for inhalant use presented with anxiety. YSAC (2010) found that 67 per cent of youth entering solvent use treatment centres reported experiencing sexual, physical and emotional abuse, including threats of neglect and abandonment.

MOOD DISORDERS

People who have mood disorders present with distress and a sense of lacking control over their feelings (Sadock & Sadock, 2007). People who use inhalants have higher rates of major depression, one type of mood disorder; in fact, major depression is the psychiatric disorder most often associated with inhalant use (Evren et al., 2006; Sakai et al., 2004; Substance Abuse and Mental Health Services Administration [SAMHSA], 2008). Major depression features markedly diminished interest or pleasure in activities, insomnia, feelings of worthlessness and suicidal ideation. Some researchers have concluded that depressive symptoms appear before inhalant use and thus major depression should be considered a risk factor for inhalant use (Evren et al., 2006; SAMHSA, 2008). However, as Rogers (2003) stated, diagnosing major depression is a "hit or miss proposition . . . odds are 50:50 that it will be accurate" (pp. 220–221). Regardless of diagnostic difficulties, there is much evidence of a strong association between major depression and inhalant use. For example, 58 per cent of youth in solvent use treatment reported feeling sad or unhappy and had serious doubts about their self-worth; at least 45 per cent had attempted suicide on average three times; and 26 per cent had lost at least one friend to inhalant use (YSAC, 2010).

PERSONALITY DISORDERS

Personality disorders are common, chronic conditions characterized by behaviours that differ from societal norms. People diagnosed with a personality disorder may experience difficulties with cognition, emotional regulation, impulse control and social functioning. It is estimated that at least 50 per cent of people with a psychiatric diagnosis also have a co-existing personality disorder (Sadock & Sadock, 2007). Having a personality disorder also predisposes the person to substance use disorders. Wu and Howard (2007) reported that 45 per cent of adults who used inhalants had a co-existing personality disorder. A retrospective study of 130 people who used solvents found that 61 per cent had a co-existing personality disorder, particularly antisocial personality disorder (Dinwiddie et al., 1990).

SCHIZOPHRENIA AND OTHER PSYCHOSES

Schizophrenia is a psychotic disorder that involves altered cognition, emotion and perception, as well as behavioural indicators that mirror those of inhalant intoxication.

Both untreated schizophrenia and inhalant use are discernible by auditory and visual hallucinations and may include verbalizations to people or objects that are not there. A person who is high on an inhalant will appear dazed, as if in another world. An episode of inhalant use can itself cause symptoms of paranoid psychosis. A case review of 22 people in treatment for inhalant use found that 14 of them had persistent paranoid psychosis (Byrne, as cited in Evren et al., 2006), although the direction of the causal relationship was not indicated, as is the case with many comorbidity studies. In a Japanese study that involved 120 people who used inhalants, Okudaira and colleagues (1996) found that although symptoms of psychosis can be a consequence of inhalant use, they are not caused entirely by the inhalant use; rather, biological predisposition remains a factor. Schaumburg and colleagues (2007) reported that symptoms of psychosis dissipate as the inhalant leaves the body. They also found that any relationship between inhalant use (of toluene products, in particular) and schizophrenia is more coincidental than causal.

The research findings to date do not yield conclusive evidence about the causal relationships between mental health problems and inhalant use. Furthermore, the data cannot be extrapolated to Aboriginal people in Canada, and even less so to Native Americans. What is clear, however, is that people with co-occurring disorders experience more stigma and problems attaining services than people with either mental health or substance use issues alone.

Case Study: A.J.

To fully conceptualize the phenomenon of inhalant use in Aboriginal populations, we must remove the Western lens and look at the issue in a more holistic manner. The story of A.J. illustrates how pre-use context and social factors, combined with grief and trauma, can play a role in inhalant use by an Aboriginal person.

> A.J. is a 14-year-old Aboriginal male from a fly-in community in northern Ontario. He was referred to residential inhalant treatment after two years of chronic inhalant use. A.J. adjusted well to the structured parts of the programming, waking each morning, completing chores, and attending school and all counselling and education sessions. He presented as humorous, communicative and very likable. However, three days after entering the program, he began a pattern of running away every night at 9:00 p.m. to siphon gasoline from cars near the treatment facility. He would stay hidden away sniffing gasoline until about 1:00 a.m., when he would return to the treatment centre. He would then go to sleep, get up in the morning and participate in programming. In a discussion about his

reasons for this nightly routine, A.J. described what happens when he sniffs. He missed his family, four of whom died in a drowning accident several years before he started using inhalants. The accident happened as he watched from the land. Sniffing helped to conjure up his deceased family members, particularly his grandmother, and memories of having tea with them before bed. He described in detail his grandmother pouring the tea and telling stories at bedtime. The hallucination evoked the same comforts he enjoyed before the deaths of his family members.

A.J.'s story reveals signs of posttraumatic stress disorder, adjustment disorder, anxiety, depression and a number of other DSM disorders. A.J. fits the profile suggested by Copur that "depressive adolescents frequently use inhalants to relieve loneliness and unhappiness" (as cited in Evren et al., 2006, p. 58). In this regard, A.J.'s behaviour fits the self-medication hypothesis. The high he experienced and the hallucinated presence of his grandmother temporarily eased his anxiety and loneliness, and allowed him to sleep. In A.J.'s view, inhalant use returned him to a homeostasis of sorts. Yet there is more to it. A.J. did not display violence, unpredictability or many of the other negative behaviours commonly linked to inhalant use. Instead, his behaviour was predictable, even scheduled. He experienced a profound sense of grief, and his inhalant use can be interpreted as the only way he knew to maintain a connection to his deceased relatives. A.J.'s story illustrates the importance of understanding the individual and environmental contexts within which inhalant use takes place. For A.J., the bedtime rituals of comfort and connection with his family were powerful drivers pushing him toward inhalant use.

Culturally Competent Psychiatric Assessment

DSM classifications of mental health problems, addictions and posttraumatic stress may have limited cross-cultural applicability (Escobar & Vega, 2006). As Tseng (2006) argued: "There is a need to consider the impact of culture on every psychiatric disorder, not only culture specific syndromes" (p. 554). Given cultural differences, it is important to remember that conclusions from a study of one population cannot be applied wholesale to another population. We have seen how the findings of inhalant use studies that focus primarily on Aboriginal people in Canada have limited generalizability. Comorbidity studies that do focus on Aboriginal populations must be culturally sensitive, reflected in how interviews are conducted, case formations developed and diagnoses made.

Most research about inhalant use is too narrowly focused, emphasizing pathology and dysfunction rather than viewing the issue within a broader context that includes environmental, cultural and, particularly for Aboriginal people, historical influences. Substance use and other mental health issues among Aboriginal people cannot be addressed without considering the historical, cultural and social context in which these issues have emerged.

Tseng (2006) posited that cultural influences on psychiatric syndromes can occur in at least six ways. Two of these influences that are particularly relevant to Aboriginal people are called the *pathogenic effect* and the *psychoselective effect*. The pathogenic effect refers to cultural influences on the formation of mental health disorders; for example, loss of cultural identity and the intergenerational impacts of residential schools on entire communities may contribute to the development of a mental health disorder in an Aboriginal person. The psychoselective effect refers to particular coping patterns that a culture chooses to deal with stress; in our case study, A.J. chose to use inhalants to cope with grief. Both of these effects are important to consider before drawing conclusions about the nature of inhalant use and comorbidities in Aboriginal populations. Tseng (2006) suggested taking a dynamic approach to understanding the individual's personal history, which includes family background, psychological development, experiences of stress and coping patterns. A culturally competent practitioner should consider how her or his world view and theoretical orientation might differ from that of an Aboriginal client, whose addiction and mental health issues exist within a particular cultural and historical context.

Treatment

PSYCHOSOCIAL APPROACHES

Studies in the United States have found that inhalant use is considered very difficult to treat. Beauvais, Jumper-Thurman and colleagues (2002) surveyed drug treatment providers and concluded that most programs were ill equipped to treat inhalant use and that providers were very pessimistic about the potential for recovery. Jumper-Thurman and Beauvais (2002) found that the period of treatment usually runs less than nine months. Few reports have identified the range of possible treatment options.

In contrast, inhalant use treatment in Canada reveals a more promising picture. One important example is the programs provided by YSAC, which are rooted in a First Nations culture-based model that takes a positive approach to treatment and reflects a belief in clients' resilience. Short and colleagues (2006) described the role of resilience in health:

> There is powerful healing energy, produced by the combination of hope and utility, that results in greater resiliency. In order to maintain health, patients need to realize that there is some meaningful thing that can be done in relation to their problems. Without a reason to act, there is no initiative. (p. 30)

YSAC program providers operate under the belief that it does not matter which came first, the mental health issue or the inhalant use. Instead, they take a holistic view of their young clients, which includes examining not only the etiology of their inhalant use, but also their inherent resiliencies and future prospects. Most YSAC centres do not employ routine psychiatric or psychological diagnostics, so DSM diagnosis of comorbidities is rare. Those centres that use psychological services do so in the limited capacity of admission reviews, staff consultations and crisis intervention. When clients exhibit symptoms consistent with DSM–defined disorders, they are not pinned with diagnostic labels or treated with pharmacological therapy. Instead, signs and symptoms of a DSM–defined disorder are generally addressed with traditional practices, such as consulting with Elders, participating in sweat lodges or fasting ceremonies and engaging in other cultural practices that acknowledge all of creation (land, animals, cosmic family, medicines and foods) and connection to ancestors.

A.J.'s case illustrates this holistic, positive approach to treatment. A.J. participated in a combination of culture-based therapies that included a memorial feast to help him honour his dead relatives and process his grief. Because wellness in Aboriginal cultures involves maintaining ongoing relationships with ancestors, it was important that A.J.'s treatment promote this spiritual connection to help him heal. After participating in this memorial feast, Aboriginal youth commonly report dreams in which their ancestors thank them for the food, offer words of encouragement in their healing journey and show them the potential for their path ahead. Rarely would Western-based therapeutic approaches help a young person experience this depth of healing or resolution of their grief, and so quickly.

From the beginning, YSAC programs have crafted a system of intervention that is anchored in Aboriginal history, current reality and culture-based healing methods. A primary value among Aboriginal peoples is the interdependent relationship with all of creation. Treatment programs begin with a culture-based intervention of connecting clients with their culture's creation story. All Aboriginal peoples have a creation story, which is the foundation for their world view. This story communicates the inherent gifts of youth, giving these young people a spiritual foundation for promoting their strengths and resilience. Following this intervention, an ongoing process facilitates further nurturing of the client's cultural identity, such as seeking out an Elder, bestowing the spirit name and clan family of the youth and using traditional medicines to support physical detoxification. Another primary value of Aboriginal people is family. Research has found that young people with strong family connections or who established healthy family connections while in treatment were 16 per cent more likely to complete treatment. A YSAC (2010) follow-up study at three, six and 12 months post-treatment found that school attendance improved by 33 per cent after treatment, 85 per cent participated in positive social activities and 51 per cent had reduced their inhalant use. As a national program, YSAC strives to monitor the impact of treatment services by collecting data for these three indicators, as well as others.

Such findings suggest that holistic, culture-based approaches to treatment may be effective in helping Aboriginal people overcome substance use problems, such as inhalant use. Erickson and Butters (2005) reported that "these national Aboriginal programs are among Canada's most innovative and promising, given the extent of Native substance use associated problems, the holistic approach, and the careful evaluation that is being done" (p. 967).

DETERRENT INTERVENTIONS

In many parts of the world, inhalant researchers and program administrators have joined together to develop community-wide deterrent interventions. These range from adding a deterrent chemical, such as a mustard-derived bitterant, to products containing inhalants to developing product substitutes. These interventions have had various levels of success. One promising intervention is the Opal Fuel Project, spearheaded by British Petroleum in Australia. British Petroleum developed Opal fuel, a brand of gasoline that has had most of its aromatic hydrocarbons removed, thus reducing its abuse potential. The fuel has been subsidized by the Australian government. In most remote Aboriginal communities, it is the only fuel sold. Australian communities have reported up to a 70 per cent reduction in sniffing after the fuel was introduced (D'abbs & Shaw, 2007). The project has been tested on a small scale in Canada, but in its current form, Opal can only be used as a fuel in warm climates (Opal Committee, 2010).

In Canada, the community of Kugluktuk in Nunavut built and distributed lockable fuel storage boxes to all households in response to a gas-sniffing crisis. This initiative is powerful on two fronts: the storage boxes limit access to substances, and using the boxes sends the message that adults in the community care about the sniffing crisis and are acting to reduce it (Canadian Press, 2013).

In addition to interventions that reduce availability, other community deterrent strategies include passing legislation or bylaws that carry strong penalties for offences relating to sale or supply; providing diversionary activities, including sport, culture and recreation; providing dedicated prevention programs beginning as early as kindergarten that include parent and community education; and supporting broader health programs that use strength-based practices to reclaim identity and cultural connections.

PHARMACOLOGICAL APPROACHES

There are few options for pharmacological treatment of inhalant use. Although recent advances in neurobiology have advanced our understanding of how substances interact with the brain's reward systems, inhalants are under-studied. This is partly due to low prevalence rates and to the inherent difficulty in conducting pre-clinical studies of self-administration in animal models. However, there are a few clinical trials involving pharmacological treatment for controlling inhalant craving. Clinical trials of the mood stabilizers buspirone and lamotrigine have shown some positive results (Muralidharan et al., 2008; Niederhofer, 2007; Shen, 2007). However, more research is needed before these treatments can be considered for use.

Conclusion

In examining inhalant use among Aboriginal populations, it is important to remember Waldram's (2004) words: "How the colonizer has maintained control of indigenous populations is through the production of knowledge about them" (p. 10). Culture-based Aboriginal programs for inhalant use may have more success than mainstream treatment programs at least partly because Aboriginal people themselves controlled knowledge production. If we do not explore what makes such programs more successful, we will lose valuable evidence about the etiologogy and evolution of inhalant use, and the potential for recovery. If we continue to focus on pathology and ignore potential and proven recovery, we do an extreme disservice to the substance use field as a whole.

To date, researchers and clinicians have mostly examined the mental health of Aboriginal people from a Western perspective, using mostly Western diagnostic tools. However, embracing other perspectives is crucial to recovery, as Short and colleagues (2006) remind us: "Mental health is not something that can be standardized and then forced upon a patient. It is a subjective victory that is uniquely defined by each person's background, life experiences and learnings" (p. 20). Aboriginal communities and treatment centres in Canada continue to win victories in the fight against inhalant use. Despite the pathological picture, they have carved out a positive path toward healing, filled with hope and belief in the inherent ability of Aboriginal people and communities to heal their own.

References

American Psychiatric Association. (2013). *Diagnostic and Statistical Manual of Mental Disorders* (5th ed.). Washington, DC: Author.

Beauvais, F., Jumper-Thurman, P., Plested, B. & Helm, H. (2002). A survey of attitudes among drug user treatment providers toward the treatment of inhalant users. *Substance Use & Misuse, 37*, 1391–1410.

Beauvais, F., Wayman, J., Jumper-Thurman, P., Plested, B. & Helm, H. (2002). Inhalant abuse among American Indian, Mexican American, and non-Latino white adolescents. *American Journal of Drug and Alcohol Abuse, 28*, 171–187.

Cairney, S., O'Connor, N., Dingwall, K.M., Maruff, P., Shafiq-Antonacci, R., Currie, J. & Currie, B.J. (2013). A prospective study of neurocognitive changes 15 years after chronic inhalant abuse. *Addiction, 108*, 1107–1114. DOI: 10.1111/add.12124

Canadian Press. (2013, May 29). Northern community fights gas-sniffing with fuel safes. Retrieved from CTV News website: www.ctvnews.ca/canada/northern-community-fights-gas-sniffing-with-fuel-safes-1.1302255

Council on Drug Abuse. (2009). *Masking the Pain or Creating It? Substance Abuse and Mental Illness.* Retrieved from www.drugabuse.ca/masking-pain-or-creating-it-substance-abuse-and-mental-illness

D'abbs, P. & Shaw, G. (2007). *Evaluation of the Impact of Opal Fuel: Executive Summary.* Retrieved from Department of Health (Australia) website: www.health.gov.au/internet/stoppetrolsniffing/publishing.nsf/Content/sniffing-pubs-opalimp

Dingwall, K., Maruff, P., Fredrickson, K. & Cairney, S. (2011). Cognitive recovery during and after treatment for volatile solvent abuse. *Drug and Alcohol Dependence, 118,* 180–185. DOI: 10.1016/j.drugalcdep.2011.03.017

Dinwiddie, S., Reich, T. & Cloninger, C. (1990). Solvent use and psychiatric comorbidity. *British Journal of Addiction, 85,* 1647–1656. DOI: 10.1111/j.1360-0443.1990.tb01655.x

Erickson, P. & Butters, J. (2005). How does the Canadian juvenile justice system respond to detained youth with substance use associated problems? Gaps, challenges, and emerging issues. *Substance Use & Misuse, 40,* 953–973. DOI: 10.1081/JA-200058855

Escobar, J.I. & Vega, W.A. (2006). Cultural issues and psychiatric diagnosis: Providing a general background for considering substance use diagnoses. *Addiction, 101,* 40–47.

Evren, C., Barut, T, Saatcioglu, O. & Cakmak, D. (2006). Axis I psychiatric comorbidity among adult inhalant dependents seeking treatment. *Journal of Psychoactive Drugs, 38,* 57–64.

Hawkins, E.H. (2009). A tale of two systems: Co-occurring mental health and substance abuse disorders treatment for adolescents. *Annual Review of Psychology, 60,* 197–227. DOI: 10.1146/annurev.psych.60.110707.163456

Howard, M.O., Balster, R.L., Cottler, L.B., Wu, L.T. & Vaughn, M.G. (2008). Inhalant use among incarcerated adolescents in the United States: Prevalence, characteristics, and correlates of use. *Drug and Alcohol Dependence, 93,* 197–209.

Ivey, A., Ivey, M., Myers, J. & Sweeney, T. (2005). *Developmental Counseling and Therapy: Promoting Wellness over the Lifespan.* Boston: Houghton Mifflin.

Jumper-Thurman, P. & Beauvais, F. (2002). *Treatment of Volatile Solvent Abusers.* Bethesda, MD: Department of Health and Human Services, National Institute on Drug Abuse.

Kelly, T., Cornelius, J. & Lynch, K. (2002). Psychiatric and substance use disorders as risk factors for attempted suicide among adolescents: A case control study. *Suicide & Life-Threatening Behavior, 32,* 301–312.

MacLean, S. (2005). "It might be a scummy-arsed drug but it's a sick buzz": Chroming and pleasure. *Contemporary Drug Problems, 32,* 295–318.

Mehta, J. (2006). Whiff of trouble. *Current Health 2, 33* (1), 23–25.

Mosher, C., Rotolo, T., Phillips, D., Krupski, A. & Stark, K. (2004). Minority adolescents and substance use risk/protective factors: A focus on inhalant use. *Adolescence, 39,* 489–492.

Muralidharan, K., Rajkumar, R.P., Mulla, U., Nayak, R.B. & Benegal, V. (2008). Baclofen in the management of inhalant withdrawal: A case series. *Primary Care Companion to the Journal of Clinical Psychiatry, 10,* 48–51.

National Inhalant Prevention Coalition. (n.d.). Damage inhalants can do to the body and brain. Retrieved from www.inhalants.org/damage.htm

Niederhofer, H. (2007). Treating inhalant abuse with buspirone. *American Journal on Addictions, 16* (1), 69.

Okudaira, K., Yabana, T., Takahashi, H., Iizuka, H., Nakajima, K. & Saito, A. (1996). Inhalant abusers and psychiatric symptoms. *Seishin Shinkeigaku Zasshi, 98,* 203–212.

Opal Committee. (2010). *Opal Fuel Trial: A Trial of Opal Fuel in a Canadian Community* (Unpublished manuscript).

Phillips, J. (2010, August). The cultural dimension in DSM-5: PTSD. Retrieved from Psychiatric Times website: www.psychiatrictimes.com/dsm-5-0/cultural-dimension-dsm-5-ptsd

Rogers, R. (2003). Standardizing DSM-IV diagnoses: The clinical applications of structured interviews. *Journal of Personality Assessment, 81*, 220–225.

Sadock, B.J. & Sadock, V.A. (2007). *Kaplan & Sadock's Synopsis of Psychiatry* (10th ed.). Philadelphia: Lippincott Williams & Wilkins.

Sakai, J., Hall, S.K., Mikulich-Gilbertson, S. & Crowley, T. (2004). Inhalant use, abuse, and dependence among adolescent patients: Commonly comorbid problems. *Journal of the Amercian Academy of Child and Adolescent Psychiatry, 43*, 1080–1088.

Schaumburg, H., Wade, L. & Masur, D. (2007). Persistent psychosis from toluene exposure; more likely coincidence than cause: A review of our experience and the literature. *Current Psychiatry Reviews, 3*, 277–280. DOI: 10.2174/157340007782408842

Shen, Y.C. (2007). Treatment of inhalant dependence with lamotrigine. *Progress in Neuro-Psychopharmacology & Biological Psychiatry, 31*, 769–771.

Short, D., Erickson, B.A. & Erickson, R. (2006). *Hope & Resiliency: Understanding the Psychotherapeutic Strategies of Milton H. Erickson*, MD. Wales, UK: Crown House.

Siqueira, L.M. & Crandall, L.A. (2007). Inhalant use in Florida youth. *Substance Abuse, 27* (4), 27–34. DOI: 10.1300/J465v27n04_04

Smye, V. & Browne, A.J. (2002). "Cultural safety" and the analysis of health policy affecting Aboriginal people. *Nurse Researcher, 9* (3), 42–56.

Substance Abuse and Mental Health Services Administration (SAMHSA). (2008). *National Survey on Drug Use and Health*. Retrieved from www.samhsa.gov/data/NSDUH.aspx

Suh, J., Ruffins, S., Robins, C., Albanese, M. & Khantzian, E. (2008). Self-medication hypothesis: Connecting affective experience and drug choice. *Psychoanalytic Psychology, 25*, 518–532. DOI: 10.1037/0736-9735.25.3.518

Tseng, W.S. (2006). From peculiar psychiatric disorders through culture-bound syndromes to culture-related specific syndromes. *Transcultural Psychiatry, 43*, 554–576. DOI: 10.1177/1363461506070781

Waldram, J.B. (2004). *Revenge of the Windigo: The Construction of the Mind and Mental Health of North American Aboriginal Peoples*. Toronto: University of Toronto Press.

Wu, L. & Howard, M. (2007). Psychiatric disorders in inhalant users: Results from the national epidemiologic survey on alcohol and related conditions. *Drug and Alcohol Dependence, 88*, 146–155. DOI: 10.1016/j.drugalcdep.2006.10.012

Wu, L.T., Pilowsky, D. & Schlenger, W.E. (2004). Inhalant abuse and dependence among adolescents in the United States. *Journal of the American Academy of Child and Adolescent Psychiatry, 43*, 1206–1214.

Youth Solvent Addiction Committee (YSAC). (2008). *Youth Solvent Addiction Committee Annual Report, 2007–2008*. Saskatoon SK: Author.

Youth Solvent Addiction Committee (YSAC). (2010). *Emilys Story: Youth Solvent Addiction Committee Report, 2010*. Saskatoon SK: Author.

ABOUT THE AUTHORS

Debra Dell is executive director of the Youth Solvent Addiction program, a collective of 11 First Nations treatment programs across Canada. She holds a master's degree in counselling psychology, and has specialized addictions training. She has been designing and delivering solvent-specific prevention and intervention programs for more than 25 years.

Carol Hopkins is executive director of the National Native Addictions Partnership Foundation. She came to this position from Nimkee NupiGawagan Healing Centre, a youth solvent use treatment centre that is founded on Indigenous culture and lifeways, where she was the founding director for 13 years. She holds a master's degree in social work from the University of Toronto. Carol is third-degree Midewiwin (the Grand Medicine Society of the Anishinabe).

Chapter 19

Our Relationship with Tobacco

LYNN F. LAVALLÉE

I am an Anishinaabe Métis woman who has never smoked cigarettes, but who has been significantly affected by nicotine addiction. My mother smoked from the time she was in her early 20s, and was first diagnosed with lung cancer at age 50. After having a third of her lung removed, and some lymph nodes, she returned from hospital, only to have her family continue to smoke in front of her. She died in 1991. Three years before she died, my father was diagnosed with chronic obstructive pulmonary disease (COPD) and quit smoking cold turkey. He later contracted tuberculosis, which was treated, but then passed on to the spirit world two years later. The autopsy demonstrated that the cancer had spread throughout his lungs and the rest of his body.

After my parents died, the only family that was left besides me was two older sisters and their children. My sisters continued to smoke and my niece and one nephew took up the habit very young. In 2012, my oldest sister was diagnosed with severe COPD with 25 per cent lung capacity. She was told to quit smoking but returned home and the cycle repeated itself—her family continued to smoke as did she. In November 2013, at age 52, she passed away. Indicative of the complicated addictions we see in Aboriginal communities, the cause of death was a lethal dose of methadone complicated by pneumonia. The methadone clinic was not aware of her severe COPD.

Unfortunately, my family's story is not unusual within Aboriginal communities. It reflects both the pervasiveness of tobacco use and its devastating health effects through the generations. This chapter provides statistics on tobacco use and related health issues in First Nations, Inuit and Métis populations, and also distinguishes between sacred and commercial tobacco use. As well, it explores effective approaches to prevention and tobacco cessation in Aboriginal communities.

Sacred Tobacco

What I describe about sacred tobacco use stems from the Anishinaabe teachings given to me by my Elders and traditional teachers over many years. Because of the diversity in teachings across Aboriginal nations in Canada, I recognize that other Aboriginal peoples' understanding of sacred tobacco may differ.

Tobacco is a sacred medicine for many Aboriginal peoples across Turtle Island,[1] although not for most Inuit or some Aboriginal peoples from more northern communities where tobacco has not traditionally been grown. I cannot address its use in other countries. Some Aboriginal people may be unaware of traditional understandings of tobacco.

Tobacco is often termed "traditional" or "sacred" when it is used as a sacred medicine, as part of ceremony, or as an offering or prayer to the Creator or our ancestors. "Commercial" tobacco, on the other hand, refers to non-traditional use (Lavallée, 2005). Some people grow their own tobacco for traditional use to ensure it is chemical-free, while others buy it from a store. Although technically tobacco is considered commercial if it is bought, commercial and sacred tobacco are distinguished by how the tobacco is used, rather than by the type of tobacco involved.

I do not discuss in detail here the use of tobacco in ceremony because that should remain an oral teaching. I can say that pipe ceremonies, one of the many types of sacred tobacco ceremonies, can only be conducted by pipe carriers, who are gifted with a pipe because of their traditional path. True pipe carriers do not purchase a pipe; the pipe comes to them.

Sacred tobacco is often offered to someone from whom we are seeking assistance, such as an Elder or traditional healer. To make this offering, a large pinch of tobacco is wrapped in a cloth bundle, referred to as a tobacco bundle or tie. Someone who is not a pipe carrier but who receives tobacco may choose to keep the tobacco, place it in a sacred fire or bury it—all practices that are much more common than smoking it. Aboriginal people who follow this traditional practice are increasingly offering tobacco as a form of consent in research, in place of signing a consent form (Lavallée, 2009; Piquemal, 2001).

---

1   The name Turtle Island originates in the historical stories of several Indigenous nations and refers to the land that is now generally known as North America.

When the first settlers arrived on Turtle Island, First Nations people introduced them to traditional tobacco. Tobacco began to be used commercially. The first tobacco company, Macdonald Tobacco (now JTI-Macdonald Corporation), emerged in Montreal in 1858 (Alberta Health Services, n.d.). This non-Aboriginal–owned corporation is now one of the three leading tobacco companies in Canada, along with Imperial Tobacco Canada and Rothmans, Benson & Hedges. While the three largest companies dominate the Canadian market and are the powerhouse of the tobacco industry in North America, other smaller Aboriginal-owned companies, including Tabac ADL and Grand River Enterprises, were established in the 1990s (Ontario Campaign for Action on Tobacco, n.d.).

Commercial Tobacco Use

While statistics vary, the overall smoking rate among Aboriginal populations is two to three times higher than that of the non-Aboriginal population. The datasets used to capture the statistics on tobacco smoking come primarily from the Canadian Community Health Survey and the Aboriginal Peoples Survey, which are both administered by Statistics Canada and focus on Aboriginal peoples not living on reserves. Statistics also come from the First Nations Regional Longitudinal Health Survey administered by the First Nations Information Governance Centre, which focuses on First Nations people living on reserves. Other studies gather more specific data or compare rates of smoking within Indigenous populations in other countries.

The most recent Statistics Canada data indicates that 32 per cent of First Nations people, 30 per cent of Métis people, 39 per cent of Inuit and 15 per cent of non-Aboriginal people smoke (Gionet & Roshanafshar, 2013). Another study (Public Health Agency of Canada, 2011) found that First Nations people living on reserves smoke more than First Nations people who do not live on reserves (43 per cent and 35 per cent, respectively). However, research in specific communities has found even higher rates of smoking. For example, Chateau-Degat and colleagues (2010) found that 84 per cent of Inuit adults in Quebec smoke commercial tobacco.

Aboriginal youth in Canada also have a higher smoking rate than non-Aboriginal youth. Elton-Marshall and colleagues (2011) found that among Aboriginal youth in grades 9 to 12 living off reserves, 25 per cent smoked compared to 10 per cent of their non-Aboriginal counterparts. These Aboriginal youth were also more likely than non-Aboriginal youth to be exposed to second-hand smoke in the home (37 per cent versus 20 per cent) and in cars (51 per cent versus 30 per cent). The higher rate of smoking in cars may be attributed in part to youth being in cars with other youth who are smoking, and to Aboriginal youth being more likely to have parents in the car who also smoke. For the period 2007–2010, Statistics Canada reported that Aboriginal children were more likely to be exposed to second-hand smoke in the home, particularly

Métis youth, whose exposure was 24 per cent compared with seven per cent for non-Aboriginal youth (aged 12 to 24 years). Smoking rates for First Nations youth living off reserves and for Inuit were not provided (Gionet & Roshanafshar, 2013).

General studies have found that people who smoke in the home also endanger other members of the household by exposing them to "third-hand smoke"—the toxic chemicals from smoking that remain in clothing, hair, furniture, dust and anything else exposed to tobacco smoke. Babies and toddlers are particularly vulnerable because of their higher respiratory rate and because they are more likely to be touching objects and putting them in their mouths (Canadian Lung Association, 2014).

Elton-Marshall, Leatherdale, Burkhalter and Brown (2013) found that although non-Aboriginal youth's susceptibility to smoking decreased from 2004 to 2008, susceptibility among Aboriginal youth stayed the same. In general, people who are younger and have lower income and education smoke more than people who are older and have a higher income and education (Reid et al., 2012). The fact that Aboriginal people tend to be younger, poorer and less educated than non-Aboriginal people may partially account for their higher smoking rates.

While smoking has declined in the non-Aboriginal population over the past few decades (Canadian Tobacco Use Monitoring Survey, 2012), the rate of decline has been slower within Aboriginal populations.

Morbidity and Mortality Related to Smoking

Not only are smoking rates higher in Aboriginal communities; morbidity and mortality related to smoking are also higher (Wardman & Khan, 2004). Rates vary substantially between First Nations, Inuit and Métis.

The Centers for Disease Control and Prevention ([CDC], 2013) classifies the following as smoking-related diseases:
• cancers of the lip, oral cavity, pharynx, esophagus, stomach, pancreas, larynx, trachea, lung, bronchus, cervix, kidney, bladder, and acute myeloid leukemia
• cardiovascular diseases, specifically ischemic heart disease, cerebrovascular disease, atherosclerosis, aortic aneurysm and other arterial diseases
• respiratory diseases, including pneumonia, influenza, bronchitis, emphysema and chronic airway obstruction.

Infants and children exposed to second-hand smoke or whose mother smoked while pregnant are at risk of low birth weight, respiratory distress syndrome and other respiratory conditions, and sudden infant death syndrome (CDC, 2013).

Wardman and Khan (2004) compared smoking-attributable mortality (SAM) in First Nations communities and non–First Nations communities in British Columbia. The study examined deaths among adults over age 34 years and infants aged one year and younger between 1997 and 2001. Age- and gender-adjusted SAM rates were higher in the First Nations population. The sam rates were 39.9 (1997) and 28.6 (2001) per 10,000 for First Nations adults, and 27.8 and 25.3 per 10,000 for non–First Nations adults. The sam rates were 6.8 and 3.6 per 10,000 for First Nations infants, and 1.4 and 1.0 per 10,000 for non–First Nations infants. First Nations tended to have higher death rates as a result of smoking compared with non–First Nations smokers, which may be due to comorbid factors, such as a higher rate of diabetes (Wardman & Khan, 2004). Although the study did not address the relationship between adverse living conditions (e.g., mould in homes and overcrowding) and higher rates of poverty in First Nations and higher mortality rates, these factors might have also played a role.

Smoking-related cancer is more prevalent in the Inuit Nanangat population compared with the rest of Canada (Carrière et al., 2012). For example, lung and bronchus cancers were the most frequent types of cancer for Inuit males (36 per cent) and Inuit females (27 per cent), compared to prostate cancer (24 per cent) for other males and breast cancer (28 per cent) for other females (Carrière et al., 2012).

In a national Statistics Canada report exploring mortality rates among Métis and status First Nations people, the rate of smoking-related morbidity was higher for Métis adults than status First Nations adults (a ratio of 1.14:0.98 for males and 1.76:1.17 for females) (Tjepkema et al., 2009).

Prevention and Cessation Programs

Although I have never smoked tobacco, I recognize the challenge people face when trying to quit, even when they know it will be detrimental to their health. Tobacco dependence, like all addictions, is complex and needs to be examined in relationship to other issues such as poverty, addictions, mental health issues and other social factors when considering the Aboriginal community. Elder Vern Harper, who worked for more than 10 years at the Centre for Addiction and Mental Health's Aboriginal Services, stated that tobacco is the hardest addiction to break: it is even worse than trying to kick heroin! As a previous heroin addict, Vern Harper spoke from the position of lived experience. He explained that tobacco is often the last addiction that someone tries to break. If that person has given up alcohol and other drugs, tobacco may be his or her only remaining vice. Many smokers have told me that they don't want to quit. For people living in poverty who have felt controlled by society, tobacco may be the one thing that they feel can't be taken away from them. A 68-year-old First Nation woman who I spoke to recently says that she has few friends on the reserve, doesn't go out, and has little money, so smoking is her only enjoyment. I could not argue with that. This reflects the complexity of tobacco addiction and the strong relationship people have with tobacco.

Helping Aboriginal people to quit smoking requires understanding why they smoke. In addition to the unique social, historical and psychological stressors that Aboriginal people experience that may be linked to smoking, physiological factors also explain why some people smoke and find it more difficult to quit. A growing body of research suggests that nicotinic acetylcholine receptors (nAChRs) mitigate nicotine reward, dependence and addiction (Wu, 2009), and that genetics play a significant role in susceptibility to nicotine (Davies & Soundy, 2009). Genetics play a role in the decision to smoke, the ability to quit and whether a person succeeds in a smoking cessation program (Davies & Soundy, 2009). People with a greater physiological susceptibility to tobacco addiction may need more intensive smoking cessation therapy. Although Aboriginal people may be wary of genetic studies because of past and continuing injustices in research, it may be useful for future research to explore a possible genetic predisposition to tobacco addiction among Aboriginal people given their higher rates of tobacco use.

Population approaches to tobacco prevention include public service announcements that address the dangers of smoking, and school-based education campaigns. These prevention and health promotion efforts should reflect Aboriginal people and Aboriginal world views. For example, a campaign run by an Aboriginal group in Canada created "Let's keep tobacco sacred!" posters. Legislation is another population approach: it includes legislating that graphic pictures and warnings be displayed on cigarette packaging, not allowing cigarette and tobacco products to be displayed in stores, and banning smoking in public places. Although provincial and municipal legislation in Canada does not extend to First Nations people living on reserves, many First Nations communities ban smoking in public places, such as bingo halls, casinos and the workplace. Federal taxation on tobacco products is also meant to deter smoking and is particularly effective for youth (Ross & Chaloupka, 2003). However, cigarettes and tobacco sold on reserves to First Nations status people are less expensive because tobacco does not carry the heavy tax burden of buying cigarettes off reserves (Elton-Marshall, Leatherdale & Burkhalter, 2013).

Individual approaches to tobacco cessation include one-on-one, group and peer counselling; motivational interviewing; and nicotine replacement therapies (NRT) in the form of gums, patches, nasal spray, inhalers and lozenges. Prescription medications such as bupropion (Wellbutrin) and varenicline (Champix) are also used in tobacco cessation therapy. The cost of NRTs and prescription medications may be similar; however, only prescription medications are covered by extended health care plans or non-insured benefits for status First Nations people. Since NRTs are generally available without a prescription, they are not covered by most health care plans.

There has been little research on the effectiveness of NRTs, prescription drugs and other smoking cessation approaches in Aboriginal populations. Only four per cent of

First Nations smokers in a British Columbia study attempted to use individual tobacco cessation approaches (Wardman & Khan, 2004). Wardman and colleagues (2007) compared perceptions of tobacco cessation therapies in First Nations people living on reserves in northern British Columbia and Saskatchewan and non-Aboriginal people affiliated with these reserves. They found that fewer Aboriginal people were willing to try bupropion or the nicotine patch, although those who sought care from a physician were more likely to consider using the drug. In addition, First Nations people who were aware that the cost of the prescription was subsidized were more willing to try drug therapy.

Studies exploring individual tobacco cessation interventions with Aboriginal people are limited. This lack of research was highlighted in a meta-analysis of smoking cessation initiatives in Indigenous populations in Canada, Australia, New Zealand and the United States (DiGiacomo et al., 2011). Only 16 articles from these countries (and only one from Canada) explored the impact of individual-level interventions. This gap illustrates the need for more research on individual-level interventions, as well as population-based interventions with Aboriginal people in Canada.

DiGiacomo and colleagues' (2011) meta-analysis did, however, reveal higher cessation rates for interventions that included NRT or bupropion compared to those that included only counselling or education. Of the studies that included NRT or bupropion, those that combined counselling and/or other supports were more effective than counselling or medication alone. Although this meta-analysis did not include studies of varenicline, non-Indigenous studies have demonstrated that varenicline is superior to bupropion followed by NRT. Studies of people using NRT patches have revealed low compliance. Pharmacotherapy is suggested for people who may be genetically predisposed to nicotine addiction (DiGiacomo, et al., 2011). A *Toronto Star* (McLean & Bailey, 2012) article suggested that Heath Canada was being tight-lipped about varenicline as a leading suspected cause of reported suicides. However, Thomas and colleagues (2013) reported no evidence of an increased risk of suicidal behaviour among people taking varenicline or bupropion for tobacco cessation. Further research may be needed, particularly about pharmacological approaches with people who might be depressed.

Studies of counselling interventions have found that more intensive interventions that are adapted to the individual's schedule are more successful (DiGiacomo et al., 2011). Support that addressed systemic barriers to accessing treatment, such as ensuring clients had transit fare or child care, and covering the costs of NRT and prescriptions increased success rates. The cost of NRTs, prescription medication and counselling is a definite barrier for Aboriginal people. Although Health Canada covers non-insured health benefits such as the costs of NRTs, prescription medication and counselling for some status First Nations people and Inuit, they may not be able to access these benefits because of the complex bureaucratic approval process. Non-status First Nations and Métis people are not covered.

DiGiacomo and colleagues (2011) also found that people who reported high levels of stress were less successful with smoking cessation. Because stress is a factor that affects success, studies have recommended including stress management in smoking cessation programs. However, adequately addressing stress may be challenging because Aboriginal people are affected by larger social and systemic issues such as poverty, colonization and dispossession (DiGiacomo et al., 2011).

The meta-analysis conducted by DiGiacomo and colleagues (2011) did not discuss the transtheoretical model of behaviour change. This model involves various stages of readiness for change: pre-contemplation, contemplation, preparation, action, maintenance and termination. The type of intervention is determined by which stage of change the person is at (Prochaska et al., 2008). The model incorporates processes of change, such as seeking and using social supports, using a decisional balance to assess the pros and cons of change and developing self-efficacy or confidence in oneself and one's ability to resist temptations to change.

One of my strongest critiques of the transtheoretical model is its lack of attention to systemic issues such as colonization, oppression, dispossession, poverty, and its emphasis on individual behaviour change rather than on a holistic, integrated approach. People with higher stress and who live with other smokers have a more difficult time quitting (2008 PHS Guideline Update Panel et al., 2008), which affects the degree to which the person feels able to quit smoking. If we simply focus on the stages of change and the individual, we fail to look at Aboriginal peoples in a holistic way. Poverty and isolation, and the sense of hopelessness and helplessness that may arise from these and other societal pressures, are very real issues that must be addressed. People working with Aboriginal clients need to be aware of these broader issues while they help them to make changes at the individual level.

Culturally Relevant Prevention and Cessation

The research literature is clear: Aboriginal communities need culturally relevant and targeted initiatives (Selby et al., 2011; Wardman et al., 2007). While the relationship that Aboriginal people have to tobacco may be similar to the relationship non-Aboriginal people have to smoking, tobacco cessation strategies used in the mainstream may not be ideal for Aboriginal people. Tobacco cessation interventions need to be culturally appropriate, but they cannot be built on studies conducted with one or two Aboriginal communities because the findings cannot be generalized to all Aboriginal people. The circumstances of First Nations people living on reserves differ from those of people living in urban areas or off reserves. For example, people living on reserves have access to cheaper cigarettes but poorer access to health care. Such differences between settings mean that tobacco cessation programs need to be tailored to each community (DiGiacoma et al., 2011). Working with the community to design an intervention ensures that the needs of the community are considered and targets potential barriers to success. Incorporating the community's cultural practices into the intervention is also essential (DiGiacoma et al., 2011).

An international example, "The village that quit smoking" (Groth-Marnat et al., 1996), illustrates how an entire community succeeded in cutting smoking rates through a culturally based smoking cessation program that it developed. In 1990, 31 per cent of adults in the Fijian village of Nabila smoked. When a medical team that had been working with the community since 1986 failed to influence the community's smoking rates, the team proposed to match the community's funds to build a community centre if the entire village abstained from smoking. Elders conducted a ceremony in which the community gathered together all the cigarettes and the smokers chain-smoked them. Afterward a formal taboo on smoking was put in effect. Further ceremonies were conducted with people who relapsed. The community maintained a very low smoking rate after the ceremony.

For Aboriginal people who come from nations where tobacco was and is a sacred medicine, approaches to prevention and cessation have often hinged on traditional teachings. For example, Cancer Care Ontario's Aboriginal Tobacco Program encourages "tobacco-wise" communities rather than "tobacco-free" communities. The program recognizes that many Aboriginal communities use tobacco in a sacred way and that tobacco may not be used to "feed a powerful and deadly addiction" (Aboriginal Tobacco Program, n.d., ¶5). The Aboriginal Tobacco Program is primarily educational, teaching the difference between sacred and commercial tobacco use through fact sheets, posters and activities, such as a photography project called Pathway to a Healthy Life, in which children from Nipissing First Nation used cameras to capture their views on the positive and negative aspects of tobacco use in their community (Aboriginal Tobacco Program, 2010).

Conclusion

Cultural understanding of tobacco as a sacred medicine differs across Aboriginal communities. Smoking prevention and cessation programs need to be culturally relevant and tailored to the needs and situation of each First Nation, Inuit or Métis community. The community needs to be involved in developing the programs. In larger urban centres, community involvement might be organized by Aboriginal agencies.

If the government is sincere about getting people to quit smoking, tobacco education and cessation programs, including counselling, NRTs and pharmacotherapy, would be widely available and accessible to Aboriginal people. Of course, the leading tobacco companies would suffer greatly, so perhaps influencing the tobacco industry is the greatest hurdle! Free tobacco cessation programs would yield a significant return for the health care system—with decreased smoking-attributed morbidity and mortality, increased quality of life and a break in the family cycle of smoking.

As we begin to role model non-smoking, our communities will inevitably follow suit. It is my dream that my niece and nephew model this behaviour for my grandnephew and break the cycle within our own family.

References

2008 PHS Guideline Update Panel, Liaisons & Staff. (2008). *Clinical Practice Guideline: Treating Tobacco Use and Dependence: 2008 Update*. Rockville, MD: Department of Health and Human Services. Retrieved from www.ahrq.gov/clinic/tobacco/treating_tobacco_use08.pdf

Aboriginal Tobacco Program. (n.d.). About us. Retrieved from www.tobaccowise.com

Aboriginal Tobacco Program. (2010). *Pathway to a Healthy Life* [video]. Retrieved from www.tobaccowise.com

Alberta Health Services. (n.d.). Tobacco industry. Retrieved from www.albertahealthservices.ca/2536.asp

Canadian Lung Association. (2014). Smoking & tobacco. Retrieved from www.lung.ca

Carrière, G.M., Tjepkema, M., Pennock, J. & Goedhuis, N. (2012). Cancer patterns in Inuit Nanangat: 1998–2007. *International Journal of Circumpolar Health*, 71, 1–8. Retrieved from http://dx.doi.org/10.3402/ijch.v71i0.18581

Centers for Disease Control and Prevention (CDC). (2013). *Tobacco-Related Mortality*. Retrieved from www.cdc.gov/tobacco/data_statistics/fact_sheets/health_effects/tobacco_related_mortality/

Chateau-Degat, M-L., Dewailly, É., Louchini, R., Counil, É., Noël, M., Ferland, A., . . . Egeland, G.M. (2010). Cardiovascular burden and related risk factors among Nunavik (Quebec) Inuit: Insights from baseline findings in the circumpolar Inuit Health in Transition cohort study. *Canadian Journal of Cardiology*, 26 (6), e190–e196.

Davies, G.E. & Soundy, T.J. (2009). The genetics of smoking and nicotine addiction. *South Dakota Journal of Medicine* (Special issue), 43–49.

DiGiacomo, M., Davidson, P.M., Abbott, P.A., Davison, J., Moore, L. & Thompson, S.C. (2011). Smoking cessation in Indigenous populations of Australia, New Zealand, Canada, and the United States: Elements of effective interventions. *International Journal of Environmental Research and Public Health*, 8, 388–410. DOI: 10.3390/ijerph8020388

Elton-Marshall, T., Leatherdale, S.T. & Burkhalter, R. (2011). Tobacco, alcohol and illicit drug use among Aboriginal youth living off-reserve: Results from the Youth Smoking Survey. *Canadian Medical Association Journal*, 183, E480–488. DOI: 10.1503/cmaj.101913

Elton-Marshall, T., Leatherdale, S. T. & Burkhalter, R. (2013). Native, discount or premium brand cigarettes: What types of cigarettes are Canadian youth currently smoking? *Nicotine & Tobacco Research*, 15, 435–443.

Elton-Marshall, T., Leatherdale, S.T., Burkhalter, R. & Brown, K.S. (2013). Changes in tobacco use, susceptibility to future smoking and quit attempts among Canadian youths over time: A comparison of off-reserve Aboriginal and non-Aboriginal youth. *International Journal of Environmental Research and Public Health*, 10, 729–741.

Gionet, L. & Roshanafshar, S. (2013). *Select Health Indicators of First Nations People Living Off-Reserve, Métis and Inuit* (Statistics Canada catalogue no. 82-624-X). Retrieved from www.statcan.gc.ca/pub/82-624-x/2013001/article/11763-eng.pdf

Groth-Marnat, G., Leslie, S. & Renneker, M. (1996). Tobacco control in a traditional Fijian village: Indigenous methods of smoking cessation and relapse prevention. *Social Science & Medicine*, 43, 473–477.

Lavallée, L. (2005, June). Sacred tobacco use in the Aboriginal community: What you should know as a researcher and practitioner. Paper presented at the Canadian National Conference on Tobacco and Health, Ottawa.

Lavallée, L. (2009). Practical application of an Indigenous research framework and Indigenous research methods: Sharing circles and Anishnaabe symbol-based reflection. *International Journal of Qualitative Methods*, 8 (1), 21–40. Retrieved from http://ejournals.library.ualberta.ca/index.php/IJQM/article/view/943/5195

McLean, J. & Bailey, A. (2012, October 4). Health Canada tight-lipped on Champix suicides. Retrieved from *Toronto Star* website: www.thestar.com

Ontario Campaign for Action on Tobacco. (n.d.). Canadian tobacco companies. Retrieved from www.ocat.org/opposition/industry.html#

Piquemal, N. (2001). Free and informed consent in research involving Native American communities. *American Indian Culture and Research Journal, 25* (1), 65–79.

Prochaska, J.O., Redding, C.A. & Evers, K.E. (2008). The transtheoretical model and stages of change. In K. Glanz, B.K. Rimer & K. Viswanath (Eds.), *Health Behavior and Health Education: Theory, Research and Practice* (pp. 97–122). San Francisco: Jossey-Bass.

Public Health Agency of Canada. (2011). *Diabetes in Canada: Facts and Figures from a Public Health Perspective.* Retrieved from www.phac-aspc.gc.ca

Reid, J.L., Hammond, D., Burkhalter, R. & Ahmed, R. (2012). *Tobacco Use in Canada: Patterns and Trends—2012 Edition.* Waterloo, ON: Propel Centre for Population Health Impact, University of Waterloo. Retrieved from www.tobaccoreport.ca/2012/TobaccoUseinCanada_2012.pdf

Ross, H., Chaloupka, F. & Wakefield, M. (2006). Youth smoking uptake progress: Price and public policy effects. *Eastern Economic Journal, 32*, 355–367.

Selby, P., Herie, M., Zawertailo, L., Dragonetti, R., Hussain, S., Czyzewski, K. & Lecce, J. (2011). *Aboriginal-Focused Resources for Commercial Tobacco Cessation: An Environmental Scan of Resources, Programs and Tools.* Retrieved from Nicotine Dependence Clinic, Centre for Addiction and Mental Health website: www.nicotinedependenceclinic.com

Thomas, K.H., Martin, R.M., Davies, N.M., Metcalfe, C., Windmejer, F. & Gunnell, D. (2013). Smoking cessation treatment and risk of depression, suicide, and self harm in the Clinical Practice Research Datalink: Prospective cohort study. *BMJ, 347.* DOI: 10.1136/bmj.f5704

Tjepkema, M., Wilkins, R., Senécal, S., Guimond, E. & Penney, C. (2009). *Mortality of Métis and Registered Indian Adults in Canada: An 11-Year Follow-up Study* (Component of Statistics Canada catalogue no. 82-003-X). Retrieved from www.statcan.gc.ca/pub/82-003-x/2009004/article/11034-eng.pdf

Wardman, D. & Khan, N. (2004). Smoking-attributable mortality among British Columbia's First Nations populations. *International Journal of Circumpolar Health, 63* (1), 81–92.

Wardman, D., Quantz, D., Tootoosis, J. & Khan, N. (2007). Tobacco cessation drug therapy among Canada's Aboriginal people. *Nicotine and Tobacco Research, 9*, 607–611.

Wu, J. (2009). Understanding of nicotinic acetylcholine receptors. *Acta Pharmacologica Sinica, 30*, 653–655. DOI: 10.1039/aps.2009.89

ABOUT THE AUTHOR

Lynn F. Lavallée, BA, MSC, PHD, is Anishinaabe Métis born in Sudbury, Ontario. She moved to Toronto as a child and grew up in the social housing development Regent Park. As a youth and young adult she faced mental health challenges. Lynn has a BA in psychology and kinesiology, an MSC in community health and a PHD in social work. She is an associate professor at Ryerson University, as well as associate director of the School of Social Work and chair of the Research Ethics Board. Her research interests include the holistic well-being of Indigenous peoples, social and political determinants of health and Indigenous research ethics.

Chapter 20

Gambling

YALE D. BELANGER[*]

Information about gambling among the Indigenous[1] peoples of North America is limited. Although the literature offers impressive prevalence studies, the formal addiction counselling literature about Indigenous peoples focuses on substance use problems and, more recently, suicide, but remains mostly silent about gambling problems and treatment options.

This gap in the research may have to do with the fact that, unlike gambling, "substance abuse conflicts with traditional Aboriginal cultural beliefs about courage, humility, generosity, and family honour, [and therefore] cultural wholeness can serve as both a preventative and a curative agent in substance-abuse treatment" (McCormick, 2009, p. 351). This statement raises a few important questions: what if the troubling behaviour reflects traditional Indigenous cultural beliefs? What if it is a historical aspect of traditional Indigenous cultures? Acknowledging that traditional games and gambling differ from modern games and gambling, which emphasize high-stakes wagering, how do we develop responsive treatment strategies that do not simultaneously undermine the cultural role of other forms of gambling?

This chapter is for anyone who wants to understand the historical context of Indigenous gambling, how these traditions have been maintained and how they may continue to influence contemporary Indigenous gambling practices. It highlights the central roles that games and gambling played in most pre-contact North American societies and seeks to offer insights from which to establish culturally unique programming to address gambling disorders among contemporary Indigenous peoples.

---

* I would like to thank Dr. David Gregory for his insightful comments after reviewing an earlier draft, which helped strengthen this chapter. Any errors in fact or interpretation are solely my responsibility.

1 This chapter uses the term "Indigenous" to refer to the original inhabitants of North America. The term "Aboriginal" is used to refer specifically to the Indigenous peoples of Canada.

A Historical and Cultural Perspective on Traditional Games

Traditionally, gambling was a common feature of most Indigenous communities in North America. The peoples' beliefs about life and reality guided their interpretation and understanding of games and wagering. Events such as sporting competitions, pow wows and rodeos included, and continue to include, traditional games and related wagering (Deiter-Buffalo, 1996). These are large gatherings for entertainment that historically were both social and political: they enabled multiple communities to interact, a process deemed essential in promoting non-hostile environments where people from different communities freely exchanged goods, rather than acquiring goods through raids and warfare (Herndon, 1979). These events were "occasions of feasting and gift giving, accompanied by singing, dancing, gambling and contests of skill" (Belanger, 2006, p. 29). Little is known about the cultural meaning of the games played by Indigenous peoples, and even less is known about the differences in gambling behaviours among these groups. Arguably, we must understand the past, by examining how different cultural groups assign different roles and meanings to gambling, before we grapple with the current state of gambling disorders among Indigenous peoples (Dieter-Buffalo, 1996). This knowledge can help us to develop culturally reflective and competent approaches to assist people who are struggling with their gambling behaviour (Duran, 2006; Raylu & Oei, 2004).

The history of Indigenous games and gambling is impressive, as Stewart Culin demonstrated with his massive 846-page inventory of Indigenous gaming practices in North America, first published in 1907 (Culin, 1907/1992). In all, he catalogued 36 games among the 229 Indigenous communities he observed. The games were divided into two general classes: games of chance and games of dexterity. Impressed with the author's ability to advance both our collective "understanding of the technology of games and of their distribution," a Culin admirer insightfully concluded that his work was an "appreciation of native modes of thought and of the motives and impulses that underlie the conduct" of Indigenous people generally (Holmes, 1907, pp. 39–40). Clearly, these ideas came to inform several generations of academics studying Indigenous gambling: in 2004, *The Encyclopedia of the Great Plains* (Wishart, 2004) characterized these games precisely as Culin had. Despite Culin's enlightened approach highlighting the complexity of both the games and the wagering practices, most writers portrayed the games as a morally reprehensible pastime: lazy individuals seeking improved living conditions through games of chance. Europeans were shocked to witness Indigenous gamblers losing their possessions, which confirmed their belief that these were the actions of uncivilized peoples (Belanger, 2006). The social acceptance by mainstream society of these attitudes led to the vilification of these activities so much so that by the time Culin's work became well known, mainstream society considered Indigenous gaming, once a hallmark of Indigenous political economies, the purview of the uncivilized. The popular misperception of all Indigenous people as inveterate gamblers persists to this day.

Games and gambling were more than simple amusements or diversions. They were often used to predict the future or to curry favour with Creation and its various manifestations; beating the odds meant that an individual had won spiritual protection (Binde, 2007; Culin, 1992). Gaming ceremonies were used to promote good hunts, secure superior harvests and assist with various curative measures and funerary customs (Culin, 1992; Gabriel, 1996; Salter, 1972). Other writers have suggested that the intensity and prevalence of Indigenous gaming practices resulted from the demand for inter-tribal competition (Binde, 2005). Few, however, have taken the opportunity to determine the importance of gaming practices to pre- and post-contact political economies, a process that would necessitate studying the influence of games and wagering techniques over trade, diplomacy, politics, education and kinship. Several studies have expanded on gaming's contemporary role in Indigenous communities (Belanger, 2006; Campbell, 1999; McGowan & Nixon, 2004; McGowan et al., 2002; Nilson, 2004; Skea, 1997). Yet the fact remains that the historical role of gaming in Indigenous societies has been only marginally explored (Belanger, 2011; Deiter-Buffalo, 1996; Guth, 1994; Heine, 1991; Lange, 2004).

Academics rarely situate games and gambling within larger Indigenous society. As a result, these studies confine the games to history, as a pre-contact phenomenon now vanished. Or they portray gaming as an affectation of modernity that Indigenous peoples embrace in order to buttress sagging economies, further demonstrating gambling's limited ties to the past. As I discuss below, recent research demonstrates the centrality of gaming to most Indigenous societies in North America, and that in certain cases, historical ways of wagering on traditional games inform modern wagering philosophies. The high incidence of gambling in these societies also suggests that contemporary individuals often do not consider their gambling behaviours problematic, since, as I have heard many people reason, "That's the way we've always done things."

Definitions of Gambling Behaviours

Many people enjoy social gambling, which the American Psychiatric Association ([APA], 2013) defines in the *Diagnostic and Statistical Manual of Mental Disorders* (DSM-5) as gambling that typically occurs with friends or colleagues and lasts for a limited period of time, with acceptable losses. The concept of an acceptable level of social gambling contrasts with an earlier conceptualization of gambling or gaming as a sin or vice. In the latter part of the 20th century, gambling behaviour came to be medicalized, so that participation at a level that became troublesome for the person gambling was identified as a disease (Rose, 1988). When a person was unable to control his or her gambling, this gambling behaviour was identified as compulsive, addicted, disordered, problem or pathological, or some combination of these (Campbell & Smith, 2003). Often used interchangeably to describe gambling behaviour, these last two terms, "problem" and "pathological," encompassed addicted or disordered behaviour, but in fact represented different concepts. Problem gambling was defined as "gambling behaviour that creates negative consequences [e.g., bankruptcy, job distress] for the gambler, others in his or her social network, or for the community" (Ferris & Wynne, 2001, p. 12). Pathological gambling was defined as the more acute expression of gambling-related problems, and was recognized as a mental disorder in the DSM-IV (APA, 1994). Pathological gambling's primary features were listed as a continuous or periodic loss of control over gambling; a progression in gambling frequency and amounts wagered, preoccupation with gambling and obtaining money with which to gamble; and continued gambling involvement despite adverse consequences (APA, 1994). The DSM-5 (APA, 2013) has reclassified and renamed pathological gambling as "gambling disorder," and has also refined the diagnosis so that a person's gambling disorder may be described as mild, moderate or severe, depending on the number of diagnostic criteria met. Because the literature cited in this chapter predates the publication of the DSM-5, the DSM-IV definition of pathological gambling is used here.

Contemporary Problem and Pathological Gambling Trends

Historically, Indigenous populations embraced games and gambling activities in ways that today's DSM-5 would clearly classify as social. Today, many Indigenous people continue to enjoy social gambling in various forms and manage their gambling behaviour without difficulty, contrary to lingering perceptions that all Indigenous people who gamble will develop a gambling disorder.

Yet the available data indicates that problem and pathological gambling behaviours are five times higher among Indigenous peoples compared with the general population. Early research found that among Indigenous peoples, the prevalence of problem gambling ranged from 5.8 per cent to 19 per cent and that of pathological gambling from 6.6 per cent to 22 per cent (Wardman et al., 2001). Wardman and colleagues also reported that the estimated lifetime prevalence rate of problem and probable pathological gambling in Aboriginal populations was 14.5 per cent, compared with 3.5 per cent in the general population. Among First Nations, the prevalence rate of problem and probable pathological gambling was an estimated 12.3 per cent, compared with 2 per cent in the general population (Volberg, 1993). U.S. research (comparable to emerging trends in Canada) confirmed increased rates of both pathological and potentially pathological gambling among American Indian populations (Cozzetto, 1995; Cozzetto & Larocque, 1996). Two Canadian studies estimated that 28 per cent of First Nations people in Alberta gambled problematically, while an additional 21 per cent were at risk of developing a problem (Hewitt & Auger, 1995).

Despite their limited nature, these studies clearly suggested that Aboriginal people in Canada are more likely than non-Aboriginal people to develop gambling addiction (Hewitt, 1994; Hewitt & Auger, 1995). Relying on an extensive literature review and five prevalence studies involving Aboriginal people, Williams and colleagues (2011) estimated the overall average rate of problem and pathological gambling among Aboriginal peoples to be between 10 per cent and 20 per cent. They cautioned, however, that the prevalence rate among different Aboriginal groups may vary considerably, from 7 per cent to 45 per cent. In identifying this problematic trend, they concluded that "the Canadian provincial problem gambling prevalence rate is in fact *best* predicted by proportion of the population with Aboriginal ancestry" (p. 21). The greater the percentage of Aboriginal people in the provincial population, the greater the prevalence of problem gambling.

Various explanations have been proposed to explain the higher rates of problem and pathological gambling among Indigenous peoples (Raylu & Oei, 2004). At the same time, there is an absence of significant research specifically about Indigenous gambling to help us determine the root causes. However, five reasons for these higher rates of problem and pathological gambling have been posited:

- Gambling's cultural acceptance in Indigenous communities is likely related to a higher participation rate (Williams et al., 2011).
- Historical forms of gambling that relied on supernatural forces to influence game outcomes suggested that humans could also influence game outcomes by treating the spirits properly (Shanley, 2000). The research at this stage is thin, but it has been suggested that this belief continues to influence Indigenous gamblers (Joukhador et al., 2004).
- Inadequate socio-economic and socio-political achievement leads to poverty, unemployment, health problems and societal marginalization, which result in high rates of mental health and substance use problems (Chansonneuve, 2007). Having a mental health or substance use problem predisposes a person to addictions such as problem gambling (Petry, 2007).
- The comparatively young average age of Aboriginal people in Canada may contribute to a trend of younger people experiencing the highest rate of problem gambling.
- Aboriginal communities have a greater availability of gambling products and gaming sites that could potentially lead to greater overall harm. For example, increased Internet access in remote communities means that Aboriginal people have easy access to gambling through online gambling sites despite the lack of physical access to video lottery terminals (VLTs), electronic gambling machines and casinos. An added "bonus" is that people may be able to gamble in the comfort of their homes, away from prying eyes.

Characteristics of Problem and Pathological Gambling in Indigenous People

Contemporary Indigenous people, like everyone else, gamble for various reasons, perhaps the most popular being that it provides escape, sometimes from overwhelming life circumstances (McGowan & Nixon, 2004). Others may gamble as a way of seeking prestige by emulating various cultural heroes' gambling exploits (McGowan & Nixon, 2004; Nixon & Solowoniuk, 2009). Many manage their gambling activities effectively, and some may restrict their activities to traditional games. Those who have difficulty managing their gambling, particularly those with moderate to severe gambling problems, may experience serious social, emotional, health and financial consequences. They may have work-related difficulties, such as lower productivity, higher absenteeism and job loss, and may experience higher rates of marital and family breakdown. McCown and Howatt (2007) identified clues that gambling behaviour is becoming problematic, including:

- health signs: sleep disturbances, weight change, poor hygiene, moodiness, headaches, various physical ailments, heart palpitations, hypertension, gastrointestinal problems
- emotional stress: depression, anxiety, secretiveness, explosiveness, excessive defensiveness, reports of suicidal or homicidal thoughts
- financial issues: unpaid or late payment of bills, selling personal or family possessions to finance gambling activities, a sudden infusion of cash, indifference to financial matters.

In addition to experiencing problems in these areas, more than half of people with gambling problems also have substance use problems, not including smoking (Black & Moyer, 1999; Zimmerman et al., 2006).

Gambling in Traditional Games According to Traditional Means

To date, little research has been devoted to the impact of culture on gambling among Indigenous people. It is assumed that cultural factors play a significant role, even if these factors are given limited attention in prevalence studies (Betancourt & López, 1993). The lack of research is largely due to difficulties studying so many different communities across Canada. There is nothing in the literature or in my own experience working with Aboriginal leaders and community members to indicate that people who exclusively gamble at traditional games will develop problem or pathological gambling behaviours. My own research indicates that this is probably true for several reasons:

- Traditional games are not played as frequently, which limits the opportunities to over-participate. These games are usually only played at pow wows or similar gatherings.
- Where traditional games are played and wagering takes place, knowledge holders, Elders or older people are usually on hand to monitor and guide the play and restrict wagering by limiting pot amounts.
- Participants frequently respect historical norms and usually only wager material possessions rather than cash (although use of cash has been increasing). As discussed below, it is also evident that the norms that historically guided these games and wagering practices, such as betting material possessions while being supervised, are still regularly practised today.

Co-existence of Traditional and Contemporary Games and Wagering Behaviour

The situation becomes more complicated with the addition of modern forms of gambling. Traditional wagering techniques when playing traditional games co-exist with modern wagering techniques when playing modern games of chance. To describe this phenomenon, I refer to a conversation I had in 2011 with a front-line addiction counsellor who works in a northern Alberta First Nation community with people who have gambling problems. She was concerned about recent trends that were emerging among youth who gambled. These young people regularly participated in traditional games after school and on weekends, such as the hand and stick games, where participants are permitted to gamble their possessions, in keeping with the games' traditions. What disturbed this counsellor was the number of young people who, upon returning home, immediately headed to the computer to go to online poker sites. In her opinion, the youth did not distinguish between the very different types of gambling. Traditional gambling is a social and spiritual activity that draws all age and gender groups together and where, traditionally, reciprocity ensured that wealth did not leave the community, but remained and circulated internally. Young people who played traditional games did so in the presence of older people, who observed their actions to ensure they learned the rules and how to wager properly. Online gambling, on the other hand, involves wagering substantial amounts of cash, is done alone and unsupervised and sees wealth removed from the community. For youth in this community, the rules and supervision involved in traditional gambling were absent when it came time to register their online poker wagers—something the youth failed to realize. They found it socially acceptable to gamble when participating in traditional games and when playing online poker games: they failed to distinguish between the two forms of gambling.

Modern games such as VLTs, bingo, lotteries and those found in casinos are now as popular as traditional games, such as stick games and horse racing. This has cultural consequences, as reported by McGowan and Nixon (2004): "Bingo, VLT playing, and casino gambling have had a significant cultural impact in many communities by replacing or reducing participation in cultural activities of a more traditional nature" (p. 12). This is an issue because there is less community monitoring of gambling behaviour with modern wagering on modern games. Also, historically, traditional wagering methods made it possible for people to wager all of their personal possessions without significant personal hardship. If a person lost a wager, the extended family would take care of him or her until, through reciprocity, the person could repay the relatives' kindness (Barsh, 1986). However, these support networks may have dwindled, leaving gamblers with great personal hardship.

Prevention and Intervention Programs

Today, Aboriginal people living in communities near larger urban centres in southern Canada can access a range of treatment options for gambling problems. Mainstream treatment is available, but if a person desires a cultural pathway, dual treatment strategies that combine Western addiction treatment with traditional healing methods are also possible, if not as yet readily available. Mainstream resources include Gamblers Anonymous and formal medical treatments and therapies. On the other hand, northern and more isolated communities, despite having easy Internet access to various forms of gambling, have limited access to treatment options.

There are few Aboriginal-led gambling intervention programs in Canada. In 2011, the Métis Nation of Ontario established a working group to explore its administrative capacity to respond to gambling-related issues. Virtually no information is available about whether Inuit are investigating Inuit-specific gambling addiction programs. Several programs for First Nations gambling treatment are funded by First Nations casino administrators in British Columbia, Saskatchewan, Manitoba and Ontario. In British Columbia, funding for the Problem Gambling Program is set at a fixed amount each fiscal year, and the program is available to all citizens, including Aboriginal people. The provincial government shares the net income from the First Nation–owned Casino of the Rockies with the First Nation and a handful of agencies treating problem gamblers. Thus, revenue the First Nation community receives is available for public health programs, which presumably could be used for gambling prevention and treatment programs. The Province of Saskatchewan and the Federation of Saskatchewan Indian Nations created the First Nations Addictions Rehabilitation Foundation "to ensure that effective and accessible education, prevention and treatment programs about problem gambling are available to First Nation people" (Belanger, 2010, p. 22). This foundation is funded from gambling revenue and addresses gambling addiction and other co-existing addictions. The Province of Manitoba allocates three per cent of annual gambling revenues generated at First Nations casinos to First Nations gambling addiction programs. In Ontario, the Aboriginal Responsible Gambling Strategy Steering Committee identified a need for provincial service plans and counselling methods to recognize and incorporate cultural features and needs.

Calls by academics and clinicians to create culturally responsible treatment programming remain unheeded by governments, and most provincial health ministries recommend that Aboriginal people with gambling problems enter mainstream programs. The reasons for this vary. For one, there is serious under-representation of Aboriginal counselling professionals nationally (Dyall, 2007). Few universities offer addiction counselling programs, and there is currently no specific program dedicated to addictive behaviour and mental health issues among Aboriginal people. Consequently, even in instances where counsellors attempt to integrate Aboriginal perspectives into their practice, there is little practical knowledge available to guide them. The stigma associated with what is perceived to be yet another Aboriginal social problem frequently leads individuals to under-report their gambling difficulties, which in turn suggests statistically that the problem is not widespread. If so, the received wisdom is that creating culturally specific programs may not be necessary and that Aboriginal people can make do with existing mainstream programming. Also, Canada does not embrace a multi-level public health strategy aimed at or involving Aboriginal peoples. This means that communities that want to develop treatment programs do so on their own and usually at their own expense, and often find it difficult to find the money needed to create these programs.

Despite funding inadequacies, several gambling education and community awareness campaigns exist. Their aims include improving public information about available services, offering Aboriginal gambling counselling and associated treatment programs, providing cultural awareness training for non-Aboriginal counsellors, ensuring access to self-exclusion (people with gambling problems voluntarily agree to be barred from casinos and/or gaming locations) and ensuring that governments prioritize gambling policy reforms with an emphasis on providing more funding for treatment programs.

Conclusion

Gambling remains an important feature in most Aboriginal communities in Canada. In an age when First Nations and non-Aboriginal casinos have become ubiquitous features of the Canadian gaming industry, Aboriginal people demonstrate higher rates of problem and pathological gambling. Currently, there is no consensus as to what causes these increased rates. However, contemporary games and wagering practices have infiltrated Aboriginal communities, and those who gamble may be transferring traditional beliefs about gambling to these modern games. However, when people play these modern games, the cultural checks and balances that prevented them from betting too much and protected them from disaster when they lost are absent.

The factors that cause Aboriginal people to gamble problematically are difficult to determine, and because of this, there is a lack of innovative, culturally reflective prevention, treatment and harm minimization. Until more is known about why Aboriginal people have higher rates of gambling problems than members of the general population, contemporary mainstream treatments offer avenues to healing. Greater understanding of the cultural meaning of gambling behaviours in different Aboriginal communities would allow this traditional knowledge to be integrated into contemporary treatments to better facilitate individual and community healing.

References

American Psychiatric Association (APA). (1994). *Diagnostic and Statistical Manual of Mental Disorders* (4th ed.). Washington, DC: Author.

American Psychiatric Association (APA). (2013). *Diagnostic and Statistical Manual of Mental Disorders* (5th ed.). Washington, DC: Author.

Barsh, R.L. (1986). Canada's Aboriginal peoples: Social integration or disintegration? *Canadian Journal of Native Studies, 14,* 1–46.

Belanger, Y.D. (2006). *Gambling with the Future: The Evolution of Aboriginal Gaming in Canada.* Saskatoon, SK: Purich.

Belanger, Y.D. (2010). First Nations gaming as a self-government imperative? Ensuring the health of First Nations problem gamblers. *International Journal of Canadian Studies, 41,* 13–36. DOI: 10.7202/044161ar

Belanger, Y.D. (2011). Toward an innovative understanding of North American indigenous gaming in historical perspective. In Y.D. Belanger (Ed.), *First Nations Gaming in Canada* (pp. 10–34). Winnipeg: University of Manitoba Press.

Betancourt, H. & López, S.R. (1993). The study of culture, ethnicity, and race in American psychology. *American Psychologist, 48,* 629–637.

Binde, P. (2005). Gambling across cultures: Mapping worldwide occurrence and learning from ethnographic comparison. *International Gambling Studies, 5,* 1–27. DOI: 10.1080/14459790500097913

Binde, P. (2007). Gambling and religion: Histories of concord and conflict. *Journal of Gambling Issues, 20,* 145–165. DOI: 10.4309/jgi.2007.20.4

Black, D.W. & Moyer, T. (1999). Study finds other psychiatric ills accompany pathological gambling. *Outcomes & Accountability Alert, 4* (8), 4.

Campbell, C. & Smith, G.J. (2003). Gambling in Canada—from vice to disease to responsibility: A negotiated history. *Canadian Bulletin of Medical History, 20* (1), 121–149.

Campbell, K. (1999). *Community Life and Governance: Early Experiences of Mnjikaning First Nation with Casino Rama* (Unpublished master's thesis). University of Manitoba, Winnipeg, MB.

Chansonneuve, D. (2007). *Addictive Behaviours among Aboriginal People in Canada.* Retrieved from Aboriginal Healing Foundation website: www.ahf.ca

Cozzetto, D.A. (1995). The economic and social implications of Indian gaming: The case of Minnesota. *American Indian Culture and Research Journal, 19* (1), 119–131.

Cozzetto, D.A. & Larocque, B.W. (1996). Compulsive gambling in the Indian community: A North Dakota case study. *American Indian Culture and Research Journal, 20* (1), 73–86.

Culin, S. (1992). *Games of the North American Indian.* Lincoln: University of Nebraska Press. (Original work published 1907)

Deiter-Buffalo, C. (1996). *The Handgame Project.* Hobbema, AB: Indian Association of Alberta.

Duran, E. (2006). *Healing the Soul Wound: Counseling with American Indians and Other Native Peoples.* New York: Teachers College Press.

Dyall, L. (2007). Gambling, social disorganisation and deprivation. *International Journal of Mental Health and Addiction, 5,* 320–330. DOI: 10.1007/s11469-007-9085-5

Ferris, J. & Wynne, H. (2001). *The Canadian Problem Gambling Index: Final Report.* Retrieved from Canadian Centre on Substance Abuse website: www.ccsa.ca

Gabriel, K. (1996). *Gambler Way: Indian Gaming in Mythology, History, and Archaeology in North America.* Boulder, CO: Johnson Books.

Guth, F.R. (1994). *Western Values Comparison in Gambling with a Comparison to North American Aboriginal Views*. Sault Ste. Marie, ON: Algoma.

Heine, M.K. (1991). The symbolic capital of honour: Gambling games and the social construction of gender in Tlingit Indian culture. *Play and Culture, 4*, 346–358.

Herndon, M. (1979). Play elements in the myth of North American Indians. In E. Norbeck & C.R. Farrer (Eds.), *Forms of Play of Native North Americans* (pp. 121–131). St. Paul, MN: West Publishing.

Hewitt, D. (1994). *Spirit of Bingoland: A Study of Problem Gambling among Alberta Native People*. St. Albert, AB: Nechi Training, Research and Health Promotions Institute.

Hewitt, D. & Auger, D. (1995). *Firewatch on First Nations Adolescent Gambling*. St. Alberta, AB: Nechi Training, Research and Health Promotions Institute.

Holmes, W.H. (1907). Games of the North American Indians. In *Twenty-fourth Annual Report of the Bureau of American Ethnology to the Secretary of the Smithsonian Institution, 1902–1903*. Washington, DC: Government Printing Office.

Joukhador, J., Blaszczynski, A. & MacCallum, F. (2004). Superstitious beliefs among problem and nonproblem gamblers: Preliminary data. *Journal of Gambling Studies, 20*, 171–180.

Lange, P. (2004). A First Nations hand game: Gambling from supernatural power. *Journal of Gambling Issues, 11*, 147–152.

McCormick, R. (2009). Aboriginal approaches to counselling. In L.J. Kirkmayer & G.G. Valaskakis (Eds.), *Healing Traditions: The Mental Health of Aboriginal Peoples in Canada* (pp. 337–354). Vancouver: UBC Press.

McCown, W.G. & Howatt, W.A. (2007). *Treating Gambling Problems*. Hoboken, NJ: John Wiley & Sons.

McGowan, V., Frank, L., Nixon G. & Grimshaw, M. (2002). Sacred and secular play among Blackfoot peoples of southwest Alberta. In A. Blasczynski (Ed.), *Culture and the Gambling Phenomenon* (pp. 241–255). Sydney, Australia: National Association for Gambling Studies.

McGowan, V. & Nixon, G. (2004). Blackfoot traditional knowledge in resolution of problem gambling: Getting gambled and seeking wholeness. *Canadian Journal of Native Studies, 24*, 7–35.

Nilson, C. (2004). *The FSIN–Province of Saskatchewan Gaming Partnership: 1995 to 2002* (Unpublished master's thesis). University of Saskatchewan, Saskatoon, SK.

Nixon, G. & Solowoniuk, J. (2009). Introducing the hero complex and the mythic iconic pathway of problem gambling. *International Journal of Mental Health and Addiction, 7*, 108–123. DOI: 10.1007/s11469-008-9153-5

Petry, N.M. (2007). Gambling and substance use disorders: Current status and future directions. *American Journal on Addictions, 16*, 1–9.

Raylu, N. & Oei, T.P. (2004). Role of culture in gambling and problem gambling. *Clinical Psychology Review, 23*, 1087–1114.

Rose, N. (1988). Compulsive gambling and the law: From sin to vice to disease. *Journal of Gambling Behaviour, 4*, 240–260.

Salter, M.A. (1972). The effect of acculturation on the game of lacrosse and its role as an agent of Indian survival. *Canadian Journal of History and Sport and Physical Education, 3*, 28–43.

Shanley, K. (2000). Lady Luck or Mother Earth? Gaming as a trope in Plains Indian cultural tradition. *Wicazo Sa Review, 15* (2), 93–101.

Skea, W. (1997). *Time to Deal: A Comparison of the Native Casino Gambling Policy in Alberta and Saskatchewan* (Unpublished doctoral dissertation). University of Calgary, Calgary, AB.

Volberg, R.A. (1993). *Establishing Treatment Services for Pathological Gamblers in Manitoba*. Winnipeg, MB: Manitoba Lotteries Foundation.

Wardman, D., el-Guebaly, N. & Hodgins, D. (2001). Problem and pathological gambling in North American Aboriginal populations: A review of the empirical literature. *Journal of Gambling Studies, 17,* 81–100.

Williams, R.J., Stevens, R.M.G. & Nixon, G. (2011). Gambling and problem gambling in North American Aboriginal peoples. In Y.D. Belanger (Ed.), *First Nations Gaming in Canada* (pp. 166–194). Winnipeg: University of Manitoba Press.

Wishart, D.J. (2004). Sports and recreation. In D.J. Wishart (Ed.), *The Encyclopedia of the Great Plains.* Retrieved from Encyclopedia of the Great Plains website: http://plainshumanities.unl.edu/encyclopedia

Zimmerman, M., Chelminski, I. & Young, D. (2006). Prevalence and diagnostic correlates of DSM-IV pathological gambling in psychiatric outpatients. *Journal of Gambling Studies, 22,* 255–262.

ABOUT THE AUTHOR

Yale D. Belanger, PhD, is an associate professor in Native American studies, and an adjunct associate professor in the Faculty of Health Science at the University of Lethbridge in Alberta. He is among Canada's leading authorities on First Nations gaming and gambling. He published *First Nations Gaming in Canada* in 2011 (University of Manitoba Press) and *Gambling with the Future: The Evolution of Aboriginal Gaming in Canada* in 2006 (Purich).

Chapter 21

Perspectives on Aboriginal Suicide: Movement toward Healing

ANA BODNAR

This chapter explores suicide, including risk and protective factors and suicide prevention initiatives among Aboriginal people in Canada, particularly youth. The suicide rate is tragically high among Aboriginal people—about 2.5 times higher than in the non-Aboriginal population (Kirmayer et al., 2007), with even higher rates among youth. Aboriginal suicide is a complex issue. It can be a response to feelings of isolation, sadness and hopelessness, which can lead to an inability to project a successful future. These feelings can be experienced on the individual and collective level, and must be understood within the larger historical and social context of the many losses experienced by Aboriginal peoples over centuries.

The Nishnawbe Aski Nation Voices of Children project, a collaborative project between Nishnawbe Aski Nation tribal councils and Voices of Children, a national organization empowering children, described the emotional reaction to suicide:

> At first, there is unbelievable shock and then pain. Then your mind
> races with a million questions: "What made them do it?" "How could
> I have helped to stop it?" There is guilt and hurt all mixed together.
> People move from disbelief and denial to being angry at others, angry
> with themselves and angry at the person who took their own life . . .
> It's hard to judge the total impact of suicides. . . . You never get used

to it. It's always there, sometimes just a matter of time before another one happens. It has a way of colouring how you look at yourself and the world. (Nishnawbe Aski Nation Youth Forum on Suicide, 1996)

Demographics

Canada has many Aboriginal communities with different languages and dialects, and with shared experiences of colonialism and its resultant intergenerational trauma. In the 2011 National Household Survey (Statistics Canada, 2013), 1,400,685 people identified as Aboriginal. Specifically, 851,560 identified as First Nations, 451,795 as Métis and 59,445 as Inuit. In general, there are large disparities in economic status between Aboriginal and non-Aboriginal people. In urban settings, Aboriginal people are about 2.5 times more likely than the general population to have economic difficulties (Siggner & Costa, 2005).

Although there is much variation in suicide rates in Aboriginal communities in Canada, the rates among youth are particularly alarming: according to Health Canada (2003), suicide and self-inflicted injuries are the leading causes of death for First Nations youth and adults up to 44 years of age. Suicide rates are five to seven times higher for Aboriginal youth than for non-Aboriginal youth (Health Canada, 2006). The suicide rate for First Nations male youth between ages 15 and 24 years is 126 per 100,000 compared to 24 per 100,000 for non-Aboriginal male youth; for First Nations females, the suicide rate is 35 per 100,000 compared to 5 per 100,000 for non-Aboriginal females (Advisory Group on Suicide Prevention, 2003). In addition, as many as 25 per cent of accidental deaths among Aboriginal youth may actually be unreported suicides (Royal Commission on Aboriginal Peoples [RCAP], 1995).

Suicide rates among Inuit youth are some of the highest in the world, at 11 times the national average (Statistics Canada, 2013). Another Statistics Canada study for the period 2004–2008 found that children and teenagers in Inuit Nunangat, the four Arctic regions that make up the Inuit homelands, were more than 30 times as likely to die from suicide as youth in the rest of Canada (Oliver et al., 2012).

Although Aboriginal peoples in Canada have much higher rates of suicide than the general population, it is important to note that there is considerable variation in suicide prevalence in Aboriginal communities, with some communities experiencing very high rates, while others have no suicides (Chandler & Lalonde, 2008).

Global Reaction to Aboriginal Suicide in Canada

In 2004, United Nations (UN) special rapporteur on the rights of Indigenous peoples, Rodolfo Stavenhagen, reported that "poverty, infant mortality, unemployment, morbidity, suicide, criminal detention, children on welfare, women victims of abuse, child prostitution are all much higher among Aboriginal people than in any other sector of Canadian society" (United Nations Commission on Human Rights, 2004, p. 2). The report added: "The Canadian Human Rights Commission views the social and economic situation of Aboriginal peoples among the most pressing human rights issues facing Canada" (p. 9). Unfortunately, since this report, the loss of life through suicide has continued to be very high. Like his predecessor, UN special rapporteur James Anaya in 2013 painted a grim picture of the conditions facing First Nations, saying Canada is facing a "crisis" when it comes to its treatment of Indigenous peoples (Mas, 2013). The seriousness of the situation is highlighted by such events as the Neskantaga First Nation declaration of a state of emergency in April 2013 in response to high rates of suicide in the northwestern Ontario community ("Suicides Prompt," 2013). The tragedy of Aboriginal suicide is unrelenting despite the efforts of many studies and programs to investigate and end it.

Suicide within a Historical and Contemporary Context

Researchers and community members are working hard to understand these high rates of suicide. The current explanatory model identifies intergenerational trauma as a key factor. In this model, suicide is understood as a response to generations of loss and trauma linked to colonialist policies (Bombay et al., 2009). These policies severely damaged communities through the dispossession of culture, land and economic well-being. One such policy was the residential school system, in which Aboriginal children were forcibly removed from their families and communities and deprived of emotional nurturing, often suffering abuse and neglect. Raised without the guidance of parents or grandparents, these children were not able to develop the appropriate life or parenting skills required to support their own children. Communities and families that experience such disruption take many years to heal, and recovery can be lengthy and complex.[1] The intergenerational trauma model may be used to guide strategies for suicide prevention, intervention and postvention.

For an explanatory model to be effective as a basis for finding solutions, it must encompass an understanding of the multiple challenges for Aboriginal people and the risk and protective factors at both the individual and community levels (Bodnar, 2005a). Not all individuals with similar stressors exhibit suicidal behaviour or complete a suicide: suicidal behaviour results from an individual's vulnerabilities in combination with pressures from the environment. Accordingly, there is significant variation among communities in rates of suicide (Chandler & Lalonde, 2008). This variation has been linked to the degree of cultural continuity in a community, which means how active a community is in self-government and in revitalizing cultural traditions. At the

---

1 For more detailed discussions about residential schools and intergenerational trauma, see chapters 3 and 5.

individual level, cultural continuity is reflected in a sense of self-continuity, that is, in a person's ability to see himself or herself as someone with an identity and a future (Chandler & Lalonde, 2008).

My clinical experiences with Aboriginal individuals and communities, along with supporting research, inform my reflections. Like others working in this field, I recognize the complexity of trying to understand and intervene in the area of Aboriginal suicide. It is crucial not only to understand the historical, theoretical and clinical contexts, but also to see how these realities are experienced and expressed by a person trying to live a good life. This chapter explores some of the issues that contribute to suicide's complexity, and suggests areas for further study and practice. With youth asking to have their voices heard and to be more empowered, planning suicide prevention strategies must involve youth input and address their needs.

Working with Youth and Adults: Clinical Experiences

My early work in the 1990s involved research, teaching, consultation and clinical work in remote territories of the Nishnawbe Aski Nation (Bodnar, 2005b; Bodnar & Devlin, 1994). I have continued to work in the Aboriginal community in research, curriculum and program development, and teaching, in remote and urban settings. This included acting as the consulting psychologist to the Aboriginal Service at the Centre for Addiction and Mental Health for many years (Menzies et al., 2010). I also provide expert assessments for residential school survivors in their claims process. Through these experiences, I have developed several reflections on Aboriginal suicide.

I worked in the Nishnawbe Aski Nation as part of the Suicide Bereavement Project based in Sioux Lookout, Ontario. For more than 20 years, suicide rates in Nishnawbe Aski Nation communities have ranged between three and 40 times higher than the national average. The communities have also experienced suicide clusters (or "copycat" suicides), which refers to two or more suicides or suicide attempts that occur in close succession in a defined geographical area. In some clusters in Nishnawbe Aski Nation communities, suicide rates reached 40 times the national average (Nishnawbe Aski Nation Youth Forum on Suicide, 1996).

The Suicide Bereavement Project was developed to help remote communities deal with grief and bereavement by supporting the chief and council, social service staff, mental health workers and other community members. The leaders and caregivers in the community were often wounded themselves, and also needed help to heal. Alongside a team of First Nations mental health professionals, I helped train community-based front-line workers in suicide prevention protocols and in coping with bereavement. We also provided counselling and developed healing circles for people who had lost family members or friends to suicide. Since many of the communities we worked in had small populations of only a few hundred people, the entire community was affected by the many losses. We would convene healing circles with adults and youth so they could share their feelings and thoughts about the suicides. The added challenge was that other suicides would follow. The community would be trying to recover from one suicide when another death would occur. This often interrupted people in their grief healing cycles, leading to patterns of complicated grieving, which could in turn lead to other mental health problems. Community members did not have a unified voice about the causes of these suicide clusters, but felt that the loss of traditional culture, poor housing conditions and lack of recreational activities were contributing factors. They reported worrying that their children were "lost" and that they were copying one another through suicide.

To promote the healing process, our team treated the young people who had contemplated or attempted suicide. We worked with groups of bereaved youth and adults following suicides in their communities, and with front-line social service providers addressing suicide issues. Also, our team worked with Elders around how to revitalize traditional healing methods, such as drumming and sweat lodges, as ways to help individuals and communities deal with the overwhelming losses by suicide. The Elders highlighted the fact that in the past, many traditional practices, such as drumming, had to be conducted in secret. Drums were hidden to avoid confiscation by various Church and government officials who entered the community. Elders discussed how many cultural losses had led to a loss of traditional grieving practices and that in the past, communities did not have to deal with such overwhelming losses. The Elders stated that traditional practices needed to be revived and additional healing strategies developed to help people recover from the overwhelming losses that were blocking the community's ability to heal.

In my work with suicidal First Nations youth, it became clear that their peer group was extremely important and could potentially be a support to youth at risk. Young people I counselled said that when they lost a peer to suicide, their own sense of security and identity was affected, putting them at further risk of suicide. They also told me that a friend's suicide served as an example of a way to cope and escape from problems or unbearable feelings. These kinds of emotional responses could lead to copycat suicides, which was very challenging for the communities because they had so many deaths to grieve.

It is important for youth to belong somewhere—with their family, their peer group or their close friends and loved ones. The importance of connection is captured in the concept of the Aboriginal "spirit of belonging" (Brokenleg & Van Bockern, 2003). When their personal relationships were disrupted, young people often presented in my office with a sense of isolation, confusion and profound loneliness. They often said that their parents and other family members had their own problems and were not able to provide support. In counselling, I saw youth who were contemplating killing themselves because a friend had died by suicide. I saw several young people who had their friends' names tattooed on their hands or arms. They often told me they wanted to follow that friend by doing the same. From their world view, the act of suicide made sense: they wanted to be with their friends. At times, they also felt guilty that they had not been able to stop their friends from completing suicide, and for this reason thought that they should join them—a form of survivor guilt. In counselling dialogues, these young people did not talk about the historical and cultural issues often discussed in the research literature; rather, they focused on their immediate personal realities and on the quality of their relationships with family, friends and romantic partners. Some youth had come to see suicide as a "normal" response to personal problems, because they had seen family members and friends attempting or actually completing suicide. They often felt isolated and experienced profound sadness and hopelessness. The counselling goal was to explore alternatives to suicide, and to support these young people in their will to live. We focused on building resilience by connecting with their strengths, promoting positive relationships, encouraging hope for the future and addressing experiences of sadness. Some of these depressed or suicidal youth were also experiencing problems with substances, such as alcohol or inhalants, further complicating the overall picture.

It was clear that the youth were suffering deeply and often did not feel they could trust or confide in adults. They felt very vulnerable to peer influence and pressure. Many had difficulties with attachment to others. In small communities, the well-being of individuals and the health of the community are powerfully linked. Thus, strategies for suicide prevention, intervention and postvention work should integrate both individual and community approaches.

Youth Voices in Manitoba: Bringing Demographics to Life

In 2004, I conducted a focus group in a remote, fly-in community in central Manitoba. The purpose was to hear from youth and community service workers about how suicide was being addressed and what additional suicide prevention strategies could be introduced. The on-reserve population was 2,000, and 1,000 off reserve. About half of the population was under 21 years old. Nine suicides—two adults and seven youth—had been reported in the community between 2001 and 2004. Clusters of suicides were reported as part of the total, but specific details were not available.

Various conclusions emerged from the focus group:
• Many community members were not aware of existing social services.
• There was a lack of outreach and a lack of effective communication channels.
• There was a lack of cohesion among service professionals when facing a suicide crisis, and services were not effective.
• In general, there was little or no discussion about suicide prevention or treatment in the community. Thus, there was a lack of emotional support following a suicide, which led to unresolved grief and increased risk for further suicides. The youth stated that in the community, "We just bury them and go on."

Youth in the focus group identified a number of key risk factors:
• difficulties in accessing social services and lack of trust in services

• lack of individuals to talk to about their problems
• lack of overall adult support, including a lack of respect for youth perspectives
• high availability of substances and potential for misuse
• abuse within the family
• lack of positive activities for youth
• lack of communication between youth and adults.

The young people were interested in learning about traditional Aboriginal cultural practices as a healing strategy. There was also interest in enhancing communication through a youth radio program and the school newspaper. These efforts would support youth by giving them a greater voice in the community and enabling them to discuss specific issues of concern. It was clear that youth felt isolated and that many adults were struggling with their own problems and were not able to support these young people. Moreover, there was only a small number of key human services professionals making strong efforts to work alongside youth to make positive changes. Overall, the entire community was suffering and often felt overwhelmed by the complexity of its problems.

Risk Factors: Mental Health Influences on Suicide

Predicting suicide is difficult and inexact because we are not able to talk to those who have completed suicide and people are reluctant to discuss the issue due to the stigma that surrounds it. However, risk factors for suicide have been identified. For example, the presence of a mental disorder is an important risk factor for suicide. It is generally acknowledged that more than 90 per cent of people who died by suicide had a psychiatric diagnosis at the time of death (Bertolote & Fleischmann, 2002).

Depression combined with social isolation and the recent loss of an intimate relationship dramatically increases suicide risk (Brown et al., 2000). There is evidence that rates of depression have generally been increasing in Western nations, with particularly high levels of depression and suicide in many Indigenous communities (Kirmayer et al., 2001, 2007). It is hard to be both young and Aboriginal in Canada. It is doubly challenging to develop a successful suicide prevention program due to the many difficulties young people face in a rapidly changing world, in addition to sharing the historical, social and economic burdens that all Aboriginal people carry.

Many studies have revealed higher than usual prevalence rates of mental health disorders among Aboriginal people in Canada. Aboriginal youth as well as mental health professionals have identified a link between substance use and a predisposition to suicidal behaviour (Kirmayer et al., 2007). It is important to keep in mind that these mental health issues occur within the larger historical, social and cultural experience of loss over generations. This broader view of mental health issues highlights the impact of intergenerational trauma in the lives of Aboriginal people. Although there is no proven causal link between intergenerational trauma and suicide, this trauma legacy may be seen as an important risk factor for feelings of sadness and hopelessness among Aboriginal people. It is difficult to find a solution to alleviate the individual and collective trauma arising from generations of harsh losses.

Protective Factors: Cultural Continuity

The variation in suicide rates in Aboriginal communities has been linked to several risk and protective factors. In British Columbia, where suicide rates in some Aboriginal communities have reached 800 times the national average, while in others suicides are virtually non-existent, Chandler and Lalonde (1998) identified cultural continuity as a protective factor against suicide.

Cultural continuity is understood as active efforts to maintain or revitalize cultural institutions and practices. This may include active negotiation for land claims and self-government, and control over education, police and fire services, health and cultural facilities. The more communities have control over these institutions and practices, the stronger the cultural continuity they experience. Chandler and Lalonde (1998, 2008) found that where specific steps were taken to preserve and revitalize culture, youth suicide rates were significantly lower.

It is important to understand how cultural continuity is linked to the decision to live or die. As Chandler (1994) noted, the linkage is located in the concept of self-continuity. Self-continuity is an essential feature of the self that allows individuals to see themselves as having a personal identity. This sense of selfhood creates stability and a continuous sense of identity over time. It contributes to the ongoing functioning of the overall social order. The sense of identity is made up of individuals' inner experiences of themselves, their social identity in terms of roles and responsibilities, and the way in which others view them. Having the desire to continue living requires a sense of being a person who has a future. Adolescence is an important period because it involves great identity change and upheaval. A successfully navigated adolescence is one in which the person comes to a stable, definitive sense of identity and sees it continuing into the future (Chandler, 1994).

Chandler and Lalonde (1998, 2008) suggested that communities with higher degrees of cultural continuity could provide at-risk youth with greater support to promote a sense of positive self-continuity. For First Nations adolescents, the sense of personal identity and self-continuity may be more fragile due to challenging social and cultural factors. When the sense of identity and self-continuity are under stress, and individuals do not have a strong sense of themselves into the future, they become more vulnerable to suicide. As discussed earlier, the Aboriginal youth I have worked with often relied on peers as their anchor in life, sometimes more than their own families. When one member of the peer group died by suicide, the sense of self-continuity of the individual at risk was affected. This was particularly true for those young people already at risk and without many significant relationships in their lives.

Bowlby (1969) used attachment theory to explain the power of the peer group for self-continuity. He posited that the patterning for a secure sense of self develops with early positive attachments to caregiver adults. Since many Aboriginal adults struggle with their own difficulties related to historical losses and intergenerational trauma, they may not be able to offer their children positive parenting and secure attachment. Aboriginal views on attachment theory include a vision where children can be raised by an extended family, where the mother–infant dyad is not the only source of security (Neckoway et al., 2007). However, many youth I spoke with told me they had little support from any of the adults they knew, and if they had only one meaningful connection in their life, it could give them a reason to stay alive.

An Elder's Views on Suicide

At the 2006 conference of the Canadian Association for Suicide Prevention, Elder Vern Harper and I presented a workshop on the complexities of suicide. Elder Harper's techniques included storytelling, traditional teachings and counselling dialogue. He drew upon traditional stories of Aboriginal people who overcame adversity and talked about how he overcame his own difficulties. In his counselling and teaching, he uses a direct and personal interactive style, which puts people at ease.

In his presentation, Elder Harper described traditional beliefs about suicide and how he helps people who are suicidal. He supports people by helping them develop a strong sense of cultural identity and pride, and emphasizes that suicide would cause a great deal of suffering for their friends and families. Elder Harper sees suicide as a direct response to the loss of cultural identity and pride (personal communication, May 15, 2006). He believes that many youth who die by suicide are confused about their beliefs and think that suicide is an escape. He explains to youth that according to traditional teachings, people who die by suicide are not released from their pain, but live in the in-between land of the living and the dead, and continue to suffer. By spending time with people, sharing stories from his own life and advising them about their day-to-day issues, as well as their spiritual concerns, he demonstrates to these young people that they are important. Essentially, Elder Harper tries to deter youth from suicide through spiritual teachings and compassionate support.

Promising Strategies in Suicide Prevention and Intervention

Several reports have reviewed suicide prevention programs and have made recommendations for effective strategies for Aboriginal communities. For example, the RCAP (1995) report described five programs in Ontario, New Brunswick, the Northwest

Territories, British Columbia and Saskatchewan. In evaluating the success of these suicide prevention programs, RCAP found that it was important for programs to be community-based, to be informed by traditional knowledge, to include community consultation, to address all levels of prevention and to have local control along with outside collaboration.

The Advisory Group on Suicide Prevention (2003) report *Acting on What We Know: Preventing Youth Suicide in First Nations* identified various elements of successful suicide prevention programs: they promote pride and control in the community; improve self-esteem and identity; transmit First Nations knowledge, language and traditions; and employ culturally appropriate methods. The report provided the following guidelines for developing suicide prevention programs for Aboriginal youth:

- The program should take a comprehensive approach that involves providing crisis services, promoting broad preventive action and community development and addressing the long-term problems and needs of the community.
- The program should be seen as a community wellness program that promotes all aspects of well-being: physical, mental, emotional and spiritual.
- Programs should be owned locally and be based on the values of the local First Nations culture.
- Strategies for suicide prevention are the responsibility of the entire community, and need the support and involvement of political, religious, family and social service groups.
- The target group should be children and youth up to their late 20s. The entire family and community should be involved.
- Suicide prevention needs to be addressed from many perspectives, including the biological, psychological, socio-cultural and spiritual dimensions of well-being.
- Suicide prevention strategies that are long term, as well as based on crisis response, are needed.
- Evaluation of suicide prevention strategies is important (p. 54).

These guidelines align with the recommendations of RCAP, the Australian National Suicide Prevention Strategy, the U.S. Surgeon General's National Strategy for Suicide Prevention and the American Academy of Child and Adolescent Psychiatry. The Advisory Group on Suicide Prevention report (2003) also includes specific suggestions for primary, secondary and tertiary prevention, described below:[2]

Primary Prevention: Education and Support
Prevention programs can educate and support people if they focus on the following:
- peer counselling groups with trained youth
- school curriculum, including teaching about positive mental, emotional and spiritual health, and cultural heritage.

2 From *Acting on What We Know: Preventing Youth Suicide in First Nations*. Health Canada, 2003. © All rights reserved. Modified and reproduced with permission from the Minister of Health, 2014.

- curriculum that covers the dangers of substance use and recognizing suicidal behaviour
- recreational and sports programs for youth to combat boredom and alienation
- workshops on life skills, problem solving and communication
- family life education, parenting skills based on culturally sensitive models
- support groups for individuals and families at risk
- cultural programs and activities for the community at large
- co-ordination among community workers, traditional helpers in health, social services and education
- training for professional and lay helpers around health promotion and suicide risk factors
- open community and town meetings to invite participation and communication of concerns.

Secondary Prevention: Intervention

Intervention programs can address the needs of people at high risk of suicide if they focus on:
- training for primary care providers, such as nurses, physicians and social workers, in suicide risk detection, crisis intervention and the treatment of depression, anxiety, substance use problems and other psychological problems
- a regional crisis hotline that is based outside the community to allow for confidentiality
- development of a crisis centre in the community or close by
- immediate crisis intervention for acute risk
- assessment and intervention services aimed at parents of at-risk youth.

Tertiary Prevention: Postvention

Postvention programs can help people if they focus on:
- helping individuals and communities address their grief and bereavement in a constructive and active manner
- providing individuals and groups with education on the process of grief and bereavement
- providing education on copycat suicides and suicide clusters
- working closely with media to promote responsible reporting of deaths by suicide
- ensuring that professional and natural caregivers are sufficiently trained in postvention techniques (Advisory Group on Suicide Prevention, 2003, pp. 56–58).

Postvention is crucial to a comprehensive suicide prevention program. People who have lost someone to suicide are obviously deeply affected by the loss and need to engage in their own process of grieving and healing. If the natural process of grieving and bereavement is interrupted or incomplete, these individuals can develop mental health difficulties associated with complicated grief.

Another report, *Aboriginal Youth: A Manual of Promising Suicide Prevention Strategies* (White & Jodoin, 2003), presents an explanatory model for suicide among Aboriginal youth. It describes 17 suicide prevention strategies and outlines examples of

Aboriginal suicide programs across Canada. It also offers culturally relevant resources for program development and suggests a step-by-step action plan to help people mobilize their groups and communities.

Two other programs, the Fraser Region Aboriginal Youth Suicide Prevention Collaborative (2012) and the Swampy Cree Suicide Prevention Team (Isaac et al., 2009), have shown the benefits of collaboration among academics, service providers, community gatekeepers and youth. The National Aboriginal Youth Suicide Prevention Strategy released by Health Canada (2013) focuses on prevention approaches that are initiated by the community, involve all stakeholders, and are strength-based and grounded in traditional Aboriginal knowledge practices.

A final note about prevention: mainstream suicide prevention programs may not work well in Aboriginal communities. One study showed that resilience training may be more effective in improving well-being than mainstream suicide prevention programs (Reynolds, 2013).

Conclusion

In my suicide prevention work over the last 20 years, and in my ongoing clinical work with Aboriginal people, I am often struck by the overwhelming and complex difficulties faced by Aboriginal people dealing with intergenerational trauma and its associated historical, social and cultural losses. It is shameful that a country as "developed" as Canada purports to be continues to lose so many Aboriginal people to suicide. It is my profound hope that the many studies on Aboriginal suicide will not be considered as purely academic work, but will translate into real change.

In my recent work with residential school survivors, I am encouraged by the healing that occurs when people overcome their suffering, including the multiple losses caused by separation from their families, communities and cultural traditions. I see healing taking place when people find ways to develop a more positive sense of personal and cultural identity, when they forge healing relationships with their families and communities. All of us in the human family thrive on being accepted and valued.

Considering suicide prevention research, the words of youth, the wisdom of Aboriginal traditions and my own work in the Aboriginal community, it is possible to help people find a life worth living by strengthening positive attachments across generations so that Elders, adults and youth can come together, as well as by building strong families. Youth have made it clear that in order to promote healing, their own voices must be heard so that their needs can be met and their wisdom acknowledged. The social, economic and intergenerational effects of historical government policies concerning Aboriginal communities must be understood in order to address suicide within the framework of intergenerational trauma. Each suicide can be viewed as a tragic expression of the history of this loss and trauma.

I am grateful for what I have learned through my work with colleagues in the Suicide Bereavement Project and in other community-based contexts over the years. The ongoing dedication of front-line workers has helped support many people in their lives, creating hope and yielding positive outcomes. May there be a clear and ongoing commitment from all levels of government to listen to and heed the voices of Aboriginal people in order to find the best ways to support healing, so that the tragedy of Aboriginal suicide can come to an end.

References

Advisory Group on Suicide Prevention. (2003). *Acting on What We Know: Preventing Youth Suicide in First Nations*. Retrieved from Health Canada website: www.hc-sc.gc.ca

Bertolote, J.M. & Fleischmann, A. (2002). Suicide and psychiatric diagnosis: A worldwide perspective. *World Psychiatry, 1*, 181–185.

Bodnar, A. (2005a). *Assessment and Planning Tool Kit for Suicide Prevention in First Nations Communities*. Retrieved from National Aboriginal Health Organization website: www.naho.ca/documents/fnc/english/FNC_SuicidePreventionToolkit.pdf

Bodnar, A. (2005b). Ode to Marie, learning with the women: My travels in First Nations country. In G.S. Harding (Ed.), *Surviving in the Hour of Darkness: The Health and Wellness of Women of Colour and Indigenous Women* (pp. 253–264). Calgary, AB: University of Calgary Press.

Bodnar, A. & Devlin, A. (1994, June). *Grief and healing in First Nations communities*. Presentation at the 2nd International Conference on Grief and Bereavement, Stockholm, Sweden.

Bombay, A., Matheson, H. & Anisman, H. (2009). Intergenerational trauma: Convergence of multiple processes among First Nations peoples in Canada. *Journal of Aboriginal Health, 5* (3), 6–47.

Bowlby, J. (1969). *Attachment and Loss. Vol. 1: Attachment*. London, UK: Hogarth.

Brokenleg, M. & Van Bockern, S. (2003). The science of raising courageous kids. *Reclaiming Children and Youth, 12* (1), 22–27.

Brown, G.K., Beck, A.T., Steer, R.A. & Grisham, J.R. (2000). Risk factors for suicide in psychiatric outpatients: A 20-year prospective study. *Journal of Consulting and Clinical Psychology, 68*, 371–377.

Chandler, M. (1994). Self-continuity in suicidal and nonsuicidal adolescents. *New Directions for Child Development, 1994, 64*, 55–70. DOI: 10.1002/cd.23219946406

Chandler, M.J. & Lalonde, C. (1998). Cultural continuity as a hedge against suicide in Canada's First Nations. *Transcultural Psychiatry, 35*, 191–219.

Chandler, M.J. & Lalonde, C.E. (2008). Cultural continuity as a protective factor against suicide in First Nations youth. [Special issue—Hope or Heartbreak: Aboriginal Youth and Canada's Future], *Horizons: Policy Research Initiative, 10*, 68–72.

Fraser Region Aboriginal Youth Suicide Prevention Collaborative. (2012). *Suicide Prevention, Intervention and Postvention Initiative*. Retrieved from Fraser Health website: www.fraserhealth.ca/media/AH_suicide-prevention.pdf

Health Canada. (2003). *A Statistical Profile on the Health of First Nations in Canada for the Year 2000: Determinants of Health, 1999 to 2003*. Retrieved from www.hc-sc.gc.ca

Health Canada. (2006). *First Nations and Inuit Health—Suicide Prevention*. Retrieved from www.hc-sc.gc.ca

Health Canada. (2013). *National Aboriginal Youth Suicide Prevention Strategy (NAYSPS): Program Framework*. Retrieved from www.hc-sc.gc.ca

Isaac, M., Elias, B., Katz, L.Y., Belik, S., Deane, F.P., Enns, M.W. & Sareen, J. (2009). Swampy Cree Suicide Prevention Team. Gatekeeper training as a preventative measure for suicide: A systematic review. *Canadian Journal of Psychiatry, 54*, 260–268.

Kirmayer, L.J., Brass, G.M., Holton, T., Paul, K., Simpson, C. & Tait, C. (2007). *Suicide among Aboriginal People in Canada*. Retrieved from Aboriginal Healing Foundation website: www.ahf.ca

Kirmayer, L.J., Macdonald, M.E. & Brass, G.M. (Eds.). (2001). *Proceedings of the Advanced Study Institute: The Mental Health of Indigenous Peoples*. Montreal: McGill University Summer Program in Social and Cultural Psychiatry.

Mas, S. (2013, October 15). UN aboriginal envoy says Canada is facing a "crisis." Retrieved from CBC News website: www.cbc.ca

Menzies, P., Bodnar, A. & Harper, V. (2010). The role of the Elder within a mainstream addiction and mental health hospital: Developing an integrated paradigm. *Native Social Work Journal, 7*, 87–107.

Neckoway, R., Brownlee, K. & Castellan, B. (2007). Is attachment theory consistent with Aboriginal parenting? *First Peoples Child and Family Review, 3* (2), 64–75.

Nishnawbe Aski Nation Youth Forum on Suicide. (1996). *Horizons of Hope: An Empowering Journey— Final Report*. Thunder Bay, ON: Nishnawbe Aski Nation.

Oliver, L.N., Peters, P.A. & Kohen, D.E. (2012). Mortality rates among children and teenagers living in Inuit Nunangat, 1994 to 2008. *Health Reports, 23* (3). (Component of Statistics Canada catalogue no. 82-003-X). Retrieved from www.statcan.gc.ca/pub/82-003-x/2012003/article/11695-eng.pdf

Reynolds, L. (2013, March 30). Suicide program a danger: Professor. Retrieved from *Winnipeg Free Press* website: www.winnipegfreepress.com

Royal Commission on Aboriginal Peoples (RCAP). (1995). *Choosing Life: Special Report on Suicide among Aboriginal People*. Ottawa: Canada Communication Group.

Siggner, A.J. & Costa, R. (2005). *Aboriginal Conditions in Census Metropolitan Areas, 1981–2001*. (Statistics Canada catalogue no. 89-613-MWE2005008). Ottawa: Minister of Industry.

Statistics Canada. (2013). *National Household Survey, 2011: Aboriginal Peoples in Canada—First Nations People, Métis and Inuit*. (Catalogue no. 99-011-X2011001). Ottawa: Minister of Industry.

Suicides prompt First Nation to declare emergency. (2013, April 18). Retrieved from CBC News website: www.cbc.ca

United Nations Commission on Human Rights. (2004). *Report of the Special Rapporteur on the Situation of Human Rights and Fundamental Freedoms of Indigenous People, Rodolfo Stavenhagen: Addendum—Mission to Canada*. Retrieved from United Nations Office of the High Commissioner for Human Rights website: http://daccess-dds-ny.un.org/doc/UNDOC/GEN/G05/100/26/PDF/G0510026.pdf?OpenElement

White, J. & Jodoin, N. (2003). *Aboriginal Youth: A Manual of Promising Suicide Prevention Strategies*. Retrieved from Centre for Suicide Prevention website: http://suicideinfo.ca

ABOUT THE AUTHOR

Ana Bodnar, CPsych, holds a doctorate in psychology from the University of Toronto and is a registered clinical psychologist with a practice in Toronto. She has worked in research, curriculum development, training and clinical consultation within Aboriginal communities for 20 years, including in remote First Nations communities, for Aboriginal organizations and as the consulting psychologist for the Aboriginal Service at the Centre for Addiction and Mental Health. She is an expert assessor for the Indian Residential School Adjudication Secretariat and is adjunct faculty at the University of Toronto. She has carried out research and training in New Zealand, Cuba and Mexico.

Chapter 22

Housing and Homelessness

JANET GASPARELLI

The statistics on Aboriginal homelessness are overwhelming. In Toronto, for example, the Aboriginal community represents approximately two per cent of the overall population, yet comprises almost 29 per cent of the homeless population (City of Toronto, 2010). In metro Vancouver, almost 28.5 per cent of people who are homeless are Aboriginal, with an overrepresentation of that population living on the streets rather than in shelters (Greater Vancouver Regional Steering Committee on Homelessness, 2010). Cities across the country have similar statistics, although thousands more people who are homeless may not be reported in the statistics because they are couch surfing, are living in overcrowded housing or the correctional system, or are in and out of hospital.

Not only are Aboriginal people overrepresented in the homeless population, they are also overrepresented in the rental housing market. According to the 2011 National Household Survey, 69 per cent of Canadians own homes (Statistics Canada, 2013). This number is in stark contrast with the Toronto Aboriginal Research Project report, which found that 79 per cent of the Aboriginal people surveyed lived in rented accommodation (McCaskill et al., 2011). This discrepancy in home ownership rates between the Aboriginal and general populations highlights a significant disadvantage to Aboriginal people given the advantages afforded homeowners (Hulchanski, 2002).

Despite Canada's housing system grossly favouring home ownership, renters have the most social need. All three levels of government have been actively engaged in homeownership initiatives since the Second World War, while public policy decisions continue to worsen the situation in the rental housing sector (Hulchanski, 2006). According to Hulchanski (2002), Aboriginal people are among the most vulnerable in urban centres as a result of deteriorating social and economic conditions, and likely because of their gross overrepresentation in the rental housing sector.

Aboriginal homelessness represents a distinct problem that requires unique intervention and prevention strategies. Although lack of affordable and adequate housing seems like an obvious cause of homelessness, factors such as addiction, poverty and public policy, around everything from social services to corrections, also strongly contribute. These issues are often intertwined, making it difficult to explore one problem without addressing the others.

Little practical literature exists on homelessness to support workers in the health, social service and justice fields. This chapter provides some background on the issues that define homelessness among Aboriginal people, and addresses practical skills and knowledge for front-line practitioners who work with Aboriginal people who are homeless.

In this chapter, most of the discussion reflects the Aboriginal situation in Toronto. However, urban centres across the country may differ from Toronto, depending on such factors as the age and gender of people who are homeless. Government policies and mainstream views affect funding strategies and therefore the programs that are available locally. This chapter also focuses mainly on homelessness in urban rather than rural settings, and how it affects the Aboriginal population, and does not address specific sub-groups, such as single men and women, or families and children, as these discussions are beyond the scope of this chapter. It is important to keep in mind that these variables may affect the generalizability of the information presented in this chapter to the Aboriginal clients with whom we work.

Defining Homelessness

For the purposes of this chapter, homelessness is characterized as a spectrum of physical living situations with living on the streets at one end of the continuum and being insecurely housed at the other (Canadian Homeless Research Network, 2012).

Most attempts to categorize homelessness focus on its severity, based on the duration and frequency of homeless periods. A common system identifies people who are homeless in one of three groups: people who are chronically homeless (often those with addiction and/or mental health problems); people who are cyclically homeless (those who find housing periodically but become homeless again due to changing circumstances); and people who are temporarily homeless (those without places to live for short periods due to fires or floods) (Casavant, 1999).

The fact that the media seldom reports on rural homelessness and overrepresents the urban experience, coupled with the dearth of statistics on homelessness in general, has resulted in a lack of recognition of rural homelessness in public perception and public policy. Canada's National Secretariat on Homelessness estimates that about

150,000 people in Canada are homeless, although other estimates put the number at 300,000 (Echenberg & Jensen, 2008), and it is not clear whether these estimates include people in rural settings.

Causes of Aboriginal Homelessness

Menzies (2005) has developed an Aboriginal-specific explanation for homelessness that is congruent with an Aboriginal world view to describe how the experience of homelessness for Aboriginal people differs from that of non-Aboriginal people. He argues that Aboriginal homelessness is a "resultant condition of individuals being displaced from critical community social structures and lacking in stable housing" (p. 8). This explanation is useful because it stresses the importance of community connection. Aboriginal world views and community structures are founded on connectedness, which is needed to sustain individual health and well-being. Thus, when people of Aboriginal heritage have no connection to their community, they have no home.

Having practised in the Toronto Aboriginal community as a front-line worker for the last several years, I have heard many Aboriginal men who are homeless describe how they have been involved with the child welfare system, and have struggled with addiction, identity issues and the effects of trauma. The Aboriginal homeless narrative is distinctly consistent. Unfortunately, limited research exists to address the underlying systemic factors that have led to the continued overrepresentation of Aboriginal people in the homeless population (Menzies, 2005).

A common misconception about homelessness is that people who are homeless find themselves in these circumstances because of their own incapacity to manage themselves (Willse, 2010). In reality, homelessness is caused by a number of structural factors, such as decrease in supply of affordable housing; discrimination; racism; and personal histories, such as loss of employment, family breakup, mental illness and substance use problems (Homeless Hub, n.d.). People who use alcohol and other drugs tend to be demonized by the general population and end up barred from social service agencies, which often results in their becoming homeless and having limited access to the services that work to prevent and alleviate homelessness (Willse, 2010).

Affordable housing and employment rates have a direct impact on homelessness, and can fluctuate with the economy. Historically, homeless populations have increased during economic downturns and decreased during economic upswings (Willse, 2010). Many of the clients I have worked with are only employed sporadically: those working in construction tend to have only seasonal work, while those employed with moving companies tend to have work depending on the demand. These ups and downs leave people with inconsistent financial resources and, ultimately, an inability to secure stable housing.

Another cause of homelessness in the Aboriginal population relates to intergenerational trauma[1] and the long-term effects of colonization (Menzies, 2005). Many clients I have worked with have been exposed to lifelong trauma. This pervasive exposure results in long-lasting wounds that the clients have not developed the skills to heal, in part because they do not have the family or community supports to help them learn these skills.

Another significant cause of Aboriginal homelessness is migration, particularly for members of a First Nation. As recently as the 1940s, most First Nations people tended to live on the lands provided to them by the government (Peters & Robillard, 2009). However, according to the 2006 census, 54 per cent of Aboriginal people now live in urban centres (Statistics Canada, 2008). While many Aboriginal people are migrating to urban centres, they also move back and forth. They go to the city for services and to their reserves to see friends and family.

Links between Health and Homelessness

According to the Chief Public Health Officer, adequate housing and good health are connected (Statistics Canada, 2008). Fallis and Murray (1990) identified a link between substandard housing or lack of housing and a diminished quality of life. Homelessness has even been found to increase the risk of death (Morrison, 2009). With such severe potential consequences as illness and death, one cannot speak about homelessness without speaking about health.

The health needs of the Aboriginal homeless population can be overwhelmingly complex. Many clients I have worked with in the shelter system have long histories of violence and abuse, alcohol and other substance use problems, mental health issues and chronic illness. Rates of physical injuries and assaults also tend to be higher among people who are homeless (Hwang et al., 2008). A recent Toronto study found that 53 per cent of the surveyed people who are homeless had sustained a traumatic brain injury (TBI) at some point in their lives, with reported rates being significantly higher for men than women. Of the Aboriginal people in the study, 61 per cent reported at least one occurrence of TBI. Among people who are homeless, experiencing a TBI is strongly associated with adverse health effects, which can lead to an increased risk of subsequent mental health and substance use problems (Hwang et al., 2008).

Specific issues, such as government policies and economics, have contributed to the perpetuation of Aboriginal homelessness. The social determinants of health comprise 14 conditions that have been found to shape health and well-being. These determinants, which include housing, are largely controlled by government policy and economics. The federal government has attempted to demonstrate its dedication to addressing these conditions by developing a reference group with the goal of advancing action on the social determinants of health. However, the government has

---

1 For more discussion about intergenerational trauma, see chapter 5.

been inconsistent in creating and implementing policies on homelessness and hous-
ing security, including those that relate specifically to Aboriginal issues. The fact that
Canada does not have a national housing strategy has been criticized by the United
Nations (Raphael et al., 2008).

Mental Health, Trauma and Identity

Research has shown that Aboriginal people disproportionately experience anxiety disorders, posttraumatic stress disorder and traumatic events (Gagné, 1998).

The residential school system, the child welfare system and the Indian Act have
been linked to the experience of trauma within Aboriginal communities (Menzies,
2006). These experiences have been so pervasive that they have engulfed generations.
The traumas of one generation are inevitably passed to the next and become intergenerational. Separation from family and community has gravely affected people's ability
to maintain balance in their lives and respond to their physical, emotional, mental
and spiritual needs; this imbalance limits their ability to attain health, well-being and
self-actualization (Menzies, 2006). As members of a community become traumatized,
they become limited in their capacity to seek, afford or maintain adequate housing.

Gagné (1998) argued that colonization is the seed of trauma within Aboriginal
communities that has resulted in political, economic and social dependence. This
dependence perpetuates and transmits cycles of violence and trauma from one
generation to the next. Colonization changed the family and community systems
of Aboriginal people and left them without a way to support one another and their
communities. Menzies (2005) described how Aboriginal men who are homeless lack
connection to their extended families and biological children.

Emotional attachment plays a significant role in belongingness. Menzies (2005)
found that Aboriginal men who are homeless experience difficulty in maintaining relationships with birth or adoptive family members, with their partners, and often even
with their own children. Because of this estrangement, they have even more difficulty
reaching out to these people in times of need.

Within the Aboriginal homeless population, there are people on one end of the
spectrum who have no connection to their family and community, while on the
other end, there are people living on the streets with their siblings, mothers, fathers
and cousins. The latter situations often involve relationships that can significantly
complicate individual intervention because every step that a person takes to choose
a healthier path for himself or herself may mean taking a step away from the family.
It becomes difficult as a clinician to encourage clients to leave the people they have
traditionally relied on.

Key indicators of intergenerational trauma include low self-esteem and a lack of a
sense of belonging, identification or affiliation with a specific community, culture or

nation (Menzies, 2006). Indicators of a nation's exposure to intergenerational trauma include a lack of appropriate holistic programs and services and a lack of support for community self-determination (Menzies, 2006). A community that has been intergenerationally traumatized can become indifferent to its own culture and may not create programs to improve its members' quality of life. It may be apathetic about its role in determining the community's future. Homelessness can be linked to the disconnection of Aboriginal people from their communities, culture and nation because of intergenerational trauma. As practitioners, we must strive to rebuild these connections.

A consistent theme of disconnection and lack of personal and collective identity pervades the research on Aboriginal communities and trauma. Colonial systems have stripped Aboriginal communities of their languages, values, beliefs and traditions, all of which are part of an individual's identity (Tafoya & Del Vecchio, 1996). Phinney (1992) described people's identity as coming from their "knowledge in a social group together with the value and emotional significance to that membership" (p. 156). Membership in an Aboriginal community is different from membership in any other community in Canada in that an external agency, the Canadian government, determines the rules and guidelines of membership. Additionally, the media continues to perpetuate negative and inaccurate images of the Aboriginal community, which only makes it more confusing for Aboriginal people to understand and develop their identity.

Aboriginal people struggle to achieve a strong sense of self-worth when the public perception of their community continues to popularize negative stereotypes (Menzies, 2005). How are people expected to develop a healthy view of themselves, their history and their ancestors if what they have learned in the education system and media portrays them as savages? Menzies (2005) surmised that this personal identity struggle results in people internalizing feelings of anger and confusion, which can affect self-esteem.

Holistic Interventions

Services for Aboriginal people who are homeless do not simply involve putting a roof over the person's head: they must address their physical, emotional, mental and spiritual well-being needs. These services include shelters, housing programs, hospitals, community health centres, friendship centres, withdrawal management programs, inpatient and outpatient treatment programs, intensive case management programs and legal services.

The City of Toronto has supported Aboriginal community initiatives that empower both the community and the clients being served. Menzies (2006) wrote that "the solution must be driven by the insights and priorities identified from within our community and not external to it" (p. 4). The Native Men's Residence (Na Me Res) in Toronto is an example of how this can be done: the residence has changed over time to accommodate the evolving needs of its residents. It began as an emergency shelter and has since expanded to provide a continuum of care to Aboriginal men who are homeless.

Finding and accessing appropriate services for clients is an essential part of their care. The Internet, service directories and co-workers can be great resources for finding out what local services are available for Aboriginal people.

HOW TO PROVIDE INDIVIDUAL INTERVENTION

A thorough assessment is an essential first step to ensuring a client-centred intervention. An assessment should include a client's previous housing experiences, including barriers to safe and affordable housing, which typically include addiction and mental health issues, although these should never be assumed. The assessment should also routinely include a question about whether the person has had a TBI, given the prevalence of these injuries among people who are homeless.

I once accompanied a young male client to an intake appointment at a community health centre where we sat with a nurse to discuss his presenting issues and concerns. It quickly became clear that this client, whom I thought I knew well, had many more health concerns than I realized. This young man indicated that he had been diagnosed with fetal alcohol spectrum disorder and hepatitis C as a child, had had a head injury as a youth, had experienced chronic pain from a physical assault, and was an intravenous drug user. Each of these conditions had significant implications for this young man's health, intervention and case planning. Had I not accompanied him to the appointment, I would have been unaware of many of the issues and barriers he was facing. And had I initially completed a thorough assessment, I would have already been aware of the issues.

Psychoeducation supports clients' ability to understand the complex variables and relationships affecting their behaviour, with visual aids often proving helpful. McIntyre-Mills (2010) suggested using mapping and picturing, as these processes provide visual examples to illustrate thought patterns and behaviours. Physical and mental health issues, such as those associated with a TBI or fetal alcohol spectrum disorder, may complicate the psychoeducational process. Clients with these issues may experience greater difficulty understanding their conditions and related symptoms without the support of visual explanations.

Physical, mental, emotional and spiritual health conditions are connected and require equal consideration to support clients to restore balance in their lives. Clients who have experienced a TBI, for example, may require significant accommodations to address their symptoms, such as difficulty thinking clearly, concentrating or remembering and following conversations or directions; feeling chronically tired and lacking energy; feeling irritable; having amplified emotionality; being depressed and/or anxious; and having trouble sleeping (Hwang et al., 2008). Clinicians and front-line workers in residential and program settings should look for patterns of troubling behaviour, such as a client receiving several warnings for sleeping in, which is a risk for being discharged from the program. Waking up in the morning might be difficult because of a TBI, not because the client is being defiant.

Identity tends to be a complicated issue within the Aboriginal community that needs to be treated gently. I once worked with a client who was adopted by a non-Aboriginal family and was raised with no connection to his birth family or community. As an adult, he no longer had a relationship with his adoptive family and had been estranged from his wife and children. While he was homeless, he stayed exclusively at the Native Men's Residence emergency shelter where he was surrounded by Aboriginal staff and traditional Aboriginal teachings, yet he vehemently separated himself from his Aboriginal background, saying he did not identify with Aboriginal people. Why, then, was he staying at an Aboriginal shelter? Providing a seamless continuum of care is essential. Clinicians should be knowledgeable about the resources available to them within both their own and neighbouring communities. Research has shown that, due to the connection between traumatic experiences and mental health issues and homelessness, providing proactive services as part of a long-term continuum of care is more effective than offering sporadic crisis-based services (Kim et al., 2010).

Finally, recognize success when it happens, both for you and your client. Success does not necessarily mean that you have supported a client to stop his or her chronic substance use, find stable housing and develop a full-time career. Many of the changes we see in clients are less dramatic and develop slowly. Take every opportunity to recognize these changes and celebrate them with the client.

HOW TO PROVIDE COMMUNITY INTERVENTION

Community intervention is an important element in stopping trauma from being transmitted to future generations. Empowering Aboriginal organizations to achieve well-being for Aboriginal people is a step in the right direction (McIntyre-Mills, 2010). Gagné (1998) suggested that breaking an Aboriginal community's cycle of political, economic and social dependence would lead to healthier communities.

To a degree, the government has recognized the need for community-based interventions. For example, the national Homeless Partnering Strategy, which began in 2007, was directed to prevent and reduce homelessness (Employment and Social Development Canada, 2013), and has funded programs ranging from addiction services to soup kitchens. The Aboriginal community was identified as a specific funding group, and the initiative required that funding proposals be community-driven.

Clinicians need to ask themselves: Are we providing crisis services only, or are we looking for long-term solutions to prevent homelessness in future generations? By working together, the community can identify priorities and strategies that are culturally and politically appropriate.

Preventing Homelessness

In the last 20 years, innovative approaches to preventing homelessness have been developed. For example, the "housing first" approach was developed and applied in New York City in the early 1990s as a way to get people off the streets and into housing. This approach differs from previous approaches in that clients are no longer required to be in treatment for mental health and substance use problems to get housing (Pathways to Housing, 2013). Tsai and colleagues (2010) found that clients who were chronically homeless improved their psychosocial skills over time, spent more days in independent housing and fewer days incarcerated using the housing first approach. These results challenge the view that people's mental health must be stable and their addictions under control before they can successfully maintain independent housing. The housing first approach could also potentially reduce clients' exposure to such risks as harsh weather and violence. The City of Toronto implemented the approach as part of its homelessness initiatives in the early 2000s.

Knowing what risks a client faces can greatly increase a clinician's abilities to successfully engage preventative strategies. For example, because research suggests that the first occurrence of TBI often precedes the first occurrence of homelessness (Hwang et al., 2008), the practitioner should consider a client's risk of homelessness if he or she sustains a TBI.

Appropriate discharge planning is another important component of homelessness prevention. Research on young adults leaving the child welfare system has demonstrated that planning transitions from one residential program to another tends to increase the likelihood of clients' making a smooth transition into adulthood and independence (Brown & Wilderson, 2010). Many clinicians in the health, social services and justice systems are implicitly involved in clients' discharge planning process. Knowledge of community organizations and their eligibility criteria facilitates appropriate referrals. Researchers describe the need for service providers to work across disciplines and to collectively address social well-being (McIntyre-Mills, 2010). This opinion is mirrored by research out of St. Michael's Hospital (2010), which suggested that "formalized partnerships and interagency collaboration can be valuable resources for improving the lives of homeless clients" (p. 1).

Safe, secure and affordable housing can be difficult to access in urban centres. This deficiency suggests that, even once people enter independent housing, they are not necessarily in a safe, secure, healthy environment. Aboriginal Legal Services of Toronto has developed a program to support clients to manage issues that arise once they have secured housing, such as dealing with unsafe premises, rental arrears and discrimination. This program has proven to be an innovative approach to supporting homelessness prevention in the City of Toronto.

According to Hulchanski (2006), government plays a central role in creating, sustaining and changing the housing system. All levels of government need to be involved in order to decrease homelessness. Although more affordable and safe housing would not hurt, Canada's housing system needs to change structurally, so as to eliminate the dichotomous relationship between homeowners and renters, and allocate equal benefits to each. The allocation of differential benefits to the advantage of the homeowner must be rectified.

Implications for Clinicians

Clinicians are essential in the healing process and play an integral role in engaging and moving clients along a healing path. Although our work is centred on the people we work with, as clinicians, we need to consider our own views and perceptions of homelessness to ensure that our practice is as unbiased as possible. It is a common belief that individual effort determines class, income, wealth, power, prestige and health (Raphael et al., 2008). Do you agree with this belief? What do you think when clients spend money on alcohol rather than basic necessities or miss visitations with their children? We must be aware of how we feel to ensure that our personal perceptions and sentiments do not negatively affect our clinical work. Clinicians run the risk of perpetuating homelessness by holding negative stereotypes and choosing to work only with clients who show more promise in the journey toward good health.

Issues of Aboriginal identity are equally complicated. Criteria for status and non-status Indians and Métis people have been imposed by federal and provincial legislation and can be discriminatory. People both within and outside Aboriginal communities can be very judgmental about who belongs in what group, according to these governmental definitions of "Aboriginality," such as the terms "status" versus "non-status" Indian. Clinicians need to determine how they define Aboriginality and how their perceptions affect their practice.

Given the history of trauma and the continued racism, discrimination and stigmatization toward Aboriginal peoples, Gagné (1998) stated that "cultural sensitivity on the part of the professional is mandatory if the cycle of trauma is to be stopped" (p. 369).

Conclusion

Aboriginal peoples are still dealing with centuries of trauma. Homelessness is one symptom of that experience and is closely linked to many other issues, including addiction, mental health and involvement in the criminal justice system. Until we end the transmission of trauma across generations, we are likely to witness increasing numbers of children, youth, women and men without homes.

There are no hard and fast rules when it comes to interventions with clients dealing with homelessness. But thorough assessments and appropriate interventions are essential starting points. In addition, you should consider the physical, emotional, mental and spiritual elements of clients' lives. Work toward balance and harmony to promote health and well-being.

Lastly, self-reflection is key. When you work within Aboriginal communities and specifically with people who are homeless, be aware of your own perceptions of the circumstances within which clients find themselves. You should be able to answer the following questions: Who is ultimately responsible for homelessness? Who is an Aboriginal person and what does that mean in relation to our practice, healing and prevention?

Aboriginal clients who are homeless often have a litany of presenting issues. If you have ever felt overwhelmed by the task of supporting these clients through their healing process, you are not alone. Remember to take one day at a time. As common as each client's story might be, each person will interact with his or her history in a different way. Use the Teachings of the Seven Grandfathers as your guide: truth, humility, wisdom, honesty, courage, love and respect.

References

Brown, S. & Wilderson, D. (2010). Homelessness prevention for former foster youth: Utilization of transitional housing programs. *Children and Youth Review, 32*, 1464–1472.

Canadian Homeless Research Network. (2012). *Canadian Definition of Homelessness*. Retrieved from Homeless Hub website: www.homelesshub.ca

Casavant, L. (1999). *Definition of Homelessness*. Retrieved from Parliamentary Research Branch website: http://publications.gc.ca/Collection-R/LoPBdP/modules/prb99-1-homelessness/definition-e.htm

City of Toronto. (2010). *2009 Street Needs Assessment: Results and Observations*. Retrieved from www.toronto.ca/legdocs/mmis/2010/cd/bgrd/backgroundfile-29122.pdf

Echenberg, H. & Jensen, H. (2008). *Defining and Enumerating Homelessness in Canada*. Retrieved from Library of Parliament website: www.parl.gc.ca/content/lop/researchpublications/prb0830-e.pdf

Employment and Social Development Canada. (2013). *Understanding Homelessness and the Strategy*. Retrieved from www.hrsdc.gc.ca/eng/communities

Fallis, G. & Murray, A. (Eds.). (1990). *Housing the Homeless and Poor: New Partnerships among the Private, Public, and Third Sectors*. Toronto: University of Toronto Press.

Gagné, M. (1998). The role of dependency and colonialism in generating trauma in First Nations citizens: The James Bay Cree. In Y. Danieli (Ed.), *International Handbook of Multigenerational Legacies of Trauma* (pp. 355–372). New York: Plenum Press.

Greater Vancouver Regional Steering Committee on Homelessness. (2010). *Homelessness in Metro Vancouver: A Comparative Community Profile*. Retrieved from Metro Vancouver website: www.metrovancouver.org

The Homeless Hub. (n.d.). *Homelessness: Causes of Homelessness*. Retrieved from www.homelesshub.ca/topics/causes-of-homelessness-199.aspx

Hulchanski, J.D. (2002). *Housing Policy for Tomorrow's Cities*. Retrieved from Centre for Urban and Community Studies, University of Toronto website: www.urbancentre.utoronto.ca/pdfs/elibrary/CPRNHousingPolicy.pdf

Hulchanski, J.D. (2006). What factors shape Canadian housing policy? The intergovernmental role in Canada's housing system. In R. Young & C. Leuprecht (Eds.), *Canada, State of the Federation 2004: Municipal–Federal–Provincial Relations* (pp. 221–247). Montreal: McGill-Queen's University Press.

Hwang, S.W., Colantonio, A., Chiu, S., Tolomiczenko, G., Kiss, A., Cowan, L., . . . Levinson, W. (2008). The effect of traumatic brain injury on the health of homeless people. *Canadian Medical Association Journal, 179,* 779–784. DOI: 10.1503/cmaj.080341

Kim, M.M., Ford, J.D., Howard, D.L. & Bradford, D.W. (2010). Assessing trauma, substance abuse, and mental health in a sample of homeless men. *Health and Social Work, 35* (1), 39–48.

McCaskill, D., FitzMaurice, K. & Cidro, J. (2011). Toronto Aboriginal Research Project. Retrieved from Toronto Council Fire Native Cultural Centre website: www.councilfire.ca/Acrobat/tarp-final-report2011.pdf

McIntyre-Mills, J. (2010). Participatory design for democracy and wellbeing: Narrowing the gap between service outcomes and perceived needs. *Systemic Practice and Action Research, 23* (1), 21–45. DOI: 10.1007/s11213-009-9145-9

Menzies, P. (2005). *Orphans within Our Family: Intergenerational Trauma and Homeless Aboriginal Men* (Unpublished doctoral dissertation). University of Toronto, Toronto.

Menzies, P. (2006). Intergenerational trauma and homeless Aboriginal men. *Canadian Review of Social Policy, 58,* 1–24.

Morrison, D.S. (2009). Homelessness as an independent risk factor for mortality: Results from a retrospective cohort study. *International Journal of Epidemiology, 38,* 877–883. DOI: 10.1093/ije/dyp160

Pathways to Housing. (2013). Our Model. Retrieved from http://pathwaystohousing.org/our-model/

Peters, E.J. & Robillard, V. (2009). "Everything you want is there": The place of the reserve in First Nations' homeless mobility. *Urban Geography, 30,* 652–680. DOI: 10.2747/0272-3638.30.6.652

Phinney, J.S. (1992). The Multigroup Ethnic Identity Measure: A new scale for use with diverse groups. *Journal of Adolescent Research, 7,* 156–176. DOI: 10.1177/074355489272003

Raphael, D., Curry-Stevens, A. & Bryant, T. (2008). Barriers to addressing the social determinants of health: Insights from the Canadian experience. *Health Policy, 88,* 222–235. DOI: 10.1016/j.healthpol.2008.03.015

St. Michael's Hospital. (2010, May/June). *Centre for Research on Inner City Health Research Flash.* Retrieved from www.stmichaelshospital.com/newsletter/crich_newsletter/crich-may-june-2010.pdf

Statistics Canada. (2008). *Aboriginal Peoples in Canada in 2006: Inuit, Métis and First Nations, 2006 Census.* (Catalogue no. 97-558-XIE). Ottawa: Minister of Industry.

Statistics Canada. (2013). *National Household Survey, 2011: Homeownership and Shelter Costs in Canada.* (Catalogue no. 99-014-X2011002). Ottawa: Minister of Industry.

Tafoya, N. & Del Vecchio, A. (1996). Back to the future: An examination of the Native American holocaust experience. In M. McGoldrick, J. Giordano & J. Pearce (Eds.), *Ethnicity and Family Therapy* (2nd ed.; pp. 45–54). New York: Guilford Press.

Tsai, J., Mares, A.S. & Rosenheck, R.A. (2010). A multisite comparison of supported housing for chronically homeless adults: "Housing first" versus "residential treatment first." *Psychological Services, 7,* 219–232.

Willse, C. (2010). Neo-liberal biopolitics and the invention of chronic homelessness. *Economy and Society, 39,* 155–184. DOI: 10.1080/03085141003620139

ABOUT THE AUTHOR

Janet Gasparelli is a member of the Six Nations of the Grand River Territory. She studied social work and social service administration at the University of Toronto and has worked in the Aboriginal community for several years doing both front-line and administrative work. Most of her experience has been working with the homeless population. She is currently program manager for the Native Men's Residence in Toronto and is dedicated to addressing intergenerational trauma at the client and organizational level.

Chapter 23

Addressing Aboriginal Family Violence: Innovation, Resilience and Empowerment

L. JANE MCMILLAN

Family violence rarely existed in Aboriginal societies pre-contact, due to strong, cohesive cultures in which individuals, families and the community were deeply interconnected (Baskin, 2006). Now the problem of family violence is one of the primary issues affecting the quality of life of Aboriginal peoples across Canada. This chapter explores family violence in Mi'kmaq communities in Nova Scotia and describes the strategies Mi'kmaq people are using to address family violence to illustrate effective approaches to tackling these complex issues in many Aboriginal communities.

Contrary to historical perceptions of the First peoples in Canada as being without law, culture, religion or governance, these First peoples had highly complex and innovative societies. The customs and values that governed them and enabled people to live and work together to flourish as nations were rooted in a strong cultural world view and were integrated into every facet of community life. When problems occurred, mechanisms were available for managing disputes and altering behaviours to reintegrate wrongdoers back into the family and community and repair harmed relations. Responsibility for maintaining peace was communal; everyone had a role to play in finding a resolution and facilitating reconciliation. Talking it out was the key strategy; every person had a voice. Elders and leaders provided guidance through teachings highlighting respectful relations. Spiritual sanctions and purification rituals helped to heal rifts between individuals, families and the community.

Colonization and subsequent colonial relations were framed by power imbalances that denigrated the cohesive Aboriginal cultures into chaos and collapse. Tools of colonialism such as the Indian Act and residential schools undermined traditional ways of life and tore apart families and communities.[1] Ongoing systemic discrimination has prevented equal participation of Aboriginal peoples in justice, education, economic and health institutions, and has created epidemic crises in mental and physical health. Today, many Aboriginal communities are confronting a wide range of complex family-related issues stemming from many factors, including historical trauma, racism, poverty, unemployment, inadequate housing, poor access to health and social services, lack of education, single parenthood, failures in the justice system and substance use problems (Sinclair et al., 2009). Spousal abuse and neglect and child abuse are issues created by these factors.

Mi'kmaq Families and Family Violence

The Mi'kmaq Nations have lived in eastern North America for more than 12,000 years and have experienced one of the longest periods of contact and colonization of any Aboriginal group in Canada. The primary social unit of the Mi'kmaq people was the extended family, or kin group. Several families grouped together to form a local community; each local community had its chief. A council of Elders made decisions on matters affecting the whole community and addressed problems that could not be resolved within families.

Oral traditions taught people how to behave honourably and avoid shame and reproach. Songs, rituals and feasting protocols reinforced ideas and values of expected proper behaviour. As in many customary law systems, Mi'kmaq people used shaming and shunning to encourage proper behaviour. Wrongdoers also faced sanctions from the spirit world. The sweat lodge was used as a purification ritual conducted prior to making major decisions, and a spiritually sick wrongdoer could seek purifying healing there with the help of a shaman or Elder. Courtship and marriage practices included extensive counselling from Elders on how to live with each other in the Mi'kmaq way. If a husband and wife did not live well together, they could easily separate (Paul, 2006); in such cases, parenting continued within the extended family networks. The community ensured that each child was cared for, providing resources to the parents and conflict resolution when these were needed (Blackstock, 2003).

In 2011, there were 13 Mi'kmaq communities in Nova Scotia and 14,958 status Indians registered to Nova Scotia bands, mostly Mi'kmaq Nations. Another estimated 10,000 non-registered Mi'kmaq people were living in Nova Scotia (Nova Scotia Office of Aboriginal Affairs, 2011). Most Mi'kmaq people still live in vibrant extended-family networks. It is fairly common for men and women to have children with multiple

---

1   For more discussion about the Indian Act and residential schools, see chapters 2 and 3, respectively.

partners, thus expanding kinship networks. According to the Nova Scotia Advisory Council on the Status of Women (2006), Aboriginal women are considerably less likely to marry, are somewhat more likely to live in common-law relationships and are more than twice as likely to be lone parents compared with non-Aboriginal women. Regardless of their marital status, Aboriginal women living on reserves are much more likely to have three or more children, while most Aboriginal women living off reserves have only one or two children. The age of first birth tends to be younger than the national average. Grandparents are frequently involved in primary care of their grandchildren, particularly when their children are employed, attending school or unable to care for their families properly due to substance use or mental health issues.

Family violence is a term "designating a constellation of harmful, exploitative, violent and aggressive practices that form in and around intimate relationships" (Blagg, 2002, p. 193). Family violence occurs regularly in Mi'kmaq communities, with incident rates varying depending on community size and location (Loppie & Wien, 2007). Statistics from Mi'kmaw[2] Family and Children's Services Family Healing Program annual reports indicate that family violence is a serious problem (Boyd-Crowther, 2007). Exact rates of violent incidents are impossible to determine because most cases are not reported to police or service providers. Factors that contribute to non-reporting include real and perceived prejudice by police, courts and community services; uncertainty concerning rights; the possibility of dual charges; fear of losing children; illiteracy; shame and self-blame; fear of retaliation; a severe lack of culturally appropriate exit options, such as housing, employment and transportation; and extended family and community political dynamics (McMillan, 2011a). However, national studies give a general indication of the extent of the problem. The Native Women's Association of Canada (2007) found that Aboriginal people in Canada are three times as likely to experience spousal abuse as non-Aboriginal people. Some research places rates of Aboriginal spousal violence as high as 80 to 90 per cent in the territories, and between 25 and 100 per cent in other parts of Canada. Violence is also more severe and more likely to be ongoing for Aboriginal people (Brownridge, 2008).

Addressing Mi'kmaq Family Violence

In 2006, a unique collaboration facilitated the development of a comprehensive, community-based participatory-action research project on family violence in Nova Scotia Mi'kmaq communities. The project was funded by the Atlantic Aboriginal Health Research Program. This collaboration originated when the Nova Scotia Advisory Council on the Status of Women sponsored a small delegation from Nova Scotia to attend the Policy Forum on Aboriginal Women and Violence in Ottawa hosted by Status of Women Canada. As a result of this opportunity, a working group

---

2   *Mi'kmaw* is another way to spell *Mi'kmaq.*

on family violence and Aboriginal communities was formed in Nova Scotia. Initially, the working group consisted of representatives from:

- Nova Scotia Advisory Council on the Status of Women
- Mi'kmaw Legal Support Network, a customary law and court worker program including translation services and justice and sentencing circles using customary Mi'kmaq conceptualizations of reconciliation, mediation and restitution
- Mi'kmaw Family Healing Centres, located in the Waycobah and Millbrook First Nations communities, which provide shelter services for Aboriginal women and outreach and education programs for Mi'kmaq people
- Steering Committee of the Mi'kmaq–Nova Scotia–Canada Tripartite Forum, a partnership between the Nova Scotia Mi'kmaq, the Province of Nova Scotia and the Government of Canada, formed to address issues of mutual concern affecting Mi'kmaq communities
- Nova Scotia Office of Aboriginal Affairs.

The working group became the Family Violence Sub-Committee of the Tripartite Forum's Justice Working Committee, and membership in the working group subsequently grew to include representation from the Nova Scotia Native Women's Association; the Nova Scotia departments of Justice, Community Services, and Health and Wellness; and the RCMP. It remains active today.

The goal of the research was to examine the characteristics of family violence and the design and implementation of culturally aligned, community-based anti-violence programs that would create meaningful, effective opportunities for prevention, intervention and resolution of family violence within Mi'kmaq communities in Nova Scotia. Additionally, we aimed to empower Mi'kmaq families and communities by involving them directly in decision making and by implementing their contributions (Archibald, 2006).

The Family Violence Research Project

Our research began with an extensive literature review focusing on feminist and anthropological theories, restorative justice, and Aboriginal peoples and the justice system. The Aboriginal student research assistants reviewed Aboriginal family violence intervention and prevention programs across the country to glean and summarize best practices. Individual members of the working group participated in national and international conferences investigating issues specific to Aboriginal family violence. The group drew on its collective knowledge to identify the considerable gaps in service at the community level with respect to family violence intervention, both within community service provider capacity and in the Canadian justice system.

After receiving approval to conduct our research from Mi'kmaw Ethics Watch (a committee appointed by the Grand Council of the Mi'kmaq Nation to establish a set of principles and protocols that will protect the integrity and cultural knowledge of the Mi'kmaq people) and from St. Francis Xavier University's Research Ethics Board, we talked with many people from many different circumstances and walks of life: youth, family violence survivors and perpetrators, Elders and other leaders, front-line workers, people with substance use problems, individuals who were employed and unemployed, and men and women. More than 150 Mi'kmaq people were formally consulted through interviews, focus groups and two major community forums.

Objectives of the community forums were to present information on family violence, encourage dialogue on the issues involved and obtain direction from the community, particularly the grassroots, in terms of appropriate responses to the problem of violence. In this way, the community provided leadership with respect to the focus and objectives of the overall research project and its outcomes. We carefully considered how best to consult with the communities on this sensitive and often highly personal subject. We worked to ensure that the forums were an opportunity to gather in a healthy way to raise awareness and discuss issues of concern in order to map how the community members perceive and experience family violence and to consider how to apply their knowledge in creating innovative, meaningful responses. We were all concerned with safety, confidentiality and creating an environment for respectful sharing. Social workers and support counsellors from Mi'kmaq Family and Children's Services (a private child welfare agency) and the Mi'kmaw Family Healing Centres volunteered their services during and after the forum in case people required immediate assistance or referrals to services.

After much discussion within the working group, we decided to pose two questions at the day-long forums: "How does family violence affect you and your community?" and "What are options for changing family violence?" We divided the large group into smaller talking circles to give people a greater opportunity to share, and gave each group a flip chart. Facilitators from the Mi'kmaw Legal Support Network and Mi'kmaw Family Healing Centres recorded responses. We presented the first question in the morning. At the end of the morning session, we asked circle members to choose the three issues from their lists they considered the most important. After lunch, we presented the second question, and again asked people to select the issues they felt were most important. We then gathered into a large group, had a thank-you ceremony, reminded people of the counselling services available to them and gave them the contact information of the researcher in case they wanted to have private discussions. Once the participants left, the working group gathered to debrief.

The community forums were very successful in helping us to gather and synthesize peoples' insights and experiences of family violence. Many people shared deeply personal stories of witnessing and experiencing violence and abuse. Heartfelt accounts of anger and frustration detailing the challenges facing their communities in overcoming widespread social problems were mixed with hopeful visions of better futures. The community forums increased our awareness of the prevalence and impact of family violence in Aboriginal communities across Nova Scotia, highlighted the urgent need for increased resources in order to effectively deal with the issues of family violence and illuminated community perceptions of the services available.

In addition to the community forums, we conducted focus groups and interviews with victims and perpetrators of violence and their extended families; front-line workers and service providers who deal with family violence prevention and intervention; police officers and justice personnel; and youth. We examined the nature and extent, and past history and present circumstances, of family violence; reactions and responses to abuse; adequacy and inadequacy of approaches; and the desired outcomes and recommendations for change. We examined the unique social-political phenomena emerging from the collective historical trauma of colonialism, residential schools, systemic discrimination and racism, as well as the very personal experiences of abuse.

We then compiled our findings and returned to the community for feedback on the best practices for prioritizing a community strategy to help families and individuals experiencing violence in ways that protected their rights, acknowledged their unique identities and customs as Mi'kmaq people, and provided satisfactory remedies in times of crisis and ongoing support for family and community healing.

Finally, we assembled our findings and the community recommendations and presented them to a wide variety of interested groups—community, government and academic organizations; and agencies, forums, task forces, symposiums, workshops and conferences—representing many perspectives, including family violence, addiction, crime prevention, adult education and policing. This range of engagement is critical to participatory-action research processes.

WHAT WE LEARNED

Overwhelmingly, the participants in this research indicated that poverty, addiction and a pervasive sense of cultural distance are the most significant factors that perpetuate family violence. Many stressed that conflicts within their communities and families do not reflect who they are as Mi'kmaq people. Again and again, from community members and service providers alike, we heard about the great need for men's programs, so that perpetrators of violence will have better opportunities to heal and break the cycles of harm. Men's problems with family violence often stem from their own experiences of violence in childhood. Perpetrators consistently reported that working with someone who speaks Mi'kmaq, "who gets life on the rez and gets where I come from," and who understood Mi'kmaq life and family dynamics had been the most effective in helping them recognize their issues and in providing support. Others noted that it will be crucial to mobilize reintegration procedures and support-network activities in each Mi'kmaq community on reserves and in urban centres. Families are a support for some, and part of the problem for others. Many identified a strong need for more community programs to help families.

Clients, service agencies and community members all want services that make sense in the Mi'kmaq context. Moratoriums on restorative justice for domestic violence, avoidance of mediation for abused women, and pro-charge and pro-conviction stances do not serve the interests of Mi'kmaq families, do not help men, and tend to contradict Mi'kmaq cultural practices and ways of being that are communally oriented (Nova Scotia Advisory Council on the Status of Women, 2006). Many participants spoke about the need to expand and sustain services for Mi'kmaq victims of family violence, and about the need for services such as family group conferencing, a healing and decision-making process designed to help parents, children and extended families come together with counsellors and service providers to create a family plan to protect and care for all family members. In all of our sessions, people said they want holistic supports, peer mediation and workshops because they think education is the best deterrent to family violence. There were many other great suggestions for ways to combat family violence. People in one community said, "Have peace talks"; others suggested "more gatherings and feasts, waltes [a customary gambling game] night or language classes" or "reach out to Elders more" and "return to the land and teachings."

Access to justice is a significant problem for Aboriginal victims and offenders. Mi'kmaq people are unlikely to turn to the Canadian justice system or mainstream service providers for help because of a general mistrust due to significant inadequacies of the justice system to meet Mi'kmaq needs caused by systemic discrimination and marginalization across race, class, poverty, language, ability and sexual orientation.[3] The Canadian justice system is seen as an institution of colonial oppression. Other deterrents include the length of time it takes to process charges; fear of losing children; placing responsibility on women in situations of family violence; zero-tolerance policies resulting in countercharges; limited culturally appropriate options in court, causing problems in giving evidence and cases to collapse; inappropriate and unenforceable conditional sentences and probation orders, or inadequate sentences; lack of culturally appropriate high-risk assessment tools; restrictions to obtaining emergency protection orders on reserves due to complicated federal and provincial jurisdictions over property rights; the financial and social costs of going to court; an inability to navigate the legal system; and pro-charge and pro-incarceration policies. (McMillan, 2011a). Victims and offenders alike are generally dissatisfied with the justice system's treatment of their cases when their disputes result in charges. While many participants in our study agreed that there are some cases that should result in prosecution, conviction and incarceration, most people want to avoid the police and courts and seek alternative intervention and mediation options to help reconcile relations or end them in a good way. Service providers also experience first-hand the inadequacies and contradictions of justice system responses to family violence incidents that help to perpetuate the problems.

Everyone agreed that organizations must work together to better meet the diverse and extensive needs of their communities. The staff of the Native Alcohol and Drug Abuse Counselling Association of Nova Scotia, who have long experience in working

---

3 For a discussion about the criminal justice system in Canada, see chapter 25.

with Mi'kmaq communities, noted that the key to establishing a positive reputation is to put respect into action by delivering consistent, reliable, responsible programming that people can count on being there when they need it. They emphasized the necessity and right that social services be available in the Mi'kmaq language and compatible with Mi'kmaq values and teachings. Timeliness is critical to dispute management, and Mi'kmaq communities are in much better positions to deal with matters immediately than are the courts or outside service agencies, but in order to do so, the responsibilities of each organization need to be clarified and communicated to everyone. Communication among service agencies, courts and health services detailing their program offerings, schedules and training is sporadic and ineffective. Additionally, the lack of a comprehensive confidentiality policy for service providers prohibits effective information sharing and perpetuates inadequate communication, which in turn diminishes the quality of service provision and client satisfaction. Program transparency and accountability suffer from poor communication to clients about goals and services. These obstacles must be addressed if effective community collaboration and legitimation of services are to occur (Dickson-Gilmore & La Prairie, 2005).

Service providers must work within the narrow mandates and funding structures of the complicated bureaucracy of Indian and Northern Affairs, the Indian Act and band politics. Their organizations are forced to compete for scarce resources and modify programs in order to meet external funding requirements; often, they operate divisively in isolation, rather than collectively or communally. Structurally, programs and organizations mirror the bureaucracies that fund them, and thus, their policies tend to be contradictory, creating gaps where individuals fall through. Agency linkages are interrupted through human resource–draining funding competitions, which are divisive, oppressive and unsustainable.

Grant-based models create circumstances in which decision making is short term and non-strategic; funders outside of the communities set the development agenda; and development is treated as primarily an economic problem, with Aboriginal culture considered as an obstacle to, rather than the framework for, healing and well-being (Jorgensen, 2007). When programs are forced to focus on the short-term fix, service provision is difficult to maintain because incremental building cannot take place. When decision making occurs remotely, a top-down approach results in which organizations have limited power to determine how their resources are used and they remain dependent on external resources. Furthermore, the evaluation processes required by funders do not take into consideration the significant time that programs need to build community trust and capacity. Families need regular, consistent opportunities for engagement with healing so that trust can be established and results observed and openly shared. A history of failed enterprises undermines community self-confidence and results in frustration and hopelessness.

Among the biggest challenges reported by Mi'kmaq service providers is breaking the "codes of silence" and encouraging people to get help. There are many obstacles to seeking help for family violence in Aboriginal communities: fear of losing children or housing; addiction; lack of trust of service providers; lack of community support; lack of comprehensive assistance and crisis follow-up; limited sustainable or culturally aligned services for victims; inadequate communication strategies regarding what help is available; shame and self-blame; fear of family retaliation; and high rates of reconciliation (McMillan 2011a).

In addition to residential schools as a mechanism for dismantling Aboriginal cultures across Canada, foster care and adoption systems were widely used to break down extended kinship networks as a strategy of assimilation. During the 1960s, 1970s and 1980s, non-Aboriginal child welfare workers held Aboriginal people responsible for the poverty, overcrowded and unsanitary housing conditions and malnutrition in which the majority of people lived, and this led to extensive adoptions or temporary placements of Aboriginal children into non-Aboriginal homes (MacDonald & MacDonald, 2007).[4] Social workers were involved in these tragedies, and are involved in the continued overrepresentation of Aboriginal youth in child welfare programs. Exposure to domestic violence under the Child Welfare Act is seen as a "failure to protect" on the part of the parent, leaving parents to be held responsible for exposing their children to continued violence if they do not leave abusive relationships. Considering the complicated situation within Aboriginal communities in which women may be unable to leave an abusive situation for numerous reasons, including isolation, fear of retribution or poverty and addiction, there is a very real threat of women being revictimized, albeit unintentionally, by the very organizations from which they sought help originally. Women often view programs such as those offered by the Mi'kmaw Family and Children's Services of Nova Scotia as too closely linked with child welfare agencies and treat them with tentativeness and fear.

Building trust is the key to effective counselling relationships, and the key to trust is time. Many participants in our research feel judged and misunderstood by service providers who have little experience in working with Aboriginal families. To build trust it is important to get to know the community and its unique characteristics and resources. Most people in dire need have difficulty scheduling and attending appointments because they have no access to public transportation, regular phone service or affordable child care. Family members may have legal conditions, such as no-contact orders or conditional sentences, which impinge on opportunities for family group conferencing. Many people living in crisis are focused on day-to-day survival; providing food for the family takes priority over cleaning houses or tending yards. Child-rearing practices, eating habits, social boundaries and kinship bonds are all culturally constructed. It can be challenging for service providers to distance themselves from their lived experiences and the qualities of life they take for granted, but such standards of evaluation can make meaningful connections with clients difficult. Literacy rates and language comprehension abilities are diverse and difficult to interpret and assess in brief encounters. Some people will have problems filling out forms, or understanding

---

4   For a discussion about the child welfare system, see chapter 4.

questions or certain concepts, but will not feel comfortable admitting this or asking for help. Taking the time to talk through administrative issues, offering choices in case management that best fit client realities, and confirming and reconfirming client understanding of their choices and responsibilities help empower people to become active participants in their well-being. Learning about the historical impacts of colonization and systemic discrimination, as well as the many attributes of Aboriginal cultural practices, helps prepare service providers for positive engagements and empathic dialogue that can help end the silences of suffering.

Finally, systemic discrimination and the intergenerational traumas brought about through centuries of attempted ethnocide, coerced assimilation, discriminatory legislation and the destruction of families, communities and culture by outsiders seeking to control Mi'kmaq rights, territory and resources have resulted in desensitization toward violence. Often little or nothing is done to address acts of violence between intimate partners: there are few services available to victims that offer meaningful help, and few consequences for perpetrators. Even though many Mi'kmaq are aware of, know of or are themselves in violent relationships, unless it is a case of extreme, life-threatening violence, it usually goes ignored and unreported. The community often agrees as a whole to let it just go away. Perpetrators take the risk of carrying out harmful acts, assuming that no one will demand that they take responsibility for their behaviour. Victims are taught to wait for other influences to take over and rebalance relationships. Local norms and values of non-interference and the desire to handle matters for themselves without outside interference facilitate the "normalization" of violence.

But violence is not a Mi'kmaq cultural norm: Mi'kmaq people and communities are horrified, angered, fearful, frustrated, confused and traumatized by acts of violence. They want them to stop. However, frequent and severe violence; feelings of helplessness; patterns of continued abuse linked with substance use; poverty and lack of effective interventions and remedies; lack of access to the Canadian justice system and its inability to provide adequate justice; and feeling distant from their culture are all experiences that people tell us are normal in their lived experiences.

Critical Paths to Prevention, Intervention and Remedy

Our research with the Mi'kmaq of Nova Scotia points to three critical paths to addressing family violence in other Aboriginal communities across Canada. First, the cultural health of First Nations requires recognition of Aboriginal rights and title, meaningful consultation and fulfilment of the fiduciary obligations of the Crown. Without rights education and the implementation of treaties, systemic discrimination and poverty will continue to contribute to, rather than limit, the Aboriginal experience of family violence. Such recognition will enhance nation-rebuilding strategies and afford opportunities for reconciliation between Aboriginal peoples, federal and provincial governments and their constituents. This is a necessary project of decolonization and cultural realignment.

The second path is to continue to improve Aboriginal access to and experiences within the Canadian justice system through expanding and improving support and legal services for Aboriginal people, including victims' and family court services, legal aid, translation services, court worker services, probation services and aftercare. Aboriginal peoples are exploring the use of traditional justice knowledge and approaches in contemporary settings and developing and using groundbreaking mechanisms for crime prevention, intervention and resolution (McMillan 2011b). The criminal justice system is cautiously absorbing these changes through modest recognition of restorative justice practices and a gradual shift toward community-based sentencing. However, most Aboriginal communities have avoided using restorative justice models to address family violence. This is due in large part to broad-based moratoriums prohibiting domestic violence cases in non-Aboriginal restorative justice programs over concerns about victim safety, power and gender inequities and re-victimization, and a pro-charge, pro-conviction stance supported by provincial domestic violence legislation and hence service providers and police (Balfour, 2008; Cameron, 2006). The creation of an Aboriginal court with powers equal to a federal court and guided by Aboriginal cultures and traditions, an idea suggested by the Marshall Inquiry (Royal Commission on the Donald Marshall, Jr., Prosecution, 1989) more than two decades ago, would help to reduce the increasing problem of over-incarceration; observe the directions of section 718.2(e) of the Canadian Criminal Code for courts to consider all reasonable sanctions other than imprisonment, with particular attention to the circumstances of Aboriginal offenders; and better reflect and respect Aboriginal sovereignty (Milward, 2012; Roach & Rudin, 2000).

The third and perhaps most important path to addressing family violence in Aboriginal communities is to alleviate the great sense of cultural distance among many Aboriginal peoples by developing and implementing programs and remedies that are meaningful to those who participate in them. The Mi'kmaq communities of Nova Scotia have told us they want customary law programs to promote prevention and provide interventions to help families in crisis. Customary law protocols rooted in Mi'kmaq ways of being and framed by Mi'kmaq rights will provide meaningful, flexible and culturally relevant mechanisms to help people work through their crises, enhance Mi'kmaq values for living right, and provide visible and serious consequences for those who commit acts of violence in Mi'kmaq communities.

Mi'kmaq customary law involves talking it out (addressing root causes), seeking and receiving counsel, Elder reprimands and teachings, shame and shunning, restitution, reintegration, reconciliation, transparency and accountability. When wrongdoings need to be corrected, the authority of the verdicts are accepted as just because they are consistent with cultural values and positively reinforced by other members of the community. Mi'kmaq customary law is not structurally adversarial; it does not create a dichotomous relationship between offender and victim. And Mi'kmaq justice is much more inclusive than the Canadian system. The Mi'kmaq approach takes care of everyone—both the wrongdoer and all who were affected by the wrongdoing—and all collaborate to design appropriate and effective remedies and compliance monitoring strategies. But this is not reflected in the services available for Mi'kmaq people as they encounter mainstream justice, and as a result, many more injustices are perpetrated.

The findings of our research support the creation of a specialized Mi'kmaq customary law program that draws on Mi'kmaq philosophies, adapted for contemporary environments, to address the problems of family violence. A holistic approach involving Mi'kmaq justice, education, health and political institutions working together to address poverty, addiction and culture loss will improve Mi'kmaq familial relations, offer cultural safety[5] and provide consistent, reliable support for people in volatile domestic situations. It will empower Mi'kmaq communities to address the problems of access to justice and to choose to live in communities where doing nothing about violence is no longer normal.

Aboriginal communities vary widely in their ability, capacity and desire to use traditional dispute-management strategies. Each community has different historical, political, familial, economic and cultural characteristics that influence how local legal consciousness is constructed. While goals and approaches will be diverse, the priorities of the process remain constant: to prioritize victim safety; to offer material and social supports for victims in a co-ordinated community response that ensures follow-up, monitors compliance with healing plans and supports reintegration for all parties; to engage in normative judgments that oppose gendered domination and violence; to work with state resources when necessary; and to operate on the premise that forgiveness is not a goal of the process, but may be an outcome (Coker, 2006).

Conclusion

The extraordinary resilience of Aboriginal people must be celebrated. In Aboriginal communities today, kinship bonds are being revitalized and celebrated in response to the imposition of mainstream approaches of colonization and assimilation that undermined the cultural significance of family. There is a surging tide of Aboriginal pride and empowerment in Canada today. The Idle No More movement reflects the strength of Aboriginal peoples' desire for well-being. The spirit of community collaboration for the protection of land and resources demonstrates the drive of Aboriginal peoples and their allies to move forward together to create and sustain nurturing environments that celebrate and perpetuate healthy families and positive identities. We all have roles to play in addressing inequality and improving access to health, education and justice. The dialogue is rich and instructive for moving from survival to prosperity, and the learning starts from within.

---

5   For a discussion about cultural safety, see chapter 30.

References

Archibald, L. (2006). *Final Report of the Aboriginal Healing Foundation. Vol. 3: Promising Healing Practices in Aboriginal Communities*. Retrieved from Aboriginal Health Foundation website: www.ahf.ca

Balfour, G. (2008). Falling between the cracks of retributive and restorative justice: The victimization and punishment of Aboriginal women. *Feminist Criminology, 3*, 101–120. DOI: 10.1177/1557085108317551

Baskin, C. (2006). Systemic oppression, violence, and healing in Aboriginal families and communities. In R. Alaggia & C. Vine (Eds.), *Cruel but Not Unusual: Violence in Canadian Families* (pp. 15–48). Waterloo, ON: Wilfrid Laurier University Press.

Blackstock, C. (2003). First Nations child and family services: Restoring peace and harmony in First Nations communities. In K. Kufeldt & B. McKenzie (Eds.), *Child Welfare: Connecting Research Policy and Practice* (pp. 331–342). Waterloo, ON: Wilfrid Laurier University Press.

Blagg, H. (2002). Restorative justice and Aboriginal family violence: Opening a space for healing. In H. Strang & J. Braithwaite (Eds.), *Restorative Justice and Family Violence* (pp. 191–205). Cambridge, UK: Cambridge University Press.

Boyd-Crowther, D. (2007). *Annual Report: Family and Community Healing Program*. Shubenacadie, NS: Mi'kmaw Family and Children's Services of Nova Scotia.

Brownridge, D. (2008). Understanding the elevated risk of partner violence against Aboriginal women: A comparison of two nationally representative surveys of Canada. *Journal of Family Violence, 23*, 353–367. DOI: 10.1007/s10896-008-9160-0

Cameron, A. (2006). Stopping the violence: Canadian feminist debates on restorative justice and intimate violence. *Theoretical Criminology, 10* (1), 49–66. DOI: 10.1177/1362480606059982

Coker, D. (2006). Restorative justice, Navajo peacemaking and domestic violence. *Theoretical Criminology, 10* (1), 20–49. DOI: 10.1177/1362480606059983

Dickson-Gilmore, J. & La Prairie, C. (2005). *Will the Circle Be Unbroken? Aboriginal Communities, Restorative Justice, and the Challenges of Conflict and Change*. Toronto: University of Toronto Press.

Jorgensen, M. (Ed.). (2007). *Rebuilding Native Nations: Strategies for Governance and Development*. Tucson: University of Arizona Press.

Loppie, C. & Wien, F. (2007). *The Health of the Nova Scotia Mi'kmaq Population*. Halifax, NS: Mi'kmaq Health Research Group. Retrieved from Union of Nova Scotia Indians website: www.unsi.ns.ca/upload/reports/ns%20rhs%20report%2007.pdf

MacDonald, N. & MacDonald, J. (2007). Reflections of a Mi'kmaq social worker on a quarter of a century work in First Nations child welfare. *First Peoples Child & Family Review, 3* (1), 34–45.

McMillan, L.J. (2011a). *Addressing Mi'kmaq Family Violence. Family Violence and Aboriginal Communities: Building Our Knowledge and Direction through Community-Based Research and Community Forums*. Retrieved from Tripartite Forum website: www.tripartiteforum.com

McMillan, L.J. (2011b). Colonial traditions, cooptations, and Mi'kmaq legal consciousness. *Law and Social Inquiry, 36*, 171–200. DOI: 10.1111/j.1747-4469.2010.01228.x

Milward, D. (2012). *Aboriginal Justice and the Charter: Realizing a Culturally Sensitive Interpretation of Legal Rights*. Vancouver: UBC Press.

Native Women's Association of Canada. (2007). *Violence against Aboriginal Women and Girls: An Issue Paper*. Retrieved from www.nwac-hq.org/en/documents/nwac-vaaw.pdf

Nova Scotia Advisory Council on the Status of Women. (2006). *Fact Sheet on Aboriginal Women*. Retrieved from http://women.gov.ns.ca/factsheets

Nova Scotia Office of Aboriginal Affairs. (2011). Aboriginal people in Nova Scotia: Fact sheets and additional information. Retrieved from www.novascotia.ca/abor/aboriginal-people/demographics

Paul, D. (2006). *We Were Not the Savages*. Halifax, NS: Fernwood.

Roach, K. & Rudin, J. (2000). *Gladue:* The judicial and political reception of a promising decision. *Canadian Journal of Criminology, 42,* 249–280.

Royal Commission on the Donald Marshall, Jr., Prosecution. (1989). *Royal Commission on the Donald Marshall, Jr., Prosecution: Digest of Findings and Recommendations.* Retrieved from Nova Scotia Department of Justice website: http://novascotia.ca/just/marshall_inquiry/

Sinclair, R., Hart, M. & Bruyere, G. (Eds.). (2009). *Wicihitowin: Aboriginal Social Work in Canada.* Halifax, NS: Fernwood.

ABOUT THE AUTHOR

L. Jane McMillan is the Canada Research Chair in Indigenous Peoples and Sustainable Communities and associate professor in the Department of Anthropology at St. Francis Xavier University in Antigonish, Nova Scotia. Jane has worked with Mi'kmaq communities for the past 19 years, conducting ethnography, researching and advocating for Aboriginal and treaty rights, community-based justice, resource regulation and economic development. She teaches Mi'kmaq and Indigenous studies, provides training and supervision around student research, co-chairs the Committee for Aboriginal and Black Student Success, and is a member of the Indigenous Peoples Research Cluster. She is also president of the Canadian Law and Society Association, and a member of the Mi'kmaq–Nova Scotia–Canada Tripartite Forum Justice Committee.

Chapter 24

Working with First Nations Youth and Families: A Psychiatrist's Perspective

PETER BRAUNBERGER

The communities of northern Ontario are culturally and politically diverse. They encompass almost 100 First Nations, four treaty groups and three major language groups. The communities are spread out over 500,000 square kilometres, and include more than 30 fly-in communities, which can only be accessed by air and in winter, by ice roads. Providing psychiatric services to youth in northern Ontario has these challenges, and also involves navigating different governments, ministries and agencies (Finlay et al., 2010).

A main concern I have in writing about psychiatric issues affecting First Nations children and adolescents is making generalizations. There may be more or less helpful ways of approaching child psychiatry practice with First Nations communities, but "essentialisms" and stereotypes must be avoided (Waldram, 2000). In addition to acknowledging a wide diversity of cultures among First Nations, it is also important to understand that a child's own awareness of and identification with his or her culture may fluctuate considerably as part of a normal developmental trajectory.

Mental health professionals and medical caregivers, psychiatrists in particular, have sometimes focused on the individual and on families at the expense of larger interpersonal networks and community. As documented in the groundbreaking report of the Royal Commission on Aboriginal Peoples ([RCAP], 1996), mental health issues that Aboriginal people experience may stem from much larger historical and ongoing political forces that continue to disempower individuals and communities. These forces include colonialist policies and institutions such as the Indian Act, residential schools and the child welfare system.[1] It is crucial for mental health professionals working with Aboriginal people to educate themselves about these larger issues and how they affect the existing power structure (CIHR Institute of Aboriginal Peoples' Health, 2011; RCAP, 1996). We must avoid mindlessly or accidentally repeating earlier experiences of intrusion, if not disempowerment.[2]

Through three case studies synthesized from my work as a child psychiatrist based in northern Ontario, I offer some tentative thoughts on the assessment and care of northern Ontario First Nations youth with mental health concerns. No case study represents any one particular youth or situation; rather, each was constructed to present a number of issues and questions across many clinical cases.

RESIDENTIAL SCHOOLS AND THE NEXT GENERATION

J was a 12-year-old Oji-Cree boy who, in an argument about going to school, had threatened to harm others with a stick. In his initial assessment at the local nursing station in his remote community, he also reported that he "heard voices" telling him what to do when he was angry. The nurse requested that J be admitted to the regional hospital for a psychiatric assessment.

When I saw J, he had missed more than half of the last school year and it seemed that this school year would be the same. School did not seem particularly important to J.[3] It soon became clear that he had made a genuine effort to go to school in the previous few weeks, but had re-experienced bullying. So he again began avoiding school. J was also anxious, if not paranoid. He had reported that people were following him and stealing his school supplies. However, his paranoid thoughts and voices faded within the first few days of being in the hospital, and without the use of medications.

J's parents reported recent irritability in J, likely correlated with a mounting pressure to attend school. But they also described J playing video games, helping out around the house and being out on the land with his father.

J was a particularly quiet youth, and he did not readily engage with me; I was concerned that he had a language or learning disorder, or perhaps even low cognitive function. However, we were at least able to assess his non-verbal skills, and he scored at the 90th percentile, which suggested more cognitive strengths than deficits.

I initially diagnosed J with adjustment disorder, meaning he had difficulty responding appropriately to the pressure to attend school from his parents and school administrators. School avoidance is often a symptom of anxiety, but J did not meet

---

1 For a more detailed discussion of the history of colonialism, residential schools and the child welfare system, see chapters 2, 3 and 4, respectively.

2 For a discussion about cultural safety training for service providers, see chapter 30.

3 Note, however, that the degree to which school involvement is a measure of healthy functioning may vary across communities and cultures (Devries et al., 2009; Fisher et al., 1999).

full criteria for a particular anxiety disorder, and although he was somewhat socially inhibited, he also had some social skills: he made eye contact and could have conversations with people. His sociability was within the wider range of what might be expected in a small northern community (Brant, 1990; Ross, 1992).

Typically, a youth displaying impulsive or angry behaviours will be assessed for attention-deficit/hyperactivity disorder (ADHD). In J's case I was never able to obtain the kind of background information, such as that provided by school records, needed for an ADHD assessment, but aside from J's anger about being expected to attend school, J's parents did not report other behaviours that pointed toward ADHD. J did not report mood symptoms. Fortunately, J had no contributing medical history, or substance use or legal problems. Overall, he appeared to be a resilient and hopeful youth.

Before a child is discharged from the hospital a treatment and safety plan is developed. Prior to J's discharge, we discussed a range of psychosocial interventions that J's parents and school might undertake, given the resources available in their remote community.

Over the next few months, however, J was admitted twice more to the hospital following significant explosive episodes. J's intermittent behaviours were thought to be a serious enough risk to others or himself that we tried a medication that sometimes helps with explosivity and impulsivity. However, it remains a general concern that in some smaller and remote communities, medication is more available than counselling, due to the cost and scarcity of experienced health care providers. For example, a trained counsellor flies into remote communities two days a month and may see up to 30 children in these two days. This scarcity of follow-up support shifts the balance away from using evidence-based psychosocial interventions and toward using medications that otherwise may be second-line or adjunct treatments.

In early appointments with J's parents, I had discussed parenting strategies to manage their son's behaviour. They didn't openly disagree with my suggestions, but they would not try them. I'm not sure why and somewhat to my surprise, we were eventually able to establish enough trust such that several appointments and phone calls later, J's parents spontaneously related a worry about their parenting. J's grandparents had attended residential schools, an experience that affected not only their parenting strategies, but also affected J's parents' confidence in listening to their own parenting instincts.[4] J's parents felt they did not know what to do, and were afraid of failing if they tried the parenting strategies we had discussed initially.

This conversation was a turning point in my understanding of how to work with J and his family. I also understood in a new way how important it is to get beyond perceptions (mine and theirs) of my role as "expert" and to develop my roles as a learner and a partner.

---

4 For more discussion about how the residential schools have affected Aboriginal people, including issues around parenting, see chapter 5 on intergenerational trauma. See also chapter 4 about the child welfare system.

As a result of our discussions, J's parents were willing to experiment with parenting techniques, tolerate small failures and keep trying, and I encouraged them in their efforts. Over time, a few small parenting successes begat more successes. J's parents became increasingly comfortable with their instincts about providing boundaries and expectations. I later learned that with less anxiety around expectations at home, and with clearer rewards and expressions of family strengths, J was back at school, did not take medication and was no longer being bullied.

More generally, parents often have good instincts about parenting their children, but they lack confidence in applying and persisting with them because such approaches may not have been used by their own parents. Their parents may have attended residential schools, removed from their families, and were never exposed to positive parenting role models.

Sometimes parents need to consider a wider range of parenting techniques. Many parenting programs based on a mainstream Western world view can be successfully adapted to First Nations contexts (Dionne et al. 2009; Houlding et al., 2012). Walkup and colleagues (2009) reported early positive outcomes for a paraprofessional mediated program for young American Indian mothers living on reservations. However, if a program is adapted for a specific cultural group, do not assume that it will be relevant to other cultural groups. These programs must be carefully considered for their appropriateness for each First Nation.

When working with Aboriginal youth who have behavioural concerns, it is essential to refer to evidence-based practice guidelines (e.g., Steiner et al., 2007), but it is also crucial to consider the historical, social and cultural roots of specific behaviours. We also need to respect community autonomy. The overall picture is one of listening, sometimes waiting, and making sure there is enough time to develop healthy, trusting partnerships.[5]

BACK NORTH, AND JUST AS ANGRY

K, almost 14 years old, was referred to us from a local child protection service's staffed home, having just "again" (her words) "broken down" (her worker's words) in yet another foster placement. K's acting out and high-risk behaviours were such that she had been in a therapeutic residential placement in southern Ontario for two years. But after just a few weeks of being back north, home, another carefully planned foster placement ended. The foster parents could not handle K's running away, self-harming (cutting) and substance use.

K was usually bright, humorous and distractible. Sometimes she used her quick wit to avoid a serious conversation, or a difficult thought or emotion. It was hard to get a clear sense of her feelings about her most recent transition, but I picked up, at least partly, a sense of relief. Sometimes it seems easier to get the foster placement breakdown out of the way. To deal with her anxiety about being rejected in her placement,

---

5 For more discussion about working with and supporting Aboriginal youth, see chapter 9.

K had acted in such a way that ensured the placement did not work.

K was a notably vulnerable youth. She was impulsive and reactive, and extremely sensitive to real or perceived criticism, becoming angry and occasionally self-harming in response. K tended to fluctuate between idealized thinking, controlling behaviours and a dismissive "why would I care?" attitude. Even in her most insightful moments, K underestimated potential harms of running away, substance use, and interacting with at-risk and opportunistic peers. These vulnerabilities, coupled with access to marijuana and alcohol, had intermittently resulted in hopelessness, suicidal statements, self-harm, suicide attempts, visits to the emergency room and hospital admissions.

Despite multiple non-Aboriginal foster and residential placements, K identified strongly with her Aboriginal heritage and readily related visits with her grandmother and her home community. But she resisted when I asked about her culture and traditions. She quickly re-engaged on a wide range of (safer) topics.

K also expressed apparent indifference to childhood trauma. In her infant and toddler years, she was exposed to intimate partner violence and substance use issues within her family, and also to her mother's own extended hospitalization for mental health problems. K's earlier clinical assessments emphasized a disorganized attachment style. Because her parents had been emotionally and physically absent, she did not learn who to turn to for comfort and how to soothe herself when faced with strong emotions. When strong emotions did arise, she would become frantic and use alcohol or other drugs, or cutting to calm herself. In recent relationships it was apparent that K continued to struggle to assert herself positively. She was too worried about what other people thought of her and she would often make unhealthy decisions because her need for approval trumped other needs.

In addition to attachment challenges, traumas, institutionalization and substance use issues, K also met criteria for ADHD and a mild learning disability. She was also old enough to legitimately expect more independence, including deciding whether or not to interact with her family.

Diagnoses and past and present behaviours suggested that K was at risk of self-harm or suicidal behaviours. But K was also negotiating several narratives and trajectories (urban/rural, traditional/mainstream Western, family/in-care, and safe/unsafe). As much as she seemed to be looking to belong, I suspect she was also seeking to find a path. When I first met her, belonging to a place ("I want to be in Thunder Bay") was probably her way of saying she wanted to be connected to family and culture. As she grew into adolescence, she was able to articulate how important her culture was to her.

In conjunction with a supportive team, the role of a psychiatrist for youth such as K is sometimes limited to walking alongside, a kind of careful waiting, advocating developmentally appropriate self-regulation skills, engaging in safety planning and only sometimes considering pharmacological options. I made genuine efforts to neither overuse nor underuse medications to help manage K's affect and behaviour, weighing the risks of medications with the risks of impulsive behaviours, and to decrease risks associated with major and frequent transitions.

However, if there was a breakthrough with K, it was due to neither medications nor counselling, although both were likely important at times. Perhaps as an almost "last option," child protection workers had re-engaged K's family about within-family placement for K. K still had a high risk of impulsive behaviour, but, as a matter of development and increasing maturity, she seemed more ready to negotiate more respectfully with an aunt than with child protection or residential staff. Some of her fighting against "institutional" processes faded, and, to my surprise and genuine thankfulness, I, K, aunty and the social worker found ourselves in a genuine partnership in which we could discuss development, personal goals, parenting and cultural identification.

As with many other youth, K found her way to young adulthood with a balance of strengths and vulnerabilities and a growing sense of possibility. Over the next few years, as child protection supports faded, K's capacity for thoughtful decision making and engagement with community (to go to school, to limit substance use, to work with a counsellor) gave us all a much more hopeful outlook.

K's risk of suicide was exacerbated when she was in the throes of frantic behaviour in response to her emotions, and she had made suicide attempts in this state. Clinicians who encounter First Nations youth in their practice need to pay particular attention to the risks of suicide within this group. For a wide range of historical, political and socio-economic reasons, First Nations youth in Canada have significantly elevated rates of suicide (MacNeil, 2008).[6] It is important to note, however, that many First Nations communities have neither a recent history of suicide, nor elevated suicide rates (Chandler & Lalonde, 1998). Although many variables contribute to the risk profile of any one youth (Lemstra et al., 2009; Novins et al., 1999), some First Nations youth may also have protective factors that lower their risk of suicide, such as family or community cohesion (Chandler & Lalonde, 1998; Freedenthal & Stiffman, 2007; Gould et al., 2003). When doing a risk assessment, it is important not to overlook the protective factors, which may come from culture, community, family or the individual. Aboriginal or not, being in care increases risk of negative mental health outcomes, including suicide (Barber & Delfabbro, 2009; Costello et al., 2003).

Despite an extensive epidemiology on youth suicide, there is still little specific research on individual intervention strategies for Aboriginal youth who are suicidal (Middlebrook et al., 2001; Storck et al., 2009). One possible model of intervention is the Zuni Life Skills Development Program, a unique variation of the American Indian Life Skills Development Curriculum (LaFromboise & Lewis, 2008). Muehlenkamp and colleagues (2009) developed a suicide prevention model incorporating the principles of the medicine wheel for at-risk college students. Community-based participatory research will be an essential first step in understanding and better supporting protective variables (Mullany et al., 2009). School-, community- and health care–based prevention programs may yet prove an important role in addressing suicide risk (Gould et al.,

---

6   For a detailed discussion about suicide, see chapter 21.

2003; White & Jodoin, 2003). It is important that each First Nation community evaluate each program to determine whether it would be relevant for their own community (Bennett et al., in preparation).

Aboriginal-specific assessment and treatment strategies for trauma and substance use issues are also in the early stages of development (Gone & Alcántara, 2007; Storck et al., 2009). Evidence-based practice guidelines remain important reference points (Cohen et al., 2010; Silverman et al., 2008). Morsette and colleagues (2009) presented positive results of a pilot study of a school-based treatment program for reservation-based American Indian youth with symptoms of posttraumatic stress disorder. Individual and group skills–based interventions are generally thought most effective in limiting substance use problems (Cheadle et al., 1995; Dixon et al., 2007; Schinke et al., 1988).

While Gone and Alcántara, (2007) suggested a general consensus on adapting mainstream mental health and substance use treatments for ethnic minorities, Wexler and Gone (2012) added that "normative assumptions that underpin standard suicide prevention interventions" should be challenged (p. 5). Adaptations of existing programs may not pay appropriate respect to a culture's conception of healing (Ngo et al., 2008; Rousseau & Kirmayer, 2009).

NORTH SOUTH WEST EAST

L was a 14-year-old girl from the most northern part of the province. She was Cree, and her family had an evangelical Christian tradition. L was living with her mother, father and several siblings, ranging from toddlers to young adults. L had earned awards for academic achievement, but had not now attended school for several months because of bullying. L initially presented to the hospital with a slow heartbeat (bradycardia) and low weight, and it became apparent that she had a restricting eating disorder and significant mood symptoms. She did not have other medical, legal or substance use issues.

L had a strong family history of depression. Her mother reported that she herself had never found antidepressants to be helpful. L and her family did not report a trauma history, although there had been a number of recent family deaths. L had previously spent time surfing the Internet and reading, but she had recently been doing much less of both. Her mother said that it had become difficult to persuade L to go with her brothers to watch them play hockey.

L reluctantly related her own sense of hopelessness. More specifically, when discussing school, she related that having been a good student was a waste of time because it would lead to nothing more than bullying. Being numb, bored and empty were added to her list of feelings and emotions. L had been superficially cutting her arms for a year, many months before anyone became aware of it.

L, like many youth with eating disorders, was intermittently harsh and critical of her parents, especially when they challenged her to eat more. In my own experience, direct rudeness toward parents is less common in northern Ontario Aboriginal teens, who are far more likely than non-Aboriginal youth to show deference to their parents (see also Brant, 1990). This rudeness was thus more likely a symptomatic process, as opposed to a sometimes normal developmental process. Perhaps understandably, L's parents felt surprised and confused and had backed off.

L presented with serious medical and mental health conditions; her irritability, isolating behaviours, self-harm and disordered eating were of genuine clinical concern. Initial assessment involved considerable discussion around specific medical risks and eating disorders in general. L's parents, who initially might have been watching and waiting, very quickly became engaged in specific discussions about meal supervision and a broader safety plan. They were reasonably quieter when discussing the causes of L's mood symptoms and diet restriction, but they took time to listen to the team's concerns.

L was ambivalent and skeptical about treatment. I had a sense that she saw too many potential conflicts (familial, religious, cultural, developmental) or traps in trusting or agreeing. I hope that L's hospital experience was eventually one of understanding and empathy, particularly around mood symptoms.

In addition to an initial safety and treatment plan, we were able to contribute to a plan that also considered strengthening developmental, interpersonal and coping skills. With L's permission, we communicated this information to the nursing station in L's community. This information was also incorporated into a follow-up plan. Risks and benefits of medications were discussed, but almost immediately L and her parents declined. Medication was left as a future option, if needed.

After only one follow-up by telepsychiatry, we lost contact. I hope that the initial discussion of issues, diagnoses and resources with L and her parents was a starting point. I also hope that a number of genuine personal and family strengths came to the fore.

Youth living in northern communities who have specialized mental health needs, such as eating disorders, face additional barriers to accessing culturally respectful, evidence-based care compared to youth from southern regions. These barriers include distance and lack of awareness of services in the first place.

High rates of hopelessness and other symptoms of depression in American Indian and Aboriginal youth are frequently reported (Jackson & Lassiter 2001; LaFromboise et al., 2010). Culture may affect how depressive symptoms are expressed. For example, if in a particular culture mental distress results in physical symptoms, such as stomach aches, or externalizing behaviours, such as acting out or self-harming, depression may be underdiagnosed (Pumariega et al., 2010). This means that clinicians have to gain experience with the culture or consult with people well versed in the culture to get a sense of how mental distress is expressed. LaFramboise and colleagues (2010) found that youth who had "bicultural competence," that is, who were comfortable with both Aboriginal and mainstream cultures, had significantly lower hopelessness scores. Difficulty with acculturation, or responding to a diversity of cultural priorities or values, might have been a significant source of stress for L.

Beals and colleagues (2005) provided examples of the limitations of using existing depression assessment protocols for youth and young adults (aged 15 to 24 years) in cross-cultural situations. They suggested using semi-structured interviews, which are more open and follow the client's lead, but incorporate standard questions and provide windows for new ideas to come up.

When a client first meets with a clinician, it can be hard to get a sense of whether the client understands what participating in treatment involves. In other words, it is hard to know whether the person is properly informed. This can be even more tricky when the person belongs to another culture, language being only one of a number of possible barriers to understanding (Pumariega et al., 2010).

Many studies have reported high rates of eating disorder symptoms in Aboriginal youth in North America (Marchessault, 2004; Neumark-Sztainer et al., 1997; Smith & Krejci, 1991). Yet relatively few youth present to our regional eating disorder service. To explain this discrepancy, we need to understand regional epidemiology; variation in vulnerability to particular mental health issues; cross-cultural validity of diagnoses and symptom profiles; stigma; and systemic and geographic barriers to care. No culturally sensitive interventions to support Aboriginal youth with eating disorders have yet been developed or assessed. Even if such interventions existed, geographic barriers to care could preclude our best efforts to be thoughtfully and consistently engaged.

Conclusion

The three case studies described in this chapter demonstrate the diversity of mental health issues and inherent strengths often seen in Aboriginal youth and families. And although a psychiatrist working in a cross-cultural context must use evidence-based treatments, a lack of such treatments specific to Aboriginal contexts means that carefully developing relationships with the individual and the family is even more important. These relationships, which involve learning, following, advocating and providing care, are defined not only by expertise, but also by respect, trust and boundaries, elements that can only be demonstrated and grown over time. I value the French writer André Gide's admonition "Do not understand me too quickly" and try to apply it to any growing relationship, cross-cultural or not.

Adapting existing evidence-based programs and therapies to suit local communities might be helpful, but the local community has to be part of the adaptation process. Only these communities can know which aspects of a program are relevant to them.

Students and practitioners of cross-cultural child psychiatry and mental health care should avoid stereotypes and generalizations: after some initial cross-cultural training, a novice practitioner may expect every First Nation person to act a certain way. But time and experience will show that there is a wide range of "normal" behaviour. Knowing this allows practitioners to consider the needs of clients more quickly and effectively. We must also come into the room as learners rather than "experts." We share the responsibility of addressing the bigger questions of quality of life, wellness and mental health with Elders, teachers, religious and spiritual leaders, parents and the youth themselves.

The experience of safety, built on confidentiality, positive regard and cultural awareness and respect, is important for clients and families. But it is also important to remember that it is the First Nations children and families who are doing most of the cross-cultural work. Out of necessity, they have learned to negotiate mainstream Western culture. I am very thankful that First Nations workers and families are willing to create a safe space for clinicians like me to learn, make mistakes and recover. They do this with gentleness and humour. All cross-cultural clinicians have to do is walk slowly and keep their eyes open!

References

Barber, J.G. & Delfabbro, P.H. (2009). The profile and progress of neglected and abused children in long-term foster care. *Child Abuse & Neglect, 33*, 421–428. DOI: 10.1016/j.chiabu.2006.03.013

Beals, J., Novins, D.K., Whitesell, N.R., Spicer, P., Mitchell, C.M. & Manson, S.M. (2005). Prevalence of mental disorders and utilization of mental health services in two American Indian reservation populations: Mental health disparities in a national context. *American Journal of Psychiatry, 162*, 1723–1732.

Brant, C.C. (1990). Native ethics and rules of behaviour. *Canadian Journal of Psychiatry, 35*, 534–539.

Chandler, M. J. & Lalonde, C. (1998). Cultural continuity as a hedge against suicide in Canada's First Nations. *Transcultural Psychiatry, 35*, 191–219.

Cheadle, A., Pearson, D., Wagner, E., Psaty, B.M., Diehr, P. & Koepsell, T. (1995). A community-based approach to preventing alcohol use among adolescents on an American Indian reservation. *Public Health Reports, 110*, 439–447.

CIHR Institute of Aboriginal Peoples' Health. (2011). *Internal Assessment for 2011 International Review—CIHR Institute of Aboriginal Peoples' Health*. Retrieved from www.cihr-irsc.gc.ca

Cohen, J.A., Bukstein, O., Walter, H., Benson, R.S., Chrisman, A., Farchione, T.R., . . . AACAP Work Group on Quality Issues. (2010). Practice parameter for the assessment and treatment of children and adolescents with posttraumatic stress disorder. *Journal of the American Academy of Child & Adolescent Psychiatry, 49*, 414–430. DOI: 10.1097/00004583-199810001-00002

Costello, E.J., Compton, S.N., Keeler, G. & Angold, A. (2003). Relationships between poverty and psychopathology: A natural experiment. *JAMA, 290*, 2023–2029. DOI: 10.1001/jama.290.15.2023

Devries, K.M., Free, C.J., Morison, L. & Saewyc, E. (2009). Factors associated with the sexual behavior of Canadian Aboriginal young people and their implications for health promotion. *American Journal of Public Health, 99*, 855–862. DOI: 10.2105/AJPH.2007.132597

Dionne, R., Davis, B., Sheeber, L. & Madrigal, L. (2009). Initial evaluation of a cultural approach to implementation of evidence-based parenting interventions in American Indian communities. *Journal of Community Psychology, 37*, 911–921. DOI: 10.1002/jcop.20336

Dixon, A.L., Yabiku, S.T., Okamoto, S.K., Tann, S.S., Marsiglia, F.F., Kulis, S. & Burke, A.M. (2007). The efficacy of a multicultural prevention intervention among urban American Indian youth in the southwest U.S. *Journal of Primary Prevention, 28*, 547–568.

Finlay, J., Hardy, M., Morris, D. & Nagy, A. (2010). Mamow ki-ken-da-ma-win: A partnership approach to child, youth, family and community wellbeing. *International Journal of Mental Health and Addiction, 8*, 245–257. DOI: 10.1007/s11469-009-9263-8

Fisher, P.A., Storck, M. & Bacon, J.G. (1999). In the eye of the beholder: Risk and protective factors in rural American Indian and Caucasian adolescents. *American Journal of Orthopsychiatry, 69*, 294–304. DOI: 10.1037/h0080404

Freedenthal, S. & Stiffman, A.R. (2007). "They might think I was crazy": Young American Indians' reasons for not seeking help when suicidal. *Journal of Adolescent Research, 22* (1), 58–77.

Gone, J.P. & Alcántara, C. (2007). Identifying effective mental health interventions for American Indians and Alaska Natives: A review of the literature. *Cultural Diversity and Ethnic Minority Psychology, 13*, 356–363.

Gould, M.S., Greenberg, T., Velting, D.M. & Shaffer, D. (2003). Youth suicide risk and preventive interventions: A review of the past 10 years. *Journal of the American Academy of Child & Adolescent Psychiatry, 42*, 386–405. DOI: 10.1097/01.CHI.0000046821.95464.CF

Houlding, C., Schmidt, F., Stern, S.B., Jamieson, J. & Borg, D. (2012). The perceived impact and acceptability of Group Triple P Positive Parenting Program for Aboriginal parents in Canada. *Children and Youth Services Review, 34*, 2287–2294. DOI: 10.1016/j.childyouth.2012.08.001

Jackson, P.B. & Lassiter, S.P. (2001). Self-esteem and race. In T.J. Owens, S. Stryker & N. Goodman (Eds.), *Extending Self-Esteem Theory and Research: Sociological and Psychological Currents* (pp. 223–254). New York: Cambridge University Press.

LaFromboise, T.D., Albright, K. & Harris, A. (2010). Patterns of hopelessness among American Indian adolescents: Relationships by levels of acculturation and residence. *Cultural Diversity and Ethnic Minority Psychology, 16* (1), 68–76. DOI: 10.1037/a0016181

LaFromboise, T.D. & Lewis, H.A. (2008). The Zuni Life Skills Development Program: A school/community-based suicide prevention intervention. *Suicide and Life-Threatening Behavior, 38*, 343–353. DOI: 10.1521/suli.2008.38.3.343

Lemstra, M., Neudorf, C., Mackenbach, J., Kershaw, T., Nannapaneni, U. & Scott, C. (2009). Suicidal ideation: The role of economic and Aboriginal cultural status after multivariate adjustment. *Canadian Journal of Psychiatry, 54*, 589–595.

MacNeil, M.S. (2008). An epidemiologic study of Aboriginal adolescent risk in Canada: The meaning of suicide. *Journal of Child and Adolescent Psychiatric Nursing, 21* (1), 3–12. DOI: 10.1111/j.1744-6171.2008.00117.x

Marchessault, G. (2004). Body shape perceptions of Aboriginal and non-Aboriginal girls and women in southern Manitoba, Canada. *Canadian Journal of Diabetes, 28*, 369–379.

Middlebrook, D.L., LeMaster, P.L., Beals, J., Novins, D.K. & Manson, S.M. (2001). Suicide prevention in American Indian and Alaska Native communities: A critical review of programs. *Suicide and Life-Threatening Behavior, 31*, 132–149. DOI: 10.1521/suli.31.1.5.132.24225

Morsette, A., Swaney, G., Stolle, D., Schuldberg, D., van den Pol, R. & Young, M. (2009). Cognitive Behavioral Intervention for Trauma in Schools (CBITS): School-based treatment on a rural American Indian reservation. *Journal of Behavior Therapy and Experimental Psychiatry, 40*, 169–178. DOI: 10.1016/j.jbtep.2008.07.006

Muehlenkamp, J.J., Marrone, S., Gray, J.S. & Brown, D.L. (2009). A college suicide prevention model for American Indian students. *Professional Psychology: Research and Practice, 40*, 134–240.

Mullany, B., Barlow, A., Goklish, N., Larzelere-Hinton, F., Cwik, M., Craig, M., & Walkup, J.T. (2009). Toward understanding suicide among youths: Results from the White Mountain Apache tribally mandated suicide surveillance system, 2001–2006. *American Journal of Public Health, 99*, 1840–1848. DOI: 10.2105/AJPH.2008.154880

Neumark-Sztainer, D., Story, M., Resnick, M.D. & Blum, R.W. (1997). Psychosocial concerns and weight control behaviours among overweight and nonoverweight Native American adolescents. *Journal of the American Dietetic Association, 97*, 598–604. DOI: 10.1016/S0002-8223(97)00154-5

Ngo, V., Langley, A., Kataoka, S.H., Nadeem, E., Escudero, P. & Stein, B.D. (2008). Providing evidence-based practice to ethnically diverse youths: Examples from the Cognitive Behavioral Intervention for Trauma in Schools (CBITS) program. *Journal of the American Academy of Child & Adolescent Psychiatry, 47*, 858–862. DOI: 10.1097/CHI.0b013e3181799f19

Novins, D.K., Beals, J., Roberts, R.E. & Manson, S.M. (1999). Factors associated with suicide ideation among American Indian adolescents: Does culture matter? *Suicide and Life-Threatening Behavior, 29*, 332–346.

Pumariega, A.J., Roth, E.M., Song, S. & Lu, F.G. (2010). Culturally informed child psychiatric practice. *Child and Adolescent Psychiatric Clinics of North America. 19*, 739–757. DOI: 10.1016/j.chc.2010.07.004

Ross, R. (1992). *Dancing with a Ghost: Exploring Indian Reality*. Markham, ON: Octopus Publishing Group.

Rousseau, C. & Kirmayer, L. (2009). Cultural adaptation of psychological trauma treatment for children. *Journal of the American Academy of Child & Adolescent Psychiatry, 48*, 954–955. DOI: 10.1097/CHI.0b013e3181b21669

Royal Commission on Aboriginal Peoples (RCAP). (1996). *Report of the Royal Commission on Aboriginal Peoples. Vol. 3: Gathering Strength*. Ottawa: Canada Communication Group.

Schinke, S.P., Orlandi, M.A., Botvin, G.J., Gilchrist, L.D., Trimble, J.E. & Locklear, V.S. (1988). Preventing substance abuse among American-Indian adolescents: A bicultural competence skills approach. *Journal of Counseling Psychology, 35* (1), 87–90.

Silverman, W.K., Ortiz, C.D., Viswesvaran, C., Burns, B.J., Kolko, D.J., Putnam, F.W. & Amaya-Jackson, L. (2008). Evidence-based psychosocial treatments for children and adolescents exposed to traumatic events. *Journal of Clinical Child & Adolescent Psychology, 37*, 156–183. DOI: 10.1080/15374410701818293

Smith, J.E. & Krejci, J. (1991). Minorities join the majority: Eating disturbances among Hispanic and Native American youth. *International Journal of Eating Disorders, 10*, 179–186.

Steiner, H., Remsing L. & Working Group. (2007). Practice parameter for the assessment and treatment of children and adolescents with oppositional defiant disorder. *Journal of the American Academy of Child & Adolescent Psychiatry, 46*, 126–141.

Storck, M., Beal, T., Bacon, J.G. & Olsen, P. (2009). Behavioral and mental health challenges for indigenous youth: Research and clinical perspectives for primary care. *Pediatric Clinics of North America, 56*, 1461–1479. DOI: 10.1016/j.pcl.2009.09.015

Waldram, J.B. (2000). The problem of "culture" and the counseling of Aboriginal peoples. In L.J. Kirmayer, M.E. Macdonald & G.M. Brass (Eds.), *The Mental Health of Indigenous Peoples: Proceedings of the Advanced Study Institute, McGill Summer Program in Social and Cultural Psychiatry* (pp. 145–158). Retrieved from McGill University website: https://www.mcgill.ca/files/tcpsych/Report10.pdf

Walkup, J.T., Barlow, A., Mullany, B.C., Pan, W., Goklish, N., Hasting, R., ... Reid, R. (2009). Randomized controlled trial of a paraprofessional-delivered in-home intervention for young reservation-based American Indian mothers. *Journal of the American Academy of Child & Adolescent Psychiatry, 48*, 591–601. DOI: 10.1097/CHI.0b013e3181a0ab86

Wexler, L.M. & Gone, J.P. (2012). Culturally responsive suicide prevention in indigenous communities: Unexamined assumptions and new possibilities. *American Journal of Public Health, 102*, 800–806. DOI: 10.2105/AJPH.2011.300432

White, J. & Jodoin, N. (2003). *Aboriginal Youth: A Manual of Promising Suicide Prevention Strategies*. Retrieved from Centre for Suicide Prevention website: https://suicideinfo.ca/Store/Publications.aspx

ABOUT THE AUTHOR

Peter Braunberger, MD, FRCPC, has been practising child and adolescent psychiatry in Thunder Bay and northwestern Ontario since 2005 when he completed his residency at McMaster University. Based at St. Joseph's Care Group in Thunder Bay, Dr. Braunberger consults to four regional Aboriginal child protection and child mental health agencies. He is also the liaison with Aboriginal communities with the Telelink Mental Health Program at The Hospital for Sick Children in Toronto. He is an assistant professor with the Northern Ontario School of Medicine, and chair of the Advocacy Committee of the Canadian Academy of Child and Adolescent Psychiatry.

Chapter 25

The Criminal Justice System: Addressing Aboriginal Overrepresentation

JONATHAN RUDIN

Aboriginal people have been overrepresented in Canadian prisons since at least the end of the Second World War (Aboriginal Justice Inquiry of Manitoba, 1991). This fact is linked, at least in part, to the strong perception in Canadian society that Aboriginal people are more prone to alcohol use, violence and criminality than other groups.

In 1998, the Supreme Court of Canada quoted from the groundbreaking work *Locking Up Natives in Canada: Report of the Canadian Bar Association Committee on Imprisonment and Release* (Jackson, 1988):

> Put at its baldest, there is an equation of being drunk, Indian and in prison. Like many stereotypes, this one has a dark underside. It reflects a view of native people as uncivilized and without a coherent social or moral order. The stereotype prevents us from seeing native people as equals. (*R. v. Williams*, 1998, ¶58)

This passage was quoted in the Court's decision in the case of *R. v. Williams* (1998), in which Mr. Williams, an accused Aboriginal person, successfully sought to have the right to question jurors concerning whether their ability to judge his case was influenced by stereotypes about Aboriginal people. In finding that Mr. Williams had this right, the Court added: "There is evidence that this widespread racism has translated into systemic discrimination in the criminal justice system" (*R. v. Williams*, 1998, ¶58).

Aboriginal people who find themselves enmeshed in the criminal justice system face this systemic discrimination at all turns: at the point of arrest, at the decision of what charges to lay, during plea negotiations, during the trial (if one is held) and at sentencing. The power of the stereotype is such that it often serves to blind those working in the criminal justice system to the life circumstances of the Aboriginal person who is before the court.

To the extent that an accused person is seen as an individual, he or she is often represented in court by only two pieces of paper: his or her prior criminal record, if there is one, and the synopsis of the offence allegedly committed. Since these documents tend not to portray the person in the best light, it is not surprising to find that Aboriginal people are overrepresented in Canadian prisons. Essentially, these documents are graphic illustrations of colonialist government policies, but they are not capable of explaining how those policies have manifested themselves in the life of the person before the court. While discrimination and stereotypes clearly play a role in understanding the phenomenon of overrepresentation, it is important to look at why the problem has persisted even though it has been recognized repeatedly by the highest court in Canada.

Overrepresentation of Aboriginal People

Aboriginal people make up less than four per cent of the Canadian population. In 2011, they represented 22 per cent of all inmates in federal prisons and 27 per cent of all inmates in provincial and territorial prisons (Dauvergne, 2012). (In Canada, sentences two years or longer are served in federal prisons, while sentences less than two years are served in provincial and territorial prisons.) Aboriginal women made up 32 per cent of women in federal prisons (Correctional Service of Canada, 2011). The percentages of Aboriginal youth in custody are even more dramatic. A study of youth in custody in Canada between 2008 and 2009 reported that 35 per cent of youth sentenced to prison were Aboriginal. Forty-four per cent of sentenced girls were Aboriginal (Calverley et al., 2010). The percentages of Aboriginal inmates have been on the rise for years for both adults and youth: we now have the highest levels of Aboriginal overrepresentation ever recorded.

The issue of overrepresentation has not gone unnoticed by legislators. In 1995, the federal government passed Bill C-41, the first large-scale, comprehensive revamping of sentencing procedures in Canada (Bill C-41, An Act to Amend the Criminal Code [Sentencing], 1995). Included in the bill was section 718.2(e) of the Criminal Code (Criminal Code, R.S.C. 1985). The section, which must be read in conjunction with the rest of section 718, states:

718.2 A court that imposes a sentence shall also take into consideration the following principles:

(e) all available sanctions other than imprisonment that are reasonable in the circumstances should be considered for all offenders, with particular attention to the circumstances of aboriginal offenders. (Criminal Code, R.S.C. 1985)

In 2003, the wording of section 718.2(e) was incorporated into section 38(2)(d) of the Youth Criminal Justice Act (YCJA) when that bill was enacted (Youth Criminal Justice Act, S.C. 2002).

While not intended solely to address Aboriginal overrepresentation, Bill C-41 also created a new type of sentence—the conditional sentence. The equivalent measure in the YCJA is called deferred custody. These measures give more flexibility in looking for alternatives to incarceration, and are available to a judge who determines that the appropriate sentence for an offender is a period of incarceration of less than two years. Rather than having the person serve the sentence in prison, the judge can order the person to serve the sentence in the community under any number of relatively strict conditions. These conditions can include punitive sanctions, such as house arrest, but also therapeutic conditions, such as requiring the person to attend and even complete a treatment program. Offenders who fail to comply with the conditions can be brought back to court and incarcerated for the remainder of their sentence.

Overrepresentation and the Supreme Court of Canada

Giving even greater impetus to judges to address Aboriginal overrepresentation, in 1999, the Supreme Court of Canada released its decision in *R. v. Gladue* (1999). The case was the first opportunity for the Supreme Court to interpret section 718.2(e) of the Criminal Code in the context of sentencing an Aboriginal offender. Building on the language used in *R. v. Williams* (1998), the Court referred to Aboriginal overrepresentation as "a crisis in the Canadian criminal justice system" (*R. v. Gladue*, 1999, ¶64). The Court also said that section 718.2(e) was Parliament's direction to judges to address the issue of Aboriginal overrepresentation to the extent that the problem could be fixed by the sentencing process.

The Supreme Court was also quite clear that section 718.2(e) of the Criminal Code singled out Aboriginal offenders because Aboriginal people found themselves before the courts quite often as the result of direct and systemic discrimination resulting from government policies and practices targeting them as a people. In other words, the reality of Aboriginal people and the causes of their offending behaviour are often rooted in long-standing governmental and societal prejudices.

R. v. Gladue (1999) and cases that followed made it clear that section 718.2(e) of the Criminal Code was neither a sentencing discount nor a so-called get out of jail free card for Aboriginal people (e.g., *R. v. Kakekagamick*, 2006, ¶34). Rather, the section required judges to sentence Aboriginal offenders based on information as to why the individual was before the court, including systemic factors, and to consider, in light of this information, sentencing options other than prison that might better address these issues. The Supreme Court noted that incarceration was particularly ineffective for Aboriginal offenders, in part because discrimination in prison against Aboriginal people was "rampant" (*R. v. Gladue*, 1999, ¶68). A recent study found that the situation facing Aboriginal offenders in the federal prison system has not improved at all since 1999, and may in fact have worsened (Office of the Correctional Investigator, 2012).

In addition, the Court said that Aboriginal overrepresentation "flows from a number of sources, including poverty, substance abuse, lack of education, and the lack of employment opportunities" (*R. v. Gladue*, 1999, ¶67). Of course, Aboriginal people are not alone among those involved in the criminal justice system who are poor, unemployed and addicted to substances. Indeed, those factors are common to many people who are before the courts. The Court went on as follows:

> It is true that systemic and background factors explain in part the incidence of crime and recidivism for non-aboriginal offenders as well. However, it must be recognized that the circumstances of aboriginal offenders differ from those of the majority because many aboriginal people are victims of systemic and direct discrimination, many suffer the legacy of dislocation, and many are substantially affected by poor social and economic conditions. (*R. v. Gladue*, 1999, ¶68)

The Royal Commission on Aboriginal Peoples (RCAP) reached a similar conclusion in a 1996 report on criminal justice, *Bridging the Cultural Divide* (RCAP, 1996). It identified the cause of Aboriginal overrepresentation to be the legacy of colonialism in Canada. It was this legacy that led Aboriginal people to being "poor beyond poverty" (RCAP, 1996, p. 46).

The Supreme Court of Canada re-examined the issue of Aboriginal overrepresentation in the case of *R. v. Ipeelee* (2012). It reaffirmed and expanded its commitment to the decision made in *R. v. Gladue* (1999). For the first time, the Court explicitly referenced colonialism as an important factor in understanding Aboriginal overrepresentation. The Court also identified sentencing judges as "the front line workers" (*R. v. Ipeelee*, 2012, ¶67) who were responsible for ensuring that systemic discrimination did not lead to unnecessary or unduly long jail sentences for Aboriginal offenders.

Aboriginal People before the Courts

Despite the important findings of the Supreme Court, the legacy of colonialism is not always easy to see. Aboriginal people coming before the courts are often not in a position to describe the impact of colonial processes on their lives, including the residential school experience, the destruction of culture and the large number of adoptions and apprehensions by children's aid societies. Rather, Aboriginal people often present only as individuals with long criminal records and a history of addiction.

Many Aboriginal people have fractured and traumatic childhoods due to a history of family and cultural dislocation. Early in their lives, some may turn to substances to cope with these traumas. By the time they come into the criminal justice system, their addictions are often firmly in place. The criminal justice system then sees a person with an addiction who is committing criminal offences, often either to support their addiction or when in the midst of the addiction. Root causes are difficult to see.

Compounding the issue is that, from a clinical point of view, many of these individuals also have concurrent mental health issues, such as posttraumatic stress disorder. From a practical point of view, however, obtaining a diagnosis of a concurrent disorder can be quite difficult for these individuals. They usually do not have a mental health professional with whom they are regularly in contact. In addition, many mental health disorders can only be clearly diagnosed after an individual has been sober for a period of time, since the symptoms of the addiction can mirror those of various mental health disorders. When a person develops an addiction prior to the diagnosis of a mental health problem, it may be very difficult to ever get a concurrent disorder diagnosis.

Similarly, many Aboriginal offenders who come before the courts may be living with fetal alcohol spectrum disorder (FASD). While there have been no large-scale prevalence studies and the condition is grossly under-diagnosed, the Public Health Agency of Canada (2007) estimates that FASD affects one in 100 babies born in Canada. It is not necessarily more prevalent in the Aboriginal population than in the general population (Pacey, 2009). However, since people with FASD are more likely to be involved in the criminal justice system and Aboriginal people are overrepresented in prison, we should not be surprised to find that Aboriginal people are overrepresented among people with FASD in the criminal justice system.

Here, too, however, diagnosis is a real problem. Confirmation of the birth mother's consumption of alcohol is required before an individual can be assessed for FASD. For people who have been separated from, and may never have known, their birth mothers, this can be difficult to obtain. Even when it is confirmed that an individual's mother consumed alcohol while pregnant, obtaining an assessment for FASD is often difficult and requires many appointments. In most provinces, FASD assessments are not readily available for people who are in custody. For people with FASD who are homeless or marginally housed, making the various appointments with doctors, psychologists and social workers necessary to complete the assessment is a challenge.

GLADUE: A MOVE TOWARD A NEW PERSPECTIVE

The difficulties in assessing FASD or in understanding the interplay between addiction, mental health and involvement in the court system brings us back to the stereotype recognized by the Supreme Court of Canada in *R. v. Williams* (1998). Without information about the circumstances of the individual's life, and without the assessments required to substantiate the existence of a concurrent mental health disorder or FASD, Aboriginal offenders often go through the system labelled as violent, recidivist, sociopathic, remorseless and incorrigible.

Aboriginal people face other stereotypes in the criminal justice system, as well. One of the most prevalent misunderstandings surrounds the question of who is an Aboriginal person. On its face, section 718.2(e) of the Criminal Code clearly applies to all Aboriginal people. The Constitution Act, 1982 defines the Aboriginal peoples of Canada as including Indians, Inuit and Métis. The term "Indian" includes both people with Indian status as recognized by the federal government and those without status. The history of Canada, however, is rife with examples of the state, or those representing the state, making arbitrary decisions about who is or is not an Aboriginal person. This sad tradition continues in the criminal justice system.

R. v. Gladue (1999) is itself a good example of this issue. The defendant, Jamie Tanis Gladue, was described to the court at her sentencing as having a Cree mother and a Métis father. She grew up in McLennan, Alberta. In a revealing exchange, when asked by the sentencing judge if McLennan was an Aboriginal community, her lawyer responded, "No, it's a regular community" (*R. v. Gladue*, 1999, ¶12).

At the time of the offence, Ms. Gladue was living in Nanaimo, B.C. When sentencing her, the judge declined to apply section 718.2(e) of the Criminal Code, despite its clear application to her as an Aboriginal person, arguing the following:

> The factor that is mentioned in the Criminal Code is that particular attention to the circumstances of aboriginal offenders should be considered. In this case both the deceased and the accused were aboriginals, but they are not living within the aboriginal community as such. They are living off a reserve and the offence occurred in an urban setting. They [*sic*] do not appear to have been any special circumstances because of their aboriginal status and so I am not giving any special consideration to their background in passing this sentence. (*R. v. Gladue*, 1999, ¶89)

The Supreme Court made it clear that this interpretation was wrong and that *R. v. Gladue* (1999) applied to all Aboriginal people as covered by section 35 of the Constitution Act, 1982, ¶90. Nevertheless, Aboriginal people coming before the courts regularly have to satisfy the image of an Aboriginal person held by counsel, crown attorneys or judges. Failing to meet these expectations often means that the provisions of section 718.2(e) (Criminal Code, R.S.C. 1985) are not applied or are minimized.

A related problem with sentencing Aboriginal people is that many people working in the criminal justice system think they know more about the offender and his or her community than they actually do. It is not unusual to hear those working in areas with many Aboriginal people who appear before the courts saying things such as, "We don't need *Gladue*; we've been doing *Gladue* years before it was decided." Having sentenced, represented or prosecuted Aboriginal people over many years does not necessarily guarantee that the individuals engaged in the process actually know the circumstances of a particular Aboriginal person.

This issue of a person not knowing what he or she does not know is particularly vexing for the criminal justice system. In sentencing Aboriginal people, judges and lawyers often rely on knowledge they have acquired through first-hand experience, but it is not clear whether the knowledge is accurate. Where does this information come from? Courts often rely on pre-sentence reports (PSRS) when sentencing individuals, particularly when prison is an option. However, PSRS tend to come from a risk-based assessment model that is not culturally sensitive (Hannah-Moffat & Maurutto, 2010). The reality is that risk-based predictive tools will assess many Aboriginal people as being at high risk to reoffend simply because they *are* Aboriginal.

Preparing a Gladue report is one way of trying to ensure that the courts have the information they need when sentencing an Aboriginal offender. Gladue reports differ from PSRS in a number of significant ways (Hannah-Moffat & Maurutto, 2010). A Gladue report is prepared specifically to provide the court with information on the life circumstances of the Aboriginal offender, including a consideration of systemic and background factors, and a discussion of possible sentencing options, particularly those that do not involve incarceration. The first Gladue reports were prepared by Aboriginal Legal Services of Toronto (ALST) and were initially developed for presentation to judges who sat in Gladue court—a court specifically established to work with Aboriginal people in conflict with the law. (Gladue courts will be discussed in more detail later in this chapter.)

Gladue reports tell the story of the Aboriginal offender in a narrative style, often beginning with the lives of parents or grandparents. The reports generally shy away from making conclusions, instead allowing those interviewed in the report to speak for themselves by way of direct quotes. This approach allows the readers of the reports to draw their own conclusions.

Gladue reports not only identify issues specific to the individual, but also provide some background information on systemic or background factors. For example, if the person's parents went to residential school, the Gladue report will discuss the history of residential schools and the concept of intergenerational trauma. Providing this context is important because it cannot be assumed that everyone working in the criminal justice system understands what has happened to Aboriginal peoples historically and how that historical experience plays out in the lives of people who are before the courts.

After discussing the life of the offender and his or her family and community, the report concludes with recommendations for sentencing. Gladue reports are not sentencing submissions; they do not take the place of defence counsel. Rather, they look at sentencing options solely in the context of the issues identified in the report. It is for the judge to weigh those options along with other sentencing concepts enshrined in the Criminal Code, such as deterrence and denunciation, two of the sentencing principles found elsewhere in section 718.

In arriving at these recommendations, the writer of the Gladue report engages the offender in the process. It is important that the report make recommendations that the individual is prepared to undertake: there is no point in setting the person up for failure. In addition, the writer works to make the recommendations as concrete as possible. For example, in most cases, it is not enough to recommend that a person receive treatment for addiction or childhood trauma. The report must also provide information about the locations and waiting lists for such programs. Where possible, the writer should supply an acceptance letter from the program. If the person must travel to attend treatment, ALST often covers transportation costs to facilitate compliance with the report's recommendations. These are features not typically found in PSRs.

The term "Gladue report" has found its way to the Supreme Court of Canada: the Court specifically referenced these reports in the decision of *R. v. Ipeelee* (2012, ¶60). Still, what constitutes a Gladue report has not yet been precisely defined. Any individual or organization can prepare a report and state that it is a Gladue report. In some provinces, pre-sentence reports for Aboriginal offenders are described as Gladue reports or as PSRs with a Gladue component. Simply calling a document a Gladue report does not guarantee that it actually has all the features described earlier. The issue of who should prepare the report and what it should look like remains contested. In some provinces, Aboriginal organizations wishing to prepare these reports sometimes face stiff opposition from probation officers who believe that only they are able to write them. As Hannah-Moffat and Maurotto (2010) concluded in their research, a Gladue report is a very different document from a PSR, whether or not that PSR has a Gladue component.

Currently in Ontario, Gladue reports prepared by individuals working for Aboriginal organizations are available in some jurisdictions but not throughout the province. It is very difficult to obtain Gladue reports in other parts of Canada, although in the wake of *R. v. Ipeelee* (2012), more provinces are seriously considering how to provide judges with this sort of relevant information. The fact that a Gladue report is not available for an Aboriginal offender does not preclude the need for relevant information to be brought to the attention of the sentencing judge, but the challenge of how that is to be done is one major reason why the promise of *Gladue* has not been fulfilled.

The Supreme Court was clear that the decision made in *R. v. Gladue* (1999) applies to any Aboriginal offender before any court in Canada. At the same time, judges have struggled in the wake of this decision to obtain the information they need to sentence Aboriginal offenders according to the guidelines set by the Supreme Court.

One response to this has been the creation of Gladue courts. These are specialized courts that focus only on Aboriginal people and deal primarily with issues of bail and sentencing. The idea behind their establishment was that if a corps of people (composed of judges, crowns, defence counsel and Aboriginal and non-Aboriginal service providers) was able to work together in a court, it might be better able to arrive at resolutions more in keeping with the spirit of *Gladue* and thus be more responsive to the needs of the Aboriginal offender.

On one level, Gladue courts are part of a broader movement in the court system over the past 20 years or so that has seen a proliferation of so-called specialty or therapeutic courts. Examples of these courts include drug treatment courts and mental health courts. In contrast, Gladue courts are not intended to be the site where change for the individual will occur. They facilitate the involvement of Aboriginal alternative justice programs and foster recognition of the existence of agencies outside of the court that are better placed to work with individuals.

By allowing Aboriginal knowledge to be recognized as a valid source of information for the court, Gladue courts have changed the court process. In doing this, they have acknowledged that this knowledge may not rest solely, if at all, with those who traditionally have status roles in the court. Employees of Aboriginal organizations and Aboriginal Elders and traditional teachers are now seen as vital partners in the court process. This development has also been seen in Australia, where Aboriginal sentencing courts have also developed, although differently than in Canada (Marchetti & Daly, 2007).

As with the term Gladue report, "Gladue court" does not have a fixed definition. At the time of writing, there are seven Gladue courts in Ontario—five in Toronto, including an Aboriginal youth court, one in Sarnia and one in London. There are initiatives underway at the local level to increase the number of Gladue courts in the province. Their development has been a local, judge-driven initiative in the particular courts, rather than a response to any particular initiatives provincially or federally. While there are no Gladue courts outside of Ontario, British Columbia has created four First Nations courts. In New Brunswick, an Aboriginal healing to wellness court has been set up at the Elsipogtog First Nation (Clairmont, 2013). There are also a number of provincial courts located on First Nations across the country. There is no question that interest in developing Aboriginal-specific courts across Canada is on the rise.

THE PATH AHEAD

Despite what appears to be increasing interest in Gladue courts and similar initiatives, we cannot ignore that rates of Aboriginal overrepresentation are rising rather than falling. At the macro level, the legislative environment in Canada over the past number of years has not been conducive to sentencing innovations. In fact, such innovations have been severely constrained and likely have contributed to the rising rates of overrepresentation. At the micro level, while specific initiatives at the level of the local court have had an impact on the sentencing of particular Aboriginal offenders, these initiatives have not reached a tipping point in the Canadian justice system.

The passing in 1995 of Bill C-41 marked a significant rethinking of punishment in Canada. The amendments were part of a broad reassessment of how sentencing should be done. While the core elements of Bill C-41 remain in place (in the context of this discussion, these elements include section. 718.2[e] of the Criminal Code and the existence of conditional sentences), more recent "tough on crime" legislation has severely impinged the ability of courts to address Aboriginal overrepresentation through the sentencing process.

A recent example of this approach is Bill C-10, the Safe Streets and Communities Act (2012). Its effect has been to restrict the ability of judges to rely on non-custodial sentencing options. This restriction has been accomplished in two ways. First, many more offences now carry mandatory minimum sentences. Conditional sentences are not available for offences with a mandatory minimum sentence, no matter how short that minimum sentence might be. Second, Bill C-10 restricted the use of conditional sentences by judges even for offences without mandatory minimum sentences by setting out a range of specific offences, both violent and non-violent, for which conditional sentences were no longer permitted.

Criminal behaviour does not come neatly packaged into obvious categories. A robbery, for example, is a theft where violence is used or threatened. While robberies are not generally eligible for a conditional sentence, the distinct criminal offences of theft and assault that make up a robbery charge *are* eligible *if* they prosecuted these as two distinct offences. Thus, the decision as to what offence to prosecute can determine whether a conditional sentence is available.

The Criminal Code has long categorized offences as summary, indictable or hybrid. A hybrid offence can be prosecuted summarily, meaning it is not viewed as a particularly serious offence, or by indictment, attracting higher sentences. It is the decision of the prosecutor whether to treat an offence as summary or indictable. Where there is no minimum sentence, the decision to proceed summarily or by indictment does not affect the lower range of sentence, just the upper range. For example, the offence of assault causing bodily harm is a hybrid offence. If prosecuted summarily, the maximum sentence available is 18 months imprisonment; if prosecuted by indictment, the maximum sentence is 10 years. Now in the Criminal Code, some offences can attract conditional sentences if they are prosecuted summarily, but conditional sentences are not possible for these offences if they are prosecuted by indictment. Foreclosing a conditional sentence does not mean that the judge must always incarcerate the person, but the options are stark—either prison or a sentence with less opportunity for the individual to be supervised in the community.

How prosecutors exercise their discretion as to what offences to prosecute is now a significant issue in attempting to address Aboriginal overrepresentation. The difficulty with the exercise of this discretion, however, is that it generally takes place behind closed doors and is not subject to challenge within the legal system. Significantly, the

Ontario Court of Appeal found in the case of *United States v. Leonard* (2012) that the Gladue principles apply to decisions of Crown attorneys in that province, although we do not yet know what that might mean in practice.

Bill C-10 is not specifically targeted to Aboriginal people. Nevertheless, the impact of these amendments is likely to be felt most directly by Aboriginal people who, based on current trends, can be expected to continue to make up an ever-increasing percentage of the Canadian jail population.

The average Canadian does not have much opportunity to comment on legislative initiatives that make up the macro level of this issue, such as getting tough on crime. Nevertheless, if politicians thought this approach did not resonate with voters they would not have pursued it with such vigour. On the micro level of the issue, how-ever, those who work with Aboriginal people who have addiction or mental health concerns and are before the courts can play a role in helping the courts arrive at sentencing options that focus on healing and reintegration, and ultimately on making communities safer. Often judges rely on custody because no other options have been provided, even though they exist in the community. Mental health professionals can provide specific options tailored to the needs of Aboriginal clients that may never have occurred to judges or lawyers.

It is not uncommon to hear a judge tell an offender who is looking at a jail sen-tence but who has presented a compelling case for, say, a non-custodial sentence, "I'm going to give you a chance and not send you to jail. But if I see you before me again you will be going to jail." Such an approach, while understandable, does not allow for an understanding of the realities of the healing process. In such a situation, the pro-fessional working with an Aboriginal offender with addiction or mental health issues has a potentially critical role to play. People involved in the justice system need to better understand what a person with addiction or mental health challenges (or both) can accomplish. Nothing is served by setting up the person to fail. Indeed, failing to comply with a court order is, in and of itself, a distinct offence in the criminal justice system. It is important, then, to try to see that bail conditions and sentences are crafted realistically. For example, it is not uncommon that, as a condition of bail or sentence, a person be required not to consume alcohol or other drugs. From the court's perspec-tive, this condition is easily justified, particularly if the offence was committed when the person was under the influence. The problem, of course, is that people with addic-tion cannot just stop because they are told they have to do so.

This does not mean that a sentence should not address addiction issues. Rather, it means that the sentence should do so in a way that the person is able and/or more likely to comply and that provides a springboard for further healing. To come up with a sentence that creates these possibilities, a judge needs to know what programs and services are available that can address the issues of the particular Aboriginal offender. Establishing what programs and services could help also requires first speaking with the offender so as to determine what he or she needs and wants in a sentence. People before the courts are often willing to say almost anything to get released from custody, so any discussion of sentencing must be a frank one that honestly engages the offender in determining what he or she can actually do. A mental health professional, particularly someone with a relationship with the Aboriginal client, can perform an invaluable service to the client and the court.

People who come back before the courts after breaching their conditional or other non-custodial sentence are often viewed as failures by others and themselves. However, what may have been one slip should not mask the progress they may have made over a number of months. For example, it would not be unusual for a person with FASD to fail to observe one of the sentencing conditions over an 18-month non-custodial sentence. If that person were to return to court, it would be very important that the court see what the person has been able to accomplish—the success, not the failure. Those who work most closely with these individuals in a treatment context often have important information for the court and should not wait to be invited to speak to the court. Instead, they should make their presence known to defence counsel, the prosecution and the judge.

A mental health professional who learns that a client has been arrested should speak to defence counsel or the Aboriginal court worker, if there is one in the court, to see how and when his or her input would be most helpful. This might be at the beginning of the process when bail is being considered or at the end when a sentence is arrived at, or both. It may be that a letter outlining the client's history with the mental health agency and programming options is all that is required; on the other hand, the professional might have to attend court to speak with the lawyers or the judge, either in an informal manner or, if necessary, by testifying. Aboriginal people before the courts need advocates, and those advocates are not exclusively or necessarily their lawyers.

Conclusion

Aboriginal overrepresentation in prisons need not be a given. We should not resign ourselves to seeing prison as increasingly the preserve of Aboriginal people. Prisons should not become the institutional replacement for residential schools and the child welfare system. There are tools that can be used for systemic change, but the change itself must be driven by individuals with knowledge about the lives and circumstances of Aboriginal people. People who work with Aboriginal offenders contending with addiction and mental health problems must become more involved in the criminal justice system. This work is too important to leave to lawyers and judges alone.

References

Aboriginal Justice Inquiry of Manitoba. (1991). *Report of the Aboriginal Justice Inquiry of Manitoba: Vol. 1. The Justice System and Aboriginal People.* Retrieved from www.ajic.mb.ca/volumel/toc.html

Bill C-10, An Act to Enact the Justice for Victims of Terrorism Act and to Amend the State Immunity Act, The Criminal Code, The Controlled Drugs and Substances Act, The Corrections and Conditional Release Act, The Youth Criminal Justice Act, The Immigration and Refugee Protection Act and Other Acts. Short Title: Safe Streets and Communities Act. (2012). 41st Parliament, 1st session. Retrieved from www. parl.gc.ca/LegisInfo/BillDetails.aspx?Language=E&Mode=1&billId=5120829

Bill C-41, An Act to Amend the Criminal Code (Sentencing) and Other Acts in Consequence Thereof. (1995). 35th Parliament, 1st session. Retrieved from www.parl.gc.ca/LegisInfo/BillDetails.aspx?Language=E&Mode=1&billId=2328308

Calverley, D., Cotter, A. & Halla, E. (2010). Youth custody and community services in Canada, 2008/2009. *Juristat, 30* (1), 5–35. (Statistics Canada catalogue no. 85-002-X). Retrieved from www. statcan.gc.ca/pub/85-002-x

Clairmont, D. (2013). The development of an Aboriginal criminal justice system: The case of Elsipogtog. *University of New Brunswick Law Journal, 64,* 160–186.

Constitution Act, 1982, Schedule B to the Canada Act 1982 (UK) (1982, c. 11). Retrieved from http://canlii.ca/t/ldsx

Correctional Service of Canada. (2011). *Aboriginal Corrections Accountability Framework Year End Report, 2010–2011.* Ottawa: Author.

Criminal Code, R.S.C. (1985, c. C-46). Retrieved from http://laws-lois.justice.gc.ca/eng/acts/C-46/FullText.html

Dauvergne, M. (2012, October 11). Adult correctional statistics in Canada, 2010/2011. *Juristat,* 1–26. (Statistics Canada catalogue no. 85-002-X). Retrieved from www.statcan.gc.ca/pub/85-002-x

Hannah-Moffat, K., & Maurutto, P. (2010). Restructuring pre-sentence reports—race, risk and the PSR. *Punishment & Society, 12,* 262–286. DOI: 10.1177/1462474510369442

Jackson, M. (1988). *Locking Up Natives in Canada: Report of the Canadian Bar Association Committee on Imprisonment and Release.* Reprinted in UBC Law Review (1988–89), *23,* 215–300.

Marchetti, E. & Daly, K. (2007). Indigenous sentencing courts: Towards a theoretical and jurisprudential model. *Sydney Law Review, 29,* 415–443.

Office of the Correctional Investigator. (2012). *Spirit Matters: Aboriginal People and the* Corrections and Conditional Release Act. Retrieved from www.oci-bec.gc.ca

Pacey, M. (2009). *Fetal Alcohol Syndrome and Fetal Alcohol Spectrum Disorder among Aboriginal Peoples: A Review of Prevalence.* Retrieved from FASD Justice website: www.fasdjustice.ca/aboriginal-peoples-and-fasd/incidence-and-prevalence-in-aboriginal-populations.html

Public Health Agency of Canada. (2007). *Fetal Alcohol Spectrum Disorder (FASD).* Retrieved from www.phac-aspc.gc.ca

R. v. Gladue, [1999] 1 S.C.R. 688.

R. v. Ipeelee, [2012] 1 S.C.R. 433.

R. v. Kakekagamick (2006), 81 OR (3d) 664.

R. v. Williams, [1998] 1 S.C.R. 1128.

Royal Commission on Aboriginal Peoples (RCAP). (1996). *Bridging the Cultural Divide: A Report on Aboriginal People and Criminal Justice in Canada.* Ottawa: Canada Communication Group.

United States v. Leonard, 2012 ONCA 622. (CanLII). Retrieved from http://canlii.ca/t/fss8m

Youth Criminal Justice Act, S.C. (2002, c. 1). Retrieved from http://laws-lois.justice.gc.ca/eng/acts/Y-1.5/page-1.html

ABOUT THE AUTHOR

Jonathan Rudin received his LLB and LLM from Osgoode Hall Law School in Toronto. In 1990, he was hired to establish Aboriginal Legal Services of Toronto (ALST) and is now its program director. He has appeared before all levels of court, which includes representing ALST before the Supreme Court of Canada in *R. v. Ipeelee*. He has written and spoken widely about Aboriginal justice. He co-wrote the Royal Commission on Aboriginal Peoples' report on justice, *Bridging the Cultural Divide*, and was a member of the Research Advisory Committee of the Ipperwash inquiry. He also teaches part time in the Law and Society Program at York University.

Part 5

Providing Services to Aboriginal Communities

Chapter 26

Urban Aboriginal People in Canada

PETER DINSDALE

The urbanization of Aboriginal people is not very well understood among the general population. The 2006 census showed that 54 per cent of Aboriginal people reside in urban areas (Statistics Canada, 2008). This is the first time in recent Canadian history that more Aboriginal people live in urban areas than elsewhere. But Aboriginal people have always lived in urban areas. In fact, it can be argued that most Canadian cities, including Toronto, Ottawa, Montreal, Winnipeg and Saskatoon, are located where they are because originally they were the point where First Nations, Métis or Inuit trading routes crossed. Aboriginal peoples have always lived in communities that today we would understand to be cities.

However, since the arrival of Europeans, Aboriginal peoples have been regulated and legislated into locations away from cities and towns. After the War of 1812, Aboriginal people were no longer needed to help in military campaigns, and it was more economical for the British to simply move them out of the way of development through force and coercion that was legislated through treaties between First Nations and the federal government. Treaties made after 1871 enabled the government to pursue agriculture, settlement and resource development of the West and the North (Aboriginal Affairs and Northern Development Canada [AANDC], 2010, ¶8). In the meantime, Aboriginal people continued to be physically separated from the rest of Canada until after the Second World War when they began to reappear in cities.

This chapter discusses the initial migrations back to urban areas and the challenges faced by those who undertook them. It also explores the current situation facing urban Aboriginal people and contemplates their future. Although this chapter is about the

Aboriginal experience of urbanization, the discussion tends to focus on First Nations because of the political issues created by the Indian Act, which applies only to status Indians and as such affects Indian reserves.[1] However, non-status Indians, Métis and Inuit have also increasingly migrated to cities from their settlement areas.

Coming Back Home

The re-emergence of Aboriginal people in cities is, in large part, a result of their participation in the First and Second World Wars. Despite the difficult relationships that existed between Canada and Aboriginal peoples, Aboriginal people fought in these wars. Fighting overseas for Canada and the British Crown, they were treated with respect and as equals, but in their homeland First Nations people still could not vote, attend university or leave their reserves without permission from the Indian agent (Furi & Wherrett, 2003). While far too often Aboriginal soldiers were given the most difficult assignments, they fought with valour and honour (Veterans Affairs Canada, 2005). They expected that when the wars ended and they returned home, they would continue to be treated as equal citizens. Instead, they were treated in the same way as when they departed—as second-class citizens. Many Aboriginal veterans were unable to attend legion halls because the Indian Act prohibited status Indians from possessing alcohol, which was served in these places (Moss & Gardner-O'Toole, 1991). While they were equal enough to fight together overseas, they were not equal in Canada (Royal Commission on Aboriginal Peoples [RCAP], 1996a).

Many veterans from First Nations found living back on reserves confining. They had fought as free men (most of the veterans were men) and wanted to continue to live that way. A few had been promoted to the rank of commissioned officer, but by law, this honour meant that they also lost their registered Indian status and could no longer live on their reserves (RCAP, 1996a).[2] The first migration from reserves to urban areas began with returning veterans wanting or needing to move out of their communities.

Push and Pull Factors

Returning veterans may have begun the first wave of migration to the cities, but there were many more migrations to come. Most academics now understand the urbanization of Aboriginal people to involve a combination of "push and pull" factors from rural communities to urban areas (United Nations Housing Rights Programme, 2010). Housing was one significant push factor. Many First Nations and Inuit communities

---

1   For a discussion about the Indian Act and how it has affected Aboriginal peoples, see chapter 2.

2   Status Indians could lose their status for other reasons, for example, marrying a non-status man or pursuing a university education. Losing their Indian status meant these people could no longer live on their reserves.

did not receive enough government funding to meet the demand for new housing units. Métis settlements received no financial support. As the housing crunch grew, multiple generations of families resided in the same dwelling. In addition, poor-quality construction meant that the houses that were built were unsuitable for long-term habitation and fell into disrepair. Mould, lack of clean or running water, poor heating and ventilation and limited housing stock all contributed to a housing crisis, which forced people to move away from their communities. They had been pushed.

Other factors pushed Aboriginal people to urban areas. The social environment in remote communities was deteriorating. While the full effects of residential schools would not be known for decades, the first effects were being felt immediately in Aboriginal communities. Entire generations of children had been taken from their families and sent to residential schools to be Christianized and assimilated. Many were abused. When they returned home and had children of their own, the absence of healing opportunities made many of them unfit to be parents, and the next generation of children suffered. This cycle of abuse created another push factor for people to move from their communities to urban areas.[3]

There were also various pull factors at play. Most First Nations communities had elementary schools but no high schools, so students had to leave to continue beyond Grade 8. In addition, opportunities for post-secondary education did not exist, so young people were drawn to cities to pursue this level of education. Community members were also pulled to urban areas by employment opportunities and health care needs, or simply by the desire to explore the world around them. Whether they were pushed or pulled, Aboriginal people continued their urban migration in earnest in the 1950s (RCAP, 1996b).

Life in the New Urban Environment

Life in the urban environment was not easy for the first waves of urban Aboriginal people. Generally, the atmosphere was hostile and racism was pervasive. Aboriginal people encountered racism in housing, employment and training, and access to services (RCAP, 1996b). They also experienced a culturally foreign environment. The physical landscape was different: trees, lakes and open space were replaced with office towers, concrete and congestion. The slower pace of life in rural Canada was replaced with the hustle and bustle of city life. The generally friendly, communal environment Aboriginal people had left behind was replaced by a cold, isolated, highly individualistic society. These first urban immigrants did not encounter a welcoming environment, but they banded together and made the cities their homes.

As more and more Aboriginal people came to the cities, they developed their own services and agencies to meet their needs. Friendship centres in Toronto, Vancouver

---

3   For a discussion about the impact of the residential schools, see chapters 3 and 5.

and Winnipeg emerged as the first expressions of urban identity and were responses to the environment in which Aboriginal people were living. These agencies acted as a refuge from foreign city life, organizing cultural gatherings, language classes, culturally specific services and friendly drop-ins. They provided a foundation for urban Aboriginal people to grow in these cities.

The network of friendship centres continued to grow as the urbanization of Aboriginal peoples spread throughout Canada. Naturally, the larger cities in Canada saw the first waves of migration; however, the change was happening in cities all over Canada. In the mid- to late 1960s, a number of regional friendship centre bodies, such as the Ontario Federation of Indian Friendship Centres, the Manitoba Association of Friendship Centres and the British Columbia Association of Friendship Centres, emerged. In the 1970s, the National Association of Friendship Centres (NAFC) was developed to represent the growing numbers of friendship centres across the country.

Today, the friendship centre movement consists of 119 local friendship centres, seven regional bodies and the NAFC (NAFC, 2012). This network provides more than 1.3 million client contacts each year (NAFC, 2009). With the demand for services growing across the country, the need for more service delivery agencies is growing.

Urban Aboriginal services were not limited to friendship centres. Many housing agencies were also developed in the 1960s. In the larger communities, Aboriginal health centres, women's programs and shelters were among the first services to be provided.

Today's Urban Challenges

Life for urban Aboriginal people is every bit as complicated today as it was for the first urban immigrants in the 1950s. Even though many urban Aboriginal people come to cities in search of better opportunities, poverty is a common experience. A study conducted by the Ontario Federation of Indian Friendship Centres in 2000 found that more than 51 per cent of all Aboriginal children in Ontario are raised in poverty (Anderson et al., 2000). It is through the lens of poverty that we can understand most of the day-to-day challenges facing urban Aboriginal people.

Any discussion of urban Aboriginal people today must acknowledge the demographic realities of this population. For example, as identified by the 2006 census (Statistics Canada, 2008), 54 per cent of Aboriginal people live in urban areas[4] and 45 per cent of Aboriginal people are under 25 years old. The 2012 Aboriginal Peoples Survey (Statistics Canada, 2013) found that 72 per cent of First Nations people live off reserves. It also found that 42 per cent of Inuit and 77 per cent of Métis aged 18 to 44 years had graduated from high school, compared with 89 per cent of the non-Aboriginal population (Statistics Canada, 2013). These statistics reveal an

---

4   Statistics from the 2011 census are not available. The accuracy of future estimates will be problematic due to changes in the delivery of the long-form census.

urban Aboriginal population that is very young, undereducated and impoverished. Recognizing this reality will help us to address the systemic challenges that urban Aboriginal people experience.

A significant aspect of the political challenges facing urban Aboriginal people is the role of First Nations, Inuit and Métis leadership. For Métis and Inuit, who do not fall under the Indian Act and do not reside on reserves, the issue of leadership in urban centres is somewhat different from that of First Nations people. Métis political leadership is based on geographic regions within each province. For example, while there is a National Métis Council, each province has a provincial body composed of councils based on region. Urban areas have their separate councils but fall within the provincial council. Inuit have ties to their respective Inuit settlement areas. The national body that plays a role in the political representation of Inuit in Ottawa is the Inuit Tapiriit Kanatami. There is also the Congress of Aboriginal Peoples, a national organization that provides a voice for non-status and off-reserve status Indians, as well as Métis and Inuit living in southern parts of Canada.

Status Indians living in urban centres are generally affiliated with a particular First Nation community, but living in an urban centre presents various challenges. One challenge is how any First Nation can effectively represent its members when they are spread across the country. For many First Nations, a majority of their members live outside of their communities, which makes it difficult for non-resident members to actively participate in community governance and policy development. However, many First Nations now conduct policy forums in major urban areas in order to include these non-resident members.

The ability of First Nations to provide services to their people, regardless of residence, is even more complicated. First Nations reserve communities have very little funding, and simply meeting the basic needs of their residents is challenging. However, some tribal councils in Western Canada are developing service delivery locations in urban areas to serve their members. Another emerging trend is the establishment of urban reserves. Due to settled land claims or successful economic development, some First Nations have enough funds to buy land and create reserves in or near major cities.

Given the diverse Aboriginal groups (status and non-status Indians, Inuit and Métis) who reside in urban centres, the simple expansion of First Nations agencies and councils to urban areas is not enough to address the broader issues facing urban Aboriginal people. While a specific service or approach on its own is fully appropriate, a much more comprehensive approach is required. Dividing the urban Aboriginal community by tribal associations (i.e., First Nations, Inuit, Métis) creates significant challenges. All urban Aboriginal people need a forum to articulate needs and policy approaches. As an entire community, urban Aboriginal people need a voice and process to be heard.

An International Perspective

As difficult as the situation appears to be for urban Aboriginal people in Canada, it is no better for urban Indigenous people anywhere else in the world. In 2007, the United Nations hosted the International Urban Indigenous Peoples and Migration Conference in Chile. Representatives from across the world gathered to discuss the current situation and approaches to urban migration. As country after country described the lack of action on urban migration, it became increasingly apparent that Canada is ahead of other nations in addressing the needs of urban Aboriginal people. One of the most significant findings from this meeting was that many Indigenous peoples are struggling just to have their individual human rights, such as the right to security, protected.

One of the biggest challenges for urban Aboriginal people in Canada is to ensure that their needs are adequately addressed when Aboriginal policies and programs are being developed. It has become politically expedient for the federal government to focus on developing programs and policies for the three main Aboriginal groups—First Nations, Métis and Inuit. While this approach is quite proper and relevant, it becomes challenging when it ignores where people live. A perfect example of this was the 2005 Kelowna Accord, which was developed between then–Prime Minister Paul Martin, the premiers and five national Aboriginal organizations—the Assembly of First Nations, Métis National Council, Inuit Tapiriit Katatami, Native Women's Association of Canada and Congress of Aboriginal Peoples. The Kelowna Accord's collaborative approach enabled all parties to shape specific approaches to education, economic development, housing, accountability and health. Conspicuously absent were any specific plans for urban Aboriginal people. This oversight was tragic not only because of the missed opportunity for so many jurisdictions to work together on critical issues for urban Aboriginal people, but also because it was possible that had the goals of the accord been implemented, the majority of Aboriginal people—urban Aboriginal people—may not have benefitted from it. Unfortunately, this type of exclusion from policy and programming debates is common. When pushed, governments suggest that urban issues are to be a lens through which issues need to be examined. All too often this lens is a blindfold.

A positive policy development was the creation of the Urban Aboriginal Strategy (AANDC, 2012). The strategy was a federal initiative launched in 1998 as a part of the government's response to the Royal Commission on Aboriginal Peoples. The purpose of the strategy was to provide funding for pilot projects in specific urban Aboriginal communities and to co-ordinate the government's responses to urban Aboriginal service needs. The Urban Aboriginal Strategy operated in 13 communities and provided support for Aboriginal people in those communities. In 2012, the federal government committed $27 million to the strategy over two years (2012–2013 and 2013–2014), but that same year, the federal office that dealt with the Urban Aboriginal Strategy was streamlined into the department's Regional Operations branch (AANDC, 2012). As of 2013, there has been no clear direction from the federal government on how this commitment has been allocated since 2012, and at the time this chapter was prepared, no further information was available.

Mental Health and Addiction Programs for Urban Aboriginal People

Theoretically, all Aboriginal people can access programs in provincially and federally funded hospitals and treatment centres. For example, an Aboriginal person can go to a hospital and receive the same treatment that any non-Aboriginal person would receive. Status Indians and Inuit can receive some health benefits that are not covered by insured hospitals and primary care and other health services; for example, some prescription drugs, eye and dental care, medical supplies and equipment, and medical transportation are covered for people who continue to be a fiduciary responsibility of the federal government through the Indian Act (Health Canada, 2012). In addition, short-term crisis intervention mental health counselling benefits are covered for status Indians and Inuit. As with all of the other benefits, the short-term mental health counselling has restrictions: the initial consultation cannot be more than two hours, the approximate number of visits allowed is 10 and services must be provided by an accredited professional. These benefits must be approved by the federal government before the person accesses them. In many cases, people wait a long time before approval is granted. Métis and non-status Aboriginal people do not have any non-insured benefits.

If an urban Aboriginal person requires help for mental health or addiction issues, it is important to find out the person's cultural identity. For a person who identifies as Aboriginal, culturally appropriate services may be available. Many urban centres offer mental health and addiction services specifically for Aboriginal people. For example, the Aboriginal Service at the Centre for Addiction and Mental Health (CAMH) in Toronto includes Elders and traditional healers who provide counselling to Aboriginal clients. CAMH has also partnered with friendship centres in Toronto to offer workshops and counselling. Many friendship centres across the country offer mental health and wellness programming in partnership with other local agencies.

Many Canadian cities have medical centres that provide mainstream Western medical care through physicians, nurses and dentists, as well as traditional Aboriginal medicine through traditional healers, Elders and ceremonies. For example, the Vancouver Native Health Society delivers medical, counselling and social services. In Ontario, the Aboriginal health access centres are located in urban centres across the province and offer primary health care in addition to traditional healing and ceremonies (e.g., Anishnawbe Health in Toronto and Wabano Centre for Aboriginal Health in Ottawa). CAMH has a specific addiction treatment program for Aboriginal men and women, but this type of service may not exist elsewhere, and many urban Aboriginal people use the standard addiction services available through provincial health care.

The View Ahead

Urban Aboriginal people continue to face many challenges. Poverty is far too pervasive and racialized in many urban areas. Too many Aboriginal children are left behind in the public education systems. Despite advances in education, there are too many Aboriginal people who are unemployed and unable to take advantage of the economic opportunities available to all Canadians. Finally, urban Aboriginal people face significant health challenges. Preventable diseases such as diabetes, addiction, HIV, hypertension and heart disease are associated with populations living in poverty and struggling to survive and are common in the urban Aboriginal population. Taken together, these are significant and preventable challenges for urban Aboriginal people. Any road forward must include targeted poverty reduction strategies.

On the positive side, there are some heartening developments in the urbanization of Aboriginal people. The first is the emergence of a middle class. This is the result of the focus that Aboriginal people have placed on education in recent years. In many large communities, a new and dynamic class of Aboriginal people with significant stable incomes is emerging. These people are staffing Aboriginal organizations and working for all levels of government. They pay property taxes; they participate in the civic life of the communities where they live; their children attend public schools. This Aboriginal middle class presents new programming and policy challenges: What types of services do its members require? How do they fit into the political structures and processes that already exist? How are they coping as urban Aboriginal people?

In addition, living in urban areas has contributed to the development of Aboriginal cultural expression. Many Aboriginal people have received teachings or cultural enrichment only after they have relocated to the cities. Often, Elders and traditional people are vibrant central figures in urban Aboriginal communities. Cultures from across Canada come together and learn from one another, which creates a renewed vision of past practices.

Finally, a new political consciousness is emerging. Too often it was believed that the only way to live as a "real" Aboriginal person was on a reserve, Métis settlement or Inuit hamlet. It was felt that Aboriginal people who moved to cities gave up some of their Aboriginal identity. Now that the majority of Aboriginal people live in urban areas, it is only natural that the identity of Aboriginal people is also an urban one. Aboriginal people increasingly accept this reality. Whether through the development of urban Aboriginal service organizations or the political reawakening of community members, a new identity is emerging that is both relevant and important.

All levels of government and Aboriginal organizations must be prepared to work meaningfully on urban Aboriginal issues. If governments and Aboriginal organizations work collaboratively, as they did when they developed the Kelowna Accord, they will need to include meaningful discussions around the urban question. How will Aboriginal political organizations represent them? Who will pay for the much-needed services? Who will deliver those services? As these questions are answered, we will be in a much better position to move forward as a country with a fully engaged urban Aboriginal population. Canada requires no less.

References

Aboriginal Affairs and Northern Development Canada (AANDC). (2010). *Treaties with Aboriginal People in Canada*. Retrieved from www.aadnc-aandc.gc.ca/eng/1100100032291/1100100032292

Aboriginal Affairs and Northern Development Canada (AANDC). (2012). Urban Aboriginal Peoples. Retrieved from www.aadnc-aandc.gc.ca/eng/1100100014277/1100100014278

Anderson, K., Blackwell, S. & Dornan, D. (2000). *Urban Aboriginal Child Poverty: A Status Report on Aboriginal Children and Their Families in Ontario*. Toronto: Ontario Federation of Indian Friendship Centres.

Furi, M. & Wherrett, J. (2003). *Indian Status and Band Membership Issues*. Retrieved from Parliament of Canada website: www.parl.gc.ca

Health Canada. (2012). *Your Health Benefits—A Guide for First Nations to Access Non-Insured Health Benefits*. Retrieved from www.hc-sc.gc.ca

Moss, W. & Gardner-O'Toole, E. (1991). *Aboriginal People: History of Discriminatory Laws*. Retrieved from Government of Canada Publications website: http://publications.gc.ca

National Association of Friendship Centres (NAFC). (2009). Programs [Web page]. Retrieved from http://mail.nafc.ca

National Association of Friendship Centres (NAFC). (2012). Our history [Web page]. Retrieved from http://nafc.ca

Royal Commission on Aboriginal Peoples (RCAP). (1996a). *Report of the Royal Commission on Aboriginal Peoples. Vol. 1: Looking Forward, Looking Back*. Ottawa: Canada Communication Group.

Royal Commission on Aboriginal Peoples (RCAP). (1996b). *Report of the Royal Commission on Aboriginal Peoples. Vol. 4: Perspectives and Realities*. Ottawa: Canada Communication Group.

Statistics Canada. (2008). *Aboriginal Peoples in Canada in 2006: Inuit, Métis and First Nations, 2006 Census*. (Catalogue no. 97-558-XIE). Ottawa: Minister of Industry.

Statistics Canada. (2013). The education and employment experiences of First Nations people living off reserve, Inuit, and Métis: Selected findings from the 2012 Aboriginal Peoples Survey. *The Daily*, November 25. (Component of catalogue no. 11-001-X). Retrieved from www.statcan.gc.ca/daily-quotidien/131125/dq131125b-eng.pdf

United Nations Housing Rights Programme. (2010). *Urban Indigenous Peoples and Migration: A Review of Policies, Programmes and Practices*. Nairobi, Kenya: United Nations Human Settlements Programme.

Veterans Affairs Canada. (2005). *Aboriginal Veterans*. Retrieved from www.veterans.gc.ca/pdf/cr/pi-sheets/Aboriginal-pi-e.pdf

ABOUT THE AUTHOR

Peter Dinsdale is an Anishnawbe and member of the Curve Lake First Nation in Ontario. He is the chief executive officer of the Assembly of First Nations. Peter has worked extensively with Aboriginal people and organizations in urban environments at the local, regional and national levels. Between 2004 and 2010, he was executive director of the National Association of Friendship Centres. Peter holds a bachelor of arts degree in political science and Native studies, and a master of arts in interdisciplinary humanities from Laurentian University in Sudbury.

Chapter 27

Providing Psychiatric and Medical Services to Remote Communities in Northern Ontario

BRUCE MINORE, JOHN HAGGARTY, MARGARET BOONE AND MAE KATT

Responding to the mental health issues that First Nations, Métis and Inuit who live in remote parts of Canada face is particularly challenging (Mental Health Commission of Canada, 2009). Due to the sparseness of the population and consequent isolation, these communities need more cross-jurisdiction care management, experience greater difficulty recruiting and retaining mental health care providers and have significantly higher service delivery costs in a generally underfunded system. If we focus only on the resulting inequities around access to services, however, we might overlook existing situational strengths such as the mental health knowledge of community members (Alberta Mental Health Board, 2006), or we might miss the need for "approaches that are attuned to the circumstances and priorities of remote communities," as noted in an Australian context by Hunter (2007, p. 91).

This chapter examines three case studies of individuals from Cree and Anishinabe communities in northern Ontario to show how one regional system, the Sioux Lookout Zone, strives to meet the needs of a geographically scattered client base. This system serves a region that shares many characteristics with other remote places in Canada in terms of population mix, physical and human health care resources and service strategies.

Characteristics of the Sioux Lookout Zone

The Sioux Lookout Zone is an administrative division of Health Canada's First Nations and Inuit Health Branch (Ontario Region). It includes 28 First Nations communities scattered amidst a vast area of boreal forest that stretches about 1,120 kilometres north of the 50th parallel and extends 640 kilometres west from the Hudson Bay coast to the Manitoba border. These communities are home to about 22,851 people. Only 53 people live in the smallest place, but 2,869 others reside in the largest settlement (Aboriginal Affairs and Northern Development Canada, 2013). To access other centres, people in these communities must travel by airplane or, in winter, over ice roads cleared across frozen lakes and rivers. Nonetheless, local residents are quite mobile, travelling readily back and forth between their homes and larger towns in the region.

The health services found in these communities are similar to those in other northern regions of the country. Only primary care is available locally and is delivered by resident nurses and by physicians who fly in, usually monthly. In addition, band members trained as community health representatives or mental health workers also provide care. These band members, along with on-call staff, are members of crisis response teams, which are formed when the need arises. Links to specialists in some disciplines, including psychiatry, are provided by Keewaytinook Okimakanak, the regional telehealth network, or by Ontario Telemedicine Network, the provincial telehealth network. A resident who needs hospitalization or to see a specialist in person must fly to a larger centre, usually Sioux Lookout, Kenora, Thunder Bay or Winnipeg.

Ontario does not include ethnic identifiers in health administration data sets, so it is not possible to develop a comprehensive picture of the mental health care needs of this population. However, based on analysis of the data subset for northwestern Ontario from a province-wide survey of mental health services for Aboriginal people, Minore and colleagues (2007) concluded that such needs are high. Their conclusion is supported by the incidence of suicide, a standard indicator of the prevalence of mental illness. In Sioux Lookout Zone communities, 13 people aged between 14 and 35 years died by suicide in 2012. Their deaths continue a tragic trend extending back to 1986 that has claimed approximately 200 lives. Each year, clinicians report having treated many people known or suspected to have attempted suicide. Communities have taken the initiative in responding to this situation. For example, the idea of creating on-call crisis response teams was a community-generated idea.

Case Studies

To elucidate mental health care delivery in remote communities, we present three clinical case studies, based on fact but using fictional names, which have aspects common to other remote communities, especially how clinical interventions are managed and how operational issues are resolved. The case studies also cast light on some unresolved concerns.

Jimmy

Jimmy was an 18-year-old living with social anxiety in a mid-sized isolated community. Over the previous year, he had become increasingly suspicious of others. He came to believe his food was contaminated and was no longer able to eat anything beyond clear soups. When the community nurse from the nursing station visited Jimmy at home, she found he had significantly deteriorated since an assessment three months earlier. As well as becoming more suspicious, he had lost weight and was talking to himself. Suspecting a psychosis, the nurse discussed Jimmy's case with the physician on call at the hospital in Sioux Lookout. Jimmy was prescribed a low dose of an oral antipsychotic.

After two weeks of poor compliance and lack of co-operation, Jimmy became agitated and assaulted his elderly grandfather late one night. Jimmy was evacuated by plane, first to Meno Ya Win Health Centre in Sioux Lookout, and then to the Thunder Bay Regional Health Sciences Centre. In Thunder Bay, Jimmy spent three weeks on the Psychiatric Intensive Care Unit, part of the Adult Mental Health Unit. When he was sufficiently stabilized, he was given open ward privileges, and remained hospitalized for a further two months. Upon his discharge, Jimmy received aftercare through the Early Psychosis Program in Thunder Bay.

Following one year in the Early Psychosis Program, a community liaison person in Thunder Bay helped Jimmy return to his remote community. Jimmy maintained his mental health with the aid of an injectible antipsychotic. He subsequently returned to Thunder Bay, completed his Grade 12 education and enrolled in the small-engine repair program at the community college in the city.

This case highlights several things about mental health care in the Sioux Lookout Zone. Jimmy's young age mirrors the preponderance of young people among mental health clients, which in part reflects the fact that about two-thirds of the population is less than 29 years old (Statistics Canada, 2012a). Jimmy's entry into the mental health care system through the nursing station and his progression from primary care to specialist programs are typical. Note particularly that the community nurse did not function in isolation, but was able to consult remotely with a physician about Jimmy's case. Another important aspect of Jimmy's care involved connecting him with services in Thunder Bay that help First Nations clients liaise with their home communities.

Isabelle

Isabelle was a 65-year-old great-grandmother who lost her husband a year before she experienced a mental health crisis. She had had brief periods of grief counselling and support within her community, but the community health nurse urged the visiting physician to assess her mental health. Isabelle was diagnosed as having clinical depression, moderate type, with significant grief. After a conflict with her son related to alcohol use, Isabelle made a suicide attempt and was flown south to the Lake of the Woods District Hospital in Kenora. Here, she was medically cleared in relation to the suicide attempt, but when staff followed up on her physical complaints, a malignancy was found in her abdomen. Isabelle was transferred to the Thunder Bay Regional Health Sciences Centre for surgery and then reassessed by a mental health worker and psychiatrist at the hospital's cancer clinic. During her hospitalization, Isabelle also met with an Aboriginal counsellor who shared sweetgrass healing ceremonies with her.

Once cancer was diagnosed, Isabelle's worsening depression was suspected to be related to the cancer, as well as her earlier grief and loss. Isabelle agreed to continue on an antidepressant medication and was offered aftercare at home for both her mental health and physical care, through her community nurse and the visiting physician. Unfortunately, upon her return home, Isabelle found that her community did not show her any regard or concern, and apparently feared discussing her now-treated cancer. Despite her best efforts, Isabelle continued to be isolated in her community and her depression returned. Due to staff turnover and issues of workload, health care providers were also unable to provide consistent support.

Isabelle's situation illustrates both positive and negative aspects of health care in the region. As in Jimmy's case, Isabelle's relatively smooth transfers between her community and hospitals point to a reasonable degree of systemic integration. There are appropriate supports in the city for clients. In Isabelle's case, these supports were provided by the hospital itself, which has well-established cultural programs offered on a routine basis, such as a room with reverse ventilation that is dedicated for sweetgrass ceremonies. However, Isabelle had negative experiences (the delay in cancer diagnosis and lack of support upon her return home) that are a direct result of inadequate health human resources at the community level. Staffing shortages demand that health care providers focus on acute care, at the expense of follow-up care, chronic care, health promotion and disease prevention activities. Although Isabelle's mental health symptoms were responded to appropriately by her local nurse and physician, her physical symptoms were missed until she was hospitalized in Kenora. Similarly, although her follow-up plan of care was fine on paper, resources were not available in her community to sustain it.

Susan

Susan was an anxious 24-year-old who had been "troublesome" since her mid-teens. At age 12, she was sexually abused by a neighbour. Her parents were unable to manage her in their home, so Susan was relocated to her grandparents' house. Through friends who also caused trouble in the community, Susan got access to narcotics, cannabis and ecstasy. After several days of heavy drug use, Susan was held overnight in the community's lock-up unit. After this forced withdrawal, Susan became anxious and socially reluctant, retreating to her bedroom. She only engaged socially when she was intoxicated by alcohol or other drugs. Susan tried several times to complete substance use programs available in the community, but she lost interest, in part because of turnover among program counsellors.

During a period of acute intoxication, Susan was sent to Sioux Lookout Meno Ya Win Health Centre, where she was treated for alcohol withdrawal and alcohol-related delirium. Urine tests showed evidence of other substances, including opiates. Susan was prescribed clonidine and discharged to her home community. She was advised to consider a videoconferencing-supported methadone program. She reluctantly agreed to participate upon court-mandated direction. Susan was also assessed by a psychiatrist who was tele-linked to her community, and was diagnosed with social phobia.

A community counsellor with training in cognitive-behavioural therapy helped Susan to engage in formal work-related activities. An occupational therapist located outside of the community, but accessible through videoconferencing, helped Susan prepare for full-time work at the band office of her First Nation. Although she had four different therapists, Susan was successfully weaned off narcotics and was able to work full time following two years in the methadone program. She consistently attended Narcotics Anonymous and Alcoholics Anonymous groups in her community.

Susan's experiences show that even complex cases can sometimes be successfully managed mainly in the home community. In Susan's case, this involved a combination of community-based workers and programs (some more successful than others) and support from a distance. Susan's experience shows that technology-mediated programs can contribute to desired outcomes, even when individual care providers change, as long as supports within the community are consistently available. Susan's experience again demonstrates the extent (and limitations) of system integration evident in the cases of Jimmy and Isabelle.

ANALYSIS OF THE CASE STUDIES

These three cases illustrate several key features of mental health care delivery in the Sioux Lookout Zone. In Jimmy's and Isabelle's cases, we see how multiple levels of jurisdiction are involved in the region's system of care and how clients move among them. Programs employing paraprofessionals and crisis workers are under First Nations control, as are all services in the five communities that are party to a health transfer agreement between the Shibogama First Nations Council and the federal government. In the rest of the communities, nursing and other primary care services are a federal responsibility. Most services accessed off reserves are funded by the provincial government. However, a wide range of programs now have been amalgamated into a joint First Nations/provincial/federal initiative. The Meno Ya Win Health Centre in Sioux Lookout integrates hospital, primary care and community health services so there is single-point access to physical and mental health care. The amalgamated health services include Nodin Child and Family Intervention Services, which provides on-site psychiatric assessment and treatment in Sioux Lookout. The centre also offers telehealth mental health services in 26 of the communities, including assessments and some types of therapy and caregiver education.

Together, these case studies show that the Sioux Lookout Zone has a functioning system of mental health care that is capable of responding to situations that vary widely in complexity and severity. Indeed, this system involves many features that Ontario's Health Quality Council has identified as characteristic of a good system: it is safe, accessible, client-centred, integrated, equitable and appropriately (albeit less than fully) resourced. There are multiple points of entry, obviously, and concerted efforts are made to provide services that are culturally appropriate, as well as evidence-based. The system uses an interdisciplinary model of care that includes both professionals and paraprofessionals in vital roles. Moreover, adopting technological advances has enabled client needs to be accommodated while significantly overcoming the dictates of place and space. Although the current system has problems—including the fact that individuals' unique mental health needs often are not recognized or treated—on balance, its strengths outweigh its weaknesses.

Strategies for Mental Health Care in Remote Settings

Certain strategies for mental health care delivery in the Sioux Lookout Zone deserve to be highlighted, since they reflect practices found in rural and remote mental health care nationally and internationally. These strategies include making primary care central, forging collaboration between and within disciplines, incorporating local people in mental health care delivery, and using technology to help deliver mental health care.

PRIMARY HEALTH CARE

Success in making primary care central to mental health care delivery has been documented in geographically isolated communities in Canada (Ryan-Nicholls & Haggarty, 2007; Stretch et al., 2009), the United States (Lambert & Hartley, 1998) and Australia (Bambling et al., 2007; Morley et al., 2007). When primary care providers have sufficient preparation and access to specialist support, this is an appropriate level of care in the majority of cases.

COLLABORATION

An interdisciplinary model of care, especially when it involves collaboration between and within disciplines, contributes to the successful delivery of mental health treatment in rural and remote communities. Resident nurses and visiting primary care physicians confer with one another and consult (independently or together) with psychiatric specialists. There is a particular expectation that highly interactive collaboration between generalist and specialist physicians in the mental health arena can go some distance toward meeting the needs of clients (Collaborative Working Group on Shared Mental Health Care, 2000). Admittedly, there are challenges to operationalizing continuous, co-ordinated exchanges, the most basic being finding the time to establish good working relations among parties with hectic schedules (Perkins et al., 2006). However, evidence suggests that a collaborative approach improves the continuity of care (Valleley et al., 2007) and client outcomes (Haggarty et al., 2008). Ideally, this approach maximizes the use of available resources.

LOCAL PEOPLE

In the Cree and Anishinabe communities of northern Ontario and in similar communities, mental health care system functioning depends on community mental health workers and other paraprofessionals or community members, such as Elders. Incorporating local people in the delivery of care in Aboriginal communities is a longstanding practice nationally (Minore et al., 2009) and internationally (Niven, 2007).

Local people bring their cultural knowledge to bear on caregiving in both clinical and non-clinical settings. This understanding of their communities can also help both resident nurses and outside professionals in their interactions with clients. It is common for First Nations people to distrust non–First Nations care providers whose Western medicine practices are thought to disregard traditional values (Maar et al., 2009). However, through their training in mental health care, paraprofessionals can both address community members' misconceptions about proposed therapeutic interventions and alert non-Aboriginal care providers to local concerns (Isaacs et al., 2010).

TECHNOLOGY

Delivery of mental health services in rural and remote communities routinely relies on technologies ranging from e-mail communications to videoconferencing. These technologies are collectively referred to as e-health or telehealth (Smith et al., 2008). In partnership with the provinces, territories and Aboriginal organizations, the federal government has supported a number of inter-jurisdictional Aboriginal telehealth mental health initiatives to facilitate assessment and treatment (Health Canada, 2004) and support training for community-based workers (Muttit et al., 2004). Multiple benefits of using telehealth in mental health care in rural settings have been documented, including increased access to care (Wagnild et al., 2006), facilitation of primary care and specialist consultation (Fenell & Hovestadt, 2005), greater clinical effectiveness (O'Reilly et al., 2007) and better cost effectiveness (Nelson & Bui, 2010). Although the use of telehealth in mental health care specifically in Aboriginal populations has not been explored extensively, there is evidence that it is well accepted (Hogenbirk et al., 2006; Shore et al., 2008).

Challenges to Mental Health Care in Remote Settings

Like its successful strategies, mental health care in remote communities has many unique aspects. We consider three of the most significant ones: limits to the use of technology, difficulties retaining qualified personnel and difficulties arising from the need to transfer clients between sometimes far-distant facilities.

TECHNOLOGY

Among care providers in Native American communities, Dick and colleagues (2007) noted a considerable lack of awareness about the proper application and operation of technology in facilitating the delivery of mental health care. Furthermore, many remote communities lack the necessary infrastructure or consistent availability of professional personnel to support optimal transmissions, which greatly constrains the use of more complex technologies such as videoconferencing. For example, having a limited number of data transmission lines can cause audio lags. These lags may result in people appearing to be speaking simultaneously, interrupting one another, which interferes with the therapeutic exchange (Hilty et al., 2009). This technological difficulty may be of particular concern in cultures where the patterns of turn-taking and conversational rhythms differ from those of Euro-Canadians, who may accept this effect more readily. Yellowlees and colleagues (2008) stated that generally, "little is known about how to deliver culturally appropriate e-mental healthcare" (p. 487). Indeed, we do not yet know if a technological interface is a neutral factor and, if it is not, how it affects interactions.

PERSONNEL

Chronic shortages in human resources continually undermine efforts to maintain robust systems of mental health care in rural and remote areas. Technology-supported services can offset this deficit to some extent, but it is not a full remedy (Chipp et al., 2008). In more remote First Nations, for example, there is a constant turnover among primary care providers. Nurses often stay in a community for only a few weeks and physicians may be locums who change monthly. Additionally, specialist care is constrained by the mix of specialists available. In northwestern Ontario, which includes the Sioux Lookout Zone, there are just two child psychiatrists serving a population of 224,034 people, of which only a tiny fraction live in Zone communities (Statistics Canada, 2012b). As a result, primary care practitioners carry a heavy burden of mental health clients. As we stated previously, it is appropriate for primary care practitioners to see these clients if they are adequately prepared and supported, but in regions with high turnover, however, neither condition may exist (Mays et al., 2009; Morley et al., 2007). This lack of preparation and support is a particular concern at the community level, where practitioners may make inappropriate decisions because they lack knowledge or confidence in their knowledge base. Poor decision making can yield detrimental results, ranging from missing clients' symptoms to ordering unnecessary transfers for assessment or treatment outside the communities. The observation by Berntson and colleagues (2005) that rural psychiatrists in Canada have to be "comfortable with a greater degree of uncertainty and risk" (p. 4) applies to all mental health care providers in remote communities.

CLIENT TRANSFERS BETWEEN SERVICES

Client transfers are frequently points of disruption when trying to create a seamless system of mental health care by integrating services in the Sioux Lookout Zone, especially when clients are returning to their communities. The client's plan of care may not arrive at the home community in a timely way or, because urban-based specialists are unaware of the available resources, may include treatment strategies that are not feasible in the client's community. The latter limitation is tied to level of preparation, as well as to the number and category of caregivers present. In general, crisis situations are well managed, but follow-up care is more problematic in communities where the few mental health care providers must focus mainly on acute cases. Having few and/ or regularly changing mental health care providers in a community can lead to early symptoms going unrecognized or clients only presenting at a clinic when they are in an acute state. As a result, mental health care providers often find themselves dealing with more complex cases.

Key Considerations for Planning and Delivering Care

Despite the challenges, mental health services in the Sioux Lookout Zone continue to evolve and improve, tapping the deep vein of resilience that has sustained the communities through a long struggle with issues such as a high suicide rate. Based on our analysis of the three case studies presented in this chapter, we offer key considerations that we hope will be useful to those responsible for planning and delivering mental health care to Aboriginal people residing in similar northern communities in Canada:

- **Systems have to function on a primary care model.** Case management should rest with primary care providers who, given proper preparation and support, can offer appropriate care themselves and/or co-ordinate referrals to specialists. This approach recognizes the strengths and limitations of the health human resources generally available and optimizes their use.

- **Resource deficits and geographical imperatives demand high levels of system-wide collaboration.** The keystone to effective primary health care delivery in any setting includes inter- and intra-disciplinary team approaches. The uniquely complex environment of separate and shared responsibilities that exists in providing health care to Aboriginal people also requires cross-jurisdictional co-operation.

- **Use telecommunications technologies when possible to overcome geographical barriers and associated time constraints.** However, technology use must not intrude on the care process; it must enhance the delivery of care. While technology-mediated care is often useful, it is not always appropriate. It should not be exclusively relied upon as a "best available" substitute, since this approach may sometimes deny clients access to the best care.

- **Continuing clinical education must be available to caregivers, and its nature and content should be dictated by the care environment.** Cultural competence and role diversity are particularly important aspects of providing care to people from remote Aboriginal communities. Training in cultural competence will always be group specific. Similarly, education regarding role diversity must be consistent with the educational and experiential backgrounds of health care team members, whether professionals or those recruited from the communities.

• **Optimize the use of community members as formal and informal players in the mental health care system.** Achieving this requires respecting and understanding the roles community members might play, as well as acknowledging and having confidence in their skills. Too often, mental health workers or community health representatives are underused or misused by health care professionals, who limit paraprofessional community members to tasks such as translating at the nursing station, rather than letting them get on with the health promotion work in the community that they have been specially prepared to do.

References

Aboriginal Affairs and Northern Development Canada. (2013). First Nation Profiles. Retrieved from http://pse5-esd5.ainc-inac.gc.ca/FNP/Main/Index.aspx

Alberta Mental Health Board. (2006). *Aboriginal Mental Health: A Framework for Alberta*. Retrieved from Alberta Health Services website: www.albertahealthservices.ca

Bambling, M., Kavanagh, D., Lewis, G., King, R., King, D., Sturk, H., . . . Bartlett, H. (2007). Challenges faced by general practitioners and allied mental health services in providing mental health services in rural Queensland. *Australian Journal of Rural Health, 15*, 126–130.

Berntson, A., Goldner, E., Leverette, J., Moss, P., Trapper, M. & Hodges, B. (2005). Psychiatric training in rural and remote areas: Increasing skills and building partnerships. *Canadian Journal of Psychiatry, 50* (9), 1–8.

Chipp, C., Johnson, M., Brems, C., Warner, T. & Roberts, L. (2008). Adaptations to health care barriers as reported by rural and urban providers. *Journal of Health Care for the Poor and Underserved, 19*, 532–549. DOI: 10.1353/hpu.0.0002

Collaborative Working Group on Shared Mental Health Care. (2000). *Shared Mental Health Care in Canada: Current Status, Commentary and Recommendations*. Retrieved from College of Family Physicians of Canada website: http://cfpc.ca/uploadedFiles/Directories/_PDFs/sharedmentalcare.pdf

Dick, R.W., Manson, S.M., Hansen, A.L., Huggins, A. & Trullinger, L. (2007). The Native Telehealth Outreach and Technical Assistance Program: A community-based approach to the development of multimedia-focused health care information. *American Indian and Alaska Native Mental Health Research, 14* (2), 49–66.

Fenell, D. & Hovestadt, A. (2005). Rural mental health services. In R.G. Steele & M.C. Roberts (Eds.), *Handbook of Mental Health Services for Children, Adolescents and Families* (pp. 245–258). New York: Kluwer Academic/Plenum Publishers.

Haggarty, J., Klein, R., Chaudhuri, B., Boudreau, D. & McKinnon, T. (2008). After shared care: Patients' symptoms and functioning 3 to 6 months following care at a rural shared mental health care clinic. *Journal of Community Mental Health, 27* (2), 47–54.

Health Canada. (2004). *Telemental Health in Canada: A Status Report*. Retrieved from Government of Canada Publications website: http://publications.gc.ca/collections/Collection/H21-236-2004E.pdf

Hilty, D., Yellowlees, P., Sonik, P., Delet, M. & Hendren, R. (2009). Rural child and adolescent telepsychiatry: Successes and struggles. *Pediatric Annals, 38*, 228–232.

Hogenbirk, J., Ramirez, R. & Ibanez, A. (2006). *KO Telehealth / North Network Expansion Project: Final Evaluation Report.* Retrieved from Centre for Rural and Northern Health Research website: www.cranhr.ca

Hunter, E. (2007). Disadvantage and discontent: A review of issues relevant to the mental health of rural and remote Indigenous Australians. *Australian Journal of Rural Health, 15,* 88–93.

Isaacs, A., Pyett, P., Oakley-Browne, M., Gruis, H. & Waples-Crowe, P. (2010). Barriers and facilitators to the utilization of adult mental health services by Australian Indigenous people: Seeking a way forward. *International Journal of Mental Health Nursing, 19,* 75–82. DOI: 10.1111/j.1447-0349.2009.00647.x

Lambert, D. & Hartley, D. (1998). Linking primary care and rural psychiatry: Where have we been and where are we going? *Psychiatric Services, 49,* 965–967.

Maar, M., Erskine, B., McGregor, L., Larose, T., Sutherland, M. & Graham, D. (2009). Innovations on a shoestring: A study of a collaborative community-based Aboriginal mental health service model in rural Canada. *International Journal of Mental Health Systems, 3* (27). DOI: 10.1186/1752-4458-3-27

Mays, V.M., Gallardo, M., Shorter-Gooden, K., Robinson-Zañartu, C., Smith, M., McClure, F., . . . Ahhaitty, G. (2009). Expanding the circle: Decreasing American Indian mental health disparities through culturally competent teaching about American Indian mental health. *American Indian Culture and Research Journal, 33* (3), 61–83.

Mental Health Commission of Canada. (2009). *Toward Recovery and Well-Being: A Framework for a Mental Health Strategy for Canada.* Retrieved from www.mentalhealthcommission.ca

Minore, B., Hill, M.E., Boone, M., Katt, M., Kuzik, R. & Lyubechansky, A. (2007). *Community Mental Heath Human Resource Issues Pertaining to Aboriginal Clients.* Retrieved from Centre for Rural and Northern Health Research website: www.cranhr.ca

Minore, B., Jacklin, K., Boone, M. & Cromarty, H. (2009). Realistic expectations: The changing role of paraprofessional health workers in Canada's First Nation communities. *Education for Health, 22* (2), 1–9.

Morley, B., Pirkis, J., Naccarella, L., Kohn, F., Blashki, G. & Burgess, P. (2007). Improving access to and outcomes from mental health care in rural Australia. *Australian Journal of Rural Health, 15,* 304–312.

Muttit, S., Vigneault, R. & Loewen, L. (2004). Integrating telehealth into Aboriginal health care: The Canadian experience. *International Journal of Circumpolar Health, 63,* 401–414.

Nelson, E.L. & Bui, T. (2010). Rural telepsychology services for children and adolescents. *Journal of Clinical Psychology: In Session, 66,* 490–501. DOI: 10.1002/jclp.20682

Niven, J. (2007). Screening for depression and thoughts of suicide: A tool for use in Alaska's village clinics. *American Indian and Alaska Native Mental Health Research, 14* (2), 16–28.

O'Reilly, R., Bishop, J., Maddox, K., Hutchinson, L., Fisman, M. & Takhar, J. (2007). Is telepsychiatry equivalent to face-to-face psychiatry? Results from a randomized controlled equivalence trial. *Psychiatric Services, 58,* 836–843.

Perkins, D., Roberts, R., Sanders, T. & Rosen, A. (2006). Far west area health service mental health integration project: Model for rural Australia? *Australian Journal of Rural Health, 14,* 105–110.

Ryan-Nicholls, K.D. & Haggarty, J.M. (2007). Collaborative mental health care in rural and isolated Canada: Stakeholder feedback. *Journal of Psychosocial Nursing and Mental Health Services, 45* (12), 37–45.

Shore, J., Brooks, E., Savin, D., Orton, H., Grigsby, J. & Manson, S. (2008). Acceptability of telepsychiatry in American Indians. *Telemedicine and e-Health, 14,* 461–466. DOI: 10.1089/tmj.2007.0077

Smith, A., Thorngren, J. & Christopher, J. (2008). Rural mental health counseling. In I. Marini & M. Stebnicki (Eds.), *The Professional Counselor's Desk Reference* (pp. 263–274). New York: Springer.

Statistics Canada. (2012a). NHS Aboriginal Population Profile, 2011 (database). Retrieved from http://www12.statcan.gc.ca/nhs-enm/2011/dp-pd/aprof/index.cfm?Lang=E

Statistics Canada. (2012b). Population and dwelling counts, for Canada, provinces and territories, and census divisions, 2011 and 2006 censuses (table). *Population and Dwelling Count Highlight Tables, 2011 Census.* (Catalogue no. 98-310-XWE2011002). Retrieved from http://www12.statcan.gc.ca/census-recensement/2011/dp-pd/hlt-fst/pd-pl/Table-Tableau.cfm?LANG=Eng&T=101&S=50&O=A

Stretch, N., Steele, M., Davidson, B., Andreychuk, R., Sylvester, H., Rourke, J. & Dickie, G. (2009). Teaching children's mental health to family physicians in rural and underserviced areas. *Canadian Journal of Rural Medicine, 14,* 96–100.

Valleley, R., Kosse, S., Schemm, A., Foster, N., Polaha, J. & Evans, J. (2007). Integrated primary care for children in rural communities: An examination of patient attendance at collaborative behavioral health services. *Families, Systems & Health, 25,* 323–332.

Wagnild, G., Leenknecht, C. & Zauher, J. (2006). Psychiatrists' satisfaction with telepsychiatry. *Telemedicine and e-Health, 12,* 546–551.

Yellowlees, P., Marks, S., Hilty, D. & Shore, J. (2008). Using e-health to enable culturally appropriate mental healthcare in rural areas. *Telemedicine and e-Health, 14,* 486–492. DOI: 10.1089/tmj.2007.0070

ABOUT THE AUTHORS

Margaret Boone is a professor emerita in nursing at Lakehead University specializing in maternal and child health, as well as an associate researcher at the Lakehead University site of the Centre for Rural and Northern Health Research. Her research has focused on northern and rural health delivery and interdisciplinary teams, primarily in the remote First Nations and rural communities of northwestern Ontario. Her research has included nationally funded projects on the continuity of care for mental health, diabetes and cancer clients in remote Aboriginal communities and the continuity of care for special needs children in northern rural communities.

John Haggarty is a graduate of McMaster Medical School in Hamilton, Ontario; the University of Ottawa (family medicine); and the University of Western Ontario (pharmacology, psychiatry) in London. He is medical director of mental health programs at St. Joseph's Care Group in Thunder Bay, where his clients include First Nations people. He is also a professor at the Northern Ontario Medical School and an adjunct professor at Lakehead University. Dr. Haggarty presents internationally and publishes on collaborative mental health, health outcomes, and Inuit and First Nations people. He is a fellow of the Royal College of Physicians of Canada, a diplomat of the American Board of Neurology and Psychiatry and a certified physician executive of Canada.

Mae Katt is a member of the Temagami First Nation on Bear Island and currently works as a nurse practitioner in Thunder Bay. From 1996 to 2000, Mae was Ontario regional director for Health Canada's First Nations and Inuit Health Branch. Previously, she was the health director for the Nishnawbe Aski Nation for six years, and spent four years as the founding co-ordinator of the Native Nurses Entry Program at Lakehead University. She is an associate researcher at the Centre for Rural and Northern Health Research at Lakehead University, leading projects that focus on access to care for Aboriginal people in Ontario.

Bruce Minore is a senior research fellow at the Centre for Rural and Northern Health Research at Lakehead University. For two decades, Bruce and his colleagues have worked with First Nations community partners, as well as Health Canada and the Ontario Ministry of Health and Long-Term Care, on projects that have a direct policy and program focus. These studies have looked at the delivery of care for specific conditions, including mental health and cancer, and at human resource issues, including the recruitment of health professionals and the appropriate use of paraprofessionals.

Chapter 28

Medical Practice in Remote Northern Ontario First Nations Communities

MICHAEL OUELLETTE

> Few individuals have good insight into the plight of native people in this province. As physicians we are privileged in this respect. We work with First Nations communities at every level. We are there when their children are born. We are with them in sickness and death. We witness their deaths, too many of which are premature. We are coroners trying to understand their excessive mortality and morbidity. We see their endless suffering. (Trusler, as cited in Kay, 2013)

Physicians have a unique and privileged position in attempting to understand human beings, society and community. The above excerpt from a letter to the Ontario College of Family Physicians written by Murray Trusler, former chief of staff of the Weeneebayko Area Health Authority, highlights this important role. On a daily basis, patients share with us their innermost secrets, stressors, sources of happiness and other intimate aspects of their lives. We listen to their stories, see their tears, watch them smile, feel their pain and experience life with them. We can then reflect on the patient experience and what it means to the person in the context of family, community and the greater social web. For a physician in a remote northern First Nation community, comparisons with health services and outcomes elsewhere in Canada are unavoidable, and what is revealed is a deep social chasm between Aboriginal peoples and other

Canadians. Many people in these communities are struggling. Some live day to day with little hope for the future. A child growing up in an isolated First Nation simply has fewer opportunities for a good life, compared to many people in our country. Those who want to understand the reasons for this gulf in opportunities and outcomes and help to eliminate it must undertake a journey that will lead to unpredictable personal change.

Each of us will view the experience of working in a remote Aboriginal community through our own personal lens. An Aboriginal medical student may have an advanced understanding of many of the relevant issues—social, political, economic and cultural—but will still find new things to learn. A non-Aboriginal physician with 25 years of clinical experience will bring different insights, perspectives and wisdom while having much to learn about culture, history and politics. All perspectives have something valuable to offer and the interactions among them can lead to the growth of all. The intention of this chapter is to present one such perspective—one way of framing the experience of medical practice in remote northern Ontario Aboriginal communities. Some important aspects of physician practice are explored through a novel lens and a physician's unique experience. This chapter is not meant to be an exhaustive and complete exploration of all elements related to medical practice, as there certainly are many other topics that deserve attention.

Conceptualizing Medical Practice in Remote Northern Ontario First Nations Communities

In 2007, Murray Trusler wrote his advocacy letter to the Ontario College of Family Physicians on behalf of the people in the Weeneebayko Area, six predominantly Cree communities along the western James Bay coast that stretch from Moosonee to Peawanuck, more than 200 kilometres away on Hudson Bay (Kay, 2013). That year, 21 First Nations youth in Kashechewan had attempted suicide.

Trusler eloquently described the experience of working in an isolated First Nations community. He identified four levels, or tiers, of involvement, commitment and insight (Figure 29-1). These tiers are progressive in scope and complexity. Trusler correlated the four tiers to the quadrants of the medicine wheel used in some First Nations traditions. The medicine wheel offers us a way to see exactly where we are in the world and in which areas we need to develop in order to realize our full potential.

In Tier 1, represented by the east quadrant of the medicine wheel, are students, residents or locums coming to the North for a unique experience. This stage is an opportunity to learn and grow. In Tier 2 (the south quadrant, associated with affectivity and feeling), the physician confronts, responds to and adapts to health inequities experienced in the North, becoming attuned to the basic needs of people and communities and the issues that affect them as the physician works in common with others and

FIGURE 29-1

Tiered Model for Conceptualizing Medical Practice in Remote Northern Ontario First Nations Communities

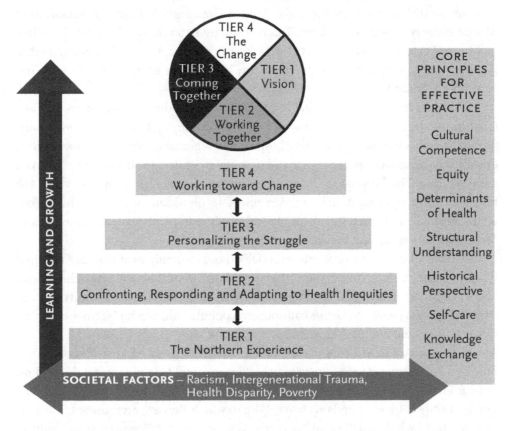

learns to work together. Some physicians will begin to personalize the struggle, incorporating it into their sense of self. A physician in Tier 3 (the west quadrant, associated with the body) becomes involved in the community and understands the enormous issues facing it, but feels powerless to create change. A physician in Tier 4 (the north quadrant, associated with the mind and understanding) analyzes the problems further and pushes for change. As Trusler (Kay, 2013) wrote, these physicians

> see a solution and attempt to make it happen. Until the Kashechewan crisis, most physicians were mired in the third group. But, with Kashechewan, it became obvious that we have the power to inform the Canadian public and enlist their support as agents of reform.

The progressive movement through each tier reflects the physician's increasing awareness of the interlacing factors that weigh upon people and the development of a holistic view of health and well-being.

TIER 1. THE NORTHERN EXPERIENCE

In 1673, on a small three-kilometre-long island where Moose River meets James Bay, the Hudson's Bay Company established Moose Fort as the second fur-trading post in North America. In 1905, the Moose Cree signed Treaty 9, establishing Moose Factory Island as a reserve. Today, roughly 1,500 mostly Cree residents live in Moose Factory (as Moose Fort is now known). Total Moose Cree membership is more than 3,000 people, which reflects the high degree of mobility of most First Nations communities.

Weeneebayko General Hospital in Moose Factory is the most northern and isolated hospital in Ontario. Built in 1949 as a 200-bed hospital and tuberculosis sanitarium, it now functions as a teaching hospital and regional referral centre for surgery, obstetrics, diagnostics, specialist care and outpatient services for the six Weeneebayko communities. The hospital is the main employer in the region and serves as the hub for health services. A full complement of 14 physicians works and lives close to the hospital, and specialists from Queen's University, University of Toronto and McMaster University visit regularly.

Medical students and residents, especially those in family medicine, are required to spend time in rural environments for some portion of their training. The unique history of Moose Factory, the natural beauty of its setting and the opportunity to work with Indigenous people make this community a popular education placement for physician trainees and many other health professionals.

Most primary health care institutions in northern, isolated First Nations communities are nursing stations. In rare cases, there are still federal hospitals located on or near First Nations lands, as in Moose Factory. Within these institutions, physicians quickly notice different standards from those to which they are accustomed. The reasons for this include small population size, resource-base differences, poor political organization and will, weak levels and organization of advocacy, regularly changing numbers of short-term professionals, chronically underfunded and inappropriately maintained infrastructure and equipment strains (Waldram et al., 2006).

Poor political organization and will can occur within any political group. Conversely, there are often very determined and passionate people working for positive change. They must work in complex political environments in which health care delivery is hindered by layers of bureaucracy imposed by Health Canada, the province, the First Nations and Inuit Health Branch and others. Progress needs to be made on this front.

Cultural Competence and Medical Training

In 2008, the Indigenous Physicians Association of Canada and the Association of Faculties of Medicine of Canada launched First Nations, Inuit, Métis Health Core Competencies: A Curriculum Framework for Undergraduate Medical Education (IPAC-AFMC Aboriginal Health Curriculum Subcommittee, 2008). Recommendations have since been carried out across Canadian medical schools. Today's students and medical residents are more informed about social and medical issues facing Aboriginal people and can use this knowledge to inform and guide their future clinical practice. The number of Aboriginal physicians is increasing, helping to reinforce efforts to improve cultural competence and ensure that Aboriginal issues have a voice in the health system.

Some medical schools now have admissions, education and residency training programs specially tailored to prepare students for practice in Aboriginal and other northern or rural communities. The Northern Ontario School of Medicine (2010) was founded in 2005 to represent and serve the culturally diverse population of Ontario's North, partly by "actively involving Aboriginal, Francophone, remote, rural and underserviced communities" (p. 3). In addition, after many years of work by Aboriginal peoples' health advocates and aided by new governmental funding, many medical schools have modified their admissions policies and altered their curricula in an effort to achieve equity in health human resources and health care delivery and better serve the needs of Aboriginal people.

The Society of Obstetricians and Gynecologists of Canada's *Guide for Health Professionals Working with Aboriginal Peoples*, which was co-ordinated by Janet Smylie (2001), a Métis family physician, identifies several important learning objectives for Canadian health professionals. These include knowing the correct names for Aboriginal groups and the traditional territories and language groups; understanding the socio-demographics of Aboriginal peoples in Canada and the significant impact on health of the challenges facing individuals and communities; understanding the disruptive impact of colonization on Aboriginal health and well-being and governmental obligations and policies regarding Aboriginal health; recognizing the need to provide health services for Aboriginal peoples close to home; and, supporting Aboriginal communities in the process of self-determination. In First Nations communities, medical students and residents can apply the knowledge and skills they have developed, guided by experienced staff physicians, nurses, allied health professionals and community members who can explain why and how this additional knowledge is important to the provision of medical care. Learners can deepen their understanding of how culture and health care are connected by participating in local cultural events, where community members can act as teachers for the medical trainee.

Technology, Telemedicine and Electronic Medical Records

Technology continues to change the way medical care is delivered in isolated communities in Canada. Airplanes and helicopters have shortened patient travel times, while the Internet, fax machines, fibre optics and other innovations have improved communication.

Telemedicine involves the use of telecommunications and information technology to provide health care at a distance; its use is expanding in remote areas. Both patients and care providers stay in their home communities, increasing the potential for improving efficiency, quality and cost savings for the health care system while reducing disruption and cost to the patient.

Electronic medical records (EMR) are another valuable tool. Patients in the North often travel long distances for tests and to see specialists. When shared EMR between care providers is possible, it can improve information flow and decrease duplication of investigations, thus improving patient safety and communication between care providers.

TIER 2. CONFRONTING, RESPONDING AND ADAPTING TO HEALTH INEQUITIES

The 14 physicians in the Weeneebayko Area Health Authority (WAHA) region are all based in Moose Factory. At times there are as many as six medical students and residents training in the region. When available, relief physicians back up those away on holiday or continuing their medical education. The physician group works closely together to cover medical services at the hospital and in the clinics in the five other communities in the WAHA zone. Optimally, physicians regularly travel to the more remote communities on a regular schedule according to population and needs. The emergency room is open 24 hours a day and must always have a doctor on duty. When emergency cases cannot be addressed in the local community, the emergency physician is available by phone or can receive air ambulance patients around the clock. The hospital also has an inpatient ward, obstetrical care and surgical services.

Practice Characteristics of Northern and Rural Family Physicians

Family physicians in northern remote communities tend to have a broader scope of practice and perform a wider range of clinical procedures than their urban counterparts. This trend strengthens as the community becomes smaller and more remote. In Moose Factory, all of the family physicians provide comprehensive medical care—outpatient, inpatient, emergency, obstetrics, home visits and so on. They deal with any patient (of any age) who walks through the door. This type of medicine is both highly challenging and quite rewarding. Adaptability, patience, courage and the ability to learn on the fly are necessary characteristics of the rural physician.

The regular flow of newer medical graduates and residents brings energy and up-to-date evidence-based knowledge. However, there is really no way to train doctors in advance for the breadth and severity of medical conditions they will inevitably encounter with unnerving regularity in isolated rural settings. They must gain this experience through practice, mentored by more senior physicians (if they are present) and continuing medical education outside the community. In settings such as these, physicians, nurses and support staff are a team in every sense of the word, and all positions are indispensable.

A Day in the ER

> As I walk into the emergency department to start my shift, the physician just completing her shift hands over the caseload from the night

before. A 15-year-old female from one of the more northern communities will be arriving by air ambulance sometime in the next few
hours. She had taken an unknown quantity of some pills and alcohol.
It is unclear whether this was a suicide attempt. There was no blood-
work available. Fortunately, her vital signs are stable for now.

As well as handling the regular caseload, physicians in the Moose Factory ER must
provide backup to the nurses in the five other WAHA communities. During the day,
expanded-scope nurses run clinics in those communities. At night, they provide
urgent/emergency care. After completing an assessment, a nurse may require physician consultation. Advice on medication or the management plan can usually be given
over the phone. The telemedicine screen can be used to obtain visual information,
for example, to view a rash. For more complicated cases, the physician may need to
arrange for air ambulance transfer to Moose Factory or a hospital in an urban centre
such as Timmins, Kingston or Toronto. This can be time-consuming and laborious—
there are often delays in transport or a lack of an accepting physician or hospital. It can
be incredibly difficult to find appropriate care and resources for some patients, such as
adolescents with mental health, suicidal or substance use issues.

Unfortunately, there simply are not enough physicians to staff each of the isolated
northern communities with a doctor. Often, the population is too small to justify a
full-time physician. Even when positions are available, they are often left unfilled.
Thus, nurses provide the bulk of medical services for these communities.[1] Expanded-
scope nursing is very demanding, highly complex and requires well-trained professionals and rather special people. This system functions well when a community is
fortunate enough to have a high-quality team of nurses. Two examples of real cases
illustrate the system at both ends of the spectrum.

Scenario 1. The ER physician in Moose Factory receives a priority phone consult
from the nurse in Attawapiskat, one of the six WAHA communities. The nurse does a
thorough medical assessment and describes symptoms consistent with a stroke. The
physician and nurse agree that the patient should be transferred to the stroke centre in
Timmins. Fortunately the weather is good and there is an air ambulance ready to pick
up the patient and transfer him within the four-hour window for him to receive the
appropriate medical treatment.

Scenario 2. The ER physician in Moose Factory receives a page to call Fort Albany,
another outlying nursing station. The nurse states that the patient has an elevated
heart rate. The patient had been in 12 hours previously, but was sent home by the nurse
on call the night before. The discharge diagnosis was heartburn, and the nurse thought
the patient was feeling better despite still having an elevated heart rate. This patient is
now feeling quite unwell. Fortunately, a few blood tests are available at the clinic. The
physician asks for any possible labs. One blood test shows severe damage to the heart

---

1   For a discussion about nursing in remote northern communities, see chapter 29.

muscle—a myocardial infarction or heart attack. The appropriate medications are given promptly and this helps to stabilize the patient briefly. The team decides to send the patient to the cardiac centre in Kingston. Unfortunately, there are delays in flights due to weather. In the 12 hours it takes to pick up the patient, his illness worsens and he now needs a breathing tube. He ends up dying in-flight.

Remote nurses are often expected to handle complex cases, alone at night, with limited laboratory technology and tests available and with air evacuation services being at the mercy of the weather. They endure high levels of stress and often suffer from burnout. They are often the eyes and ears for the physician, and they are vital to quality care for patients in the North.

Recruitment and Retention

Rural and remote areas across the country face significant physician shortages. Government strategies to attract physicians to these areas include salary incentives, improved continuing medical education access and resources, recruitment drives and supports for locum physicians (Heng et al., 2007). Developing an effective physician services recruitment and retention strategy is an essential component of remote hospital administrative work and must include much more than salary incentives.

Factors that affect retention rates in rural and remote practice include personnel shortages, locum relief and time away from work; unmet family needs, a desire for an urban lifestyle or spousal employment needs (Pong et al., 2007); and quality of housing, schools, and social, cultural and recreational resources. Since physicians with a good sense of their needs will choose appropriate work locations and be able to advocate for those things that will help to keep them in the area, facilitating this self-knowledge would be a helpful institutional approach. When the physician is not mindful of these and similar self-care issues, the result can be a short stay in remote communities due to reasons such as burnout, loneliness and depression. Although some people thrive in this practice environment, it is not for everyone and can certainly stress the health and wellness of the physician.

Early and repeated exposure to rural communities by medical trainees has been found to increase the likelihood of the physician entering rural practice (Easterbrook et al., 1999). Rural practitioners are also more likely to be from rural backgrounds (Chan et al., 2005). In 1990, the Ontario government established the Northeastern Ontario Family Medicine Program in Sudbury and the Family Medicine North Program in Thunder Bay. The mandate of these two residency programs is to supply the North and underserviced communities with physicians. This model has been successful; nearly two-thirds of all person-years of medical practice by graduates of these programs have taken place in such communities (Heng et al., 2007).

Working in the North, one quickly realizes the importance of recruitment and retention of high-quality colleagues, including nurses, social workers, dieticians, lab technologists and other professionals. The smaller and more isolated the community, the more important this is. Staff spend significant amounts of time with one another:

they work with one another in the day and socialize at night. The camaraderie and team building that occur as a result of living and working in such close proximity can be one of the most satisfying aspects of practice in more remote locations. Collegiality encourages retention. Once a group gains stability, a momentum is created that allows it to begin tackling the larger community health issues.

Health Inequities

It is well known that Aboriginal people—no matter where they live in Canada—experience dramatic health challenges. Data also consistently shows that living in rural, remote communities compounds these issues. Although Aboriginal people are heterogeneous with respect to culture, language and geography, they tend to uniformly experience higher rates of diabetes, heart disease, strokes, tuberculosis, skin infections and many other diseases. Compared with national averages, the Aboriginal infant mortality rate is two to four times higher (Smylie et al., 2010), and suicide rates are five to seven times higher for First Nations youth and 11 times higher for Inuit youth (Health Canada, 2006). Life expectancies are five to 15 years less on average (Statistics Canada, 2010). These are just some of the many statistics that continue to prove the sad and deplorable truths of inequity (Adelson, 2005; Reading & Wien, 2009).

It is one thing to read statistics like these in newspaper reports or hear about them in high-profile reports such as the 2011 Coroner's report on the suicide crisis experienced in Pikangikum, Ontario, between 2006 and 2008 (Ontario Ministry of Community Safety and Correctional Services, 2011). It is quite another to experience and witness these tragic occurrences on a daily basis as a physician. Comparing one's previous medical experiences in Canada or internationally with circumstances in the North is unavoidable. For the physician, seeing fellow human beings struggle like this can be difficult.

Canada has been criticized by the United Nations Committee on Economic, Social and Cultural Rights for its treatment of Aboriginal people. The UN Human Development Report, which ranks well-being from 187 member states, ranked Canada eleventh (United Nations Development Programme, 2013). After visiting Canada in 2013, the UN Special Rapporteur on the Rights of Indigenous Peoples, James Anaya, stated:

> From all I have learned, I can only conclude that Canada faces a crisis when it comes to the situation of indigenous peoples of the country. The well-being gap between aboriginal and non-aboriginal people in Canada has not narrowed over the last several years. (Anaya, 2013, ¶5).

To begin to understand the health and disease experienced by Aboriginal peoples, one must see them in the conditions in which they live. A physician educated in the determinants of health knows that one cannot separate the patient from the social, economic and physical environment (Mikkonen & Raphael, 2010; Raphael, 2009). These determinants of health are increasingly being recognized as even more important than factors such as medical care and personal health behaviours. Canada has been a leader in these areas of study and advocacy. Despite this work, remote northern Aboriginal communities still suffer some of the worst health outcomes in Canada, and the physician may achieve a better degree of understanding of why.

TIER 3. PERSONALIZING THE STRUGGLE

By this stage, the physician has lived in the community long enough to gain more insight into the daily lives and resultant health outcomes of his or her patients, through home visits and repeat visits, and shopping alongside them at the grocery store. Respecting, attending and participating in local cultural events creates common interests and helps build relationships and galvanize friendships. When extended families of 20 to 40 people gather at the hospital to celebrate a birth or support one another in death, the physician has the honour of being present and sharing in those times with patients. If the physician is fortunate, he or she may begin to gain acceptance in the community—trust is earned. This process requires patience and perspective. It is made easier by recognizing that the effects of colonization, the residential school system, systemic racism and local history may affect one's relationships with patients.

At this point, it is not uncommon for the physician to reflect on his or her first patient encounters. These could very well have been short, with patients answering with single words and a steely, blank stare. It is common for doctor and patient to end an encounter in mutual frustration, misunderstanding and unfulfilled expectations. The naïve practitioner becomes cognizant of cultural barriers and over time builds trust with patients. Now the patient begins to open up about painful abuse at home, depression and substance use issues—the real reasons for the prior visits. The patient may stop the doctor at the grocery store, smiling, "Hey, can you take a look my elbow?" The therapeutic alliance strengthens and the doctor forges deeper connections to the people and the community. It becomes possible to move cautiously toward aspirations of creating some kind of meaningful and lasting change. However, the realities are complex and do not admit quick fixes. One must temper one's exuberance to be more effective and avoid future disappointment.

Community Well-Being
The Community Well-Being Index developed by Indian and Northern Affairs Canada (now Aboriginal Affairs and Northern Development) uses Statistics Canada census data on education, labour force, income and housing to come up with a socio-economic well-being score for each Canadian community. This data is then used to help measure the quality of life of First Nations and Inuit communities relative to other communities. The index reveals a significant disparity in well-being between Aboriginal and other Canadian communities. Of the "bottom 100" Canadian communities in 2006, 96 were First Nations and one was Inuit. Only one First Nations community ranked among the "top 100"

Canadian communities (Aboriginal Affairs and Northern Development Canada, 2010).

Although deepening connections with the community strengthen one's resilience, it is during this third stage that a physician may start to feel disillusioned. With such severe inequities, the differences may sometimes feel too great to bridge. Vacations and trips to one's home community serve to reinforce the stark contrasts. Continually confronting the practice implications of a lack of co-ordination of funding, programming or administrative and professional support wear on the will. Conversations among colleagues may start to head toward feelings of hopelessness. Are we making any progress? Are things ever really going to change? Energy and willpower may give way to discouragement, inaction and even depression. Burnout becomes a very real concern for many. Thoughts of leaving are coupled with feelings of guilt about abandoning the community.

At this point, some will choose to move on to entirely different professional opportunities. Those who have been mindful of their experiences and have done their best to grow and provide high-quality, caring medicine have already been of value to the system and to the people they served. Some physicians will stay longer. Others may stay committed to the issues, but choose another practice location. All who have made it to this point will have been affected by their experience in a deep and profound way.

TIER 4. WORKING TOWARD CHANGE

In 2005, Kashechewan became the centre of national media attention. Drinking water contaminated with *Escherichia coli* bacteria caused many of the citizens to become ill and prompted mass evacuations. Then, in late 2011, the media focused on Attawapiskat. Leadership in the community declared a state of emergency as winter approached and many citizens, including newborn babies and older people, had inadequate and unsafe housing. Some people were living in wooden shacks, with space heaters and without running water or functional sewage services. The headlines read "Attawapiskat housing crisis," but those familiar with the housing in Attawapiskat and many other First Nations communities across Canada knew these issues are more extensive and long-standing than the word "crisis" connotes.

Physicians, including Murray Trusler, were at the centre of advocacy for the people of Kashechewan. Much of the initial media coverage of the issue and resultant action was due in part to the actions of the community doctors working in concert with the local chief, politicians and other active community members. Again, in Attawapiskat, reporters looked to local physicians as a reliable source of information on the state of housing and overall health. When physicians discuss issues pertaining to health, people listen. The public understands that doctors live and work right in these communities, alongside the people. Doctors are in a natural position to communicate this reality.

The media coverage of Aboriginal issues comes in waves. It often provokes strong responses—for a short time. For most of the Canadian population, these issues are forgotten when they are not being covered by the media. Many Canadians are disconnected from Aboriginal issues. Some blame Aboriginal people for their plight and think they must solve their own problems. Others recognize the challenges, agree that help is needed and want to assist, but simply do not know what to do.

Physicians in Tier 4 view health-related issues in a broader context that includes both present and historical social, political, environmental and cultural factors. They understand that the health of the individual is inseparable from that of the community and nation. These physicians give the issues a deeper analysis while also working for change, and become engaged as communicators of the current reality to the wider audience. There is a great need for individual leadership and engagement as active agents of change. The disillusionment often encountered by physicians in Tier 3 is overcome through active participation in the solutions that will move Aboriginal people toward better health.

Role of the Physician

The German pathologist and politician Rudolf Virchow asserted that "physicians are the natural attorneys of the poor" (Ackerknecht, 1953, p. 243). He understood the opportunities and responsibilities we have to advocate for the underprivileged in society. Physicians today have support in this task from many important allies—in health care, government, public policy and law, and in professions such as nursing, social work and teaching—who aim to create systems change and social innovation.

Physicians can contribute to improving conditions in Aboriginal communities in many ways. Awareness of Aboriginal health issues is the essential starting point. Education on Aboriginal health issues for medical students and residents creates a necessary base of knowledge. Medical associations and colleges have a responsibility to incorporate and prioritize Aboriginal issues on their agendas. Physicians may also choose to practise in an underserviced Aboriginal reserve community. This can be done as a learner, a locum or in a contractual position. When physicians are present in these communities, the result is a higher standard of health care. Physicians can also act as advocates, communicating pertinent issues. For real progress to be achieved, improved collaboration is needed between the Aboriginal community, health advocates, elected officials, policy-makers, the business community and others. Physicians should also support efforts for self-determination of health services for Aboriginal people.

However, if we are to improve the health of Aboriginal people in Canada, doctors (Aboriginal and non-Aboriginal) are only part of the solution. The Canadian public and governments must first agree that this inequality is unjust and unacceptable. They must then develop a viable plan to move forward and provide the resources necessary to implement that plan successfully.

Conclusion

Life on an isolated First Nations reserve is much different from life for the average Canadian. The physician experiences these realities in a unique way. As our patients share with us their strength, courage, pain and sadness, we gain an appreciation for the multitude of factors that create and influence life, health and happiness for those who call these isolated communities home. However we choose to integrate this knowledge and experience into our view of the world, these experiences will have a profound effect on how we continue to live as individuals, physicians and Canadians.

Seeing this aspect of Canada from the four-tiered perspective reflected in the medicine wheel reveals truths to those who participate. Deep, emotive experiences can occur at any stage—during the first day as a medical student or at any point in a physician's career. Revelation of these truths can be intensely moving—perhaps enough so to move us to action.

References

Aboriginal Affairs and Northern Development Canada. (2010). *First Nation and Inuit Community Well-Being: Describing Historical Trends (1981–2006)*. Retrieved from www.aadnc-aandc.gc.ca

Ackerknecht, E.H. (1953). *Rudolph Virchow: Doctor, Statesman, Anthropologist*. Madison: University of Wisconsin Press.

Adelson, N. (2005). The embodiment of inequity: Health disparities in Aboriginal Canada. *Canadian Journal of Public Health, 96* (Suppl. 2), S45–61.

Anaya, J. (2013). Statement upon conclusion of the visit to Canada. Retrieved from http://unsr.jamesanaya.org/statements/statement-upon-conclusion-of-the-visit-to-canada

Chan, B.T.B., Degani, N., Crichton, T., Pong, R.W., Rourke, J.T., Goertzen, J., . . . McCready, B. (2005). Factors influencing family physicians to enter rural practice: Does rural or urban background make a difference? *Canadian Family Physician, 51*, 1246–1247.

Easterbrook, M., Godwin, M., Wilson, R., Hodgetts, G., Brown, G., Pong, R. & Najgebauer, E. (1999). Rural background and clinical rural rotations during medical training: Effect on practice location. *Canadian Medical Association Journal, 160*, 1159–1163.

Health Canada. (2006). *First Nations and Inuit Health: Suicide Prevention*. Retrieved from www.hc-sc.gc.ca

Heng, D., Pong, R.W., Chan, B.T., Degani, N., Crichton, T., Goertzen, J., . . . Rourke, J. (2007). Graduates of northern Ontario family medicine residency programs practise where they train. *Canadian Journal of Rural Medicine, 12*, 146–152.

IPAC-AFMC Aboriginal Health Curriculum Subcommittee. (2008). *First Nations, Inuit, Métis Health Core Competencies: A Curriculum Framework for Undergraduate Medical Education*. Retrieved from Association of Faculties of Medicine of Canada website: www.afmc.ca/pdf/CoreCompetenciesEng.pdf

Kay, J. (2013, January 10). What's wrong with remote native reserves? Let's ask a veteran doctor who worked there. Retrieved from *National Post* website: http://fullcomment.nationalpost.com/2013/01/10/jonathan-kay-whats-wrong-with-remote-native-reserves-lets-ask-a-doctor-who-worked-there-for-43-years/

Mikkonen, J. & Raphael, D. (2010). *Social Determinants of Health: The Canadian Facts.* Toronto: York University School of Health Policy and Management. Retrieved from www.thecanadianfacts.org

Northern Ontario School of Medicine. (2010). *Strategic Plan 2010–2015.* Retrieved from www.nosm.ca/strategicplan.aspx

Ontario Ministry of Community Safety and Correctional Services. (2011). *The Office of the Chief Coroner's Death Review of the Youth Suicides at the Pikangikum First Nation 2006–2008.* Retrieved from www.mcscs.jus.gov.on.ca

Pong, R.W., Chan, B.T., Crichton, T., Goertzen, J., McCready, W. & Rourke, J. (2007). Big cities and bright lights: Rural- and northern-trained physicians in urban practice. *Canadian Journal of Rural Medicine, 12,* 153–160.

Raphael, D. (2009). *Social Determinants of Health: Canadian Perspectives* (2nd ed.). Toronto: Canadian Scholar's Press.

Reading, C. & Wien, F. (2009). *Health Inequities and Social Determinants of Aboriginal Peoples' Health.* Retrieved from National Collaborating Centre for Aboriginal Health website: www.nccah-ccnsa.ca

Smylie, J. (2001). A guide for health professionals working with aboriginal peoples: Cross cultural understanding. *Journal of the Society of Obstetricians and Gynecologists of Canada, 23,* 54–68.

Smylie, J., Fell, D. & Ohlsson, A. (2010). A review of Aboriginal infant mortality rates in Canada: Striking and persistent Aboriginal/non-Aboriginal inequities. *Canadian Journal of Public Health, 101,* 143–148.

Statistics Canada. (2010.) *Aboriginal Statistics at a Glance: Life Expectancy.* Retrieved from www.statcan.gc.ca

United Nations Development Programme. (2013). *Human Development Report 2013. The Rise of the South: Human Progress in a Diverse World.* Retrieved from http://hdr.undp.org

Waldram, J.B., Herring, D.A. & Young, T.K. (2006). *Aboriginal Health in Canada: Historical, Cultural and Epidemiological Perspectives* (2nd ed.). Toronto: University of Toronto Press.

ABOUT THE AUTHOR

Michael Ouellette is a First Nations family physician, born and raised in northern Manitoba. After working as a chiropractor in Cross Lake First Nation, he returned to Winnipeg to complete his doctor of medicine degree at the University of Manitoba. He then completed his medical residency at Mount Sinai Hospital in Toronto. Having practised as both a chiropractor and a medical physician in isolated northern First Nations communities for several years, Dr. Ouellette developed a personal vision of what it means to live and work as a physician in the North—recognizing the profound importance and necessity of people working together and coming together in common purpose.

Chapter 29

Working in Northern Nursing Stations

BAIBA ZARINS

Health care professionals have always taken great interest in providing health care in varying locations. Nursing in remote areas offers great opportunities to engage in expanded point-of-care autonomous nursing practice. In some cases, this means being the sole health care provider in the community. Working in remote areas gives nurses the opportunity to fulfil their desire to improve health care within a broad scope of practice. Rural and remote communities face many challenges in recruiting and retaining nurses. Challenges arise in the areas of compensation, housing, professional development and quality of work life. Other challenges include serving very small populations scattered across large geographical areas, being geographically isolated and having little social and economic interaction with urban areas (Canadian Institute for Health Information [CIHI], 2007).

Finding ways to address these unique challenges is crucial, since in 2000, 18 per cent of registered nurses (RNs) practised in rural, remote and northern communities, where 22 per cent of Canadians live (CIHI, 2002). An analysis of 2006 Ontario data found that 70.5 per cent of the provincial RN workforce lives and works in urban regions. Of those living in rural areas, 3.8 per cent commute to work in the largest cities, 3.3 per cent work in mid-sized cities, and 3.3 per cent work in rural areas (CIHI, 2007). The number of nurses in these communities is declining, while the number of people living in rural and small towns is increasing. This trend is not changing (CIHI, 2002).

By sharing the innovative collaborative model described in this chapter, I hope to encourage health care organizations in other parts of the country to explore ways to work with remote communities to provide health care human resources. The common goal of providing health care should not be limited by geographical or cultural boundaries.

Establishing and Promoting the James Bay Program

The experiences outlined in this chapter are based on a health human resource planning model developed between a large urban health care centre in Toronto, the University Health Network (UHN), which is composed of several teaching hospitals, and remote First Nations communities in northern Ontario. The James Bay Program was set up to redress the nursing shortage in remote First Nations communities in northeastern Ontario (Ferguson-Paré et al., 2010). Staff from the UHN area spent between four and eight weeks and longer in remote settings, and staff from the remote communities worked in urban health care environments for two-week periods. Once the program was established, it was marketed to both urban and remote nursing staff as a learning opportunity. An internal website within the UHN described the program and the application process. Staff who had already participated in the program posted journal reflections, presentations and photo journals to share their personal experiences with potential participants.

Alexandrea Mason-Harty and Jennifer Taylor were among the first nursing participants in the James Bay Program in 2008. For this chapter, they have graciously provided excerpts from their journals. These excerpts describe their personal impressions of working in the remote North,[1] and exemplify the experiences of the more than 60 UHN staff who, as of 2012, have participated in the program.

Preparing for Work in Remote Communities

Once a nurse decides to pursue remote-location nursing, having realistic expectations ensures a positive experience for both the nurse and the remote community. Vast amounts of information are readily available through the Internet. However, the most meaningful information is garnered through conversations with other health care staff who have worked in similar remote locations.

For the James Bay Program, interested nurses can access an internal UHN website that gives detailed information about each remote community hospital or station placement. It describes staffing complements, typical staffing schedules, travel and accommodation, and provides specific skill competency checklists and web links to relevant resources. Other material, such as photos and previous traveller presentations, provide additional information that is reviewed and discussed as part of the

---

1 These observations are personal observations and do not necessarily represent the views of UHN or the program's remote location partner agencies.

decision to participate in the program.

Nurses who decide to pursue a remote-location placement must sign a service contract, which is also agreed to by all stakeholders (e.g., unit or hospital management, union representatives, human resources). The contract outlines the terms and details of employment. The following list provides potential points to consider for negotiation in the service contract:

• adherence to local collective agreements in respect to rate of pay, seniority, benefits, as well as periodic performance review
• transportation costs or provision of a travel allowance
• northern/remote nursing allowance (a specific additional payment to offset higher living costs in remote communities)
• schedule of work (e.g., master set rotation, self-scheduling), work hours (full-time, part-time, casual, job-share) and employment expectations (e.g., on-call, remote fly-in for staff coverage, callbacks)
• initial orientation to workplace and surroundings (length of time, evaluation, probation period)
• opportunities for professional development (e.g., academic courses, conferences, computer access to relevant information and services)
• vacation allowances (hours, financial support for scheduled fly-outs)[2]
• housing (shared, private, supported, subsidized), housing provisions (furnished, unfurnished), length of time housing is provided.

Both public and private health care staffing agencies, as well as academic institutions, offer courses to prepare for nursing in rural and remote communities. Learning about Aboriginal culture and history and developing cultural competence, in addition to learning about the specific First Nations communities the nurse will visit, are extremely important. Gaining knowledge and experience in clinical areas such as advanced cardiac life support (both adult and pediatric), triage assessment, obstetrics and family medicine prior to departure is also highly recommended.

If the remote nursing position is connected to a hospital or private agency, pre-departure briefings can answer any questions or concerns nurses may have about travel and work issues. It is important to discuss preparing for sensory and physical isolation, cultural sensitivity, scope of practice expectations, nursing skill assessment and strategies for adapting to the new environment (e.g., nutrition, physical activity, social communication). Nurses should find out how they can communicate with friends and family: is there e-mail or telephone access? They should also consider ways to document the experience, such as keeping a journal, taking photographs or posting a social media blog. Physical and psychological preparations are of the utmost importance in ensuring a successful remote nursing placement (Martin Misener et al., 2008). Insightful advice from one of the first nurses to participate in our program was to

---

2   UHN staff are not permitted vacation shifts during their short-term placements. However, worked shifts are incorporated into overall accrued vacation entitlements.

adequately prepare for physical and psychological challenges, but more importantly, to embrace wonderful work experiences with an "open mind and an open heart."

Travelling to and between Remote Communities

Travel to remote communities entails use of smaller aircraft, either fixed-wing or helicopter. Weight restrictions and baggage allowances ensure the safety of both aircraft and travellers, so adherence to these rules is essential. When travelling north or between remote locations, layered clothing helps to accommodate changing cabin temperatures and local climates along the journey. Pack overnight essentials in a carry-on bag in the event of baggage loss or unexpected flight delays. These essentials include:

• change of clothing, personal toiletries
• money (there may not be banking machines or debit card kiosks)
• snacks (in event of flight delays, cancellations).

The flights can be very long and stressful to the novice traveller. Many communities are one to two hours' flight time away from the nearest city or town and are not accessible by road. Transportation in remote areas is weather dependent; aircraft can be grounded due to poor take-off or landing conditions. In water-access communities, transportation is subject to seasonal thaws and freeze-up, which affect the community's accessibility. Depending on the season, modes of ground transport range from canoe and motorboat to snowmobile, all-terrain vehicle and car or truck.

Investigating weather patterns will ensure that nurses bring appropriate clothing and footwear. Waterproof boots for the muddy spring thaw or fall rains are a necessity, as are warm insulated boots for extreme winter temperatures. Having a separate pair of indoor shoes avoids tracking dirt, mud or snow into your work or housing facility.

The Nursing Station or Hospital

Health care centres in remote communities vary in size and capacity. They range from referral hospitals with inpatient beds, surgical suites, clinics and emergency services to very remote stand-alone day clinics with a limited number of inpatient beds.

> The hospital is quaint and they only have what is necessary. There is no permanent local physician, but monthly 'fly-ins' who stay for approximately a week. There are a few rooms for the inpatients, a kitchen, a bathing room, a birthing room, an autoclave room, a main supply room, an x-ray room, a pharmacy, a maintenance room, a few

clinic rooms for those for the walk-in clinic and for the medical doctor to assess, a trauma room, and yes a lab—I'll be spinning my own blood! By the end of these four weeks, I hope I'll feel like the ultimate omni nurse! — *Alexandrea*

Staffing complements vary. The more remote settings may have four to six advanced practice nurses and registered nurses who perform the roles of physician, pharmacist, lab technician, occupational therapist and social worker. Contact with a physician is available via remote communication or on scheduled fly-ins. As Jennifer reflects with amazement, "I am really impressed and overwhelmed at the added skills these nurses must possess. I overhear one staff nurse say to another: 'Is there a doctor this week?' I *am* nervous." Larger remote hospitals have more staff, with on-site physicians and robust health care teams. Remote settings also follow a slower pace, and have different process and documentation systems. For example, blood work may be sent to labs in different locations in the province, and results may take days to obtain. In this setting, all health care staff become very adept at clinical assessment and resource management.

There are no computer entry and/or label printers, simply paper requisitions with corresponding specimen stickers. Most documents are hand written, and every procedure has a documentation process of phone calls and faxes. How enlightening it is to recognize the advantages of informatics and yet still appreciate the varying complexity of this hospital's processes. I have to quickly learn the processes of the Medevac system (designed to evacuate acute patients via airplane), physician telephone consults and monthly physician consults at the hospital. — *Alexandrea*

Meals are social gatherings for sharing stories and taking breaks. In most locations, the hospital acts as a social centre for health care personnel and community service providers, such as ambulance crews and local police agencies.

Some of the staff are locals, and others are "city folk" who are up here on contract. It takes but five minutes to go through the entire hospital, a drastic contrast to the hospitals of Toronto. As my first week came to an end, I came to realize that the hospital was the "hot spot" where the nurses and sometimes the paramedics would come to socialize. — *Alexandrea*

Lengths of stay and shifts vary among remote centres. Most have some degree of "on-call" opportunity for physicians and nurses, as day clinics close for the night and become 911 call centres for after-hours emergencies. Short-term placement nurses may assume these advanced roles once they have acclimatized to nursing within a higher degree of autonomous practice.

> The hospital is located in the middle of town. It has approximately 16 to 18 inpatient beds. About seven of those beds hold chronic patients—a kind of nursing home. The other half of the hospital is a clinic that is open daily until 6 p.m. One staff RN is assigned to the hospital area. She works with two health care aides who are local Cree. They all work 12-hour shifts. There are usually/hopefully three or four RNs working in the clinic every day for eight hours. On weekends there is one 12-hour duty RN seeing clinic patients and working in the hospital. There is usually, but not always, a doctor on duty at the clinic from Monday to Thursday during the day. The doctor sees clinic patients with a pre-booked appointment. A nurse will assess a client and decide whether the person needs to see a physician and then books the appointment. A nurse who needs a doctor's assistance must page the on-call physician who is working at a hospital south. When necessary, patients are sent by a Medevac plane to a receiving hospital. It could be Moosonee, Timmins, Kingston—anywhere where there is a bed. — *Jennifer*

A frequently noted observation is a lack of continuity of care, which often happens when health care staff work on short-term contracts or rotations. Lack of continuity means that patients often have difficulty complying with their health care plans (Tarlier et al., 2007). Unfortunately, staff may be inadequately prepared or trained for work in remote health care stations, which affects levels of engagement and understanding to elicit mutually respectful therapeutic relationships. These factors may influence the level of person-centred holistic care (which incorporates both traditional and mainstream Western medicine approaches) and follow-up care. Nurses become sensitive to the challenges people have in accessing health care services and knowing about available community service agencies or preventative care programs. Often nurses are not prepared for the conditions they encounter upon arrival, and are surprised at the differences between remote nursing stations or northern hospitals and large urban hospitals.

> [The hospital][3] does not have a CT scanner. Patients are flown out for most tests and procedures such as chemotherapy. The cost of a Medevac transfer is $10,000. The x-ray technician works Monday to Friday during the day only. Blood work is drawn by the nurses and sent to different labs in the province. It can take several days to get

---

3 Square brackets within journal entries indicate that text has been omitted or changed to protect anonymity.

results. Everything up here works at a much slower pace than in the south. I became a much more patient nurse. — *Jennifer*

Diabetes is at epidemic proportions here. It is very poorly controlled up here for many reasons. Patients here receive oral hypoglycemics. The isolation and transportation costs make access to health care difficult. There is a shortage of health care staff as well. Some would describe the care as "rudimentary." — *Jennifer*

Nursing Skills

The fundamental nursing process encompasses assessment, planning, implementation and evaluation. Applying these fundamentals to remote environments entails diagnostic reasoning, critical thinking and patient care management. These unique opportunities foster therapeutic relationships of respect and mutual understanding for both practitioner and care recipient.

I assess my patients, diagnose accordingly, and prescribe and fill the treatment according to the clinical guidelines. What autonomy! An experience that allowed me to completely utilize my clinical skills learned in school, and an experience every nurse should acquire. — *Alexandrea*

Nurses working in remote communities must also embrace the rich traditional knowledge and wisdom found in First Nations' ways of knowing, which place importance on language, storytelling, values and experience. Often both traditional and mainstream Western knowledge sets can be incorporated into nursing practice to acknowledge the experience and cultural context of every individual in a collaborative partnership.

Nurses contemplating northern outpost nursing should possess excellent physical assessment skills. As well, they would do well to educate themselves about the customs and values of First Nations people. First, as a sign of respect, and second, to avoid frustration. A nurse must be very patient. A high priority is placed on politeness here. — *Jennifer*

The Aboriginal population is comparatively young, and many young people are having, or already have, children. Having obstetric and pediatric experience is definitely useful for nurses in remote communities.

To date, the majority of patients seen at the clinic appear to be babies. I have never seen such gorgeous babies and children in my life. Teen pregnancy is high here. Most women in their 20s have as many as six children. I met a young woman who was 24 and had two babies in one year—January and December. Women in their 40s are grand-mothers many times over. — *Jennifer*

I see patients young and older. My prenatal patients are very new to me, and thus I have L. accompany me until I am comfortable. I only briefly reviewed prenatal information prior to my arrival—I wish I knew such a majority of my patient population would be pregnant. — *Alexandrea*

Emergency room skills are also an asset:

At 0700 hrs. a trauma patient arrives by ambulance. He was found bleeding and running naked in the snow. It is at least -20°C outside. He has sustained many self-inflicted lacerations and is covered in blood. I learn to suture very quickly—a very useful skill. While sutur-ing this fellow, many of his relatives come and go freely in and out of the trauma room. A flash goes off over my shoulder; the family are taking pictures! I find out later that this is normal. — *Jennifer*

First Nations Peoples

Health care providers seek to assist all individuals, families and communities when and where necessary with care and sensitivity. Through exposure to different cultures, providers become introspective and analytical, reflecting on their own beliefs, attitudes and behaviours. In remote communities, this includes Aboriginal people and the community at large. By taking the time to have meaningful interactions, staff and patients create an atmosphere of inclusion and wisdom.

How would I describe the local First Nation people? Shy, reserved, maybe even aloof. A visitor must make the effort to greet and intro-duce themselves. I found my outgoing personality along with years of ER nursing a definite asset. Within a few days I found people were warmer, waving and smiling to me while I was out for my walks. — *Jennifer*

The children tend to be more open and sociable. Some nurses seem to be very accepted within the community. I learn that many agency nurses come and stay only briefly, thus people have reason to be suspicious and cautious of new faces. There must be very few dark-skinned people who come here, as some of the children would ask me if I painted my skin. I love the objective simplicity of a child's thought process. — *Alexandrea*

I meet the inpatients, some of whom are Elders of the community. . . . I soon learn one is the "community's Elder," as she was once the hospital cook and fed the young school children. Now, the hospital is her home. Day to day, hour by hour you can observe her demeanor as she swings from mood to mood. She sings praises and hymns at the top of her lungs in the morning, hugging and dancing with anyone within proximity, providing a warm and inviting ambiance. Often the evenings are full of tears, a sense of loneliness, self-comforting fetal positions and sleep. Her life reflects care, empathy, unity and contentment; she only remembers some of it since the surgery. Another resident emits the light-hearted simplicity of a schoolgirl. She is an adult. She steers around the hospital in her electric wheelchair, taking cigarette breaks, conversing with the residents and friends who stop by the hospital. She is always smiling.

All the Elders have a story to tell. — *Alexandrea*

Working with First Nations people can highlight differences in ways of working, which can be perplexing to anyone who does not understand the cultural context and complexities of remote communities.

The First Nation hospital staff are interesting, or some might dare to say, eccentric. . . . Generally though, they are excellent and work hard. The nursing staff are careful not to upset or offend the Cree staff. We NEED them! — *Jennifer*

Community spirit, the feeling of interdependence and an overall deeper sense of understanding are highlighted when tragedies happen, and reflect the community's resilience.

One family recently fell victim to a fire, but the community has been collaboratively working to fundraise so the family can get back to common ground. Collections are taken up in the convenience stores, and roasts are held in their honour. . . . Larger festivities are

> sometimes held in the neighboring community. Despite the violence, there is a strong sense of unity. In life you take the good with the bad, but concentrate on the good. — *Alexandrea*

Historical context, housing, education, employment, access to health care and local governance all affect the overall health status of any community, but are particularly important in remote environments. As they strive to provide quality care, visiting nurses bear witness to the effects these complex factors have on the individuals seeking health care.

> After the first week, I become very conscious that non-compliance and apathy are major barriers of care for the community. Many clients are appreciative of the care and the treatment, while others simply nod and smile in agreement while continuing their destructive habits—smoking while pregnant, [eating] high-fat and sugary snacks, lack of glucose monitoring, suicide and consistent binge drinking (to an extent that would kill others). I recall one of D.'s night shifts with a self-inflicted gunshot victim—did I mention it was self-inflicted? — *Alexandrea*

> I am interested in how the nurses cope . . . with what they see; the extreme poverty, alcohol abuse and patient non-compliance. . . .

> Other nurses have expressed their frustration to me as they feel their efforts are somewhat fruitless when the only person who appears to care about clients' well-being is the caregiver. Sadly, I can attest to such situations, but I feel nothing is done in vain. — *Alexandrea*

> I have noticed that obesity among children is common here. I had a 12-year-old patient with hypertension. Apparently, despite education and information, parents insist on giving their children Carnation evaporated milk. As well, few mothers breastfeed their new babies. I was told the reason for the evaporated milk was to keep their weight up for survival. I guess some beliefs are ingrained into the psyche. — *Jennifer*

Health care staff understand they have little influence on the larger socio-economic circumstances of the community. Once nurses are personally exposed to these complexities, they can reflect on the larger challenges facing Aboriginal communities:

> I have heard so many Canadians lament that Aboriginals have free education and do not take advantage of it. I have come to see that this

is an extremely uninformed statement. This is much easier said than done and a complex problem. . . . I wonder with increased exposure to media and the world will there be increased apathy and frustration amongst the young people. My new term: "emotional poverty."
— *Jennifer*

Remote Locations

The following observations about remote Aboriginal communities illustrate the realities and necessities of daily life in remote communities:

The town is empty today. . . . S. and I venture in and meet the local priest. He is a slight elderly looking man with a radiant smile. He tells us that he is originally from Quebec. He has been in [this community] for 35 years. He speaks French, Latin, English, Cree and Ojibwa! The community population is 1,200. There is a public health department, Canada Post and the band office. There is the hospital, ambulance station and NAPS—the reserve police. Court is held about twice a year. — *Jennifer*

Many of the homes are construction trailers. Some homes are prefabs with aluminum siding. No brick homes in sight. Very few homes have windows that are not boarded up or have plastic covering them. The staff tell me that some of these homes have 15 family members living in them. — *Jennifer*

The "Ice Highway" is the frozen river/bay. It opens usually in February for a few weeks. You can drive your truck from [. . .], and from there anywhere you want. Once the ice melts the isolation resumes. — *Jennifer*

Going to a store in the North is very different, for me, than in Toronto. I am forced to refrain from my usual habit of just browsing and buying what I want. Here I have to carefully plan my shopping. I really have to take into account $$$, adequate nutrition and attempting to have variety. It is very easy to fall into a diet of processed sugar and carbohydrates. — *Jennifer*

We stop at the [. . .]. It is the big store in [this community]. It serves as a grocery, hardware and clothing store. The store has about eight to 10 aisles. I brought $20 with me to buy a case of water and candy. I got up to the cashier—$47 for one case of water!!! Back to the shelf went the water. A loaf of bread is $5.99 and a small bag of apples is $10. — *Jennifer*

Accommodation

Housing is difficult to both acquire and manage, especially in smaller remote communities. Nurses should prepare to embrace simple comforts of remote life, as Alexandrea describes:

> The air is cool, clean and refreshing, and my goose bumps testify the difference between 22°C here compared to 22°C in Toronto. The lodge will be my home for the next four weeks—a shared kitchen, a bedroom with satellite television and a bathroom (THANK GOODNESS MY OWN BATHROOM!) Simplicity can be wonderful.

> I learn that the other nurses in the lodge are only there as a necessity, as their homes were flooded and are currently in the process of restoration. I also note the absence of a familiar container—there is no recycling here. As the day progresses, I introduce myself to my fellow roommates and settle in by cleaning.

Social Isolation

Social isolation can be a concern for anyone unfamiliar with remote work environments. People working in remote locations have different strategies to bridge this emotional longing for familiar interaction:

> One nurse tells me that Facebook and the Internet help her cope. She calls her children almost every day. At the end of April she is leaving on vacation for a few weeks to visit family and friends. D., a nurse practitioner, purchases many phone cards and calls her daughter in Sault Ste. Marie, as well as friends and relatives around the globe. — *Jennifer*

> The nurses from the Philippines say they cope by flying home for several weeks twice a year. The nurses live within a short walking distance of each other and the hospital. They get together frequently to gossip

and vent. I find myself spending hours on the Internet, reading and calling my family to buy me more phone cards. — *Jennifer*

Over the past month there has been a group of construction workers here renovating the hospital. They left yesterday very anxious to return home to southern Ontario. The staff nurses are sullen and a little withdrawn at their departure. They had made new friends. I have come to accept that encounters are transient; it is a given fact. I was grateful that the guys left all of the nurses 2 cases of water each— THANK YOU!!!! — *Jennifer*

Getting to know the community and taking part in community activities can also help alleviate isolation. Social events with other transient workers helps to build a sense of community among workers:

Every Thursday was volleyball night at the school. It was an eight-minute bike ride for J. and I. Our roommates tend to occupy themselves within the lodge. We would meet up at the gym with the paramedics, who were also young professionals up here on contract. This was a great social gathering as mothers, daughters, fathers, and sons came to play for fun and sometimes fundraise for local events and/or families in need.

The weekly event was something for me, and surely others, to anticipate, as I was accustomed to the metro life of endless gym memberships and local sports clubs. In [. . .], there were very few options—no malls, no plazas, no community centers, no fast food restaurants, no community pools, just a lot of free time, loose dogs, one local grocery store, a couple convenience stores and the dike. — *Alexandrea*

I try to occupy myself by exploring the reserve—which only took about an hour and half to walk. The walk to the dike is much longer, as there is only a wide road surrounded by green—I walked for hours and eventually turned back as sunset approached and the mosquitoes . . . oh how I loathe mosquitoes. Other days I ride the dirt trails to see where it takes me—a few dead ends, beautiful picturesque scenes, the power generator, the dump and nature everywhere. I eventually have to stop my long walks, as there has been a wolf spotting, and back in my room I quickly pass my time by reading, sleeping and watching the Olympics. One of the hospital security guards is kind enough to offer a boat ride to [. . .]; unfortunately I was working on his days off. — *Alexandrea*

Spending time in remote communities can give travelling health care staff a new sense of perspective:

> The simplicity and scarce options for socialization emphasize how fortunate and ungrateful many Torontonians are, as I recall friends and acquaintances stating, "There's nothing to do." It is a statement I care never to hear again. — *Alexandrea*

Returning to Urban Settings

Nurses who have spent time in remote communities leave with different perspectives on their role as health care providers, the importance of team and the people they have come to know.

> At the meeting, we are offered permanent nursing positions. It is very tempting. We are told that that many RNs who return to the south come back, as they find the increased autonomy nurses have here difficult to relinquish. — *Jennifer*

> We are waiting to go to the airport and it is time to say our goodbyes. The staff have been so accommodating over the past month. I am rather surprised at the many hugs I get from the local Cree I have come to know. They don't talk a lot, but do hug very tightly. We are invited back. — *Jennifer*

> We arrive back in Toronto around 6:30 p.m., looking ridiculous in our snow gear and big Sorel boots. I never anticipated that when I returned to Toronto the bombardment of sensory overload would be an obstacle. It took three days before I could get used to driving my car again. I thought Tim Hortons would be the first thing I would want. Instead, it was raw vegetables I craved. They took on a whole new meaning. For a week I was fascinated by their colours and texture. Something to crunch is a thrill. — *Jennifer*

> I have become aware of the amount of garbage I deposit on the curb each week. During my adventure up North I only accumulated one green bag of waste. — *Jennifer*

Conclusion

Reflecting on their experiences in the North, urban nurses who were part of the James Bay Program expressed their appreciation of and respect for the culturally rich environments they visited and the scope of nursing practice they encountered. In their debriefing sessions, nurses particularly remarked on how these placements enhanced their skills in physical assessment, suturing, casting and pharmacology, as well as in providing holistic, patient-centred health care. As staff attested, remote nursing entails complex and broad knowledge and skills. They appreciated the greater autonomy and increased resourcefulness they developed in understanding the complexities of remote health care. The enriched professional and personal growth is at the core of these positive experiences. Many of these nurses went on to acquire further education and skill, which they used in subsequent placement opportunities. Nurses who participated in the program developed a spirit of collegiality, inquiry and cultural appreciation that lasted well beyond the placement. In Jennifer's words, "My only advice is if you decide to go North, go with an open mind and an open heart."

References

Canadian Institute for Health Information (CIHI). (2002). *Supply and Distribution of Registered Nurses in Rural and Small Town Canada*. Retrieved from www.cihi.ca

Canadian Institute for Health Information (CIHI). (2007). *Workforce Trends of Registered Nurses in Canada, 2006*. Retrieved from www.cihi.ca

Ferguson-Paré, M., Mallette, C., Zarins, B., McLeod, S. & Reuben, K. (2010). Collaboration to change the landscape of nursing: A journey between urban and remote practice settings. *Canadian Journal of Nursing Leadership, 23* (Special issue), 87–98.

Martin Misener, R., MacLeod, L.M., Banks, K., Morton, A.M., Vogt, C. & Bentham, D. (2008). "There's rural, and then there's rural": Advice from nurses providing primary healthcare in northern remote communities. *Canadian Journal of Nursing Leadership, 21* (3), 54–63.

Tarlier, D.S., Browne, A.J. & Johnson, J. (2007). The influence of geographical and social distance on nursing practice and continuity of care in a remote First Nations community. *Journal of Nursing Research, 39*, 126–148.

ABOUT THE AUTHOR

Baiba Zarins is project manager of global practice at the University Health Network (UHN) in Toronto, where she facilitates staff initiatives to local, remote and international destinations. She also manages an innovative second-degree BSCN nursing program in a collaboration between Nipissing University and four Toronto-based health care organizations. Select nursing students in this program have also participated in remote First Nations community placements to enhance their experiential nursing education. Baiba's 25 years of experience as a registered nurse has included clinical practice, teaching and administrative portfolios in acute and long-term care settings. Her interests include research into innovative nursing education teaching and learning pedagogies.

Chapter 30

Improving the Health of Indigenous People through Health Practitioner Training

ALEXANDRA KING AND MALCOLM KING

The Indigenous peoples of Canada—First Nations, Inuit and Métis—are underserved and under-represented in health care. This contributes to the relatively poor health status they experience compared with the general population. One step on the path to improving the health of Indigenous people is to increase the number of health practitioners who are Indigenous; another is to provide cultural safety training in all health practitioner training programs. Programs that prepare practitioners to work with Indigenous people need to examine the historical context of these populations, as well as region-specific knowledge, harm reduction strategies and the social determinants of health. Well-designed, locally oriented training is an excellent way for health practitioners to learn about the role of traditional knowledge and practices in promoting the wellness of Indigenous people.

Increasing the number of Indigenous health practitioners and training all practitioners to work with Indigenous people in a culturally safe and appropriate way will help to create a health system that better meets the needs of Indigenous people and result in improvements in Indigenous health (King, 2005; Royal Commission on Aboriginal Peoples, 1996). A national dialogue with First Nations, Inuit and Métis communities confirmed the need for more culturally appropriate health care that reflects the needs and world views of Indigenous peoples (CIHR Institute of Aboriginal Peoples' Health, 2011).

Equity Targets for Indigenous People in Health Care

Distrust of the health care system, rooted in historical as well as more recent events, is common among Indigenous people, and can prevent them from seeking help when they are sick. Indigenous people may be more likely to seek help when health practitioners are Indigenous because they see them as allies in a foreign world.

In 1996, the Royal Commission on Aboriginal Peoples (RCAP) recommended that 10,000 Aboriginal health practitioners be trained to provide for the health needs of Aboriginal people in Canada. The rationale is rooted in equity: Indigenous people should be able to participate in the delivery of programs aimed at promoting and improving their own health and wellness. Equity targets are easy to set: if four per cent of the population is Aboriginal, then four per cent of health practitioners should also be Aboriginal (King, 2005).

The number of Indigenous health practitioners, even now, falls far short of this equity target, despite a number of university and college programs that have been created to help reduce the gap (Aboriginal Nurses Association of Canada, Canadian Association of Schools of Nursing & Canadian Nurses Association, 2009). As part of its overall social accountability and responsibility strategy, the Association of Faculties of Medicine of Canada (2008), with leadership from the Indigenous Physicians Association of Canada, decided to endorse increasing the number of Aboriginal physicians in this country. Similar strategies have been developed by schools of nursing and other health-related professions. For example, the Aboriginal Nurses Association of Canada is working with the Canadian Association of Schools of Nursing and the Canadian Nurses Association to increase the number of First Nations, Inuit and Métis nurses (2009).

Other strategies for increasing the number of Indigenous people working in health care include removing barriers to primary and secondary education, and addressing other social determinants of health. Facilitating retraining and mature entry into a health care career, as well as providing local or on-site training programs, may also help to reduce the equity gap.

Cultural Safety in Training Programs and in Practice

Indigenous health workers can help to increase cultural safety for clients and patients. Cultural safety is a concept developed by Irihapeti Ramsden, a Maori nurse in New Zealand. Health practitioners who work in a culturally safe way acknowledge and respect cultural differences, practise self-reflection and are familiar with the culture's skills, knowledge and attitudes (Papps & Ramsden, 1996). Knowing a culture's social and political history helps health practitioners understand why norms may differ among clients and patients, and also facilitates empathy. This sensitivity can improve health practitioners' interactions and relationships with clients and patients, which can lead to better health outcomes, and ultimately benefit the community (Brascoupé & Waters, 2009).

Many Canadian health care training programs have embraced cultural competence—having knowledge about other cultures—but often do not address cultural safety. Cultural safety goes beyond cultural competence by analyzing power imbalances in society. In a health care context, cultural safety acknowledges the power differential inherent in the relationship between health provider and client and the impact of privilege on health and relationships. Students should have a thorough grounding in the principles of cultural safety. Learning about cultural humility (Tervalon & Murray-Garcia, 1998) and cultural resonance (Manson et al., 2009) can also support health practitioners in working with Indigenous people.

Being Indigenous does not in itself guarantee that the health practitioner will provide culturally safe services. Indigenous health practitioners who have grown up in a non-Indigenous environment may need to learn about their own culture or other Indigenous cultures, just as do most non-Indigenous practitioners. However, having an Indigenous presence in the health care system can help to improve the health of Indigenous people.

Most health care training programs reflect a mainstream Western orientation. By including cultural safety training, these conventional programs can teach students the value of careful reflection and cultural integration. Given the diversity of Indigenous cultures, everyone has something to learn from cultural safety training—including Indigenous health practitioners.

Key Elements of Training

In addition to providing cultural safety training, all formal training programs should incorporate the elements discussed below.

INDIGENOUS VALUES

Students in every area of health care, at every level of education, need to understand key Indigenous values. Two of these values are relationships and respect. Relationships pertain to how we relate, not only to other people such as family and friends, but also to our community, to our Elders, to our ancestors and future generations, to our land, and to so much else. Relationships are fundamental and are often valued more than an individual's immediate goals. The second value, respect, means accepting others as they are, without passing judgment. Respect also includes non-interference, a basic Indigenous ethical principle, which means promoting positive interpersonal relationships by discouraging coercion of any kind (Brant Castellano, 2004). In a clinical context, these values mean that health practitioners must be sensitive in the advice they provide and how they provide it. The approach should be collaborative, not directive.

HISTORICAL CONTEXT AND REGION-SPECIFIC KNOWLEDGE

Canada has approximately 630 First Nations communities, as well as Inuit living mostly in northern areas and Métis living mostly in Ontario and the western provinces. Training programs need to emphasize this diversity to provide an accurate historical context and avoid generalizations about Indigenous peoples. Identity is a complex construct; Indigenous peoples often struggle with generalizations—too much or too little priority placed on Indigenous world views.

Indigenous peoples in each region of Canada have experienced colonization differently. With these differences come unique legal and treaty status and variations in experiences of the residential schools and the child welfare system.[1] These features are layered upon the unique cultures of Indigenous peoples, both as they existed originally and as they have been changed through colonization. Training programs should require students to learn about the history of the particular region in which they will be working.

It is important to learn about the region's current situation, politics, economics, priorities and challenges. Local health services, both mainstream and traditional, vary by location, but can be leveraged to improve the delivery of mental health and addiction services. Programs should provide students access to websites, newspapers and administrative offices of First Nations, Inuit and Métis communities, and ideally offer mentoring relationships.

Training should also prepare students to work with Indigenous people living in urban centres. Students need to be prepared to respect and learn about the unique background of each person they encounter, and to understand that urban Indigenous people cannot be approached from a pan-Indigenous perspective. Learning about friendship centres, Indigenous service organizations and agencies providing services in various cities and regions across the country will also prepare students to support their clients when they enter practice.

CAUSES OF POOR HEALTH

Poor health is rooted in the social determinants of health (Marmot, 2007), especially among Indigenous peoples. These determinants include the classic socio-economic indicators: income, education, employment, living conditions, social support and access to health services (Ottawa Charter for Health Promotion, 1986).

---

1   See chapter 3 for a discussion about the residential school experience. See chapter 4 for a discussion about experiences in the child welfare system.

The health of Indigenous people is also affected by a range of cultural, political and historical factors, including racism, loss of language, loss of connection to the land, environmental deprivation, and spiritual, emotional and mental disconnectedness (King et al., 2009).

The disparities between Indigenous and non-Indigenous peoples are widest in the areas of mental health and addiction (Kirmayer et al., 2009). Indigenous people in Canada experience a higher rate of suicide-related issues than the general population. In the First Nations Regional Health Survey (First Nations Information Governance Centre [FNIGC], 2012), 13 per cent of First Nations adults living on reserves reported having attempted suicide at some point in their lives; of these, 51 per cent reported that their attempt occurred during adolescence, and four per cent attempted suicide in childhood. Among Inuit living in northern regions, the suicide rate is more than 11 times that of the general population. Tjepkema and colleagues (2009) found elevated death rates related to alcohol and external causes, including suicide and accidents, among registered Indians and Métis compared with the general population.

The First Nations Regional Health Survey (FNIGC, 2012) reported high rates of smoking and binge drinking among First Nations adults and youth living on reserves. Substance misuse and problem gambling were also issues. A regional health survey of Métis (Sanguins et al., 2013) provided evidence of depression, anxiety disorders and substance use problems. The 2007–2008 Inuit Health Survey (Inuit Health Survey, 2010) reported that smoking addiction was prevalent among Inuit. A study by the National Coordinating Centre for Aboriginal Health (2010) found elevated rates of fetal alcohol spectrum disorder among Indigenous people.

High rates of mental health and addiction problems among Indigenous people are linked to the residential school experience. In Canada, multiple generations of Indigenous children experienced residential schools. This resulted in collective traumas, which include disrupted family and community structures; the loss of parenting skills as a result of institutionalization; patterns of emotional response that reflect the lack of warmth and intimacy in childhood; the perpetuation of physical and sexual abuse experienced by children in the schools; the loss of Indigenous knowledge, languages and traditions; and the systemic devaluing of Indigenous identity (Kirmayer et al., 2003). Although the residential schools have ceased to exist, their legacy lives on, as children continue to be taken by the child welfare system, and thus continue to be separated from their families, communities and identities. At present, almost half of all children in foster care in Canada are Aboriginal, yet only 4.3 per cent of the general population is Aboriginal (Statistics Canada, 2013). This trauma, combined with generally poor social determinants of health, has led to high rates of mental health and addiction issues among these children.

Indigenous people often do not access care until their condition is advanced, be it acute or chronic (FNIGC, 2012). As a result, care is focused on treating immediate health problems. However, successful treatment requires addressing the underlying social determinants of health, such as poverty and substandard living conditions. It is next to impossible for people to adhere to medical and lifestyle regimens when their lives are chaotic and they lack control over their environment. Training needs to prepare students for a wise-practice treatment model that involves a multidisciplinary approach with a strong focus on social work.

HARM REDUCTION

Harm reduction within a health care context typically means reducing the negative consequences of drug use or risky sexual behaviours. It can also be applied to mental health problems and to health care approaches, such as chronic disease management.[2] The importance of harm reduction in the context of mental health and addiction among Indigenous people cannot be overstated. While some people embrace an abstinence model, many others need a more flexible approach. This may involve varying degrees of harm reduction with frequent reassessment, which may eventually translate into abstinence.

A harm reduction approach to a high-risk activity involves analyzing the activity's critical components in order to identify individual or interdependent components that result in negative consequences. The analysis examines barriers to stopping the activity using a non-judgmental and culturally appropriate approach. The practitioner can then help the client consider alternatives to the high-risk activity. There are at least two critical contributors to this process: first, clients themselves must be actively involved. They are more aware of the barriers they face and possible ways to mitigate harm. They also know what alternative practices might be best and how to implement them. A second key contributor to the process is the health professionals and others who normalize harm reduction. A combination of senior-level and front-line people from different fields contributes to developing a truly multidisciplinary approach.

Ideally, all mental health and addiction professionals working with Indigenous people would have some harm reduction training. Unfortunately, opportunities for this training may be scarce. Some professional organizations offer courses in specific aspects of harm reduction (e.g., methadone or Methadose maintenance treatment), and there are harm reduction conferences that delve into a range of issues.

LOCALLY ORIENTED AND IN SITU TRAINING

Locally oriented training is important; for example, educational opportunities exist for learning about the Treaty 6 Cree context in Edmonton or the Six Nations/Mississauga context in Hamilton, Ontario. Ideally, a significant portion of formal training takes place in situ, for example, taking a program to an accessible community, such as Hobbema, near Edmonton, or Ohsweken, near Hamilton. Students should be introduced

---

2   See chapter 8 for a discussion about harm reduction.

to key people in the community, such as Elders and community health workers, and have access to local information. Learning to leverage the strengths of each agency through cross-agency co-ordination is key in providing mental health and addiction care and will lead to improvements in health service delivery and, ultimately, in people's health. The myriad of programs and workers can overwhelm anybody, let alone someone struggling with mental health or addiction issues. It is important to appreciate the client's perspective and to protect privacy, which can be compromised when client information is transferred among agencies.

In situ training should also address protocol. Expectations and practices of health practitioners may differ depending on the community. Students should be given many different experiences with Indigenous people in different communities to help them understand the unique realities and diversity of each community.

Longer-term in situ training programs teach students how to establish therapeutic alliances and evaluate and reflect upon management plans. They should promote building relationships with individuals and families, as well as with communities. Trainees should understand that they are in a privileged position and that their contribution should go beyond just providing health services. For example, to reciprocate the teachings and knowledge received from a community, a trainee might offer to speak about mental health or about career possibilities at a community meeting, school or youth gathering. The specifics need to be negotiated with each community, but will help in establishing a relationship.

In situ training should provide opportunities to interact with and even shadow traditional healers and Elders. Each brings different skills and techniques, but generally they approach wellness in a wholistic[3] manner that focuses on spiritual as well as mental and physical health. These experiences help students understand the important role traditional healing can play. It is important that trainees develop their practice in a way that provides systemic support for traditional knowledge and Indigenous medicines in the development of individualized treatment plans.

Creating a Health System That Reflects Indigenous Values and Needs

Canada needs more health practitioners—Indigenous and non-Indigenous, traditional and mainstream—who are competent in providing culturally safe and appropriate health services for Indigenous people. It is important to create an Indigenous-friendly environment within the health care system. Indigenous health practitioners who are grounded in both their own culture and mainstream Western culture play a key role in making the health care system more culturally safe. The Native Mental Health Association of Canada (2007) points out that it is important to promote culturally

---

3   We spell "wholistic" with a *w* to emphasize the concept of wholeness.

appropriate capacity building, guided by cultural safety standards, to prepare and equip mental health practitioners.

Non-Indigenous health practitioners often lack knowledge of Indigenous culture and social structures. Collaborating with Indigenous community health workers and addiction counsellors is an effective way for non-Indigenous health practitioners to provide culturally safe services to Indigenous clients. The Royal Commission on Aboriginal Peoples (1996) noted that Indigenous people highly value the practical experience and cultural awareness that Indigenous paraprofessionals can provide. When health practitioners are non-Indigenous (as most are), combining their knowledge, skills and judgment with the cultural and community awareness of Indigenous paraprofessionals is considered the only workable means of delivering culturally appropriate health services to Indigenous peoples in the North (Minore & Boone, 2002).

INTEGRATING INDIGENOUS HEALING AND MAINSTREAM TREATMENT APPROACHES

Despite a disproportionately high burden of mental health problems, Indigenous people underuse mainstream mental health services (FNIGC, 2012; Kirmayer et al., 2009). It has been suggested that Indigenous people experience limited success with this approach to mental health treatment because it does not value their ways of knowing, especially those pertaining to health and wellness. Indigenous mental health constructs are fundamentally different from the dominant Western paradigm (Lavallée & Poole, 2010). Furthermore, counselling Indigenous people using the mainstream paradigm may perpetuate colonial oppression (Duran & Duran, 1995).

Indigenous concepts of mental health incorporate intersecting themes of community, cultural identity, wholistic approaches and interdependence. Culturally appropriate counselling can be provided by integrating these themes into a Western treatment model. Stewart (2008) suggested that practitioners working with Indigenous clients incorporate fundamental Indigenous values—demonstrating respect and non-interference and not being judgmental—and that they use the medicine wheel, which emphasizes balance in life and healing. An Aboriginal mental health best practices working group recommended three features of culturally appropriate mental health services for Indigenous people (Smye & Mussell, 2001). These services should:
• be culturally relevant and safe (i.e., respectful of the diverse cultures of individuals, families and communities)
• be strength-based
• integrate traditional healing approaches with Western models to complete the circle of care.

Collaborative, culturally safe services that integrate clinical approaches with traditional Indigenous healing have been hailed as promising approaches to reducing the high rates of mental health problems in Indigenous communities in Canada. In their study of a community-based Indigenous mental health care model in a rural, high-needs environment, Maar and colleagues (2009) found positive outcomes that included improved quality of care and cultural safety. Maar and Shawande (2010) reported that integrated care resulted in positive experiences for clients and health practitioners, and concluded that traditional healing approaches can be successfully integrated with clinical mental health services. There are many examples of nursing programs, particularly in the western provinces, that integrate collaborative work with communities in both in situ training and developing regional knowledge (Gregory & Barsky, 2007).

Indigenous health practitioners who use traditional teachings generally focus their counselling strategies on reducing alienation and introducing positive cultural experiences (Durie, 2001; McCormick, 1995). Traditional teachings and knowledge provide a basis for developing a positive self-image and a healthy identity. Elders play a key role in helping Indigenous people regain positive identities (Letendre, 2008). Menzies and colleagues (2010) described the work of an Elder who was a full partner with a mainstream mental health team in a clinical setting. Many clients have indicated that this two-pronged approach gives them the best of both worlds: they gain insight into their problems from both an Indigenous perspective and a Western clinical perspective. Indigenous health practitioners, with their greater knowledge of Indigenous cultures and ways of knowing, play an important role in helping the health care system meet the needs of Indigenous people.

This integrated approach to care is reflected in the social work graduate program at the University of Regina. It prepares students to be clinical practitioners skilled in Indigenous approaches to therapy and to be sensitive to issues facing Indigenous communities. Fundamental to the program is an understanding of traditional Indigenous spirituality, culture and healing, and how these traditions can be incorporated into contemporary settings (University of Regina, n.d.).

Conclusion

Indigenous society is inherently different from mainstream society. There is a connection to land and community, and a cultural continuity that define Indigenous identity. For Canada's health care system to better meet the needs of Indigenous people, all health practitioners must be trained to provide culturally safe services that reflect Indigenous values. In such a system, the mix of health workers and skill sets would differ from that of the current health care system, which reflects a mainstream Western perspective: there would be fewer doctors, nurses and social workers, and more healers and health promoters. This would lead to a redefinition of health and an expansion of health care services.

The health burdens that Indigenous people experience, particularly mental health and addiction problems, suggest that an "equity-plus" approach is justified: more health care resources than those determined by equity targets should be provided to address these higher health burdens. The challenge, however, is to quantify the benefits of increasing the number of Indigenous health practitioners. More research is needed to establish the significance of cultural competence and cultural safety approaches in terms of improved health outcomes. Knowledge about what works and what doesn't—from promising practice to good practice—needs to be developed and then translated and scaled up for the wider benefit of both Indigenous and non-Indigenous people (King, 2011).

References

Aboriginal Nurses Association of Canada, Canadian Association of Schools of Nursing & Canadian Nurses Association. (2009). *Cultural Competence and Cultural Safety in Nursing Education: A Framework for First Nations, Inuit and Métis Nursing.* Retrieved from www.anac.on.ca

Association of Faculties of Medicine of Canada. (2008). IPAC–AFMC Indigenous health education initiatives. Retrieved from www.afmc.ca/pdf/IPAC-AFMC%20Indigenous%20Health%20Education%20Initiatives-e.pdf

Brant Castellano, M. (2004). Ethics of Aboriginal research. *Journal of Aboriginal Health, 1,* 98–114.

Brascoupé, S. & Waters, C. (2009). Cultural safety: Exploring the applicability of the concept of cultural safety to Aboriginal health and community wellness. *Journal of Aboriginal Health, 5,* 6–41.

CIHR Institute of Aboriginal Peoples' Health. (2011). *Internal Assessment for 2011 International Review—CIHR Institute of Aboriginal Peoples' Health.* Retrieved from www.cihr-irsc.gc.ca

Duran, E. & Duran, B. (1995). *Native American Postcolonial Psychology.* Albany: State University of New York Press.

Durie, M. (2001). *Mauri Ora: The Dynamics of Māori Health.* Auckland, New Zealand: Oxford University Press.

First Nations Information Governance Centre (FNIGC). (2012). *First Nations Regional Health Survey (RHS) Phase 2 (2008/10): National Report on Adults, Youth and Children Living in First Nations Communities.* Retrieved from www.fnigc.ca

Gregory, D. & Barsky, J. (2007). *Against the Odds: An Update on Aboriginal Nursing in Canada.* Retrieved from University of Lethbridge website: www.uleth.ca

Inuit Health Survey. (2010). *Inuit Health Survey 2007–2008—Nunavut.* Retrieved from Centre for Indigenous Peoples' Nutrition and Environment website: www.mcgill.ca/cine

King, M. (2005). Commentary on training Aboriginal health professionals in Canada. Retrieved from the Alberta Network Environments for Aboriginal Health Research website: www.neahr.ualberta.ca

King, M. (2011). Scaling up the knowledge to achieve Aboriginal wellness. *Canadian Journal of Psychiatry, 56,* 73–74.

King. M., Smith, A. & Gracey, M. (2009). Indigenous health part 2: The underlying causes of the health gap. *The Lancet, 374,* 76–85. DOI: 10.1016/S0140-6736(09)60827-8

Kirmayer, L.J., Simpson, C. & Cargo, M. (2003). Healing traditions: culture, community and mental health promotion with Canadian Aboriginal peoples. *Australasian Psychiatry, 11* (Suppl.), 15–23.

Kirmayer, L.J., Tait, C.L. & Simpson, C. (2009). The mental health of Aboriginal Peoples in Canada: Transformations of identity and community. In L.J. Kirmayer & G.G. Valaskakis (Eds.), *Healing*

Traditions: The Mental Health of Aboriginal Peoples in Canada (pp. 3–35). Vancouver: UBC Press.

Lavallée, L.F. & Poole, J.M. (2010). Beyond recovery: Colonization, health and healing for Indigenous people in Canada. *International Journal of Mental Health and Addiction, 8*, 271–281.

Letendre, A.D. (2008). *Aboriginal Female Sexual Health in a Context of Cervical Cancer and Cervical Cytology Screening with Reference to the Cree and Cree-Métis of Northern Alberta* (Doctoral dissertation). Retrieved from OCLC WorldCat database. (Accession no. 695977515).

Maar, M. & Shawande, M. (2010). Traditional Anishinabe healing in a clinical setting: The development of an Aboriginal interdisciplinary approach to community-based Aboriginal mental health care. *Journal of Aboriginal Health, 6*, 18–27.

Maar, M.A., Erskine, B., McGregor, L., Larose, T.L., Sutherland M.E., Graham, D., . . . Gordon, T. (2009). Innovations on a shoestring: A study of a collaborative community-based Aboriginal mental health service model in rural Canada. *International Journal of Mental Health Systems, 3.* DOI: 10.1186/1752-4458-3-27

Manson, S.M., Naquin, V. & Matsuoka, J.K. (2009). *Indigenous Mental Health in the United States: Toward Culturally Resonant Best Practices.* Retrieved from National Association of State Mental Health Program Directors website: www.nasmhpd.org/meetings/presentations/Commissioner2009_W/SperoManson.pdf

Marmot, M. (2007). Achieving health equity: From root causes to fair outcomes. *The Lancet, 370*, 1153–1163. DOI: 10.1016/S0140-6736(07)61385-3

McCormick, R. (1995). Culturally appropriate means and ends of counselling as described by the First Nations people of British Columbia. *International Journal for the Advancement of Counselling, 18*, 163–172. DOI: 10.1007/BF01407960

Menzies, P., Bodnar, A. & Harper, V. (2010). The role of the elder within a mainstream addiction and mental health hospital: Developing an integrated paradigm. *Native Social Work Journal, 7*, 87–107.

Minore, B. & Boone, M. (2002). Realizing potential: Improving interdisciplinary professional/para-professional health care teams in Canada's northern Aboriginal communities through education. *Journal of Interprofessional Care, 16*, 139–147.

National Coordinating Centre for Aboriginal Health. (2010). *Fetal Alcohol Syndrome & Fetal Alcohol Spectrum Disorder among Aboriginal Canadians: Knowledge Gaps.* Retrieved from www.nccah-ccnsa.ca

Native Mental Health Association of Canada. (2007). *Charting the Future of Native Mental Health in Canada: Ten-Year Strategic Plan, 2008–2018.* Retrieved from http://nmhac.ca

Ottawa Charter for Health Promotion. (1986). Retrieved from World Health Organization website: www.who.int

Papps, E. & Ramsden, I. (1996). Cultural safety in nursing: The New Zealand experience. *International Journal for Quality in Health Care, 8*, 491–497. DOI: 10.1093/intqhc/8.5.491

Royal Commission on Aboriginal Peoples. (1996). *Report of the Royal Commission on Aboriginal Peoples. Vol. 3: Gathering Strength.* Ottawa: Canada Communication Group.

Sanguins, J., Bartlett, J.G., Carter, S., Hoeppner, N., Mehta, P. & Bassily, M. (2013). *Depression, Anxiety Disorders, and Related Health Care Utilization in the Manitoba Metis Population.* Winnipeg, MB: Manitoba Metis Federation.

Smye, V. & Mussell, B. (2001). *Aboriginal Mental Health: "What Works Best"—A Discussion Paper.* Retrieved from Simon Fraser University website: www.sfu.ca

Statistics Canada. (2013). *National Household Survey, 2011: Aboriginal Peoples in Canada—First Nations People, Métis and Inuit.* (Catalogue no. 99-011-X2011001). Ottawa: Minister of Industry.

Stewart, S.L. (2008). Promoting Indigenous mental health: Cultural perspectives on healing from Native counsellors in Canada. *International Journal of Health Promotion and Education, 46*, 12–19. DOI: 10.1080/14635240.2008.10708129

Tervalon, M. & Murray-Garcia, J. (1998). Cultural humility versus cultural competence: A critical distinction in defining physician training outcomes in multicultural education. *Journal of Health Care for the Poor and Underserved, 9*, 117–125.

Tjepkema, M., Wilkins, R., Senécal, S., Guimond, E. & Penney, C. (2009). Mortality of Métis and Registered Indian adults in Canada: An 11-year follow-up study. *Health Reports, 20* (4). (Statistics Canada catalogue no. 82-003-XPE). Ottawa: Minister of Industry.

University of Regina. (n.d.). Faculty of Social Work—Programs. Retrieved from www.uregina.ca/socialwork/programs/

ABOUT THE AUTHORS

Alexandra King, MD, FRCPC, a member of the Nipissing First Nation (Ontario), did her medical training at the University of Toronto, the University of Alberta and the University of British Columbia. She is undertaking an advanced research degree at Simon Fraser University. She plans to focus on Indigenous health by combining clinical practice with research, in the areas of social determinants of health, HIV/AIDS, health systems and resiliency.

Malcolm King, PhD, a member of the Mississaugas of the New Credit First Nation, is a health researcher at Simon Fraser University and scientific director of the CIHR Institute of Aboriginal Peoples' Health. Starting in basic science, his current research focuses on airborne disease transmission, as well as the respiratory health inequities facing Aboriginal people. At the CIHR, he leads the development of a national health research agenda aimed at improving wellness and achieving health equity for Aboriginal peoples. Malcolm received a National Aboriginal Achievement Foundation award for health research in 1999.

Chapter 31

The Story of the Aboriginal Healing Foundation

MICHAEL DEGAGNÉ

The Aboriginal Healing Foundation (AHF) was created in 1998 through a contribution agreement between a nationally representative board of directors comprising Aboriginal people and the federal government in response to the profound effects of colonial disempowerment highlighted in the 1996 report of the Royal Commission on Aboriginal Peoples (RCAP) (AHF & Minister of Indian Affairs and Northern Development, 1998). The mission of AHF was to encourage and support Aboriginal communities in building and reinforcing sustainable healing processes capable of addressing the legacies of the residential school system in Canada. AHF worked as a liaison between mainstream resources and Aboriginal peoples with an Aboriginal board of directors steering it in its mission. During its 15-year mandate, AHF funded more than 1,500 projects to help Aboriginal people and their communities.

This chapter outlines the historical impetus and context that led to the formation of AHF, including the Indian residential school system in Canada, the Aboriginal healing movement and RCAP. It describes AHF's funding, activities, mandate, structure, vision and principles. Three examples of projects funded by AHF are presented to serve as a model for addressing Aboriginal mental health and addiction issues in Canada: the Nuu-chah-nulth Chiefs and Tribal Council's Mental Wellness Team in Ahousaht, B.C.; the Eyaa-Keen Centre in Winnipeg, Manitoba; and the Aboriginal Survivors for Healing in Charlottetown, P.E.I.

The Indian Residential School System

Canada's Indian residential school system was a formal partnership from 1892 to 1969 between the federal government and agencies of the Presbyterian, Roman Catholic, United and Anglican churches. The system was intended to acculturate and assimilate Aboriginal people to Christian morality and the Canadian economic and legal systems— and as Duncan Campbell Scott, a senior official of Indian Affairs, phrased it in 1920, to absorb "Indians" into the "body politic" (as cited in Leslie & Maguire, 1978, p. 114). Removed from their homes and from the influence and care of parents and community, Aboriginal children were institutionalized in industrial-based boarding schools and submitted to a daily regimen of cultural indoctrination. All students experienced loneliness and fear, and many suffered physical and sexual abuse. This experience has had a lasting and deleterious impact on many Aboriginal individuals and communities.

Generations of Indian residential school students were submitted to the notion of the white man's moral and intellectual superiority (Wesley-Esquimaux & Smolewski, 2004). The internalized shame engendered by this project of racial denigration was compounded by the physical and sexual abuse of children by their presumed caregivers. The Indian residential school, as a hierarchical institution governing every aspect of day-to-day life, modelled authoritarian and exploitative relationships. Not only were the children powerless by virtue of their age; they were also extracted from a politically and socially dominated group whose adults were themselves identified by legislation as wards of the state. Wesley-Esquimaux and Smolewski (2004) outlined the many effects of unresolved trauma that Aboriginal people experienced as a result of the institutional abuses, including:
• lateral violence and abuse (when an oppressed group turns on itself and members begin to violate one another)
• suicide
• crime
• depression
• poverty
• alcohol use problems and other addictions
• lack of parenting skills
• lack of capacity to build and sustain healthy families and communities.

According to Wayne Spear (2002), "As noted in the 1991 Manitoba Justice Inquiry, the residential school 'is where the alienation began'—alienation of Aboriginal children from family, community, and from themselves" (¶18). As the testimony of survivors makes abundantly clear, the Indian residential school system did little or nothing to prepare students for life either on reserves or in general society. For many people who attended residential schools, and for their children and grandchildren, life afterwards became a suspension between these two worlds[1] (Assembly of First Nations, 1994; Battiste & Barman, 1995; Haig-Brown, 1988; Miller, 1996; Milloy, 1999; Regan, 2010).

---

1 For a more detailed discussion about residential schools, see chapter 3.

It is important to understand that the residential school system is only one entry in the catalogue of historical abuses, and that others include the banning, through legislation, of ceremonial practices and the imposition of Indian Act governance systems. Aboriginal peoples suffered the expropriation of their land and material resources, their systems of traditional governance and their right to self-determination. These legislated deprivations by an aggressive colonial power created deep emotional and, many would say, spiritual, wounds (Wesley-Esquimaux & Smolewski, 2004).

Despite courageous individual instances of resistance and non-compliance, Aboriginal people were continually deprived of the ability to care for themselves. The trauma of being so thoroughly disempowered contributed to the shame, despair, dependence, addiction and violence that are still observed today (AHF, 2006).

The Aboriginal Healing Movement

Beginning around 1950, the systemic impoverishment and oppression of Aboriginal communities prompted the growth of Aboriginal political consciousness and the Aboriginal healing movement (AHF, 2006). Specifically, the political and healing movements arose as interrelated radical efforts to identify the root causes of poverty and community dysfunction (e.g., addiction, unemployment, violence, family breakup) and reverse the damaging effects of colonial policies. These movements were influenced by the highly visible Aboriginal rights movement (including the American Indian movement in the United States and the National Indian Brotherhood in Canada). The healing movement was also nurtured and influenced by three less visible but equally powerful currents, as described below.

THE REVIVAL OF TRADITIONAL SPIRITUALITY AND CULTURES

Many communities reintroduced old ceremonies, practices and teachings, such as smudging, the sweat lodge, the sacred pipe, fasting and vision quests. Ceremonies for naming, healing, reconciliation and personal or collective commitment have also been used to reassert the community's role in its internal well-being. More broadly, traditional Aboriginal cultures have brought shape, energy, key principles and ways of working to the healing movement. The National Native Alcohol and Drug Abuse Program is an excellent example of a treatment program that uses traditional spiritual and cultural teachings.

THE ADDICTIONS AND HUMAN POTENTIAL MOVEMENTS

The addictions and human potential movements began in the 1950s to raise critical awareness of widespread self-medication among Aboriginal people and to promote more empowering responses to colonization. These efforts led to the introduction of personal growth and healing as a primary line of action in community life and included a host of strategies and programs for addressing substance use problems, sexual abuse, violence and personal growth.

Alcoholics Anonymous (AA) was particularly influential and helpful for many Aboriginal people and communities. AA's notion of a lifelong, structured path of wellness, as well as its emphasis on a higher power, has inspired many to embark on the "red road" of the Aboriginal healing movement. Many Aboriginal communities have taken AA concepts and practices, such as the 12 steps, and integrated them into healing approaches better suited to Aboriginal community realities and conditions than mainstream urban approaches to running AA meetings.

THE HOLISTIC FOCUS ON HEALTH AND WELLNESS

Influenced by the addictions and human potential movements, the Aboriginal healing movement adopted a holistic focus on health and wellness rather than sickness—a significant departure from the medical model. This focus yielded successful efforts to convince governments of the importance of funding proactive mental health and wellness initiatives, for example, the Brighter Futures and Building Healthy Communities programs. Viewed from this holistic perspective, health is more than just the absence of disease. The healing movement asserts that our primary energy and thinking should be poured into building a healthy life in all its aspects, rather than trying to root out sickness or problems.

The Aboriginal healing movement has also adopted the holistic idea that the healing of individuals requires the healing of families and communities—a "whole person, whole community" approach that involves the mental, emotional, physical and spiritual well-being of individuals and families, as well as the political, economic, social and cultural well-being of communities. In this approach, individual problems such as alcohol addiction or sexual abuse cannot be isolated and dealt with apart from the rest of human and community development.

A significant milestone in the growth and impact of the Aboriginal healing movement was unquestionably the establishment in 1982 of the National Native Alcohol and Drug Abuse Program. This program established a core group of Aboriginal and non-Aboriginal people, and a number of organizations, such as the Nechi Training Centre and the National Association of Native Treatment Directors, as leaders and experts in healing alcohol and other substance use problems. Initially focused primarily on addiction, the movement expanded its scope over time to increasingly address the complete legacy of residential school abuse. Particularly important in this development was AFN National Chief Phil Fontaine's willingness in 1990 to speak publicly of the abuse he suffered as a student at the Sagkeen Indian Residential School (Frum, 1990). At this time, the residential school system's legacy of physical and sexual abuse began to enter Canadians' discussions about Aboriginal people.

The Royal Commission on Aboriginal Peoples

When the federal government of Brian Mulroney appointed RCAP in August 1991, there was relatively little understanding of the pervasive effects of residential schools, either within the government or among the Canadian public. RCAP held hearings across the country and analyzed Aboriginal issues extensively. In November 1996, it issued its final five-volume, 4,000-page report, featuring more than 100 pages of detailed recommendations.

The report (RCAP, 1996) concluded that the residential schools were "opportunistic sites of abuse" (p. 351) requiring "much more public scrutiny and investigation" (p. 366). Specifically, it recommended a public inquiry, public hearings and additional "research and analysis of the breadth and effects" (RCAP, 1996, p. 366) of Indian residential school government policies and practices. The report also recommended investigating and identifying abuse and that governments and the responsible churches take remedial action to relieve conditions created by the residential school experience. This remedial action included "apologies by those responsible; compensation of communities [to assist them in designing and administering programs to] help with the healing process and rebuild their community life; and funding for treatment of affected individuals and their families" (RCAP, 1996, p. 367). As one researcher noted, the RCAP report, along with academic studies and histories written by former students, provide "stark testimonials" that "reveal the systemic long-term violence that characterized [Indian residential school] policy and practice" (Regan, 2010, p. 37). The history and legacies of residential schools underline a profound need for healing of the First Nations, Métis and Inuit communities directly affected by the intergenerational experience of residential schools, as well as of the nation that allowed this systemic and systematic perpetration of abuse.

The Aboriginal Healing Foundation

On January 7, 1998, in response to the RCAP report, the federal government, under the leadership of Prime Minister Jean Chrétien, announced the creation of a $350-million healing fund to address the legacy of residential school abuse. On March 31, 1998, AHF was established to oversee this fund. It signed a funding agreement with the federal government, with an 11-year mandate ending in March 2009. Additional funding of $40 million from Prime Minister Paul Martin's federal government and $125 million from the 2007 Indian Residential School Settlement Agreement enabled AHF to extend 134 contribution agreements to March 31, 2010. Funding for a network of 12 regional healing centres was also extended to the end of 2013 (AHF, 2012, 2013).

The mandate of AHF was to encourage and support Aboriginal people in sustaining healing processes that address the legacy of physical and sexual abuse they experienced in the residential school system. This mandate was articulated in the original funding agreement between the federal government and a committee appointed by the five national Aboriginal political organizations: the Assembly of First Nations, Inuit Tapirisat of Canada (later the Inuit Tapiriit Kanatami), Métis National Council, Congress of Aboriginal Peoples and Native Women's Association of Canada. AHF's policy was formulated by a governing board of directors, and its main activities were to provide funds for healing projects, promote awareness of healing issues and needs, and nurture a broad public environment supportive of reconciliation and healing. AHF was accountable both to the federal government and to Aboriginal peoples through its funding agreement and through its board, eight members of whom were nominated by the representative Aboriginal organizations and seven of whom were nominated by Aboriginal people at large.

Although AHF reported to the Minister of Indian Affairs, it was not an Indian Affairs program. Established as a private corporation under Canada's Corporations Act, AHF was one of several arms-length institutions set up by the Chrétien government in the late 1990s to achieve non-political long-term policy objectives. The AHF board of directors was bound by the funding agreement with Canada, as well as by the federal laws governing private corporations; however, a great deal of discussion and effort went into articulating the character of the relationship between Aboriginal communities and AHF, and contrasting this relationship to the often toxic one between Aboriginal people and the federal government. As a delegated funding authority, AHF developed a collaborative approach that stood in sharp contrast to the paternalistic approach of government-delivered programs. AHF continuously revised its funding process to accommodate community needs, concerns and criticisms. In part this evolution was informal, rooted in community visits and conversations. The relationship was also formalized through AHF's code of conduct, ethical guidelines and communications strategy,[2] which explicitly and publicly itemized the principles and practices to which the organization would try to adhere in its partnership with Aboriginal communities.

Between 1998 and 2001, the start-up years, AHF staff, guided by the board of directors, crafted a broad range of detailed policy instruments governing everything from how to review proposals to how to achieve fairness in funding distribution. The Aboriginal communities were at the centre of this discussion, by virtue of the fact that the board members lived in these communities and that AHF undertook dozens of regional gatherings and community visits and responded to all concerns. Unique among funding organizations, AHF allocated resources for helping communities develop funding proposals and critique its processes as it did so (Spear, in press; Wadden, 2008). AHF provided toll-free telephone guidance to prospective applicants, and also proactively went across Canada to gather practical suggestions on how it might better achieve its vision. This open, collaborative approach was grounded in transparency and the cultivation of trust.

AHF envisioned a world in which those affected by the legacy of abuse experienced in residential schools were able to address their unresolved traumas, break intergenerational

---

2   These documents are available on the Aboriginal Healing Foundation website at www.ahf.ca.

cycles of abuse, achieve reconciliation in their full range of relationships and enhance their capacity as individuals, families, communities, nations and peoples to sustain their well-being and that of future generations. At the root of this work was revitalizing the community relationships disrupted by the imposition of colonial educational, political and social arrangements. Addiction was viewed as an understandable way of coping with pain in the absence of knowing how to cope in a more nurturing manner.

To realize this vision, AHF funded various categories of projects promoting awareness, addressing the roots of destructive behaviours and teaching life skills (Table 32-1).

TABLE 32-1

AHF-Funded Projects

PROJECT CATEGORY	PERCENTAGE OF GRANTS ALLOCATED
healing activities (e.g., healing circles, day treatment services, sex offender programs, wilderness retreats, on the land programs, elder support networks)	65%
prevention and awareness (e.g., education and training materials, sexual abuse awareness)	13%
building knowledge (e.g., resources for increasing knowledge about the legacy of residential school abuse)	8%
training activities	6%
honouring history (e.g., memorials, commemorations, documentation)	3%
assessing needs	3%
project design and set-up	1%
conferences	1%

From *2012 Annual Report of the Aboriginal Healing Foundation* (p. 17), 2012, Ottawa: Aboriginal Healing Foundation. © 2012 by Aboriginal Healing Foundation. Reprinted with permission.

Because of its funding agreement with the federal government, AHF could only fund activities that addressed the intergenerational legacy of physical and sexual abuse arising from the residential school system. Specifically, AHF's funding agreement (AHF & Minister of Indian Affairs and Northern Development, 1998) stated that the AHF could not fund:
• capital infrastructure (buildings)
• advocacy on behalf of survivors
• litigation-related activities
• compensation
• language and culture programs.

PRINCIPLES OF THE ABORIGINAL HEALING FOUNDATION

In the report *Promising Healing Practices in Aboriginal Communities* (Archibald, 2006), AHF attributed a large part of its success to the following principles of its mandate:

- **Independent Aboriginal governance and operating structure.** The entirely Aboriginal 17-member board of directors had both elected and appointed members. Some members were appointed by national Aboriginal organizations, and others were elected from the Aboriginal community at large. The federal government retained two seats, both of which were filled in practice by Aboriginal employees of the government. The board had an unusually high level of autonomy: once its mandate was specified in the funding agreement with the federal government, it received its entire initial $350-million grant in a lump sum up front. The independent Aboriginal governance and operating structure produced a high level of trust among Aboriginal communities, which felt that AHF was addressing their concerns.
- **Mandatory and meaningful participation of survivors.** All projects required the support of survivors in the community, and survivors had to participate in the oversight of all projects. AHF ensured this involvement by requiring letters of support from applicants, as well as by monitoring projects through an ongoing reporting regimen.
- **Community control over who receives support and how healing is defined.** The recipient of AHF funding defined the healing needs of the community and determined who should receive services. The needs of the community were not prescribed by AHF.
- **Funding decisions based on ability.** The project management team had to have sufficient background and experience to manage the project funds and to deliver services to survivors. Ability was assessed through a review of applicants' credentials and past work. When possible, AHF encouraged project teams to form formal partnerships with established organizations that themselves had a proven record of managerial competence.
- **Focus on the intergenerational legacy of the residential school system.** Children of residential school students carry a legacy of intergenerational trauma, having grown up under the influence of behaviours learned at the schools. While Aboriginal communities have acute needs for many kinds of social services funding, from housing to addiction to recreation, AHF focused its funding on promoting healing from the legacy of the residential schools, which included the descendants of former students.
- **Lasting benefits to the healing of survivors.** Projects with only short-term benefits to survivors, particularly if they focused only on individuals rather than communities, were not funded. Projects had to have long-term benefits to survivors in the transfer of knowledge or skills. Long-term benefits derive from initiatives that address root causes of dysfunction and thereby restore the ability of the community to leverage its human and cultural resources to initiate change. Benefits were assessed according to both quantitative and qualitative criteria, such as the number of community members engaged in a healing project and participants' reports indicating that they had benefited from a program. These and other data were collected by AHF from funded

projects. Unfortunately, AHF was itself only a temporary service delivery instrument supporting long-term community engagement and development. While some community projects secured private or public funds (provincial or municipal), many expired when AHF funding ended.

- **Accountability.** Projects had to be accountable to survivors, to the community where the project took place and to the target group that benefited from the project. Furthermore, the AHF board sought opportunities to make public presentations and to consult with Aboriginal people on the organization and delivery of funding and other services.

BEST PRACTICES: THREE AHF-FUNDED PROJECTS

AHF identified the following best practices of its funded projects:
- survivor-driven, community-based
- front-end, long-term planning
- thoughtful staff selection and support
- small-scale projects addressing concrete community needs, rather than mega-projects
- community-oriented goals focused on people and participation (Archibald, 2006).

These best practices are also defined as projects that engage broad community participation (e.g., young and old, male and female) and that produce an observable positive change in community behaviours. Best practices serve as a model for future Aboriginal mental health and addiction service delivery and provide multiple benefits, including healthy communities and reduced costs in the broader justice and health care systems.

Of the more than 1,500 projects funded by AHF, the following three examples provide an overview of the organization's work and illustrate its best practices.

1. Ahousaht

Ahousaht, a small Nuu-chah-nulth coastal village of 1,000 residents in British Columbia, had witnessed more than 100 youth suicide attempts in a matter of months. The Nuu-chah-nulth chief reached out to the tribal council's mental wellness team (MWT) to come to the community to help the youth. A unique approach to healing resulted from that AHF-funded partnership between the Ahousaht band and the MWT. The MWT, composed of Elders and professional, Western-trained mental health counsellors, assessed the community based on informal sources of knowledge about the community. The team determined that the adults were exhibiting violent behaviours associated with alcohol and other drug addiction, such that the community was unsafe for youth between dusk and dawn.

One morning at 6:00 a.m., the MWT began drumming at the four corners of the community. The MWT came day after day at 6:00 a.m. until, after about one month, the adults started to come out of their homes to see and eventually interact with the

MWT counsellors and Elders. It took several months for the dialogue between community members (adults and youth) to become strong enough for the MWT to suggest a community meeting to discuss the community's key strength—its culture.

The dialogue allowed the community to reflect on its vision of a healthy, safe community and evolved to a point where community members asked the chief to take action against the drug dealers and bootleggers in the community. With the support of the community, the chief and tribal council approached each of the known offenders and offered two options: to be banished from the community permanently or to leave the community immediately for pre-arranged addiction treatment and to return once they completed treatment.

The majority chose the second option. When they finished treatment, these community members were welcomed back to the community in a healing community ceremony. This project dramatically reduced youth suicide attempts in Ahousaht. *The Ahousaht Story: Healing the Past, Creating a Future* (Chambers, 2006) is a film that shares insights into the community and its healing.

This project demonstrated the following AHF principles:

- **Community control over who receives support and how healing is defined.** In this community-driven project, the community controlled the technique of establishing dialogue and chose a culturally appropriate response. Action was not taken until the community supported it. Furthermore, the community decided on the options given to the drug dealers and bootleggers, as well as the means of reintegrating those individuals back into the community.
- **Funding decisions based on ability.** The project drew on the expertise of professional Western-trained mental health counsellors where appropriate and leveraged existing community strengths.
- **Lasting benefits to the healing of survivors.** A focus on the long term, combined with a community-health perspective, led to targeting the drug dealers and bootleggers for help, instead of merely targeting the "sickness" of the addicted.

The experiences in Ahousaht illustrate the power of culturally safe mental wellness services. They also highlight the viability of this partnership model of healing for Aboriginal communities.

2. Eyaa-Keen Healing Centre

The Eyaa-Keen Healing Centre in Winnipeg, Manitoba, is a private non-profit organization run by a volunteer Aboriginal board of directors. Mel and Shirley Chartrand received an AHF development assistance grant in 1999 and opened the centre in 2000. The centre offers therapeutic trauma treatment and "psychological rehabilitation" programs and services to address the needs of Aboriginal adults seeking new ways, behaviours and disciplines to help them become better parents, workers, leaders and mentors within their families and society. The focus is on the spiritual, mental, emotional and physical well-being of Aboriginal people. Diverse Aboriginal clients from across Manitoba (including Ojibwe, Cree, Oji-Cree, Dakota and Dene) travel to the

Eyaa-Keen Healing Centre to receive services. According to the centre's unpublished annual report prepared for AHF in 2012, 1,532 participants were served in 2012, 1,184 in 2011 and 1,285 in 2010.

Before the Chartrands created and delivered this innovative behavioural health program, they healed themselves. "Psychologists couldn't heal me, it was something that I had to do for myself," said Shirley in the annual report. And so the Chartrands set out on their personal journeys to find ways to become healthy in a holistic manner. From this experience, they determined that it was their mission to assist others in their journey to restore peace of mind, strengthen personal and professional skills, and become grounded and connected. Their vision was to assist others in becoming *eyaa-keen*, the Ojibwe word for "being self" or "being natural."

The Eyaa-Keen Healing Centre training programs develop participants' caregiving skills, abilities and discipline. The centre offers in-residence programs lasting from three to 10 days, as well as hour-long "day programs." Its in-residence programs are conducted in group and one-on-one settings with therapists and trainers. All programs use the same processes, but the day programs are more flexibly structured to fit the needs of individual participants.

One older woman who attended the program looked back on her life of alcohol addiction, abuse and domestic violence, from her childhood to her adult years. She said she was an intergenerational survivor of the residential schools. She realized that her own lack of knowing how to relate to others or how to demonstrate love and nurturing was at the root of her addiction—a common legacy of the residential school experience. She said that she had left home and became a parent at a very young age, and admitted that, not knowing any better, she had repeated many of the same mistakes her parents had made. The patterns from her childhood were repeated in her adult years.

Life changed for her when she became a grandmother. Wanting her grandchild to have a better life, she was motivated to begin healing, and attended training programs at Eyaa-Keen. Although she sometimes fell back on old habits and old ways of thinking, she kept attending: first, an intensive three-day in-residence program, then a five-day program and eventually the 10-day program, which she attended twice. "You get out of it what you put into it!" she said.

Following her attendance at Eyaa-Keen, her decision making was clearer, and her relationship with her family and friends improved. She had a peaceful feeling inside and no longer carried the pain and sadness of the past with her. Her newly gained confidence was evident in her ability to conduct an interview. As a new band counsellor in her community, she was working to help others. Her advice to other survivors: "There is hope for a good life, but each person has to make a commitment to work at it."

Eyaa-Keen has enjoyed a high level of support from Aboriginal communities. While the AHF funds have ended, the project continues, although the Chartrands anticipate scaling down their staff and service levels in the absence of alternative funding.

This project demonstrated the following AHF principles:

- **Focus on the intergenerational legacy of the residential school system.** Eyaa-Keen targets intergenerational survivors of the residential schools, thereby developing expertise in serving that client base.
- **Lasting benefits to the healing of survivors.** By focusing on caregiving, Eyaa-Keen addresses the care received by the next generation and helps to break the intergenerational cycle of abuse.

3. Aboriginal Survivors for Healing

The Aboriginal Survivors for Healing (ASH) program in Charlottetown, P.E.I., opened in 2000 to provide counselling, traditional healing methods, men's and women's eight-week healing groups, and training of support workers to assist survivors of residential schools, and of subsequent abuses. Most ASH clients are former students (or the Mi'kmaq, Maliseet and Passamaquoddy descendants of the former students) of the Shubenacadie Indian Residential School, the only officially recognized Indian residential school in Canada's Atlantic region.

According to founding director Tarry Hewitt, one key to the success of ASH is staff stability and programming continuity. Hewitt believes that consistent staffing establishes a safe and confidential environment in which clients can trust and respect staff and thus benefit from programs offering healing and reassurance.

The AHF funding allowed the ASH project to support Aboriginal abuse survivors in healing from mental health and addiction issues. Dale Sylliboy, a long-time counsellor with ASH, uses traditional methods, such as weekly healing circles and keeping a reflective journal. In the men's and women's weekly healing circles, participants share breakfast or lunch and then take turns speaking about their life journeys, in some instances passing an eagle feather, the holder of which receives the respectful attention of the circle. Healing circles are typically opened and closed by an Elder or other individual respected by the community, and last as long as the participants want, sometimes into the evening.

Many abuse survivors report that the sharing and dialogue help. Survivors often have difficulty understanding the problems they currently face in their lives, and so they must recall the time when the abuse started. They talk about the learned behaviours from residential school and how they passed those behaviours on to their children. Descendants of survivors are often angrier than the direct survivors because they typically know even less about what happened in the past and how it affects their present. Sharing can be extremely emotionally difficult for many survivors, but in the healing circle, they learn to sort through their pain and let it go.

Participants share a different topic during the circle each week, for example, what does it mean to be a good parent? Many survivors cannot answer that question at first. In the circle, they recall their family and childhood before the residential schools, learning lessons from their traditional community activities and family structure.

At the end of the eight-week session, the group performs a traditional ceremony.

The survivors then burn their journals and begin as new people; the group celebrates its journey with a feast.

The ASH project shares traditional ways and teachings with Aboriginal participants and encourages them to use those teachings to help others. The women in particular have a strong unity of sisterhood and support one another. Often, they bring new members into the circle. Survivors are thereby empowered to become mentors and healers, which is difficult, but also very rewarding, as Sylliboy described:

> The problems people face in their lives today are due to the neglect and abuse of the past, but if people face and own the problems and these issues from the past, life will get easier. The scars will always be there, as scars don't go away—but life will go on in a new way. (as cited in Miller, 2007, p. 3)

The future of ASH is uncertain; however, the project has secured funding from federal and provincial agencies and is likely to continue.

Several AHF principles play a key role in making the ASH project successful:

• **Mandatory and meaningful participation of survivors.** Much of ASH's programming is directly targeted at survivors. As noted, survivors often become mentors and healers, participating in project decisions and implementation. Over time, therefore, the project became increasingly survivor-driven.

• **Focus on the intergenerational legacy of the residential school system.** ASH focuses explicitly on this intergenerational legacy.

• **Lasting benefits to the healing of survivors.** With its holistic, wellness-based approach, ASH produces deep, long-term psychological benefits for survivors.

The partnership between AHF and ASH allowed the Aboriginal community of P.E.I. to access culturally relevant methods of healing. With the help of government funding, the ASH project continues to help Aboriginal people retrieve traditional knowledge and address mental health and addiction issues arising from residential school abuse.

Conclusion

AHF provided significant and sustained funding to support the healing movement in Canada. During its 15 years in operation, it built upon the earlier work of the Aboriginal healing movement and forged important and productive partnerships with Aboriginal communities. These partnerships allowed AHF to provide vital funds to help residential school survivors and their descendants address the mental health issues arising from disempowerment and abuse. The principles developed to guide AHF's work had been spoken of for decades: community-based interventions by and for Aboriginal people, building on existing strengths and respectful support from outside Aboriginal communities. Although AHF has closed its doors, the success of the many people and organizations it has helped to support will continue. The positive effect of this work, and the principles that helped guide it, can serve as an example for other organizations that are committed to delivering healing programs to Aboriginal communities into the future.

References

Aboriginal Healing Foundation (AHF). (2006). *Final Report of the Aboriginal Health Foundation. Vol. 1: A Healing Journey—Reclaiming Wellness.* Retrieved from www.ahf.ca

Aboriginal Healing Foundation (AHF). (2012). *2012 Annual Report of the Aboriginal Healing Foundation.* Retrieved from www.ahf.ca

Aboriginal Healing Foundation (AHF). (2013). *2013 Annual Report of the Aboriginal Healing Foundation.* Retrieved from www.ahf.ca

Aboriginal Healing Foundation (AHF) & Minister of Indian Affairs and Northern Development. (1998). *Funding Agreement.* Retrieved from www.ahf.ca

Archibald, L. (2006). *Final Report of the Aboriginal Healing Foundation. Volume 3: Promising Healing Practices in Aboriginal Communities.* Retrieved from Aboriginal Health Foundation website: www.ahf.ca

Assembly of First Nations. (1994). *Breaking the Silence: An Interpretive Study of Residential School Impact and Healing as Illustrated by the Stories of First Nations Individuals.* Ottawa: Author.

Battiste, M. & Barman, J. (Eds.). (1995). *First Nations Education in Canada: The Circle Unfolds.* Vancouver: UBC Press.

Chambers, B. (Producer). (2006). *The Ahousaht Story: Healing the Past, Creating a Future.* Canada: Filmwest Associates.

Frum, B. (Host). (1990, October 30). Phil Fontaine's shocking testimony of sexual abuse. In M. Starowicz (Producer), *The Journal.* Retrieved from CBC Digital Archives website: www.cbc.ca/archives/categories/politics/parties-leaders/phil-fontaine-native-diplomat-and-dealmaker/shocking-testimony-of-sexual-abuse.html

Haig-Brown, C. (1988). *Resistance and Renewal: Surviving the Indian Residential School.* Vancouver: Tillacum Library.

Leslie, J. & Maguire, R. (Eds.). (1978). *The Historical Development of the Indian Act* (2nd ed.). Ottawa: Department of Indian Affairs and Northern Development.

Miller, J. (2007). Aboriginal survivors for healing. *Healing Words, 5* (2), 3. Retrieved from Aboriginal Healing Foundation website: www.ahf.ca

Miller, J.R. (1996). *Shingwauk's Vision: A History of Native Residential Schools.* Toronto: University of Toronto Press.

Milloy, J. (1999). *A National Crime: The Canadian Government and the Residential School System, 1879–1986.* Winnipeg: University of Manitoba Press.

Regan, P. (2010). *Unsettling the Settler Within: Indian Residential Schools, Truth Telling and Reconciliation in Canada.* Vancouver: UBC Press.

Royal Commission on Aboriginal Peoples (RCAP). (1996). *Report of the Royal Commission on Aboriginal Peoples. Vol. 1: Looking Forward, Looking Back.* Ottawa: Canada Communication Group.

Spear, W. (in press). *Full Circle: A Story of the Indian Residential School System's Legacy, the Aboriginal Healing Foundation, the Indian Residential School Settlement Agreement and the Unfinished Work of Hope, Healing, Reconciliation and Change.* Montreal: McGill-Queen's University Press.

Spear, W.K. (2002). *Canada's Indian Residential School System.* Retrieved from http://waynekspear.com/2010/03/10/canada's-indian-residential-school-system/

Wadden, M. (2008). *Where the Pavement Ends: Canada's Aboriginal Recovery Movement and the Urgent Need for Reconciliation.* Vancouver: Douglas & McIntyre.

Wesley-Esquimaux, C. & Smolewski, M. (2004). *Historic Trauma and Aboriginal Healing.* Retrieved from Aboriginal Healing Foundation website: www.ahf.ca

ABOUT THE AUTHOR

Michael DeGagné, BSC, MA, PhD, has 25 years of public sector leadership experience. His academic credentials include a bachelor of science degree in biology from the University of Toronto, a master's degree in administration from Central Michigan University, a PhD in educational administration from Michigan State University and a master of laws degree from York University's Osgoode Hall. Since 1998, he was executive director of the Aboriginal Healing Foundation. He has also served as chairman of Ottawa's Queensway Carleton Hospital and is a member of the board of directors of the Mental Health Commission of Canada. He currently serves as president and vice-chancellor of Nipissing University in North Bay.

About the Editors

Peter Menzies, BA, BSW, MSW, PhD, is a member of the Sagamok Anishnawbek First Nation. He is a private consultant working primarily with First Nations communities in Ontario. Before establishing his private practice, Peter spent 14 years building culturally congruent mental health and addiction programs in partnership with urban and rural First Nations communities through the Centre for Addiction and Mental Health in Toronto. Peter is an assistant professor in the Department of Psychiatry at the University of Toronto and an adjunct professor in the Faculty of Social Work at Laurentian University in Sudbury. He received the Centre for Equity in Health and Society's Entrepreneurial Development and Integration of Services Award in 2005, and the Kaiser Foundation's Excellence in Indigenous Programming Award in 2011.

Lynn F. Lavallée, BA, MSc, PhD, is Anishinaabe Métis born in Sudbury, Ontario. She moved to Toronto as a child and grew up in the social housing development Regent Park. As a youth and young adult she faced mental health challenges. Lynn has a BA in psychology and kinesiology, an MSc in community health and a PhD in social work. She is an associate professor at Ryerson University, as well as associate director of the School of Social Work and chair of the Research Ethics Board. Her research interests include the holistic well-being of Indigenous peoples, social and political determinants of health and Indigenous research ethics.

Index